Awards and Honors for Geoffrey Stone's *Perilous Times*

Los Angeles Times Book Prize for History, 2004

Robert F. Kennedy Book Award, 2004

Lysander Spooner Award for Advancing the Literature of Liberty, 2005

Harry J. Kalven Freedom of Expression Award, presented by the ACLU, 2005

Honorable Mention for the American Bar Association's Silver Gavel Award,
2005

American Political Science Association's Gladys M. Kammerer Award, 2005

Goldsmith Book Prize, presented by Harvard's Shorenstein Center on the Press,
Politics, and Public Policy, 2005

Hugh M. Hefner First Amendment Award, 2005

Scribes Award for Best Book of the Year in Law, 2005

Notable or Best Books of the Year

Washington Post Best Book of 2004

New York Times Notable Book of 2004

Los Angeles Times Best Book of 2004

Chicago Tribune Best Book of 2004

Philadelphia Inquirer 10 Best Books of 2004

Christian Science Monitor Best Book of 2004

More Praise for *Perilous Times*

"Scholarly in its depth, yet accessible to lay readers, *Perilous Times* is a book for all times and places." —Alan M. Dershowitz, *Boston Globe*

"Mr. Stone is a constitutional scholar and a zealous defender of free speech, but he is also a great storyteller." —Jonathan Karl, *Wall Street Journal*

"The book's material is rich and analyzed with great clarity and depth. . . . Stone's book will serve as an invaluable guide as we watch the actions of the government in the coming years." —Michael Riccardi, *Legal Intelligence*, Philadelphia

"This is great, dramatic, and absorbing legal history at its best—beautifully written, highly accessible, and critically important for our time." —Jonathan Cole

"*Perilous Times* is magisterial, timely, and wise. . . . By placing a spotlight on restrictions of freedom amidst war, Stone has done an extraordinary public service—and produced a classic in the process." —Cass Sunstein

"A remarkable compendium." —David M. Skover, *Legal Times*

"Sometimes a book just hits the intellectual spot. . . . As terrorists from abroad pose a continuing and dangerous threat to our safety, we act at our peril if we respond at home without recalling our past history that Stone describes with such clarity." —Floyd Abrams

"Geoffrey Stone's outstanding book alarms as much as it clarifies. As the current administration flouts the Constitution in genuinely groundbreaking ways, it is also exposing us to dangers hitherto unknown."
—Stephen Holmes, *The New Republic*

"Comprehensive and consistently readable, this enlightening book arrives at a time when national political debate should be at a fever pitch."
—*Publishers Weekly*

Perilous Times

FREE SPEECH IN WARTIME

FROM THE SEDITION ACT
OF 1798 TO THE
WAR ON TERRORISM

GEOFFREY R. STONE

For information about permission to reproduce selections from this book, write to
Permissions, W. W. Norton & Company, Inc., 500 Fifth Avenue, New York, NY 10110

Manufacturing by RR Donnelley, Harrisonburg, VA
Book design by Abbate Design
Production manager: Anna Oler

Library of Congress Cataloging-in-Publication Data
Stone, Geoffrey R.
Perilous times : free speech in wartime from the Sedition Act of 1798 to the war on
terrorism / Geoffrey R. Stone. — 1st ed.
p. cm.
Includes bibliographical references and index.
ISBN 0-393-05880-8 (hardcover)
1. Freedom of speech — United States — History. I. Title.
JC591.S76 2004
323.44'3'0973 — dc22

2004017871

ISBN 978-0-393-32745-8 pbk.

W. W. Norton & Company, Inc., 500 Fifth Avenue, New York, N.Y. 10110
www.wwnorton.com

W. W. Norton & Company Ltd., Castle House, 75/76 Wells Street, London W1T 3QT

2 3 4 5 6 7 8 9 0

W. W. NORTON & COMPANY

NEW YORK • LONDON

ALSO BY GEOFFREY R. STONE

First Amendment, 2nd Edition
with Louis Seidman, Cass Sunstein, and Mark Tushnet
(2003)

Constitutional Law, 5th Edition
with Louis Seidman, Cass Sunstein, and Mark Tushnet
(2001)

Eternally Vigilant: Free Speech in the Modern Era
with Lee Bollinger
(2001)

The Bill of Rights in the Modern State
with Cass Sunstein and Richard Epstein
(1992)

FOR NANCY

"Those who won our independence believed . . .

courage to be the secret of liberty."

JUSTICE LOUIS D. BRANDEIS
(Whitney v. California 1927)

CONTENTS

LIST OF ILLUSTRATIONS

ACKNOWLEDGMENTS

THIRTY YEARS AGO, I had the unique privilege and great good fortune to learn at first hand from two of the twentieth century's most influential and generative thinkers about free speech—Professor Harry Kalven Jr. and Justice William J. Brennan Jr. They were inspiring and demanding mentors who helped shape my views, while insisting that I question them constantly. I hope this book would have pleased them.

I also had the good fortune to work on this project with splendid student research assistants. Shana Wallace, Kelsi Brown Corkran, Patrick Curran, Angela Russo, David Geary, and Justin Sandburg of the University of Chicago Law School and Jake Kreilkamp and Jason Husgen of New York University School of Law were enthusiastic, energetic, and challenging at every step of the way. Shana and Kelsi were truly my partners in this venture, and I am especially grateful to them for their remarkable intelligence, diligence, and encouragement.

Over the past two years, I had the opportunity to test and refine my ideas in a series of workshops, conferences, and lectures. This is an essential part of the academic process, and I was fortunate to be able to explore the implications of this subject in many venues, including the 2004 William J. Brennan Jr. Lecture at the University of California at Berkeley and at the University of Virginia; New York University's 2003 Jacob K. Javits Distinguished-Scholar-in-Residence Lecture; New York University's 2002 Lewis Rudin Lecture; the 2002 Keynote Address for the Supreme Court Historical Society; the University of Chicago's "Chicago's Best Ideas" Lecture Series (2003 and 2004); faculty workshops at Harvard, the University of Chicago, New York University, and the New York School of Law; conferences at the University of Missouri, the Italian Constitution Society, and

Cardozo Law School; and lectures to the Chicago Council of Lawyers and the American Constitution Society.

Several excerpts from this work have already seen the light of day. These include *Judge Learned Hand and the Espionage Act of 1917: A Mystery Unraveled*, 70 University of Chicago Law Review 335 (2003); *The Origins of the Bad Tendency Test: Free Speech in War Time*, 2002 Supreme Court Review 411; *Abraham Lincoln's First Amendment*, 73 New York University Law Review 1 (2003); *Civil Liberties in Wartime*, 28 Journal of the Supreme Court Historical Society 215 (2003); and *Free Speech in World War II: "When Are You Going to Indict the Seditionists?"* 2 International Journal of Constitutional Law 334 (2004).

I received generous research support from the University of Chicago Law School's Harry Kalven Jr. Faculty Research Fund and Russell Baker Scholars Fund and New York University Law School's Faculty Research Fund, Lewis Rudin Faculty Fund, and Jacob K. Javits Distinguished-Scholar-in-Residence Fund.

Throughout this process, I gained invaluable insight from many friends and colleagues who were most generous with their criticisms. I am particularly grateful to Albert Alschuler, Kathy Anderson, Rachel Barkow, Emily Buss, Jonathan Cole, Mary Anne Case, Jim Chandler, David Currie, Norman Dorsen, Clayton Gillette, Ingrid Gould, Bernard Harcourt, Glen Hartley, Mary Harvey, Jill Hasday, Stephen Holmes, Dennis Hutchinson, Lillian Kraemer, Larry Kramer, Daryl Levinson, Saul Levmore, Deborah Malamud, Geoffrey Miller, Bill Nelson, Richard Pildes, Eric Posner, Richard Posner, Stephen Schulhofer, Julie Stone, Mollie Stone, David Strauss, Cass Sunstein, Art Sussman, Pat Swanson, Adrian Vermeule, Christina Wells, and Iris Marion Young.

I also benefited enormously from the constant support and advice of Lynn Chu, a brilliant and creative literary agent; Bob Weil, whose wisdom and editorial comments improved this work immeasurably; and Ruth Mandel, who was always a pleasure in our common quest for the perfect illustrations. Many others at Norton contributed in important ways to this project. In particular, I am grateful to Brendan Curry, Nancy Palmquist, Erin Sinesky, Anna Oler, and Otto Sonntag.

Most of all, though, I am grateful to Nancy, my most astute reader, my most fervent supporter, and my very best friend. As with so much that is fine in my life, you made this possible.

Perilous Times

WAR FEVER

"Uncle Sam" at War

"**M**Y COUNTRY, right or wrong!"
"Love it or leave it!"
"Better Dead than Red!"

War excites great passions. Thousands, perhaps millions, of lives are at risk. The nation itself may be at peril. If ever there is a time to pull out all the stops, it is surely in wartime. In war, the government may conscript soldiers, commandeer property, control prices, ration food, raise taxes, and freeze wages. May it also limit the freedom of speech?

It is often said that dissent in wartime is disloyal. This claim puzzles civil libertarians, who see a clear distinction. In their view, dissent in wartime can be the highest form of patriotism. Whether, when, for how long, and on what terms to fight a war are among the most profound decisions a nation encounters. A democratic society must debate these issues throughout the conflict. Dissent that questions the conduct and morality of a war is, on this view, the very essence of responsible and courageous citizenship.

At the same time, however, dissent can readily be cast as disloyal. A critic who argues that troops are poorly trained or that the war is unjust may make a significant contribution to public discourse. But he also gives "aid and comfort" to the enemy. The enemy is more likely to fight fiercely if it is confident and believes its adversary divided and uncertain. Public disagreement during a war can strengthen the enemy's resolve.

War generates a powerful mass psychology. Emotions run high. Spies, saboteurs, and terrorists lurk around every corner. *Our* way of life is imperiled. Anything that increases the danger to *our* troops—*our* sons and daughters—is feared and despised. The thought that a loved one or friend has put life and limb at risk for an unworthy cause is intolerable. We are just; our enemy is cruel, immoral, inhuman. Loyalty is the order of the day.

In such an atmosphere, the line between dissent and disloyalty is elusive, and often ignored. As we shall see, the United States has a long and unfortunate history of overreacting to the perceived dangers of wartime. Time and again, Americans have allowed fear and fury to get the better of them. Time and again, Americans have suppressed dissent, imprisoned and deported dissenters, and then—later—regretted their actions. This book is first and foremost about why this happens and how we can break this pattern as we look to the future.

"CONGRESS SHALL MAKE NO LAW . . ."

THE PARADIGM violation of the First Amendment is a law forbidding citizens to criticize their government's policies. In the entire history of the United States, the national government has never attempted to punish opposition to government policies, *except* in time of war. Of course, the government routinely regulates speech in many ways—it restricts obscenity, prohibits false advertising, limits the size of billboards, and regulates campaign contributions. But it prohibits political dissent *only* in wartime. In peacetime, in times of relative tranquillity, which (by my count) make up roughly 80 percent of our history, the United States does not punish individuals for challenging government policies. This is a little-noted, but critical, fact. It reveals a great deal about our constitutional traditions and makes clear that, in order to understand free speech, we must understand free speech in wartime.

IMAGINE FOR A MOMENT that you are a U.S. senator and the nation has been drawn ineluctably into a war. The president proposes a new law forbidding any person "to criticize the conduct of the war or to advocate the cause of the enemy." This legislation, he says, is essential to the national security. Would you support the president? What questions would you ask?

Because much of this inquiry turns on the First Amendment, we need to clear away some of the constitutional underbrush. "Congress shall make no law

. . . abridging the freedom of speech, or of the press."* Note that the First Amendment limits only "Congress." It would thus appear that the president of the United States, the state of California, the city of Philadelphia, and General Motors are free to abridge "the freedom of speech" to their hearts' content. Only Congress is constrained.

But this still covers a lot of ground. Because war is a national event, government regulation of "free speech in wartime" turns largely on laws made by Congress. In fact, however, the First Amendment is not so limited. Through a complex process of constitutional amendment and judicial interpretation, the Constitution has come to mean that "*Government* shall make no law abridging the freedom of speech, or of the press"—that is, the First Amendment constrains not only Congress but also the president, the state of Montana, the city of Pittsburgh, the University of Nebraska, and police officers in Phoenix.†

On the other hand, like other provisions of the Constitution, the First Amendment restricts *only* the government. It does not restrict private individuals or institutions. If Columbia University, a private institution, fires a teacher for being a member of the Socialist Party, its action does not violate the First Amendment. If a mob tars and feathers a speaker for praising the enemy, it does not violate the Constitution. Private individuals and institutions have no legal capacity to violate the First Amendment.

WHEN WE TURN AGAIN to the text of the First Amendment, it may seem self-evident that the proposed law is unconstitutional. According to the dictionary, "abridge" means to contract, abbreviate, or reduce. A law forbidding any person to "advocate the cause of the enemy" would seem clearly to "abridge" the freedom of speech.

But it is not so simple. The dictionary does not dictate the meaning of the Constitution. Suppose an intruder breaks into your home in the middle of the night.

---

* The full text reads, "Congress shall make no law respecting an establishment of religion, or prohibiting the free exercise thereof; or abridging the freedom of speech, or of the press; or the right of the people peaceably to assemble, and to petition the Government for a redress of grievances."

† The Supreme Court has never construed the word "Congress" as limiting the First Amendment only to the legislative branch. Moreover, as early as 1925 the Court reasoned that the First Amendment restricts the states as well as the federal government by virtue of the Fourteenth Amendment, which provides, "No State shall make or enforce any law which shall abridge the privileges or immunities of citizens of the United States; nor shall any State deprive any person of life, liberty, or property, without due process of law. . . ." See *Gitlow v. New York*, 268 US 652 (1925).

Using a bullhorn, she demands that you oppose the proposed law. Can she be punished? Would such punishment "abridge" her freedom of speech? No one, I suppose, would make such a claim. This suggests that "the freedom of speech" must be defined. Yes, the government may not abridge "the freedom of speech." But what *is* "the freedom of speech" that may not be abridged? Presumably, it does not include the right of a speaker to trespass upon private property at 3:00 A.M. with a loudspeaker in order to shatter the sleep of a senator.

In deciding whether any particular law abridges the First Amendment, we need to know *why* the Constitution protects the "freedom of speech," but not the "freedom to eat," the "freedom to jog," or the "freedom to manufacture widgets." Several theories have been advanced to explain the constitutional protection of free expression.

Some judges and scholars reason that the First Amendment is an essential corollary of self-governance. In a pure monarchy, the king decides. He need not consult his subjects, and they need not be well informed about income redistribution, environmental policy, or the wisdom of tax cuts. Robust discussion of such matters may be of interest to some of the king's subjects, but it is not a constitutional necessity.

In a self-governing society, however, the citizens themselves must decide whether to support or oppose particular policies and candidates. "Should I vote for or against the candidate who favors gun control, gay marriage, and the war in Iraq?" To meet the responsibilities of democracy, individuals must have access to a broad spectrum of opinions, ideas, and information. For the government to censor public debate because *it* thinks a particular speaker unwise or ill informed would usurp the authority of citizens to make their own judgments about such matters and thus undermine the very essence of self-government. As the philosopher Alexander Meiklejohn put the point, the First Amendment requires "that no suggestion of policy shall be denied a hearing because it is on one side of the issue rather than another."[1]

A related, but slightly different, theory regards the constitutional protection of free speech as indispensable to the maintenance of a political and intellectual environment in which individuals can develop the capacity to deal with sharp differences of opinion, perspective, and understanding. By allowing for ambiguity and conflict in the public sphere, the First Amendment promotes the emergence of character traits that are essential to a well-functioning democracy, including tolerance, skepticism, personal responsibility, curiosity, distrust of authority, and independence of mind.[2]

The First Amendment may also help check the danger that public officials will attempt to manipulate public discourse in order to preserve their authority. This is one of the greatest threats to democracy. Ordinarily, constitutional law presumes that government officials will fulfill their responsibilities in good faith and that their actions are constitutionally permissible. Without such a presumption, government would come to a standstill.

In some circumstances, however, this presumption may be unwarranted. Because public officials are only human, they may sometimes be tempted (consciously or unconsciously) to suppress criticism in order to promote their policies and perpetuate their power. When this danger exists, there is good reason to suspend the usual presumption of constitutionality and insist upon a *compelling* justification for the government's action. The best example is when public officials attempt to punish speech that challenges them or their policies. The First Amendment guards against such abuse by declaring such laws presumptively *unconstitutional*.[3]

The guarantee of free expression may also help preserve a constructive balance between stability and change. Government suppression of dissenting and nonconforming views substitutes "force for reason." It produces a sense of alienation on the part of those who are censored and casts doubt on the legitimacy of government action. Because people are more likely to accept adverse decisions if they feel they have had a fair hearing, the constitutional protection of free speech promotes the long-term cohesiveness of society.[4]

The First Amendment also furthers the day-to-day "search for truth." In the words of Justice Oliver Wendell Holmes, "the best test of truth is the power of the thought to get itself accepted in the competition of the market."[5] The core idea here is that in *all* areas of decision making—including not only whether to support a particular political candidate but also whether to have children, enlist in the army, contribute to one's church, buy a Saab, or go to law school—the "best" way for individuals to reach the best decisions for themselves is for them to consider all competing ideas, opinions, and perspectives, without government interference. This is, in effect, an argument against government paternalism in the realm of ideas and information. Of course, the constitutional protection of free speech does not *ensure* that individuals will always, or even usually, make the "right" decisions. But this theory presumes that it is better for each of us to decide these things for ourselves than for government to decide them for us.[*]

Finally, the First Amendment protects individual self-fulfillment. As human beings, we have an inherent need to speak our mind; express our emotions, passions, fears, and desires; create music, art, dance, and fiction; and share ideas and experiences with others. On this view, the freedom of speech, like the freedom of

---

[*] This does not mean that government cannot make *acts* unlawful. For example, the government may make it a crime for a draftee to refuse induction into the army. A more difficult question is whether the First Amendment protects an individual who makes a speech *encouraging* draftees to refuse induction. Can there be a constitutional right to encourage others to act unlawfully? As we shall see, this is a central question of First Amendment theory.

religion, protects our integrity as individuals and helps ensure that our lives are not "meager and slavish."[6]

These reasons for according constitutional protection to free speech are not always consistent with one another. Sometimes they point in different directions. Abstract art, for example, may facilitate individual self-fulfillment, but perhaps not self-governance. A commercial advertisement for mouthwash may further the "marketplace of ideas," but perhaps not the goal of democratic "character building." Moreover, each of these rationales is legitimately open to question. In very general terms, however, they reflect the primary values the First Amendment is thought to serve.

IDENTIFYING THESE VALUES may clarify why we should be uneasy about laws that restrict the freedom of speech. But it does not tell us *which* laws are unconstitutional. To get at that question, we should consider some of the reasons why government might want to limit free expression, focusing particularly on free speech in wartime:

- A newspaper may disclose information that is useful to the enemy, such as invasion plans or the vulnerabilities of the navy.
- Moral condemnation of the war may lead people to refuse induction into the army or even to blow up military installations.
- Antiwar dissent may strengthen the enemy's resolve and make it more difficult for the nation to achieve victory or negotiate a just peace.
- Persistent criticism of the nation's leaders in wartime may demoralize citizens and weaken their will to fight.
- Dissent may persuade people to vote for political candidates who will end the war, even though those in authority are certain this is contrary to the national interest.
- Critics may disseminate *false* information, such as inflated casualty counts, in an effort to mislead the public and turn people against the war.

For which of these reasons, if any, would you, as a U.S. senator, support the government's suppression of dissent? Once a nation commits itself to war and puts its young men and women in harm's way, should it be able to insist on unity in order to minimize the number of casualties and maximize the prospects for success? What should we make of the ancient maxim *Inter arma silent leges*, "In time of war the laws are silent"? Do you agree with Chief Justice William Rehnquist that in time of war the balance between freedom and order must shift "in favor of order"?[7]

EVEN AT THIS POINT, we can identify a few key principles that have shaped the Supreme Court's understanding of the First Amendment. Only with a sense of these background principles can we determine how much, if at all, they should "shift" in wartime. Three such principles are critical for our purposes:

No government paternalism in the realm of political discourse. The government may not suppress dissent merely because *it* thinks that a speaker's opinions or values are wrong, misguided, or improper. Similarly, it may not censor dissent because it fears it might persuade citizens to vote for antiwar candidates. The explanation is simple: under the First Amendment, it is for citizens to make such decisions, after hearing all the arguments. It is not for government to prevent citizens from contemplating their legal and political options by keeping them in the dark and shutting down public debate.

Punish the actor, not the speaker. When dissent increases the risk that listeners or readers will commit unlawful acts, the government *ordinarily* must direct its punishment at those who act unlawfully, rather than at those who dissent. For example, the government ordinarily may not prohibit speech condemning a war on the plea that such speech might inadvertently "cause" others who turn against the war to refuse induction or blow up induction centers. This is less obvious than the "no paternalism" principle. Not surprisingly, the Supreme Court did not warm to this principle quickly or easily.

As we will see, in debating the circumstances in which government may punish speakers for "causing" others to commit criminal acts, judges, legislators, and presidents have wrestled with such elusive concepts as whether the speaker *expressly advocated* unlawful conduct, whether she *specifically intended* to instigate unlawful acts, whether she *should have known* that her speech might trigger criminal acts, and whether her speech created a *"clear and present danger"* that such acts would follow.

This principle lies at the very core of the struggle to define the limits of free speech in wartime. Although many considerations support this principle, it is worth noting two at the outset of our inquiry. First, free speech is fragile. The direct benefit to any particular person of expressing a dissenting view is relatively slight. Unless she is a person of unusual power and influence, her individual voice is unlikely to have much immediate impact on public opinion or government policy. But the cost to her of being imprisoned for her speech is potentially staggering. Thus, she is easily "chilled" in her willingness to sign a petition, march in a rally, or speak on a soapbox if doing so risks criminal prosecution.

Moreover, this effect is multiplied across society. Even though many citizens may share the same dissenting point of view, they may all *individually* be "chilled" in their willingness to express their opinion if they fear punishment for doing so. Thus, without a robust protection for free speech, we may wind up with an impoverished public debate. Recognizing the fragility of free speech helps explain the "punish the actor, not the speaker" principle. Unless individuals are secure in their knowledge that they will not be punished for their dissent, even though others might act unlawfully, they may forgo their rights, to the detriment of democracy.

Second, the problem of pretext plays an important role in explaining this principle. As we have already noted, public officials are sometimes tempted to suppress speech that criticizes them or threatens their power. Because the "no paternalism" principle is well established, public officials will rarely argue that dissent should be prohibited merely because it criticizes them or their policies. But to achieve the same effect, they can argue that dissent is "dangerous" to the nation because it will trigger disorder and even violence. They might argue, for example, that criticism of the war must be suppressed, not because the ideas are "wrong," but because it will stir people to refuse induction, block troop trains, or bomb military installations. The second principle ("punish the actor, not the speaker") is directed, in part, at this concern.

Low-value speech. The "punish the actor, not the speaker" principle is inapplicable to certain categories of expression that the Supreme Court has held to have only "low" First Amendment value. As the Court explained in 1942,[8]

> There are certain well defined and narrowly limited classes of speech, [such as the obscene and the libelous, that] are no essential part of any exposition of ideas and are of such slight social value as a step to truth that any benefit that may be derived from them is clearly outweighed by the social interest in order and morality.

For these categories of "low" value expression, such as obscenity, false statements of fact, commercial advertising, and threats, the Court has upheld expansive forms of government regulation. (Consider, from this perspective, the relevance of *falsity* in the earlier example concerning inflated casualty counts.) As we will see, a critical question is whether express advocacy of unlawful conduct for political purposes falls within the realm of "low" value speech under the First Amendment.

These three principles will most directly inform our inquiry. They are not exhaustive; they do not deal with a host of First Amendment issues. But they do frame the central questions in defining the appropriate limits of free speech in wartime.

THE LESSONS OF HISTORY

THE UNITED STATES has attempted to punish individuals for criticizing government officials or policies only during six episodes in our history. At the end of the eighteenth century, when the United States was on the verge of war with France, Congress enacted the Sedition Act of 1798, which made it a crime for any person to publish or utter any disloyal statement against the government of the United States, the Congress, or the president, with the intent to bring them into contempt or disrepute.

Sixty years later, during the Civil War, President Lincoln suspended the writ of habeas corpus.* Subsumed within that controversy were arrests for speech critical of the administration, including the infamous conviction by military tribunal of Clement Vallandigham, a national leader of the Copperheads, who was imprisoned and then exiled because he publicly condemned the president, the Emancipation Proclamation, the draft, and the war.

During World War I, the federal government prosecuted some two thousand individuals for their opposition to the war and the draft. Those convicted under the Espionage Act of 1917 and the Sedition Act of 1918 were routinely sentenced to terms ranging from ten to twenty years in prison. Under the Wilson administration, any genuine debate about the merits of the war was effectively squelched. Even Eugene Debs, who received a million votes as the Socialist Party candidate for the presidency in 1912, was sentenced to ten years in prison for publicly denouncing the war and conscription.

Twenty-five years later, during World War II, the central civil liberties issue was the internment of 120,000 individuals of Japanese descent. But this was not the only such issue to arise during the "Good War." To the contrary, as we will see, at the prodding of Franklin Roosevelt, the federal government also attempted to stifle criticism by prosecuting, denaturalizing, or deporting those who questioned the war, especially American fascists.

The Cold War, which followed hard on the heels of World War II, marked perhaps the most repressive period in American history. In an aggressive effort to uncover subversion, the federal government initiated abusive loyalty programs,

---

* A petition for a writ of habeas corpus is a request by an individual asking a judge to determine the legality of his detention by the government. Suspending the writ of habeas corpus prohibits judges from reviewing the legality of an individual's detention or ordering his release if the detention is unlawful.

legislative investigations, and criminal prosecutions of the leaders and members of the Communist Party of the United States. It was an era scarred by the excesses of the House Un-American Activities Committee and the rampage of Senator Joseph McCarthy.

In the 1960s and 1970s, during the Vietnam War, there were massive antiwar demonstrations, widespread acts of civil disobedience, and instances of serious political violence. The FBI carried out a far-reaching program to "expose, disrupt and otherwise neutralize" dissident political activities, the federal government sought to enjoin the *New York Times* and the *Washington Post* from publishing the "Pentagon Papers," and antiwar protesters were prosecuted for expressing contempt for the American flag and burning draft cards. It was a time fraught with tension and marked by street protests, student strikes, teach-ins, violence at the 1968 Democratic National Convention, and the shooting of students at Kent State University.

In each of these episodes, the nation faced extraordinary pressures—and temptations—to suppress dissent. In some of these eras, national leaders cynically exploited public fears for partisan political gain; in some, they fomented public hysteria in an effort to unite the nation in common cause; and in others, they simply caved in to public demands for the repression of "disloyal" individuals. Although each of these episodes presented a unique challenge, in each the United States went too far in sacrificing civil liberties—particularly the freedom of speech.*

MOST BROADLY, this book is about Americans struggling to fulfill the daunting responsibilities of self-governance in the most perilous of times. More specifically, it is about some of the most interesting characters in American history. It is about presidents who have faced the challenge of balancing liberty and security in times of great national crisis. It is about John Adams, Thomas Jefferson, Abraham Lincoln, Woodrow Wilson, Franklin Roosevelt, Harry Truman, Lyndon Johnson, Richard Nixon, and George W. Bush.

It is also about those justices of the Supreme Court who have struggled to define an appropriate role for the judiciary in time of war. It is about Samuel Chase, who was almost impeached for his conduct on the bench in enforcing the

---

* Although this work focuses on freedom of speech rather than on civil liberties more generally, the central lessons apply across the board. Indeed, several chapters address broader civil liberties questions, such as the suspensions of habeas corpus during the Civil War and the internment of Japanese Americans during World War II.

Sedition Act of 1798, and Roger Taney, whose judicial order in 1861 President Lincoln flagrantly ignored. It is about Oliver Wendell Holmes and Louis Brandeis, who first breathed life into the First Amendment after World War I, and Felix Frankfurter, Robert Jackson, Hugo Black, and Earl Warren, who wrestled with the limits of free speech for Nazis and Communists.

It is also about those who have dissented in times of high drama. It is about Matthew Lyon, the first man prosecuted under the Sedition Act of 1798; Emma Goldman and Mollie Steimer, who fiercely opposed American intervention in World War I; William Dudley Pelley, the self-proclaimed "Hitler of America" during World War II; Eugene Dennis, the leader of the Communist Party at the height of the Cold War; Lillian Hellman and Dalton Trumbo, who suffered under the blacklist; David Paul O'Brien, who burned a draft card; and Daniel Ellsberg, who purloined the Pentagon Papers. Some of these men and women were individuals of great moral courage and integrity; some were fools, or worse.

This book is about heroes and villains (as to which is which, we may not always agree), and many people in between. Most fundamentally, though, this book is about Americans, for as we shall see it is "the people themselves," and not only our presidents, judges, and congressmen, who must preserve the spirit of liberty in times of crisis.[9]

THE "HALF WAR"
WITH FRANCE

The First First Amendment

Republicans Burning John Jay in Effigy

*T*HE YEARS BETWEEN 1789 and 1801 marked a critical period in American history. In an atmosphere of fear, suspicion, and intrigue, the nation's new Constitution was put to a test of its very survival. Bitter internal conflicts buffeted the young nation, even as it found itself dangerously embroiled in a fierce struggle between the French Republic and imperial Britain.[1]

It was in this political cauldron that the United States first faced the challenge of reconciling the First Amendment with the felt necessities of wartime. The ensuing conflict led Congress to enact the Alien and Sedition Acts of 1798, revealed sharp divisions in the nation's nascent understanding of "the freedom of speech," and yielded fundamental lessons that have shaped our national values to this day.

We tend to romanticize the "founding fathers," but they were subject to petty jealousies, partisan squabbling, and deep distrust, especially of one another. Moreover, they were unsure of the constitutional system they had put in place. It was, after all, an experiment. As they embarked upon an adventure in self-governance, they had no precedents to guide them. When the issue was war and peace, they disagreed bitterly over how much to risk on an untested idea.

As we have seen, one goal of the First Amendment is to foster the development of certain values and character traits among citizens, values and traits that are essential to a well-functioning self-governing society—tolerance, skepticism, independence of mind, critical judgment, distrust of authority. Today, perhaps more than we appreciate, we have integrated many of these values into our national character and gained confidence in our constitutional system. But in America's first decade, at a time when almost all nations were run by monarchies, the First Amendment had not yet had time to do its work. For the founding generation, the First Amendment was unexplored terrain.

In the contest over the Sedition Act of 1798, the nation confronted a profound test of its commitment to "the freedom of speech." The themes that emerged in this struggle have returned in different forms throughout our history. Although the context changes from 1798 to 1861 to 1917 to 2004, the most fundamental questions recur. Are those who dissent in time of war "disloyal"? Do the demands of war justify the suppression of dissent? How do we distinguish the "real" necessities of war from the partisan exploitation of a crisis? Can we rely upon judges and jurors to preserve civil liberties in the highly charged atmosphere of wartime?

As the founding generation worked its way through these issues, it began to articulate and test the fundamental tenets of the freedom of speech.

THE LYON OF VERMONT

IN 1764, FIFTEEN-YEAR-OLD Matthew Lyon sailed from Ireland in a disease-ridden ship to start life anew as an indentured servant in the colony of Connecticut. An untutored and impertinent youth, Lyon's indenture ended abruptly after he threw a mallet at the head of his master. Over the next several years, Lyon married and, with his young wife, made the arduous journey through western Massachusetts to the wilderness of the Green Mountains. With the approaching Revolution, he threw in his lot with Ethan Allen's Green Mountain Boys, a citizens' militia founded in 1770 in Bennington, Vermont. In 1775, Lyon fought with this militia in the legendary attack on Fort Ticonderoga, and the following year he was commissioned a second lieutenant in the Continental Army.

Upon his return from the war, Lyon helped draft Vermont's new constitution, the first to abolish property qualifications for voting, and was elected to a series of local political offices. At the same time, he added to his growing prosperity by establishing a sawmill, a tavern, an iron foundry, and a paper mill. He was the first American to use wood pulp in the production of paper, a major advance that could have made him wealthy. But Lyon declined to seek a patent, explaining, "[I]f this discovery should prove advantageous to mankind we shall be glad to bid the world—welcome to it."[2]

Lyon soon became enmeshed in the political divisions that emerged after the Revolution. In Vermont, these divisions erupted in disputes over the property rights of Tories whose land had been confiscated during the Revolution. Vermont's social and economic elite maintained that these confiscations violated the common law and that the former owners could lawfully evict the settlers who had developed the land during the Revolution. Vermont's "self-made" men—newcomers like Matthew Lyon—insisted that the settlers were entitled to compensation for the value they had added to the land by clearing forests, building dams, constructing roads, and defending the land against attack. Never one to mince words, Lyon attacked his "privileged" opponents as "landjockies and overgrown landjobbers."[3]

Lyon put himself forward for election to the first Congress. He was defeated in 1791, 1793, and 1795, but his persistence paid off in 1797, when he finally defeated his Federalist opponents. In these campaigns, Lyon openly challenged the national leader of the Federalist Party, the patrician Secretary of the Treasury Alexander Hamilton, accusing him of "screwing the hard-earnings out of the poor people's pockets" to enable the government to "vie with European Courts in frivolous gaudy appearances." Lyon's adversaries were equally harsh, casting him as a person whose "conscience is too calous for compunction."[4]

Even before his election to Congress, Lyon worked hard to popularize republicanism in Vermont. In 1793, he launched a weekly newspaper, the *Farmers' Library*, to counter the anti-Republican sentiment that flooded Vermont from neighboring states.[5] Lyon saw the fundamental issue of the age as the struggle between republicanism and monarchism. Like other Republicans, he professed a deep faith in the common man and viewed monarchist Britain as a continuing threat to the United States.

COARSE, BOMBASTIC, AND IRISH, Congressman Lyon was a natural target for the more refined Federalists. He was the first, and perhaps the only, former indentured servant ever to serve in Congress.[6] Lyon immediately excited the ire of the Federalists. Following British tradition, the House of Representatives sent a committee each year to call on the president to formally request his attendance at the House's response to his opening address to Congress. Lyon ridiculed this ceremony as pompous, un-American frippery.

The Federalist congressman John Allen of Connecticut snapped back that Lyon's attitude reflected his lowly Irish birth. The Vermont frontiersmen retorted that he had no objection to gentlemen of "high blood" wasting their time with this "boyish piece of business," and cheerfully conceded that he himself could not claim to be "descended from the bastards of Oliver Cromwell" or those who "hanged the witches."[7] Lyon's impertinence infuriated the Federalists. William Cobbett, editor of the Federalist *Porcupine's Gazette*, penned a satire describing "the Vermont Lyon" as "more clamorous" than "the African lion" and more like a "bear" in appearance.[8] Lyon was subjected to a barrage of insults, leading eventually to an ugly incident on the floor of the House. After the Federalist congressman Roger Griswold of Connecticut disparaged Lyon's military record,* a seething Lyon spat in his face.[9] That brought down on Lyon the full wrath of the Federalist Party. Congressman Robert Goodloe Harper condemned Lyon's action as "a personal outrage" and the House appointed a special committee to determine whether Lyon should be expelled for "gross indecency."[10]

After two weeks of highly partisan bickering, the Federalists failed to muster the two-thirds majority necessary for expulsion.[11] Although the Republicans agreed that Lyon's conduct had been unfortunate, they argued that censure rather than expulsion was the appropriate remedy. The Federalists protested that the Republicans had sacrificed principle to the "ambition of party." Lyon became a national sensation, caricatured as "Spitting Matt," the "most pitiful, low-breed blackguard that has ever been heard of in America."[12]

After the House failed to expel Lyon, Congressman Griswold exacted his own vengeance. On the floor of the House, he attacked Lyon with a hickory walking stick, severely beating him about the head and leaving him bruised, with "blood running down his face."[13] The House rejected a motion to expel them both, with Federalists overwhelmingly opposing Griswold's expulsion. James Madison observed that this "affair" had been bad for the nation in "every way," and Congressman Edward Livingston summed up the episode by noting that members of Congress had expressed "their abhorrence of abuse in abusive terms, and their hatred of indecent acts with indecency."[14] It was the temper of the times.

A year later, as the nation armed for war with France, the Federalists enacted the Sedition Act of 1798, perhaps the most grievous assault on free speech in the history of the United States. The act prohibited any person from writing, publishing, or uttering anything of a "false, scandalous and malicious" nature against

---

* When Lyon was a second lieutenant in the Continental Army in 1776, his company revolted under the threat of an Indian attack. Lyon was cashiered. Although he was later reinstated and promoted to captain, this incident haunted his political career. In a reference to this event, *Porcupine's Gazette* ridiculed Lyon in August 1797 for his alleged "cowardice" during the Revolution, and asserted he had been condemned to "wear a wooden sword." Lyon warned that if anyone should insult him in this manner again he would not let it "pass with impunity." (The "wooden sword" image was apparently a denigrating reference to Lyon's Irish heritage and/or a symbol of cowardice.) Griswold triggered the incident in Congress when, in the course of an already unpleasant exchange, he insultingly asked Lyon whether he would be wearing a "wooden sword." *Curious Anecdote*, Porcupine's Gazette 3 (Aug 1, 1797); 7 *Annals of Congress* at 1023 (cited in note 7); id at 1015.

Matthew Lyon and Roger Griswold Battle in Congress

the government of the United States. Lyon opposed the legislation, warning that under this act people would have to "hold their tongues and make toothpicks of their pens."[15] Later that summer, during his campaign for reelection, Lyon wrote a letter to the editor of *Spooner's Vermont Journal* in response to a scathing attack that accused him of being a "corrupt Jacobin."*[16] Lyon's reply fumed that under President Adams "every consideration of the public welfare" was "swallowed up in a continual grasp for power, in an unbounded thirst for ridiculous pomp, foolish adulation, and selfish avarice." For this assertion, Matthew Lyon became the first person indicted under the Sedition Act of 1798.[17]

---

* The term "Jacobin" was derived from the name of a church in Paris where a group of radicals first met during the French Revolution. In the United States at this time "Jacobin" was "a scare word intended to denote the anarchy in France in 1793–1794." Smith, *Freedom's Fetters* at 177 (cited in note 16).

ON WAR FOOTING

NO SINGLE FOREIGN EVENT affected the United States more profoundly in the 1790s than the French Revolution and its social, political, and diplomatic repercussions. After the Revolution of 1789, most Americans hailed the new Republic's commitment to *"liberté, fraternité, égalité."* Over the next several years, however, France exploded with religious conflict, civil war, and economic chaos. With the executions in 1793 of Louis XVI and Marie Antoinette, France spiraled into the "Reign of Terror." The new French government sought to suppress dissent, de-Christianize the nation, and impose a rigid system of economic egalitarianism.

Fearing the spread of revolution, a pro-monarchist coalition, including England, Spain, Austria, the Netherlands, and Prussia, declared war on France. By 1794, however, France had repelled the invaders, and by 1797 it had taken the offensive and seized modern-day Belgium, the Rhineland, and the Italian peninsula. Napoleon's victories made France the dominant military power in Europe. A mighty French army threatened to cross the Channel to England.

The United States, eager to maintain its growing international commerce, strained to preserve a precarious neutrality. President Washington in 1793 proclaimed it the "duty and interest of the United States" to "pursue a conduct friendly and impartial towards the belligerent Powers."[18] By refusing to support either the British or the French, the United States incurred the enmity of both. The British navy seized American ships and impressed American seamen into its service, bringing the United States and England to the brink of war. Desperate to avoid a break with England, Washington sent John Jay to London. In 1794, Jay negotiated a treaty that ensured cordial Anglo-American relations.[19]

The Jay Treaty affronted the French, however, who charged that it betrayed America's long-standing alliance with France. France then launched its own campaign against American shipping and declared that captured American seamen would be treated as pirates. Between June 1796 and June 1797, French corsairs seized 316 ships flying the American colors.

IN THE MEANTIME, sharp political divisions had begun to emerge in the United States.[20] In 1796, in the first contested presidential election, John Adams, the candidate of the Federalist Party, defeated Thomas Jefferson, the leader of the Republican Party, by a scant three electoral votes. Both Federalists and Republicans had reservations about Adams. Alexander Hamilton expressed doubts about

Adams's "character," and James Madison observed that Adams had "made himself obnoxious to many" because of his peculiar "political principles"* and "extravagant self-importance."[21] Adams was persnickety, irascible, and grandiose. As one commentator put it, Adams could "never be said to possess a lovable disposition."[22]

After Adams's election, Uriah Tracy, a Federalist senator from Connecticut, wrote Hamilton that he feared the breakup of the union. Another Federalist leader, Oliver Wolcott, expressed grave misgivings about the new president, depicting him as "a man of great vanity" and "of far less real abilities than he believes he possesses." Wolcott darkly predicted a civil war in which "we shall divide" into Federalists and Republicans. Republicans were equally pessimistic. Former Senator John Taylor warned Thomas Jefferson that secession must be considered an option and that Virginia and North Carolina might have to declare "their separate existence."[23]

Rumors ran rampant in Philadelphia, then the nation's capital. The president was informed of plots to burn the city, and a riot erupted between patriots and a band of men wearing the tricolor of France. Jefferson observed that the capital "was so filled with confusion . . . that it was dangerous going out."[24]

At a special session of Congress shortly after his inauguration, Adams reported that France had treated "us neither as allies nor as friends, nor as a sovereign state." He declared it essential for the United States to "convince France and the world that we are not a degraded people, humiliated under a colonial spirit of fear." Although promising a renewed effort to negotiate, Adams asked Congress to establish a provisional army and to expand the navy to protect American commerce and defend the nation against possible invasion.[25]

The president then sent an American legation consisting of John Marshall, Elbridge Gerry, and Charles Cotesworth Pinckney to Paris to try to settle American differences with France. The French Directory refused to meet with them, and in the notorious XYZ Affair, three agents of Talleyrand, the minister of foreign affairs, demanded a huge bribe for the Directory and a loan to France as conditions of any further negotiations. To this demand, Pinckney replied, "No, no; not a sixpence." Two months later, Talleyrand contemptuously informed the envoys that negotiations were at an end.

When Adams learned of these developments, the most pressing question for

---

* In his *Defence of the Constitution*, written in 1786–87, and *Discourses on Davila*, in 1791, Adams made plain that, in his view, there was much to be said for a hereditary rather than an elective chief of state. In the first session of Congress, he advocated semiregal designations for the president, such as "His Highness." All this made him a "tempting target" for those who accused him of "monarchical leanings." Marcus Cunliffe, *Elections of 1789 and 1792*, in Schlesinger and Israel, eds, 1 *History of American Presidential Elections* at 23–24 (cited in note 19).

him was whether the United States should declare war. From the very outset of the crisis, Vice President Jefferson insisted that war with France would be calamitous. Such a war, he feared, would drive the United States into the arms of England and deliver a deathblow to the forces of republicanism. He believed that if the United States could stand apart from the European conflict, France might defeat England and thus secure republicanism "once and for all in America." At the opposite end of the cabinet, Secretary of State Timothy Pickering favored an immediate declaration of war against France and a military alliance with England.[26]

Adams was in a state of turmoil. In early March 1798, he began drafting a message to Congress arguing that the "accumulation of Injury, outrage and Insult" inflicted upon the United States by France demanded "an immediate Declaration of War." By mid-March, however, his anger had subsided. Having concluded that the United States had little to gain from war with France, and being uncertain whether the American people would support such a war, Adams prepared a more temperate message. But because he had given up all hope of a rapprochement with France, he called for immediate defense measures and urged Congress to show "zeal" in its "defence of the national rights."[*][27]

When the full details of the XYZ correspondence came to light,[†] Americans were outraged at the arrogance of the French.[28] A wave of patriotic fervor swept the nation. Adams placed the United States into a "virtual state of undeclared war."[29] As Congress would do many times in the future in similar circumstances, it gave the president everything he asked for, and more. It ordered additional warships, appropriated funds to fortify the nation's harbors, established the Department of the Navy, expanded the army by adding twelve new regiments of infantry, authorized the navy to attack armed French ships, and abrogated all treaties with France. An aging George Washington was recalled from Mount Vernon to assume command of the nation's military forces. With the approach of war, the man who had won the presidency by only three electoral votes became a national hero. Whenever he appeared in public, he was greeted with huzzas. The nation was on war footing.

---

[*] Jefferson described Adams's address as "insane" and urged Republicans to delay any military action. Letter from Thomas Jefferson to James Madison, Mar 21, 1798, in Ford, ed, 8 *Works of Thomas Jefferson* at 386 (cited in note 23).

[†] The Republicans, distrustful of Adams's report of the developments in France, demanded that he present to Congress the documents on which he based his conclusion that peace could not be attained. When Adams publicly released the dispatches, which disclosed that the American envoys had been treated with contempt by Talleyrand's agents, the tactic backfired on the Republicans and generated enormous support for the President. See Smith, *Freedom's Fetters* at 7 (cited in note 16); Elkins and McKitrick, *The Age of Federalism* at 587–88 (cited in note 26).

John Adams

"A MERE BUGBEAR"?

THE IMPENDING WAR with France was hugely popular among Americans, most of whom rallied to the cause. Bands played, cannon roared, and flags unfurled in patriotic fervor. In this atmosphere, the nation's commitment to civil liberties was quickly rationalized out of existence.

To understand the bitterness of the debate over the Alien and Sedition Acts of 1798, it is necessary to appreciate the emergence of political parties. The framers of the Constitution had not anticipated political parties and had warned sternly against the perils of faction.[30] But party structures began to emerge naturally during Washington's first administration as the consequence of long-standing disagreements between merchants and farmers, creditors and debtors, northerners and southerners.[31]

The Federalists, led by Alexander Hamilton, and the Republicans, steered by Thomas Jefferson and James Madison, differed sharply in their attitudes toward government finance, centralization of authority, and popular government. Federalists distrusted the ignorance, passions, and prejudices of the common man. They feared that democracy could readily lapse into anarchy and believed that a governing elite was necessary to lead the nation. Although the "people" might express their views at the ballot box, their representatives, once elected, had the responsibility to govern.[32]

A central mission of the Federalist Party was to save the nation from the perils of democracy. To Federalists, the paramount end of government was to "protect the rights of property and the tranquility of society."[33] The Federalist Party drew its support largely from the propertied interests—merchants, bankers, shippers, financiers, and large landowners. It was committed to long-term economic growth and a strong central government.

Republicans, by contrast, held an ardent faith in popular government.[34] They feared tyranny more than anarchy, and valued liberty more than security. They advocated a government directly responsive to the will of the people, without the oversight of a ruling class. Consisting largely of artisans, mechanics, and farmers, the Republican Party distrusted the nation's commercial and financial interests and envisioned a decentralized republic that would stand as a symbol to all the world of the triumph of individual liberty.[35]

The division between Federalists and Republicans grew increasingly acrimonious over the crisis in Europe. Republicans saw the French Revolution as an extension of the American promise of liberty, republicanism, and democracy.

Federalists saw it as a menacing harbinger of disorder, licentiousness, and atheism; it was, to them, a clear and present danger to the established order.[36]

Republicans feared the allure of British laws and customs; Federalists feared the contagion of Jacobin values and ideas. Each party feared that the other posed a threat to its vision of America. Republicans feared that Federalists wanted to mimic British conventions and entrench formal class distinctions in the United States; Federalists feared that Republicans sought to plunge the nation into an American reign of terror in which the unthinking masses would seize political power, confiscate private property, and corrupt religion.[37]

The political tension and mutual suspicion soon reached fever pitch.[38] Thomas Jefferson wrote Edward Rutledge, the Republican governor of South Carolina, "[P]assions are too high at present. . . . Men who have been intimate all their lives, cross the street to avoid meeting, and turn their heads another way, lest they should be obliged to touch their hats." Another contemporary observed that by April 1798 the "dominant party scorned . . . even the appearance of moderation toward their opponents. . . . Friendships were dissolved, tradesmen dismissed, and custom withdrawn from the Republican party; the heads of which . . . were recommended to be closely watched, and committees of Federalists were appointed for that purpose." A month later, there were anti-Republican riots in Philadelphia. Benjamin Bache described the situation on May 10, 1798: "The passions of our citizens which have been artfully inflamed by war speeches . . . burst out in . . . tumultuous meetings and riots."[39]

THE ANTAGONISM BETWEEN THE PARTIES came to a head in the rancorous congressional debates in spring 1798 over Adams's proposed defense measures. Federalists were quick to embrace the president's call to strengthen the nation's defense. Republicans were skeptical. Fearing that a large military buildup would make war with France inevitable, increase the authority of the president, and deepen the national debt, they opposed every significant measure put forth by the Federalists. But because the Federalists had working majorities in both houses of Congress, most Federalist proposals were quickly enacted by a (more or less) straight party vote.*[40]

A careful review of these debates reveals important patterns of discourse that

---

* Until March 1798, the Republicans had a majority in the House of Representatives. With the disclosure of the XYZ papers, however, several Republicans simply went home, leaving the Federalists with a working majority.

have been repeated throughout American history in times of real or perceived national crisis.

At the outset of the debate over the president's war policy, Republicans charged that Federalists were exaggerating the danger and that the steps they proposed would precipitate, rather than avoid, a perilous and unnecessary war. Congressman Albert Gallatin of Pennsylvania, the leader of the House Republicans,* derided Federalist fears of a French invasion as "as a mere *bugbear*," and Congressman Richard Brent observed that he was no more apprehensive of a French invasion than he was of being "transported before night into the moon."[41] The implication was that Federalists were cynically inflating the threat to American interests in order to further their partisan ends.

The Federalists were appalled. Congressman Robert Goodloe Harper of South Carolina pronounced it "extremely probable" that France would send its well-trained army against the United States, and warned that the nation must prepare immediately for war. "Long John" Allen of Connecticut roared that once France had settled its score with England, it would surely turn its might against the United States, and that unless the nation prepared immediately for war, he looked "for nothing but bloodshed, slaughter, pillage, and a complete subjection to France."[42]

Although agreeing that the United States had legal and moral grounds to declare war, Republicans insisted that the nation would suffer more if it provoked a full-scale war than if it went on quietly suffering the French depredations of American commerce. The European war was drawing to a close, they argued, and it would not serve American interests to escalate the stakes. Congressman John Nicholas of Virginia maintained that if the United States could just avoid getting embroiled in the conflict, "we might escape it altogether."[43]

Federalists responded that national honor, as well as self-defense, demanded military action. Congressman Allen questioned whether Republicans loved their country,[44] and Congressman Harper accused Republicans of seeking to preserve a peace of "vile submission." War, he said, is not the greatest evil that can befall a nation. A greater evil is to be "subjected to tribute and plunder."[45] Congressman William Edmund charged Republicans with being "so degraded" that they were

---

* Gallatin arrived in the United States from Geneva, Switzerland, in 1780. Because he still had a French accent, he was a ready target for Federalist attack. On one occasion, *Porcupine's Gazette* derided Gallatin with the following story: "When Mr. Gallatin rose from his seat . . . there was an old farmer sitting beside me. . . . 'Ah, ah!' says he, 'what's little Moses in Congress?' I sharply reprimand him for taking one of our representatives for a Jew: but to confess a truth, the Gentleman from Geneva has an accent not unlike that of a wandering Israelite." Quoted in Rosenfeld, *American Aurora* 56 (cited in note 13).

willing to receive whatever "boon we can beg" from the French. He demanded a more "manly course of conduct." [46]

In a pattern that became all too common in later American history, Federalists raised the specter of internal subversion. Congressman Samuel Sitgreaves of Pennsylvania maintained that the government must "destroy the cankerworm that is corroding in the heart of the country," and Harrison Gray Otis of Massachusetts warned that "an army of soldiers would not be so dangerous to the country, as an army of spies and incendiaries scattered through the Continent."[47]

Blurring the line between dissent and treason, Federalists accused Republicans of disloyalty. Congressman Harper charged that Republicans were attempting to prepare "the people for a base surrender of their rights" and were intentionally taking positions that would lead to the "destruction of the country." He asked just what "masters" they served.[48] Congressman Jonathan Dayton of New Jersey was even harsher. In a statement that reveals as much about class divisions as about patriotism, he suggested that Gallatin was not concerned about a French invasion, because he shared the principles of "the furious hordes . . . which threaten this country with subjugation." Gallatin would watch "our dwellings burning" with "the calmness of indifference."[49]

Republicans were outraged. Congressman Nicholas charged that whenever anyone disagreed with the Federalists, he was immediately "branded with treason." Congressman William Giles of Virginia labeled the Federalist attacks "indecent," and Edward Livingston of New York accused the Federalists of spewing "a most uncommon strain of calumny."[50]

Robert Williams of North Carolina complained that the Federalist strategy of character assassination was intended to destroy the "freedom of debate," and Gallatin accused the Federalists of attempting to intimidate their opponents into silence. Anticipating twentieth-century objections to Woodrow Wilson, Joseph McCarthy, and Richard Nixon, Gallatin observed that, in the view of the Federalists, the only way a Republican could prove he was not an agent of France was to support the Federalist proposals. It shocked Gallatin that any member of Congress could suppose it appropriate to attack "the character of another member" in order to coerce him to support a measure he opposed. He declared that his constitutional duty was to follow his own judgment, not to be cowed by threats or calumny. Nicholas asked, "Why are we sent here if we are not freely to exercise our opinions?"[51]

THE FEDERALISTS' TACTIC of accusing their adversaries of conspiring with the French did not begin or end with the congressional debates.

Their newspapers decried the Republican "traitors." The leading Federalist journal, Philadelphia's *Gazette of the United States*, coined the statement "He that is
not for us, is against us." President Adams charged that "the agents of a foreign
nation" have "a party in this country, devoted to their interest." The Republicans,
he said, supported measures that "would sink the glory of our country and pros-
trate her liberties at the feet of France." Such persons were deserving only of "our
contempt and abhorrence."[52] Alexander Hamilton wrote that Republicans had
made "unremitting efforts" to divert the affections of Americans "from their own
to a foreign country."[*53]

In this crisis, the Federalists saw—and seized—the opportunity to strike a critical blow at the Republicans. By discrediting Jefferson and his colleagues as disloyal and treasonable, they attempted to entrench themselves as the nation's
dominant party. By leveraging a moment of high patriotism, they managed to
enact a legislative program designed to cripple, perhaps even destroy, the Republican Party.[†54]

THE ALIEN ACTS: "ALL IS DARKNESS, SILENCE, MYSTERY, AND SUSPICION"

A THEME THAT RECURS throughout the history of war in the
United States is the status of aliens. After all, who is more likely to be "disloyal"
than a noncitizen, a person with no formal allegiance to the nation? With fears
about the French in 1798, the Germans in World War I, the Japanese and Ger-

---

[*] The Federalist fear that France had agents in the United States who were plotting to subvert
the national interest was not an idle one. A critical part of France's armory was diplomatic treachery,
which it had used with great effect to undermine the governments of Holland, Switzerland, and
Venice. Congressman Otis was undoubtedly sincere in warning that, in the fate of those nations, "we
might read our own." Indeed, the dispatches from the American envoys in France related a conversation in which Agent Y had warned the envoys, "[T]he diplomatic skill of France, and the means
she possesses in your country, are sufficient to enable her, with the French Party in America, to
throw the blame which will attend the rupture of the negotiations on the Federalists . . . and you may
assure yourselves this will be done." The "French Party in America" was, of course, the Republicans.
Miller, *Crisis in Freedom* at 7 (cited in note 11); 8 *Annals of Congress* at 1482 (cited in note 36)
(Congressman Allen reading a portion of the dispatches).

[†] Hamilton suggested, for example, that the "spirit of patriotism" that now prevailed could be
used to destroy the Republicans so that "there will shortly be *national unanimity*." Letter from
Alexander Hamilton to Rufus King, June 6, 1798, in Syrett, ed, 21 *Papers of Alexander Hamilton* at
490 (cited in note 23).

mans in World War II, and Muslims in the War on Terrorism, the United States has long wrestled with the question whether noncitizens enjoy constitutional rights.

To Federalists, the greatest *internal* danger facing the nation was the rapidly growing foreign-born population. Between 1790 and 1798, a wave of foreigners entered the United States, especially from France, Ireland, and Germany. Federalists saw these immigrants, many of whom had fled tyrannical governments, as a nest of potential disloyalty and future Republican strength. Federalists like Harrison Gray Otis feared that immigrants would "contaminate the purity . . . of the American character." He was appalled at the prospect that the "turbulent and disorderly of all parts of the world" would come to America to "disturb our tranquility." Rufus King complained that such immigrants "are hardly landed in the United States, before they begin to cavil against the Government." Robert Goodloe Harper stormed that it is "high time we should recover from the mistake . . . of admitting foreigners to citizenship." He argued that "*nothing but birth* should entitle a man to citizenship."[55]

The first Congress had authorized immigrants to obtain citizenship after only two years of residence. Because these new citizens tended to flock to the Republican Party, the Federalists lengthened the requirement to five years in 1795. Then, in the spring of 1798, in an atmosphere of rampant nativism and war fever, the Federalists extended the residence requirement to fourteen years—the longest in American history.[*][56]

At the same time, the Federalists also enacted two alien acts. The Alien Enemies Act provided that, in the case of a *declared* war, citizens or subjects of an enemy nation residing in the United States could be detained, confined, or deported at the direction of the president. Adopted with bipartisan support, this act has remained a permanent part of American wartime policy. By definition, enemy aliens have an allegiance to a nation with which we are at war. It is therefore reasonable, within limits, to fear that enemy aliens may be potential spies and saboteurs.

But the Federalists did not regard the Alien Enemies Act as sufficient to their needs. They also enacted the much more controversial Alien Friends Act as an "emergency" measure that would expire on the final day of President Adams's

---

[*] By denying new immigrants U.S. citizenship for fourteen years, the act did not prevent them from voting, because the qualifications for voting, even in federal elections, are determined by state law. But the extended residence requirement did prevent these individuals from holding federal office, and it also served as a discouragement to immigration. The Naturalization Act was repealed by the Republicans in 1802.

term of office. The act empowered the president to seize, detain, and deport *any* noncitizen he deemed dangerous to the United States.[57] This was so without regard to whether the United States was at war with the individual's native land. Moreover, the noncitizen had no right to a hearing, no right to be informed of the charges against him, and no right to present evidence on his behalf. The act vested the final decision exclusively in the president.*

Republicans attacked the act as a xenophobic betrayal of the nation's most fundamental principles. Congressman Williams observed that whenever governments want "to make inroads upon the liberties of the people" they trump up "an alarm of danger." He objected that no amount of danger could ever justify assigning such an "arbitrary power to the President."[58] Albert Gallatin asserted that "no facts had appeared, with respect to alien friends, which require these arbitrary means to be employed against them," and demanded that, if supporters of the bill possessed such facts, they "lay them before the House." Moreover, even if such a danger existed, it should be addressed by conventional laws, without adopting such an extreme measure. Gallatin warned that if such a law was appropriate for alien friends, it might later be directed at citizens. He defied supporters of the act to point to "a single clause in the Constitution which . . . would not equally justify a similar measure against citizens of the United States." Although acknowledging that the rights of aliens may in some respects be limited, Gallatin noted that the Constitution did not limit only to citizens the right to trial by jury, the writ of habeas corpus, or the right to due process of law.[59]

Congressman Livingston warned that as little as "a careless word, perhaps misrepresented, or never spoken, may be sufficient" to trigger the act; "no innocence can protect" against the dangers of false accusation; surrounded by spies and informers, "the unfortunate stranger" will never know "of the accusation, or of the judgment, until the moment it is put in execution." With "no indictment; no jury; no trial; no public procedure; no statement of the accusation; no examination of the witnesses in its support; no counsel for defence; all is darkness, silence, mystery, and suspicion."[60]

The Federalists were unfazed. Congressman Otis replied that the act was necessary because "the times are full of danger, and it would be the height of madness not to take every precaution in our power." Congressman Harper accused Republicans of objecting to the act because "it puts a hook into the nose

---

* The First Amendment implications of such legislation are complex. Although the Alien Friends Act was not directed *expressly* at speech, judgments about a person's "dangerousness" are often predicated upon his expression, beliefs, and associations. The act therefore had inescapable implications for the free speech of noncitizens.

of persons who are leagued with the enemies of this country."[61] To the Republican charge that the Alien Friends Act violated the Constitution, Congressmen Gordon and Otis replied that the Constitution gave no rights to aliens. As Otis put the point, aliens "cannot complain of any breach of our Constitution."[62]

This infuriated the Republicans. James Madison described the act as a "monster," while Thomas Jefferson labeled it "detestable." Congressman Livingston fumed that "neither common law, common justice, nor the practice of any civilized nation, will permit this distinction." Indeed, he argued, the Constitution makes no distinction "between citizen and alien." "All are entitled to the same equal distribution of justice, to the same humane provision to protect their innocence; all are liable to the same punishment that awaits their guilt." "We never," he observed, inquire whether a person "is a citizen, before we give him a public trial by jury."

Livingston declared that the danger of the Federalists' thinking would not "stop here," for the "same arguments" of "necessity" they advanced to justify denying these rights to aliens could also be invoked to deny these rights to citizens. He warned that "either in this, or some other shape, this will be attempted."*[63] Livingston cautioned that the people of the United States "will resist this tyrannic system." Indeed, he added, they "ought not to acquiesce," for if "we exceed our powers, we become tyrants, and our acts have no effect." He predicted that the act would lead to "tumults, violations, and a recurrence to first revolutionary principles."[64]

To the Federalists, this was nothing less than treason. Congressman Christopher Champlin of Rhode Island charged Livingston "with a derangement of intellect," and Congressman John Kittera accused him of having called "upon the people to resist this law." Having never "heard a doctrine more fraught with heresy," he called for the immediate passage of a "strong sedition bill." Congressman Otis declared that if Livingston "insisted upon evidence of seditious dispositions in our country," he need look only "to his own speech." Exclaiming that he "could hardly believe" his ears, Otis declared that Livingston was himself ready to "join in an insurrection." Such, he said, is "evidence of the contagion of the French mania." He concluded that "when a mind like that of the gentleman is so easily infected, no better evidence need be required of the necessity of purifying the country from the sources of pollution."[65]

---

* And, indeed, during the Civil War (with Lincoln's suspensions of the writ of habeas corpus), World War II (with Roosevelt's incarceration of eighty thousand Japanese Americans), and the War on Terrorism (with Bush's indefinite detentions without judicial review of American citizens accused of being "enemy combatants"), this came to pass.

THE ALIEN FRIENDS ACT was indeed a "monster." To put the most vulnerable members of society at the mercy of presidential fiat, with no right to due process, to counsel, or independent judicial review, was a betrayal of the spirit, if not the letter, of the Constitution. The government could have achieved its *legitimate* goals in dealing with aliens without stripping them of fundamental procedural protections. The decision to deny noncitizens those protections was petty and intolerant. Like the attack on aliens during the post–World War I Red Scare, the internment of eighty thousand Japanese Americans during World War II, and the secret detention of hundreds, perhaps thousands, of noncitizens during the "War on Terrorism," the Alien Friends Act did not do the nation proud.

Although no alien was ever deported under the act, the very existence of the act had a corrosive effect. Apprehensive French immigrants fled the country, and the flow of immigrants into the United States trickled to a halt. Those French and Irish immigrants who remained in the United States went out of their way not to attract attention. Médéric Louis Elis Moreau de St. Méry, a French scholar and former member of the French assembly, who ran a bookstore in Philadelphia, captured the spirit of the times when he observed that "everybody was suspicious of everybody else: everywhere one saw murderous glances."[*][66]

THE SEDITION ACT OF 1798: "FRAUGHT WITH THE MOST SERIOUS MISCHIEFS"

TO UNDERSTAND THE SEDITION ACT of 1798, it is essential to appreciate the Federalist view of "the freedom of speech." In short, the Federalists had little faith in free and open debate. As Congressman James A. Bayard observed, confidence that truth prevails over falsehood is "a fine moral sentiment,

---

[*] The primary reason for the underenforcement of the Alien Friends Act was President Adams's decision to accord the act a less expansive interpretation than the extreme Federalists demanded. Indeed, over the objections of Secretary of State Pickering, Adams maintained that the broad powers bestowed by the act ought to receive a "strict construction." On the other hand, Adams was willing to enforce the act against individuals he considered dangerous, and he signed blank warrants for the arrests of several aliens under the act, none of whom was ever apprehended. Letter from John Adams to Timothy Pickering, Oct 16, 1798, in Charles Francis Adams, ed, 8 *The Works of John Adams* 607 (Little, Brown 1853).

but our limited knowledge of events [does not] verify it." Federalists believed that the common man was easily manipulated and misled. They feared that even one Jacobin could "alarm a whole country with ridiculous fears of government." The Federalist *Philadelphia Gazette* warned that if "the alarm is caught by the weak," it will soon be "spread by the foolish" like a "contagious disease."[*][67]

After witnessing the violent aftereffects of the French Revolution, Federalists had no doubt of both the power and the danger of public opinion. Congressman John Allen recounted that "at the commencement of the Revolution in France, those loud and enthusiastic advocates for liberty and equality took special care to occupy and command all the presses." The Jacobins understood that the press was especially potent in holding sway over "the poor, the ignorant, the passionate, and the vicious." "Over all these classes," Allen noted, "the freedom of the press shed its baneful effects," and "the virtuous, the pacific, and the rich, were their victims."[68]

Judge Alexander Addison warned his Federalist colleagues that "speech, writing and printing are the great directors of public opinion, and public opinion is the great director of human action." "Give to any set of men the command of the press," and you "give them the command of the country." It was thus essential for the Federalists to control the Republican press to ensure that "the high priests of Jacobinism" did not lead the people astray.[69]

To the Federalists, these dangers were not theoretical. They saw the Republican press as dishonest, abusive, and utterly irresponsible. As early as 1796, Abigail Adams, who rarely failed to act as her husband's eyes and ears, condemned Republican newspapers as "the offspring of faction and nursed by sedition." Federalists characterized Republican newspapers as pestilent compilers of slander, calumny, and falsehood. Their entire mission, the Federalists charged, was to deceive the public. The *Albany Centinel* accused Republicans of propagating nothing but "lies and liars, as a hot day breeds maggots or musketoes."[70]

Alexander Hamilton took it to be a maxim of the Jacobins that "no character, however upright, is a match for constantly reiterated attacks, however false." "The public mind," he explained, "fatigued" by the struggle to resist "the calumnies which eternally assail it," eventually embraces "the opinion that a person so often accused cannot be entirely innocent."[71] Federalists worried that constant attacks on the reputations of public officials would drive "our wisest and best

---

[*] Indeed, The Federalists denied there were two sides to the questions that divided them and the Republicans. As Judge Alexander Addison observed, "truth has but one side, and listening to error and falsehood is indeed a strange way to discover truth." Miller, *Crisis in Freedom* at 79 (cited in note 11).

public officers . . . from their stations" and that their successors would be obscure and venal men "without virtue or talents." President Adams complained that the Republican press went to "all lengths of profligacy, falsehood and malignity in defaming our government," and demanded that the "misrepresentations which have misled so many citizens . . . must be discountenanced by authority."[72]

There was some merit to these concerns. The most prominent of the Republican newspapers, the *Aurora*, was edited by Benjamin Franklin Bache of Philadelphia. The grandson of Ben Franklin, Bache, who had been raised by his grandfather in Paris, was well educated, temperamental, and self-righteous. At a time of scurrilous journalism, Bache was a master of the art. He once described President Adams as "blind, bald, crippled, toothless [and] querulous," and he accused even the revered George Washington of reveling in neomonarchical ceremony, dipping into the public treasury, and incompetent soldiering.[73]

Bache proclaimed that if ever a nation has been "debauched by a man, the American Nation has been debauched by Washington." At various times, he referred to Washington's manner, carriage, and clothing as "apish," "monarchical," "pompous," and "tawdry." When Washington stepped down as president— in part to escape Bache's unrelenting attacks—Bache castigated him as "the source of all the misfortunes of our country." In January 1797, Washington complained that the *Aurora* had assailed him with "malignant industry and persevering falsehoods" in order to "weaken, if not destroy, the confidence of the Public."[74] Bache's motives were not entirely base. He believed in a polity based on principle, not men, and felt a responsibility to bring even George Washington down to human scale.[75]

Republicans applauded Bache as a fervent advocate for the public good; Federalists despised him as a seditious scoundrel and accused him of being Talleyrand's agent. In 1797, Bache was physically assaulted by a young Federalist, who was later rewarded with a government position. A year later, a mob of drunken Federalists attacked Bache's home and terrorized his wife and children. In June 1798, even before passage of the Sedition Act, the Federalists had Bache arrested and charged with "libeling the President & the Executive Government," without even bothering to specify the publications in question.*[76]

Venom was not the exclusive province of Republicans. The most prominent Federalist paper, the *Gazette of the United States*, announced that its mission was to oppose the "the raging madness of Jacobinism."[77] Its editor, John Fenno, char-

---

* A few months later, bankrupted by the cost of defending himself in this prosecution, Bache died of yellow fever. The Federalists rejoiced at his death. Bache's widow married William Duane, and together they continued to publish the *Aurora* with the same tone and direction as before. See Pasley, *"Tyranny of Printers"* at 102–4 (cited in note 6); Miller, *Crisis in Freedom* at 96–97 (cited in note 11).

acterized critics of the Adams administration as "dismal cacklers," "propagators of calumny," and the "worst and basest of men."[78] William Cobbett, who edited the Federalist *Porcupine's Gazette*, exceeded all others in the art of vilification. He once accused Bache of being an "abandoned liar" and suggested that he be dealt with like "a Turk, a Jew, a Jacobin, or a Dog."[79]

To what extent should government officials have to tolerate such abuse? Is it necessary for "the freedom of speech, or of the press" to allow individuals to vilify the president and members of Congress with attacks on their character, conduct, and motives? What would be lost if Benjamin Bache had been prohibited from ridiculing Adams as "blind, bald, crippled, toothless [and] querulous" or accusing Washington of "reveling in neo-monarchical ceremony" and "incompetent soldiering"?

THE CENTERPIECE OF the Federalists' legislative program of 1798 was the Sedition Act:

> SEC. 2. . . . That if any person shall write, print, utter or publish . . . any false, scandalous, and malicious writing or writings against the government of the United States, or either house of the Congress of the United States, or the President of the United States, with intent to defame [them], or to bring them [into] contempt or disrepute; or to excite against them [the] hatred of the good people of the United States, . . . then such person . . . shall be punished by a fine not exceeding two thousand dollars, and by imprisonment not exceeding two years.[80]

In this act, the Federalists (and the U.S. government) declared war on dissent.* In its bitter debate over this legislation, Congress first began to explore the mean-

---

* The Sedition Act as enacted was actually less extreme than some versions that had been proposed and debated in Congress. One bill, for example, would have defined as "seditious" any expression that stated or implied that officers of the government had enacted laws because of motives that were hostile to the liberties of the people. Alexander Hamilton cautioned against hurrying this bill through Congress for fear of establishing a "tyranny." His objection, however, was based less on a concern for freedom of speech than on a fear that it might inflame citizens against the Federalists. See Smith, *Freedom's Fetters* at 109–10 (cited in note 16); Curtis, *Free Speech* at 63 (cited in note 80).

ing of the First Amendment. Although no consensus emerged at the time about that meaning, the debate and the subsequent experience under the act played a central role in shaping the future of American constitutional law.

Albert Gallatin was the first to throw down the gauntlet. The act, he charged, could be understood only as a deliberate attempt by the Federalists "to perpetuate their authority." He recalled that laws against political criticism had been used time and again by tyrants "to throw a veil on their folly or their crimes" and to "satisfy those mean passions which always denote little minds." The "proper weapon to combat error," he argued, "is truth."[81]

Gallatin reasoned that this sort of legislation could be justified in the United States only if it was necessary to save the country. The supporters of the law must therefore "prove that the President dare not, cannot, will not, execute the laws, unless the abuse poured upon him from certain presses is suppressed." Gallatin challenged the Federalists to demonstrate that there existed such "alarming symptoms of sedition" as would make it necessary to adopt such an "extraordinary measure" for suppressing the freedom of speech, and of the press.[82]

Federalists responded that the act was indeed necessary. Harrison Gray Otis declared that the nation's very existence was endangered by that "crowd of spies and inflammatory agents" who had spread across the nation "fomenting hostilities" and "alienating the affections of our own citizens." The *Massachusetts Mercury*, a Federalist newspaper, argued that the act was justified because the nation was plagued by "parricidal miscreants" who were "preying on the vitals of the country." Congressman John Allen justified the act on the ground that a treasonable conspiracy of Republican congressman and editors was attempting to "ruin the Government by publishing the most shameless falsehoods" and by inciting the people to "insurrection."[83]

To prove this conspiracy, Allen, as if scripting a scene for Joseph McCarthy 150 years later, pointed to several items of "evidence," including a "false" accusation in the *Aurora* that the Adams administration had failed to exhaust all reasonable efforts to negotiate a peaceful settlement with France; Congressman Livingston's speech several days earlier in which he had put forth the "false idea" that the same concerns that had led Congress to enact the Alien Friends Act could lead it to enact similar legislation against citizens; a "false" statement in the *Aurora* that it was no longer clear whether there was more "liberty to be enjoyed at Constantinople or Philadelphia"; and an article in the *Aurora* designed, in Allen's words, to make the proposed Sedition Act "odious among the people" by "falsely" asserting that it would render it "criminal to expose the crimes, the official vices or abuses, or the attempts of men in power to usurp a despotic authority."[84]

In light of such "proof," Allen asked, "who can doubt the existence" of a "conspiracy against the Constitution, the Government, the peace and safety of this country?" Such utterances were "calculated to destroy all confidence in the government." The First Amendment, Allen assured his colleagues, "was never understood to give the right of publishing falsehoods and slanders, nor of exciting sedition, insurrection, and slaughter, with impunity. A man was always answerable for the malicious publication of falsehood; and what more does this bill require?"[85]

THE REPUBLICANS RESPONDED to this defense of the act. Gallatin conceded that some of the statements Allen had quoted were objectionable, but he observed that "in almost every one of them there was a mixture of truth and error." Did Allen fear that "error could not be successfully opposed by truth," and did the Federalists believe that the nation had fallen to such a state that they required "the help of force" in order to counter "the opinions of those who did not approve all their measures"? Gallatin noted the irony that Allen would chastise the *Aurora* for questioning whether there was more freedom in Constantinople than in Philadelphia, while at the same time avowing "principles perfectly calculated to justify" the *Aurora*'s query.[86]

Gallatin added that Allen's evidence of a dangerous "conspiracy" consisted entirely of writings or speeches "expressing an opinion that certain measures of Government have been dictated by an unwise policy, or by improper motives, and that some of them were unconstitutional." Supporters of the act apparently believed that every critic of the Adams administration "is seditious, is an enemy, not of the Administration, but of the Constitution." That notion, Gallatin charged, is "subversive" of the Constitution itself.[87]

Congressman Nicholas argued that the Sedition Act would deprive the people of "information on public measures" that is the "life and support of a free Government." Like Gallatin, he conceded that some printers might "abuse" the liberty of the press, but he maintained that the "great check" on calumny must be the "sound understanding of the people." Congressman Nathaniel Macon warned Federalists that this law would "produce more uneasiness, more irritation, than any act which ever passed the Legislature of the Union," and asserted that the act is "in direct opposition to the Constitution."[88]

The Federalists were incredulous. Congressman Otis was at a loss to understand the alarm caused by the bill, which he described as "perfectly harmless." Congressman Samuel Dana of Connecticut declared it absurd to suggest that the framers of the First Amendment had intended "to guarantee, as a sacred principle, the liberty of lying against the Government." Congressman Harper maintained that the Republicans could not possibly believe that the Constitution authorized "persons to throw, with impunity, the most violent abuse upon the

President and both Houses of Congress." He said that he could never be persuaded that the Constitution could be violated "by a law to punish, on conviction before a jury, the publication of false, scandalous, and malicious libels."[89]

Republicans replied that the matter was not so simple. Gallatin conceded that under the act a defendant would be acquitted if he proved the truth of his assertions. But, he observed, the act was directed against "writings of a political nature, libels against the Government," and it "was well known that writings, containing animadversions on public measures, almost always contained not only facts but opinions." Certainly, many of the examples offered by Congressman Allen fit this description. How, Gallatin asked, could the truth of such opinions be proved?

As an illustration, Gallatin posited an individual who believed, as did he, that the proposed legislation was unconstitutional. Suppose that individual decided to publish his opinion and the administration prosecuted him under the act. Would a jury, Gallatin asked, "composed of the friends of that Administration," hesitate to declare "the opinion ungrounded, or, in other words, false and scandalous, and its publication malicious?" In the "present temper of the parties" could the accused convince such a jury "that his opinion was true?"[90]

Congressman Nicholas added that under the Sedition Act the government could readily "torture into an offence" almost any criticism of its measures. As a result, printers would be "deterred from printing anything" that might offend "a power which might so greatly harass them." Printers would even be "afraid of publishing the truth," for it might not always be possible "to establish the truth to the satisfaction of a court of justice," especially one that might be hostile to their views. Nicholas warned that this legislation risked suppressing "every printing press . . . which is not obsequious to the will of Government."[91]

The essence of this challenge was that the threat of punishment for "false and malicious" statements can easily be manipulated to chill the willingness of printers and others to criticize the government. The direct "benefit" any particular speaker gains from criticizing the government is relatively slight, and, standing alone, he is unlikely to change public opinion. Thus, the risk of punishment for such criticism can effectively silence dissent. Unless terms like "false" and "malicious" are narrowly and clearly defined, the chilling effect of such legislation is potentially powerful and pernicious.

THE FEDERALISTS EMPHATICALLY rejected the Republican plea that the Sedition Act violated the First Amendment. The most forceful argument was offered by Congressman Harrison Gray Otis, who maintained that "every independent Government" necessarily has the authority to "preserve and defend itself against injuries and outrages which endanger its existence." The First Amendment, he argued, did not deny the United States the power to defend itself against false and malicious attacks.[92]

Otis held that the language of the First Amendment—"Congress shall . . . make no law abridging the freedom of speech, or of the press"—had "a certain and technical meaning." He set forth two propositions to support his conclusion that the Sedition Act did not violate this "meaning." First, the framers of the First Amendment had borrowed its language from England, where the freedom of speech meant "nothing more than the liberty of writing, publishing, and speaking one's thoughts, under the condition of being answerable to the injured party, whether it be the Government or an individual, for false, malicious, and seditious expressions," and where the freedom of the press meant nothing more than "an exemption from all previous restraints."[*][93]

To support this claim, Otis quoted Blackstone's *Commentaries*, perhaps the most influential legal treatise of the day, which summarized the law of England in 1769:

> The liberty of the press consists in laying no *previous* restraints upon publications, and not in freedom from censure for criminal matter when published. To subject the press to the restrictive power of a licenser . . . is to subject all freedom of sentiment to the prejudices of one man, and make him the arbitrary and infallible judge of all controverted points in learning, religion, and government. But to punish (as the law does at present) any dangerous or offensive writings, which, when published, shall on a fair and impartial trial be adjudged of a pernicious tendency, is necessary for the preservation of peace and good order, of government and religion, the only solid foundations of civil liberty.[94]

Otis argued that the First Amendment incorporated Blackstone's definition of "the freedom of speech, or of the press," and that under that definition the Sedition Act was plainly constitutional.

Second, Otis held that the act was consistent with "the laws of the several States." He noted that many state constitutions contained guarantees similar to the First Amendment and that the states had never understood those guarantees to forbid the punishment of "defamatory and seditious libels." Otis reasoned that if the Sedition Act violated the First Amendment, then these similar state laws necessarily infringed the state constitutions. This, he said, was implausible, for it

---

[*] A previous or prior restraint traditionally consisted of "a system in which publication of a newspaper or book was illegal unless approved by the government in advance." Publication without prior approval of the licensing authority was itself a crime. Kermit L. Hall, ed, *The Oxford Companion to the Supreme Court of the United States* 669 (Oxford 1992).

had never been thought the case. He expressed "astonishment" that there should be such an outcry against a law that was "perfectly analogous to the laws and usages under which" all members of Congress had "been born and bred." Although efforts had been made to delude the people into believing that the Sedition Act threatened the loss of a "darling privilege," these were "idle terrors" because the act did not in any way assault the "immemorial laws and customs of the country."[95]

Republicans attacked Otis's interpretation of the First Amendment as "preposterous." Gallatin charged that it was an "insulting evasion" of the Constitution to tell the people that "we claim no power to abridge the liberty of the press," but "if you publish anything against us, we will punish you for it." Nicholas emphasized that the First Amendment states clearly that "Congress shall make no law abridging the freedom of speech, or of the press," not that "Congress may pass laws punishing speech that is licentious or pernicious," terms he deemed "so indefinite" that they would enable the meaning of the First Amendment to be "arbitrarily controlled."*[96]

DISAGREEMENT OVER THE "RIGHT" interpretation of the First Amendment in 1798 continues to this day. Some scholars argue that the framers had been "nurtured" on the "narrow conservatism" of Blackstone and that the "ways of thought of a lifetime are not easily broken." On this view, the proposition that the framers of the First Amendment intended to abolish the crime of seditious libel seems doubtful, at best.[97]

Other scholars, however, certainly the substantial majority, echo Gallatin's judgment that Otis's position was untenable. They point out that the mischief the framers sought to prevent could not have been licensing, because licensing had expired in England in 1695 and in the colonies by 1725. There was simply no reason to enact a constitutional amendment to settle an issue that had been "dead for decades."[98] These scholars argue that what most fundamentally con-

---

* Congressman Nathaniel Macon added that the best way to discern the meaning of the First Amendment was to consider the opinions expressed "when it was under discussion in the different States." He then quoted several statements during the ratification process to illustrate that "it was never understood that prosecutions for libels could take place under the General Government; but that they must be carried on in the State courts, as the Constitution gave no power to Congress to pass laws on this subject." See 8 *Annals of Congress* at 2151 (cited in note 36). For support of Macon's view, see Akhil Reed Amar, *The Bill of Rights: Creation and Reconstruction* 36–37 (Yale 1998).

cerned the framers was the crime of seditious libel, which had been used, often over vehement objection, both in England and in the colonies, to suppress political dissent.[99]

In fact, the framers of the First Amendment had no common understanding of its "true" meaning. They embraced a broad and largely undefined constitutional principle, not a concrete, well-settled legal doctrine. It was an aspiration, to be given meaning over time. As Benjamin Franklin observed, referring to the First Amendment, "few of us" have any "distinct Ideas of its Nature and Extent."[100] But anyone who thought seriously about the issue had to begin with seditious libel. It was too important, too controversial, to ignore.[101]

To understand the origins of the law of seditious libel, one must go back more than seven hundred years, to a 1275 statute that outlawed "any false news or tales whereby discord . . . may grow between the king and his people." Violations of this statute were punished by the king's council sitting in the "starred chamber." Although the essence of the crime as fixed by the statute of 1275 was the falsity of the libel, by the early seventeenth century English courts had held that even a *true* libel could be criminally punished. An English court explained why this should be so: "If people should not be called to account for possessing the people with an ill opinion of the government, no government can subsist. For it is very necessary for all governments that the people should have a good opinion of it."[102] A true libel was especially pernicious because, unlike a false libel, the dangers of truthful criticism cannot be defused by disproof. It was thus an oft-quoted maxim that "the greater the truth the greater the libel."

Seventeenth-century English judges punished as seditious libel any "written censure upon any public man whatever for any conduct whatever, or upon any law or institution whatever."[103] As one commentator has observed, "no single method of restricting the press was as effective as the law of seditious libel."[104] There was ample reason for the framers of the First Amendment to be wary.

Moreover, although the framers had been "nurtured" on William Blackstone, they were not necessarily enamored of him. An antirepublican Tory, Blackstone believed that human laws, like scientific laws, were the creation of God, waiting to be discovered, just as Isaac Newton had discovered the laws of gravity. In Blackstone's view, the sovereign could do no wrong. "The king," he wrote, "is not only incapable of doing wrong, but even of thinking wrong."[105]

Although not a strict monarchist, Blackstone was no democrat. He argued that it would be well "if the mass of mankind will obey the laws when made, without scrutinizing too nicely into the reasons of making them." Jeremy Bentham denounced Blackstone's *Commentaries* as "nonsense upon stilts," and Thomas Jefferson complained that Blackstone was responsible for "the degeneracy of legal science." He once observed that Blackstone had "done more towards the suppression of the liberties of man than all the millions of men in arms of Bonaparte." James Wilson, a signer of both the Declaration of Independence and the Constitution, castigated Blackstone's philosophy as damnable.[106]

Ultimately, however, the disagreement between Federalists and Republicans over the meaning of the First Amendment was less about Blackstone than about their divergent visions of government and class. Federalists believed that the governors were superior to the people and must not be subjected to censure that might diminish their authority.[107] Republicans believed that the governors were servants of the people, who therefore had a right and a responsibility to question and criticize their judgments. As the legal scholar David Currie has explained, Republicans in general and Gallatin and Nicholas in particular developed in the debates over the Sedition Act of 1798 the single most important insight about free expression—that it is indispensable "to the political process."[108]

The difference between Republicans and Federalists in this respect is neatly captured in the competing observations of Congressmen Thomas Claiborne and Robert Goodloe Harper. Arguing that the Sedition Act was "fraught with the most serious mischiefs," the Republican Claiborne expressed confidence that "the people would do what is right if they are not oppressed." The Federalist Harper, on the other hand, expressed hope that "attempts to sow discontent" would prove ineffectual because "the good sense and patriotism of the people" would shield the nation against sedition. But he was not confident this would be so, "and lest it should not," he supported the Sedition Act.[109]

The Federalists had the votes. On July 10, 1798, the House approved the Sedition Act by a straight party vote of 44 to 41.[110] On July 14, President Adams signed the act into law.

Federalists celebrated not only the enactment of this legislation but also its "liberalization" of the common law. Three procedural questions had played a central role in the historical debates over seditious libel. First, must the government prove that the defendant maliciously *intended* to cause sedition, or was it sufficient for the government to prove that the speech had a seditious tendency? Common-law judges had held that proof of malicious intent was unnecessary. Second, was truth a defense? English judges had rejected truth as a defense, arguing that truth increased the danger. Third, who should determine whether the publication was seditious—judge or jury? Common-law judges had held that the judge should decide this question and that the jury's function was limited to determining the underlying facts, such as whether the defendant had uttered the words in question.*[111]

---

* These issues were central to the prosecution of John Peter Zenger in New York in 1735, the most famous seditious libel prosecution of the colonial period. Zenger, the publisher of the New

The Sedition Act provided that malicious intent was an essential element of the crime, that truth was a defense, and that the jury should decide whether the speech had a seditious effect. Federalists could therefore boast that the 1798 act had eliminated those aspects of the English common law that had been particularly controversial in the seventeenth and eighteenth centuries. Federalists proclaimed the new legislation "a wholesome and ameliorating interpreter of the common law."[112]

These reforms were small consolation to the Republicans. They knew full well that the defense of truth would be of little value in prosecutions based on political opinions and that the other procedural changes would not shield them against Federalist judges and juries. As the New York *Time Piece* observed three days after the act took effect, Americans would now all have to "sing to the same tune!"[113] And, indeed, as the Republicans feared, the procedural reforms of the act proved wholly illusory.

"THE REIGN OF WITCHES"

IMMEDIATELY AFTER PRESIDENT ADAMS signed the Sedition Act into law, most Republican editors continued to criticize both the act itself and the administration.[114] Many citizens also protested the act. A public meeting in Suffolk County, New York, resolved that the act impaired the right of "every citizen" to publish his "opinions respecting the propriety" of government officers and measures. Twelve hundred citizens of Northampton County, Pennsylvania, signed a petition objecting that if the press is "to be open only" to those in power, and "the doors shut against their political opponents," the consequence will be "inimical to the genius of a republican government."[115]

The Kentucky and Virginia Resolutions, drafted secretly by Thomas Jefferson and James Madison, respectively, were adopted by the Kentucky and Virginia legislatures in the fall of 1798. These resolutions reflected the Republicans' grim conclusion that to save republicanism from the Federalist onslaught, they had to strengthen the states as "bastions of safety" from repressive federal legislation.[116]

York *Weekly Journal*, had been charged with seditious libel by the governor general of New York, whom he had criticized. Zenger argued that truth should be an absolute defense and that the jury, rather than the judge, should decide the questions of seditious tendency and intent. Although these propositions were rejected by the trial judge, the jury, responding to the popularity of Zenger's cause, disregarded the judge's instructions and returned a verdict of not guilty.

The resolutions argued that the Constitution was a compact between the states that limited the federal government to certain enumerated powers, and that the federal government could not be the final arbiter of the scope of the powers delegated to it by the states. They reasoned that when the federal government exceeded its powers, the states retained the authority to protect their "rights and liberties" under the compact. The Virginia Resolutions declared that the Sedition Act violated the First Amendment because it was "levelled against that right of freely examining public characters and measures" that is the "only effectual guardian of every other right."[117]

The Kentucky and Virginia legislatures invited other states to join with them in declaring the Sedition Act "void, and of no force." None accepted the invitation, and ten repudiated the resolutions. The Maryland House of Delegates, for example, condemned the resolutions as "highly *improper*" because "no State government . . . is competent to declare an act of the Federal Government unconstitutional." Delaware dismissed the resolutions as "not fit subject for . . . further consideration," while Vermont reproached Virginia and Kentucky for encroaching on a power "exclusively vested in the judiciary courts of the Union." Even more bluntly, Theodore Sedgwick called the resolutions "little short of a declaration of war."[118]

A year later, Madison wrote a detailed report on the Sedition Act for the Virginia legislature. In this report, Madison disputed the Federalist interpretation of the First Amendment, arguing that, whatever the peculiarities of English history, it made no sense to construe the First Amendment as prohibiting only prior restraints. "It would seem a mockery," he observed, "to say that no law should be passed preventing publications from being made, but that laws might be passed for punishing them in case they should be made." In other words, he asked, how can it possibly make sense to prohibit the government from denying a license to speech because it is "seditious," if the government remains free to punish the speech once it is uttered?

Madison maintained that fundamental differences between English and American political institutions rendered the British conception of free speech inapposite to the United States. He explained that, in the seventeenth and eighteenth centuries, when the English common law of seditious libel evolved, the rulers— kings and lords—were deemed the "superiors" of the people. In such a system, it was appropriate to require citizens to treat their rulers with respect and to prohibit criticism of their decisions. But in the United States "a greater freedom of animadversion" is essential because government officials are "responsible to their constituents," who may quite properly bring them "into contempt or disrepute" if they "fail to live up to their trusts." Madison concluded that the Sedition Act was unconstitutional because it undermined "the responsibility of public servants and public measures to the people" and embraced the "exploded doctrine 'that the administrators of the Government are the masters, and not the servants, of the people.' "[119]

THE ENMITY THAT MARKED the congressional debates of 1798 also infected Federalist enforcement policy. The Federalists continued to identify the Adams administration with the Constitution and to construe criticism as disloyalty. Federalist mobs threatened Republican congressmen, editors, and citizens, and in a few instances Federalist militia beat or whipped Republican editors and cut down Republican "liberty poles."*[120]

Federalist newspapers pressed for vigorous enforcement of the Sedition Act, evincing no inkling of understanding that in the long run they might be placing their own liberties in jeopardy. The *Albany Centinel,* for example, proclaimed that "it is patriotism to write in favor of our government" and "sedition to write against it." The New York *Gazette* demanded that Republican editors be "ferreted out of their lurking places and condemned" to punishment.[121] The New York *Commercial Advertiser* declared that anyone who inveighed against the Sedition Act "deserves to be suspected" of sedition. The *Salem Gazette* explained that the "safety of our nation depends" on the Sedition Act, and William Cobbett, the editor of *Porcupine's Gazette,* dutifully compiled a list of seditious newspapers for the benefit of government prosecutors.[122]

The Adams administration was eager to enforce the act. Secretary of State Timothy Pickering led the charge. Grim-faced and single-minded, Pickering was zealous in his hunt for Jacobin influences. He exemplified the most rigid form of "extreme Federalism." Even to Abigail Adams, never at a loss for caustic comment, he was a man "whose manners are forbidding, whose temper is sour and whose resentments are implacable." In Pickering's view, the Sedition Act was not a threat to free speech but an essential measure to exterminate the "pests of society and disturbers of order and tranquility."[123]

To his Federalist contemporaries, Pickering was the "man of the hour." He was perfectly suited to saving the nation from the perils of Jacobinism. Every morning, Pickering closely scrutinized Republican newspapers for any hint of sedition and vigorously encouraged a network of spies and informers to keep him personally apprised of their suspicions.[124] Federalists praised him as "the Scourge of Jacobinism"; Republicans despised him as the "Federalist ogre."[125]

In an era described by Thomas Jefferson as "the reign of witches," the Feder-

---

* The use of liberty poles dates to around 1765. The Sons of Liberty, a group organized by Samuel Adams to protest British taxes, rallied in town squares around tall poles on which they flew their flag. The idea quickly spread throughout the colonies. Many towns erected such poles, which were often more than a hundred feet tall, as a symbol of resistance to the British.

Secretary of State Timothy Pickering

alists issued seventeen indictments for seditious libel—fourteen under the Sedition Act and three under the common law. The Federalist enforcement strategy was aimed directly at the presidential election of 1800. Pickering's objective was to silence every leading Republican newspaper as the contest between Adams and Jefferson drew nigh. Pickering prosecuted four of the five most influential Republican journals, as well as several lesser Republican newspapers. As a result of these prosecutions, two Republican newspapers folded and several others were compelled to suspend operations while their editors were in jail.[*][126]

THE TRIAL OF MATTHEW LYON

DURING THE CONGRESSIONAL DEBATES over the Sedition Act, Matthew Lyon predicted that the act "very likely would be brought to bear on me the very first." This was a sensible prediction, for by the time Congress adjourned in the summer of 1798 Lyon was one of the most despised Republicans in the nation. His "uncouthness" and "fractious insolence" had made him both the butt of jokes and the object of loathing. A popular humorist portrayed him to highly appreciative audiences as the "Beast of Vermont" in his production of "Rugged Mat, the Democrat." The *Albany Centinel* accused Lyon of trying to "excite mobs" to overthrow the government. All along the route from Philadelphia to Vermont, Lyon was taunted, hissed, and hooted by Federalist crowds. In Trenton, a local band serenaded him with the "Rogue's March." In New Brunswick, a huge throng greeted him with insults. In New York City, he was jeered at his hotel. The Federalist *Gazette of the United States* cheerfully warned Lyon that this was nothing compared "to the honors which await him, on his return to his own district in Vermont."[127]

---

[*] Pickering's first target was John Daly Burk, a "wild" Irishman who had transformed the New York *Time Piece* into one of the mostly staunchly Republican papers in the nation. Pickering already had Burk in his sights when, in July 1798, Burk allegedly declared that he hoped the French would invade the United States and "put to the guillotine" every "scoundrel in favor of this Government." On Pickering's orders, Burk was arrested by federal marshals on a warrant, signed by John Adams, charging him with seditious libel. While Adams and Pickering dithered over whether to prosecute Burk for sedition or deport him under the Alien Friends Act, Burk fled to Virginia, where he took up an assumed name and went into hiding as the preceptor of a college. Ironically, Burk was killed in a duel in 1808 after he affronted a Frenchman by damning the French as "a pack of rascals." Miller, *Crisis in Freedom* at 99, 102 (cited in note 11). See generally id at 97–102; Smith, *Freedom's Fetters* at 173 (cited in note 16); Lawson, *Reign of Witches* at 31 (cited in note 35).

Because Republicans and Federalists were almost evenly divided in the House of Representatives, the congressional elections of 1798 were bitterly contested. A tip one way or the other could determine the outcome of pivotal national issues. A criminal prosecution for sedition of one of the nation's best-known Republicans while he was in the midst of his reelection campaign was sure to incite political passions.[128]

When Lyon returned to Vermont in the summer of 1798, his political prospects were uncertain. He had lost three of the four previous elections, his district was predominantly Federalist, and the publicity he had received from Philadelphia was surely not all to his credit. To counter unremitting Federalist attacks on him, Lyon published a letter in *Spooner's Vermont Journal*, explaining why he rejected the "principle of Presidential infallibility." In this letter, Lyon sharply criticized John Adams and his administration, declaring that under President Adams "every consideration of the public welfare" was "swallowed up in a continual grasp for power." Although the letter was published before Adams signed the Sedition Act, Lyon read it to audiences several times thereafter in his campaign speeches in Vermont. In those speeches, Lyon also quoted a letter written by Joel Barlow, an expatriate American poet, to the effect that Congress should have sent Adams to "a mad house" for the way he had dealt with the French.[129]

Although Lyon expected his enemies to indict him under the Sedition Act, he was not silenced. To the contrary, he defiantly established a new magazine — the *Scourge of Aristocracy and Repository of Important Political Truths*. In the October 1, 1798, issue, Lyon accused the Federalists of "falsehood, detraction and calumny" and proclaimed that the "great object" of the *Scourge* "shall be to oppose truth to falsehood, and to lay before the public such facts as may tend to elucidate the real situation of this country." When the executive, he added, puts forth a proposition "injurious to my constituents and the Constitution, I am bound by oath . . . to oppose it; if outvoted, it is my duty to acquiesce — I do so; But measures which I opposed [in Congress] as injurious and ruinous to the liberty and interest of this country . . . you cannot expect me to advocate at home."[130]

On October 3, 1798, the federal Circuit Court for the District of Vermont convened in Rutland. In charging the grand jury, Associate Justice William Paterson of the U.S. Supreme Court[*][131] explained the Sedition Act and advised the grand jurors to pay careful attention "to the seditious attempts of disaffected per-

---

[*] The Judiciary Act of 1789 required that the justices of the Supreme Court serve also as judges of the local circuit courts. This proved very burdensome on the justices, and in the Judiciary Act of 1869 Congress established a separate circuit court judiciary, although the justices retained nominal circuit-riding duties. Congress finally ended the practice entirely in 1891.

Congressman Matthew Lyon

sons to disturb the government." They replied, "[W]e solemnly feel what the Honorable Judge has so powerfully expressed, that licentiousness more endangers the liberties and independence of a free Government than hosts of invading foes." On October 5, the grand jury indicted Matthew Lyon for sedition.[132]

The indictment charged that Lyon, with "malicious" intent "to bring the President and government of the United States into contempt," had violated the Sedition Act both by accusing the Adams administration of fostering "ridiculous pomp, foolish adulation, and selfish avarice" and by quoting the statement in Barlow's letter that Congress should have sent Adams to "a mad house."[133]

Acting as his own attorney,[134] Lyon argued that the Sedition Act was unconstitutional, that he had not spoken maliciously, and that his statements were true.*[135] Justice Paterson rejected out of hand Lyon's constitutional objection and

---

* To prove the truth of his assertion that the administration was pompous and avaricious, Lyon asked Justice Paterson whether he had not frequently "dined with the President, and observed his

then instructed the jurors that they "must render a verdict of guilty" if Lyon had made his remarks with the intent to render the president "odious and contemptible" and bring him "into disrepute." After an hour's deliberation, the jury returned a verdict of guilty.[136]

The next day, Justice Paterson prepared to impose sentence. He asked Lyon whether he had anything to say. Lyon informed the court that because of the depression of 1798 he had lost most of his wealth and could not raise more than $200 in cash. Paterson expressed sympathy, but told Lyon he had to make an example of him. He then sentenced Lyon to four months in jail, a fine of $1,000, and court costs of $60.96.* Paterson ordered further that Lyon would remain in jail, even beyond his four-month sentence, unless and until the fine and costs were paid.[137]

Not expecting to be thrown into jail, Lyon was stunned. The most he had anticipated was a minor fine and a reprimand. But the sentence was only the beginning. From that moment on, Lyon was subjected to a long series of indignities. He was not permitted to return to his lodgings to procure his papers or given time to arrange his affairs, but was taken immediately into custody. Instead of being imprisoned in his home county of Rutland, where the trial had taken place, he was dragged on a humiliating two-day journey, under armed guard, to a jail in Vergennes, forty-four miles away.

Jabez Fitch, the marshal in charge of Lyon's imprisonment and one of his most bitter Federalist enemies, seized every opportunity to add to the prisoner's misery. Fitch confined Lyon in a cell that Lyon described as "the common receptacle for horse-thieves, money-makers, runaway-negroes, or any kind of felons." In the corner of the cell was a "necessary" that, in Lyon's words, afforded "a stench about equal to the Philadelphia docks in the month of August." There was nothing "but the iron bars to keep the cold out." Thus, Lyon had to "walk smartly with [his] great coat on, to keep comfortably warm." Lyon's constituents were outraged by his treatment and threatened to break into the jail to free him, but Lyon dissuaded them, vowing that he would rather "suffer any kind of death here . . . than be taken out by violence."[138]

On October 14, Lyon wrote a lengthy letter to Senator Stevens T. Mason of Virginia. He informed Mason, "[T]he jury was composed of men who had been accustomed to speak ill of me." He reported that, on learning of the indictment,

---

ridiculous pomp and parade?" Although this was a most peculiar tactic, Justice Paterson responded that he "had sometimes, though rarely, dined with the President," but had "never seen any pomp or parade." Rather, he had seen only "a great deal of plainness and simplicity." Wharton, *State Trials* at 335 (cited in note 17).

* The sum of $1,000 in 1798 is the equivalent of approximately $15,000 in 2004.

his friends in Rutland had urged him to flee, but he had refused to do so because he "had done no wrong." He reminded Mason of his prediction that he would be the first person prosecuted under the Sedition Act, and observed that perhaps that was for the best because he, who had been "a football for dame fortune" all his life, was "best able to bear it."[139]

Federalists were overjoyed with Lyon's conviction. The *Albany Centinel* prayed that "the good God grant this may be the case of every Jacobin"; the *Salem Gazette* cheered that "the vile career of the beast of the mountain" has ended in disgrace; and the *Gazette of the United States* celebrated Lyon's conviction as the triumph of law over the "unbridled spirit of opposition to government." Republicans, of course, were of a different mind. The *Aurora* hailed Lyon as a martyr of "a law framed directly in the teeth of the Constitution," and Jefferson wrote that federal judges are now "objects of national fear."[140]

Undaunted by his plight, Lyon launched a vigorous reelection campaign from jail. For the first time in American history, a candidate for Congress championed his cause from a federal prison. Lyon's letter to Senator Mason appeared throughout the nation. Lyon appealed to the American sense of justice, and as he attacked his Federalist persecutors he "ceased to appear as a barroom brawler" and took on the mantle of a "Republican hero suffering unmerited punishment for having upheld freedom against his enemies."[141] Lyon's imprisonment even inspired his followers to express their anger in verse. One Z. Porter offered the following tribute to Lyon (the "fighting" he refers to was the Revolutionary War):

> . . . Our rulers can feast on six dollars pr day
> the poor Must be taxt their extorsion to pay
> And if I Should unto them any Thing say
> They would trump up a Bill of Sedition.
> . . . We soon may disown before it be long
> that while we were fighting we fought for a wrong
> if knaves will Oppress us and make themselves strong
> By the help of a Bill of Sedition.[142]

Several thousand Vermonters signed a petition asking President Adams to pardon Lyon. They declared themselves loyal Americans who had been unjustly deprived of their representative to Congress. When the Reverend John C. Ogden presented this petition to Adams, the president asked whether Lyon himself had sought the pardon. When informed he had not, Adams refused to receive the petition, stating that "penitence must precede pardon."[143]

When the ballots were counted, Lyon won a stunning victory. He almost doubled the votes of his Federalist opponent. Republicans were jubilant. Jefferson exultantly wrote Madison, "Lyon is re-elected!" Federalists were furious. The *Commercial Advertiser* lamented that "our national councils" will again be "disgraced by that vile beast." After learning of his reelection, Lyon wrote a letter to his supporters from jail, thanking them for their confidence and declaring that his only offense had been to refuse to sacrifice the trust of his constituents to "those who wish to see a luxurious court . . . fattening on the labours of the farmer and the poor mechanic."[144]

That still left the matter of the $1,000 fine. Senator Mason wrote Lyon on November 10, 1798, that he and Lyon's fellow Republicans had agreed that his "personal suffering" was much more than what he "ought to bear in the common cause of Republicanism." Because the fine was the only part of the sentence in which others could share, Lyon's colleagues decided "that it should be paid by subscription among the enemies of political persecution." Jefferson, Gallatin, Madison, and James Monroe were among those who contributed to this fund.

At the same time, with the active support of his Vermont constituents, Lyon sought to raise sufficient cash to pay his fine by raffling off his property, including his home, farm, and books. A race ensued between Vermont and Virginia for the honor of securing Lyon's release. In the end, they raised twice the necessary amount, so each group paid half of the fine.[145]

At eight on the morning of February 9, 1799, after four months in jail, Lyon was reluctantly released by his Federalist captors. Even then, he was not safe. Warned that his enemies were preparing to prosecute him for the "seditious" letters he had written from jail, he announced before setting foot outside his cell, "I am on my way to Congress." Because members of the House are privileged from arrest while en route to the nation's capital, this statement shielded Lyon from any Federalist attempt to rearrest him.[146]

Lyon's return trip to Philadelphia was triumphant. A huge crowd cheered him as he stepped from his cell, then accompanied him in a jubilant procession to Middlebury, nearly twelve miles away. In Timouth, Lyon was hailed as "our brave representative, who has been suffering for us under an unjust sentence." In Bennington, a large throng celebrated Lyon's victory, and Anthony Haswell, a Republican journalist, who nine months later was himself prosecuted under the Sedition Act, sang a song he had penned for the occasion. The final stanza proclaimed,[147]

> Come take the glass and drink his health,
> Who is a friend of Lyon,
> First martyr under federal law
> The junto dared to try on.

When Lyon arrived in Philadelphia to take his seat in Congress, the Federalist *Porcupine's Gazette* snarled that he "looks remarkably well for a gentleman just out of jail." It added, caustically, "happy must the nation be where it is but a single step from the *dungeon* to the *Legislature!*" To celebrate Lyon's return, a group of Republicans held a party where, according to a Federalist wag, they got as drunk as they "generally do whenever they get a chance to swig."[148]

The Federalists in Congress moved immediately to expel Lyon from the House because of his conviction under the Sedition Act. In the ensuing debate, Congressman Nicholas argued that Lyon's conviction was unwarranted, because he had been prosecuted for statements of political opinion. Nicholas asked the Federalists whether they truly believed that "opinions can be false." "Men's opinions," he argued, "are as various as their faces, and the truth or falsehood of those opinions are not fit subjects for the decision of a jury." Albert Gallatin followed up by analyzing every statement for which Lyon had been convicted to demonstrate that each was a statement of opinion "not susceptible of proof by evidence." Gallatin concluded that Lyon had been tried for political reasons that violated the Constitution. The vote on the motion for expulsion followed straight party lines, with 49 in favor and 45 opposed. Because a two-thirds majority is necessary to expel a member of the House, Lyon (once again) retained his seat.[149]

THE TRIAL OF THOMAS COOPER

LYON WAS THE FIRST PERSON prosecuted under the Sedition Act, but hardly the last. Thomas Cooper, in contrast to Lyon, was born to a wealthy family in 1759 in Westminster, England. He received a classical education and then studied law, chemistry, and other natural sciences at Oxford. He tried his hand for a while at politics and business, before staking out his claim as a public advocate for the abolition of slavery. He soon ran head-on into the tide of repression that swept England during the French Revolution, however, so he set sail for the United States in 1794.

Upon his arrival, Cooper set up to practice both law and medicine in Pennsylvania. In 1797, Dr. Joseph Priestley, an eminent scientist and longtime friend of John Adams, wrote the president recommending Cooper for a position in government. Neither Priestley nor Cooper ever received a reply.

Over the next two years, Cooper became increasingly active in American politics. As editor of the Northumberland, Pennsylvania, *Gazette*, he wrote an essay that sharply criticized Adams and his administration. The essay was republished and widely circulated. It implied that Adams was a "power-mad despot" and an enemy "of the rights of man." Furious, Adams told Timothy Pickering that it "ought to be prosecuted."[150]

Shortly thereafter, an anonymous "communication" appeared in the October 26, 1799, issue of the Reading *Weekly Advertiser*, inquiring whether the Thomas Cooper who had recently criticized the Adams administration was the same Thomas Cooper who had applied to the president two years earlier for a government appointment. The anonymous missive revealed that in his job application Cooper had stated that his "political sentiments" would be "agreeable to the President." The "communication" added that after the president had "rejected Cooper's application with disdain," Cooper, acting out of "disappointment and revenge," had viciously attacked the president. It characterized Cooper's essay as "cunning and insidious" and demanded he answer these charges.[151]

Cooper saw this publication as an underhanded effort by the Adams administration to impugn his integrity and his credibility as a critic. Because the information in the anonymous communication could have come only from Adams, Cooper decided to explain to the public how he could have applied for a position with the administration in 1797, but then come to criticize the administration only two years later. He therefore published a handbill in which he set out the above facts, and then continued,

> Nor do I see any impropriety in making this request [the application for a government appointment] of Mr. Adams. At that time he had just entered into office; he was hardly in the infancy of political mistake: even those who doubted his capacity thought well of his intentions. Nor were we yet saddled with the expense of a permanent navy, or threatened, under his auspices, with the existence of a standing army. Our credit was not yet reduced so low as to borrow money at eight per cent. in time of peace. . . .[152]

For publishing this statement, Cooper was charged under the Sedition Act "with having published a false, scandalous and malicious attack on the character of the President of the United States, with an intent to excite the hatred and contempt of the people of this country against the man of their choice." The trial convened in April 1800 in Philadelphia. Supreme Court Justice Samuel Chase was the presiding judge. The trial, a major political event, took place in the nation's capital during the heat of the presidential campaign. Its national significance was underscored by the presence in the courtroom of Secretary of State Pickering, the secretaries of war and the navy, and Congressman Robert Goodloe Harper, who had played a central role in drafting the Sedition Act.[153]

In stating his case, Cooper, who represented himself, denied that his essay, which had triggered the anonymous communication, had "originated from any motives of revenge." He observed that two years had elapsed after his unsuccessful application for a presidential appointment before he wrote anything about "the politics of this country." Moreover, he had "published nothing which truth will not justify" and his motives were "honest and fair." [154]

Cooper expressed concern that he might not receive a fair trial. He pointed out that the country was "almost equally divided, into two grand parties," one of which "wishes to increase, the other to diminish, the powers of the executive"; one of which thinks the people have "too much, the other too little, influence on the measures of government"; one of which is "friendly, the other hostile, to a standing army and a permanent navy"; one of which "thinks the liberties of our country endangered by the licentiousness, the other, by the restrictions of the press." He argued that in such circumstances the members of each party will inevitably "view with a jealous eye the positions of the other" and that "there cannot but be a bias of the partisans of the one side, against the principles and doctrines inculcated by the other." In a trial under the Sedition Act, he feared, such a bias would have devastating consequences.[155]

Cooper conceded the "necessity of a certain degree of confidence" in the president. But this "confidence ought not to be unlimited," and it ought to be earned, not imposed "by sedition laws." Cooper added that, "in the present state of affairs, the press is open to those who will praise" the president, but not to those who criticize him. The president's critics, he argued, must speak "in fear and trembling, and run the hazard of being dragged like myself before the frowning tribunal, erected by the Sedition Law."[156]

Cooper then went through his handbill line by line in order to prove that his statements were not false. For example, with respect to his statement that Adams had hardly been "in the infancy of political mistake" when Cooper applied for a government position, Cooper asked the jury whether the nation had "advanced so far on the road to despotism" that "we dare not say our President may be mistaken." Is the president, he asked, "blessed with political infallibility"? He added, "I know that in England the king can do no wrong, but I did not know till now that the President of the United States had the same attribute."

Cooper then turned to his statement that the nation had been "saddled with the expense of a permanent navy." The truth of this statement he thought self-evident. He asked whether it was really necessary for him to "enter into a detail of authorities to prove that the sun shines at noon-day." According to the report of the trial, Cooper "went on to argue at great length, from a copious collection from the public documents of the day," that the other statements in his handbill were true.[157]

After Cooper rested his defense, the prosecutor exclaimed that Cooper's defense was "one of the most extraordinary" he had ever seen. "It is," he said, "no less than to call into decision whether Thomas Cooper [or] the President of the United States . . . is best qualified to judge whether the measures adopted by our government are calculated to preserve the peace and promote the happiness of

Thomas Cooper

America."[158] Stating the Federalists' view of self-governance, the prosecutor argued that "those who are qualified and who have been appointed for the purpose" can judge the wisdom of these measures "for the nation," and it is not for Cooper or others "to raise surmises and suspicions of the wisdom and design of measures of this kind, which he cannot know sufficient of to explain, or the people to understand."[159] This argument paled before Justice Chase's charge to the jury.

BORN IN 1741 in Somerset County, Maryland, Samuel Chase was the son of an Episcopal clergyman, a classical scholar who made sure his only son received a splendid education. At the age of eighteen, Chase went off to Annapolis to study law. He soon became a prominent lawyer and was elected to the colonial legislature. He was an ardent advocate of American independence and one of the leaders of the Sons of Liberty, who protested the Stamp Act in 1765 by breaking into government offices, destroying the stamps, and burning the stamp collector in effigy. Colonial officials denounced the twenty-four-year-old firebrand as a foul-mouthed radical.

In 1774, Chase was appointed a delegate from Maryland to the Continental Congress. Two years later he was one of the signers of the Declaration of Independence. After a minor financial scandal and some business reverses, Chase became chief judge of the General Court of Maryland in 1791. Abrasive, arrogant, and overbearing, Chase had many admirers, but few intimate friends. In 1796, President Washington appointed him to the Supreme Court of the United States.

In the trial of Thomas Cooper, Justice Chase blocked the defense at every turn. He consistently ruled against Cooper on the admissibility of evidence offered to establish the truth of his statements or his lack of personal malice against the president. When Cooper sought to introduce into evidence newspaper reports of Adams's speeches to prove what the president had said, Chase ruled them inadmissible on the theory that the only way Cooper could prove what the president had said was by presenting authenticated copies of Adams's statements. Chase lectured the defendant that writing about the president is a risky business and if Cooper had made the mistake of relying on newspaper accounts, rather than authenticated copies, he would just have to take the consequences. When Cooper asked for a continuance so he could obtain authenticated copies of Adams's statements, Chase denied the request.

Chase's most memorable improprieties, however, were in his charge to the jury. He began by informing the jury that "if a man attempts to destroy the confi-

Justice Samuel Chase

dence of the people in their officers," he saps the very "foundation of the government." He accused Cooper of attempting to "arouse the people against the President so as to influence their minds against him on the next election." Chase
volunteered that there could be no doubt of the defendant's motives, because he
had made clear in his own defense that his motives, "were to censure the conduct
of the President."

Responding to Cooper's defense, Chase went through the handbill line by
line to explain to the jury why it violated the Sedition Act. To Cooper's statement
that Adams had called for a standing army, Chase responded that "we cannot
have a standing army in this country," because the Constitution expressly
declares that "no appropriation shall be made for the support of an army longer
than two years." There can thus be a standing army in the United States only if
"the Constitution is first destroyed." Chase concluded that Cooper's accusation
was therefore "directly calculated to bring" the president "into contempt with the
people, and excite their hatred against him," because it implied that Adams
sought to destroy the Constitution.[160]

Similarly, Chase characterized as a "gross attack upon the President"

Cooper's statement that in the early days of Adams's presidency "our credit was not yet reduced so low as to borrow money at eight per cent. in time of peace." "Can this be true?" Chase asked the jury sarcastically. "Can you believe it? Are we now in time of peace? Is there no war? No hostilities with France? Has she not captured our vessels and plundered us of our property to the amount of millions? . . . Have not we armed our vessels to defend ourselves, and have we not captured several of her vessels of war? Although no formal declaration of war has been made, is it not notorious that actual hostilities have taken place? And is this, then, a time of peace?" Cooper, Chase declared, "has published an untruth, knowing it to be an untruth."[161]

The justice went further. "Take this publication in all its parts," he declared, "and it is the boldest attempt I have known to poison the minds of the people." He then submitted the case to the jury members, reminding them that, in his defense, Cooper "must prove every charge he has made to be true; he must prove it to the marrow." Chase added that "if he asserts three things, and proves but one, he fails; and if he proves but two, he fails in his defence, for he must prove the whole of his assertions to be true." Not surprisingly, the jury returned a verdict of guilty. Chase then sentenced Cooper to six months in prison and a fine of $400.[162]

President Adams thought the Cooper matter had gone too far. He was inclined to pardon Cooper in order to put the whole mess behind him. But Cooper would not ask for clemency, or accept a pardon, unless the president first acknowledged his own breach of good faith in leaking the circumstances of Cooper's job application. This Adams would not do.[163]

Imprisonment did not silence Cooper. Only a week after he was sentenced, he published an account of his trial in which he asked the public to consider whether those responsible for his confinement merited reelection. He declared that the lesson of his conviction was that, under the Federalist administration, citizens should "hold their tongues, and restrain their pens, on the subject of politics."*[164]

---

* Several years after his release from jail, Cooper was appointed a judge in Pennsylvania, where he served without distinction from 1804 to 1811. He was ignominiously removed from office for a stunning array of misconduct, including imprisoning a Quaker who refused for religious reasons to remove his hat in court, issuing warrants not under oath, and abusively harassing counsel, witnesses, and parties from the bench. Cooper then found work as a chemistry professor at Dickinson College, the University of Pennsylvania, and South Carolina College, where he also served as president. Toward the end of his career, Cooper repudiated the natural rights philosophy of Thomas Jefferson, became an advocate of the moral and economic virtues of slavery, and fiercely defended the right of the southern states to secede from the Union. See Dumas Malone, *The Public Life of Thomas Cooper, 1739–1839* (Yale 1926).

THE TRIAL OF JAMES CALLENDER

HAVING HAD HIS WAY in Pennsylvania, Justice Chase headed next to Virginia, where he planned to try James Thomson Callender, perhaps the most vitriolic of the Republican journalists. Chase was determined to demonstrate that the Sedition Act could be enforced even in Virginia, despite its presumptuous resolutions.[165]

James Callender was a Scotsman who had been expelled from England. He had built a reputation as a scathing critic of the British government, which he once likened to a "mass of legislative putrefaction."[166] In this spirit of colorful invective, Callender turned his attention to the Federalists. Variously described as "a little reptile" and as "a dirty, little toper with shaved head and greasy jacket,"[167] Callender was often down-at-the-heels and frequently drunk. He was once physically ejected from the halls of Congress because he was "covered with lice and filth."[168] Nonetheless, his ability to write with rare verve made him a great asset to the Republicans. Jefferson both encouraged Callender and supported him financially.

Even before the Sedition Act, Federalists had demanded action against Callender. The *Gazette of the United States* characterized him as the "scum of party filth" and charged that he deserved "the benefit of the gallows." A ditty sung frequently at Federalist gatherings in the spring and summer of 1798, to the tune of "Yankee Doodle Dandy," accused Callender and Bache of treason:

Tom Callender's a nasty beast,
Ben Bache a dirty fellow;
They curse our country day and night,
And to the French would sell her.
Fire and murder, keep it up,
Plunder is the dandy;
When some folks get the upper hand,
With heads they'll be so handy.[169]

In *The Prospect before Us*, a pamphlet advocating the election of Jefferson over Adams in 1800, Callender charged that the "reign of Mr. Adams . . . has been one continued tempest of malignant passions." Indeed, the president "has never opened his lips, or lifted his pen without threatening and scolding; the grand object of his administration has been to exasperate the rage of contending parties, to calumniate and destroy every man who differs from his opinions."

Callender accused Adams of contriving "a French war, an American navy, a large standing army, an additional load of taxes, and all the other symptoms and consequences of debt and despotism." "Take your choice," Callender concluded, "between Adams, war and beggary, and Jefferson, peace and competency."[170]

A Federalist informant sent Justice Chase a copy of *The Prospect before Us*. After deciding that the pamphlet violated the Sedition Act, Chase headed to Virginia, noting that Callender should be "hanged." Callender was promptly arrested and indicted. The arrest created immediate unrest in Virginia. Affidavits circulated stating that Justice Chase intended to "teach the lawyers in Virginia the difference between the liberty and the licentiousness of the press" and that he had ordered the marshal to exclude all Republicans from the jury.[171]

Callender's prosecution became a national sensation.[172] The courtroom was filled to capacity. Callender's lawyers, among the most accomplished in Virginia, argued that the Sedition Act was unconstitutional. Justice Chase disagreed, reaffirming his decision in the prosecution of Thomas Cooper. Callender's attorneys then sought a continuance to give them time to gather evidence and summon witnesses, some of whom were hundreds of miles away. Chase denied the motion. Callender's attorneys argued that the Sedition Act should be construed to apply only to false statements of fact and not to statements of political opinion. Chase ruled otherwise, branding Callender's statements "false," without regard to whether they were "opinions."[173] Throughout the proceedings, Justice Chase was intemperate, rude, partial, and contemptuous to Callender's counsel.[174] After several hours of abuse, Callender's attorneys withdrew. As a formal review of the proceeding later concluded, the entire trial was marked by "manifest injustice" and "repeated and vexatious interruptions of . . . counsel." It was all over quickly. The jury brought in a verdict of guilty.[175]

Justice Chase sternly lectured Callender on the evils of sowing "discord among the people" and asserted that Callender's attack on Adams was "an attack upon the people themselves." He explained that to believe Adams capable of the "atrocities" charged by Callender necessarily implied that the people who had elected him "must be depraved and wicked." He then sentenced Callender to nine months in jail and a $200 fine.[176]

The Republican press condemned Chase's conduct as "reprehensible." The *Aurora* offered up an unfinished couplet: "Cursed of thy father, scum of all that's base, Thy sight is odious, and thy name is ———." Callender used his time in jail to write the second volume of *The Prospect before Us*, which intensified his attack on John Adams, whom he now described as a "wretch," "an unprincipled oppressor," and "a repulsive hypocrite." He also went after Chase, calling him a "detestable and detested rascal." When Chase wrote Callender in reply that he planned to beat him after his release from prison, Callender vowed, "[I]n case of attack, I'll shoot him."*[177]

"PERSECUTIONS AND PERSONAL INDIGNITIES"

FROM JULY 1798 TO MARCH 1801, when the Sedition Act expired, the Federalists arrested approximately twenty-five well-known Republicans under the act. Fifteen of these arrests led to indictments. Ten cases went to trial, all resulting in convictions. In addition, the Federalists initiated several common-law prosecutions for seditious libel.[178] The prosecutions of Lyon, Cooper, and Callender are among the most infamous, but others are worthy of note to give a fuller sense of the times.

Like Matthew Lyon, Anthony Haswell was a veteran of the Revolution. He was the postmaster general of Vermont and editor of the *Vermont Gazette*. Friends of Lyon asked Haswell to publicize the lottery to raise funds to pay Lyon's fines. He readily agreed. The notice read, "Your representative . . . is holden by the oppressive hand of usurped power in a loathsome prison, suffering all the indignities which can be heaped upon him by a hard-hearted savage, who has, to the disgrace of Federalism, been elevated to a station where he can satiate his barbarity on the misery of his victims." It asked citizens to participate in Lyon's lottery to help raise the "ransom" that was needed to "bring liberty to the defender of your rights."

The Federalists charged that this statement violated the Sedition Act. Although already in poor health, Haswell was arrested by Jabez Fitch, the same "hard-hearted savage" who had arrested Lyon. Fitch dragged Haswell from his home "at a very early hour," forced him to ride sixty miles in a chill rain, and had him "thrown into a filthy prison at midnight, notwithstanding his entreaties to be permitted to dry his clothes." Although a friend offered to post bail for Haswell, Fitch vetoed the offer.

Supreme Court Justice William Paterson presided at Haswell's trial. Paterson virtually directed a verdict of guilty, charging the jury members that it was their responsibility to preserve the Constitution "from the malicious attacks of unprincipled sedition." The jury convicted, and Patterson sentenced Haswell to two months in jail and a fine of $200. When Haswell's sentence expired, a crowd of more than two

---

* After he regained his freedom, Callender turned against Jefferson and unleashed upon him the same venom he had earlier directed at Adams. Callender died in 1803 in a drunken seizure when he fell off a ferry and drowned in the James River. See Miller, *Crisis in Freedom* at 220 (cited in note 11).

thousand citizens gathered to celebrate his freedom and express indignation at his imprisonment. Indeed, the area's residents postponed their annual Fourth of July celebration until July 7, the day of Haswell's release, so they could commemorate the nation's independence and Haswell's liberation as a single event.[179]

THE MOST SEVERE SENTENCE LEVIED UNDER the Sedition Act was imposed on David Brown, a vagabond radical who wandered from town to town preaching the evils of the Federalist government. In Dedham, Massachusetts, a group of local Republicans, inspired by Brown, erected a liberty pole. Affixed to the pole was a placard reading, "No Stamp Act, No Sedition Act, No Alien Bills, No Land Tax, downfall to the Tyrants of America; peace and retirement to the President; Long Live the Vice-President." Fearing that such liberty poles, which had been used to inspire the American Revolution, would rally dissent against the administration, a mob of Federalists chopped down the Dedham pole.

Although Brown was generally regarded as a harmless crank,[180] Dedham was the home of Fisher Ames, one of the most repressive of Federalists. To raise a liberty pole in Ames's backyard was certain to court disaster. As Ames observed at the time, "the liberty-pole is down," but the "devil of sedition is immortal, and we, the saints, [have] an endless struggle to maintain with him." The government instituted an all-out search for Brown. Ames proclaimed that "the government must display its power *in terrorem*." Republicans were outraged. The Boston *Independent Chronicle* noted that during the Revolution a pole surmounted with a message criticizing the government was celebrated as a "Liberty Pole," but "now they are called Sedition Poles and . . . suppressed by Government." [181]

Brown was arrested, indicted, and tried in June 1799. Justice Chase presided over the prosecution. Although Brown pleaded guilty, Chase insisted on hearing all the prosecution's witnesses in order to make out a full case against the "wandering apostle of sedition."[182] He then demanded that Brown disclose the names of all those who had aided him or subscribed to his writings. Brown refused. Furious at this contumacy, Chase sentenced Brown to a fine of $450 and eighteen months in prison.*[183]

---

* Not only was Brown given the most severe sentence imposed under the act, but when he could not afford to pay the fine at the end of his term, President Adams refused to release him from jail. As a result, Brown remained in jail for twenty months. See Smith, *Freedom's Fetters* at 268 (cited in note 16).

––––––––––

ONE OF THE MOST SKILLFUL of the Republican polemicists, William Duane was born in America but spent his youth in Ireland, England, and India, where he founded the Calcutta *World*. In 1794, the British governor general, persuaded that Duane's reports showed too much sympathy for the French Revolution, ordered him to leave India because he had advocated "the democratic principles of Tom Paine."[184]

In 1796, Duane returned to America and accepted a position with Benjamin Bache's Philadelphia *Aurora*. After Bache died of yellow fever in 1798, Duane married Bache's widow, Margaret, and assumed the editorship of the *Aurora*, continuing Bache's biting criticism of the Adams administration. By 1800, Duane was a critic of national influence and the toast of Republicans. He was honored at a Republican dinner in Philadelphia as the "scourge" of his nation's "enemies."[185]

Needless to say, Federalists did not share this view. Shortly after Duane took over the *Aurora*, a Federalist mob bushwhacked him, but as it was readying him to be tarred and feathered a group of Republicans came to his rescue. In February 1799, the Federalist authorities in Philadelphia indicted Duane on trumped-up charges that he had "willfully and maliciously stirred up a seditious riot" by circulating a petition calling for the repeal of the Alien Friends Act. After only thirty minutes of deliberation, the jury acquitted him. The Federalists were furious. A month later, thirty members of Philadelphia's volunteer cavalry dragged Duane from the *Aurora*'s office and beat and whipped him until he was unconscious.

In July 1799, Duane charged in the *Aurora* that the British exercised undue and improper influence in the State Department. After consulting the president, who heartily encouraged prosecution, Timothy Pickering directed the federal district attorney to pursue the matter. Duane was promptly indicted under the Sedition Act. The prosecution was hastily abandoned by order of the president, however, when Duane revealed that he had an authenticated letter from John Adams making the very same charge.[186]

As the election of 1800 approached, the Federalists were increasingly desperate to disable critics like Duane and to find ways to ensure Adams's reelection. In January 1800, Federalist Senator James Ross introduced a bill in the Senate to create a "Grand Committee of Thirteen," which would decide in secret session which candidate had won the electoral votes of any contested states in the upcoming presidential election. The committee's composition was designed to ensure that it would be dominated by Federalists.[187] Convinced that this bill was intended to manipulate the outcome of the election, three Republican senators provided a copy of the bill to Duane, who published it in the *Aurora*.[188] Duane charged that the bill was a telling example of "faction secretly working."[189]

The Federalist senators decided to punish Duane for publishing this report and for accusing them (however accurately) of improper motives. Because a criminal prosecution under the Sedition Act would take too long to achieve their goal, they cooked up instead a new Senate committee to punish Duane for his effrontery.

Republicans criticized this innovation as a "star chamber" proceeding and objected that Duane had been perfectly within his rights to publish the text of a bill that had been introduced in Congress. Moreover, they argued that Congress had no constitutional authority to punish a citizen for challenging its conduct or motives and that the proposed procedure denied Duane's constitutional right to due process of law. By a straight party vote, the Federalists rejected these arguments and, without conducting any hearing, condemned Duane for a "high breach of the privileges of this House."[190]

The Senate then invited Duane to appear in person to offer evidence in "mitigation" of his offense, but it refused to permit Duane's lawyers to present evidence of the truth of his assertion or to question the constitutionality of its action. Duane announced that he was bound by his "most sacred duties to decline" to participate in so lawless a proceeding, and promptly went into hiding. To the utter vexation of the Federalists, Duane continued surreptitiously to edit the *Aurora*, which maintained its drumbeat criticism of Adams and his party.[191]

Years later, recalling the fear inspired by the Sedition Act, Jefferson reflected that "no person who was not a witness of the scenes of that gloomy period, can form any idea of the afflicting persecutions and personal indignities we had to brook."*[192]

---

* Other noteworthy victims of Federalist prosecutions for seditious libel included Charles Holt, the twenty-eight-year-old editor of the New London, Connecticut, *Bee*, who was convicted under the Sedition Act for writing that Americans had a "natural and just abhorrence for standing armies"; Abijah Adams, the bookkeeper for the Boston *Independent Chronicle*, which had editorialized that members of the Massachusetts legislature had violated their oaths of office when they refused to endorse the Virginia and Kentucky Resolutions; and Luther Baldwin, a hapless New Jersey Republican of absolutely no repute, who was convicted for drunkenly observing that he didn't care if the local cannon, which were giving President Adams a sixteen-gun salute, "fired thro' his a——." Bee 1–2 (May 21, 1800); Smith, *Freedom's Fetters* at 373–84 (cited in note 16); *A Beacon for the Seditious*, Massachusetts Mercury 1 (Apr 9, 1799); Clyde Augustus Duniway, *The Development of Freedom of the Press in Massachusetts* 144–45 (Burt Franklin 1969). Miller, *Crisis in Freedom* at 120–23 (cited in note 11); Greenleaf's New Daily Advertiser (Oct 15, 1798), excerpted id at 113–14.

"WE ARE ALL REPUBLICANS—WE ARE ALL FEDERALISTS"

ALTHOUGH THE SEDITION ACT was purportedly enacted as a war measure to strengthen the nation in its impending war with France, it served primarily as a political weapon to strengthen the Federalists in their "war" with the Republicans. The Federalists designed the act to expire on March 3, 1801—the last day of Adams's term of office. The stated rationale for this limitation was that the act was a temporary, emergency measure to deal with an immediate crisis. But it was also intended to ensure that the act would not be turned against the Federalists in the event Jefferson defeated Adams in the election of 1800. Although Federalist editors and speakers were as guilty as their Republican counterparts in their resort to innuendo, hyperbole, and false statement, not a single Federalist was ever indicted under the act.[*][193]

Whatever the initial motivation for the Sedition Act, the concerns about wartime security soon became a pretext for securing political advantage. During the liberty pole incident in Dedham, for example, the Federalist *Salem Gazette* published a letter protesting the "plan of the Jacobins" to win a "majority in our next Legislature." The fear was not that the liberty pole would undermine the nation's defense or incite a violent insurrection but that it would rally citizens to the Republican cause.[194]

In a series of essays in the *Boston Gazette*, Fisher Ames made this perfectly clear. Ames alerted fellow Federalists that Republicans intended to "spread the infection" by gaining control in the next "elections of the house of representatives."[195] The Jeffersonians intended to establish a "mobocracy," he warned, and one of their "pestilent designs" was to gain control of the state governments in 1799. Ames cautioned that this was only the first step of their plan. Their ultimate goal was to seize control of the federal government in the elections of 1800. Ames railed that Jacobins were "everywhere in movement, preparing every engine of power and influence, to transfer the country, its liberty, and property, at the next election of president and vice-president, into the hands of men equally destitute of private virtue and public spirit." If such characters ever attained a majority,

---

[*] One of the more revealing features of the Sedition Act was that it expressly protected the president and the Congress against sedition, but not the vice president, who just happened to be Jefferson.

they would "overturn, and overturn, and overturn, till property shall take wings, and true liberty and good government find their graves."

Ames exhorted his Federalist colleagues that unless they defeated the "rabble," they would have to prepare their swords within the next two years. Like most Federalists, he had no confidence at all in the electoral process. He argued that "no nation" can rely on the "political discernment of its citizens, to discover and repel the danger to its liberty and independence." To protect the people from being duped by the Republicans at the polls, the government must be armed "with force enough" to keep "watch in our stead."[196]

THE FEDERAL BENCH, WHICH CONSISTED entirely of Federalists, joined the campaign against republicanism with such fervor as to taint its capacity to conduct impartial trials.[*][197] Although Samuel Chase stood alone in the scale of his impropriety, many judges fanned political passions, applied the Sedition Act to further partisan interests, and actively cooperated in ferreting out potential violators.

The Supreme Court did not rule on the constitutionality of the Sedition Act in this era,[†] but Federalist judges and justices were unanimous in upholding it. Justice Iredell offered the standard argument in favor of the act. In the course of his charge to a grand jury in May 1799, he conceded that the meaning of "the freedom of the press, if it had been a new subject," might "admit of some controversy." But "so far as precedent, habit, laws, and practices are concerned, there can scarcely be a more definite meaning." That meaning, he explained, was set forth in Blackstone's *Commentaries*, which made clear that although the government could not require a license to publish, it could punish "any dangerous or offensive writings." Iredell asserted that this made sense, as did the Sedition Act, because if you "take away from a Republic the confidence of the people . . . the whole fabric crumbles into the dust."[198]

Of all the Federalist judges, Chase was the one Republicans most feared and

---

[*] In part because of the conduct of the federal judges in the Sedition Act cases, the Republicans opposed the notion that the Supreme Court is the final arbiter of the meaning of the Constitution. This helps explain the Virginia and Kentucky Resolutions, which sought a different mechanism to determine whether federal laws were unconstitutional by allowing states to oppose laws they thought violated the terms of their compact.

[†] Because the Supreme Court was composed entirely of Federalist justices, Republicans had no incentive to seek review in the Supreme Court.

loathed. They referred to Chase's behavior in sedition trials from 1798 to 1800 as "Chase's Bloody Circuit." Like Timothy Pickering, Chase made it his personal mission to destroy those whose political opinions threatened his vision of the United States. Chase dreaded "the licentiousness of the press," and thought it the most "certain means of bringing about the destruction" of republican government.[199]

In 1804, the House of Representatives voted a bill of impeachment against Justice Chase. The articles of impeachment found that, in the trial of James Callender, Chase had committed misconduct in his rulings and in his "rude and contemptuous" treatment of the prisoner's counsel. The articles declared that the trial had been marked by "manifest injustice, partiality and intemperance."[200] Only considerations of Chase's age, the presence of a block of Federalist senators, and the determination of a handful of Republican senators to avoid any hint of impeachment for "political reasons" saved Chase from conviction by the required two-thirds majority.[*][201]

AS EVENTS PLAYED OUT in the final years of the eighteenth century, a full-scale war with France was avoided. After the summer of 1798, there was a gradual easing of tensions. Although most Federalists expected war in the spring of 1798, they hesitated because they were unsure of sustained public support, especially if England fell to the French. More important, France did not want war with the United States. Its goal was to reorient American foreign policy, not to precipitate a full-scale military conflict. After the French suffered reverses in Europe and the Near East, Talleyrand let it be known that he was open to renewed negotiations.[202]

Most Federalists feared that Talleyrand was merely manipulating American public opinion to foster division, but Adams decided to take him at his word. Over the opposition of most Federalists, he sent a peace mission to Paris in November 1799.[203]

Once Adams reopened negotiations, the French threat began to dissipate. It could no longer serve as a rallying cry for military expenditures or the suppression

---

[*] The Senate's failure to convict Chase was an important victory for President Jefferson's policy of reconciliation and has served over the years as a salutary precedent because it implicitly established the proposition that federal judges may not be impeached merely for taking judicial positions that are unpopular with the prevailing opinion. In that sense, it has measurably strengthened the federal judiciary as an independent branch of government. See Currie, *Constitution in Congress* at 31–36 (cited in note 31); Richard Ellis, "The Impeachment of Samuel Chase," in Michael R. Belknap, ed, *American Political Trials* 57, 71–72 (Greenwood 1994).

of the "Jacobin menace." For many Federalists, however, the fear of Jacobinism and the clamor for a military buildup had become obsessions they could not relinquish. As the elections of 1800 approached, leaders of the Federalist Party, furious at Adams for sending a peace delegation to France, began searching for ways to replace him as the party's candidate for president. The more conservative among them concluded that Adams had gone soft on both the external and internal dangers threatening the nation. When Adams ordered the demobilization of the army in the spring of 1800, his enemies within the party set out to destroy him.[204]

As relations among Federalists deteriorated in a web of plots and conspiracies, Adams raged against his foes. He aimed his most bitter barbs at Alexander Hamilton, whom he described as "the greatest intriguant in the world" and "a man devoid of every moral principle." Adams's former intimates believed him unhinged and savaged him publicly as well as privately. Speaking of Adams, Theodore Sedgwick, his longtime ally, said that "every tormenting passion rankles in the bosom of that weak and frantic old man." Fisher Ames decried Adams's "extravagant opinion of himself," his "ignorance of parties and characters," and his "pride" and "caprice."[205]

In October 1800, Hamilton circulated his infamous *Letter concerning the Public Conduct and Character of John Adams*, in which he announced that Adams "does not possess the talents adapted to the Administration of Government" and that "there are great and intrinsic defects in his character, which unfit him for the office of Chief Magistrate." Hamilton averred that Adams lacked "sound judgment" and "steady perseverance," but possessed "a vanity without bounds, and a jealousy capable of discoloring every object." Many Federalists feared that Hamilton had gone too far and that his hatred of Adams bordered on the fanatical. Noah Webster charged that Hamilton was destroying the party, and the New London *Bee* complained that Hamilton's attack included "the most gross and libelous charges against Mr. Adams that have ever yet been published." The Republicans gleefully asked why the administration did not prosecute Hamilton under the Sedition Act. The Federalist Party was visibly disintegrating.[206]

When the votes were finally tallied, Jefferson had defeated Adams and the Republicans had won a substantial majority in the House of Representatives. In attempting to steer a "sensible middle course," Adams had managed to offend everyone.[207] But he did restore the peace. Adams later wrote, "I desire no other inscription over my gravestone than 'Here lies John Adams, who took upon himself the responsibility of the peace with France in the year 1800.'"[208] The "revolution of 1800" was complete.*

---

* Jefferson received 73 electoral votes to Adams's 65. The makeup of the House of Representatives shifted from a strongly Federalist majority of 63 to 43 to a substantial Republican majority of

THE SEDITION ACT EXPIRED on March 3, 1801, the final day of Adams's term of office. The net effect of the act had been to "stir up a nest of hornets." Even though the three most influential Republican editors—Cooper, Callender, and Duane—were all in jail by 1800, the act did not dampen the vigor of the Republican opposition. John Quincy Adams later observed that the act had "operated like oil upon the flames."[209] The Sedition Act alienated a substantial majority of the American people, gave those who supported the Republican cause a powerful issue of principle around which to rally, and hastened the downfall of the Federalist Party.[210] In this respect, the Sedition Act of 1798 teaches a critical lesson: the protection of freedom must come ultimately from *the people themselves.* As the legal scholar Larry Kramer has observed, "nothing can vouchsafe the rightness" of what our governmental institutions do, nothing can ultimately "save them from partiality and blindness, other than democratic challenge, scrutiny, and revision."[211]

A fundamental test for the new nation was whether it could peacefully transfer power from one faction to another. In 1800, the nation seemed to be "tottering on the edge of chaos." No one knew for sure whether the election of 1800 would trigger civil war. The Alien and Sedition Acts had left Republicans, and especially Virginians, afraid that a Federalist victory in 1800 would spell the demise of republicanism and their liberty. With the Kentucky and Virginia Resolutions, and rumors that Virginia and other states were stockpiling arms, Federalists feared that a Republican victory would lead to an era of state-sponsored Jacobinism. There was good reason to believe that, like the Federalist Party, the nation would simply disintegrate. But beneath the abusive rhetoric and venomous invective, it turned out that Federalists and Republicans shared a deeper allegiance to the Constitution than even they had suspected.[212]

In his inaugural address in March 1801, President Jefferson was conciliatory. He observed, "During the contest of opinion through which we have passed, the

---

65 to 41. Jefferson's victory ushered in a prolonged period of Republican control of the federal government. From 1801 until 1825, through the presidencies of Jefferson, Madison, and Monroe, the Republicans dominated national politics. Looking back on the election of 1800, Jefferson spoke of "the revolution of 1800" as "as real a revolution in the principles of our government as that of 1776 was in its form; not effected indeed by the sword, as that, but by the rational and peaceable instrument of reform, the suffrage of the people." Schlesinger and Israel, eds, 1 *History of American Presidential Elections* at 101 (cited in note 19). See Sharp, *American Politics in the Early Republic* at 248, 278 (cited in note 1).

Thomas Jefferson

animation of discussions . . . has sometimes worn an aspect which might impose on strangers unused to think freely and to speak and to write what they think." He urged Americans to "reflect that, having banished from our land that religious intolerance under which mankind so long bled and suffered, we have yet gained little if we countenance a political intolerance as despotic, as wicked, and capable of as bitter and bloody persecutions." "Every difference of opinion," he observed, "is not a difference of principle. . . . We are all republicans—we are all federalists."

Jefferson added, "If there be any among us who would wish to dissolve this Union or to change its republican form, let them stand undisturbed as monuments of the safety with which error of opinion may be tolerated where reason is left free to combat it." Noting that the nation was "in the full tide of successful experiment," he conceded that "sometimes it is said that man cannot be trusted with the government of himself." But, he asked, "can he, then, be trusted with the government of others?"

After setting forth what he deemed "the essential principles of our government," including "the diffusion of information," the "arraignment of all abuses at the bar of public reason," and the "freedom of the press," Jefferson proclaimed that "should we wander" from these principles "in moments of error or alarm, let us hasten to retrace our steps and to regain the road which alone leads to peace, liberty, and safety."[213]

As one of his first official acts of office, Jefferson pardoned all those who had been convicted under the Sedition Act and freed those still in jail, noting that he considered the act "to be nullity as absolute and as palpable as if Congress had ordered us to fall down and worship a golden image."*[214]

Forty years later, on July 4, 1840, Congress repaid all of the fines paid under the Sedition Act, with interest, to the legal representatives of those who had been convicted. The congressional committee report declared that the Sedition Act had been passed under a "mistaken exercise" of power and was "null and void." The unconstitutionality of the act, the report announced, had been "conclusively settled."[215]

More than a century after Congress's action, the Supreme Court, in its landmark 1964 decision in *New York Times v. Sullivan*,[216] celebrated the "profound national commitment to the principle that debate on public issues should be uninhibited, robust, and wide-open," noting that it may well include "vehement, caustic, and sometimes unpleasantly sharp attacks on government and public officials." The Court added that "this is the lesson to be drawn from the great controversy over the Sedition Act of 1798, which first crystallized a national awareness of the central meaning of the First Amendment." It concluded that, "although the Sedition Act was never tested in this Court, the attack upon its validity has carried the day in the court of history."[217]

"THERE IS NO SUCH THING AS A FALSE IDEA"

WHAT SHOULD WE LEARN from this episode? The threat of imminent war with France fostered a climate of fear, anxiety, and suspicion.

---

* Like Hamilton and Adams, Jefferson worried about the licentiousness of the press. He differed from the Federalists primarily in his view that regulation of the press was a matter for the states rather than for the federal government. During his presidency, Jefferson expressed the opinion that "a few prosecutions of the most prominent offenders would have a wholesome effect in restoring the integrity of the presses." Miller, *Crisis in Freedom* at 231–32 (cited in note 11); Pasley, *"Tyranny of the Printers"* at 258–319 (cited in note 6).

Given the recent history of France, which had successfully undermined other governments by promoting domestic subversion, accusations of disloyalty were inevitable and rampant. Such charges were leveled both at aliens, whose loyalty could easily be called into question, and at Republicans, whose opposition to war measures could readily be cast as treasonable efforts to undermine the nation's defenses and weaken its will to fight.

The glory of the American Revolution was still fresh in the national memory. The sights and sounds of martial music, waving flags, patriotic parades, and men in uniform stirred the blood and quickened the imagination. In this atmosphere of high anxiety and fevered patriotism, the nation rallied in support of bold new legislation designed to strengthen the military, ferret out and destroy potential subversives, and crush disloyalty. The cautions voiced by Republicans were swept aside as the self-interested protests of a suspect faction. Circumstances were ripe for the aggressive suppression of dissent.

But what was actually *wrong* with the Sedition Act of 1798? After all, as the Federalists argued, the act was clearly an advance over the English common law. If this episode was regrettable, what should we do differently in the future? What lessons should we learn?

Perhaps most obviously, when we act in the heat of war fever, we may overreact against those who question the need for military action. Fear, anger, and an aroused patriotism can undermine sound judgment. The congressional debates in 1798 reveal how easily a nation can slide from disagreements about policy to accusations of disloyalty. The consequence is not only the suppression of individual dissent but the mutilation of public discourse and government decision making.

Moreover, as the events of 1798 illustrate, those in power may exploit a threat to the nation's security to serve their partisan ends. A time-honored strategy for consolidating power is to inflate the public's fears, inflame its patriotism, and then condemn political opponents as "disloyal." A national crisis (real, fabricated, or imagined) invites this strategy.

The struggle over the Sedition Act should also cause us to question whether we can count on judges and jurors to protect our civil liberties in moments of high national anxiety. Although the circumstances in 1798 were unique in that the Federalists had appointed all sitting federal judges, the conduct of those judges is nonetheless revealing. Because federal judges are guaranteed life tenure, are professionally trained to be impartial and independent of the elected branches, and understand that they have a special responsibility to enforce the Constitution and laws of the United States in an objective and evenhanded manner, they can play an important role in preserving constitutional rights even in the face of social, political, and military pressures.

But even the best and most well-intentioned judges cannot separate themselves *entirely* from their own political, social, philosophical, and personal beliefs. Judges live in the same world as the rest of us, and they are subject to the same fears, passions, and uncertainties. Thus, in times of national crisis, judges will not always be inclined or able to preserve civil liberties when they are under assault. In a self-governing society, citizens must not sit back passively and expect judges and jurors to make the hard decisions for them. To preserve constitutional liberties, citizens must educate themselves and play an active role in the political process. In the long run, a passive citizenry will be a citizenry that has forfeited rights.

We should also learn from this episode to be skeptical of confident assurances that courts can readily distinguish between "malicious" intent and "legitimate" dissent. Inquiries into a speaker's subjective intent are elusive, at best. If a speaker condemns a president as ill informed and incompetent, is his intent "maliciously" to obstruct the president's policies or "legitimately" to criticize him for failing in his official responsibilities? As the Republicans warned during the debates over the Sedition Act, and as the judgments of juries in the Sedition Act prosecutions suggest, this is a difficult line to tread. Jurors are much more likely to find "malice" when they disagree with a speaker's views. This is too fine a thread on which to rest the constitutional protection of free expression.

The Sedition Act controversy should also cause us to look askance at self-serving government assertions that its "real" reason for punishing dissent in wartime is to protect the national security. Republican criticism of the Adams administration surely could have dampened enthusiasm for the military buildup and made it more difficult for the government to muster troops, build ships, and provision the army. But it also could have changed public opinion about the nature of the French threat and legitimately called the administration's leadership into question. The "real" purpose of the government in attempting to suppress such criticism might be to stifle political opposition, it might be to protect the national security, and it might be some combination of the two. This is critical. Suppressing speech because it is dangerous to the national interest is one thing; suppressing it because it threatens a partisan interest is something else entirely. As the events of 1798 demonstrate, it is often difficult to tell the difference.

One lesson of this episode is unmistakable. The very concept of a false political *opinion* is incompatible with the First Amendment. Although Republicans understood this throughout the Sedition Act controversy, Federalists (including Federalist judges) rejected this proposition.

In perhaps its single most important sentence on the freedom of speech, the Supreme Court declared in 1974 that "under the First Amendment there is no such thing as a false idea."[218] What does this mean? It does not mean that some ideas are not better than others, or that we must always act as if all ideas are of equal worth. Rather, it means that *conclusive* judgments about which ideas are good and which are bad, which are true and which are false, are not to be made by the government, by a judge, by a jury, or even by a majority vote of the people. As the Court explained, "however pernicious an opinion may seem, we depend for its correction not on the conscience" of legislators or judges or voters "but on the competition of other ideas."[219]

Thus, we can act on the "good" idea that we should go to war with France, but we cannot act on the "good" idea that no one may question that decision, or challenge its premises, or criticize its supporters. The First Amendment, in other words, places out of bounds any attempt to freeze public opinion.

But why should this be so? If we are convinced that a war is justified, why shouldn't we ban speech that attacks the war as unwise or immoral? Why can't we act on our judgment that such claims are false? A simple answer would be that we don't *need* to ban "bad" ideas, because we are confident the people will not embrace them if they are allowed to consider them in free and open debate. But we shouldn't believe that. We know that knowledge, people, and debate are imperfect, and that at least sometimes people will accept and act upon "bad" ideas if they are free to do so. So, that is not the explanation.

It is, rather, that we are balancing two competing risks. On the one hand, there is the risk that, if permitted to consider all ideas, the people will sometimes embrace bad ones. On the other hand, there is the risk that, if given the power to suppress ideas they believe to be "false," the people will sometimes suppress ideas that would better be left open to continued debate and deliberation.

In choosing between these risks, and deciding whether the people, acting through their government, should be able to declare certain ideas "false," we must consider the nature of human nature. As history teaches, people are prone to intolerance. We have a need to believe that we are right, to believe "that we know that we know," to silence those who disagree, and, in the words of Justice Holmes, to "sweep away all opposition."[220]

If the people can act on this instinct, there is every danger they will do so. It is not inherent in human nature to be skeptical, self-doubting, and tolerant of opposing ideas. We are naturally inclined to enforce what is "right," rather than to abide ideas that, again in the words of Justice Holmes, "we loathe and believe to be fraught with death." The First Amendment, on this view, cuts *against* human nature. It demands that we be better than we would be.[221]

The Supreme Court has it right. The danger of repression is greater than the danger of debate. For our nation to declare that "under the First Amendment there is no such thing as a false idea" is, in effect, to embrace ambivalence, to foster an ongoing reexamination of our beliefs, and to insist upon tolerance of those opinions we might too readily dismiss.[222] It is, in short, to insist upon the right to doubt. That is the most fundamental lesson of the Sedition Act of 1798.

SPADRE BLUFFS

AND WHAT OF MATTHEW LYON? After his reelection and release from prison, Lyon was ready for a change. As he wrote John Adams on the day both of their terms of office expired, he was done with the "base" and "cruel" calumnies of politics. At the age of fifty, Lyon was ready to withdraw from public life. He and his family decided to head west to Kentucky, where he sought respite from the "persecutions" of partisan strife.[223]

Lyon settled his affairs in Vermont, deeded a significant parcel of land to the town for a public library, and moved on to the western frontier. On a bluff overlooking the Cumberland River, he and his clan established a new community. He quickly developed several successful businesses—trading along the Mississippi River, provisioning the army, building ships, selling books, and operating a paper mill and a cotton gin.

Despite his business ventures, Lyon found politics irresistible. In 1803, he was elected to represent his Kentucky district in Congress, a position he held until 1811. He became a man of respectable bearing, making up for his "great defects of education" by his "openness of temper and force of mind."[224] He emerged as a strong voice in the House, fighting for democratic reforms in the rules of Congress and in the governance of the western territories.

During this phase of his career, Lyon ironically found himself allied with traditional Federalist positions on such issues as the sanctity of contract and respect for property rights.[225] As time went on, he became increasingly alienated from the Republicans, particularly on matters of international trade and foreign affairs. When he opposed the War of 1812, Republicans in Kentucky branded him a Tory, a Federalist, and a British partisan, and cast him out of office.

In 1816, Lyon suffered business reverses and fell into dire financial straits. He brought his plight to the attention of President Monroe, who appointed him to the humble position of U.S. factor to the Cherokee Indians, at Spadre Bluffs, Arkansas. At the age of seventy-one, Lyon undertook this post with characteristic vigor. His responsibility was to oversee an isolated trading post, buying goods from the Indians, such as fur and buffalo horns, and selling them products to help develop their economy. Lyon lived in a cabin and slept on bearskins on the floor. He became an avid advocate for the Indians and persuaded the U.S. gov-

ernment to supply the Cherokees with a cotton gin so they could learn to cultivate the land. In 1822, however, to Lyon's bitter disappointment, the government
reneged on its agreement.[226]

In his seventy-seventh year, Lyon loaded a flatboat with furs, pelts, and Indian
goods and set off from Spadre Bluff down the Mississippi River to New Orleans.
On arriving there, he exchanged these products for the ironware and machinery
necessary to establish a cotton gin in Spadre Bluff. The round trip, which he
made in frigid winter conditions, covered more than three thousand miles.[227] On
August 1, 1822, at the age of seventy-seven, Matthew Lyon died at his lonely trading post in Arkansas.

2

THE CIVIL WAR

Mr. Lincoln's First Amendment

Antidraft Protest Turns Violent, New York, 1863

*F*OR SIXTY YEARS FOLLOWING the election of 1800, the U.S. government did not attempt to silence criticism of national leaders or policies. Although this was an often stressful era, the government adhered to the consensus about free speech that had emerged from the struggle over the Sedition Act of 1798.

The Civil War, however, revived the conflict over free speech in wartime. As the war raged and casualties mounted into the hundreds of thousands, dissent took many forms, ranging from thoughtful criticism to vicious invective and mob violence. Abraham Lincoln was subjected to the most ill-tempered and vituperative denunciation ever directed at a president of the United States. By sapping public morale, demoralizing soldiers, and emboldening those who would resort to unlawful acts of resistance, Civil War dissent fractured the North as no war has divided the nation before or since.

Although Lincoln suspended the writ of habeas corpus* in an effort to maintain civil order, he resisted the temptation to enact a new Sedition Act. Whether for reasons of practical politics or constitutional principle, he declined to censor criticism of him or his administration. Often called a "tyrant" for his conduct of the war, Lincoln struggled to leave unpunished even the most vicious utterances. And in those instances when he did approve the suppression of dissent, he offered

---

* The writ of habeas corpus enables an individual who has been detained by government officials to seek a judicial determination of the legality of his detention. If the writ of habeas corpus is suspended, no court may review the legality of detention or order the individual's release if the detention is unlawful.

thoughtful explanations of his judgments and posed serious questions about the appropriate limits of free speech in wartime.

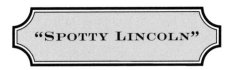

"SPOTTY LINCOLN"

THE CONFLICT WITH MEXICO began in the 1830s with the Texas war of independence, a war that thrilled the nation. Americans ardently "remembered the Alamo." Following the annexation of Texas in 1845, war with Mexico seemed inevitable. President Polk sent a contingent of troops to the Rio Grande to protect Texas from invasion. Shortly thereafter, Polk reported to Congress that the Mexican army had attacked American citizens. On May 11, 1846, the United States declared war. In a burst of patriotic fervor, three hundred thousand young men volunteered in response to Polk's call to arms.

By the time Abe Lincoln, a newly elected congressman, arrived in Washington, the war had been raging inconclusively for twenty months. Members of his party accused the president of instigating the war in order to expand American territory and strengthen the slavery faction in the United States. Congressman Robert Toombs of Georgia called upon Congress to put a halt to the president's lust for Mexican land, and Congressman Smith of New York charged Polk with invading Mexican territory "to which we had no manner of claim."[1] The president insisted that Mexico had started the war by attacking American citizens on American soil.

The new congressman from Illinois was determined to enter the fray. Only two weeks after he was sworn in, Lincoln boldly presented a series of questions, known as the "spot" resolutions, which demanded that the president inform the House "whether the particular spot on which the blood of our citizens" was first shed "was or was not" on American soil.[2] Receiving no response from the White House, Lincoln took the floor of the House to challenge the president personally. He characterized Polk's justification for military action as dishonest and warned that if Polk refused to respond to his resolutions he would have to conclude that the president "was deeply conscious of being in the wrong." He declared that the president's explanation of his policies was like "the half insane excitement of a fevered dream" and charged that Polk was a "completely bewildered man" without even a "conception" of how or when the war would end.[3]

Lincoln's constituents accused him of disloyalty and charged that he had betrayed the thousands of young men who had fought bravely for their country. His former supporters resented his implication that they and their fallen comrades had risked—and sacrificed—life and limb in an unworthy cause. Critics condemned his speech in the House as the work of an "imbecile" and embraced resolutions denouncing "slanderers of the President." The press attacked his "dastardly and treasonable assault upon President Polk" and tagged him the "second Benedict Arnold." Mocking his "spot" resolutions, the press ridiculed him as "spotty Lincoln."[4] Although Lincoln had planned to run for reelection, this was now out of the question.

FIFTEEN YEARS LATER, President Lincoln faced a grave dilemma. On May 1, 1863, Clement Vallandigham, a former congressman and one of the most prominent of the antiwar "Peace Democrats," delivered a rousing speech to a large gathering in Mount Vernon, Ohio. Vallandigham described the Civil War as "wicked, cruel, and unnecessary," blamed it on Lincoln and the Republicans, and called it a war "for the freedom of the blacks and the enslavement of the whites." The speech brought cheers from the largely antiwar, anti-Lincoln crowd. Without consulting the president, General Ambrose Burnside ordered a company of infantry to arrest Vallandigham, who was charged with making "treasonable utterances" and promptly tried and convicted by a military commission, which sentenced him to imprisonment for the remainder of the war.[5]

Citizens throughout the Union protested this action. Mass demonstrations erupted in almost every major Northern city. The Democratic press declared the government's conduct a crime against the Constitution, and even some Republicans criticized Vallandigham's arrest and detention. The president received petitions beseeching him to reverse the military commission. For Lincoln, in the light of his own experience, this posed a dilemma with exquisite personal resonance.

"ABRAHAM AFRICANUS THE FIRST"

TO APPRECIATE THE FREE SPEECH issues that arose during the Civil War, it is necessary to understand the extraordinary crises that faced the new president. To most Southerners, slavery was not an evil, but the essential basis of peace and prosperity, a "necessity to prevent blacks from degenerating into barbarism, crime, and poverty."[6] Southerners resented the moral condemnation of slavery as an insult to Southern honor. On the subject of slavery, declared the *Charleston Mercury* in 1858, "the South and the North . . . are not only two Peoples" but two "hostile Peoples."[7]

The presidential election of 1860 was the culmination of nearly a century of sectional conflict. Southerners insisted upon a candidate who would guarantee the extension of slavery into the territories. They therefore rejected the Democratic nominee, Stephen A. Douglas, whose support of popular sovereignty would have left their interests in doubt by allowing new states to reject slavery, and backed John C. Breckinridge, splitting the Democratic Party. Citizens voted along strict sectional lines, leading to the election of the Republican candidate, Abraham Lincoln, who won only 40 percent of the popular vote and whose support was limited almost entirely to the North and the West.

Despite repeated warnings from Southerners that a Republican victory would leave the nation "crimsoned in human gore,"[8] Lincoln did not expect any serious effort to dissolve the Union. The "people of the South," he opined, "have too much of good sense, and good temper, to attempt the ruin of the government."[9] Six weeks after his election, however, amid fireworks, marching bands, and celebratory rallies, South Carolina announced its secession from the Union. Submission to a Republican administration, wrote one South Carolinian, would mean "the loss of liberty, property, home, country—everything that makes life worth having."[10] The other states of the lower South soon followed South Carolina's lead.

The lame-duck administration of President James Buchanan did nothing to counter these developments. In December 1860, in an address that has aptly been described as one of the most "unfortunate" in U.S. history,[11] Buchanan blamed the crisis on the Republicans' "incessant and violent agitation of the slavery question" and declared that although secession was unconstitutional, the national government had no power "to coerce a State into submission."[12] Pro-secessionist forces seized most of the federal forts in the South, and in early February of the new year, a month before Lincoln's inauguration, South Carolina, Georgia, Florida, Alabama, Mississippi, and Louisiana lost no time in meeting in Montgomery, Alabama, to establish the Confederate States of America.

In this critical period of transition, many in the North urged conciliation in order to preserve the Union. The powerful newspaper editor Horace Greeley advised that the North should let the South "go in peace."[13] Although Lincoln remained firm in opposing the extension of slavery to the territories, he gave his express approval to an offer of compromise that would have guaranteed "slavery in the states against any future interference by the federal government."[14] Before this proposal could be acted upon, however, Confederate guns opened fire on Fort Sumter in early April of 1861. For the next four years, the twenty-three states of the Union and the eleven states of the Confederacy* were locked in one of his-

---

* The original secessionist states were later joined by Virginia, North Carolina, Texas, Arkansas, and Tennessee.

tory's most brutal conflicts. Some 620,000 soldiers lost their lives in the Civil War, dwarfing the human cost of any other American conflict.

Lincoln confronted a tangled knot of complications common to most civil wars, including sharply divided loyalties, fluid and often uncertain military and political boundaries, and easy opportunities for espionage and sabotage. He also faced a unique set of additional dilemmas because of his need to retain the loyalty of the border states, address divisive questions of race, slavery, and emancipation, and impose conscription for the first time in the nation's history. Bitter disagreement, even within the Union, was inevitable.

UPON ASSUMING OFFICE, Lincoln was desperate to nurture the precarious loyalty of Delaware, Maryland, Kentucky, and Missouri—the four slave states that had not yet seceded. If these four states left the Union, they would add almost 50 percent to the military manpower of the Confederacy. Maryland was especially vital because it surrounded the nation's capital on three sides (with Virginia on the fourth).[15]

The gravity of the challenge in Maryland was apparent even before Lincoln's inauguration. While en route to Washington, Lincoln had to pass through Baltimore, a port city teeming with secessionist sympathizers. Multiple assassination threats caused Lincoln reluctantly to cancel a public appearance and sneak though Baltimore "like a thief in the night."[16] Rumors quickly spread that he had donned a Scotch plaid hat and a long military cloak to disguise his appearance. This was not true, but the Democratic press had a field day. The Baltimore *Sun* chided, "[H]ad we any respect for Mr. Lincoln, . . . the final escapade by which he reached the capital would have utterly demolished it." Suggesting that Lincoln was a buffoon and a coward, the *Sun* added, "[W]e do not believe the Presidency can ever be more degraded" than it already has been by him, "even before his inauguration."*[17]

A month later, shortly after the attack on Fort Sumter, the Sixth Massachusetts Volunteers attempted to march through Baltimore in order to reach the nation's capital. A mob of Confederate sympathizers attacked the soldiers, causing sixteen deaths and widespread rioting. To prevent additional Union troops from entering the city, the mayor ordered the destruction of all railroad bridges connecting Baltimore with the North. Suddenly, the nation's capital was isolated and its citizens were gripped by fear.[18] On April 27, to restore order in Baltimore

---

* Lincoln always regretted the way he "skulked" into Washington as "a source of shame and regret to me." Sandburg, 2 *Abraham Lincoln* at 205–6 (cited in note 17).

and enable Union forces to protect Washington, Lincoln suspended the writ of habeas corpus and declared martial law in Maryland.[*][19]

Soon thereafter, in the course of arresting suspected secessionists, Union soldiers seized John Merryman, a cavalryman who had allegedly burned bridges and destroyed telegraph wires during the April riots. Merryman immediately filed a petition for a writ of habeas corpus, seeking his release from military detention. The judge assigned to hear Merryman's petition was Roger B. Taney, chief justice of the United States.[†]

BORN IN MARYLAND IN 1777, Taney was raised in the conservative tradition of the Southern landed aristocracy. He established himself as a protégé of President Andrew Jackson, who appointed him attorney general of the United States in 1831. Four years later, Jackson appointed Taney chief justice of the Supreme Court, succeeding John Marshall. In 1857, Chief Justice Taney attempted to end the nation's agony over slavery by holding in the *Dred Scott* case[20] that Congress had no power to ban slavery in the territories and that members of the African race were not citizens of the United States and were therefore not entitled to any of "the rights and privileges" guaranteed by the Constitution. Often described as the greatest legal and moral blunder in the Court's history, this decision inflamed the national crisis and led the abolitionist William Lloyd Garrison to deride the Constitution as "a covenant with death, and an agreement with hell."[21]

Shortly after the assault on Fort Sumter, Taney expressed his hope "that the North, as well as the South, will see that a peaceful separation, with free institutions in each section, is far better than the union of all the present states under a military government, and a reign of terror."[22] He therefore welcomed the opportunity to consider Merryman's petition. On May 26, 1861, Taney ruled in *Ex parte Merryman* that only Congress was authorized to suspend the writ of habeas corpus and that Lincoln's executive order was therefore unconstitutional. Moreover, because Merryman was not a member of the military forces of the United States, and because the civil courts in Maryland were open and functioning, Taney held that ordinary judicial process, rather than military authority, had jurisdiction over the matter. Taney therefore issued a writ of habeas corpus and commanded General George Cadwalader, who was in charge of Fort McHenry

---

[*] The order was narrow in scope, encompassing only those areas that would cut off travel routes to and from Washington, D.C.

[†] The justices still "rode circuit" and heard cases individually at the local level.

Justice Roger Taney

and who had custody of Merryman, to appear before him with "the body of John Merryman" in order to comply with whatever the "Court shall determine." [23]

Taney's attack on Lincoln's order was celebrated throughout the Confederacy. In the North, it quickly became a critical part of the anti-administration literature. The decision was condemned, however, by the pro-administration press. The Washington *Evening Star* complained that it palpably ignored the "existing state of the country." The *New York Times* added that Taney's action presented "the ungracious spectacle" of a judicial officer who is "eager . . . to exculpate a traitor."[24]

Lincoln flatly refused to comply with the chief justice's ruling.[25] When the U.S. marshal arrived at Fort McHenry to serve the writ on Cadwalader, he was refused entrance to the fort. Taney was stymied. Although noting that the marshal technically had legal authority to seize Cadwalader and bring him forcibly before the court, Taney recognized that the marshal "will be resisted in the discharge of that duty by a force notoriously superior" to his own and, "such being the case, the Court has no power under the law." He concluded that all he could do was to "reduce to writing" the reasons under which he had acted and report them to the president, in the hope that he will "perform his constitutional duty to enforce the laws; in other words to enforce the process of this Court."[26] Lincoln ignored Taney's "report."

Given the frantic and fearful state of the Union at this moment, there was no meaningful public opposition either to Lincoln's suspension of the writ of habeas corpus or his disregard of Taney's decision.[27] Merryman was released several weeks later. Although charged with treason, he was never tried, because the government recognized that no Maryland jury would convict him.[28]

MATTERS WERE SIMILARLY GRIM in Missouri and Kentucky. A month after the fall of Fort Sumter, the Missouri governor publicly called for secession. Federal troops marched into St. Louis, triggering a riot in which several citizens were killed. Large areas of the state soon became a battleground in which arson, ambush, and murder were common.[29] Missouri, a state that had been riven by violence throughout the 1850s, seemed headed for a civil war within its own borders. To restore order, local military commanders sharply restricted civil liberties.[30] In August 1861, John C. Frémont, the Union commander of the Western Department, summarily declared martial law in St. Louis County and announced that the slaves of all Missouri rebels would immediately be freed. Lincoln, who was trying to keep Missouri in the Union, promptly superseded Frémont's order.[31]

The situation in Kentucky proved little better. More than 40 percent of the men from Kentucky who participated in the Civil War fought for the South. The families and friends of these men were bitterly divided in their loyalties. In September 1861, Lincoln observed wearily, "[T]o lose Kentucky is nearly the same as to lose the whole game. Kentucky gone, we can not hold Missouri, nor, as I think, Maryland. These all against us, and the job on our hands is too large for us. We would as well consent to separation at once, including the surrender of this capital."[32]

In an effort to suppress pro-secessionist forces in these border states, Lincoln placed Secretary of State William Seward in charge of internal security, granting him authority to arrest all persons suspected of disloyalty in those areas where habeas corpus had been suspended.[33] Although these actions triggered some protest, for the most part they were approved by the public as effective means of quelling disorder.[34] In the spring of 1862, Lincoln explained that harsh measures had been necessary in the early days of the rebellion because "every department of the Government [had been] paralyzed by treason."*[35] He responded to criticism of his actions with a medical analogy, noting that a limb must sometimes be amputated to save a life, but that a life must never be given to save a limb.[36] Once order had been established, Lincoln directed the release of these prisoners upon an oath of loyalty to the Union. The *New York Tribune* rejoiced that "the reign of lawless despotism is ended."[37]

THROUGHOUT THE WAR, Lincoln maintained that his only goal was to preserve the Union. If states could secede at will whenever they disagreed with the judgments of the majority, there could be no Union, no lasting democracy, and the great American experiment would fail. This, rather than slavery, was the issue that motivated many, perhaps most, Northerners.[38] By the summer of 1862, however, the Union had become increasingly polarized on the issue of emancipation. Abolitionists had grown impatient with the president's inaction. William Lloyd Garrison complained that Lincoln was "nothing better than a wet rag," and Frederick Douglass accused Lincoln of "allowing himself to be . . . the miserable tool of traitors and rebels." Horace Greeley attacked the president mercilessly in the *New York Tribune* for his failure to act decisively.[39]

---

* Congress and the Lincoln administration also experimented with loyalty oaths. A month after Fort Sumter fell, Congress enacted, without debate, a loyalty-oath statute, which Lincoln signed into law on August 8. The statute covered persons "in any way connected with the central government." Because of its perceived, and actual, ineffectiveness, Congress adopted "a tougher, 'ironclad' test oath" in July 1862. This, too, resulted in no prosecutions. Hyman, *More Perfect Union* at 175–77 (cited in note 25).

As the conflict wore on, Republicans came increasingly to view the fate of the nation as tied to the fate of slavery. As Representative George Julian of Indiana declared in January 1862, "the mere suppression of the rebellion will be an empty mockery of our sufferings and sacrifices, if slavery shall be spared."[40] By mid-1862, almost all Republicans shared this view.[41] This was due in part to the moral claims of abolition and in part to the practical judgment that emancipation would weaken the South and thus hasten an end to the war.

Democrats, on the other hand, vehemently opposed emancipation. Representative Samuel Cox of Ohio warned that Ohio soldiers would not fight "if the result shall be the flight and movement of the black race by millions northward."[42] Many Northerners shared this fear. In the summer of 1862, violent antiblack riots exploded in several Northern cities. Even some Republicans conceded the difficulty of the issue. Senator Lyman Trumbull of Illinois admitted, "[T]here is a very great aversion . . . against having free negroes come among us. Our people want nothing to do with the negro."[43] In the face of such "aversion," Lincoln reiterated, "My paramount object in this struggle *is* to save the Union, and is *not* either to save or to destroy slavery." He added, "If I could save the Union without freeing *any* slave I would do it, and if I could save it by freeing *all* the slaves I would do it; and if I could save it by freeing some and leaving others alone I would also do that."[44]

On September 22, 1862, five days after the North's victory at Antietam, Lincoln announced the Emancipation Proclamation. Over objections that the proclamation would alienate the border states and strengthen the Democrats, Lincoln concluded that it was an essential step to bring the war to a close and restore the Union. The proclamation declared that unless the rebel states returned to the Union by January 1, 1863, their slaves would "be then, thenceforward, and forever free."[*45]

The antiwar Democrats, or Copperheads,[†] bitterly protested the proclama-

---

* Lincoln became convinced that emancipation in the Confederate states would both weaken the South and strengthen the Union ranks. He therefore issued the Emancipation Proclamation on strict military grounds in his capacity as commander in chief. Critics pointed out what they saw as the hypocrisy implicit in the proclamation: it purported to free the slaves *only* in those areas over which Lincoln had no effective authority. Lincoln defended himself on the ground that the proclamation was constitutionally justified under the "war power" and that he could assert this power only to serve military ends. In the ninety-nine days between Lincoln's preliminary announcement and the date the proclamation finally took effect, there was much speculation and uncertainty about whether Lincoln would actually issue the proclamation.

† The term "copperhead" was originally coined as an epithet to liken the Democrats to the venomous snake. After several years, the Democrats proudly accepted the label and began wearing badges that resembled copper pennies.

"Emancipation"

tion. In their view, it fundamentally transformed the purpose of the war. The goal was no longer to restore the Union but to destroy the South. The Copperheads made this their central issue in the 1862 elections. They denounced emancipation, declaring that there must be "no more bloodshed to gratify a religious fanaticism."[46] Democrats in Illinois and Ohio branded the proclamation "another advance in the . . . highway of tyranny."[47]

A Democratic editor in Ohio charged that the proclamation was "monstrous, impudent, and heinous" because "it declares those 'equal' whom God created unequal." The Democratic governor of New York, Horatio Seymour, condemned emancipation as "bloody" and "barbarous."[48] The *New York World* declared that Lincoln was "adrift on a current of racial fanaticism." Other Democratic newspapers maintained that the proclamation violated the Constitution and would render "the restoration of the old Constitution and Union impossible."[49] Many Union soldiers shared these views. One volunteer wrote his fiancée, "It is not for the emancipation of the African race I fight. I want nothing to do with the negro. I want them as far from me as is possible to conceive."[50]

In the fall elections of 1862, the Democrats scored dramatic victories at both the state and the federal levels, including a gain of thirty-four seats in the House of Representatives.[51] Newly elected Copperhead legislatures in Illinois and Indiana lost no time enacting resolutions demanding an armistice and the retraction of the Emancipation Proclamation.*[52]

THE CHALLENGE OF RAISING AN ARMY posed another serious obstacle. The attack on Fort Sumter galvanized the North into action. On April 15, 1861, Lincoln called 75,000 militiamen into service to quash a rebellion "too powerful to be suppressed by the ordinary course of judicial proceedings."[53] As a "tidal wave of patriotism engulfed the North,"[54] volunteers raced forward to join the army and to claim their share of glory. A year later, however, after a succession of military defeats and disappointments, Lincoln called for an additional 300,000 volunteers. This time, there was no rush to the battlements. As the casualty lists lengthened and the grim realities of combat set in, many states had to resort to local conscription to meet their quotas.

Conscription triggered violent resistance. Mobs murdered two enrollment officers in Indiana, and the army had to send troops into Pennsylvania, Wisconsin, Ohio, and Indiana to restore order. On September 24, 1862, Lincoln issued a proclamation suspending the writ of habeas corpus and declaring martial law in these areas for "all persons discouraging volunteer enlistments, resisting militia

---

* In the summer of 1863, Lincoln responded directly to the anti–Emancipation Proclamation movement:

> You say you will not fight to free negroes. Some of them seem willing to fight for you; but no matter. Fight you, then, exclusively to save the Union. I issued the Proclamation . . . to aid you in saving the Union. . . . I thought that in your struggle for the Union, to whatever extent the negroes should cease helping the enemy, to that extent it weakened the enemy in his resistance to you. Do you think differently? I thought that whatever negroes can be got to do, as soldiers, leaves just so much less for white soldiers to do in saving the Union. Does it appear otherwise to you? But negroes, like other people, act upon motives. Why should they do anything for us if we will do nothing for them? If they stake their lives for us, they must be prompted by the strongest motive—even the promise of freedom. And the promise, being made, must be kept.

A year after he signed the proclamation, Lincoln reported to Congress that "of those who were slaves at the beginning of the rebellion, full one hundred thousand are now in the United States military service, about one-half of which number actually bear arms in the ranks." Foote, *Civil War* at 640 (cited in note 36); Nicolay and Hay, *Abraham Lincoln* at 166, 172 (cited in note 15).

drafts, or guilty of any disloyal practice affording aid and comfort to the Rebels."[55] Secretary of War Stanton imprisoned hundreds of alleged draft resisters without benefit of trial. Protest groups marched under banners declaring, "We won't fight to free the nigger."[56]

The adoption of an unprecedented national conscription law on March 3, 1863, gave the antiwar movement further impetus.* Reflecting sharp class differences within society and a sense that financial resources were as necessary as soldiers, the Conscription Act allowed a draftee to hire a substitute or pay a commutation fee of $300.† The impact of the Conscription Act was evident in its operation. Of the 255,373 individuals first called in the draft, 86,724 avoided service by paying the commutation fee, 117,986 hired substitutes, and 4,316 did not show up at all. Thus, only 46,347 of the original 255,373, or 18 percent, actually entered the ranks.[57]

Both the draft and the exemptions incited furious opposition.‡ Democratic newspapers warned that the draft "would force white working men to fight for the freedom of blacks who would come north and take away their jobs."[58] The government's often heavy-handed efforts to enforce conscription outraged many citizens. Soldiers charged with carrying out the draft conducted house-to-house searches and brutally broke up antidraft demonstrations.[59]

Even more violent protests exploded in the cruelly hot summer of 1863. Mobs killed several enrollment officers, and antidraft, antiblack violence erupted in Boston, Newark, Albany, Chicago, and Milwaukee. In July, four days of rioting in New York City left 105 people dead. Led by Irish immigrants, it was the worst riot in American history. Rioters burned a black orphanage to the ground,

---

* Alexis de Tocqueville had predicted that the United States would never use conscription: "In America conscription is unknown . . . forced recruitment is so contrary to the ideas and so foreign to the habits of the people of the United States that I doubt that one would ever dare to induce it into the laws." Alexis de Tocqueville, *Democracy in America* 213 (translated and edited by Harvey C. Mansfield and Delba Winthrop, Chicago 2000).

† In some communities, men who were eligible for the draft contributed to "draft insurance clubs" that would hire substitutes or purchase commutation for those who were called. In other communities, churches or community groups raised funds to enable their members to escape conscription.

‡ The Confederacy initiated conscription a year earlier, in March 1862. This prompted violent protests in the South as well as in the North. Several times during the war, Confederate President Jefferson Davis, acting pursuant to legislative authorization, declared martial law and suspended the writ of habeas corpus. Protests against martial law were so vehement, however, that sixteen months into the war the Confederate Congress withdrew from President Davis the authority to suspend the writ.

destroyed black homes, randomly beat passing blacks, and then lynched them on lampposts.*[60]

To add to these problems, General Meade's failure at Gettysburg in July 1863 to destroy Lee's retreating army left Lincoln despondent. As Lincoln wrote Meade, "I do not believe you appreciate the magnitude of the misfortune involved in Lee's escape." The "war will be prolonged indefinitely." Lincoln's recognition that he had failed to win the war on the field of battle heightened his fear that he would lose it on the home front. Lincoln confided to Senator Charles Sumner that he was more worried about "the fire in the rear" (meaning the Democrats) than about "our military chances."[61] There were many signs to support this concern. The Republican governor of Indiana, for example, warned the secretary of war that the Democratic legislatures of Indiana and Illinois were threatening to pass resolutions recognizing the Confederate States of America and urging the states of the Northwest to sever their ties to the New England states.

Orestes Augustus Brownson, an influential essayist, philosopher, and abolitionist, wrote Senator Sumner, "I do not believe in Mr. Lincoln at all. . . . He is thickheaded; he is ignorant; he is tricky, somewhat astute, in a small way, and obstinate as a mule. Even the good measures that he is willing to adopt lose all their value by his adopting them out of season and in an unstatesmanlike manner. Is there no way of inducing him to resign . . . ?" Congressman Julian observed, "[T]he country is going to hell, and the scenes witnessed in the French Revolution are nothing in comparison with what we shall see here."[62] Richard Dana, author of *Two Years before the Mast* and an ardent Republican, wrote from

---

* According to one eyewitness, after the government sent twenty thousand "weatherstained and dusty soldiers" into New York City to put down the riot, the fighting was brief but bloody:

There was some terrific fighting between the regulars and the insurgents; streets were swept again and again by grape, houses were stormed at the point of the bayonet, rioters were picked off by sharpshooters . . . men were hurled, dying or dead, into the streets by the thoroughly enraged soldiery; until at last, sullen and cowed and thoroughly whipped and beaten, the miserable wretches gave way . . . and confessed the power of the law.

Foote, *Civil War* at 637 (cited in note 36). This riot was the subject of Martin Scorsese's 2002 film *Gangs of New York*.

Washington, "[T]he most striking thing is the absence of personal loyalty to the President. It does not exist."[63]

Lincoln's renomination and reelection in 1864 became precarious. No incumbent president had been renominated since 1840, and none had been reelected since Andrew Jackson in 1832. The *Detroit Free Press* reported that "not a Senator can be named as favorable to Lincoln's renomination." Supreme Court Justice David Davis, a strong supporter of the president, confessed in private that "the politicians in and out of Congress . . . would put Lincoln aside if they dared."[64]

Although Lincoln was, in fact, renominated at the Republican convention in June 1864, a succession of Union defeats that summer at Spotsylvania, Cold Harbor, and Petersburg led to the collapse of Northern morale. When Lincoln then spurned peace negotiations on terms that would have required him to abandon emancipation, he was widely accused of fighting the war for the sole purpose of abolition, a charge he emphatically denied. The Democratic press lambasted Lincoln, arguing that "tens of thousands of white men must yet bite the dust to allay this Negro mania of the President." Democrats charged that Lincoln favored miscegenation and labeled him "Abraham Africanus the First." He was called "the Widowmaker," who had "sent half a million white men to their graves" because he "loves his country less, and the Negro more."[65]

The Democratic Party platform of 1864 condemned the government's "arbitrary military arrest[s]" and pledged an immediate "cessation of hostilities" with a view to restoring the federal Union.[66] The Democrats confidently nominated General George B. McClellan, whom Lincoln had earlier dismissed as commander of the Army of the Potomac, as their candidate for president. In the belief that Lincoln was certain to lose, Republican leaders quietly began considering plans to convene a new party convention to nominate someone else as their party's candidate for president.[67] Horace Greeley wrote, "Mr. Lincoln is already beaten," so we must have "another ticket to save us from utter overthrow."[68] Senator Sumner mused that there was "no way of meeting the difficulties from the candidacy of Mr. Lincoln unless he withdraws."[69] In late August, Lincoln predicted, "I am going to be beaten," and "*badly* beaten."[70]

Against this background, Lincoln confronted the question of free speech in wartime.

CLEMENT VALLANDIGHAM AND GENERAL ORDER NO. 38

AS A REPUBLICAN, Lincoln was politically committed to the principle of free speech. Republicans had tied themselves to this position in the decades leading up to the Civil War, when a fierce controversy raged over the free speech rights of abolitionists.[71] Southern states equated the advocacy of abolition with incitement to slave revolt. A North Carolina law, for example, declared it unlawful for any person to circulate any pamphlet the "evident tendency whereof is to cause slaves to become discontented with the bondage in which they are held."[72] A Virginia law made it a crime for any member of an "anti-slavery society" to "advocate or advise the abolition of slavery."[73]

From its founding in 1854, the Republican Party maintained that such laws violated the right of free expression.* After nominating John C. Frémont for president in 1856, the party's campaign slogan was "Free Speech, Free Press, Free Men, Free Labor, Free Territory, and Frémont."[74] In 1860, Republican senators unanimously supported a resolution stating that "free discussion of the morality and expedience of slavery should never be interfered with by the laws of any State, or of the United States; and the freedom of speech and of the press, on this and every other subject of domestic and national policy, should be maintained inviolate. . . ."[75]

The depth of the Republicans' commitment to free speech was severely tested during the Civil War. Critics of the administration, especially the Copperheads, attacked Lincoln as repressive and autocratic and furiously protested the suspension of habeas corpus, the draft, the conduct of the military campaign, and emancipation. To many Republicans, such critics were nothing less than abettors of the rebellion. Like the Federalists in 1798, some Republicans demanded that the government suppress "disloyal" dissent and seize "treasonable" newspapers. The *Philadelphia Inquirer* urged the president to take action against the "organs of treason," declaring, "If there be a point when patience ceases to be a virtue, the Federal Government has reached that point, in the toleration of treasonable presses existing north of the Potomac. . . . Shall we hesitate in such a crisis, and split hairs, about possible abuses of authority when all authority is threatened with annihilation?"[76]

IN MARCH 1863, Lincoln appointed General Ambrose Burnside the Union commander of the Department of Ohio. According to *Harper's Weekly*, Burnside was "a very handsome man." He was "tall and stout, with a flashing eye and a sonorous voice" — "the very *beau idéal* of a soldier."[77] Born in 1824 in a log cabin

---

* After the Kansas-Nebraska Act of 1854 repealed earlier compromises that had excluded slavery from these territories, the antislavery forces established the Republican Party to oppose the extension of slavery. The leaders of this faction chose the name "Republican" because they claimed to be the direct political descendants of Thomas Jefferson's original Republican Party, which by then had evolved into the pro–states' rights Democratic Party.

in Liberty, Indiana, Burnside received a seminary education and then set himself up as a tailor. His father, a state senator, got him a cadetship at West Point, where he rubbed elbows with George McClellan, Stonewall Jackson, and others who would later play key roles in the Civil War.

Burnside invented a new breech-loading rifle and signed a lucrative contract to make arms for the Buchanan administration. The deal went bust, however, and Burnside was soon bankrupt. McClellan, then the vice president of the Illinois Central Railroad, hired Burnside as the company's treasurer. When the Civil War broke out, Burnside, though not a very able general, rose quickly through the ranks.

Smarting from his devastating defeat at Fredericksburg in 1862 and his embarrassing dismissal as commander of the Army of the Potomac, Burnside wrote Lincoln, "I ought to retire to private life."[78] Instead, Lincoln ordered Burnside to assume command of the Department of Ohio, a position from which he presumably could not get into much trouble. But Burnside, a man of "zealous and impulsive character,"[79] soon grew concerned about disloyal persons who might give aid and comfort to the enemy. He was appalled to discover that newspapers in Ohio were full of "treasonable expressions" and that "large public meetings were held, at which our Government authorities and our gallant soldiers in the field were openly and loudly denounced for their efforts to suppress the rebellion."[80]

Although he did not begin to understand the reasons for disaffection in this part of the nation,* Burnside fully appreciated the efficacy of force. So, in April 1863, without Lincoln's knowledge or approval, he declared martial law† and issued General Order no. 38, which announced (among other things) that "the habit of declaring sympathies for the enemy will not be allowed in this Department."[81] Burnside thus established himself as the ultimate arbiter of treasonable expres-

---

* Although westerners (during the Civil War the "West" consisted of what we would today consider the Midwest) had enthusiastically supported Lincoln at the outset of the war, they suffered huge losses in the first two years of the conflict and many had grown disillusioned. The 1863 conscription law promised to have an especially severe effect on western farmers, and the West had not shared in the general prosperity that the war economy had brought to the Northeast. Perhaps most important, many westerners feared that the Emancipation Proclamation would lead to a heavy migration of freed blacks to the states of the West. See Donald, *Lincoln* at 417–18 (cited in note 49)

† According to Chief Justice Rehnquist, "whatever the theory of martial law might be, its consequences . . . during the Civil War were quite apparent. Statements critical of the government, whether appearing in the press or made in the course of political oratory, were punished by fine and imprisonment. Homes of suspects could be broken into without warrants. And none of this was in accordance with laws enacted by any legislature or city council. Martial law was the voice of whichever general was in command." Rehnquist, *All the Laws But One* at 73–74 (cited in note 15)..

General Ambrose Burnside

sions. He assumed that it was for the military to define the boundaries of legitimate dissent, that any criticism of the administration was treasonable, and that
civil officials and civil courts had failed in their duty to suppress such expression.
Burnside's issuance of General Order no. 38 precipitated the Civil War's most celebrated arrest and prosecution for disloyal speech.

CLEMENT VALLANDIGHAM WAS one of the most forceful cham-
pions of the Copperheads. He was tall, dashing, and magnetic, with bright blue
eyes, a Roman nose, and a closely trimmed dark beard. He was born in 1820 in
New Lisbon, Ohio. His father, a Presbyterian minister, could trace his lineage
directly to Huguenots who had been driven from France for their religious convictions. Vallandigham attended Jefferson College and the Union Academy. He
then taught school, practiced law, edited the *Dayton Western Empire*, served in
the state legislature, and, after several losing campaigns, won election to Congress in 1858.

A gifted orator who strongly endorsed popular sovereignty as the best way to
preserve the Union, Vallandigham saw abolitionists as Jacobins who were determined to destroy the comity of the nation's diverse sections. Because abolitionists were particularly active in Ohio, he was well acquainted with the
movement and argued vehemently that abolitionist clergymen should stay out
of politics and that abolitionist politicians should steer clear of Christian doctrine. A staunch advocate of the Jeffersonian philosophy of a limited federal
government, Vallandigham argued that Congress should not "meddle" with
slavery either in the states or in the territories. He attacked Republicans for
what he saw as their contempt for the Constitution and their blinding belief that
the cause of abolition rose above the law. Such lawlessness, he stressed, breeds
"more lawlessness."[82]

After the final meeting of Congress before Lincoln's inauguration, Vallandigham, then a Congressman from Ohio, wistfully wrote his wife that it had
been a day of "tribulation and anguish," concluding, "[W]hen the secession has
taken place, I shall do all in my power first to *restore* the Union, if it be possible;
and failing in that, then to mitigate the evils of disruption." Once hostilities
divided the nation, Vallandigham opposed the war, the draft, the military arrest of
civilians, the suspensions of habeas corpus, and the Emancipation Proclamation.
He blamed Lincoln and the abolitionists for the war. In his view, the Southern
states could not be "forced back into a Union they abhorred." A "true nation," he
contended, "must be built upon good-will and trust, not on force, distrust and

self-styled superiority." He wrote pessimistically that events had proceeded so far that it might be too late for anything but a peaceable separation.*[83]

Vallandigham was both reviled and admired for his views. The Republican press cast him as "disloyal," "treasonable," "a champion of Jeff Davis," "a contemptible traitor," a "pro-slavery apologist," a "cold-blooded, mean-spirited coward," and a "secessionist." He was compared to Benedict Arnold and Aaron Burr.[84] Ohio Republicans, with the active assistance of Lincoln and his cabinet,† gerrymandered Vallandigham into defeat in the 1862 congressional elections, but he did not leave quietly. In his farewell speech to the House on January 14, 1863, he boldly set forth his "indictment of the war" and his proposals for peace.[85]

In that address, he asserted that he was a more faithful Unionist than the Republicans, who were fighting for abolition rather than for Union. What, he asked, had they accomplished? He replied, "Let the dead at Fredericksburg and Vicksburg answer." The solution, he argued, was to "stop fighting" and to initiate immediate negotiations for reunion. He dismissed out of hand the objection that peace would preserve slavery. "I see more of barbarism and sin" in the "continuance of this war," he observed, than in "the sin and barbarism of African slavery." The "experiment" of war "has been tried long enough."[86]

After Vallandigham completed this speech, Congressman John Bingham of Ohio, a fierce proponent of emancipation, replied that if we "strip these words of all disguise" they simply mean that "this Government has no power to defend itself against armed rebellion." Thaddeus Stevens, a radical Republican from Pennsylvania, accused Vallandigham of treason.[87]

Although Vallandigham held fiery views, he consistently counseled compliance with the law: "No matter how distasteful constitutions and laws may be," he

---

* Vallandigham maintained that he was loyal to the United States and the Constitution and that the effort of Republicans to equate loyalty to the United States with loyalty to the Lincoln administration and its policies was itself a concept disloyal to the Constitution. He denied that radical Republicans had the right to "impose their definition of loyalty upon the country." Vallandigham was not "pro-slavery." Like Senator Stephen Douglas, he opposed slavery. But he did not believe that the national government should impose that view on states with a different position. Klement, *Limits of Dissent* at 323 (cited in note 46).

† President Lincoln, Secretary of War Stanton, and Secretary of the Treasury Chase (a former governor of Ohio) all worked to persuade General Robert Schenck to challenge Vallandigham. Lincoln told Schenck that he could do the nation "a greater service by sidetracking Vallandigham than by leading a brigade on the battlefield," and he assured him of a military promotion. Klement, *Limits of Dissent* at 102–5 (cited in note 46).

declared, "they must be obeyed."[*88] In March 1863, he made a speech to the Democratic Union Association in New York during which he denounced the Conscription Act and warned that if the president failed to listen to the people, even more violence might be visited upon the nation.[89] The next day, the *New York Times* reported that Vallandigham had advocated resistance to the Conscription Act. Vallandigham immediately wrote a letter to the *Times* denying this assertion. Correcting the record, he stated,

> I expressly counseled the trial of all questions of law before our judicial Courts, and all questions of politics before the tribunal of the ballot box. I am for obedience to all laws—obedience by the people and by men in power also. I am for a free discussion of all measures and laws whatsoever, as in former times, but for forcible resistance to none. The ballot box and not the cartridge box is the instrument for reform and revolution. . . . [†90]

IN APRIL 1863, after the end of his term in Congress, Vallandigham traveled to Columbus for the state Democratic convention. He hoped to receive the party's nomination for governor, but did not make much headway. In an effort to bolster his candidacy, Vallandigham decided to challenge General Order no. 38.[91]

---

[*] Vallandigham "vigorously combated disloyal activity." In one address, he predicted that men will not enlist to fight a war for emancipation. "It is easier," he said, "to die at home." He added, "I beg pardon, but I trust I am not 'discouraging enlistments.' If I am, then first arrest Lincoln, [Secretary of War] Stanton, and [General] Halleck," in whose hands the war is "a most bloody and costly failure," his implication being that they had done more to "discourage enlistments" than he could ever do. James G. Randall, *The Civil War and Reconstruction* 391 (D. C. Heath 1937); Foote, *Civil War* at 631 (cited in note 36)

[†] Three days later, Vallandigham made a similar comment in a speech at Dayton, Ohio. As reported in the *Dayton Empire*, Vallandigham said,

> He was for obedience to all laws, and for requiring the men in power also to obey them. He would try all questions of Constitution and law before the courts, and then enforce the decrees of the courts. He was for trying all political questions by the ballot. He would resist no law by force; he would endure almost every other wrong as long as free discussion . . . and a free ballot remained. . . . We had a right to change Administrations, and policies and parties, not by forcible revolution, but by the ballot-box. . . .

Vallandigham, *Life of Clement L. Vallandigham* at 239 (cited in note 83).

On May 1, in Mount Vernon, Ohio, Vallandigham rode in a "parade four miles long of wagons, buggies, carriages, horsemen, and a six-horse float holding thirty-four pretty flower girls, one for each State in the Union."[92] Before a huge throng, estimated at between 15,000 and 20,000, Vallandigham gave a spirited two-hour address in which he attacked General Order no. 38 and defended the constitutional right of the people to debate the policies of the national administration.[93]

Calling the war "wicked, cruel, and unnecessary," Vallandigham depicted the conflict as "a war for the freedom of the blacks and the enslavement of the whites," characterized General Order no. 38 as a "base usurpation of arbitrary authority," and argued that "the sooner the people inform the minions of usurped power that they will not submit to such restrictions upon their liberties, the better."[94] He asserted that his "right to speak and criticize was based upon 'General Order No. 1'—The Constitution of the United States," and urged citizens to use "'the ballot-box' to hurl 'King Lincoln' from his throne."[95] The speech brought rousing cheers from the crowd, many of whom sported copperhead pennies in their buttonholes.

Without consulting his superiors, General Burnside ordered Union soldiers to arrest Vallandigham. Acting in a manner reminiscent of Jabez Fitch's treatment of Matthew Lyon and Anthony Haswell, a contingent of more than a hundred soldiers arrived at Vallandigham's home at two-thirty in the morning of May 5, broke down his front door, seized him from his bedroom, and carted him off to prison in Cincinnati. Vallandigham was then brought before a five-member military commission and charged with "publicly expressing, in violation of general Orders No. 38, . . . sympathy for those in arms against the government of the United States, and declaring disloyal sentiments and opinions with the object and purpose of weakening the power of the government in its efforts to suppress an unlawful rebellion."[96]

During his two-day trial, Vallandigham argued that the military had no lawful authority over a civilian and protested that he was being persecuted for mere "words of criticism of the public policy, of the public servants of the people." His speech, he averred, "was an appeal to the people to change that policy, not by force but by free elections and the ballot-box. It is not pretended that I counselled disobedience to the Constitution or resistance to law or lawful authority. I never have. I have nothing further to submit."[97]

The military commission found Vallandigham guilty as charged, holding that his speech at Mount Vernon "could but induce in his hearers a distrust of their own Government and sympathy for those in arms against it, and a disposition to resist the laws of the land." Although the commission was unwilling to put Vallandigham before a firing squad, it recommended his imprisonment in "close confinement" for the duration of the war. Burnside promptly accepted this recommendation and designated Fort Warren in Boston Harbor as the place of Vallandigham's incarceration.[98]

Clement Vallandigham

General Burnside later explained his actions:

> If I were to find a man from the enemy's country distributing in my camps speeches of their public men that tended to demoralize the troops, or to destroy their confidence in the constituted authorities of the government, I would have him tried, and hung if found guilty, and all the rules of modern warfare would sustain me. Why should such speeches from our own public men be allowed? . . . [M]y duty requires me to stop license and intemperate discussion, which tends to weaken the authority of the government and army. . . . There is no fear of the people losing their liberties; we all know that to be the cry of the demagogues, and none but the ignorant will listen to it. . . .[99]

Vallandigham immediately filed a petition for a writ of habeas corpus in federal district court, arguing that he had been denied his constitutional rights to due process of law, to a public trial by an impartial jury, to confront the witnesses against him, and to compulsory process to summon witnesses in his behalf. Although no suspension of the writ of habeas corpus was in effect in this area at this time, Judge Humphrey H. Leavitt denied Vallandigham's petition.[100]

Judge Leavitt reasoned that "the court cannot shut its eyes to the grave fact that the war exists, involving the most imminent public danger, and threatening the subversion and destruction of the constitution itself." "Self-preservation," he added, "is a paramount law," and this is "not a time when any one connected with the judicial department" should in any way "embarrass or thwart the executive in his efforts to deliver the country from the dangers which press so heavily upon it." In the face of a rebellion, "the president . . . is invested with very high powers," and "in deciding what he may rightfully do" under these powers, "the president is guided solely by his own judgment and discretion, and is only amenable for an abuse of his authority by impeachment."[101]

Turning to the specific circumstances before him, Judge Leavitt observed that "artful men, disguising their latent treason under hollow pretensions of devotion to the Union," had been "striving to disseminate their pestilent heresies among the masses of the people." General Burnside had thus acted reasonably in perceiving "the dangerous consequences of these disloyal efforts" and in resolving, "if possible, to suppress them." Leavitt concluded that those who criticize the government in time of crisis "must learn that they cannot stab its vitals with impunity."*[102]

CERTAINLY A SPEECH LIKE VALLANDIGHAM'S would have been punished under the Sedition Act of 1798. On its face, his address in Canton was not appreciably different from the pamphlets, speeches, and publications of Matthew Lyon, James Callender, or Thomas Cooper in that earlier era. However, unlike the judges enforcing the Sedition Act, Judge Leavitt did not even offer the pretense that Vallandigham's speech was "false" or "malicious," though Leavitt's characterizations of the speech as "heretical," "disloyal," and "treasonous" may have implicitly covered the same ground.

His primary argument, though, relied on his assessment of the dangerousness of the speech to the Union and the high degree of deference he accorded the commander in chief. His opinion reads, not as an independent effort to interpret the First Amendment to ensure that constitutional rights are respected, but as a collaborative effort to support the president in meeting his grave responsibilities

---

* The Supreme Court declined to review the merits of the decision of the military commission. See *Ex parte Vallandigham*, 68 (1 Wall) US 243 (1863).

in wartime. The role of the judiciary, in his view, is to serve as a junior partner, rather than as a critical check on the executive.

As Judge Leavitt read the Constitution, at least in wartime, "[s]elf-preservation" is the "paramount law," rising above even the Constitution. In such times, no "one connected with the judicial department" should in any way "embarrass or thwart the executive in his efforts to deliver the country from the dangers which press so heavily upon it." He acknowledged that there might be a check on the unconstitutional exercise of authority by the president, but insisted that that check could be enforced only by Congress's impeachment power rather than by the judiciary's interpretation of the Constitution.

Leavitt thus raised a fundamental question about the appropriate role of the judiciary in wartime. Even if we trust and rely upon judges to enforce the Constitution in ordinary times, should they yield that duty in time of war? Is the Constitution effectively suspended, at least insofar as the courts are concerned, when war, in Leavitt's words, threatens "the subversion and destruction of the constitution itself"?

There are basically two arguments in favor of this proposition, as construed by Leavitt. The first asserts that the ordinary guarantees of the Constitution are fine in periods of tranquillity, but that the freedom of speech, the freedom of religion, the right to due process of law, the right to counsel, and the right to trial by jury (to name just a few of the relevant rights) should not be allowed to interfere with the government's duty to prevent "the subversion and destruction of the constitution itself." This is a *balancing* argument. These rights are valuable, and we can and should protect them in ordinary times, but everything is relative. These rights may become inconvenient, perhaps even treacherous, in time of peril. Although the government ordinarily must respect these rights, it may override them when necessary, and few circumstances pose a more compelling necessity than wartime. (It was a fear of just this sort of argument in 1798 that led Republicans to object to the Alien Friends Act as the first step down the road to denying citizens, as well as aliens, their rights in wartime.)

The second argument underlying Judge Leavitt's position turns on the relative *institutional competence* of judges relative to executive and legislative branch officials in striking the proper balance between civil liberties and military necessity. Under this view, we trust judges to enforce the guarantees of the Constitution in ordinary times, when they are capable of weighing constitutional liberties against competing governmental interests, but they lack the expertise necessary to make those judgments when the nation is at war. In wartime, assessment of the dangers is said to be beyond the experience and ability of judges, who should leave such matters to the commander in chief and the Congress. When times return to normal, courts can resume their ordinary responsibilities.

In response to these contentions, "civil libertarians" might argue that constitutional rights are constitutional rights, whether we are at peace or at war. Unless the Constitution expressly provides for their limitation in time of war (as it does with respect to the suspension of the writ of habeas corpus in cases of rebellion or invasion), the fact of war is simply irrelevant to the protection of these rights. More modestly, civil libertarians might argue that the special circumstances of wartime are *relevant* in assessing whether the government has sufficient justification to limit constitutional rights, but that this inquiry must be undertaken with due regard to the importance of the rights and with a healthy skepticism of the government's claim that these rights must be sacrificed in order to fight the war.

Civil libertarians will insist further that constitutional rights are often *most* important in time of war, and that any effort to limit them in such circumstances should be approached with *heightened* concern. Consider the freedom of speech. The decision of a nation to go to war and its continuing judgments about the conduct of the war, the morality of using certain tactics or weapons, the effectiveness of the nation's leaders, the value of the war to the national interest, whether the war has grown too costly in lives and national treasure, and whether it is time to negotiate or even withdraw—are all matters of profound public importance. To stifle free speech about such questions at the very height of wartime is arguably to suppress the right when it is *most* critical to the well-being of society.

With respect to the claim of relative institutional competence, civil libertarians have to concede that war is not the usual state of affairs and that it may indeed involve complex issues of military strategy, diplomacy, and secrecy that are beyond the usual experience of courts. On the other hand, military officials have less experience than judges in dealing with civil liberties. Just as judges might too quickly dismiss claims of military necessity because of their lack of expertise, military officials might too quickly dismiss constitutional guarantees when they are merely inconvenient. In such circumstances, civil libertarians would reply to Judge Leavitt that courts in wartime should carefully consider military judgments, but should not abdicate their responsibility to interpret and enforce the Constitution. Needless to say, this debate has continued through all subsequent conflicts, including the War on Terrorism.

ALTHOUGH THE USUALLY VOLUBLE Vallandigham declined to plead his case to the military commission, he was quick to plead it to the public. Like Matthew Lyon, who argued his cause from a jail cell in Vermont, Vallandigham issued a succession of statements from his prison cell in Ohio, declaring, for example, "I am here in a military bastille for no other offense than my political opinions."[103] Newspapers across the nation were quick to champion his cause. His arrest triggered a riot in Dayton, his hometown, where a Democratic mob burned to the ground the building occupied by the local Republican newspaper. Similar mass demonstrations followed in almost every major Northern city, reflecting the vehemence of the Democratic press.

The *Albany Argus*, for example, charged that Vallandigham's arrest and conviction were a "crime against the Constitution." The *Detroit Free Press* declared sarcastically that if speakers may be jailed "because they are opposed to the war, or the conduct of it, [then] the polls may be closed, or voters excluded from them, for the same reason. If it is disloyal to make a speech against the war, it is doubly disloyal to vote for men who are opposed to it."[104]

A month after Vallandigham's arrest, the Ohio Democratic Convention nominated him for governor. The convention adopted a resolution maintaining that rights guaranteed to the people "by their Constitution are their rights in time of war as well as in times of peace, and of far more value and necessity in war than in peace, for in peace, liberty, security, and property are seldom endangered, in war, they are ever in peril." Democrats, such as Congressman Daniel Voorhees of Indiana, charged that Lincoln had effectively reintroduced the Sedition Act of 1798, but without even the authority of an act of Congress to support him and without the procedural protections of due process.*[105]

Not everyone condemned Burnside's prosecution of Vallandigham. Some Republican officials and newspapers praised General Order no. 38 and Vallandigham's arrest and conviction. The *Cincinnati Commercial*, for example, argued that "Order 38 . . . is not designed to abridge the liberty of the individual, where that liberty is not used to the detriment of the Government." The *Chicago Tribune* reasoned that although free speech must be tolerated as a "harmless right" in times of peace, such toleration is not appropriate "in times of war and revolution."[106] Senator John Sherman of Ohio found it "remarkable" that "a

---

* Chief Justice Rehnquist has neatly described the differences between prosecution under a sedition statute and the prosecution of Vallandigham under martial law:

Vallandigham was not only tried by a military commission, rather than a jury, but the charge upon which he was tried was that he violated an order issued by Burnside — an order that forbade the expression of sympathy for the enemy. A [federal] criminal trial in a civil court must be based on a charge that the defendant engaged in conduct prohibited by an Act of Congress. . . . Burnside's order had no such pedigree; it . . . originated with Ambrose Burnside. . . . Martial law was the voice of whichever general was in command.

Rehnquist, *All the Laws But One* at 68, 74 (cited in note 15). See also id at 86 (explaining the Roman legal maxim *Nulla poena sine lege*, which prohibits any "punishment except pursuant to established law").

nation in the midst of a great war should concern itself at all with protective procedures" for loyal citizens, much less "openly disloyal ones."[107]

Other Republican voices, however, were critical. The New York Tribune noted that the Constitution does "not recognize perverse opinions, nor unpatriotic speeches, as grounds of infliction." The New York Evening Post hailed free speech as essential to "popular Government" and declared that "no governments and no authorities are to be held as above criticism." The Bedford Standard announced that we must "have faith in the power of truth, and oppose those we believe to be in error with the weapon of truth." Even the Republican senator Lyman Trumbell of Illinois denounced Burnside's action because "we are fighting for the . . . preservation of the Constitution, and all the liberties it guarantees to every citizen."[108] Indeed, one of the most impressive features of this controversy was that many Republicans added their voices to those of Democrats in condemnation of the suppression of free speech. This was a far cry from the rampant partisanship of the Sedition Act debate, and a promising development in the maturation of American democracy.

GENERAL BURNSIDE, HOWEVER, was unfazed. Disregarding the public furor he had created, only a month after Vallandigham's conviction he ordered Union soldiers to close the Chicago Times, which had sharply criticized the Lincoln administration and the arrest of Vallandigham. The Chicago Times had long been a thorn to Republicans. Indeed, the Republican governors of Illinois and Indiana had complained to Secretary of War Stanton that the Chicago Times had done "incalculable injury" to the Union cause. Over the past several months, the Chicago Times had denounced emancipation as "a monstrous usurpation" of authority,[109] editorialized that Negroes were destined to be "mere hewers of wood and drawers of water to a superior and dominant race,"[110] characterized Vallandigham's arrest as "the funeral of civil liberty," and declared that Union soldiers were "indignant at the imbecility that has devoted them to slaughter for purposes with which they have no sympathy."[111] General Burnside defended his order suppressing the Chicago Times by citing its "repeated expression of disloyal and incendiary sentiments."[112]

The man responsible for these "sentiments" was Wilbur Fiske Storey, the forty-year-old publisher and editor of the Chicago Times. In Carl Sandburg's description, Storey was "tight-lipped" and "short-spoken." He "cultivated suspicion as a habit, looked men over with a cold glitter of eye, boasted he had no friends, and seemed to count that day lost which brought him no added haters." He had single-handedly made the Chicago Times a "sensational, fearless, devious" newspaper that served as "the voice of the extremist enemies of the Lincoln administration."[113]

Upon learning of Burnside's action, Storey immediately sought relief from federal judge Thomas Drummond, who promptly issued a temporary restraining order prohibiting Burnside from taking any action against Storey or the *Chicago Times* until a full hearing could be held on the matter. He explained that this is "a government of law and a government of the Constitution, and not . . . a government of mere physical force."[114]

The next morning, in direct disregard of Drummond's order, Burnside commanded his troops to seize and close the office of the *Chicago Times*. He justified this action on the ground that "freedom of discussion and criticism, which is proper . . . in time of peace, becomes rank treason when it tends to weaken . . . confidence" in the government in time of war.[115] This action triggered angry public protests and irate demands that the administration rescind the closing of the *Chicago Times*. A noon meeting of prominent Chicagoans, presided over by the mayor, voted unanimously that the president should revoke the suspension. Later that evening, a crowd of twenty thousand, including many Republicans, gathered to protest Burnside's action and to celebrate the news that the Illinois legislature had denounced the general for his conduct.[116]

ABRAHAM LINCOLN AND THE FREEDOM OF SPEECH

PRESIDENT LINCOLN WAS SURPRISED and embarrassed by Burnside's arrest of Vallandigham. According to John Nicolay and John Hay, Lincoln's secretaries, if the president had "been consulted before any proceedings were initiated," he probably "would not have permitted them."*[117] Indeed, given his own intemperate criticisms of President Polk during the Mexican War, Lincoln was surely in an uncomfortable position. Vallandigham was not the type of agitator Lincoln expected the military to arrest. The president's security policy was aimed at deserters, draft dodgers, and bridge burners. Val-

---

* Several weeks later, Lincoln admitted publicly, "I do not know whether I would have ordered the arrest of Mr. Vallandigham." Gideon Welles, Lincoln's secretary of the navy, declared that the arrest "was an error on the part of Burnside," and members of Lincoln's cabinet doubted that the arrest was necessary and questioned the legitimacy of trying him before a military commission. Letter from Abraham Lincoln to Erastus Corning and Others, June 12, 1863, in *Abraham Lincoln: Speeches and Writings* at 462 (cited in note 45). See Donald, *Lincoln* at 420 (cited in note 49); Rehnquist, *All the Laws But One* at 67 (cited in note 15).

landigham was a national leader of the Democratic Party. His arrest compelled Lincoln to consider just how far he was prepared to go in allowing the suppression of dissent.[118]

Although Lincoln was vexed with Burnside for acting so imperiously, he decided he would do more harm than good if he directly repudiated Burnside's action. Lincoln did not want to undermine the authority of his generals, and he did not want to encourage the "secessionist element" in the North. At the same time, however, Lincoln was concerned that Vallandigham's imprisonment would be "a constant source of irritation and political discussion."[119]

He therefore sought a middle ground. He wired Burnside that he could count on the administration's support,* but to minimize the political fallout he ordered Burnside to commute Vallandigham's sentence from imprisonment to banishment to the Confederacy.†[120] The president decided that exile would "excite far less sympathy" for Vallandigham and might even "damage his prestige" among his followers.[121] He publicly defended this decision by reasoning that the purpose of imprisoning Vallandigham was not punishment, but to prevent him from causing any further injury to the military. Exile, he explained, was a more humane and "less disagreeable" means of "securing the same prevention."[122]

The president's solution may have been brilliant in theory, but it did not defuse the situation. Democratic editors launched blistering attacks against Lincoln. The *Iowa City State Press* praised Vallandigham's nobility, the *Ashland Union* predicted a dictatorship, and the *Crisis* characterized Lincoln's refusal to free Vallandigham as a terrible blunder. Other Democratic editors used such phrases as "Caesar," "usurper," "demagogue," "tyrant," and "dictator" to deride the president. The *Dubuque Herald* declared that "a crime has been committed" against the "right to think, to speak, to live," and the *Detroit Free Press* complained that Vallandigham had been punished "for no crime known to law." At a huge rally in New York, one speaker proclaimed that if Lincoln did not release

---

* Lincoln wrote Burnside, "All the cabinet regretted the necessity of arresting . . . Vallandigham, some perhaps, doubting, that there was a real necessity for it—but, being done, all were for seeing you through with it." The cabinet took up the Vallandigham matter at its meeting on May 19, 1863. The general view was that Burnside's action "had been a mistake," but that now that it had been done "there was no way to back down." Letter from Abraham Lincoln to Ambrose E. Burnside, May 29, 1863, in Basler, ed, 6 Collected Works of Abraham Lincoln at 237 (cited in note 100); Rehnquist, All the Laws But One at 67 (cited in note 15).

† Burnside protested this decision. He argued that the military commission had fully discussed the option of banishment and decided against it. He added that a change in the sentence would imply a criticism of the validity of the military trial. Lincoln rejected this plea.

Vallandigham, "free speech dies, and with it our liberty, the constitution and our country." Another speaker sarcastically recalled Lincoln's own denunciation of Polk and accused him of rank hypocrisy.[123]

The Republican press chimed in as well. The New York *Independent* criticized the president's "great mistake," the *Anti-Slavery Standard* chastised his "blunder," and the New York *Sun* observed that although "the Union can survive the assaults" of the South, "it cannot long exist without free speech."[124] According to Nicolay and Hay, no other act of the administration was "so strongly criticized" or created "so deep and so wide-spread" a feeling of opposition among the general public.[125]

Democrats held protest meetings in almost every Northern city to denounce the president's tactics. The most important of these meetings was held in Albany on May 16, 1863. The leaders demanded to know whether the Civil War was being waged to restore the Union or "to destroy free institutions" in the North. At the end of the meeting, the participants drafted ten resolutions against the Lincoln administration. The "Albany Resolves" insisted that Lincoln honor the liberties of citizens, assailed the military's "arbitrary" arrests and use of military commissions to try civilians, and charged that Vallandigham had been unconstitutionally convicted and exiled for criticizing the government. On May 19, after the Albany Resolves had been ratified by all present, the presiding officer, Erastus Corning, sent them to President Lincoln, requesting that he give them his "earnest consideration."[126]

THE ALBANY RESOLVES afforded Lincoln an opportunity to explain his position to the public. He prepared a lengthy and carefully crafted reply for public dissemination. His goal was to quell the rising tide of public outrage. His response merits careful attention because it provides us with rare insight into his views of free speech in wartime.

After crediting the patriotism of the authors of the Albany Resolves, Lincoln challenged their assertion that Vallandigham's arrest, conviction, and banishment were unconstitutional. At the outset, though, Lincoln made an important concession:

> It is asserted . . . that Mr. Vallandigham was . . . seized and tried "for no other reason than words addressed to a public meeting, in criticism of the . . . Administration, and in condemnation of the Military orders of the General." Now, if there be no mistake about this; if this assertion is the truth and the whole truth; if there was no other reason for the arrest, then I concede that the arrest was wrong.[127]

Thus, if Vallandigham had done nothing more than criticize his administration, his arrest "was wrong." This was both an important statement of principle and a possible way to distinguish his attack on Polk from Vallandigham's attack on him. Why was Vallandigham's speech different?

> But the arrest, as I understand, was made for a very different reason. Mr. Vallandigham avows his hostility to the War on the part of the Union; and his arrest was made because he was laboring, with some effect, to prevent the raising of troops; to encourage desertions from the army; and to leave the Rebellion without an adequate military force to suppress it. He was not arrested because he was damaging the political prospects of the Administration, or the personal interests of the Commanding General, but because he was damaging the Army, upon the existence and vigor of which the life of the Nation depends. He was warring upon the Military, and this gave the Military constitutional jurisdiction to lay hands upon him. If Mr. Vallandigham was not damaging the military power of the country, then his arrest was made on mistake of fact, which I would be glad to correct on reasonably satisfactory evidence.[128]

Thus, in Lincoln's view, Vallandigham was arrested not for his political criticism but for attempting to obstruct the activities of the military. But even if this was so, Vallandigham was merely *speaking*. Why not leave the speaker free and punish only those who actually refused induction or deserted? Turning to that question, Lincoln argued that it was appropriate to hold a speaker responsible for the unlawful acts of others:[129]

> Long experience has shown that armies cannot be maintained unless desertions shall be punished by the severe penalty of death. . . . Must I shoot a simple-minded soldier boy who deserts, while I must not touch a hair of a wily agitator who induces him to desert? This is none the less injurious when effected by getting a father, or brother, or friend, into a public meeting, and there working upon his feeling till he is persuaded to write the soldier boy that he is fighting in a bad cause, for a wicked Administration. . . . I think that in such a case to silence the agitator, and save the boy is not only constitutional, but withal a great mercy.[130]

Lincoln turned finally to two critical questions: How should the Constitution apply in wartime? And if we compromise our liberties in wartime, will we lose them forever?

> [T]he Constitution is not, in its application, in all respects the same, in cases of rebellion or invasion involving the public safety, as it is in time of profound peace and public security. The Constitution itself makes the distinction [in the habeas

corpus provision]; and I can no more be persuaded that the Government can constitutionally take no strong measures in time of rebellion, because it can be shown that the same could not be lawfully taken in time of peace, than I can be persuaded that a particular drug is not good medicine for a sick man, because it can be shown not to be good food for a well one. Nor am I able to appreciate the danger apprehended by [those who drafted the Albany Resolves] that the American people will, by means of military arrests during the Rebellion, lose the right of Public Discussion, the Liberty of Speech and the Press, . . . throughout the indefinite peaceful future, which I trust lies before them, any more than I am able to believe that a man could contract so strong an appetite for emetics during temporary illness as to persist in feeding upon them during the remainder of his healthful life.[131]

At almost exactly the moment Lincoln was circulating his reply to the Albany Resolves, Ohio Democrats were meeting in Columbus to nominate Clement Vallandigham, who was now in exile, for governor. The delegates also approved twenty-three resolutions that challenged the legality of the Emancipation Proclamation and Lincoln's suspensions of habeas corpus, condemned the conviction and banishment of Vallandigham, and demanded his release from exile. On June 22, the Ohio Democrats sent a delegation to Washington to present these resolutions to the president. On June 25, Judge Mathias Birchard, the chairman of the delegation, handed the resolutions to Lincoln in a brief meeting at the White House.

Four days later, Lincoln published his reply. Although this message covered much of the same terrain as his June 12 response to the Albany Resolves, it elaborated his understanding of the Vallandigham situation:

You claim . . . that according to my own position in the Albany response, Mr. V. should be released; and this because, as you claim, he has not damaged the military service, by discouraging enlistments, encouraging desertions, or otherwise. . . . I certainly do not *know* that Mr. V. has specifically, and by direct language, advised against enlistments, and in favor of desertion, and resistance to drafting. We all know that combinations, armed in some instances, to resist the arrest of deserters, began several months ago. . . . These had to be met by military force, and this . . . has led to bloodshed and death. And now . . . I solemnly declare my belief that this hindrance, of the military, including maiming and murder, is due to the course in which Mr. V. has been engaged, in a greater degree than . . . to any other one man. These things have been . . . known to all, and of course known to Mr. V. . . . When it is known that the whole burthen of his speeches has been to stir up men against the prossecution [sic] of the war, and that in the midst of resistance to it, he has not been known, in any instance, to counsel against such resistance, it is next to impossible to repel the inference that he has counselled directly in favor of it."[132]

WE SHOULD NOW ASK, What standard would Abraham Lincoln apply in deciding whether criticism of the government can be punished in wartime? Lincoln clearly accepted that the Constitution governs in time of war. He did not argue that the Constitution is irrelevant. He was equally clear, however, that the application of the Constitution may be different in time of war than in time of peace. He justified this conclusion by invoking the habeas corpus provision of the Constitution, which states that the writ of habeas corpus may be suspended "when in time of Rebellion or Invasion the public Safety may require it."

A careful reading of these letters suggests several interesting propositions about Lincoln's views of free speech in wartime. Lincoln conceded that if Vallandigham had been convicted "for no other reason" than his criticism of the administration, then his "arrest was wrong." This is an important concession. It states unequivocally that, even in wartime, the government may not punish a speaker merely for criticizing its policies, programs, or actions.

But Lincoln asserted that this was *not* the situation in Vallandigham's case. Rather, "the arrest, as I understand, was made for a very different reason." Vallandigham was arrested "because he was laboring, with some effect, to prevent the raising of troops; to encourage desertions from the army; and to leave the Rebellion without an adequate military force to suppress it." What does this mean? One possibility is that Lincoln meant to suggest that Vallandigham was

---

* Lincoln then turned his sights directly on the Ohio Democrats. In effect, he asserted that by nominating Vallandigham as their candidate for governor, "[Y]our own attitude . . . encourages desertion, resistance to the draft and the like, because it teaches those who incline to desert, and to escape the draft, to believe it is your purpose to protect them. . . ." To rebut this inference, he invited them to declare that use of military force to suppress the rebellion is constitutional and that they will do everything in their power to support the military forces of the Union. He promised that if they made such a declaration, he would lift Vallandigham's sentence of exile. Judge Birchard responded to this part of Lincoln's reply. He expressed surprise that Lincoln would impugn the loyalty of those who disagreed with him and argued that Vallandigham's rights were his by virtue of the Constitution, not by the grace of the president. Lincoln, Reply to the Ohio Democratic Convention, June 29, 1863, in *Abraham Lincoln: Speeches and Writings* at 469–70 (cited in note 45). Klement, *Limits of Dissent* at 189 (cited in note 46).

Abraham Lincoln

properly convicted because he had *expressly advocated* desertion and refusal of duty. (As we shall see, this turns out to be an important consideration in the law of the First Amendment.)[133]

Lincoln probably believed that Vallandigham had expressly advocated unlawful conduct. Explicit calls for draft evasion and desertion were not uncommon during the Civil War. Moreover, as we saw earlier, in March 1863 the *New York Times* inaccurately reported that Vallandigham had counseled resistance to the Conscription Act. It was this article that triggered Vallandigham's angry letter to the editor reaffirming that he was "for obedience to all laws" and for "forcible resistance to none."[134] The inaccurate *Times* article apparently was known to Lincoln, and may have shaped his assumptions about Vallandigham's speech in Ohio.[135]

Of course, if Lincoln believed this, he was almost surely wrong. Express advocacy of law violation was wholly out of character with Vallandigham's long record as a speaker.[136] Indeed, the most credible witness to the Ohio speech, Congressman S. S. Cox, testified before the military commission that Vallandigham had *not* counseled resistance to the law, and there was no evidence to the contrary.*

On the other hand, Lincoln did not insist that Vallandigham had expressly advocated unlawful conduct. The Ohio Democrats explained that, contrary to Lincoln's apparent assumption in his June 12 message, Vallandigham had not expressly advocated draft resistance or desertion. They therefore argued that, according to Lincoln's "own position in the Albany response, Mr. V. should be released." Lincoln was clearly taken aback by this contention. He defensively conceded, "I certainly do not *know* that Mr. V. has specifically, and by direct language, advised against enlistments, and in favor of desertion, and resistance to drafting." Lincoln was a careful lawyer. If he had thought that express advocacy

---

* At the proceeding before the military commission, neither of the two prosecution witnesses who had been sent by Burnside to "spy" on Vallandigham's speech testified that Vallandigham had expressly advocated unlawful action. Moreover, one of these witnesses conceded that Vallandigham had told the crowd that "he would not counsel resistance to the military or civil law." Congressman Cox testified on Vallandigham's behalf that Vallandigham had "warned against violence and revolutions" and said that "by the powerful means of the ballot-box all might be remedied that was wrong of a public nature, and the courts would remedy all grievances of a private personal nature." Cox denied that Vallandigham had said "anything . . . at all looking to forcible resistance of either law or military orders." Transcript of the Trial of Clement L. Vallandigham before the Military Commission, May 6–7, 1863, in Vallandigham, *Life of Clement L. Vallandigham* at 274–75, 278 (cited in note 83). See also Rehnquist, *All the Laws But One* at 66 (cited in note 15).

of unlawful conduct was *essential* to the legitimate suppression of Vallandigham's speech, at this point in the debate he would either have conceded that the conviction was "wrong" or sought additional facts. That he did neither suggests that he did not think express advocacy essential.

Although Lincoln may not have thought express advocacy of unlawful conduct essential to conviction, he clearly placed great importance on Vallandigham's *intent*. Indeed, a critical, if unstated, assumption of Lincoln's June 12 message was that Vallandigham could not constitutionally be punished if he did not *intend* to incite unlawful conduct. This assumption is evident both in Lincoln's use of the word "laboring" and in his assurance that Vallandigham's conviction would have been "wrong" had it been based only on criticism of the administration. Had Vallandigham merely been negligent in condemning the war because members of the audience might have been demoralized by his criticisms, he could not be accused of *laboring* to bring about this effect.

Nonetheless, that still left Lincoln with the problem of finding *intent*. And that is precisely where he turned next. Lincoln argued that the harm caused by Vallandigham's speeches was "of course known to Mr. V." Lincoln thus relied on circumstantial evidence to justify his characterization of Vallandigham's intent: "When it is known that the whole burthen of his speeches has been to stir up men against the prossecution [*sic*] of the war, and that in the midst of resistance to it, he has not been known, in any instance, to counsel against such resistance, it is next to impossible to repel the inference that he has counselled directly in favor of it."

Lincoln did not argue that Vallandigham was guilty merely because he *should have known* that one effect of his speeches might have been to generate discontent and perhaps eventually "cause" some listeners to desert or refuse induction. He clearly understood that such a position would contradict his earlier insistence that Vallandigham could not be punished for merely criticizing his administration, for *any* criticism of Lincoln's war-related policies could ultimately "cause" some men to desert or refuse to serve in the army.

To escape this dilemma, Lincoln again sought a middle ground. He argued that Vallandigham could justly be held responsible, not because his speech criticized the administration, but because, knowing the danger he was creating, he did not "counsel *against*" unlawful resistance to the law. In effect, under Lincoln's reasoning, Vallandigham could criticize the administration and its policies, even if he knew his speech might cause others to commit unlawful acts, as long as he mitigated the danger by making clear to his listeners that he was not advising them to violate the law. This is an ingenious argument, but it has no fair application to Mr. V., who consistently counseled *against* unlawful resistance, a fact of which the president presumably was unaware.

Two final points merit attention. Lincoln clearly thought that the *gravity* of the harm mattered. That is why he emphasized in his June 29 letter to the Ohio Democrats that "hindrance of the military, including maiming and murder, is due" more to the speeches of "Mr. V." than to "any other one man." This is a powerful condemnation (whether well founded or not) and suggests that Vallandigham's banishment was justified in part because of the *extraordinarily* dangerous impact of his public speeches.

Finally, there is Lincoln's famous hypothetical about the "simple-minded soldier boy." This example has been praised as a "stroke of genius."[137] How, after all, could the president shoot a "simple-minded soldier boy" for deserting, while not touching "a hair of a wily agitator who induces him to desert"? In fact, one can easily quarrel with this reasoning, if not with Lincoln's gift for simile. If the soldier boy is truly "simple-minded," then perhaps the government should not execute him for desertion.[138] That would be a "great mercy" *without* sacrificing anyone's right to criticize the government. To limit speech merely to "protect" the most susceptible members of the audience runs the risk, as Justice Frankfurter once observed, of reducing "the adult population" to seeing and hearing "only what is fit for children."[139]

WHATEVER THE DEFICIENCIES in Lincoln's analysis, his responses to the Albany Resolves reflected a serious effort to think through hard First Amendment questions at a level of detail and with a degree of precision that was unprecedented. Although the debates over the Sedition Act of 1798 were often eloquent and insightful, they never approached this level of analytical rigor. These letters show Lincoln not only as a brilliant politician and rhetorician but as an impressive constitutional lawyer as well.

So, to return to the original question, what constitutional "standard" did Lincoln embrace for the restriction of speech in wartime? We can infer that Lincoln would have upheld a restriction of speech if two conditions were satisfied: (1) the speaker specifically intended to cause unlawful conduct, and (2) the speech was likely seriously to interfere with the war effort. Lincoln concluded that Vallandigham met the first criterion because Mr. V. must have been aware of the unlawful consequences of his speeches, but (allegedly) did nothing to discourage them, thus giving rise to an inference that he *specifically intended* to cause such consequences. Lincoln concluded that Vallandigham met the second criterion because, in Lincoln's view, Mr. V.'s speeches had already caused grievous harm to the military.

Certainly, one can disagree with Lincoln's interpretation of the facts. But if this is the *standard* that Lincoln contemplated in these messages, it represented a substantial step forward from the Sedition Act of 1798.*

Lincoln's letters to Erastus Corning and the Ohio Democrats were published throughout the nation and read by as many as ten million people.[140] John Nicolay and John Hay described them as among the most successful of Lincoln's state papers in terms of their "impression upon the public mind."[141]

However successful these letters may have been at soothing the public, the protests against Burnside's actions did not pass unnoticed in the White House. When Burnside closed the *Chicago Times* a month after he arrested Vallandigham, Lincoln responded decisively.[142] Secretary of War Stanton immediately wrote Burnside that the president "directs me to say that in his judgment it would be better for you to take an early occasion to revoke that order" because the "irritation produced by such acts is in his opinion likely to do more harm than the publication" of the newspaper. Stanton added that, in the future, on such questions as "the suppression of newspapers not requiring immediate action the President desires to be *previously* consulted."[143] Burnside promptly lifted his closure order, and the *Chicago Times* resumed publication.[144]

And what of Vallandigham? What was his response to Lincoln's letters? Vallandigham was outraged at Lincoln's "insinuation" that he had been arrested for attempting "to prevent the raising of troops and to encourage desertion from the army" and that he was "responsible for numerous acts of resistance to the draft and to the arrest of deserters, causing 'assassination, maiming and murder.'" He branded as "absolutely false" Lincoln's charge that he had "at any time, in any way, . . . disobeyed or failed to counsel obedience to the lawful authority." His "sole offense," he reiterated, had been "words of criticism of the public policy of the Administration, addressed to an open and public political meeting of my fellow-citizens of Ohio lawfully and peaceably assembled."[145]

Ironically, the exiled Mr. V. was not welcome in the Confederacy because he still considered himself a loyal citizen of the Union. He escaped the South by running the Union blockade and made his way to Bermuda and from there to Canada. In the interim, he was nominated in absentia as the Democratic candidate for governor of Ohio. He campaigned vigorously, but unsuccessfully, from across the border.

---

* Of course, it is impossible to know whether this is the "standard" that Lincoln contemplated. We know only that he was prepared to exile an individual whose expression (he believed) satisfied these conditions. We do not know that he would *not* have banished or punished others whose speech did not satisfy one or both of these conditions. Certainly, not every person arrested during the Civil War for his expression met these conditions. One of Lincoln's failings in this regard is that he never made sufficiently clear to his subordinates the ground rules that were to govern such matters.

A year later, Vallandigham returned to the United States, "wearing false hair on his face and a large pillow strapped beneath his waist coat," in disregard of the warning that the original sentence of imprisonment would be imposed if he violated the terms of his commutation. Having by then learned the lessons of experience, Lincoln chose to ignore Vallandigham's presence, though he did keep him under watch.*[146]

Vallandigham was given a hero's welcome among Democrats, and the *Fort Wayne Sentinel* even predicted his election as the next president of the United States. Although this did not come to pass, Vallandigham did play a pivotal role in the 1864 Democratic Party convention in Chicago. He was instrumental in drafting the party's key platform planks condemning Lincoln's "suppression of freedom of speech and of the press" and pledging an immediate "cessation of hostilities."[147] The "cessation" plank, which was designed to restore the Union with slavery intact, proved calamitous to the party's presidential candidate, General George McClellan, who tried desperately to disown it.[148] Despite Lincoln's pessimism about his own reelection in the fall of 1864, the stunning news that Sherman had taken Atlanta suddenly recast the president as a victorious leader. Lincoln decisively defeated McClellan, with 55 percent of the popular vote and an electoral vote majority of 212 to 21.[149]

After the war, Vallandigham returned to Ohio and became a leading critic of the Radical Republicans. He helped form the "New Departure" wing of the Democratic Party, which maintained that the Democrats could return to power only by fully accepting the results of the Civil War and Reconstruction and looking to the

---

* Upon learning of Vallandigham's return to Ohio, Lincoln drafted a letter to Governor Brough of Ohio and General Heintzelman, who had succeeded Burnside, directing them to "consult together freely, watch Vallandigham and others closely, and, upon discovering any palpable injury or imminent danger to the Military proceeding from him, them, or any of them, arrest all implicated. Otherwise, do not arrest without further order; meanwhile report the signs to me from time to time." After writing the letter, however, Lincoln decided not to send it. According to Nicolay and Hay, Lincoln explained in conversation that "the only question to decide was whether he could afford to disregard the contempt of authority and breach of discipline shown" in Vallandigham's return to the United States. On balance, he decided that Vallandigham's presence "could not but result in benefit to the Union cause to have so violent and indiscreet a man go to Chicago," where the Democrats were holding their 1864 convention, "as a firebrand to his own party." As it turned out, Lincoln's judgment proved right because Vallandigham helped persuade the Democrats to embrace the "cessation" plank of their platform that proved disastrous to the party. Moreover, it was clear that any effort to rearrest Vallandigham would have provoked general and violent resistance. Draft of letter from Abraham Lincoln to John Brough and Samuel Heintzelman, June 20, 1864, in Basler, ed, 7 *Collected Works of Abraham Lincoln* at 402 (cited in note 142); Nicolay and Hay, 7 *Abraham Lincoln: A History* at 359–60 (cited in note 79); Vallandigham, *Life of Clement Vallandigham* at 363 (cited in note 83). See id at 355, 361.

future.[150] After losing a bid in 1868 for election to the Senate, Vallandigham resumed his law practice, earning considerable renown for his skill as a trial lawyer.

He died on June 17, 1871, at the age of fifty-one, while getting ready for a murder trial in Hamilton, Ohio. Mr. V. accidentally shot himself to death in his hotel room while preparing to demonstrate in court how his client's alleged victim could accidentally have shot himself to death.[151]

"PLEASE SPARE ME THE TROUBLE"

NO DISCUSSION OF FREE SPEECH during the Civil War would be complete without some consideration of Lincoln's suspensions of habeas corpus. In any constitutional system, there exists an inevitable tension between the aspiration for government constrained by law and the need for discretionary authority to respond to immediate crises.[152] Lincoln faced this tension more acutely than any other American president.

The writ of habeas corpus, the "Great Writ," was fundamental to the framers of the Constitution and held a hallowed place in American law and myth long before the Civil War. A writ of habeas corpus is a judicial mandate directing a government official to present an individual held in custody to the court so that it can determine whether his detention is lawful. The Supreme Court has characterized the writ of habeas corpus as a "fundamental instrument for safeguarding individual freedom against arbitrary and lawless" government action.[153] The writ had been suspended only a few times prior to the Civil War, and then only in very localized circumstances.*

Lincoln suspended the writ on eight separate occasions. As we have seen, he did so first in April 1861 after the riots in Baltimore. With the nation's capital isolated from the rest of the Union, Republicans demanded action. A Republican senator advised Lincoln to "take possession of Baltimore at once." Another influential Republican warned that "the fall of Washington would be most disastrous" and urged that, if necessary, Baltimore be "laid in ruin." Members of the cabinet insisted on decisive and immediate action. Lincoln's private secretaries revealed years later that the stress of this crisis put Lincoln in a severe "state of nervous tension."[154]

Because there was scant precedent for the suspension of habeas corpus, Lin-

---

* The writ of habeas corpus had been suspended very briefly at the end of the War of 1812 by General Andrew Jackson in New Orleans and during Dorr's Rebellion in Rhode Island in 1842.

coln turned for guidance to Attorney General Edward Bates. Bates, in turn, delegated the assignment to an assistant, Titian J. Coffey, who prepared an inconclusive memorandum. Coffey cited Matthew Hale and William Blackstone, who described martial law "as no law at all," and Joseph Story's *Commentaries on the Constitution*, which assumed that only Congress had the constitutional authority to suspend the writ of habeas corpus. This was hardly encouraging. Nonetheless, and despite the legal uncertainty, Lincoln decided to act. On April 27, he suspended the writ of habeas corpus in those areas of Maryland that could be used by secessionists to block access to and from Washington.[155]

CHIEF JUSTICE TANEY did not find the matter uncertain at all. As we have seen, he ruled in *Ex parte Merryman*[156] that the president had no independent authority to suspend the writ of habeas corpus. Indeed, Taney "supposed it to be one of those points of constitutional law upon which there was no difference of opinion . . . that the privilege of the writ could not be suspended, except by act of congress." To support this judgment, Taney invoked the text of the Constitution,*[157] Chief Justice Marshall's opinion in *Ex parte Bollman*,[158] Joseph Story's *Commentaries on the Constitution*,[159] and President Jefferson's application to Congress for authority to suspend the writ of habeas corpus when he found it necessary to deal with the Aaron Burr conspiracy. In Taney's judgment, the matter was without doubt: "the president has exercised a power which he does not possess under the constitution."[160]

Taney intended this decision to be a decisive rejection of Lincoln's use of excessive executive authority. It was not. Lincoln's supporters challenged Taney's construction of the text and his understanding of constitutional history. Moreover, they argued that the rebellion involved treasonable activity on so vast a scale that the ordinary criminal process was simply inadequate to deal with the situation. Exceptional measures were essential and, hence, lawful.[161]

Lincoln argued the matter on his own behalf in a special address to Congress on July 4, 1861. He maintained that although the Constitution was "silent" on whether suspension of the writ of habeas corpus is a presidential or congressional power, the "war power" and the president's constitutional role as commander in chief placed upon the president the responsibility to defend the nation against

---

* Taney noted that Article I, section 9, clause 2, of the Constitution, which deals primarily with the legislative power, is the only provision of the Constitution that mentions suspension of the writ of habeas corpus. He therefore reasoned that this was a power assigned exclusively to the Congress. The relevant provision of Article I, section 9, provides, "The Privilege of the Writ of *Habeas corpus* shall not be suspended, unless when in Cases of Rebellion or Invasion the public Safety may require it."

imminent destruction.[162] He asserted that Chief Justice Taney's interpretation of the Constitution would allow "all the laws, *but one*, to go unexecuted, and the government itself go to pieces, lest that one be violated." This, he implied, was implausible.[163] Acknowledging that it was uncertain whether his actions were "strictly legal or not," Lincoln insisted that they were undertaken in circumstances of "public necessity." He also hastened to assure Congress that the authority he had assumed had "been exercised but very sparingly."[164]

Two years later, in his replies to Erastus Corning and the Ohio Democrats, Lincoln offered a more compelling rationale for his suspension of habeas corpus. He began by reminding his readers that when he first assumed office secessionist "sympathizers pervaded all departments of the Government" and "hoped to keep on foot among us a most efficient corps of spies, informers, suppliers, and aiders and abettors of their cause." Although he himself revered "the guaranteed rights of individuals," he reluctantly came to the conclusion that "strong measures" were "indispensable to the public safety."[165]

Lincoln then explained that he had decided to suspend the writ of habeas corpus because the ordinary civil courts were inadequate to deal with the challenge then facing the nation:

> Civil courts are organized chiefly for trials of individuals, or, at most, a few individuals acting in concert; and this in quiet times, and on charges of crimes well defined in the law. . . .
>
> Ours is a case of rebellion . . . and the provision of the Constitution that "the privilege of the writ of habeas corpus shall not be suspended, unless when, in cases of rebellion or invasion, the public safety may require it," is *the* provision which specially applies to our present case. The provision plainly attests the understanding of those who made the Constitution, that ordinary courts of justice are inadequate to "cases of rebellion"—attests their purpose that, in such cases, men may be held in custody whom the courts, acting on ordinary rules, would discharge. . . . Indeed, arrests by process of courts, and arrests in cases of rebellion, do not proceed . . . upon the same basis. The former is directed at the . . . ordinary . . . perpetration of crime; while the latter is directed at sudden and extensive uprisings against the Government. . . .[166]

Lincoln also rejected the arguments that only Congress could suspend the writ and that the suspension of habeas corpus is constitutional only in the specific "localities where rebellion actually exists." With respect to the first issue, Lincoln contended that although the Constitution "does not expressly declare who is to decide," by "necessary implication, when Rebellion or Invasion comes, the . . . commander-in-chief . . . is the man who holds the power, and bears the responsibility" of making the decision.[167] With respect to the second issue, Lincoln argued that once a rebellion exists, the writ may be suspended whenever and wherever the public safety requires such action, whether or not the rebellion had reached that particular locale.[168]

It is interesting to contrast Lincoln's defense of his suspension of habeas corpus in 1861 with his analysis in 1848 of Polk's initiation of the Mexican War. Lincoln's friend and law partner, William Herndon, wrote Lincoln after his vitriolic attack on Polk. Disagreeing with Lincoln's position, Herndon argued that if it is necessary to repel an invasion, the president must have the constitutional authority to invade another country, and that the president must be the "sole judge" of whether such a necessity exists. In a letter to Herndon on February 15, 1848, Lincoln adamantly rejected this view:

> Allow the President to invade a neighboring nation whenever he shall deem it necessary to repel an invasion, and you allow him to do so *whenever he may choose to say* he deems it necessary for such purposes, and you allow him to make war at pleasure. Study to see if you can fix *any limit* to his power in this respect after having given him so much as you propose. If to-day he should choose to say he thinks it necessary to invade Canada to prevent the British from invading us, how could you stop him? You may say to him, "I see no probability of the British invading us"; but he will say to you, "Be silent; I see it, if you don't."
>
> The provision of the Constitution giving the war-making power to Congress was dictated, as I understand it, by the following reasons: kings had always been involving and impoverishing their people in wars, pretending generally, if not always, that the good of the people was the object. This our convention understood to be the most oppressive of all kingly oppressions, and they resolved to frame the Constitution that no one man should hold the power of bringing this oppression upon us. But your view destroys the whole matter and places our President where kings have always stood.[169]

Substitute "suspend the writ of habeas corpus" for "invade a neighboring nation," and Lincoln has almost perfectly made the case against himself. The better view, as argued by Chief Justice Taney, is that the president does not have the constitutional authority to suspend the writ of habeas corpus. The long English struggle to shift the power to suspend the writ to Parliament and the framers' deep suspicion of unchecked executive power strongly suggest that "they would have been unlikely to give the president the exclusive, final word about his own power to deprive citizens of their liberty without legal process."[170]

Right or wrong, Lincoln's blatant defiance of Chief Justice Taney's order in *Merryman* did not generate any appreciable public outcry.* No doubt, the public agreed

---

* Indeed, even Democratic newspapers tended to support the president's action. The question whether Lincoln had a legal right simply to disobey Taney's order is different from the question

with the president that this was no time to quibble over strict adherence to the Constitution. The absence of any resistance to this initial assertion of aggressive executive authority eased the way for Lincoln to proceed on other fronts as well. Only a few weeks later, he suspended the writ in Florida. His most extreme suspension order, in September 1862,[171] was applicable *nationwide* and declared that "all persons . . . guilty of any disloyal practice . . . shall be subject to martial law."[172]

Although there were several accomplished constitutional lawyers in Congress, the legislative branch proved much less concerned than the chief justice about its prerogatives with respect to the suspension of habeas corpus. Congress silently deferred to the president and then, in 1863, enacted legislation to ratify his actions and to authorize future suspensions of the writ.[173] Once suspension of the writ and declaration of martial law had been accepted by Congress and the public, the administration felt free to employ these tactics at will to enforce conscription, combat draft resistance, and defy judicial orders that might otherwise have interfered with government policy.[174]

William Seward was widely quoted in the Democratic press as having commented to the British minister, "I can touch a bell on my right hand and order the arrest of a citizen in Ohio. I can touch the bell again and order the imprisonment of a citizen of New York, and no power on earth but that of the President can release them. Can the Queen of England, in her dominions, say as much?" These arrests, usually at night, "spread fear and hate" among those who dissented from the administration's policies.[175]

IT IS UNKNOWN exactly how many civilians were arrested by military authorities during the Civil War.[176] Estimates range from 13,000 to 38,000.[177] Most of these arrests were in the border states and, as the war moved south, in the states of the Confederacy; most were for such offenses as draft evasion, trading with the enemy, bridge burning, and other forms of sabotage. Although phrases and words like "treasonable language," "Southern sympathizer," "disloyalty," and "inducing desertion" appear occasionally in the prison records, relatively few individuals were arrested for their political beliefs or expressions.[178]

Of those arrested for disloyal speech, a few were persons of influence, Vallandigham being the most prominent. Most, however, were men of obscurity,

---

whether he had a legal right to suspend the writ of habeas corpus. It is certainly arguable that even if the suspension was lawful Lincoln had a legal obligation to defend his action in the courts. For an excellent discussion of this question, see Farber, *Lincoln's Constitution* at 188–92 (cited in note 12).

whose outbursts hardly threatened the war effort. David Lyon of Illinois, for example, was arrested for saying that "anyone who enlists is a God Damn fool," William Palmer of Ohio for writing that "not fifty soldiers will fight to free Negroes," and Jacob Wright of New Jersey for saying that anyone who enlists is "no better than a goddamned nigger." These arrests were invariably initiated at low levels of authority, and these detainees were as a rule quickly released (ordinarily within a month or two) upon taking an oath of allegiance to the Union.[179]

Lincoln generally learned of these arrests, if at all, only after the fact, and he was almost always displeased. He believed that such speakers posed no real threat to the Union and feared that their arrests needlessly polarized the public. By 1863, Lincoln had grown weary of dealing with such arrests. On May 17, he made clear that "unless the *necessity*" for such arrests was "*manifest* and *urgent*," he "preferred they should cease."[180] As in the Vallandigham case, however, Lincoln did not act decisively to prohibit such arrests. He chose to defer to the judgment of his commanders.[181] Lincoln's exasperation with these incidents is perhaps best captured by his reaction to General John M. Schofield's arrest of a newspaper editor in St. Louis. Lincoln wrote Schofield, "Please spare me the trouble this is likely to bring."[182]

Another event that reveals Lincoln's sense of these issues arose out of General Ewing's decision in August 1863 to evacuate four Missouri counties whose residents had assisted the Confederate guerrilla leader William Quantrill in his murderous raid on Lawrence, Kansas.[183] Although Lincoln approved Ewing's evacuation order, he stipulated, "[Y]ou will only arrest individuals, and suppress assemblies, or newspapers, when they may be working *palpable* injury to the Military," and "in no other case will you interfere with the expression of opinion in any form."[184]

Thus, although dissenters were sometimes harassed and arrested by military authorities, in general the opposition was left free to criticize Lincoln, his policies, and his administration. At the very least, Lincoln recognized that excessive suppression of dissent could backfire and prove politically counterproductive.[185] According to Nicolay and Hay, Lincoln took "the greatest care . . . to restrain . . . any abuse of this tremendous power." They recalled that he "watched over this with increasing vigilance as the war went on."*[186]

---

*Interestingly, the experience in the Confederacy was, if anything, more civil libertarian. The Confederate Congress, for example, refused to grant President Davis broad authority for the suspension of habeas corpus, and the Confederate states tended to be somewhat more tolerant of political dissent than their Union counterparts. See Mark E. Neely Jr., *Southern Rights: Political Prisoners and the Myth of Confederate Constitutionalism* 27, 87–91 (Virginia 1999).

SHORTLY AFTER THE CIVIL WAR ended, the Supreme Court finally had occasion to consider the constitutionality of Lincoln's use of military tribunals to try civilians. Military authorities in Indiana seized Lambdin Milligan for allegedly conspiring to engage in criminal acts to aid the Confederacy. He was tried by a military tribunal, convicted, and sentenced to death. In *Ex parte Milligan*,[187] the Supreme Court held that the government could not constitutionally use military tribunals in this manner, even in time of war or insurrection, if the civil courts were open and functioning, as they were in Indiana. To justify such action, the Court added, "necessity must be actual and present; the invasion real, such as effectually closes the courts and deposes the civil administration."[188] In his opinion for the Court, Justice David Davis explained, "The Constitution . . . is a law for rulers and people, equally in war and in peace, and covers with the shield of its protection all classes of men, at all times, and under all circumstances. No doctrine, involving more pernicious consequences, was ever invented by the wit of man than that any of its provisions can be suspended during any of the great exigencies of government."[189]

DESPOT, LIAR, USURPER, THIEF, MONSTER, PERJURER, IGNORAMUS, SWINDLER, TYRANT, FIEND, BUTCHER, AND PIRATE

AS SUGGESTED BY the *Chicago Times* incident, there were instances in which the administration attempted to restrict the press without suspending the writ of habeas corpus. Shortly after the attack on Fort Sumter, for example, the administration tried to censor news dispatches by assuming control of the telegraph wires. To avoid this, reporters often just sent their dispatches by mail, which was slower, but not subject to any significant censorship.[190]

After General McClellan assumed command of the Army of the Potomac, correspondents were given broad access to information and considerable leeway to disseminate news concerning military engagements, as long as they did not publish information that would directly benefit the enemy, such as information about troop movements. Throughout the war, the press asserted the right to disseminate even news of troop movements if the information came from a source other than government officials.

In March 1862, the House Judiciary Committee undertook an investigation of military censorship of the telegraph. The committee concluded that the telegraph "should be left as free from Government interference as may be consistent with the necessities of the Government in time of war." It further resolved that "the Government shall not interfere with free transmission of intelligence by telegraph, when the same will not aid the enemy in his military or naval operations." [191]

FOR THE MOST PART, efforts to suppress anti-administration newspapers proved futile because of the permeability of the North–South border, which made it easy for secessionists to circulate anti-Lincoln newspapers in the North. This does not mean that the government did not try, however.

After the rout of the Union army at Bull Run in July 1861, the Democratic press demanded that Lincoln end the war quickly on negotiated terms. Republicans were outraged. In August, a New York grand jury sought "advice" about whether it could indict newspapers "for being disloyal." The grand jury acknowledged that "free governments allow liberty of speech and of the press to their utmost limit," but asserted that "there is, nevertheless, a limit." Declaring five New York newspapers guilty of disloyalty, the grand jury inquired of the federal court whether these presses could be indicted and punished. Although the court never responded to this query, Postmaster General Montgomery Blair excluded all five newspapers from the United States mail.[192]

Throughout the war, the administration made sporadic efforts to restrict the Democratic press.[193] According to one estimate, some three hundred Democratic newspapers were suspended for at least a brief period during the war, usually for expressing sympathy for the enemy or criticizing the administration.[194] In 1861, for example, General Frémont clamped down on "disloyal" newspapers in Missouri as part of his imposition of martial law. He prohibited the dissemination of the five newspapers listed by the New York grand jury, suppressed two newspapers that had published false statements about military movements, and arrested the editors of the *St. Louis News* for criticizing his handling of a military matter. The editors were released when they promised not to publish any further articles that would be harmful to the government.[195]

The administration also attempted to control the "secessionist" press in Maryland. Some of these newspapers were stridently anti-Union. The *Daily Exchange*, for example, described the war as "a wicked and desperate crusade"; the *South* announced that it had been established "to further the Confederate cause in Maryland and to secure the secession of that state from the Union"; and the *Daily Republican* (actually, a Democratic paper) attacked the administration as "the Despotism of Lincoln and Co." In September 1861, Postmaster General Blair barred all three of these newspapers from the U.S. mail. When the editors of these papers continued their attacks on the administration, Secretary of War Stanton ordered their arrests. The editors were briefly imprisoned, but upon their release they renewed their anti-administration tirades. In 1862, the military authorities in Maryland officially suppressed these and other "treasonable" newspapers.[196]

Such incidents were not confined to the border states. Two Iowa editors, John Mahoney of the *Dubuque Herald* and David Sheward of the *Fairfield Constitution and Union*, were arrested in 1862 by order of Stanton and shipped off to Old Capitol Prison in Washington, where they remained for three months without ever being charged with a crime. After taking an oath of allegiance to the Union, they were released, and promptly resumed their attacks on the administration. One of Mahoney's first editorials upon his return to Iowa called Lincoln a "tyrant" and asked pointedly, "Are you, as soldiers, bound by patriotism, duty or loyalty to fight in such a cause?"[197]

In 1863, Albert Boileau, editor and publisher of the *Philadelphia Evening Journal*, wrote an editorial that compared Jefferson Davis with Abraham Lincoln, concluding that the comparison is "quite damaging to the intellectual capacity of the Federal President." Boileau was arrested at his home on orders of General Schenck. Upon writing a letter of apology to Schenck, and promising not to "write, print, or publish any articles having such dangerous character" in the future, Boileau was released. He was excoriated by the Democratic press for his cowardice and for enabling the government "to establish another precedent for lawless despotism."[198]

In addition to such formal government actions against anti-administration newspapers, there were more informal incidents in which Union soldiers and "loyal" citizens, outraged by the utterances of Democratic newspapers, attacked their offices and, occasionally, their editors. At one time or another, Democratic newspaper offices were savaged by mobs in Kansas, Ohio, New Hampshire, and Massachusetts. A Republican mob in Portsmouth, New Hampshire, demanded that the editor of the *States and Union* display the American flag, and the editor of the *Essex County Democrat* was dragged from his home, covered with a coat of tar and feathers, and ridden through town on a rail. [199] Although Democrats as well as Republicans were occasionally guilty of such actions (recall the attack on the local Republican newspaper after the arrest of Vallandigham), the military was certainly not evenhanded in its protection of pro-administration and anti-administration newspapers.*

---

* On several occasions, soldiers joined mob efforts to destroy newspaper offices. The tendency was to discipline those soldiers who participated in "attacks on antiwar papers," but not those "who attacked anti-administration presses." Finkelman, *Civil Liberties and the Civil War* at 1376 (cited in note 185). See Harper, *Lincoln and the Press* at 151–52, 197–98, 230–33 (cited in note 60).

Although such efforts to restrain Democratic criticism occurred sporadically, the anti-administration press generally was given considerable latitude. As one scholar has observed, "Lincoln's defenders have often pointed to the shrill criticism of the president found in the Northern Democratic press . . . as proof that dissent was never really stifled."[200]

A review of the tolerated criticism confirms this observation. The *New York Daily News*, one of the newspapers subjected to Postmaster General Blair's exclusion order, reappeared some eighteen months later as an evening paper. During the 1864 presidential campaign, referring to Lincoln, the *Daily News* editorialized that "no influence except compulsion can induce any respectable proportion of the people to cast their votes for that compound of cunning, heartlessness and folly that they now execrate in the person of their Chief Magistrate."[201]

Harper's Weekly, which steadfastly supported Lincoln, collected a list of the invectives that had been used publicly to castigate the president. The list included the epithets "despot," "liar," "usurper," "thief," "monster," "perjurer," "ignoramus," "swindler," "tyrant," "fiend," "butcher," and "pirate."[202] The "Lincoln Catechism," a widely distributed attack on the president, offered such lessons as the following:

> Q: What is the meaning of the word "traitor"?
> A: One who is a stickler for the Constitution and the laws.
> Q: What is the meaning of the word "law'"?
> A: The will of the President.
> Q: Have the people any rights?
> A: None but such as the President gives.
> Q: Is it disloyal to believe in the Union as it was?
> A: It is.[203]

Lincoln's criticisms of President Polk during the Mexican War, in which he alluded to Polk as "a bewildered and miserably perplexed man," were often thrown back at Lincoln by the Democratic press. They repeatedly reminded Lincoln of his hope for Polk: "God grant that he may be able to show there is not something about his conscience more painful than all his mental perplexity."[204] The "Lincoln Catechism" asked, "What should be done to Abraham Lincoln if he believed now as he did in 1848?" It replied, "The king can do no wrong."[205]

The resuscitated *Daily News* specialized in verse. In midsummer 1864, it published the following:

> The night was heavy and murk, the moon shone dusky and red.
> The air had an odor of sulphurous smoke and of corpses newly dead.

And I saw in fact or a dream, or both confused in one,
A dance and a revel and a maniac rout too hideous for the sun;
And out of it came a cry:
Blood! Blood! Blood! Let the witches cauldron boil with a nation's tears for water!
Blood! Blood! Blood! Slabby and thick as mud, to sprinkle the hungry soil for
   the carnival of slaughter![206]

Until the very end of the war, the *Daily News* kept up this drumbeat of vituperation. It scoffed at all reports of Union victories and repeatedly asserted the
inevitability of the North's defeat. Nonetheless, it was left free to publish.

In 1863, the *New York Evening Express* published a scathing attack on the
draft, arguing that "conscription is a horror." "It is slavery, accursed slavery, in its
most frightful form." The Democratic press accused the president of "operating
a slaughterhouse." In 1864, the *Chicago Times* editorialized about its old neme-

"King Lincoln's Suspension of Habeas Corpus"

sis, General Burnside, describing him as "the butcher of Fredericksburg" and the "assassin of . . . liberty." It added that Burnside "was not the head butcher and assassin; he was only the creature, the mean instrument, the puppet, the jumping-jack of the principal butchers and assassins."[207]

A verse screed of more than two hundred lines titled "The Devil's Visit to Old Abe" was often reprinted in Democratic journals. It began as follows:

> With a beard that was filthy and red,
> His mouth with tobacco bespread,
> Abe Lincoln sat in the gay white house,
> Awishing that he was dead—
> Swear! Swear! Swear!
> Till his tongue was blistered o'er,
> Then in a voice not very strong
> He slowly whined the Despot's song;
> Lie! Lie! Lie![208]

The *Bangor Democrat*, which had been sacked by angry citizens in 1861 for its "disloyal" utterances, soon reopened and published this verse in 1863:

> You saw those mighty legions, Abe,
> And heard their manly tread;
> You counted hosts of *living* men—
> Pray—can you count the *dead*?
> Look o'er the proud Potomac, Abe,
> Virginia's hill along;
> Their wakeful ghosts are beck'ning you,
> Two hundred thousand strong.[209]

The Newark *Evening Journal* belittled Lincoln and his policies. In 1864, military officials finally tried to throttle the paper after it published the following editorial:

> It will be seen that Mr. Lincoln has called for another half million of men. Those who desire to be butchered will please step forward at once. All others will please stay home and defy Old Abe and his minions. . . . We hope that the people of New Jersey will at once put their feet down and insist that not a man shall be forced out of the State to engage in the abolition butchery, and swear to die at their own doors rather than march one step to fulfill the dictates of that mad revolutionary fanaticism, which has destroyed the best Government the world ever saw. . . . Let the people rise as one man and demand that this wholesale murder shall cease.[210]

The editor of the *Evening Journal*, E. N. Fuller, was charged with inciting insurrection and discouraging enlistments. He was tried in a criminal (rather than a military) proceeding and convicted. Although this editorial came perilously close to *expressly inciting* unlawful conduct, Fuller was sentenced only to pay a fine. He then went immediately back to his paper, editorializing shortly thereafter that the president "has betrayed his country and caused the butchery of hundreds of thousands of the people . . . in order to . . . put in force a fanatical, impracticable idea."[211]

Surely, Lincoln did not enjoy such caustic criticism, but he kept it in perspective and did not overreact. One anecdote is revealing. After Lincoln announced the Emancipation Proclamation in September 1863, he was subjected to a torrent of often ugly calumny. According to the *Springfield* (Massachusetts) *Republican*, someone sent him a pile of negative editorials. Lincoln later told a friend, "[H]aving an hour to spare on Sunday I read this batch of editorials, and when I was through reading I asked myself, 'Abraham Lincoln, are you a man *or a dog?*'" Although the editorials were "bitter in their criticisms upon him," Lincoln "smiled very pleasantly as he spoke of them, though it was evident that they made a decided impression upon his mind."[*][212]

---

[*] In the spring of 1864, Republicans in Congress attempted to expel Representative Alexander Long of Ohio, who had made a speech on the floor of the House stating that the war was "wrong" and "in violation of the Constitution." In support of the motion for expulsion, Representative Spalding declared, "No citizen can be permitted to utter sentiments, in time of war, that shall distract and dishearten our own soldiers." Opponents of the motion argued that Long's "views should be controverted by arguments" rather than silenced by expulsion. The motion to expel was amended to one of censure, which then passed the House, with Republicans generally voting for the motion and Democrats generally voting against. One factor that persuaded Republicans to amend the resolution was the strongly negative reaction of the press, including many Republican papers. Cong Globe, 38th Cong, 1st Sess 1580–81, 1577 (Apr 12, 1864); id at 1577 (Representative Eldridge); id at 1549 (Apr 11, 1864) (Representative Kernan). See Curtis, *Free Speech* at 345–46 (cited in note 71); Hyman, *More Perfect Union* at 174–75 (cited in note 25); *The Freedom of Debate*, Evening Post 2 (Apr 11, 1864); *How the Rebellion Is Abetted — The Folly of the House*, New-York Times 4 (Apr 13, 1864).

"EVEN AT THE DARKEST MOMENTS"

AT THE OUTSET of the Civil War, the United States had had little experience with the freedoms of speech and press in wartime. The sixty years since the Sedition Act of 1798 had seen no significant federal restrictions of political dissent, and there was thus no settled understanding of the appropriate limits of such expression.[213] Some constitutional scholars of the era thought there was something "exquisitely absurd" in the notion that a civil war could be "waged under the protection of the Bill of Rights."[214] Others held that the Constitution should "apply as if nothing going on since Sumter was different from what obtained earlier."

Critics have argued that Lincoln became an uncompromising tyrant during the course of the war.[215] Certainly, there were serious abuses in the suspensions of habeas corpus. But keeping in mind the extraordinary complexities of a civil war, the well-founded anxieties about sabotage, desertion, and draft evasion, and the nation's relative immaturity in dealing with radical dissent in wartime, it can fairly be said, on balance, that the nation suffered only a very limited—and largely unsystematic—interference with free expression during the Civil War.[216] The Lincoln administration did not enact a sedition act, it left most dissent undisturbed, and those speakers it did arrest for seditious expression were almost always quickly released.[217]

The greatest danger to robust political dissent during the Civil War came not from Lincoln, who exercised considerable restraint, but from his military commanders, who too often acted on the assumption that war substitutes the rule of force for the rule of law.[218] Lincoln should have done more to keep his military commanders in check. But, on the whole, the man who once claimed the right to excoriate a sitting president for his "misguided" wartime policies demonstrated an admirable respect for free expression—even when he was the target of attack. Moreover, the impressive public regard for free speech in this era played a critical role in keeping repression in check. Even many Republicans defended the rights of Vallandigham and other dissenters, in the belief that assaults on free expression "ultimately threatened the liberty of all."[219]

In his devotion to keeping "the country whole so that democracy could not be said to have failed," [220] Lincoln charted a middle course that melded his sense of the practical with his commitment to the law.[221] He claimed for himself—as president—powers both unprecedented and extraordinary, but he took care to root these assertions of authority in the Constitution. Even at the darkest moments of the conflict, Lincoln never asserted that the Constitution was suspended in time of war, and he never lost sight of the nation's fundamental values.*[222] Most striking was Lincoln's persistent concern for harmonizing liberty and power through constitutional discourse and his unflinching insistence that "the Constitution mattered."[223]

---

* It was often argued in the eighteenth and early nineteenth centuries that the executive could act outside the authority of the Constitution in times of grave crisis. Representing this view, Charles Sumner declared that constitutional rights must be "superseded by war which brings into being other rights which know no master." Cong Globe, 37th Cong, 2d Sess 2196 (May 19, 1862). Lincoln's approach was more moderate, for he strained to connect his actions to the terms of the Constitution itself. See Jill Elaine Hasday, *Civil War as Paradigm: Reestablishing the Rule of Law at the End of the Cold War*, 5 Kan J U Law & Pub Pol 1, 2–4 (1996).

WORLD WAR I

"Clear and Present Danger"?

The Masses, *August 1917*

*T*HE CARNAGE WAS HORRIFYING. In the spring offensives of 1915, the Allies lost 240,000 men and the Germans 140,000, with no net change in position. The following summer, the British suffered 60,000 casualties on *a single day* in the battle of the Somme. Between the outbreak of war in Europe and the decision of the United States to enter the conflict in the spring of 1917, there was continuing debate about the nation's best course of action.

Most Americans believed that the war in Europe did not implicate vital interests of the United States. President Wilson's proclamation that America should remain neutral was greeted warmly throughout the nation. What finally drew the United States into the war was the German submarine blockade. Unlike the British, who could deny the Axis essential supplies by laying minefields in the narrow shipping routes to Germany, the Axis had to resort to submarine warfare to cut off shipping to England and France, which had broad access to the sea. These blockades infuriated the neutrals, who maintained that they were entitled under international law to trade freely with all belligerents.

On February 2, 1915, Germany announced that it would treat the waters around the British Isles as a war zone in which no ship would be immune from attack. On May 7, a German U-boat sank the British liner *Lusitania*, on its way from New York to Liverpool. Among the 1,200 passengers who drowned were 128 Americans, sending a shudder of outrage through the United States. President Wilson promptly ordered his cabinet to plan for rearmament.[1]

Many Americans feared that this step would lead the nation into a bloody and unnecessary war. Although they valued the "freedom of the seas," they did not find it a sufficiently compelling reason to spill American blood on the battlefields of Europe. The more sensible course, they argued, was simply to stand aside, forgo trade with the belligerents, and let the storm pass. Many saw the conflict not as a war to make the world "safe for democracy" but as a war to protect the interests and investments of the wealthy.

Because of the outrage caused by the sinking of the *Lusitania*,[*] Germany restricted its submarine attacks. But two years later, in January 1917, it announced that, in order to limit the continued shipment of munitions and supplies to the Allies, it would sink without warning all ships in a broad area around England and France. By March 20, German submarines had sunk three American vessels. On April 2, Woodrow Wilson—who had won reelection the preceding fall on the slogan that he had "kept America out of war"—sought a declaration of war because Germany had thrown "to the winds all scruples of humanity." Echoing John Adams in 1798, he proclaimed that the United States could not "choose the path of submission and suffer the most sacred rights of our nation and our people to be ignored or violated."[2]

The voices of dissent were immediate and sharp. On April 4, during Congress's debate over the war resolution, Republican Senator George Norris of Nebraska stated that "we are about to put the dollar sign upon the American flag" and that "we are committing a sin against humanity and against our countrymen."[3] The administration's proposal to reinstitute the draft triggered bitter attacks. Champ Clark, the Democratic Speaker of the House, objected that "there is precious little difference between a conscript and a convict," and Senator James Reed, recalling the draft riots during the Civil War, warned that reinstitution of the draft "will have the streets of our American cities running red with blood."[†][4]

Unlike Lincoln, Woodrow Wilson was a man with little tolerance for criticism. In seeking a declaration of war, he cautioned that "if there should be disloyalty, it will be dealt with with a firm hand of stern repression."[5] In proposing the Espionage Act of 1917, the first federal legislation against disloyal expression since the Sedition Act of 1798, he insisted that disloyalty "was not a subject on which there was room for . . . debate." Disloyal individuals, he explained, "had sacrificed their right to civil liberties."[6] In these and similar pronouncements, he set the tone for what was to follow.[‡]

---

[*] The sinking of the *Lusitania* became a central theme in the American understanding of its justification for entering the war. It has largely been forgotten that almost two years elapsed between that event and the American declaration of war.

[†] One measure of the depths of opposition to World War I is that some 300,000 men evaded the draft during the course of the war.

[‡] In his speech requesting a declaration of war, Wilson also observed that Germany "has filled our unsuspecting communities and even our offices of government with spies and set criminal intrigues everywhere afoot against our national unity of counsel, our peace within and without, our industries and our commerce." Six members of the Senate and fifty members of the House voted against the declaration of war. 65th Cong, Spec Sess, in 55 Cong Rec S 104 (Apr 2, 1917).

Wilson understood that, if allowed to fester, antiwar dissent could undermine morale and make it more difficult for the nation to prosecute the war successfully. If citizens became disillusioned with the war, they would be more reluctant to serve in the military, commit their financial resources, and support the effort politically. Wilson knew that war is not merely a battle of armies but also a contest of wills. Defeat could come from collapse of the home front as well as from failure in the trenches. He knew that the resilience of the nation's determination to fight was as important to military success as its capacity to train and equip its army.

A key question in World War I was whether the United States could punish public opposition to the war because it might sap the nation's resolve and thus the war effort. For the first time, this question implicated not only the president and the Congress but the Supreme Court as well. It was during World War I that the Court for the *first time* attempted to make sense of the First Amendment. How would the Court reconcile the necessities of wartime with the constitutional promise that "Congress shall make no law abridging the freedom of speech, or of the press"? In a series of decisions in the spring and fall of 1919, the Court fretted over fire in a crowded theater and "clear and present danger," and established dismal precedents that took the nation half a century to overcome. Yet it was in these decisions that we find the origins of the First Amendment as we know it today.

A MERE "SLIP OF A GIRL"

SHE WAS TWENTY YEARS OLD, but looked much younger. At four feet nine inches and less than ninety pounds, she was a mere "slip of a girl." She had a round face, short, curly black hair, and a habit of clenching her fists when she was angry. When the judge entered the courtroom, she refused to rise. When the prosecutor asked whether she believed in law, she demanded he explain what he meant by "law." When the judge was about to pronounce sentence, he scornfully asked, "What have you to say?" She turned her back to the judge and proclaimed, "I do not believe in any authorities."

In 1913, Mollie Steimer arrived at Ellis Island with her parents and her five brothers and sisters, part of the flood of immigrants fleeing poverty and anti-Semitism in csarist Russia. Two days after her arrival, the fifteen-year-old went to work in a grimy garment factory amid the crowded tenements of New York's Lower

East Side. Faced with continuing hardship and bleak prospects for the future, she began to explore radical literature, discovering the works of Michael Bakunin, Peter Kropotkin, and Emma Goldman. She soon became involved in trade union activities. By the age of nineteen, she was a committed anarchist.

Steimer believed in a new social order in which no group would govern any other, private property would be abolished, and people would no longer divide themselves into warring nations. Her dedication to this ideal was so deep that she vowed to "devote all my energy, and, if necessary, render my life for it."

With the outbreak of the Russian Revolution in 1917, Steimer threw herself into political action. She joined a group of young anarchists who published a clandestine Yiddish journal, *Der Shturm* (The Storm). A year later, the group launched a new publication, *Frayhayt* (Freedom). Enlarging upon Thomas Jefferson's observation that "that government is best which governs least," the group's standard became "that government is best which governs not at all."

The *Frayhayt* group included a dozen young workers, men and women of eastern European Jewish origin. They met regularly at 5 East 104th Sreet, where several of them, including Steimer, shared an apartment. They printed *Frayhayt* on a hand press and distributed it secretly at night. Because of the paper's strident antiwar, anticapitalist stance, secrecy was essential.

In the summer of 1918, the United States sent a contingent of marines to Vladivostok. The *Frayhayt* group saw this as a move to crush the Russian Revolution. They printed two leaflets opposing the intervention in Russia, one in Yiddish, the other in English, asserting that "there is only one enemy of the workers of the world and that is CAPITALISM." The leaflets called for a general strike to protest the government's action. After distributing these leaflets throughout the city, Steimer threw the remainder from a washroom window on an upper floor of the building in which she worked. As they floated to the street below, they were retrieved by passing workmen, one of whom summoned the authorities.

Two army sergeants entered the building and discovered an informant who implicated Steimer and the other members of the group. Steimer was arrested, and the police raided the group's Harlem headquarters, ransacked the apartment, and arrested and beat the other members of the group. Steimer and four of her comrades were charged under the Espionage Act of 1917 and the Sedition Act of 1918 with conspiracy to publish disloyal material intended to obstruct the war and cause contempt for the government of the United States.

The trial opened on October 10, 1918, in the federal courthouse in New York. Two weeks later, the judge sentenced Mollie Steimer to fifteen years in prison.[7] Her case eventually reached the Supreme Court of the United States.

Mollie Steimer

WAR OPPONENTS: JANE ADDAMS, EUGENE V. DEBS, AND EMMA GOLDMAN

AMERICANS OF GERMAN ANCESTRY, who made up almost 25 percent of the population in 1917, did not relish the prospect of war between the United States and Germany. The awkwardness of their position was made painfully evident shortly after the sinking of the *Lusitania*, when some German Americans echoed the German government's claim that the liner was carrying arms to Britain. (The *Lusitania* was indeed carrying 173 tons of munitions.) President Wilson furiously replied that "there are citizens of the United States, born under other flags, . . . who have poured the poison of disloyalty into the very arteries of our national life." He added that such "disloyalty . . . must be crushed" out of existence.[8]

Pacifists and internationalists also opposed our entry into the war. Jane Addams and Crystal Eastman, for example, despised war as an archaic and immoral means of resolving international conflict and ridiculed the "pathetic belief in the regenerative results of war."[9] Addams, renowned for her settlement work with the poor, was one of the most respected figures in the United States. *Harper's Bazaar* effused that she walked "in the paths which only the great-spirited may tread."[10] Having founded Hull House in Chicago "to investigate and improve the conditions in the industrial districts of Chicago,"[11] her achievements were lauded throughout the world.

In her 1907 book, *Newer Ideals of Peace*, Addams hopefully predicted that we were entering into a new world order in which international cooperation would replace militarism. Just as she saw immigrants from many different nations living together in relative harmony in urban America, she envisioned nations embracing a new spirit of international cooperation. Less than a decade later, as the ravages of war decimated Europe, she did her best to foster peace and to persuade the United States not to join the slaughter. In January 1915, 165 women's groups formed the Woman's Peace Party, with Jane Addams as president. Three months later, Addams sailed to The Hague to chair a meeting of 1,336 women from twelve nations, including belligerents and neutrals alike, to demonstrate that peaceful discussion among enemies was possible even in time of war.

On her return to the United States, Addams addressed an overflow audience in Carnegie Hall. She called for the immediate mediation of the conflict and warned her audience that war feeds on itself, for as a war progresses, deaths mount, hatreds deepen, and the need for vengeance grows. To achieve peace, she concluded, "human understanding . . . must come to the fore."[12]

The Socialists also opposed America's entry into the war. The Socialist Party had demonstrated its political clout in 1912 when its candidate for president, Eugene V. Debs, received almost a million votes. With a sharper edge than the pacifists, the Socialists maintained that war was a capitalist tool contrived by industrialists to boost armament sales and enforce social order, while bringing only misery, demoralization, and death to the working class.[13]

Born in 1855 in Terre Haute, Indiana, Debs left school at age fourteen to become a paint scraper for the Terre Haute and Indiana Railroad. He found his mission among the rail workers. In the 1870s he became an active labor organizer, in the 1880s he organized several national unions, and in 1893 he united the various brotherhoods into the American Railway Union. The following year, the ARU, which had grown to 150,000 members, initiated the largest strike in U.S. history, paralyzing the nation's rail system. The federal government obtained an injunction against the strike, and Debs was convicted of contempt of court for refusing to comply with the injunction. The strike eventually collapsed, and Debs spent six months in prison.

During his incarceration, Debs began to embrace the ideas of socialism. His release from prison in 1895 was an extraordinary political event. Debs spoke to a crowd of 100,000 supporters who had gathered in Chicago to celebrate his freedom. In this speech, he launched his effort to unify the socialist factions in the

United States. By 1904, the Socialist Party of America was the third-largest political party in the nation. Under Debs's leadership, the SPA played a significant role in the Progressive Era, supporting woman's suffrage, workplace safety, restrictions on child labor, and the rights of workers to unionize and to strike.

Tall and gaunt, with an intense expression and a commanding manner, Debs was one of the greatest orators in American history. According to one observer, Debs "lifted audiences out of their personal preoccupations; he communicated his earnestness, his conviction, his humor, his love for his fellow man; he fired men and women with a vision of a new brotherhood that was possible, that was coming." He combined an infectious sense of comradeship with the "uncompromising resolve of the indomitable revolutionist." [14]

In a blistering speech in Ohio, Debs condemned the war:

> Wars throughout history have been waged for conquest and plunder. . . . The feudal barons of the Middle Ages, the economic predecessors of the capitalists of our day, declared all wars. And their miserable serfs fought all the battles. . . . And that is war in a nutshell. The master class has always declared the wars; the subject class has always fought the battles. The master class has had all to gain and nothing to lose, while the subject class has had nothing to gain and all to lose—especially their lives.[15]

Anarchists like Mollie Steimer also opposed the United States's participation in World War I. Mostly recent European immigrants, the anarchists were more radical—and more militant—than the Socialists. The Socialists wanted to seize the state's power; the anarchists wanted to eliminate the state.[16] Alexander Berkman, an anarchist leader, told a mass rally in New York City, "When the time comes we will not stop short of bloodshed to gain our ends."[17]

This was no empty rhetoric. In 1892, after a private army of Pinkertons shot striking steelworkers at the Carnegie steel plant in Homestead, Pennsylvania, Berkman set out to kill Henry Clay Frick, Carnegie's manager. Berkman saw Frick, whose elegant mansion still graces New York's Fifth Avenue, as a symbol of capitalist oppression. He was certain that if he could assassinate Frick he would rouse "the people" to action. He failed on all counts. Although he managed to shoot Frick (who quickly recovered), he did not awaken the masses. He did, however, serve fourteen years in prison for attempted murder.*[18]

---

* Berkman was not a man to underestimate. He was a serious intellectual, a tireless speaker, and a passionate advocate of anarchist causes. After the United States finally deported him to Russia in 1919, H. L. Mencken wrote that "with him goes a shrewder and a braver spirit than has been seen in public among us since the Civil War." Avrich, *Anarchist Portraits* at 200–7 (cited in note 7).

Berkman's colleague, Emma Goldman, known in the press as Red Emma and the High Priestess of Anarchism, was the most prominent anarchist of the era. Born in Lithuania, Goldman immigrated to the United States in 1885. Deeply moved by the Haymarket Square trial of Chicago anarchists in 1886,* she soon embraced the ideals of anarchism. Goldman defined anarchism as "the philosophy of a new social order based on liberty unrestricted by man-made law — the theory that all forms of government rest on violence, and are therefore wrong and harmful, as well as unnecessary."[19]

A charismatic speaker, Goldman quickly rose to national and international prominence. She was determined to prod the public out of its complacent acceptance of prevailing political, economic, and social norms. She spoke rapidly, in a simple, blunt style. Her orations "lifted audiences from their seats, either in passionate support or passionate hostility."[20]

Goldman vehemently opposed U.S. participation in World War I, arguing that American intervention would serve only to protect "the vilest plutocracy on the face of the globe."[21] Because of her eloquence, determination, and radicalism, Francis Caffey, the U.S. attorney for the Southern District of New York, warned in 1917 that Goldman was "an exceedingly dangerous woman."[22] Her essay called "The Promoters of the War Mania," published in *Mother Earth*[†] in March 1917, just three months before she and Berkman were arrested for

---

* On May 1, 1886, the labor movement began a nationwide strike in support of the eight-hour workday. On May 3, several people were shot at a riot at the McCormick Harvester plant in Chicago when police tangled with protesters. The following day, a mass meeting was held in the Chicago Haymarket to protest the shootings. When police ordered the demonstrators to disperse, a bomb was thrown, killing eight police officers. This became known as the Haymarket Riot. Eight suspected anarchists were arrested and tried for the crime. All were convicted, and Judge Joseph Gary sentenced seven of them to death; the eighth was given a fifteen-year sentence. Four were thereafter hanged by the state, one committed suicide in prison, and the sentences of the two others who had been sentenced to death were commuted to life in prison. On June 26, 1893, Governor John Peter Altgeld of Illinois pardoned the three who were still alive. With aid from Clarence Darrow, among others, Altgeld determined that the trial had been riddled with abuses, ranging from jury packing to blatantly biased rulings by Judge Gary. The entire prosecution, he concluded, had been tainted by an effort on the part of the Chicago business community to arouse popular passion and prejudice against the labor movement. Altgeld knew that pardoning the three surviving defendants would destroy him politically, and it did. He said that "no man has the right to allow his ambition to stand in the way of the performance of a simple act of justice." See Harry Barnard, *Eagle Forgotten* (Bobbs-Merrill 1938); Paul Avrich, *The Haymarket Tragedy* (Princeton 1984).

† *Mother Earth* was an anarchist monthly published by Berkman and Goldman. It included works by such authors as Maxim Gorky, Leo Tolstoy, Eugene O'Neill, Peter Kropotkin, Margaret Sanger, and Ben Hecht.

obstructing the draft,* is illustrative of the anarchist response to the call for American involvement:

> At this critical moment it becomes imperative for every liberty-loving person to voice a fiery protest against the participation of this country in the European mass murder. [It] is unthinkable that the American people should really want war. During the last thirty months they have had ample opportunity to watch the frightful carnage in the warring countries. . . .
>
> We are told that the "freedom of the seas" is at stake and that "American honor" demands that we protect that precious freedom. What a farce! . . . The only ones that have benefited by the "freedom of the seas" are the exploiters, the dealers in munition and food supplies. . . . Out of international carnage they have made billions. . . .
>
> Militarism and reaction are now more rampant in Europe than ever before. Conscription and censorship have destroyed every vestige of liberty. . . . The same is bound to take place in America should the dogs of war be let loose here. . . .[23]

IN A TONE REMINISCENT of the Federalists in 1798, those who campaigned for the United States to declare war attacked the patriotism of those who advocated neutrality. Eugene Debs and Emma Goldman would have expected no less, but even Jane Addams was savaged. Wherever she went, she was stalked by charges of disloyalty. She was publicly booed, her speeches were canceled, and the press abandoned her. She was blacklisted by the Daughters of the American Revolution, who accused her of conspiring against the United States.[24] As a British visitor remarked, before 1915 "it was unsafe to mention Jane Addams's name in public speech unless you were prepared for . . . a storm of applause." A few years later, "her popularity had swiftly and completely vanished."[25]

---

* The United States declared war in early April. A month later, Congress passed the Conscription Act, which was to go into effect on June 5. From mid-May to mid-June, Goldman and others sponsored a series of mass rallies to protest the draft. In mid-June, she was arrested and prosecuted for her participation in these events. In her address to the jury, on July 9, Goldman maintained that "love of one's country" does not require "blindness to its . . . faults," and that for America to "make the world safe for democracy," it "must first make democracy safe in America." She was convicted and sentenced to prison. She was later deported as part of the postwar Red Scare. *Mother Earth*, founded in 1906, went out of existence shortly after Goldman's arrest. *Goldman v. United States*, 245 US 474 (1918); Emma Goldman, Address to the Jury, in Barnett, *Words That Changed America* at 159, 163 (cited in note 81).

Emma Goldman and Alexander Berkman

For 120 years, from the expiration of the Sedition Act of 1798 until America's entry into World War I, the United States had no federal legislation against seditious expression.[26] The lessons of 1798 had carried the nation through the War of 1812, the Mexican War, the Civil War, and the Spanish-American War.[27] But by World War I the lessons had been forgotten.

In a provision drafted largely by Woodrow Wilson, the 1916 Democratic Party platform expressly condemned any group or individual who might undermine national unity. When questioned about "tolerance" at a Flag Day event, Wilson proclaimed that there should be no tolerance for those who "inject the poison of disloyalty into our most critical affairs." Americans should teach such people "once and for all that loyalty to this flag is the first test of tolerance." As the nation moved closer to war, administration officials increasingly expressed concern that the government needed new ways to restrict "warfare by propaganda."[28] As early as 1916, the president cited the need for new legislation to suppress disloyal activities.[29]

It is ironic that Woodrow Wilson took so strident a position on this issue. Only four years before his election to the U.S. presidency, while serving as president of Princeton, Wilson published his influential *Constitutional Government in the United States*, in which he stated what might be taken as quite a different view:

> We are so accustomed to agitation, to absolutely free, outspoken argument for change, to an unrestrained criticism of men and measures carried almost to the point of license, that to us it seems a normal, harmless part of the familiar processes of popular government. We have learned that it is pent-up feelings that are dangerous, whispered purposes that are revolutionary, covert follies that warp and poison the mind; that the wisest thing to do with a fool is to encourage him to hire a hall and discourse to his fellow citizens. . . . Agitation is certainly of the essence of a constitutional system, but those who exercise authority under a non-constitutional system fear its impact with a constant dread and try by every possible means to check and kill it, partly no doubt because they know that agitation is dangerous to arrangements which are unreasonable. . . .[30]

Just as Lincoln's view of inherent presidential powers shifted significantly from 1848 to 1861, Wilson's view of the respect due "agitation" in a democracy changed dramatically after he assumed the presidency. Indeed, the day after Wilson's 1916 address to Congress, the cabinet asked Attorney General Thomas Gregory to prepare legislation to deal with disloyalty. The proposed legislation was presented to Congress in mid-1916, but not acted upon until Congress declared war a year later.[31]

THE ESPIONAGE ACT OF 1917

LESS THAN THREE WEEKS after it voted a declaration of war, Congress began debate on what would become the Espionage Act of 1917. It is generally assumed today that the Espionage Act was intended by Congress to suppress virtually all criticism of the war and the draft. This was not so. In fact, Congress intended the act to have a more limited focus.

We also assume today that in 1917 Congress would not have been sensitive to the issue of free expression. We think of this sensitivity as a recent development, fostered primarily by the opinions of the Supreme Court. In fact, however, Congress took its constitutional responsibilities quite seriously and expressly rejected several key provisions proposed by the Wilson administration. But, as we shall see, as the war progressed, and the nation was whipped into a fever pitch of patriotism, the Wilson administration and the federal courts distorted the Espionage Act in order to suppress a broad range of political dissent.

Although directed primarily at such matters as espionage and the protection of military secrets, the original bill included three sections directly relevant to free speech in wartime. For the sake of convenience, I shall refer to them as the "press censorship" provision, the "disaffection" provision, and the "nonmailability" provision. An understanding of the debate over these three provisions is essential to understanding what went wrong in the United States over the next eighteen months.

AS PRESENTED TO CONGRESS, the "press censorship" provision would have declared it unlawful for any person in time of war to publish any information that the president had declared to be "of such character that it is or might be useful to the enemy." The provision added that "nothing in this section shall be construed to limit or restrict any discussion, comment, or criticism of the acts or policies of the Government."[32]

The "disaffection" provision would have declared it unlawful for any person in time of war (a) willfully to "make or convey false reports or false statements with intent to interfere with the operation or success" of the military forces of the United States or "to promote the success of its enemies," or (b) willfully to "cause or attempt to cause disaffection in the military or naval forces of the United States."[33]

The "nonmailability" provision would have granted the postmaster general authority to exclude from the mails any writing or publication that violates "any of the provisions of this act" or is otherwise "of a treasonable or anarchistic character."[34]

The press censorship provision provoked the most heated discussion. The Wilson administration's support of this provision triggered a firestorm of protest from the press, which objected that it would give the president the final authority to determine whether the press could publish information about the conduct of the war. The American Newspaper Publishers' Association protested that this provision "strikes at the fundamental rights of the people, not only assailing their freedom of speech, but also seeking to deprive them of the means of forming intelligent opinion." The association added that "in war, especially, the press should be free, vigilant, and unfettered."[35]

Individual newspapers were equally critical. The New York Times assailed the provision as "high-handed" and "Prussian," asserting that "the newspaper or the individual who criticizes or points out defects in policies . . . with the honest purpose of promoting remedial action . . . is not a public enemy."[36] The Milwaukee News characterized the press censorship provision as a "glaring attempt . . . to muzzle the press,"[37] and the Philadelphia Evening Telegraph declared that there should be no "power in this country . . . to control the voice of the press, or of the people, in honest judgment of the acts of public servants."[38]

When the press censorship provision was first presented to the House on April 30, 1917, Representative Edwin Webb of North Carolina, the chairman of the House Judiciary Committee, initiated the debate by complaining that the nation's newspapers had unfairly "created the impression" that the bill abridged the First Amendment. He sternly reminded the press that, "in time of war, while men are giving up their sons and while people are giving up its money," the press should be willing to give up its right to publish what the president "thinks would be hurtful to the United States and helpful to the enemy."[39]

Webb added that we are in "one of those situations where we have to trust somebody." Just as we trust the president, as commander in chief, with the fate of our boys in uniform, so too must we trust him to prescribe what information "would be useful to the enemy."[40] Echoing this view, Senator Lee Overman of North Carolina argued that "the good of society is superior to the right of the press to publish what it pleases," and "if the activities of newspapers were a hindrance in the prosecution of the war, their curtailment would not be unconstitutional."[41] Representative Andrew J. Volstead of Minnesota asked pointedly how the nation would feel if American troops were "sent to the bottom of the sea as a result of information" published because Congress had failed to enact this provision. "It is utterly ridiculous," he declared, "for anybody to contend that this provision is unconstitutional."[42]

Opposition to the provision was fierce. Representative Simeon Fess of Ohio warned that "in time of war we are very apt to do things" we should not do.[43] Senator Hiram Johnson of California reminded his colleagues that "the preservation of free speech" is of "transcendent importance" and that in times of stress "we lose our judgment."[44] Representative Fiorello La Guardia of New York characterized the provision as a "vicious precedent,"[45] and Representative William Wood of Indiana warned that it could become "an instrument of tyranny."[46] Representative Thomas Schall of Minnesota proclaimed that "America is not made of the stuff that has to be coddled along with tales of winning to make her fight." All that is needed is to "tell her the truth."[47]

Describing the provision as "un-American," Representative Martin B. Madden of Illinois protested that "while we are fighting to establish the democracy of the world, we ought not to do the thing that will establish autocracy in America."[48] Senator William Borah of Idaho charged that the provision "brazenly" disregards a fundamental provision of our Constitution,[49] and Senator Henry Cabot Lodge of Massachusetts expressed concern that the government officials who would administer the provision would naturally be inclined to use their authority to censor legitimate public criticism.[50] Representative Medill McCormick of Illinois added that it was appalling to think that if an epidemic were to break out in the Army the proposed provision would authorize the president to prohibit anyone from "drawing public attention to the condition of the troops."[51]

Proponents of the provision invoked the clause guaranteeing that "nothing in this section shall be construed to limit or restrict any discussion, comment, or criticism of the acts or policies of the Government." Opponents replied that it was impossible effectively to criticize the "policies of the Government" without discussing the information on which the criticism was based. At times, the debate grew heated. At one point, Representative Webb accused Representative Madden, who was questioning the constitutionality of the provision, of "taking the part of the newspapers," to which Madden replied, "I am taking the part of the American people."[52]

When it began to appear that the press censorship provision would go down to defeat, President Wilson made a direct appeal to Congress, stating that the "authority to exercise censorship over the press . . . is absolutely necessary to the public safety."[53] Members of Congress were unmoved. Representative Ira Hersey of Maine angrily replied that "we, the Congress of the United States," are now "importuned by the executive . . . to enact unconstitutional laws, to place in the hands of the President unlawful powers, to grant to him the . . . authority to take away from the citizen the protection of the Constitution."[54]

On May 31, the House defeated the provision by a vote of 184 to 144, with 36 Democrats joining the Republican opposition.[55] This effectively ended consideration of the "press censorship" provision for the duration of the war.[56]

THE "NONMAILABILITY" PROVISION also generated controversy.[*] Several members of Congress objected to granting the postmaster general broad authority to exclude political material from the mails. Senator Charles Thomas of Colorado, for example, argued that this provision would enable postmasters to exclude "legitimate" as well as illegitimate publications and would produce "a far greater evil than the evil which is sought to be prevented."[57] Representative Meyer London of New York declared the provision a "menace to freedom," adding that "there is nothing more oppressive . . . than a democracy gone mad."[58]

---

[*] This was not the first time Congress had considered regulating the content of the mails. In 1835, President Andrew Jackson proposed legislation that would have prohibited "the circulation in the Southern States, through the mail, of incendiary publications intended to instigate the slaves to insurrection." Congress rejected Jackson's proposal. After the Civil War, Congress enacted and the Supreme Court upheld a statute prohibiting the mailing of advertisements for illegal lotteries. See James D. Richardson, ed, 3 *The Messages and Papers of the Presidents* 175–76 (U.S. Congress 1900); David P. Currie, *The Constitution in Congress: Descent into the Maelstrom, 1845–1861* Prologue (Chicago, forthcoming 2005); Russel B. Nye, *Fettered Freedom: Civil Liberties and the Slavery Controversy, 1830–1860* 67–85 (Michigan State 1963); *Ex parte Jackson*, 97 US 727 (1877).

And Senator Borah cautioned that "it is perfectly useless to talk about stopping the dissemination and interchange of thought and views upon these questions," because "the more you dam up the stream the more liable you are to have a flood when it breaks over."[59]

There was particular concern about the words "treasonable" and "anarchistic." This led to a lengthy and rather remarkable debate over the meaning, or lack of meaning, of these terms.[60] Representative Johnson objected that this provision would be subject to the whim of whoever "happens to be high in the Post Office Department."[61] As if to illustrate the point, Representative Joe Eagle of Texas, quoting a letter from the Socialist Party, made clear his view that "they have a perfect right to say" that the party "strongly affirms its allegiance to the principle of internationalism," but not that the war against Germany "cannot be justified."[62]

After vigorous debate, Congress amended the "nonmailability" provision to replace the phrase "treasonable or anarchistic character" with the much narrower phrase "containing any matter advocating or urging treason, insurrection or forcible resistance to any law of the United States."[63] It is noteworthy that as a result of this amendment, only *express advocacy* of unlawful conduct could fall within this clause. Statements that were "treasonable" or "anarchistic," but did not *expressly advocate* "treason, insurrection or forcible resistance," could not be excluded from the mails. As we shall see, this was a critical distinction in later debates about the meaning of the Espionage Act, and this amendment provides important insight into Congress's intended meaning.

THE "DISAFFECTION" PROVISION, which turned out to be the most important provision of the bill, received less attention. But even this provision was amended in a significant manner. The potential difficulties were made clear in hearings before the House Committee on the Judiciary. Gilbert Roe, a distinguished attorney who represented the Free Speech League, testified that this provision was even more troublesome than the Sedition Act of 1798. He explained that the 1798 act had at least purported to recognize the defense of truth. Under the "disaffection" provision, however, truth was no defense. Every effort to discuss or criticize the war could be "brought under the ban." To illustrate the magnitude of the problem, Roe noted that "the people . . . retain their right at the next election to return to Congress Senators and Representatives . . . who are opposed to the continuation of the war." How, he asked the committee, is any voter "to form an intelligent opinion" on this question "unless there is the fullest discussion permitted of every phase of the war, its origin, its manner of prosecution, and its manner of termination?" Without such free discussion, the very essence of the democratic process is impaired.[64]

Professor Emily Balch of Wellesley College also testified against this provision. Balch warned that because the disaffection provision would be enforced in wartime, it was essential to guard against "war hysteria." Representative Thaddeus Caraway of Arkansas assured Balch that "it is the intent to cause disaffection" and not the intent to "right a wrong" that makes a statement criminal. Balch was not comforted. She explained that if an individual criticized the conduct of the war in order to "right a wrong" (by arguing, for example, that the war was immoral or the generals were inept), a prosecutor could argue that the statement contributed to "disaffection" and that the defendant should have expected that result. Representative Richard Whaley of South Carolina reminded Balch that this was not entirely up to the prosecutor. A jury, after all, would have to decide whether the defendant *intended* to cause disaffection. Professor Balch presciently replied that "in time of war a jury . . . is no less liable to hysteria than those higher up."[*][65]

In light of these concerns, the Judiciary Committee found the term "disaffection" to be "too broad," "too elastic," "too indefinite."[66] To narrow and clarify the provision, it replaced the phrase "cause or attempt to cause disaffection" with "cause or attempt to cause insubordination, disloyalty, mutiny, or refusal of duty."[67] Representative Webb explained that "to make it a crime to create disaffection" in the military "might subject a perfectly innocent person to punishment." A mother, for example, might write her son to "tell him the sad conditions back home." Webb insisted that this amendment would "protect the honest man," but "get the dishonest fellow who deliberately undertakes to spread disloyalty."[68]

AFTER NINE WEEKS of grueling debate, Congress enacted the Espionage Act of 1917. With the various emendations, including the elimination of the "press censorship" provision and the narrowing amendments to the "disaffection" and "nonmailability" provisions, the relevant part of the act made it a crime, when the nation is at war, for any person (a) willfully to "make or convey false reports or false statements with intent to interfere" with the military success of the United States or "to promote the success of its enemies"; (b) willfully to "cause or attempt to cause insubordination, disloyalty, mutiny, or refusal of duty, in the military or naval forces of the United States"; or (c) willfully to "obstruct the recruit-

---

* Emily Balch joined the faculty of Wellesley College in 1896 after studying at Bryn Mawr, Harvard, and the University of Chicago. Like Jane Addams, she was a delegate to the International Congress of Women at The Hague in 1915. She was a founding member of the Women's International League for Peace and Freedom. Balch wrote numerous scholarly works, including *A Study of Conditions of City Life* (1903), *Approaches to the Great Settlement* (1918), and *One Europe* (1947). In 1918, she was dismissed from her faculty position at Wellesley because of her antiwar activities. In 1946, at the age of seventy-nine, Balch was awarded the Nobel Peace Prize.

ing or enlistment service of the United States." Violations were punishable by prison sentences of up to twenty years.[69] The act also authorized the postmaster general to exclude from the mails any writing or publication that is "in violation of any of the provisions of this act" or that contains "any matter advocating or urging treason, insurrection or forcible resistance to any law of the United States."[70]

As the congressional debate suggests, the legislation, as enacted, was not a broadside attack on all criticism of the war. It was, rather, a carefully considered enactment designed to deal with specific military concerns. Although Congress's stance in enacting the Espionage Act could hardly be characterized as civil libertarian, its elimination of the press censorship provision (over the strong objections of the president) and its significant amendments to both the "disaffection" and "nonmailability" provisions reflected a genuine concern for the potential impact of the legislation on "the freedom of speech, or of the press."

Indeed, throughout the congressional debates there were expansive statements about the importance of free speech, even in wartime. Representative London declared, "If there are any treasonable thoughts in the minds of the American people, I want them expressed; if there is any discontent with the war, I want to hear it." He conceded that complaints about the conduct of the war or about "a shortage of food" or "incompetence in high places" might encourage the enemy. But, he asked, "shall we suppress them or shall we find compensation in the opportunity to have wrongs righted by the curing power of free discussion?"[71] Senator Thomas Sterling of South Dakota, a strong supporter of the act, assured his colleagues, "There is in this bill no prohibition on criticism . . . of any of the acts or operations or policies of the Government, or any of its representatives."[72] And even Representative Webb, the chairman of the House Committee on the Judiciary, emphasized that under the act "it is no crime to call the flag a dirty rag."[73]

But what would the act mean in practice? Would passing out antiwar leaflets be regarded as a willful "attempt to cause insubordination" in the armed forces? Would a public speech denouncing the draft be deemed a willful obstruction of "the recruiting or enlistment service of the United States"?

Much would depend on the attitude and approach of the Wilson Justice Department. The administration was clearly disappointed in the legislation. Not only had Wilson's personal appeal to Congress been rebuffed, but a year later Attorney General Thomas Gregory complained to the American Bar Association that when the war broke out the administration had "secured the passage of the Espionage Act, but most of the teeth which we tried to put in it were taken out."[74]

In light of the president's often caustic statements about disloyalty, and the attorney general's evident disappointment in the legislation, there was little reason to expect much prosecutorial restraint. Any doubt on this score was erased when Attorney General Gregory, referring to war dissenters, declared in November 1917, "May God have mercy on them, for they need expect none from an outraged people and an avenging government."[75]

"A DIVIDED, FEARFUL, AND INTOLERANT NATION"

BECAUSE THERE HAD BEEN NO direct attack on the United States, and no direct threat to America's national security, the Wilson administration needed to create an "outraged public" in order to arouse Americans to enlist, contribute money, and make the many other sacrifices war demands. This was the first and perhaps the greatest challenge to the administration. Not surprisingly, this led to one of the most fiercely repressive periods in American history.

To excite the public to a state of "outrage," Wilson resorted to rhetoric that directly echoed the cries of the Federalists in 1798. He decried the "sinister intrigue" that was being "actively conducted in this country" by "dupes of the Imperial German government," and warned that the German government had agents in the United States "in places high and low."[76]

To build public support and patriotic fervor, Wilson established the Committee on Public Information (CPI), under the direction of George Creel, a progressive journalist and public relations expert. Creel, who also chaired the nation's Board of Censors, saw himself as the nation's educator. His goal was to generate enthusiasm for the war.[77] Under his direction, the CPI produced a flood of pamphlets, news releases, speeches, newspaper editorials, political cartoons, and even motion pictures. As Frank Cobb, editor of the *New York World*, observed, the government "conscripted public opinion" as it "conscripted men and money and materials" and, having conscripted it, then "mobilized it" and "taught it to stand at attention and salute."[78] As the conflict wore on and American casualties mounted, the need to instill a sense of national purpose and dampen criticism became ever more imperative.[*]

This poses an interesting question. Surely, the government is free to tell its own side of the story and to attempt to promote a sense of national unity and

---

[*] The situation became especially acute after the 1918 midterm elections, when Wilson appealed personally for a vote of confidence from the electorate, but the voters instead elected Republican majorities in both houses of Congress.

commitment to the war effort. The question raised by the activities of the CPI is how far the government should go in this effort. This may not be a *constitutional* question. It would have to be a very extreme case to imagine a court holding that the government's own speech violates the First Amendment because it has, in effect, swamped the marketplace of ideas. As a constitutional matter, we tend to give broad leeway to the government's own propagandizing, and there is no judicial precedent declaring government speech itself unconstitutional under the First Amendment.* But even if there is no constitutional barrier to government advocacy of its own policies, there are certainly limits on how far the government *should* go. The line between responsible advocacy and irresponsible manipulation of public opinion may not be legally enforceable, but it is critical as a matter of sound governance, especially in wartime.

In World War I, Creel's efforts concentrated on two main themes: feeding hatred of the enemy and promoting loyalty to the nation.[79] The CPI produced war movies, such as *The Kaiser: The Beast of Berlin,* that depicted unspeakable German atrocities. Its pamphlets, speeches, and editorials included vitriolic attacks on German culture, false charges that Germans and German Americans were orchestrating criticism of the Wilson administration, and incendiary attacks on the loyalty of those who questioned the war.

Creel's propaganda campaign intensified divisions that had been building within American society for decades. Over the past quarter century, with new waves of immigration, divisive issues of national identity had begun to surface. During the Civil War, there was a general acceptance that Americans (except blacks) were *entitled* to their constitutional liberties. But by the early years of the twentieth century many "established" Americans, fearing that the nation had been inundated by an alien tide, were hostile to the claims of these newer, often eastern European arrivals.[80] Many of the most radical opponents of the war, especially anarchists like Mollie Steimer, Emma Goldman, and Alexander Berkman, were seen as interlopers who had no loyalty to the United States and who should go back where they belonged.

When the war came, it—and the CPI—unleashed new demands for conformity and blind allegiance. Although hatred of the enemy proved a powerful force, even

---

* The one clear exception concerns the "establishment clause" of the First Amendment, which has been interpreted as prohibiting the government from engaging in *religious* propagandizing. It may also be that the First Amendment would prohibit the government from using public resources directly to support *partisan* goals, for example by giving public money directly to the Democratic Party, but not to the Republican Party, because the government wants to promote the election of Democrats.

more potent was the demand that every person prove his loyalty. As the nation was whipped into a fury of patriotism, citizens increasingly looked askance at "strangers," and many communities went so far as to ban German-language teaching and German-language books.

Not all politicians beat a quick retreat in the face of this campaign. Senator Robert La Follette of Wisconsin, for example, took the floor of the Senate to challenge the "campaign of libel and character assassination" that had been directed against those who opposed the war. He charged that citizens and senators alike had been subjected to intimidation and vituperation by "the war party in this country." The goal, he maintained, was "to throw the country into a state of terror, to coerce public opinion, to stifle criticism, and suppress discussion of the great issues involved in this war."

La Follette conceded that "in time of war the citizen must surrender some rights for the common good," but he argued that this did not include the "right of free speech." To the contrary, even "more than in times of peace it is necessary

"Beat Back the Hun!"

that the channels for free public discussion . . . shall be open and unclogged" so that citizens may freely discuss "every important phase of [the] war," including its causes, the manner in which it is being conducted, and "the terms upon which peace should be made." La Follette concluded that "it is no answer to say that when the war is over the citizen may once more resume his rights," for "now is precisely the time when the country needs the counsel of all its citizens."[81]

His plea went unheeded. Over the next year, a torrent of mistrust and hysteria burst across the nation. Government propaganda united most of the public in common cause and common hatred. There was widespread, and unfounded, fear that swarms of German spies and saboteurs roamed the country. A crusading spirit settled upon the land. One patriot warned that "if Germany wins the war . . . German soldiers will be bayoneting American girls and women . . . rather than take the trouble to shoot them."[82]

In the first month of the war, Attorney General Gregory asked loyal Americans to act as voluntary detectives and to report their suspicions directly to the Department of Justice.[83] The results were staggering. Each day, thousands of accusations of disloyalty flooded into the department. Adding to the frenzy, the CPI encouraged citizens to form voluntary associations dedicated to informing the authorities of possible disloyalty.

The largest of these citizen groups, the American Protective League, quickly enlisted more than 200,000 members.* APL members ferreted out disloyalty whenever and wherever they could find it. They reported thousands of individuals to the authorities on the basis of hearsay, gossip, and slander. The leadership of the APL consisted primarily of conservative men of means—bankers, insurance executives, factory owners. Other volunteer organizations were the Knights of Liberty, the Boy Spies of America, the Sedition Slammers, and the Terrible Threateners.[84]

In April 1918, Attorney General Gregory boasted that the assistance of these volunteer organizations "enables us . . . to investigate hundreds of thousands of complaints and to keep scores of thousands of persons under observation. We have representatives at all meetings of any importance."[85] H. L. Mencken observed sadly that "between Wilson and his brigades of informers, spies, volun-

---

* To his credit, President Wilson was uneasy about this effort. In June 1917 he told Gregory, "[I]t seems to me it would be very dangerous to have such an organization operating in the United States." Gregory insisted, however, that the Justice Department needed the assistance of such organizations, and Wilson relented. Letter from Woodrow Wilson to Thomas W. Gregory, June 4, 1917, excerpted in Peterson and Fite, *Opponents of War* at 19 (cited in note 56).

teer detectives, perjurers and complaisant judges . . . the liberty of the citizens has pretty well vanished in America."[86]

The activities of these organizations went well beyond the reporting of alleged disloyalty. With implicit immunity, they engaged in wiretaps, breaking and entering, bugging offices, and examining bank accounts and medical records. Vigilantes ransacked the homes of German Americans. In Oklahoma, a former minister who opposed the sale of Liberty bonds was tarred and feathered. In California, a brewery worker who had made pro-German remarks was tarred and feathered and then chained to a brass cannon in a city park. In Texas, six farmers were horsewhipped because they declined to contribute to the Red Cross. In Illinois, an angry mob wrapped an individual suspected of disloyalty in an American flag and then murdered him on a public street.[87]

By the end of the war, the excesses of these organizations finally began to generate negative public reaction, and the Department of Justice attempted, with little success, to restrain their operations. A memo to all U.S. attorneys noted that the "protection of loyal persons from unjust suspicion . . . is quite as important as the suppression of actual disloyalty."[88] After a minister in Cincinnati was seized by a group of masked men and whipped when he was about to speak at an antiwar rally, President Wilson declared that he had "no sympathy with the men who take . . . punishment into their own hands." Such men, he said, are not "worthy of the free institutions of the United States."[89] Matters had gotten so far out of hand, however, that such pleas were essentially ignored.[*90]

By the late summer of 1918, even the pro-administration press began to question the activities of these organizations. In one instance, Attorney General Gregory used these groups in a series of mass raids designed to round up "slackers"—individuals who had failed to register for the draft. The intimidating and

---

[*] The use of private associations in this manner was not unprecedented. In the last decade of the eighteenth century in England, immediately following the French Revolution, a similar phenomenon occurred:

> Voluntary societies were established in London and throughout the country, for the purpose of aiding the executive government in the discovery and punishment of seditious writings or language. . . . These societies . . . were busy in collecting evidence of seditious designs, often consisting of anonymous letters, often of the report of informers, liberally rewarded for their activity. . . . Every unguarded word . . . was reported to these credulous alarmists, and noted as evidence of disaffection. Such associations were repugnant to the policy of our laws and dangerous to the liberty of the press.

Thomas Erskine May, 2 *The Constitutional History of England* 143–44 (Crosby 1964).

harassing nature of the raids triggered a public outcry. The *New York World* protested that the raiders had brought "Amateur Prussianism" to New York City and that their conduct had shamed "the very spirit of American institutions."[*91]

After the war ended, Assistant Attorney General John Lord O'Brian conceded that these associations were one of the "chief embarrassments" generated by the "war mania." Because of their excessive zeal, they "interfered with the civil rights of many people" and contributed greatly "to the oppression of innocent men." In this respect, O'Brian observed, "the systematic and indiscriminate agitation against what was claimed to be an all-pervasive system" of disloyalty did serious damage to the American people. Even George Creel, writing years later, agreed that these associations were "hysteria manufacturing bodies, whose patriotism was, at the time, a thing of screams, violence and extremes."[92]

Wilson, Gregory, and Creel had helped create not only an "outraged public" but also "a divided, fearful, and intolerant nation."[93] It was in this atmosphere of accusation and suspicion that federal judges were called upon to interpret and apply the Espionage Act of 1917.

THE LEGAL CONTEXT

FACED WITH A FRUSTRATED and aggressive Justice Department and an increasingly hysterical public, how would courts construe the Espionage Act of 1917? How would they, in the words of Senator Thomas, distinguish "legitimate" from "illegitimate" speech?[94] And, more immediately, what factors would shape their answers to these questions?

The federal judiciary was, of course, a product of the times. The predominant view during this era was that civil liberties were intended for respectable, law-abiding citizens. This did not bode well for those whose views could readily be labeled "disloyal," "radical," or "seditious." Moreover, the legal profession in this era was both politically and jurisprudentially conservative. Bar associations

---

[*] The most notorious of these raids occurred in New York City in early September of 1918. For three days, members of the American Protective League "blanketed the city, stationing themselves at subway entrances, patrolling parks and squares, and guarding the ferries and bridges. More than 20,000 hapless men, accosted on the streets, were hauled off to armories or to jail, often at bayonet-point." In one instance, all the exits to a theater were blocked and all playgoers who could not produce draft cards were arrested. Polenberg, *Fighting Faiths* at 84 (cited in note 7). See Goldstein, *Political Repression* at 112 (cited in note 4)

tended to embrace the fierce patriotism of the war effort, and lawyers who criticized the war—or even defended war critics—were subjected to ostracism and occasionally even formal discipline.* Judges who bucked the dominant attitudes of their profession could expect to be treated no less harshly.[95]

Moreover, there was as yet no deeply rooted commitment to civil liberties within the legal profession, and no well-developed understanding of the freedom of speech. Before the Espionage Act, there was scant judicial precedent on the meaning of the First Amendment.[96] (None of the prosecutions under the Sedition Act of 1798 had reached the Supreme Court, nor had any of the speech issues that arose during the Civil War.) State and lower federal courts had occasionally interpreted the First Amendment (or a state constitutional equivalent), but free speech claims had not fared very well.

Most judges continued to assume that the First Amendment implicitly incorporated the English common law. As we saw in chapter 1, Blackstone insisted in 1769 that the freedom of speech meant only that the state could not impose "previous restraints" upon speech, such as by licensing. As long as the state eschewed previous restraints, it was free to punish speech that could "be adjudged of a pernicious tendency" and was "destructive of the ends of society."[97] Courts following this approach often waxed eloquent about the value of free speech in the abstract, but rarely held government restrictions of speech unconstitutional.[98]

This approach to the First Amendment was roundly criticized in the scholarly commentary.[99] Drawing on the controversy over the Sedition Act of 1798, prominent late nineteenth- and early twentieth-century scholars disputed the assumption that the Constitution's framers had intended to import the English common law of free speech. Professor Henry Schofield of Northwestern, for example, argued that a central goal of the American Revolution "was to get rid of the English common law on liberty of speech and of the press." He chastised judges for forgetting "that the founders . . . are not distinguished" for their acceptance of the English common law, but for their "adaptation of . . . it to a new career of popular freedom." Schofield argued that speech about matters of public concern should generally be immune from regulation.[100]

Professor Thomas Cooley of the University of Michigan reasoned that although publications could be punished under the English common law because

---

* The Illinois Bar Association, for example, adopted a resolution declaring that it would be unpatriotic and unprofessional for a lawyer to defend an alleged draft evader, a resolution for which Attorney General Thomas Gregory stated his admiration. In Texas, a German-born lawyer was disbarred for saying, "Germany is going to win this war, and . . . I hope she will." A Chicago attorney was accused of subversion when, acting on behalf of his client, he challenged the constitutionality of the draft law. See Gregory, 4 ABA J at 314 (cited in note 74).

of their "tendency . . . to excite disaffection with the government," this principle was wholly "unsuited" to the "people of America," for "[r]epression of full and free discussion is dangerous in any government resting upon the will of the people." Cooley argued that political expression must be protected from restriction unless it is made with the "evident intent and purpose . . . to excite rebellion and civil war." Moreover, because the danger of repression is especially great "in times of high party excitement," even "violent discussion" of public issues must be protected.[101] Elaborating on this view, Professor Ernst Freund of the University of Chicago observed that "freedom of political discussion is merely a phrase if it must stop short of questioning the fundamental ideas of politics." He concluded that free speech finds its limit only in express "incitement to crime and violence."[102]

More than most judges of this era, for whom the freedom of speech was only an occasional subject of concern, these scholars had thought long and hard about the origins of the First Amendment and the insights gained from the debate over free speech in 1798, Lincoln's tolerance of dissent during the Civil War, and the practical and political consequences of limiting free expression. They had probed far beyond the simple invocation of Blackstone. But there had as yet been little opportunity for the legal scholarship or the experiences of 1798–1800 and 1861–65 to shape legal doctrine.

JUDGES BOURQUIN, AMIDON, AND HAND

IT WAS AN OPEN QUESTION whether federal judges would follow the limited judicial precedents or the more speech-protective analyses of the legal scholars. For almost 120 years, the United States had eschewed federal legislation directly suppressing criticism of the government. One might imagine that against that background—and with the experience of 1798 in mind—these judges would have narrowly construed the Espionage Act to avoid constitutional doubts. As it turned out, however, without firm precedent protecting the freedom of speech, few federal judges had either the inclination or the fortitude to withstand the mounting pressure for suppression. They, and the First Amendment, were swept away in a tide of patriotic fervor.

A few judges did take a courageous stand in favor of free speech, however, and we should acknowledge their contributions. Not surprisingly, each of these judges had a strong streak of personal independence.

Federal District Judge George Bourquin of Montana had been a teacher, cowboy, miner, and engineer before turning his attention to the law. After reading law, and practicing for a time in Butte, he was elected judge of the state court for Silver Bow County and was then appointed to the federal bench by President Taft in 1912. Six years later, he presided over the prosecution of Ves Hall, who was alleged to have said in a series of encounters at a picnic, in a hotel kitchen, and in a saloon that he hoped "Germany would whip the United States" and that "the United States was only fighting for Wall Street millionaires." The government charged Hall with violating the Espionage Act.

Judge Bourquin directed a verdict of acquittal, finding that Hall's comments could not be held to violate the act. Bourquin explained that none of Hall's remarks could be deemed "false reports" or "false statements" within the meaning of the act, because they were statements of opinion and belief, rather than false statements that could reasonably be proved "true" or "false."[*] With respect to the provision declaring it a crime for any person willfully to "cause or attempt to cause insubordination, disloyalty, mutiny or refusal of duty in the military or naval forces," Bourquin observed that no one claimed that Hall's comments had caused any such consequence.

Bourquin explained that an "attempt" is an effort specifically intended to commit a specific crime, which effort fails, but which is nonetheless "of sufficient magnitude and proximity" to its purpose that it can fairly be said to have been "reasonably calculated" to accomplish its goal. Noting that Hall's comments had been made at a Montana village of some sixty people, sixty miles from the nearest railway, and that no soldiers or sailors were within hundreds of miles, Bourquin concluded that any inference that Hall had intended his remarks to interfere "with the operation or success of the military," or that they were reasonably likely to have that effect, would be "unjustified, absurd and without support in the evidence." Bourquin offered that the most likely consequence of Hall's speech was "a broken head."

Judge Bourquin emphasized that Congress had not intended the Espionage Act to suppress general "criticism or denunciation, truth or slander, oratory or gossip, argument or loose talk," but only specific acts that Congress had "denounced as crimes." It had not made "disloyal utterances" criminal unless

---

[*] During World War I, in contrast to the era of the Sedition Act of 1798, courts tended to construe the false-statement provision narrowly. Most courts held that a "false report or statement . . . means a statement as to some past or existing fact," rather than statements of opinion, prophecy, or hope. In some cases, however, the government prosecuted under the false-statement provision statements about the general causes or motives of the war that historians later concluded were true. See Hilton, 28 Southwestern Soc Sci Q at 217 (cited in note 82); Carroll, 17 Mich L Rev at 644–45 (cited in note 37).

Judge George Bourquin

they met the specific requirements of the act. Having grasped the lessons of the Sedition Act of 1798, Congress, had "not ventured to denounce as crimes [mere] slanders and libel of Government and its officers." Such, Bourquin concluded, is "the genius of democracy and spirit of our people."[103]

;

JUDGE CHARLES FREMONT AMIDON was born in upstate New York in 1856, the son of ardent supporters of Abraham Lincoln. After attending Hamilton College, he moved to Fargo, Dakota Territory, in search of new challenges and opportunities. He was appointed principal of the local high school, but his passion for justice and his delight in intricate intellectual problems soon drew him to politics and the law. After Amidon served several years as a private practitioner and city attorney, President Grover Cleveland appointed him to the federal bench in 1896. Tall, lean, and white-haired, Judge Amidon was a man of impressive grace and dignity.[104]

During his thirty-two years on the federal bench, Amidon came to be regarded as one of the most progressive judges of his generation. Possessed of a quick and curious mind, he maintained a lively correspondence with some of the leading figures of his day, including Theodore Roosevelt, Learned Hand, Felix Frankfurter, Robert La Follette, and Zechariah Chafee. Amidon believed that judges should remain actively involved in "actual life" and lamented that much judge-made law had "emanated from men living in a law library." In his view, no judge could wisely "apply law to life" without "the first-hand knowledge" that comes from experience.[105]

In a series of decisions in 1917 and 1918, Judge Amidon argued forcefully against a broad construction of the Espionage Act. In one case, a farmer, E. H. Schutte, was alleged to have stated that "this is a rich man's war and it is all a damned graft and a swindle." The United States charged Schutte with violating the Espionage Act. Amidon dismissed the indictment because there was no evidence that Schutte's comments had been made to an audience containing men who were in the armed forces or eligible for the draft.[106] Another case involved John Wichek, a North Dakota banker who had stated that "banks having large holdings of Liberty Bonds are unsafe to keep money in." Amidon instructed the jury that it could not convict unless Wichek had directly affected the attitude of individuals eligible to serve in the armed forces.[107]

Judge Charles Fremont Amidon

Judge Amidon expressed his general philosophy about these issues in another prosecution, involving an individual who had spoken bitterly in opposition to war profiteering. He observed that "the only way you can produce a change in any political . . . condition is for the people who suffer from that condition to say that the people who are inflicting the sufferings are doing wrong, and speak right out plainly on that subject."[108]

BY FAR THE MOST IMPORTANT DECISION in which a federal district judge held fast against a broad construction of the Espionage Act was *Masses Publishing Co. v. Patten*.[109] The *Masses* was a monthly "revolutionary" journal that regularly featured a remarkable collection of writers, poets, playwrights, and philosophers, including Max Eastman, John Reed, Vachel Lindsay, Carl Sandburg, Bertrand Russell, Louis Untermeyer, and Sherwood Anderson. Iconoclastic, impertinent, and confrontational, it was a handsome journal, "with bright-colored covers and oversize pages filled with bold drawings and lively social satire, political criticism and intellectual commentary."[110]

Irving Howe once described the *Masses* as "a combination of Circus, nursery, and boxing ring—for almost everything that was then alive and irreverent in American culture."[111] In it, you could find brilliant artists, cartoonists, journalists, propagandists, and writers of fiction, all poking fun at the genteel tradition that had dominated American culture and challenging conventional wisdom, moral prudishness, and literary timidity.

So iconoclastic and progressive was the publication that in the summer of 1917 Postmaster General Albert Burleson ordered its August issue excluded from the mails, exercising his authority under the Espionage Act. The *Masses* sought an injunction to prohibit the local postmaster from refusing to accept the August issue for mailing.[112] The postmaster argued that four cartoons and four pieces of text violated the Espionage Act, thus justifying the order of exclusion.[113]

Illustrative of these was a cartoon drawn by Henry J. Glentenkamp entitled "Conscription" and a poem by Josephine Bell entitled "A Tribute." The poem, a "tribute" to Emma Goldman and Alexander Berkman, who were then in jail for opposing the war and the draft, included the following illustrative verse:

Emma Goldman and Alexander Berkman
Are in prison tonight.
But they have made themselves elemental forces
Like the water that climbs down the rocks:
Like the wind in the leaves;
Like the gentle night that holds us;
They are working on our destinies;

"Conscription"—from the August 1917 issue of The Masses

They are forging the love of the nations; . . .
Tonight they lie in prison.[114]

The postmaster argued that the cartoons and text violated the Espionage Act in that they willfully caused or attempted "to cause insubordination, disloyalty, mutiny or refusal of duty in the military or naval forces" and obstructed "the recruiting or enlistment service of the United States."[115] Judge Learned Hand granted the injunction and thus prohibited the postmaster from excluding the *Masses* from the mail.

Judge Hand fully appreciated the significance of this case for him personally. Hand knew he was then under consideration for promotion to the court of

---

[*] In July 1917, Amos Pinchot wrote President Wilson to protest Burleson's decision to exclude the *Masses* from the mails. Wilson's reply indicated that Burleson had "made it clear to the President that he would enforce the Espionage Act . . . as he saw fit and that his resignation might follow any attempt at interference." Scheiber, *Wilson Administration* at 36–37 (cited in note 1).

appeals, a promotion he richly deserved and much desired. When he learned he had been assigned the case, he wrote his wife that if the case were not quickly settled, his decision would go against the government, and then "whoop-la your little man is in the mud." He added that "there are times when the old bunk about an independent and fearless judiciary means a good deal."[116]

Judge Hand began his opinion by observing that in time of war Congress might have the power to "forbid the mails to any matter which tends to discourage the successful prosecution of the war." But he reasoned that he did not need to resolve the First Amendment issue because, in his judgment, the act did not cover the material published in the *Masses*.

Hand conceded the postmaster's claim that "to arouse discontent and disaffection among the people with the prosecution of the war and with the draft tends to promote a mutinous and insubordinate temper among the troops." But he argued that to read the word "cause" so broadly would involve "necessarily as a consequence the suppression of all hostile criticism, and of all opinion except what encouraged and supported the existing policies."[117] Hand observed that such an approach "would contradict the normal assumption of democratic government" and would be "contrary to the use and wont of our people." Thus, "only the clearest expression of such a power justifies the conclusion that it was intended." Hand held that the language of the statute did not require such an interpretation.[118]

This step in Hand's opinion has been the subject of considerable debate.[119] Hand's reasoning posed two important questions. First, as of 1917, was it reasonable for Hand to assert that a broad prohibition of all criticism that "could arouse discontent and disaffection" during a war would be "contrary to the use and wont of our people"? The answer, as of that time, has to be yes. The clearest example to the contrary was the Sedition Act of 1798, but by 1917 no one invoked that episode as a positive example. To the contrary, it was consistently referred to in the debates over the Espionage Act as a prime example of governmental excess and a mistake to be avoided. In the years since 1800, there had never been *any* federal legislation restricting this sort of speech in wartime or otherwise. And although the military prosecution of Clement Vallandigham during the Civil War might fit this description, it was a relatively isolated event that was regarded more as an embarrassment to Lincoln than as a precedent to be followed.

Second, was it reasonable for Hand to assert that the wording of the Espionage Act did not *require* the interpretation advocated by the postmaster general? Again, the answer has to be yes. Congress had eliminated the press censorship provision, narrowed the disaffection provision, and restricted the nonmailability provision. Hand could reasonably conclude that Congress had not intended the act to prohibit all criticism that "could arouse discontent and disaffection among

Judge Learned Hand

the people." Had Congress wanted to prohibit all such expression, it could surely have said so.*

What Congress did say in the Espionage Act was that it wanted to restrict expression *only* if it willfully undermined or attempted to undermine the effectiveness of the nation's armed forces. Although the precise line between speech that falls within that prohibition and speech that falls beyond it is far from clear, there can be no doubt that Congress meant there to be some such line.

The challenge for Judge Hand, then, was to separate "legitimate" from "illegitimate" speech under the act. Judge Bourquin focused on the law of attempt to draw this line, arguing that there must be a relatively tight causal connection between the speech and the feared consequences. Hand took a different approach.

Judge Hand began his analysis of this question by asserting that it "has always" been recognized that "one may not counsel or advise others to violate the law." Words, he observed, "are not only the keys of persuasion, but the triggers of action, and those which have *no purport but to counsel the violation of law* cannot by any latitude of interpretation be a part of that public opinion which is the final source of government in a democratic state."[120]

Hand conceded that speech falling short of express advocacy of unlawful conduct could have negative consequences. "Political agitation," he admitted, "may . . . stimulate men to the violation of law." But "to assimilate agitation, legitimate as such," with express advocacy of "violent resistance, is to disregard the tolerance of all methods of political agitation which in normal times is a safeguard of free government." This "distinction," he emphasized, "is not a scholastic subterfuge, but a hard-bought acquisition in the fight for freedom."[121]

Hand thus concluded that "if one stops short of urging" others to violate the law, "one should not be held to have attempted to cause its violation." "If that not be the test," he cautioned, "I can see no escape from the conclusion that under this [act] every political agitation which can be shown to be apt to create a seditious temper is illegal." He declared his confidence that "Congress had no such revolutionary purpose in view."[122] Applying this approach to the facts of *Masses*, Hand held that neither the cartoons nor the text crossed the line of *express advocacy* of unlawful conduct.

JUDGES BOURQUIN, AMIDON, AND HAND each made a serious effort to articulate a principled interpretation of the Espionage Act that would reserve to

---

* Indeed, Congress did say so a year later in the Sedition Act of 1918. See text accompanying notes 199–239.

the government the ability to achieve its most essential goals, while at the same time reserving to the people the opportunity for robust political debate. Like the Republicans in 1798, these judges understood that freedom of speech is not a mere personal privilege of the individual but a fundamental element of the dem-ocratic process even in wartime. By requiring a tight causal connection between speech and harm, or concrete evidence of a direct impact on individuals in the armed forces, or express advocacy of law violation, Judges Bourquin, Amidon, and Hand sought, each in his own way, to construe the Espionage Act so that "every political agitation which can be shown to be apt to create a seditious tem-per" would not automatically be deemed unlawful.

Each of these judges was taken to task for his position. Senator Thomas J. Walsh of Montana, chairman of the Senate Judiciary Committee, described Judge Bourquin's decision in *Hall* as "notorious" and predicted that it would unleash those who would "assist the cause of our enemies."[123] The day after Bourquin's ruling, Governor Sam V. Stewart of Montana announced that the cit-izens of his state were so furious that they might resort to violence. "Feeling is running high," he declared, predicting "some killing as a result of the . . . *Hall* case." The editor of the *Helena Independent* called for Bourquin's removal from the state; the managing editor of the newspaper declared that "Montana is fed up with Bourquin" and that impeachment would take too long.[*][124]

Only days after the *Hall* decision, Governor Stewart called the Montana leg-islature into emergency session and demanded legislation curbing seditious utter-ances, lest the people "may be provoked into becoming a law unto themselves."[125] The new Montana statute, passed in only nine days, declared it a crime for any person to "utter, print, write or publish any disloyal, profane, violent, scurrilous, contemptuous, slurring or abusive language" about the form of government, the Constitution, the military forces, or the flag of the United States.[126]

Judge Amidon was similarly pilloried. He was castigated in the North Dakota press, denounced by the president of the state bar association, ostracized by friends and associates, and threatened in letters and phone calls.[†][127]

Judge Hand suffered as well. Attorney General Gregory charged that Hand had gutted the Espionage Act,[128] and Hand's opinion in *Masses* was promptly and

---

* Judge Charles Crum, a state court judge in Montana, testified as a character witness in Hall's behalf. As a result of this action, the Montana legislature impeached him because he "was guilty of aiding and abetting draft dodgers and criticizing American participation in the war." Murphy, *Ori-gin of Civil Liberties* at 201 (cited in note 6).

† Amidon wrote Chafee that after he had directed a verdict of acquittal in an Espionage Act prosecution, he was hardly spoken to when he "met prominent business men whose feelings had been outraged." Letter from Charles Fremont Amidon to Zechariah Chafee (Dec 8, 1920).

emphatically reversed by the court of appeals.[129] Referring to his opinion in *Masses*, Hand wistfully "bid a long farewell to my little toy ship which set out quite bravely on the shortest voyage ever made."[130] He was passed over for the court of appeals appointment, which went to a less distinguished jurist. Hand reflected later, "The case cost me something, at least at the time," but added, "I have been very happy to do what I believe was some service to temperateness and sanity."[131]

The circulation of the *Masses* dropped sharply because of its inability to move through the mails. Only a few days after the decision of the court of appeals upholding the order of the postmaster, seven of its editors and staff were indicted for conspiracy to violate the Espionage Act. By the end of the year, the *Masses* was out of business.*[132]

THE TRIUMPH OF "BAD TENDENCY"

FEW OTHER JUDGES followed the lead of Bourquin, Amidon, and Hand.[133] Rather, most judges during the war were determined to impose severe sentences on those charged with disloyalty, and no details of legislative interpretation or appeals to the First Amendment would stand in the way. These judges were operating in a feverish atmosphere, not conducive to careful judicial reflection.[134]

John Lord O'Brian, the head of the War Emergency Division of the Department of Justice, observed shortly after the war that "immense pressure" had been brought to bear on the department "for indiscriminate prosecution" and for "wholesale repression and restraint of public opinion." It was, he added, in this atmosphere of excessive passion, patriotism, and clamor that the laws affecting free speech received the "severest test thus far placed upon them in our history."[135] In this setting, the Department of Justice invoked the Espionage Act of 1917 to prosecute more than two thousand dissenters during the war for allegedly disloyal, seditious, or incendiary speech.[136]

The prevailing approach in the lower federal courts, first clearly articulated by the court of appeals in *Masses*,[137] is well illustrated by the decision of the U.S. Court of Appeals in *Shaffer v. United States*.[138] In *Shaffer*, the defendant was

---

* Among those indicted were Max Eastman, John Reed, Josephine Bell, and Henry Glinkerkamp. The *Masses* defendants were tried twice. Each trial ended in a hung jury. A successor publication, the *New Masses*, appeared from 1927 to 1947.

charged with mailing copies of a book, *The Finished Mystery*, in violation of the Espionage Act. The book contained the following passage, which was specified in the indictment:

> Standing opposite to these Satan has placed . . . a certain delusion which is best described by the word patriotism, but which is in reality murder, the spirit of the very devil. If you say it is a war of defense against wanton and intolerable aggression, I must reply that . . . it has yet to be proved that Germany has any intention or desire of attacking us. . . . The war itself is wrong. Its prosecution will be a crime. There is not a question raised, an issue involved, a cause at stake, which is worth the life of one blue-jacket on the sea or one khaki-coat in the trenches.[139]

Shaffer was convicted, and the court of appeals affirmed, with the following reasoning:

> It is true that disapproval of the war and the advocacy of peace are not crimes under the Espionage Act; but the question here . . . is whether the natural and probable tendency and effect of the words . . . are such as are calculated to produce the result condemned by the statute. . . .
> Printed matter may tend to obstruct the . . . service even if it contains no mention of recruiting or enlistment, and no reference to the military service of the United States. . . . The service may be obstructed by attacking the justice of the cause for which the war is waged, and by undermining the spirit of loyalty which inspires men to enlist or to register for conscription in the service of their country. . . .
> It is argued that the evidence fails to show that [Shaffer] committed the act willfully and intentionally. But . . . he must be presumed to have intended the natural and probable consequences of what he knowingly did.[140]

This "bad tendency" approach was embraced by almost every federal court that interpreted and applied the Espionage Act during World War I.[141] As Gilbert Roe and Emily Balch had predicted in their testimony to the House Judiciary Committee in 1917, these judges and juries were "swayed by wartime hysteria."[142] Consider the following:

- Rose Pastor Stokes, a Russian immigrant who had worked as a cigar maker for twelve years before becoming editor of the socialist *Jewish Daily News*, was convicted under the act for saying, "I am for the people and the government is for the profiteers," during an antiwar statement to the Women's Dining Club of Kansas City. Her speech was later published in the *Kansas City Star*. Although there were no soldiers—indeed, no men—in her intended audience, the government argued that she had violated the act because "our armies . . . can operate and succeed only so far as they are supported and maintained by the folks at home," and Stokes's statement had the tendency to "chill enthusiasm, extinguish confidence, and retard cooperation" of mothers, sisters, and sweethearts. She was sentenced to ten years in prison.[143]

- J. P. Doe, the son of a chief justice of the Supreme Court of New Hampshire, was convicted for mailing a "chain" letter to "friends of immediate peace," stating that Germany had not broken a promise to end submarine warfare. Although this was clearly a matter of historical interpretation, the government argued that this statement "would have a direct tendency to obstruct the recruiting and enlistment service."[144]

- Thirty German Americans in South Dakota were convicted for sending a petition to the governor demanding reforms in the Selective Service procedure. The signers of the petition "threatened" to vote the governor out of office if he did not meet their demands. The government charged that the defendants had willfully obstructed the recruiting and enlistment service.[145]

- The Reverend Clarence H. Waldron was convicted for distributing a pamphlet stating that "if Christians [are] forbidden to fight to preserve the Person of their Lord and Master, they may not fight to preserve themselves, or any city they should happen to dwell in." The government charged that in distributing this pamphlet Waldron had attempted to cause insubordination and to obstruct the recruiting service. He was sentenced to fifteen years in prison.*

- Robert Goldstein was convicted under the act for producing and exhibiting a motion picture about the American Revolution. *The Spirit of '76* depicted Paul Revere's ride, the signing of the Declaration of Independence,

---

* The government was especially aggressive in its prosecution of clergymen who supported peace or conscientious objection. As the *New York Times* observed, Justice Department officials had warned that "disloyalty fostered by certain religious sects has been growing in the United States." The government "regards the preaching of opposition to the aims of this particular war as of seditious nature, and . . . several . . . preachers and Sunday school teachers have been indicted for disloyal utterances, and many others . . . have been warned to desist from criticizing the nation's war motives." Special Assistant Attorney General John Lord O'Brian declared that "the most dangerous type of propaganda . . . is religious pacifism, *i.e.*, opposition to the war on the ground that it is opposed to the word of God." *Warn Seditious Pastors*, New York Times 16 (Mar 31, 1918); letter from John Lord O'Brian to Representative Edwin Y. Webb, in 65th Cong, 2d Sess (Apr 16, 1918), in 56 Cong Rec S 5542 (Apr 24, 1918).

and Washington at Valley Forge. But it also included a scene portraying the Wyoming Valley Massacre, in which British soldiers bayoneted women and children. The government charged that this was an attempt to promote insubordination because it negatively portrayed America's ally in the war against Germany. In upholding the seizure of the film, the trial judge explained, "History is history, and fact is fact. There is no doubt about that." But, he added, "this is no time" for "those things that may have the tendency or effect of sowing . . . animosity or want of confidence between us and our allies." Goldstein was sentenced to ten years in prison.*[146]

In 1919, Assistant Attorney General O'Brian explained that the Espionage Act "was not directed against disloyal utterances." Rather, it was intended "to protect the process of raising and maintaining our armed forces from the dangers of disloyal propaganda."[147] But in the hands of the Justice Department and the federal judiciary, the act became an efficient tool for the blanket suppression of all "disloyal utterances."†

None of these defendants expressly advocated insubordination, refusal of service, or any other unlawful conduct. But by questioning the legality, morality, or conduct of the war, each of their statements increased the likelihood of unlawful conduct. As these cases illustrate, under the "bad tendency" interpretation of the act, it was impossible to oppose the war without running the risk of being convicted of attempting to obstruct the war effort. Against the background of these convictions, and the severity of these sentences, no sensible person would dare criticize the Wilson administration's policies. As Professor Zechariah Chafee concluded, under the bad tendency test, "all genuine discussion" of the justice and wisdom of continuing the war became "perilous."[148]

---

* One of the more extreme of the Espionage Act prosecutions was that of Walter Matthey of Iowa, who, according to Attorney General Gregory, was sentenced to a year in jail for "attending a meeting, listening to an address in which disloyal utterances were made, applauding some of the [disloyal] statements made by the speaker . . . and contributing 25 cents." Department of Justice, *Report of the Attorney General of the United States for the Year 1922* 437 (Governmental Printing Office 1922).

† The Committee on Public Information played an active role in persuading Americans to accept such limitations of their civil liberties. Its *War Cyclopedia*, a collection of terms and phrases designed to help Americans understand the war, explained that restrictions of speech, embodied in the Espionage Act prosecutions, were both proper and constitutional. Freedom of speech in wartime, the booklet intoned, rests "largely with the discretion of Congress." 8 *United States Committee on Public Information, the Red, White, and Blue Services: War Cyclopedia: A Handbook for Ready, etc.* 101 (1918), excerpted in Lawrence, 21 Wayne L Rev at 47 (cited in note 95).

THE DEATH OF FREE SPEECH: "WHAT IS AN ATTEMPT?"

To WHAT EXTENT did this sweeping application of the Espionage Act faithfully reflect the intent of Congress? As we have seen, Congress did not intend the act to prohibit "all genuine discussion" of the war. Rather, it intended to declare unlawful *only* those actions that willfully caused or attempted "to cause insubordination, disloyalty, mutiny or refusal of duty in the military or naval forces" or obstructed the "recruiting or enlistment service of the United States." The prevailing interpretation of the Espionage Act ignored the critical qualification in the statute that to violate the act the speech must have some direct relation to "the military or naval forces" or "the recruiting or enlistment service of the United States."

Shortly after the war, Assistant Attorney General O'Brian noted that this "evolution" in the meaning of the act presented "an interesting example of the process of judicial interpretation." He explained that initially "there was uncertainty as to whether the phrase 'military and naval forces' included only men actually mustered in, or whether it included also men within the draft ages." But as the war proceeded, the federal courts, with "substantial unanimity," embraced a very "broad view" of this "slenderly worded" provision. O'Brian concluded that the standard by which speech was found to violate the act was "judicial, not legislative in creation."[149]

Thus, a first objection to the prevailing interpretation of the Espionage Act is that it disregarded an essential limitation in the statute. A more faithful interpretation—one that would have accorded greater protection to the freedom of speech—would have insisted that, in order for expression to fall within the scope of the prohibition, it must be directed at members of the armed forces, or at least those eligible to serve.

BUT THERE IS A DEEPER OBJECTION. Because there were essentially no instances in which the government could prove that dissident speech had *actually* caused insubordination, mutiny, refusal of duty, or obstruction of the recruiting or enlistment service, almost every prosecution was framed as an "attempt."[150] This necessarily raised the question, posed by Judge Bourquin, "what constitutes an attempt"?

The law of criminal attempt is one of the most perplexing features of the criminal law.[151] As Bourquin noted in *Hall*, however, it is well settled that to establish an "attempt" the prosecution must prove both that the defendant had the *specific intent* to bring about an unlawful act and that she came *sufficiently close to success* to warrant government intervention. Both elements are essential. Specific intent without proximity does not constitute an attempt, nor does proximity without specific intent.[152]

The element of specific intent is essential because one "cannot attempt . . . to do an act without the intent to do the act."[153] This seems self-evident, but it is critical. An individual who negligently or even recklessly creates a danger is not guilty of attempt.[154] If a homeowner saws a limb off a tree, and the limb falls on a passerby, the homeowner may have been negligent, but she did not "attempt" to maim or kill the passerby.

Did the defendants convicted under the Espionage Act specifically intend to cause insubordination, refusal of duty, or obstruction of the recruiting or enlistment service of the United States? No doubt, some did. But few, if any, *expressly advocated* such conduct, so how did the government prove their intent? In a few instances, the government was able to present letters or other statements of the defendants to prove specific intent to cause unlawful conduct. But in the vast majority of cases, there was no such evidence.[155] To bridge this gap, the government invoked the doctrine of *constructive intent*.

As illustrated by the opinion in *Shaffer*, the federal courts typically held that the defendant could be *"presumed to have intended* the natural and probable consequences of what he knowingly did."[156] In theory, this principle is well known to the law of attempt. If an individual puts poison in the drink of an intended victim, or shoots a handgun directly at an intended victim from a distance of five feet, he can be found to have "attempted" murder, even if the intended victim spilled the drink or the gun misfired, because the defendant could reasonably be "presumed to have intended the natural and probable consequences of what he knowingly did." In these circumstances, it is reasonable to infer specific intent, even in the absence of any direct evidence of intent, because the nature of the act is such that it is difficult to imagine any *other* intent that would reasonably explain it.[*]

Now suppose that an individual delivers an impassioned address on a street corner in lower Manhattan in the winter of 1918 in which she proclaims that the draft is unjust because it serves only the interests of Wall Street and is not "worth the life of one blue-jacket on the sea or one khaki-coat in the trenches." On the basis of these facts, can one reasonably presume that the defendant *intended* to cause insubordination or refusal of duty in the armed forces?

Surely not. In this situation, there are *many* possible consequences of the

---

[*] Of course, if the defendant does have an alternative explanation, she is free to present evidence to that effect. But in the absence of such evidence, it is reasonable to presume a specific intent to murder.

speech that the defendant might have intended. Most obviously, her intent might have been to persuade others to oppose the war through *lawful* means (for example, by signing petitions, handing out leaflets, and supporting antiwar candidates). It would be unreasonable to presume that this speaker's *specific intent* was to incite unlawful conduct. (Of course, her specific intent *might* have been to incite criminal acts, but it would not be reasonable to presume this without substantial additional evidence.) What the federal courts did during World War I was to allow juries to infer specific intent from the bare *possibility* that the speaker might have had such an intent. That is not the law of attempt, and it was not the intended meaning of the word "attempt" in the Espionage Act of 1917.[157]

INQUIRIES INTO AN INDIVIDUAL'S subjective intent are always elusive, especially when political speech is at issue. Even in normal times, such inquiries risk confusing the unpopularity of an individual's views with the criminality of his intent. There is every danger that jurors will leap to the conclusion that defendants whose views they abhor must have had a criminal intent. This danger is particularly acute when a nation is at war. Jurors are expected to represent the views of their community. But in the heat of wartime, the community may be only one step ahead of the mob. Reflecting on the experience during World War I, Zechariah Chafee observed that in wartime neither judges nor juries can reliably "look into the heart of a speaker or writer and tell whether his motives are patriotic or mean."[158]

Judge Amidon put the point well in a letter to Chafee:

> Only those who have administered the Espionage Act can understand the danger of such legislation. . . . Most of the jurymen have sons in the war. They are all under the power of the passions which war engenders. [During this period, otherwise] sober, intelligent business men . . . looked back into my eyes with the savagery of wild animals, saying by their manner, "Away with this twiddling, let us get at him." Men believed during that period that the only verdict in a war case, which could show loyalty, was a verdict of guilty.[159]

This does not mean that it is impossible fairly to convict a defendant of attempt to obstruct recruitment. But it does mean that in order to do so consistent with the traditional protections of the criminal law of attempt it is necessary to follow the lead of either Judge Bourquin or Judge Hand. Bourquin dealt with this problem by insisting on a close relation between the speech and the unlawful action. He argued that for the government to prove the defendant's specific intent by inference from the "natural consequences" of his speech, it must demonstrate that those consequences were connected to the speech in the same way that intent to murder is connected to the poison in the glass or the firing of the gun.

In *Masses*, Judge Hand offered an alternative approach. He reasoned that inquiries into specific intent are so perilous, and that it is so easy erroneously to infer specific intent in times of national crisis, that in order to avoid "the suppression of all hostile criticism" the government should have to prove that the defendant *expressly advocated* unlawful conduct. Hand did not deny that some speakers might specifically intend to cause unlawful conduct even though they refrained from expressly advocating such conduct—the "Marc Antony" problem.[160] But he concluded that without a test that was objective, easily applied, and difficult to evade, prosecutors, judges, and jurors would leap too quickly to the inference that unlawful intent accompanies disloyal sentiment.[161] Moreover, Hand understood that without the assurance of a clear, unambiguous rule focusing precisely on the words used, citizens would be afraid to speak their minds for fear of being accused of harboring an unlawful intent.

At first blush, Judge Hand's approach may seem extreme. But it was more consonant with the common law than the "bad tendency" approach. As far back as Blackstone, it was recognized that even when a defendant's speech "caused" another to commit a criminal act, the defendant was not guilty of an offense unless he "does yet procure, counsel or command another to commit a crime."[162] As Hand observed in another opinion, in cases involving an alleged attempt by one person to cause another to commit an unlawful act, "the rule has always been that, to establish criminal responsibility, the words uttered must amount to counsel or advice or command to commit the forbidden acts."[163] That is, they must amount to express advocacy of unlawful conduct.[164]

THE SECOND ELEMENT of the law of attempt is the requirement of *proximity* between the speech and the unlawful act. That is, an individual who specifically intends to cause a criminal act is not guilty of an "attempt" under the criminal law unless the speech is likely directly to cause (as opposed to in a roundabout or distant manner, with many intermediate steps) the unlawful act to occur. This is so because bad intentions are not, in and of themselves, the concern of the criminal law. As Professor Joseph Beale observed more than a century ago in his seminal article on this subject, "human laws are made, not to punish sin, but to prevent crime."[165]

Thus, even if an opponent of the draft specifically intends to persuade men to refuse induction into the army, he should not be held guilty of an "attempt" unless his speech is likely to be the "proximate cause" of such conduct. This is not a simple judgment. The question of how much "proximity" is necessary to constitute an attempt has vexed the legal system for centuries.*[166] It has been said, for example, that the act "must come dangerously near to success,"[167] that it "must come sufficiently near completion to be of public concern,"[168] that it must come "very near to the accomplishment of the act,"[169] and that there must be a "harm which is foreseen as likely to follow."[170] There exist no simple or concrete rules in this area of the law. As Justice Holmes once remarked, "every question of proximity must be determined by its own circumstances, and analogy is too imperfect to give much help."[171]

But under *any* of the usual formulations of the standard, it is difficult to see how the test could be satisfied in the circumstances of most Espionage Act prosecutions. Recall, for example, the prosecutions of Rose Pastor Stokes, J. P. Doe, and Robert Goldstein. Even if they specifically intended to cause draft-eligible men to refuse induction, their speech could hardly be said to be the "proximate cause" of any particular individual's decision to resist induction into the army. Of course, if the test is merely whether the speech *increases* the probability that some person might someday refuse induction, then *every* criticism of the war or the draft could be transmogrified into an "attempt," which was precisely Judge Hand's concern. As Zechariah Chafee noted at the time, "the assassin of President McKinley may have been influenced by the denunciatory cartoons" published in "the Hearst newspapers, but the artist" did not "attempt" to commit the murder.[172]

THE CRUCIAL POINT HERE is *not* that Congress (necessarily) lacked the constitutional *authority* to declare all disloyal utterances unlawful, but that it did not seek to *exercise* that authority when it forbade any person to cause or "attempt" to cause insubordination, disloyalty, or refusal of duty.[173] If Congress intended to forbid all disloyal utterances, it could have done so in plain lan-

---

* *Black's Law Dictionary* defines "proximate" as "Immediate; nearest; direct, next in order. In its legal sense, closest in causal connection." It defines "proximate cause" as "That which, in a natural and continuous sequence, unbroken by any efficient intervening causes, produces the injury, and without which the result would not have occurred." Henry Campbell Black, *Black's Law Dictionary* 1391 (West 4th ed 1968).

guage.[174] That is not what it did when it enacted the Espionage Act of 1917.[175] But, by failing to respect the well-settled boundaries of the legal concept of "attempt," this is how the federal courts interpreted the act.

Except in the decisions interpreting the Espionage Act, the legal concept of attempt has never encompassed actions where the *only* measure of criminality was that the defendant could reasonably have foreseen that his speech would increase the probability that others might commit criminal acts. War fever turned dissent into disloyalty, and disloyalty into crime.

Interestingly, even Blackstone's *Commentaries* supported Judges Hand and Bourquin on the meaning of "attempt." Anticipating Hand, Blackstone consistently used such terms as "commands," "advises," "procures," and "counsels" in defining when an individual could be guilty of attempting to solicit a crime. And anticipating Bourquin, Blackstone explained that for an accused to be guilty of causing another to commit a crime, he must have set in motion events "which probably *could not fail* of their mischievous effect." He cites as an example an individual who "incite[s] a madman to commit murder."[176] This is a far cry from mere "bad tendency."

That the federal courts in this era departed from the prevailing understanding of the law of attempt is made even clearer by Francis Wharton's *Treatise on Criminal Law*, then the leading authority on the subject. Wharton observed that words "belong to a domain which criminal courts cannot invade without peril to individual freedom."[177] He therefore expressly rejected the proposition that speech could constitute a criminal attempt merely because of bad tendency and constructive intent:

> [W]e would be forced to admit, if we hold that solicitations to criminality are generally indictable, that the propagandists . . . of agrarian or communistic theories are liable to criminal prosecutions; and hence the necessary freedom of speech and of the press would be greatly infringed. It would be hard, also, . . . to defend, in prosecutions for soliciting crime, the publishers of Byron's *Don Juan* . . . or of Goethe's *Elective Affinities*. . . . [T]o make bare solicitations or allurements indictable as *attempts*, not only unduly and perilously extends the scope of penal adjudication, but forces on the courts psychological questions which they are incompetent to decide, and a branch of business which would make them despots of every intellect in the land.[178]

What occurred in the federal courts in 1917–18 was not the result of confusion over a technical point of law. It was, rather, the consequence of war hysteria. The doctrinal confusion was the effect, not the cause, of the problem, and it illustrates that even courts can be swept away in the riptide of war fever. The ordinary safeguards of the criminal law—which should have shielded most defendants in Espionage Act prosecutions—were forfeited in the rush to lock dissenters behind bars.*[179]

"ANTIWAR EXPRESSION . . . HAD LITTLE CHANCE"

CRIMINAL PROSECUTION UNDER the Espionage Act was only one of several tools used to suppress dissent during World War I. As we have seen, the act's "nonmailability" provision gave the postmaster general authority to exclude from the mail any publication that violated the substantive provisions of the act or that advocated "treason, insurrection or forcible resistance to any law of the United States."

As evidenced by *Masses*, Postmaster General Albert Burleson construed this provision broadly, and the courts granted him a high level of deference. Burleson announced that newspapers "cannot say that this Government is the tool of Wall Street or of munitions makers" and that nothing can be mailed that might "interfere with enlistments . . . or the sale of authorized bonds."[180] Burleson ordered the exclusion from the mails, not only of the *Masses*, but also of the *Internationalist Socialist Review*, the *Milwaukee Leader*, the *Gaelic American*, the *Irish World*, Thorstein Veblen's *Imperial Germany and the Industrial Revolution*, Lenin's *Soviets at Work*, the *Nation*, and scores of other books, magazines, and newspapers.†[181]

---

* Indeed, the Supreme Court had made all this abundantly clear a quarter century before the Espionage Act. In *Hicks v. United States*, 150 US 442 (1893), the defendant was charged with encouraging his companion to shoot a third person. The defendant had not *expressly* incited the shooting, and it was unclear from his words whether he had specifically intended to cause the act. The trial judge instructed the jury that "if the deliberate and intentional use of words has the *effect* to encourage one man to kill another, he who uttered these words is presumed by law to have intended that effect." This was, of course, the "bad tendency/constructive intent" test. The jury returned a verdict of guilty. The Supreme Court overturned the conviction, holding that the jury instruction was "erroneous" because it confounded the intent to use the words used with the intent to cause the shooting. The Court reasoned that although the accused "no doubt intended to use the words he did use," he did not necessarily intend his language "to be understood . . . as an encouragement to act." The Court held that the jury should not have been left free to convict "regardless" of the defendant's actual "intention." In other words, the combination of bad tendency and constructive intent was insufficient under the criminal law. Id at 449.

† It is difficult to measure the impact of Burleson's policies because the number of publications banned from the mails substantially understates the amount of expression suppressed. Faced with

Such fierce ideological adversaries as Theodore Roosevelt and Upton Sinclair agreed that Burleson was suppressing legitimate criticism. Roosevelt complained that Burleson had made it dangerous "for any man . . . to speak the truth, if that truth be unpleasant to the governmental authorities."[182] Sinclair, author of *The Jungle*, wrote President Wilson that although "it is hard to draw the line . . . as to the amount of ignorance permitted to a governmental official," there could be no doubt but that "Mr. Burleson is . . . on the wrong side of any line that could be drawn by anyone."[183] The moderate *New York World* asserted that "the bureaucrats of the Post Office Department . . . seem determined to set up an intellectual reign of terror in the United States."[184] Even the president occasionally thought Burleson had gone too far, although he did not rein him in.* From the time the Espionage Act was enacted, Burleson had virtually complete discretion to control the circulation of publications through the mail.

Shortly before the armistice, Congress passed the Alien Act of 1918,[185] which authorized the government to deport any alien who was a member of an anarchist organization. The act was born of many of the same impulses as the Alien Acts of 1798. Under the 1918 act, the entire deportation process was made administrative in nature. No judge or jury had to find that the potential deportee held anarchist beliefs or was a member of an anarchist organization. The entire process was now administrative, and there was no right of appeal. The preliminary investigation, a critical stage of the proceeding, was conducted in secret, with no right to counsel. Even naturalized citizens were swept within this scheme.[186] Once an individual was deported, "all mistakes and wrongs were covered by the intervening ocean."[187] In 1918 alone, the United States deported 11,625 individuals under this act.[188]

Efforts to suppress disloyalty were not confined to the federal government. State and local officials aggressively punished dissent. Eleven states enacted new

---

Burleson's policies, many publications moderated their editorial comment. For example, in October 1917, Abraham Cahan, the distinguished editor of the Yiddish *Daily Forward*, announced that "the paper will henceforth publish war news without comment and will not criticize the allies, in order to avoid suspension of mailing privileges." New York Times (Oct 7, 1917).

* Wilson now and then made suggestions to Burleson, such as the admonition that he use "the utmost caution and liberality in all our censorship," but "the Postmaster General usually had the last word in censorship matters." On two occasions, one involving an issue of the *Nation* and another involving an issue of Norman Thomas's pacifist *World Tomorrow*, Wilson did override Burleson's orders of exclusion. More often, though, Burleson simply ignored Wilson's reservations and persisted in his campaign to cleanse the mails of all "disloyal" publications. The responsibility for restraining the postmaster general rested "squarely upon Woodrow Wilson." Wilson realized this, but generally did nothing. Letter from Woodrow Wilson to Albert Burleson, Oct 11, 1917, in Roy Stannard Baker, 7 *Woodrow Wilson: Life and Letters* 301 (Doubleday, Doran 1939); Murphy, *Origin of Civil Liberties* at 96–103 (cited in note 6); Scheiber, *Wilson Administration* at 30–31, 36–37, 39 (cited in note 1).

sedition statutes, and dozens of cities passed laws prohibiting disloyal expression.[189] Most states established "councils of defense" to generate enthusiasm for the war and ferret out disloyalty. These councils pressured individuals to buy Liberty bonds. If they failed to do so, their names were publicly posted, they were threatened with revocation of their licenses to do business, and, in some instances, their property was seized and sold at auction to buy bonds.[190] The Pittsburgh Symphony was forbidden to perform Beethoven, and the Los Angeles public schools prohibited any discussion of the virtues of peace. In such an oppressive climate, "[a]ntiwar expression . . . had little chance" to survive.[191]

"THE FIRST AMENDMENT HAD NO HOLD ON PEOPLE'S MINDS"

ALTHOUGH SOME AMERICANS were concerned about the suppression of dissent, they tended to remain silent. There was not yet a strong consensus about the importance of civil liberties, and, as the Harvard law professor Zechariah Chafee later observed, "the First Amendment had no hold on people's minds."[192] At a time when the government was championing the responsibility of citizens to sacrifice their freedom in order to secure military victory, any action that seemed to question the justice or wisdom of the war was deemed disloyal.

A small group of individuals, however, attempted to educate the public about the value of civil liberties. People like Gilbert Roe and Emily Balch argued that it was appropriate for citizens to criticize the government, even in wartime, and that for the government to punish individuals for questioning its policies betrayed a fundamental lack of confidence in the American people and the democratic system.

Perhaps the most serious challenge facing civil libertarians was the ease with which most citizens distanced themselves from socialists, pacifists, anarchists, German Americans, aliens, and other dissenters. Most Americans saw dissenters as "un-American" and found no reason to care about their rights. The deeply rooted nativist association between aliens and alien ideologies compounded the problem. As in 1798, many Americans during World War I connected radical ideas with alienism and "un-Americanism," and the Wilson administration exploited that connection. The president of the American Bar Association stated a common view at the time: "[W]e should start the fires under our melting pot and keep them burning, until every man, whether born in this country or out of it, has either become thoroughly and wholly American, or, if he is incapable or refuses to become American, is driven back to the country from which he came."[193]

Unless civil libertarians could persuade mainstream Americans that free speech was fundamental to the American system, that self-governance depended on free and robust debate, that in different circumstances a different administration could turn against them, and that a commitment to civil liberties must protect even those who oppose the dominant view, they had scant chance of countering the government's war on dissent.

The organization that most effectively represented civil liberties during World War I was the National Civil Liberties Bureau, which later evolved into the American Civil Liberties Union. The driving force behind the NCLB, which was established in mid-1917, was Roger Baldwin, a pacifist social worker who strongly opposed the war and the draft. The NCLB built upon the earlier work of the Free Speech League, which had actively defended the rights of anarchists, agnostics, atheists, and supporters of birth control.

The goal of the Free Speech League, led by Theodore Schroeder and Gilbert Roe, had been to attract broad public support for free speech by demonstrating its importance to all segments of society. Others active in the league included Margaret Sanger, the outspoken proponent of birth control; Lincoln Steffens, the muckraking journalist and author of The Shame of the Cities; and Emma Goldman, who was not only the nation's most notorious champion of anarchism but also a fiery critic of economic inequality, religion, and all forms of government coercion.

The core principle of the Free Speech League was that government could not legitimately restrict speech because it feared the ideas espoused. In 1916, H. L. Mencken described Theodore Schroeder as having "done more for free expression in America than any other" individual.[194] The Free Speech League provided a critical example to the emerging NCLB, which relied heavily on the experience of league members in formulating its own legal and political agenda.[195]

Under Roger Baldwin's leadership, the NCLB challenged Espionage Act prosecutions, protested mob violence against dissidents, generated publications and public events to educate Americans about the meaning of civil liberties, and offered legal support to those charged with disloyal expression. In mid-1918, the War Department accused the NCLB of defending traitors and threatened its leaders with prosecution under the Espionage Act.[196] The Justice Department warned Americans that if they contributed to the NCLB they would hinder the war effort.[197]

When the government banned the Masses and fifteen other journals from the mails, the NCLB sent four volunteer attorneys, including Clarence Darrow, to plead (unsuccessfully) with Postmaster General Burleson and President Wilson to adopt a less repressive policy. As a consequence of this effort, Burleson denied mailing privileges to the NCLB, including, ironically, an NCLB pamphlet on the freedom of speech. In August 1918, federal agents raided the NCLB's New York offices.[198]

By the end of the war, free speech in America was approaching a low point in American history. The dominant mood of the public was repressive to a degree that is hard for contemporary Americans to imagine. Frustration with the climate of repression led many prominent writers and artists to flee the United States for the bohemian tolerance of Paris's Left Bank. Most Americans, however, had little sympathy for the civil liberties of dissenters.

It is instructive to compare World War I and the Civil War in this respect. During the Civil War, many Republicans defended the free speech rights of Copperheads. No such phenomenon occurred during World War I. This was due in part to the large influx of immigrants during the preceding forty years. Many anarchists, socialists, and other radicals came from these immigrant groups, and most Americans viewed these immigrants from eastern and southern Europe with scorn, fear, and concern. Because they did not see them as truly "American," they dismissed their claims to American rights and liberties. Moreover, Abraham Lincoln did not persecute his critics. Woodrow Wilson aggressively stifled dissent. The difference was palpable.

THE SEDITION ACT OF 1918: "WHEN DID IT BECOME WAR UPON THE AMERICAN PEOPLE?"

EVEN WITH THE "BAD TENDENCY" test well entrenched and the number of prosecutions of dissenters climbing daily, the Department of Justice sought to amend the Espionage Act to close what it described as a few loopholes in the original legislation. In the spring of 1918, Attorney General Gregory asked Congress to amend the act to prohibit any person from interfering with the government's efforts to borrow funds for the war and to clarify that the act prohibited attempts to obstruct recruiting and enlistment, as well as actual obstruction of such activities.[199]

In April, the attorney general urged the American Bar Association to support these amendments. Pointing to the recent lynching of a German American suspected of disloyalty, Gregory argued that such incidents occurred because otherwise law-abiding citizens believed that existing laws were inadequate to deal with disloyalty and therefore felt justified in taking the law into their own hands. He complained that Congress had taken the "teeth" out of what the administration had proposed a year earlier. "We got what we could," he explained, but it was not enough. He advocated greater "protection of the nation against the insidious propaganda of the pacifist." To demonstrate the inadequacy of enforcement of the 1917 act, Gregory sharply criticized Judge Bourquin's decision in the *Hall* case.

Gregory insisted that to avoid similar "mistakes" in the future, Congress had to make the Espionage Act "more drastic." Unless citizens are satisfied that disloyal individuals will not be allowed to roam free, he warned, and "unless the hysteria, which results in the lynching of men, is checked, it will create a condition of lawlessness from which we will suffer for a hundred years."[200]

What seems remarkable today about this address to the ABA is that instead of seeking federal authority to protect dissenters from mob violence, or urging state and local officials to prevent such violence, Gregory sought to expand the prohibition of dissent. This takes the idea of the "heckler's veto" to new extremes. In the "heckler's veto" situation, the government cannot constitutionally silence the speaker. But if other citizens threaten violence because *they* do not like what the speaker is saying, the government can claim that by punishing the speaker it is merely preserving order. If the government is allowed to do this in order to prevent a hostile audience response, rather than to punish those who act violently, then the government in "effect transfers the power of censorship to the crowd." The net result is the suppression of constitutionally protected speech.

In addition, the more the government acts in this manner, the more it encourages the speaker's opponents to use or threaten to use violence in order to silence unpopular expression. The proper—constitutionally required—response of the government is not to cater to the "heckler's veto" but to protect the speaker.* As Professor Chafee aptly observed, "doubtless some governmental action was required to protect [dissenters] from mob violence, but incarceration for a period of twenty years seems a very queer kind of protection." [201]

Still, the amendments to the 1917 act proposed by the attorney general were relatively narrow. Although some members of the House complained that the Espionage Act was already too broad,[202] the House adopted Gregory's proposed changes with almost no debate. The Senate Judiciary Committee, however, took it upon itself to go far beyond Gregory's recommendations, resulting in the most repressive legislation in American history.

AS WE HAVE SEEN, after Judge Bourquin's decision in *Hall*, Senator Henry Myers of Montana drafted a new state sedition statute. When the "brief amendments" proposed by Attorney General Gregory reached the Senate Judiciary Committee, Myers proposed similar legislation for the United

---

* Since the civil rights demonstrations of the 1960s, the Supreme Court has consistently rejected hostile audience arguments for punishing expression. See, for example, *Edwards v. South Carolina*, 372 US 229 (1963) (holding that civil rights demonstrators could not be convicted for breach of the peace because of the danger that audience members might become violent in opposing them); *Cox v. Louisiana*, 379 US 536 (1965) (same); *Gregory v. City of Chicago*, 394 US 111 (1969) (same).

States.[203] Senator Thomas Walsh, also of Montana, presented the radically altered bill to the Senate, explaining that the impetus for the committee's draft was Judge Bourquin's "notorious" decision in *Hall* and the violent response that followed. Walsh argued that because dissenters would be "emboldened" by decisions like *Hall* to make "disloyal and seditious utterances," Congress had to ensure that "no possible means of escape would present themselves" to such persons.[204]

The new amendment, which became known as the Sedition Act of 1918, forbade any person, "when the United States is in war,"

- to willfully utter, print, write, or publish any disloyal, profane, scurrilous, or abusive language about the form of government of the United States, or the Constitution of the United States, or the military or naval forces of the United States, or the flag of the United States, or the uniform of the Army or Navy of the United States,
- or to use any language intended to bring the form of government of the United States, or the Constitution of the United States, or the military or naval forces of the United States, or the flag of the United States, or the uniform of the Army or Navy of the United States into contempt, scorn, contumely or disrepute,
- or to willfully display the flag of any foreign enemy, or to willfully urge, incite, or advocate any curtailment of production in this country of any thing or things necessary or essential to the prosecution of the war, or to willfully advocate, teach, defend, or suggest the doing of any of the acts enumerated in this section, or by word or act to support or favor the cause of any country with which the United States is at war or by word or act oppose the cause of the United States.[205]

The debate in Congress over the Sedition Act of 1918 was striking in several respects. First, almost every member of Congress found it necessary to proclaim his loyalty to the nation and his disdain for anyone who might harbor doubts about the justness of the American cause. There was a strong undercurrent of repression even within Congress. At one point, Senator Henry Cabot Lodge of Massachusetts complained, "I have become a little weary of having Senators get up here and say to those of us who happen to think a word had better be changed" that we "are trying to shelter treason."[206] After declaring his opposition to the Sedition Act of 1918, Senator Hiram Johnson of California observed that what "has transpired again and again," both "in this Chamber" and "all over this land," is that any person who does "not subscribe *instanter*" to every effort to suppress dissent has by "that very token" been deemed "an enemy of his country."[207]

Second, although the proposed Sedition Act of 1918 clearly posed serious constitutional questions, the debate tended to fixate on the vagaries of meaning of such terms as "calculate," "favor," "resist," "inflame," "incite," and "scurrilous."[208] This is noteworthy, not because the meaning of such words is unimportant, but because one has the sense that by focusing so narrowly on these particulars, the members of Congress were trying to avoid the more fundamental questions raised by the legislation.[209]

Third, throughout the debate, supporters of the act argued that it was necessary to prevent even greater evils that would befall the nation if it were not adopted. As Senator William Borah noted, "I know this is a drastic law, and I would not support it . . . unless I believed it necessary to prevent things far worse."[210] These "things far worse" ranged from fears of mob violence by citizens who would be outraged by the failure of the federal government to punish dissenters, to concerns that, in the absence of such legislation, the government might have to convene military tribunals to deal with disloyalty.[211]

Despite the "drastic" terms of the proposed legislation, several members of Congress maintained that it did not go far enough. Senator James Hamilton Lewis of Illinois, for example, offered an amendment to the effect that any citizen found to be disloyal "shall forfeit his citizenship" and all of his property.[212] Other members of Congress expressed their impatience with any talk of "rights." Senator Albert B. Fall of New Mexico declared that the traditional procedural protections accorded criminal defendants simply did "not apply to this present situation."[213] Senator Kenneth McKellar of Tennessee announced that "if we cannot reason with men to be loyal, it is high time we forced them to be loyal," adding that "a man who has no more sense than to think that some other government is greater or better than the American Government, or that some other constitution is greater or better than the American Constitution, ought not to be in this country."[214]

Attorney General Gregory's claim that the new legislation was necessary to curb mob violence echoed throughout the debates. Senator Lee Overman of North Carolina argued that "the people of this country are taking the law in their own hands" because "Congress is not doing its duty."[215] Anyone listening to the debate might have concluded that "the best of all possible ways to protect freedom of speech was to abridge it."[216]

To be sure, there had been several vicious beatings and even one lynching, to which we will turn in a moment, but there was no persuasive evidence linking these acts to the government's failure to indict people for seditious speech. Certainly, passage of the Sedition Act would discourage some inflammatory utterances, but the more basic reason for the legislation was simply to squelch dissent that others found offensive.

AT THE HEIGHT of the Senate debate, a mob in Collinsville, Illinois, lynched Robert Prager for suspected disloyalty. Later that day, the Department of Justice issued a statement that "until the Federal Government is given power to punish persons making disloyal utterances" government officials "fear more lynchings." The next day, Senator Overman read to the Senate a telegram from the mayor of Collinsville stating that "the lynching of Robert Prager was the direct result of a widespread feeling in this community that the Government will not punish disloyalty."[217]

On April 8, Senator Lawrence Sherman of Illinois offered a more informed version of the incident. A mob of drunken coal miners, in a mood "masquerading in the guise of patriotism," had piled out of a saloon set on lynching Prager. Sherman called the mayor's telegram "a disgrace" and "an indication of the abject cowardliness of the mayor." Why, he asked, "did not he protect the victim? He is anxious to place his failure to perform his duty to the lack of law." Sherman explained that rather than halt the mob, the Collinsville "constabulary" had simply allowed it to "wreak its bloody purpose upon the helpless victim."

As a sad footnote, Sherman added that Prager was not "disloyal." To the contrary, he had registered for the draft and was in every way loyal to the United States. He was, however, a German immigrant and a socialist, and was thus taken for a traitor by his ill-informed, "patriot" neighbors. Sherman concluded that "such laws as the one proposed here will not change conditions; they will not make less frequent mobs of that kind and the consequent tragedies. What we want here, what we must have, is a more awakened public sentiment."[*][218]

THE POTENTIAL REACH of the proposed Sedition Act bothered some congressmen. Although every member of Congress accepted the need to convict dangerously disloyal individuals, several raised questions about who else might be swept up by the act. Senator Charles Thomas of Colorado wondered whether the act would cover a soldier from whom he had just received a letter complaining that his dependents were suffering because he had not received his pay.[219] Senator Gilbert M. Hitchcock of Nebraska asked whether advocates of woman's suffrage

---

* In one of the more "amusing" moments in the debate, Senator Jacob Gallinger of New Hampshire responded to the Prager lynching by observing, apparently with a perfectly straight face, that because such mobs are usually "inflamed by strong drink," it might be helpful to reduce the availability of grain for the manufacture of beer. 65th Cong, 2d Sess, in 56 Cong Rec S 4771 (Apr 5, 1918).

might be held to violate the act on the theory that they brought the Constitution "into disrepute" because they criticized it for not granting the right of suffrage to women?[220] Others wondered whether proposals for peace would fall within the act because they might be said to encourage the enemy.[221]

The fundamental question, of course, was whether the Sedition Act was consistent with the Constitution. In support of the legislation, Senator Borah argued that if our soldiers can risk their lives to protect "our form of government, our Constitution and our flag," then it is not "too much to ask complete devotion upon the part of those who remain at home to the things for which our boys are fighting and dying upon the western front."[222] Senator Miles Poindexter of Washington expressed exasperation that, "regardless of its effect upon the war," some people attached so much importance to the right of free speech, "while at the same time we take men's bodies, conscript them into the Army," and "subject them to the dangers of the firing line." "I should like to know," he asked, "what distinction there is . . . while we are taking their bodies . . . if we also take away from them somewhat of this license of speech which is so much defended?"[223]

Senator Thomas Hardwick of Georgia offered a reply:

> We are in this war. We ought to prosecute it vigorously. . . . But it is by no means necessary . . . in the prosecution of that war to . . . sacrifice . . . American liberties. . . . [I]n times of war people grow hysterical, and when people grow hysterical even executives, even legislative bodies, are not exempt from the contagion of hysteria. It is better to move along slowly; it is better . . . not to confer powers that are so broad that they are not only capable of abuse but liable to abuse; that are so broad that . . . honest, loyal American citizens may be persecuted.[224]

Senator James Vardaman of Mississippi added that "the fevered state of the public mind at this time prevents calm, dispassionate discussion and fearless reasoning." This act, he argued, reflects a "lack of confidence in the intelligence and patriotism of the American people."[225] Even former President Theodore Roosevelt weighed in. Roosevelt lambasted the "foolish or traitorous persons who endeavor to make it a crime to tell the truth," adding that the people of the United States are the president's "fellow citizens," not his "subjects," and that it is their duty to "tell the truth" about him and "to oppose him" when he serves them badly.[226] He defiantly announced that if Congress enacted the Sedition Act, he would personally "give the government the opportunity to test its constitutionality."[227]

Senator Sherman likened the act to the suspension of habeas corpus and argued that the proposed Sedition Act was unconstitutional because the government was empowered to suspend the writ of habeas corpus only in cases of rebellion or invasion. In the present circumstances, he observed, "there is neither in this country."[228]

THE ANALOGY TO the Sedition Act of 1798 did not pass unnoticed. Senator James A. Reed of Missouri asked his colleagues to note how closely the pending bill paralleled the "old" Sedition Act. He added pointedly that the proposed legislation was even worse, for "a conviction under the old sedition law" required the government to prove falsity and malice, whereas the new Sedition Act "omits both of those important qualifying terms."[229]

Senator Joseph France of Maryland then proposed an amendment to the pending bill to the effect that "nothing in this act shall be construed as limiting the liberty . . . of any individual to publish or speak what is true, with good motives and for justifiable ends."[230] Although the France amendment was initially rejected in the Senate by a vote of 31 yeas to 33 nays, the Senate later adopted the amendment by unanimous vote. On April 24, however, the conference committee recommended against the amendment.

Senator Overman, the Senate manager of the bill, explained that the France amendment had been dropped on the advice of Assistant Attorney General O'Brian, who had protested that it would interfere with the prosecution of cases under the act. The "most dangerous type of propaganda," O'Brian maintained, "is religious pacifism, *i.e.*, opposition to the war on the ground that it is opposed to the word of God." He explained that it would be impossible to convict people who advocated this view unless "motive is irrelevant" under the act. He added that another dangerous "class of propaganda" opposed the war on the ground that "this war is one between capitalists and the proletariat." In this situation, O'Brien argued, as in the case of religious pacifism, the speaker's motive is "not treasonable." He therefore urged the conference committee to reject the France amendment.*[231]

Supporters of the amendment were furious. Senator Reed declared it "strange that we have just defeated an amendment" that would have done nothing more than protect a right that was protected even under "the abominated and execrated sedition law of 1798."[232] Senator Johnson of California charged that it would be a travesty for Congress to deny the American people the right to speak what is true, with good motives and for justifiable ends. He mocked O'Brian's explanation, not-

---

* Assistant Attorney General Alfred Bettman had persuaded O'Brian that the France amendment would render the act useless because it would require actual proof of motive. The most serious problem was that many war critics had perfectly "good" motives. As Bettman conceded, even socialists wanted to promote human happiness, and certainly "the promotion of human happiness is a good motive." Letter from Alfred Bettman to John Lord O'Brian, Apr 15, 1918, excerpted in Polenberg, *Fighting Faiths* at 33 (cited in note 7).

ing that it was based on the premise "that certain people quote the Bible in a particularly inappropriate way, and in that fashion indulge a propaganda that ought not to be tolerated." Johnson thundered, "Yes, . . . [this] is war. . . . But, good God, . . . when did it become war upon the American people?"[233]

In a particularly sharp exchange, reminiscent of the charges leveled by the Federalists in 1798, Senator Overman accused supporters of the France amendment of attempting to "throw a cloak of protection around every spy in this country."[234] The amendment was defeated. Disgusted, Senator France intoned that Western civilization had not seen "in any country since the dark ages any criminal statute so repressive."[235] The Sedition Act of 1918 was approved in the Senate by a vote of 48 to 26 and in the House by a vote of 293 to 1.[236] On May 16, President Wilson signed it into law.*

ALTHOUGH HE HAD OPPOSED the France Amendment, John Lord O'Brian acknowledged the "sweeping character" of the new legislation and declined to defend its constitutionality.[237] Attorney General Gregory, concerned about the potential impact of the Sedition Act, immediately issued a circular to all U.S. attorneys, warning that the new law "should not be permitted to become the medium whereby efforts are made to suppress honest, legitimate criticism of the administration or discussion of Government policies."[238]

A few months later, Gregory issued another circular, declaring that no additional cases should be submitted to grand juries under the Sedition Act without the prior approval of the attorney general. According to O'Brian, however, "the general publicity given the statute . . . fanned animosities into flame, vastly increasing the amount of suspicion and complaints throughout the country." This led to "a large increase" in the number of prosecutions.[239] With passage of the Sedition Act in the summer of 1918, the government had put in place the perfect instrument to suppress dissent.†

---

* The president sought Attorney General Gregory's advice on the matter. Gregory, in turn, asked Assistant Attorney General Alfred Bettman for his opinion. Bettman said the act contained several very important provisions, notably those initially requested by the Department of Justice. He said the additional provisions prohibiting various forms of seditious speech "will have the advantage of calming [the public] clamor" for greater repression and "ought have no consequences detrimental to the best interests of the country" if "administered with some discretion." Letter from Alfred Bettman to John Lord O'Brian, May 10, 1918, excerpted in Polenberg, *Fighting Faiths* at 35 (cited in note 7).

† Because the Sedition Act was enacted so late in the war, there were relatively few prosecutions under it. For an example of such a prosecution, see *Abrams v. United States*, 250 US 616 (1919).

THE U.S. SUPREME COURT: "CLEAR AND PRESENT DANGER"?

IN 1919, THE SUPREME COURT was in firmly conservative hands. The values and experiences of the justices led most of them to hold anarchists, socialists, and other "radical" dissenters in contempt. This was not a Court likely to take a bold stand in favor of those who condemned capitalism and denounced the established order.[240]

Schenck v. United States[241] was the Supreme Court's first significant decision interpreting the First Amendment. *Schenck* was decided in March of 1919, after the signing of the armistice. The defendants had been charged with conspiring to obstruct the recruiting and enlistment service by circulating a pamphlet to men who had been called and accepted for military service.[*]

The pamphlet argued that the draft was unconstitutional, described a conscript as "little better than a convict," and intimated that conscription was a "monstrous wrong" designed to further the interests of Wall Street. It urged readers not to "submit to intimidation" and warned that if "you do not assert and support your rights, you are helping to deny or disparage rights which it is the solemn duty of all citizens and residents of the United States to retain." It encouraged readers to join the Socialist Party, write their congressmen to protest conscription, and "petition for the repeal of the act."

The defendants were convicted at trial because the "natural and probable tendency" of the pamphlet was to dampen the willingness of men to serve in the armed forces and because the jury could reasonably infer that the defendants intended to cause the natural and probable consequences of their actions.[242] It was, all in all, an unexceptional case under the Espionage Act.

Justice Oliver Wendell Holmes wrote the opinion for a unanimous Court— upholding the conviction. Justice Holmes began by addressing the question of intent. "Of course," he opined, "the document would not have been sent unless it had been intended to have some effect, and we do not see what effect it could be expected to have upon persons subject to the draft except to influence them to obstruct the carrying of it out."[243]

---

[*] The defendants had obtained the names of these men from the local newspaper, which had published the list. According to the record in the case, only a few inductees actually received the pamphlet, and there was no evidence that any of them were influenced by it.

This is a puzzling statement. The pamphlet expressly called upon readers to support the repeal of the draft through lawful political means. It did not expressly advocate obstruction of the draft. Of course, the defendants could reasonably have "expected" that some readers might be moved to refuse induction, and that the defendants sent the pamphlets to men who had already been drafted certainly supports the inference that they might have hoped to inspire some of them to refuse induction. But that was not what they advocated, so it is unclear why this *must* have been their "intent."

Justice Holmes next asked whether the pamphlet was protected by the First Amendment. He answered that question in the following passage, one of the most famous in the annals of American legal history:

> We admit that in many places and in ordinary times the defendants, in saying all that was said in the circular, would have been within their constitutional rights. But the character of every act depends upon the circumstances in which it is done. The most stringent protection of free speech would not protect a man in falsely shouting fire in a theater, and causing a panic. . . .
>
> The question in every case is whether the words used are used in such circumstances and are of such a nature as to create a clear and present danger that they will bring about the substantive evils that Congress has a right to prevent. It is a question of proximity and degree. When a nation is at war many things that might be said in time of peace are such a hindrance to its effort that their utterance will not be endured so long as men fight and no Court could regard them as protected by any constitutional right. . . .[244]

Like President Lincoln fifty-five years before, Justice Holmes stated clearly that war matters. In later opinions, Holmes explained that although "the principle of the right to free speech is always the same," the government's power to restrict speech is greater in time of war "because war opens dangers that do not exist at other times."[*][245]

It is noteworthy that Holmes first invoked his famous "false cry of fire" hypothetical to argue against an "absolutist" interpretation of the First Amendment. With this example, he rejected the possibility that the First Amendment means what it *appears* to say. If the statement "Congress shall make no law abridging the freedom of speech or of the press" is taken literally, then even a

---

[*] Woodrow Wilson held a similar view. In a letter to Max Eastman, he observed that "a time of war must be regarded as wholly exceptional" and that it is "legitimate to regard things which would in ordinary circumstances be innocent as very dangerous" in time of war. He conceded, though, that the line is "exceedingly hard to draw." Letter from Woodrow Wilson to Max Eastman, Sept 18, 1917, in Roy Stannard Baker, 7 *Woodrow Wilson: Life and Letters* 273 (Doubleday, Doran 1939).

"false cry of fire" would be protected by the First Amendment. But, as Holmes reasoned, even "the most stringent protection of free speech" would not reach so far. The First Amendment is thus not to be taken literally; its practical meaning will turn on the proper construction of the phrase "the freedom of speech, or of the press."

Justice Holmes also used his "false cry of fire" example to answer the question, When is speech not "protected" by the First Amendment? Holmes derives his "clear and present danger" test directly from the "false cry" hypothetical. Why can the false cry of fire be punished? Because it creates a clear and present danger of panic. Hence, this is the test for restricting speech under the First Amendment.

At first blush, this standard seems much more speech protective than the "bad tendency" test. Whereas the latter required only a remote connection between the speech and the harm, Holmes's "clear and present danger" test (as illustrated by the "false cry of fire" hypothetical) implied an immediate and reflexive connection between the speech and the harm. This test calls to mind Judge Bourquin's approach in *Hall*, which insisted on a close connection between the speech and the feared harm. This seems promising.

BEFORE WE LEAP TO THAT CONCLUSION, though, it is worth noting the very different starting points for analysis used by Judge Hand in *Masses* and Justice Holmes in *Schenck*. Whereas Hand began by defining what speech the Constitution *must* protect, Holmes began by defining what speech it does *not* protect. Hand's opinion resonates with the values of the First Amendment; Holmes's reads like a halfhearted analysis of a rather pedestrian issue.

Moreover, there is an interesting omission in Holmes's use of his "false cry of fire" example to set the terms of the First Amendment. Holmes did not consider whether the power of his hypothetical was due to the tight connection between speech and harm or to the fact that the speech in his example was "false." Suppose the cry of fire were "true." It would still create a clear and present danger that people would be trampled in the rush to the exits. But the true cry of fire would be protected speech, *even though* it creates a clear and present danger. A step is clearly missing in Holmes's analysis. Even if Holmes is right that "false" speech can be punished when it creates a clear and present danger, it does not necessarily follow that "true" speech should be punished in those circumstances. The positive value of the speech may outweigh the danger it creates, *even if the danger is clear and present*.

In any event, it is unclear whether Holmes applied the "clear and present danger" standard in *Schenck*. On the face of it, he seemed to embrace that standard. But if that test, as elucidated by the "false cry of fire" example, had been applied in *Schenck*, the Court would have *reversed* the conviction. Although the circulation of the pamphlet satisfied the "bad tendency" test, it did not pose a clear and present danger in any way analogous to Holmes's "causing a panic" paradigm. Unlike the danger created by the false cry of fire, the danger in *Schenck* had nothing "clear" or "present" about it.

Strange as it may seem to us today, the most reasonable inference is that Holmes did not intend the phrase "clear and present danger" to reflect a change in the "bad tendency" test.* More likely, he simply approved that test under a different name.[†246] Any doubt on this score was erased only a week later, when the Court handed down its decisions in *Frohwerk v. United States*[247] and *Debs v. United States*.[248]

JACOB FROHWERK WAS A COPY EDITOR who helped prepare and publish a series of antiwar, antidraft articles in the *Missouri Staats Zeitung*, a German-language newspaper. He was convicted under the Espionage Act of conspiring to cause disloyalty, mutiny, and refusal of duty in the military and naval forces of the United States. He was sentenced to ten years in prison. The Court, again in an opinion by Justice Holmes, unanimously affirmed the conviction.

One of the articles declared it a "monumental and inexcusable mistake to send our soldiers to France," stated that our participation in the war "appears to be outright murder without serving anything practical," and lauded "the unconquerable spirit . . . of the German nation." Another article deplored the recent draft riots in Oklahoma but, according to Justice Holmes, did so "in language that might be taken to convey an innuendo of a different sort." Indeed, the article wondered whether anyone would "pronounce a verdict of guilty" upon a young

---

* Indeed, if Holmes had intended to adopt a standard different from the one under which the defendants had been tried and convicted, he would not have *affirmed* the convictions. Clearly, the defendants had not been tried under the "clear and present danger" standard, which did not yet exist. Thus, if Holmes had intended to adopt a new standard, he would have remanded the case to the federal district court for a new trial, which would then have applied the *correct* constitutional standard. But Holmes did not remand; he merely affirmed the convictions.

† David Rabban has demonstrated quite convincingly that Holmes based his thinking in *Schenck* on his early work on criminal attempts, most particularly on his book *The Common Law*. As Rabban concludes, Holmes "did not use the words *clear and present danger* as a protective alternative to the bad tendency test." To the contrary, "both clear and present danger and bad tendency were roughly equivalent measures of proximity used by Holmes to determine whether an act should be punished as a criminal attempt." Rabban, *Forgotten Years* at 286 (cited in note 96).

man who "stops reasoning and follows the first impulse of nature: self-preservation. Although describing draft resistance as "technically . . . wrong" and "ill advised," the article suggested that those who resisted in this way were "more sinned against than sinning."[249]

Holmes gave short shrift to the First Amendment issue:

> It may be that all this may be said or written even in time of war in circumstances that would not make it a crime. We do not lose our right to condemn either measures or men because the country is at war. It does not appear that there was any special effort to reach men who were subject to the draft. . . . But we must take the case on the record as it is, and on the record it is impossible to say that it might not have been found that the circulation of the paper was in quarters where a little breath would be enough to kindle a flame and that the fact was known and relied upon by those who sent the paper out.[250]

Thus, only a week after *Schenck*, Justice Holmes made no reference to clear and present danger. Instead, he appeared to invoke a new "little breath that could kindle" standard.

DEBS, OF COURSE, involved Eugene V. Debs, the national leader and spiritual father of the Socialist Party. In 1912, Debs had received almost a million votes in his campaign as Socialist Party candidate for the presidency of the United States. One of every sixteen voters supported him. A major national figure, Debs strongly opposed both conscription and U.S. intervention in the war. On June 16, 1918, to demonstrate his support of those who had been jailed for their opposition to the war, Debs visited three Socialists who were imprisoned in Canton, Ohio, for violating the Espionage Act. Only a short distance from the prison, he made a bold and provocative speech to a crowd of some twelve hundred listeners. Although his address dealt mainly with the history and ideals of socialism, he also spoke about the three "martyrs for freedom":

> I have just returned from a visit over yonder [pointing to the workhouse], where three of our most loyal comrades are paying the penalty for their devotion to the cause of the working class. [Applause]. They have come to realize, as many of us have, that it is extremely dangerous to exercise the constitutional right of free speech in a country fighting to make democracy safe in the world. [Applause]. I realize that, in speaking to you this afternoon, there are certain limitations placed upon the right of free speech. I must be exceedingly careful, prudent, as

Eugene Debs

to what I say, and even more careful and prudent as to how I say it. [Laughter]. I may not be able to say all I think; [Laughter and applause] but I am not going to say anything that I do not think. [Applause]. . . . [Our three comrades] are simply paying the penalty, that all men have paid in all the ages of history for standing erect, and for seeking to pave the way to better conditions for mankind. [Applause]. . . . They tell us that we live in a great free republic; that our institutions are democratic; that we are a free and self-governing people. [Laughter]. This is too much, even for a joke. [Laughter]. But it is not a subject for levity; it is an exceedingly serious matter.[251]

For this speech, Debs was arrested, tried, and convicted under the Espionage Act for obstructing the recruiting and enlistment service of the United States. He was sentenced to a prison term of ten years.[252]

The Supreme Court, speaking once again through Justice Holmes, unanimously rejected Debs's claim that his conviction violated the First Amendment. According to Holmes, the main theme of the speech was a celebration of socialism and a prophecy of its ultimate success. He made clear that "with that we have nothing to do." But, he added, if "one purpose of the speech, whether incidental or not does not matter, was to oppose [the] war, . . . and if, in all the circumstances, that would be its probable effect, it would not be protected." Observing that Debs had praised several persons who had been convicted of encouraging others to refuse induction, Holmes concluded that Debs's First Amendment claim had in practical effect been "disposed of" in *Schenck.* [253]

Holmes emphasized that the jury members had been "most carefully instructed that they could not find the defendant guilty for advocacy of any of his opinions unless the words used had as their natural tendency and reasonably probable effect to obstruct the recruiting service, and unless the defendant had the specific intent to do so in his mind." As in *Frohwerk*, Justice Holmes made no reference to clear and present danger.[*254]

University of Chicago law professor Harry Kalven aptly observed that "although the American traditions of political and intellectual tolerance are enormously indebted to Justice Holmes for the contributions his pen and prestige are to make during the next decade, the awkward fact is that the legal tradition gets off to a limping start" with his opinions in *Schenck, Frohwerk,* and *Debs.*[†255]

THE TRANSFORMATION OF JUSTICE HOLMES: "I HOPE I WOULD DIE FOR IT"

IN ONE OF CONSTITUTIONAL LAW'S more memorable coincidences, Oliver Wendell Holmes and Learned Hand met by chance on a train as each was traveling to his summer home in June of 1918. They soon began an exchange of letters about the freedom of speech. Hand argued that "opinions are at best provisional hypotheses, incompletely tested," so "we must be tolerant of opposite . . . opinions by the very fact of our incredulity of our own." Holmes replied that he generally agreed with Hand, but offered one point of disagree-

---

* In the 1920 presidential campaign, Debs again received almost one million votes, even though he ran the campaign from his prison cell. A popular campaign button showed Debs in prison garb, standing outside the prison gates, with the caption "For President—Convict No. 9653."

† In 1923, Justice Brandeis confided to Felix Frankfurter, then a law professor at Harvard, "I have never been quite happy about my concurrence in [the] *Debs* and *Schenck* cases." Brandeis confessed, "I had not then thought the issues of freedom of speech out—I had thought at the subject, not through it." Holmes himself was less than happy with these decisions. Within a year, he admitted that he "greatly regretted his misfortune" in having the "disagreeable task" of writing these opinions. Urofsky, 1985 Sup Ct Rev at 323–24 (cited in note 262); Rabban, *Forgotten Years* at 294 (cited in note 96) (quoting letters in the spring of 1919 from Holmes to Harold Laski, Sir Frederick Pollock, and Baroness Moncheur).

ment. Free speech, he maintained, "stands no differently than freedom from vaccination," a "freedom" that the majority could readily override.[256] The gap between them was substantial.

OVER THE MORE THAN SEVENTY YEARS between Oliver Wendell Holmes's publication of The Common Law in 1881 and Learned Hand's publication of The Spirit of Liberty in 1952, Holmes and Hand were two of the most dominant intellectual forces in American law. Born in Boston in 1841, Holmes, the son of a prominent essayist and poet, served in the Union army in the Civil War. He was wounded three times—at Antietam, Ball's Bluff, and Chancellorsville—twice almost fatally. He carried throughout his life the vivid memories of his military experience.

After returning to Boston, Holmes attended Harvard Law School and embarked upon the practice of law. He found himself increasingly drawn to scholarship, however, and in 1881 he published The Common Law, often called the greatest work of American legal scholarship. In this work, which laid the foundation for the sociological, realist, and economic schools of jurisprudence, Holmes argued that law was both an instrument and a consequence of natural selection and that it was gradually evolving toward a consistent policy of avoiding unjustified harms. "The life of the law," he wrote, "has not been logic: it has been experience." His approach was historical and eclectic. He argued that "the law embodies the story of a nation's development through many centuries" and that "it cannot be dealt with as if it contained only the axioms and corollaries of a book of mathematics."[257]

The text clearly reflected Holmes's passion for the law. In what other profession, he asked, "does one plunge so deep in the stream of life—so share its passions, its battles, its despairs, its triumphs?"[258] In 1882, he was appointed to the Supreme Judicial Court of Massachusetts; twenty years later, President Theodore Roosevelt appointed him to the Supreme Court of the United States.

Holmes was courtly, gregarious, intellectually combative, supremely self-confident, and profoundly skeptical. He was a brilliant conversationalist. As one old friend recalled, "his talk would always bubble and sparkle from him, a stream of seriousness and laughter, imagination and philosophy, in which enthusiasm was undying."[259] Walter Lippmann observed that Holmes's home was one of the few bright spots in Woodrow Wilson's Washington. "When you enter it," he noted, "it is as if you had come into the living stream of high romance. You meet the gay soldier who can talk of Falstaff and eternity in one breath, and tease the universe with a quip." His presence, Lippmann added, "is an incitement to high risks."[260]

Tall, slender, and angular, Justice Holmes sported a magnificent silver mustache, the wings of which swept exuberantly upward. He was the picture of judicial grace and dignity. His dress and manner were old-fashioned. He regularly wore a tall hat, a stiff collar, a morning coat with a boutonniere in his lapel, and striped trousers.

Holmes possessed a striking judicial style. His opinions were among the most eloquent in the history of the Supreme Court. He once commented that his "way of writing a case is to get into a spasm over it." It is, he observed, "dyspeptic but thrilling."[261] Justice Brandeis complained that "when Holmes writes, he doesn't give a fellow a chance—he shoots so quickly."[262]

By the time they chanced upon one another on the train in June 1918, Hand and Holmes had known each other for several years. Hand frequently called on Holmes when he visited Washington, and Holmes valued the younger man's "good opinion very highly."[263] Born in Albany in 1872, Hand was thirty years Holmes's junior. As a young man, following the traditions of his family, Hand turned naturally to the law. He was soon bored by law practice, however, and was delighted when President William Howard Taft appointed him, at the tender age of thirty-seven, to the federal bench.

In his more than fifty years as a federal judge, Hand wrote some four thousand judicial opinions. He was a master craftsman. His opinions set the highest standards for clarity of expression and analytical precision. He was the greatest judge of the twentieth century never to sit on the Supreme Court. Although Hand was on several occasions within a hair's breadth of such an appointment, each time circumstances conspired against him.

A stocky, barrel-chested man with a square, rugged face, stiff gray hair, thick bushy eyebrows, and large, piercing eyes, Hand had an unparalleled capacity to work through even the most complex legal questions with creativity and modesty. Like Holmes, he displayed both skepticism and open-mindedness, qualities that were deeply embedded in his character and his judging. He was intolerant of absolutes and relentless in his search for understanding. He constantly questioned his own work and was often driven by self-doubt. In private discourse, as well as in his opinions, he never ceased interrogating. In his own words, "the spirit of liberty is the spirit which is not too sure that it is right."[264]

Hand did not suffer from hero worship, but "his admiration, even idolatry, of Holmes was extreme."[265] He described Holmes as "the epitome of what a judge should be" and "the example of all that I most cherish."[266] That Hand, a man of modest temperament, pursued his disagreement with Holmes about free speech was certainly out of character. Only the most deeply held convictions led Hand to "do battle" with his hero, "the most revered judge and legal philosopher in the land."[267]

Although these two great jurists shared a friendship, a deeply-rooted sense of skepticism, and a common judicial philosophy, they approached the issue of free speech from very different perspectives and experiences. Hand saw the protection of free expression as a "hard-bought acquisition in the fight for freedom," whereas Holmes, the old soldier, emphasized the necessities of wartime. As Holmes had written almost forty years earlier in *The Common Law*, "No society has ever admitted that it could not sacrifice individual welfare to its own existence. If conscripts are necessary for its army, it seizes them, and marches them, with bayonets in their rear, to death. . . . If a man is on a plank in the deep sea which will float only one, and a stranger lays hold of it, he will thrust him off if he can. When the state finds itself in a similar position, it does the same thing."[268] To Holmes, this was perfectly natural.

SHORTLY AFTER THE SUPREME COURT announced its decision in *Debs* in March 1919, Hand resumed his correspondence with Holmes. Hand observed that, in his understanding, "the rule of responsibility for speech" has never depended merely upon "reasonable forecast" of harm. Hand argued further that to rely too heavily on intent is "dangerous" because "the cases actually occur when men are excited," when "juries won't much regard the difference between the probable result of the words and the purposes of the utterer." A perplexed Holmes replied that he didn't "quite get" Hand's point. He denied that there was much difference between Hand's test in *Masses* and his own approach in *Schenck, Frohwerk,* and *Debs,* noting that he didn't "know what the matter is" or "how we differ."[269]

A month later, Professor Ernst Freund, a prominent scholar at the University of Chicago, published a biting attack in the *New Republic* on Justice Holmes and his opinions in *Schenck, Frohwerk,* and *Debs.* Freund argued that "the peril resulting to the national cause from toleration of adverse opinion is largely imaginary" and is certainly "slight compared with the permanent danger of intolerance to free institutions." He was also critical of Holmes's use of the "false cry of fire" example to anchor his analysis of the First Amendment. Freund asserted that Holmes's approach must constitute "unsafe doctrine if it has to be made plausible by a parallel so manifestly inappropriate."

Freund chastised Holmes that "to know what you may do and what you may not do, and how far you may go in criticism, is the first condition of political liberty; to be permitted to agitate at your own peril, subject to a jury's guessing at motive, tendency and possible effect, makes the right of free speech a precarious gift." He was especially concerned about the capacity of a jury to protect dissenters. Staking out a position similar to Hand's, Freund maintained that only "direct" provocation to some specific criminal act should be subject to government proscription.[270]

Learned Hand read Freund's piece with "undisguised delight."[271] He imme-diately sent Freund an appreciative note. "Your article in last week's *New Repub-lic*," he wrote, "was a great comfort to me." "I had supposed that in holding such views about the Espionage Act I was in a minority of one in the profession, and that is rather too slim a party to carry a banner." He added that he had been frus-trated in his correspondence with Justice Holmes on the subject, observing, "I was chagrined that Justice Holmes did not line up on our side; indeed, I have so far been unable to make him see that he and we have any real differences and that puzzles me a little."[272]

Holmes, on the other hand, was quite miffed at Freund. In a letter to Harold Laski, he characterized Freund's essay as "poor stuff." Nonetheless, he was defensive. Although insisting that restrictions of speech "were proper enough while the war was on," he admitted that he had "hated" writing "the Debs case and still more those of the other poor devils." He complained that he simply "could not see the wisdom of pressing" those prosecutions, and con-ceded, "I think it quite possible that if I had been on the jury I should have been for acquittal."[273]

Throughout the summer of 1919, Holmes continued to stew about the mat-ter. He complained that *Debs* had generated "a lot of jaw about free speech," and snapped that "if a man thinks that in time of war the right of free speech carries the right to try to impede by discourse the raising of armies" then he "had better not monkey with the buzzard." But he also fretted that federal judges had "been hysterical about the war."[274]

Later that summer, Justice Holmes read Professor Zechariah Chafee's article "Freedom of Speech in War Time," in the June issue of the *Harvard Law Review*. Chafee argued that the challenge was to define "where the line runs" between protected and unprotected expression, and declared that Holmes had missed a "magnificent opportunity" to draw the line firmly in *Schenck*, *Frohwerk*, and *Debs*. Nonetheless, Chafee maintained that in stating the "clear and present dan-ger" standard in *Schenck* Holmes had laid the foundation for a powerful legal principle: speech can be punished only at "the point where words will give rise to unlawful acts." This, he observed, was the most important lesson of Holmes's "false cry of fire" example.*[275]

Toward the end of the summer, Holmes's close friend Harold Laski, who had

---

* In the immediate aftermath of the war, strong efforts were made at Harvard to silence Chafee and to get him expelled from the Harvard Law School faculty. Dean John Wigmore of the North-western University Law School played a critical role in urging Chafee's dismissal. The Harvard Oversees Committee voted 6 to 5 not to fire Chafee. In general, academia did not stand up very well to the pressures of the war. The Committee on Academic Freedom in Wartime of the Ameri-

read and admired Chafee's article, invited Holmes and Chafee to join him for tea. Laski had just published *Authority in the Modern State*, dedicated to Holmes and Felix Frankfurter, in which he argued that "where the conscience of the individual is concerned, the state must abate its demands, for no mind is in truth free once a penalty is attached to thought." Laski asserted that freedom of thought should be "absolute" and that "the greatest contribution that a citizen can make" is to contribute to public understanding.[276]

In the meantime, as this round-robin of correspondence and conversation continued, Hand made clear to Chafee that he was unimpressed by Holmes's First Amendment opinions:

> I am not wholly in love with Holmesey's test, . . . [for] once you admit that the matter is one of degree, [you] give to Tomdickandharry, D.J., so much latitude that the jig is at once up. Besides . . . the Nine Elder Statesmen have not shown themselves wholly immune from the "herd instinct" and what seems [clear and present] to-day may seem very remote next year even though the circumstances surrounding the utterance be unchanged. I own I should prefer a qualitative formula, hard, conventional, difficult to evade.[277]

By this, Hand of course meant his test of *express advocacy* of unlawful conduct.

By the fall, Holmes had begun to rethink the issue of free speech.[278] On October 26, 1919, he wrote Laski, "I fear we have less freedom of speech here than they have in England. Little as I believe in it as a theory I hope I would die for it, and I go as far as anyone whom I regard as competent to form an opinion, in favor of it."[279] The next day, the Supreme Court heard argument in *Abrams v. United States*.[280]

THE DEFENDANTS IN *ABRAMS*, a group of young Russian-Jewish emigrants, had fled Russia between 1908 and 1913 to escape the czar's harsh,

---

can Association of University Professors, for example, declared that professors could legitimately be fired for "propaganda" tending to lead to draft resistance and that professors of Teutonic origin should "refrain from public discussion of the war." *Committee on Academic Freedom War Time Bulletin* 30 (Feb–Mar 1918), excerpted in Walter P. Metzger, *Academic Freedom in the Age of the University* 230 (Columbia 1955). See Jerold S. Auerbach, *The Patrician as Libertarian: Zechariah Chafee, Jr. and Freedom of Speech*, 42 New Eng Q 518, 524–25 (1969); Peter H. Irons, *"Fighting Fair": Zechariah Chafee, Jr., the Department of Justice, and the "Trial at the Harvard Club,"* 94 Harv L Rev 1205 (1981).

Professor Zechariah Chafee

anti-Semitic policies. Jacob Abrams, Mollie Steimer, Hyman Lachowsky, Samuel Lipman, and Jacob Schwartz lived in the tenements of East Harlem in New York City. They were self-proclaimed socialists and anarchists who had been deeply moved by the Bolshevik overthrow of the czar.

Before the Russian Revolution, czarist Russia had been allied with the United States in the war, but when the Bolsheviks seized power in 1917 they signed a peace treaty with Germany. The following summer, the United States sent a contingent of marines to Vladivostok and Murmansk.° Abrams and his comrades perceived this expedition as an attempt to "crush the Russian Revolution." In protest, they distributed several thousand copies of each of two leaflets, one of which was written in English, the other in Yiddish. The leaflets, which were circulated secretly and thrown from a window, called for a general strike.

The first leaflet maintained that the president's "cowardly silence" about the American intervention in Russia "reveals the hypocrisy of the plutocratic gang in Washington." It declared that "there is only one enemy of the workers of the world and that is CAPITALISM," and that it would be criminal for the workers of America to fight "the workers' republic of Russia." The leaflet ended, "Awake! Awake, you Workers of the World! REVOLUTIONISTS."

The second leaflet, in Yiddish, was headed, "Workers—Wake Up!!" It exhorted Russian emigrants to "spit in the face of the false, hypocritic military propaganda," which has fooled "you so relentlessly, calling forth your sympathy, your help, to the prosecution of the war." It warned that the money "you have loaned" to the United States for the war effort by buying Liberty bonds is being used to "make bullets not only for the Germans but also for the Workers Soviets of Russia," and it cautioned munitions workers that "you are producing bullets, bayonets, cannon, to murder not only the Germans, but also your dearest, best, who are in Russia and are fighting for freedom." The leaflet declared that "our reply to this barbarous intervention" in Russia "has to be a general strike!" It concluded, "Woe unto those who will be in the way of progress. Let solidarity live! The Rebels."[281]

The defendants were arrested by the military police. After a highly public and very controversial trial that called to mind the prosecutions under the Sedition Act of 1798 and was tainted by the judge's anti-alien, anti-Semitic, and anti-Bolshevik sentiments,[282] the defendants were convicted of conspiring to violate

---

° The stated purpose of the mission was to maintain an eastern front against Germany, but the true motivation was never clear. Newton Baker, the secretary of war, protested that the intervention violated international law. See Polenberg, *Fighting Faiths* at 36–42 (cited in note 7); Murray, *Red Scare* at 41–45 (cited in note 191).

the Sedition Act of 1918. The overall flavor of the trial is captured in Judge Henry DeLamar Clayton's remarks just prior to sentencing:

> These defendants took the stand. They talked about capitalists and producers, and I tried to figure out what a capitalist and what a producer is as contemplated by them. After listening carefully to all they had to say, I came to the conclusion that a capitalist is a man with a decent suit of clothes, a minimum of $1.25 in his pocket, and a good character. And when I tried to find out what the prisoners had produced, I was unable to find out anything at all. So far as I can learn, not one of them ever produced so much as a single potato. The only thing they know how to raise is hell, and to direct it against the government of the United States. But we are not going to help carry out the plans mapped out by the Imperial German Government, and which are being carried out by Lenine and Trotsky. I have heard of the reported fate of the poor little daughters of the Czar, but I won't talk about that now. I might get mad. I will now sentence the prisoners.[283]

The defendants were sentenced to prison terms ranging from three to twenty years.[284]

The Supreme Court affirmed the convictions on two counts: one charging conspiracy "to incite, provoke or encourage resistance to the United States" (count 3); the other charging conspiracy to urge curtailment of the production of war materials with intent to "cripple or hinder the United States in the prosecution of the war" (count 4). Speaking for the Court, Justice John H. Clarke summarily rejected the defendants' First Amendment argument, noting simply that "this contention is sufficiently discussed and is definitely negatived" in *Schenck* and *Frohwerk*.[285] Indeed, this seemed unassailable.

Surprisingly, Justice Holmes, joined by Justice Louis Brandeis, dissented. Holmes began his dissent by noting, "I never have seen any reason to doubt that . . . *Schenck*, *Frohwerk* and *Debs* were rightly decided." Although reaffirming that the power of government to restrict speech "is greater in time of war than in time of peace because war opens dangers that do not exist at other times," he made clear that "as against dangers peculiar to war, as against others, the principle of the right to free speech is always the same." It is, he announced, "only the present danger of immediate evil or an intent to bring it about that warrants Congress in setting a limit to the expression of opinion."[286]

Turning to the defendants,[287] Holmes declared that "nobody can suppose that the surreptitious publishing of a silly leaflet by an unknown man, without more, would present any immediate danger that its opinions would hinder the success of the government arms or have any appreciable tendency to do so."[288] In this case, Holmes maintained, "sentences of twenty years imprisonment have been imposed for the publishing of two leaflets that I believe the defendants had as much right to publish as the Government has to publish the Constitution of the United States now vainly invoked by them."[289]

Holmes then offered one of the most eloquent statements ever made on the freedom of speech:

> Persecution for the expression of opinions seems to me perfectly logical. If you have no doubt of your premises or your power and want a certain result with all your heart you naturally express your wishes in law and sweep away all opposi-tion. . . . But when men have realized that time has upset many fighting faiths, they may come to believe even more than they believe the very foundations of their own conduct that the ultimate good desired is better reached by free trade in ideas—that the best test of truth is the power of the thought to get itself accepted in the competition of the market, and that truth is the only ground upon which their wishes safely can be carried out. That at any rate is the theory of our Constitution. It is an experiment, as all life is an experiment. Every year if not every day we have to wager our salvation upon some prophecy based upon imper-fect knowledge. While that experiment is part of our system I think that we should be eternally vigilant against attempts to check the expression of opinions that we loathe and believe to be fraught with death, unless they so imminently threaten immediate interference with the lawful and pressing purposes of the law that an immediate check is required to save the country. . . . I regret that I cannot put into more impressive words my belief that in their conviction upon this indictment the defendants were deprived of their rights under the Constitution of the United States.[290]

THE IMMEDIATE REACTION to Holmes's dissenting opinion in *Abrams* was mixed.[291] It received both great acclaim and sharp criticism. The most forceful criticism came from Dean John H. Wigmore, a distinguished legal scholar at Northwestern University, and long a friend of Holmes. In a widely read essay in the *Illinois Law Review*,[292] Wigmore assailed Holmes and Brandeis as "obtuse" and "blind to the crisis" facing the nation. He dismissed Holmes's comment that there was no danger in "the surreptitious publishing of a silly leaflet by an unknown man," because "what is lawful for one is lawful for a thou-sand more." If there were a thousand more like Jacob Abrams, Mollie Steimer, and their comrades, then "every munitions factory in the country could be stopped by them."[293]

Wigmore derided the suggestion that freedom of speech meant "that those who desire to gather and set in action a band of thugs . . . may freely go about pub-licly . . . proposing a plan of action for organized thuggery, and enlisting their con-verts, yet not be constitutionally interfered with until the gathered band of thugs actually sets the torch and lifts the rifle." In time of war, Wigmore argued, the freedom of speech, whatever it may mean in time of peace, must be suspended because in such an emergency all rights must be subordinated to the struggle for national survival. The real danger facing the nation was not that government would suppress dissent but that a "misplaced reverence" for free speech would protect the "treacherous thuggery" of "impatient and fanatical minorities."[294]

Holmes dismissed Wigmore's attack as mere "bosh," noting that it displayed "sentiment rather than reasoning" and that Wigmore had "grown rather dogmatic" over the years.[295] He favored the more enthusiastic reviews, such as that of Professor Karl Llewellyn, who described the *Abrams* dissent as "a landmark in the law."[296]

Although the explanation for Holmes's sudden passion for the freedom of speech remains a wonderful mystery, there can be little doubt that his reading in the summer of 1919 and his discussions with Hand, Chafee, and Laski sparked a change in his thinking. In this sense, the shift in Holmes's views of the First Amendment was itself a splendid illustration of the "marketplace of ideas" in action.

WHAT, THOUGH, WAS THE RATIONALE for Holmes's revitalized "clear and present" danger test? Why should that be the standard? One argument might be that the test "balances" competing speech and government interests. Because free speech is important to our constitutional system, the government should not be able to limit that freedom unless there is an even more important interest on the other side of the balance—unless there is an "emergency" in which the danger is both "clear" and "present."

The test might also be explained as an effort to mark off a broad area of protected expression in order to address Judge Hand's concern in *Masses* that the government should not be able to render unlawful "every political agitation which can be shown to be apt to create a seditious temper." Viewed in this way, the "clear and present danger" test serves the same goal as the "express advocacy" test, though in a different way. Unlike the "bad tendency" test, which enables the government to eliminate almost all criticism, the "clear and present danger" test, stringently applied, would leave most criticism untouched, while at the same time allowing the government to restrict speech in very narrowly defined circumstances constituting an "emergency."

The test can also be understood as an attempt to reduce the risk of improper government motivation—that is, the risk that, in the guise of preventing "harm," the government is actually suppressing speech because it disapproves of the message. Under this view of the test, the existence of a clear and present danger cor-

Justice Oliver Wendell Holmes

roborates the government's claim that it has a legitimate, indeed compelling, reason to limit speech and thus helps rebut any concern that the real motive for the restriction is the government's *disagreement* with the dissenter's views.[297]

WHATEVER THE RATIONALE of the *Abrams* "clear and present danger" standard, the significance of Holmes's dissent in *Abrams* was plain: with it, "the free speech tradition divides sharply."[298] Both Justice Holmes and the majority now appealed to *Schenck* as the critical precedent. Holmes read his *Abrams* version of clear and present danger back into *Schenck*, claiming it was there all along and that the majority had irresponsibly departed from settled precedent. The majority emphasized the outcome in *Schenck*, arguing that the phrase "clear and present danger" had never meant anything different than "bad tendency." This division within the Court was evident in several post-*Abrams* decisions in which the Court, over the dissents of Holmes and Brandeis, consistently upheld World War I convictions under the Espionage and Sedition Acts.

In *Schaefer v. United States*,[299] for example, the Court affirmed the convictions of three men associated with the Philadelphia *Tageblatt*, a German-language newspaper, for the offense of translating several articles from English-language newspapers in such a way as to reflect a pro-German bias. Justice Joseph McKenna's opinion for the Court condemned the "strange perversion" of the First Amendment being invoked by those who would "debase" the "morale of our armies."[300] In dissent, Justice Brandeis, joined by Justice Holmes, warned that "to hold that such publications can be suppressed . . . subjects to new perils the constitutional liberty of the press." He cautioned that, especially in time of war, "an intolerant majority, swayed by passion or by fear," is prone "to stamp as disloyal opinions with which it disagrees."[301]

In *Pierce v. United States*,[302] four Albany socialists were convicted of violating the "false statement" provision of the Espionage Act for circulating a pamphlet asserting that, despite all of Wilson's rhetoric about democracy, "this war began over commercial routes" and was being fought to decide whether "the Allied Nations or . . . the Central Empires have the superior right to exploit undeveloped countries." In his opinion for the Court affirming the convictions, Justice Mahlon Pitney echoed Justice Chase and the other judges who had upheld the Sedition Act of 1798, reasoning that "common knowledge . . . sufficed to show" that the defendants' "statements as to the causes that led to the entry of the United States into the war . . . were grossly false." In his dissenting opinion, Justice Brandeis, joined by Justice Holmes, observed that the causes of war are complex and that even "historians rarely agree" about such matters. Thus, such statements are necessarily "matters of opinion and judgment, not matters of fact to be determined by a jury." Brandeis added that "to hold that a jury may make punishable" such statements of opinion by "declaring them to be false statements of fact" would deny to those who would dissent from government policy all "freedom of criticism and of discussion in times when feelings run high."[303]

Gilbert v. Minnesota[304] involved a conviction under a state law that made it a crime to teach or advocate "that men should not enlist in the military or naval forces." Joseph Gilbert was indicted for making a speech in which he said that "we were stampeded into this war by newspaper rot to pull England's chestnuts out of the fire." Justice McKenna affirmed the conviction, noting that "every word that [Gilbert] uttered in denunciation of the war was false, was deliberate misrepresentation of the motives which impelled it, and the objects for which it was prosecuted." He added that "it would be a travesty on the constitutional privilege he invokes to assign him its protection." Justice Brandeis dissented on the ground that the Minnesota statute interfered "with the right of a citizen of the United States to discuss" matters of national policy.[305]

These decisions left no doubt as to the Supreme Court's understanding of the First Amendment at this time: while the nation was at war, "serious, abrasive criticism" was "beyond constitutional protection." As Harry Kalven sadly observed, these decisions "are dismal evidence of the degree to which the mood of society" can "penetrate judicial chambers."[306] On the other hand, although Justices Holmes and Brandeis had not yet won any converts within the Court, their dissenting opinions "lent prestige and eloquence to a counterview" that would eventually win the day.*[307]

---

* This brings us to the remarkable saga of Victor Berger. Berger was the first Socialist elected to Congress, serving from 1911 to 1913. Several years later, he became the editor of the *Milwaukee Leader*, an antiwar German American newspaper. In September 1917, Postmaster General Burleson deprived the *Leader* of its second-class mailing privileges and blocked all first-class mail addressed to the *Leader*. Several months later, Berger was indicted under the Espionage Act. The indictment was based on several editorials in the *Leader* that said, among other things, that the United States was in the war because the Allies were washed up and that their obligations to us would be worthless. Shortly before his indictment, Berger was nominated as the Socialist candidate in Wisconsin for the U.S. Senate. He was defeated, but received more than 100,000 votes, despite the criminal charges pending against him. In the deliberations over the Sedition Act of 1918, senators from every part of the political spectrum denounced Berger as "disloyal," or worse. In November 1918, however, before his criminal trial began, Berger was elected to Congress from the Fifth District of Wisconsin, handily defeating both the Democratic and the Republican candidates. The next month, he was tried, convicted, and sentenced to twenty years in prison by Judge Kenesaw Mountain Landis. While his appeal was pending, Berger presented himself to Congress to be sworn in, but the House of Representatives refused to seat him. In December 1919, the governor of Wisconsin ordered a special election to find a replacement for Berger. Berger was again elected,

THE DEPARTMENT OF JUSTICE: JOHN LORD O'BRIAN AND ALFRED BETTMAN

CRITICAL TO THE PROTECTION of civil liberties in wartime is the stance of the Department of Justice. If the attorney general exercises restraint and good judgment, and insists on such values in his subordinates, he may keep the pressures for repression under control. As the nation's chief law enforcement officer, the attorney general can help set the tone for the entire nation. The Department of Justice during World War I played a curiously uneven role in both exacerbating and moderating the suppression of dissent.

Several key figures in the Department of Justice were dedicated to the preservation of civil liberties (at least by the standards of the day),[308] but they too often lost control of the situation. They underestimated both the divisions in the nation and the extraordinary forces the administration itself had unleashed. Not only was the public swept up in a wave of suppression, but prosecutors, judges, members of Congress, and other federal, state, and local officials were carried along with it. In such circumstances, it proved impossible to maintain fine distinctions between "legitimate" and "illegitimate" dissent.[309]

Reflecting on this era shortly after the end of the war, John Lord O'Brian, the very able and thoughtful Buffalo lawyer who served as head of the War Emergency Division of the Department of Justice, maintained that it had been the department's view throughout the war that the "expression of private or public opinion relating to matters of governmental policy . . . must not be confused with wilful attempts to interfere with our conduct of the war," and "that there should be no repression of political agitation unless of a character directly affecting the safety of the state."[310]

O'Brian reported that "immense pressure" had been brought to bear on the department for "indiscriminate prosecution" and "wholesale repression" of pub-

---

by an even greater margin than before. On January 10, 1920, the House again refused to seat him.

Meanwhile, the *Milwaukee Leader* case reached the Supreme Court. The Court, with Justices Brandeis and Holmes dissenting, upheld the decision of the postmaster general to exclude the *Leader* from the mail. See *Milwaukee Social Democratic Publishing Co v. Burleson*, 255 US 407 (1920). On January 13, 1921, however, the Court reversed Berger's criminal conviction because Judge Landis had made a series of highly inflammatory and prejudicial pretrial statements about Germans and German Americans. See *Berger v. United States*, 255 US 22 (1921). On December 3, 1923, after the Department of Justice had at last dropped its Espionage Act charges against Berger, he finally took his seat in the House, without a single dissenting vote.

lic opinion. Although the atmosphere had been "charged with suspicion and rumors," he insisted that the department had been committed to "American standards of fair play" and to weeding out prosecutions that "were essentially *de minimis*."[311] Nevertheless, the laws "affecting 'free speech' received the severest test thus far placed upon them in our history."[312]

According to O'Brian, the proper test under the Espionage Act was whether, "assuming unlawful intent to be shown, . . . the utterances complained of would have the natural and reasonable effect of producing the result aimed at by the statute." Was this interpretation of the act consistent with the First Amendment?

Three distinct approaches to the First Amendment emerged in this era. First, as O'Brian suggested, the inquiry might focus on the speaker's *intent*. Under this view, criticism of the government is not protected by the First Amendment if the speaker intends to cause others to violate the law. This approach emphasizes the moral culpability of the speaker. In the words of Judge Charles Wolverton, in an unpublished opinion that O'Brian thought stated the argument particularly well:

> A citizen is entitled to fairly criticize men and measures . . . with a view, by the use of lawful means, to improve the public service, or to amend the laws by which he is governed. . . . But when his criticism extends or leads by willful intent to the incitement of disorder and riot, or to the infraction of the laws of the land . . . it overleaps the bounds of all reasonable liberty accorded to him by the guarantee of the freedom of speech.[313]

Second, as Judge Hand suggested in *Masses*, criticism of the government may be protected by the First Amendment unless the speaker *"expressly advocates"* unlawful conduct. This approach focuses on what the speaker actually says. It asserts that what matters most is not the intent of the speaker but the "value" of his speech. If the speaker makes a useful contribution to public discourse, then it should not matter whether he does so with a "good" or a "bad" intent. On the other hand, as Hand argued, express advocacy of criminal conduct is not a "valuable" contribution to public debate, because it betrays the central premise of the First Amendment—that the appropriate way to achieve political change is by public discourse, not by force and violence. On this view, speech that expressly advocates unlawful conduct is not protected by the First Amendment and may therefore be punished.*

---

* As Judge Hand put it in *Masses*, it "has always" been recognized that "one may not counsel or advise others to violate the law as it stands." Words, he observed, "are not only the keys of persuasion, but the triggers of action, and those which have no purport but to counsel the violation of law cannot by any latitude of interpretation be a part of that public opinion which is the final source of

Third, as Justice Holmes suggested in *Abrams*, the inquiry might focus on the degree of danger created by the speech. Under this view, criticism of the government is protected by the First Amendment unless it creates a clear and present danger of serious harm. This approach assumes that what matters most is neither the value of the speaker's words nor his intent. Rather, the government may interfere with free expression if, but only if, it has a compelling interest in doing so — that is, only if the expression poses a clear and present danger of serious harm.*

In the abstract, each of these approaches is principled, coherent, and defensible. In theory, at least, each could enable the government to restrict especially dangerous, valueless, or morally culpable expression, without necessarily endangering "that public opinion which is the final source of government in a democratic state." As applied, however, these approaches may produce quite different outcomes. It is probably the case that none of the Espionage Act defendants could have been convicted under Justice Holmes's stringent "clear and present danger" standard; [314] few, if any, could have been convicted under Judge Hand's "express advocacy" standard; but more than one thousand were in fact convicted under O'Brian's intent standard.

There are obvious objections to the "intent" standard. It allows an individual to be punished even though his speech contributes positively to public debate. Consider Charles Schenck. The pamphlet he distributed included strong, but reasoned, arguments against conscription. It never expressly advocated unlawful conduct. To the contrary, it exhorted readers to sign a petition calling for repeal of the draft. Suppose Schenck's unexpressed intent had been to induce some men to refuse induction. Is that a sufficient reason to punish his speech, given its value to public debate? Is there any compelling reason to treat him differently from some other speaker who distributes precisely the same pamphlet without the "bad" intent?

Moreover, Schenck's pamphlet did not create a clear and present danger (as defined by Justice Holmes in *Abrams*) or, indeed, any significant danger of interfering with the war effort. Even if we stipulate that his pamphlet might have caused

---

government in a democratic state." 244 F 535, 540 (SD NY 1917). Endorsing this position, Chief Justice Rehnquist has argued that "if freedom of speech is to be meaningful, strong criticism of government policy must be permitted even in wartime," and that "advocacy which persuades citizens that a law is unjust is not the same as advocacy that preaches disobedience to it." Rehnquist, *All the Laws But One* at 178 (cited in note 1).

* The seriousness or gravity of the harm might enter the analysis in at least three different ways: (a) the law could require that there be a clear and present danger of at least a minimally serious harm; (b) it could require that there be a clear and present danger of a very grave harm; or (c) it could provide that the degree of clarity and presence necessary to justify the restriction should vary according to the relative gravity of the harm.

a few men to refuse induction, it seems doubtful that the harm is sufficiently grave to justify prohibiting what on its face is a valuable contribution to public discourse.

On the other hand, as Judge Wolverton argued, if we know beyond a reasonable doubt that Schenck specifically intended to cause his readers to violate the law, there must be some lingering unease about allowing him to shield his conduct behind the protection of the First Amendment. In this respect, John Lord O'Brian's precise statement of what he regarded as the proper test is illuminating. As he put it, speech is punishable if, "*assuming unlawful intent to be shown,* . . . the utterances complained of would have the natural and reasonable effect of producing the result aimed at by the statute."

Note that, in this statement, O'Brian described "unlawful intent" and "bad tendency" as distinct elements of his test, both of which must be present. He did not imply that intent could be inferred from bad tendency. As we have seen, however, this was *not* the way the test was applied in practice. Rather, federal courts routinely conflated these two elements and allowed juries to infer criminal intent from bad tendency. This distinction is critical to understanding both the position of the Department of Justice and the application of the Espionage Act in practice.

O'BRIAN'S STATEMENT OF THE STANDARD accurately reflected the position of the highest officials of the Department of Justice. In its briefs for the United States in *Schenck, Frohwerk, Debs,* and *Abrams,* all of which were submitted by O'Brian and Special Assistant Attorney General Alfred Bettman, the department consistently defined the standard in this manner.

In these briefs, O'Brian and Bettman invariably rejected Judge Hand's proposed requirement of express advocacy of unlawful conduct. In their brief in *Debs,* for example, they stated that Debs "seems to contend" that because he did not expressly advocate unlawful conduct in words that were "direct, plain, and unmistakable," his speech was constitutionally protected. They argued that this position would leave the government in the untenable position of being "powerless to punish any incitement to lawlessness, however intentional and however effective, so long as it is concealed in veiled, indirect, or rhetorical language." They rejected this as an implausible construction of the Espionage Act and an unsupportable interpretation of the First Amendment.[315]

On the other hand, O'Brian and Bettman insisted that in order to convict an individual under the Espionage Act, the government had to prove *both* that the defendant had a "specific, willful, criminal intent" *and* that he used language having "a natural and reasonably probable tendency" to cause the harms forbidden by the law.[316] In *Schenck,* for example, they emphasized that Schenck had distributed the circular to "men who had been accepted by the draft boards and were simply awaiting the orders to report for duty." This, they reasoned, "is itself sufficient to support the verdict of the jury" that Schenck's intent was "to influence the conduct of persons subject to the draft and to influence that conduct in relation to the draft." Any claim that the defendants were engaged in "legitimate political agitation" for the repeal of the draft was "negatived" by this fact.[317] O'Brian and Bettman never asserted, or even implied, that the requisite intent could be inferred from the mere bad tendency of the leaflets.

Similarly, in *Debs* they expressly endorsed the district judge's jury instruction that neither "disapproval of war" nor "advocacy of peace" is a crime under the Espionage Act unless the government proves that the defendant had "the specific, willful, criminal intent" to bring about a violation of the law *and* that the words used had "a natural and reasonably probable tendency" to cause a violation.[318] Moreover, in their effort to demonstrate the sufficiency of the evidence on the issue of intent, O'Brian and Bettman invoked Debs's prior statements and speeches to prove his specific intent to encourage draft evasion in his speech in Ohio. They never argued that Debs's intent could or should be inferred from the mere bad tendency of the speech itself.

This suggests that, at least in its highest reaches, and at least in its arguments before the Supreme Court, the Department of Justice clearly understood the difference between specific intent and bad tendency and saw them as separate and distinct elements of the law.* This is certainly more in line with the common-law doctrine of attempts, and more consistent with the intent of Congress in 1917, than the "bad tendency" test that was actually applied by the federal courts.

This also sheds new light on the Court's opinions in *Schenck*, *Frohwerk*, and *Debs*.[319] Whatever else one might think of those opinions, if one reads them in the light of the government's briefs, it would appear that Justice Holmes was not embracing the most extreme version of the "bad tendency" standard, which essentially equated all criticism of the war with unlawful intent, but was instead following the lead of the Department of Justice and treating proof of specific intent as a distinct evidentiary requirement. A careful reading of the opinions bears this out.[320]

---

* Because the Justice Department was highly decentralized, O'Brian and Bettman exercised only modest control over the nation's prosecuting attorneys. There was thus great variation from district to district in the standards applied by federal prosecutors. That makes it quite possible that O'Brian and Bettman held to a position that differed quite significantly from those adopted and employed by their subordinates. See John Lord O'Brian, *New Encroachments on Individual Freedom*, 66 Harv L Rev 1, 12 (1952) ("The United States Attorneys of the various districts exercised a large measure of discretion in instituting prosecutions and, not immune to popular alarm and hysteria, sometimes became overzealous in their activities").

BUT EVEN IF WE ACCEPT this characterization of the Justice Department's position, significant problems remain. As already noted, the intent test gives scant weight both to the positive value of the speaker's contribution to public debate and to the gravity, or lack of gravity, of the harm. Moreover, even if we stipulate specific intent, the second component of the Justice Department's test—bad tendency—fails to satisfy the proximity requirement of the common law. Recall that, for an act to constitute an attempt under the common law, it "must come dangerously near to success,"[321] or "sufficiently near completion to be of public concern,"[322] or "very near to the accomplishment of the act."[323] Few, if any, of the Espionage Act prosecutions met this test of proximity.

Beyond all this, however, the Justice Department's "intent" test failed to provide adequate protection to the freedom of speech during World War I. However morally gratifying it may be to punish speakers who have an "evil" intent, such a standard inevitably fails in practice. As Emily Balch and Gilbert Roe made clear in the congressional debates over the Espionage Act, judges and jurors cannot reliably distinguish between "good" and "evil" intent in a wartime atmosphere of fear, suspicion, and patriotic fervor.

Under the best of circumstances it is difficult to prove a defendant's subjective intent. It is particularly dangerous to undertake this inquiry when jurors and judges are already inflamed against the defendant because of the "disloyalty" of his views. As Zechariah Chafee observed, it is especially "in times of popular panic and indignation that freedom of speech becomes important as an institution, and it is precisely in those times that the protection of the jury proves illusory."[324]

In his amicus curiae brief to the Supreme Court in *Debs*, Gilbert Roe of the Free Speech League argued that the Espionage Act effectively prevented "public discussion of the war" because juries were routinely allowed to infer intent from bad tendency. As a result, "the constitutional guarantee of free speech and free press is wiped out."[325] In their reply brief, O'Brian and Bettman responded as follows:

> Mr. Roe claims, that by reason of the temper of the public during a war, a law directed at obstruction of the prosecution of the war will inevitably be applied so as to suppress all critical discussion of the war, and that the Espionage Act, as applied by courts and juries, has produced that effect. . . . [But if this be so,] then the vice, if any, . . . must either . . . [fall] exclusively within the domain of the legislative branch, or must be one which the President alone, by act of executive clemency, can correct.[326]

Interestingly, this response does not attempt to rebut Roe's characterization of the situation. Rather, it rests on a crabbed conception of constitutional law. Assuming, as the brief for the United States does, that "Congress has not the power to punish belief or opinion as such," and that "the right to criticize the Government's policies and actions" is "essential to democracy,"[327] why is it self-evident that the act does not violate the First Amendment if its effect *in actual practice* is to suppress public discussion of the war? This is the closest the Justice Department came in this era to acknowledging a fundamental gap in its understanding of the First Amendment.[328]

PERHAPS THE MOST ASTUTE ANALYSIS of these issues at the time was the largely overlooked convocation address delivered at Columbia University in 1921 by the University of Chicago Law School dean James Parker Hall. Dean Hall began his analysis by observing that no one disputes that express "incitations to crime" may be forbidden. But, like Judge Hand, he then recognized that, in order to circumvent such a rule, "shrewder" people, "instead of urging resistance to the draft," will condemn the draft as "tyrannical" and describe the dangers of battle "in colors as lurid and frightful as imagination can conceive them." Hall predicted that these "shrewder" people would claim that they were attempting only to influence public opinion to repeal the draft law and that, so long as they "did not *directly* counsel *resistance*" to the law, their political agitation must be protected by the First Amendment.[329]

Hall explained that this posed a serious dilemma, for one could hardly argue that "in war time men can lawfully be forbidden to attempt in good faith to secure changes in the laws." He observed that, to escape this dilemma, the "genuine believer in constitutional government" would argue that if the speaker "intends . . . to induce evasions of the draft," he may be punished, but if he "intends only to influence public opinion to bring about a change of law," he is protected by the Constitution.[330]

Hall then noted that although this distinction might be theoretically sound, there is a serious question whether "it really work[s] in practice."[331] Here we encounter the "problem" of the jury, for "if public opinion favors the war," jurors will be "impatient of adverse criticism and almost certain to regard it as inspired by improper motives." In short, jurors will believe that those who oppose the war are "disloyal." In such circumstances, the defendant will be condemned "because what he says is disliked, rather than because he actually intends to induce unlawful conduct."[332]

Hall thus concluded that "once you grant that you can punish a speaker not merely for literally direct incitement," but for language intended to incite, some cases are "sure to . . . be decided erroneously," and this approach will inevitably "cut off some useful criticism." Hence, "we have to choose between competing goods and ills."

Hall then reasoned that "in ordinary times" the interest in free discussion "so plainly outweighs all possible gains from its suppression" that only express incitement may be forbidden. But "during an important war," the "state may lawfully limit the ordinary freedom of speech" if this is necessary to the effective prosecution of the war, and this is so even if this limitation will be "susceptible of . . . abuse."[333]

Thus, Dean Hall meticulously traced the logical steps in the argument from the "bad tendency" test to Judge Hand's opinion in *Masses*, to the concerns of Gilbert Roe and Emily Balch about intent, to the arguments of O'Brian and Bettman. In the end, he found that it all comes down to a "choice" between a "speedier successful ending of the war" and a "freer public discussion of it."[334]

Of course, one can disagree with Hall's judgment about which of these is the more important interest, or even with how he defines the "choice." (Keep in mind that "a freer public discussion" may in fact lead to "a speedier successful ending of the war," so the "choice" he poses misses a critical element of the equation.) But even if one agrees with the "theoretical correctness" of his assessment, there is an additional factor: Does the experience during World War I, for which we can now exercise the advantage of hindsight, bear out his "choice"?

Hall himself addressed this question. What of the possibility, he asked, that the wartime restrictions of speech "were not really needed, but were the product of an excitement and quasi-panic that deprived men of the power of judging in calmness" what restrictions were needed? This question can be answered, he said, only by considering "the states of mind" of those who were in the circumstances they confronted. "One who is repelling assault and battery," for example, "is not required at his peril to judge of the proper limits of self-defence with the detachment of a bystander." Rather, "in appraising the correctness of his decision, the court will take into account his naturally excited state of mind," for "he need only decide as well as could fairly be expected . . . under such circumstances of provocation and excitement."[335]

Hall conceded that "during the late war, men of average intelligence and credulity believed there was much greater danger from pro-German and treasonable activities than was in sober truth the case." But, by analogy to the assault and battery example, he maintained that, "considering the emergency," the "temper of the country," the "stress of war," and the "imperfect information available" at the time, it "seems impossible to say" that the government's actions were in their "essential features unreasonable."[336]

Dean Hall may be correct that, viewed from within the circumstances of

World War I, the actions of the government were not "unreasonable." But is that the right question? Our concern is not whether we should hold Wilson, Gregory, Creel, or O'Brian criminally or civilly liable for their conduct but whether we should expect government to do better the *next* time it faces this "choice." If the government's actions during World War I were "reasonable" in the circumstances, but nonetheless failed to meet our aspirations as a nation, our goal should be to come closer to those aspirations in the future. That, most fundamentally, is the challenge at the heart of this inquiry.[*]

THE RED SCARE OF 1919–1920

WITH THE SIGNING OF the armistice on November 11, 1918, the victorious Americans were eager to return to the routine of their lives. It was not to be. Within a matter of weeks, the nation plunged headlong into the ferocious Red Scare of 1919–20.

The end of the war meant the end of a wartime economy. Industrial production fell at the same time that several million "doughboys" returned home. During the war, labor had maintained a truce with management. Labor was now ready to reassert itself, and management was prepared, indeed eager, to engage labor in full-scale battle in order to end economic liberalism once and for all.[337] Major and often violent strikes exploded across the nation. And the Espionage and Sedition Act prosecutions continued to grind forward.[†]

---

[*] It may be useful briefly to describe the experience in England during World War I. In the first year of the war, there was no consensus in England that any censorship of dissent was consistent with the democratic system, even if that dissent could be of comfort to the enemy or demoralizing to the nation. As the war progressed, however, and the intensity of dissent mounted, His Majesty's Government tended to allow the "patriotic" elements to deal with the problem. That is, whenever dissenters attempted to stage a protest, gangs of "patriots" would break up the event, with increasing levels of violence. For the most part, the government officials did nothing to protect the protesters. Largely in this way, the government was able to keep formal prosecutions of dissent to a minimum, but at the same time prevent dissenting voices from gaining any powerful momentum. See generally Brock Millman, *Managing Domestic Dissent in First World War Britain* (Frank Cass 2000); Panikos Panayi, *The Enemy in Our Midst: Germans in Britain during the First World War* (Berg 1991); J. Lee Thompson, *Politicians, the Press, and Propaganda: Lord Northcliffe and the Great War, 1914–1919* (Kent 1999).

[†] In the six months after the armistice, the federal government dropped most, but not all, of its pending prosecutions under the Espionage and Sedition Acts. See Goldstein, *Political Repression* at 140 (cited in note 4).

Citizens groups, like the American Protective League, remained firmly in place, and there were suddenly new enemies. The Russian Revolution generated deep anxiety in a nation already on the edge. An English journalist described the mood in the United States as "feverish" and "hag-ridden by the spectre of Bolshevism."[338] The American press was consumed with stories depicting Bolshevik rule as a compound of slaughter, confiscation, and disorder. Cartoonists portrayed Bolsheviks holding smoking guns, bombs, and a hangman's noose. One newspaper even claimed that the Bolsheviks in Petrograd had a guillotine that could chop off five hundred heads an hour.[339]

The Russian Revolution reenergized not only the patriot groups but also the American radical movement. Socialist Party membership grew by almost a third from the summer of 1918 to the summer of 1919.[340] Anarchist publications like *The Blast* celebrated the Russian Revolution and called for a communist upheaval in the United States. The Socialist Party split apart in a bitter struggle for power. Although Eugene Debs, still in prison, anchored the moderate wing of the party, many members, led by John Reed and Benjamin Gitlow, broke away to form the more radical Communist Labor Party, which advocated the overthrow of capitalist rule.

Against this background, a series of extraordinary events triggered the period of intense public panic that degenerated into the Red Scare. In January of 1919, some 35,000 Seattle shipyard workers struck for higher wages and shorter hours. When management refused to negotiate, the Seattle Central Labor Council called a general strike. The public was sent into a panic as citizens tried desperately to stock up on food, medicine, and clothing. The city was paralyzed. The mayor declared the strike part of an international plot to initiate a revolution in the United States. The *Cleveland Plain Dealer* announced that the Bolshevik "beast" had now come "into the open," and the *Chicago Tribune* warned that "it is only a middling step from Petrograd to Seattle."[341]

The next two months brought repeated, but unsubstantiated, rumors of thwarted bombing attempts. Then, on April 28, 1919, a bomb arrived at the office of the Seattle mayor. No one was injured, but the following day a bomb exploded at the home of a former U.S. senator in Atlanta, injuring two people. Two days later, the post office in New York discovered thirty-four bombs in the mail. They were addressed to Postmaster General Burleson, Justice Oliver Wendell Holmes, Senator Lee Overman, Attorney General A. Mitchell Palmer, and John D. Rockefeller, among others. This triggered a firestorm of outrage, fear, and demands for intensified security measures.

The next day, riots broke out in New York, Boston, Cleveland, and other cities as citizens and police clashed with radical May Day protestors. In Cleveland, more than a hundred May Day protesters were wounded by gunshots and two died. Newspapers across the nation warned that these events were mere "dress rehearsals" for what was to come. On May 6, at a victory pageant in Washington, D.C., a sailor fired three shots into the back of a member of the audience who refused in respect to the flag, and the crowd cheered.

On June 2, bombs exploded simultaneously in eight cities across the nation, killing two people. One of these bombs demolished part of the home of Attorney General Palmer, who immediately declared the bombings an "attempt of an anarchist element in the population to terrorize the country." Large-scale citizens groups, such as the American Legion and the Ku Klux Klan, demanded action. In several instances, these groups took matters into their own hands, harassing suspected anarchists and communists, raiding the offices of radical organizations, and, in one particularly gruesome incident, mutilating, torturing, and then hanging a member of the International Workers of the World.[342]

A subcommittee of the Senate Judiciary Committee was hastily convened to investigate "anti-American radicalism."[343] At the close of the hearings, which were reported daily in the national press, the subcommittee concluded that bolshevism was the "greatest current danger facing the Republic" and called for stringent sedition legislation to deal with the crisis. The New York Times reported, in a front-page headline, "Mass Terror of Bolsheviki!"[344]

In March 1919, the New York legislature convened the Lusk Committee to investigate the scope, tendencies, and ramifications of seditious activities.[345] The committee launched a series of raids on the headquarters of radical organizations and seized huge quantities of radical literature, documents, and mailing lists. When asked the purpose of the raids, Lusk replied, "Names."[346] The publicity-seeking Lusk Committee and various citizens groups tarred a wide range of institutions and individuals with the "radical" label and accused them of being tools of the Bolsheviks. The targets of these accusations included the University of Chicago, Vassar, Yale, and Barnard (because they taught Marxism); the National League of Women Voters, the Nation, the New Republic, Thorstein Veblen, Jane Addams, Roscoe Pound, John Dewey, Clarence Darrow, and Senators William Borah, Robert M. La Follette, and George Norris (because they questioned the legitimacy of the inquiry).[347]

Three major labor confrontations in the fall of 1919—a police strike in Boston, a nationwide strike of steelworkers, and a mine workers strike involving 400,000 miners in defiance of a federal order—led to ever more hysterical claims. The New York Tribune warned that thousands of strikers, "red-soaked in the doctrines of Bolshevism, clamor for the strike as a means of . . . starting a general red revolution in America."[348]

From the fall of 1919 through the spring of 1920, Attorney General Palmer, eyeing a run for the White House, made the suppression of radicalism a personal crusade. Declaring that radical expression threatens the "constant spread of a disease of evil thinking,"[349] Palmer established the General Intelligence Division (GID) within

Attorney General A. Mitchell Palmer

the Bureau of Investigation and appointed a young J. Edgar Hoover to gather and coordinate information relating to radical activities. Hoover quickly created an elaborate card system including the names of more than 200,000 individuals suspected of radical activities, associations, or beliefs. The GID fed the Red Scare by aggressively disseminating sensationalized and often fabricated or exaggerated charges that Communists and other radicals had instigated violent strikes and race riots.[350]

In response to public demands for the deportation of radical aliens, the GID unleashed a legion of undercover agents and confidential informants to infiltrate radical organizations. The goal was to gather additional names for deportation.[351] In November, the GID conducted its first major roundup of aliens. Approximately 650 people were arrested on suspicion of radicalism, many of whom merely happened to be in the wrong place at the wrong time. On December 21, 1919, the United States deported 249 of these individuals. The public demanded more. The *New York World* proclaimed that "America has risen in her might and delivered a blow that reached the very soul of the incorrigible fanatics," while the *Portland Oregonian* declared that this is "only a good beginning."[352]

On January 2, 1920, the government rounded up an additional 4,000 suspected radicals in a series of raids in thirty-three cities. The general procedure was to make dragnet arrests in pool halls, cafés, bowling alleys, and other places thought to be "radical hangouts."[353] Virtually every leader of every local communist organization was taken into custody. American citizens were turned over to local authorities for prosecution under state syndicalist laws; aliens were held for deportation. The public was ecstatic. The *Washington Post* expressed the dominant sentiment: "There is no time to waste on hairsplitting over infringement of liberty."[354] Attorney General Palmer predicted more than 2,700 deportations based on the January 2 raids. (In the end, there were 3,000.) In public statements, Palmer described those captured in these raids as typified by "sly and crafty eyes, . . . lopsided faces, sloping brows and misshapen features," which sheltered "cupidity, cruelty, insanity and crime."[355]

State and local governments exceeded the federal government in the virulence of their antiradical activities. With the encouragement of Attorney General Palmer, many states enacted criminal anarchy or criminal syndicalism statutes prohibiting any person from advocating the overthrow of government. Thirty-two states enacted laws prohibiting any person from displaying the Red flag as a symbol of opposition to organized government. In 1919–20, at least 1,400 individuals were arrested under such legislation, and at least 300 were convicted and sentenced to terms of imprisonment ranging up to twenty years.[356]

Judge Learned Hand wrote Justice Holmes,

> [T]he merry sport of Red-baiting goes on, and the pack gives tongue more and more shrilly. . . . I own a sense of dismay at the increase in all the symptoms of apparent panic. How far people are getting afraid to speak . . . I don't know, but I am sure that the public generally is becoming rapidly demoralized in all its sense of proportion and toleration. For men who are not cock-sure about everything and especially for those who are not damned cock-sure about anything, the skies have a rather sinister appearance.[357]

In April 1920, acting on the recommendation of the Lusk Committee, the New York legislature expelled its five Socialist members. The legislature defended its action on the ground that the Socialist Party was unpatriotic and disloyal. In September, all of the expelled assemblymen were reelected by their constituents.[358]

This event marked the beginning of the end of the Red Scare. The action of the New York legislature was seen as extreme, and faintly ridiculous, even by the standards of the day. The growing recognition among the public that the danger of widespread, systematic, organized violence had been largely exaggerated, combined with national exhaustion from almost four years of national hysteria, began to dampen the frenzy.

The first direct challenge to the authority of the Department of Justice came from Judge George Bourquin. Uncowed by the fierce reaction to his decision two years earlier in *Hall*, Bourquin in February 1920 granted a writ of habeas corpus to block the deportation of an alien accused by the government of being a "Red."

In *Ex parte Jackson*, Bourquin held that government agents had flagrantly violated the deportee's constitutional rights when they seized him during a raid on a union meeting and at his home:

> There was no disorder save that of the raiders. [Acting without a warrant, these agents], mainly uniformed and armed, overawed, intimidated, and forcibly entered, broke, and destroyed property, searched persons, effects and papers, . . . cursed, insulted, beat, dispersed, and bayoneted union members. . . . [They] perpetrated a reign of terror, violence and crime against citizen and alien alike, and whose only offense seems to have been peaceable insistence upon and exercise of a clear legal right. . . .
>
> Assuming petitioner is of the so-called "Reds," . . . he and his kind are less of a danger to America than are those who indorse [sic] or use the methods that brought him to deportation. These latter are the mob and the spirit of violence and intolerance, . . . the most alarming manifestation in America today. . . .[359]

As the tone of public discourse began to soften, Attorney General Palmer's campaign to persuade Congress to enact an even more restrictive version of the Sedition Act of 1918 fell on deaf ears.[360] On May 28, 1920, a group of distinguished lawyers and law professors, including Ernst Freund, Felix Frankfurter, and Roscoe Pound, published a *Report upon the Illegal Practices of the United States Department of Justice.* This *Report* carefully documented that without legal authorization the department had ordered wholesale arrests of suspected "radicals," that it had unlawfully held them incommunicado, and that agents provocateurs had actively engaged in unlawful entrapment.[361] The attorney general was promptly called to testify before the House Rules Committee. Palmer stated, "I apologize for nothing that the Department of Justice has done in this matter. I glory in it. I point with pride and enthusiasm to the results of that work."[362] His presidential ambitions were dashed.

On June 23, 1920, Judge George Anderson of the Massachusetts Federal District Court, relying on briefs submitted by Zechariah Chafee and Felix Frankfurter, ordered the discharge of twenty aliens who were being held for deportation because of their membership in the Communist Party. Judge Anderson concluded that there was no evidence that the Communist Party of the United States had advocated the overthrow of the government by force or violence. He went on to criticize the Department of Justice for its use of undercover spies and for its persistent abuses in not following proper legal procedures. Judge Anderson described the typical raid this way:

> The arrested aliens, in most cases perfectly quiet and harmless working people, many of them not long ago Russian peasants, were handcuffed in pairs, and then, for the purposes of transfer on trains and through the streets of Boston, chained

together . . . exposed to newspaper photographers. . . . The picture of a non-Eng-
lish-speaking Russian peasant arrested, . . . held for days in jail, then for weeks in
the city prison, . . . and then summoned for a so-called "trial" before an inspector,
assisted by the Department of Justice agent under stringent instructions . . . to
make every possible effort to obtain evidence of the alien's membership in one of
the proscribed parties, is not a picture of a sober, dispassionate, "due process of
law" attempt to ascertain and report the true facts.[363]

This essentially put an end to the deportations.[*][364] Even the conservative
Christian Science Monitor commented that, "in the light of what is now known,
it seems clear that what appeared to be an excess of radicalism . . . was certainly
met with . . . an excess of suppression." In response to claims that Palmer's actions
were justified because of a public fear "of the spread of bolshevism" and "the dastardly bomb outrages," Senator Walsh of Montana observed that it is "in such
times that the guarantees of the Constitution as to personal liberties" are of special value, and if "the Constitution is not a shield" in those times, then "the
economiums which statesmen and jurists have paid it are fustian."[†][365]

Charles Evans Hughes summarized the Red Scare in these terms in June
1920: "We have seen the war powers, which are essential to the preservation of
the nation in time of war, exercised broadly after the military exigency has passed.
. . . and we may well wonder in view of the precedents now established whether
constitutional government as heretofore maintained in this republic could survive another great war even victoriously waged."[366]

"THE MATURER JUDGMENT OF POSTERITY"

MANY THEMES PLAYED OUT in the actions taken by the Wilson
administration during World War I. The government found it necessary to bal-

---

[*] Another hero of this episode was Assistant Secretary of Labor Louis F. Post, who ordered the
release of more than a thousand individuals unlawfully detained during the Red Scare. Post bril-
liantly defended his actions in a hearing before the House Rules Committee. He pointed out,
among other things, that the searches of thousands of homes in the Palmer raids had turned up
only three weapons capable of being fired. See Carrington, 5 Green Bag 375 (cited in note 342).

[†] The Red Scare had a devastating effect on the Socialist and Communist Parties, both of
which lost almost 70 percent of their members from October 1919 to April 1920. Ironically, "the
government persecution drove the more moderate members out . . . and left behind those most
inclined to conspirational activities." Goldstein, *Political Repression* at 162 (cited in note 4).

ance a broad range of conflicting interests. It needed to rally the people and sustain public morale; channel nativist fears of aliens, socialists, and anarchists; "Americanize" a new generation of immigrants during a period of intense political and social turmoil;[367] restrain vigilante "justice" and mob violence; deflect demands that the nation intern all enemy aliens and establish military tribunals to prosecute persons charged with disloyalty;* cabin powerful conservative forces that sought to manipulate charges of disloyalty to destroy the critics of capitalism; assuage the incessant demands of "superpatriots" for ever more repressive government action; and, of course, win the war.[368]

The challenge proved daunting. But even before the war, President Wilson laid the foundation for an era of repression. Wilson did not use the loyalty issue in a cynical effort to destroy his political opponents. Rather, his goal was to squelch disharmony that might impede his mission of making "the world safe for democracy." But his emotional invocations of disloyalty fed the natural fears of a nation under stress.[369]

Moreover, like Lincoln, Wilson too often overlooked the heavy-handed behavior of federal officials who acted in his name. He allowed his subordinates to inflame public hysteria, which he did little to control, and he permitted his administration to support private groups that intimidated and harassed war critics.[370] When individuals raised concerns about the suppression of civil liberties, the Wilson administration resorted to invocations of patriotism and accusations of disloyalty to stifle those concerns. The nation, after all, was at war, and Wilson took the position that it was not asking too much for people to put aside their criticisms so that the war could be prosecuted successfully.†

---

* In "the light of past experience" during the Civil War, the Department of Justice was determined to avoid the use of military tribunals to deal with citizen disloyalty. To achieve this goal, the department thought it essential for the civil law system effectively to control potential disorder. The administration also wanted to keep the internment of enemy aliens within reasonable bounds. President Wilson did not want to intern enemy aliens indiscriminately, but wanted to permit those who would "conduct themselves in accordance with law" to "be undisturbed in the peaceful pursuit of their lives and occupations." O'Brian, 42 Rep NY St Bar Assn at 276, 285–86 (cited in note 26). See also Gregory, 4 ABA J 305 (cited in note 74).

† It is useful to contrast the security measures favored by the Wilson administration with those imposed by the Lincoln administration. Unlike the Civil War measures, which Lincoln initiated mostly by executive order, Wilson's program rested in large part upon congressional approval. Moreover, whereas Lincoln relied upon the suspension of habeas corpus and martial law, Wilson relied upon the more conventional processes of criminal prosecution, thus providing more procedural regularity and greater protection of procedural rights. On the other hand, during the Civil War most prisoners were released quickly, usually as soon as the immediate danger had passed. The Espionage Act, by contrast, authorized severe terms of imprisonment. The differences in approach

The responsibility for what occurred during World War I rests less with the Congress that enacted the Espionage Act of 1917 than with the Wilson administration, which sought to exploit and manipulate public opinion; the Department of Justice, which may have meant well, but too often lacked the authority and the discipline to fulfill its aspirations; the postmaster general, who abused his authority; the federal judiciary, which rashly interpreted and applied the law, routinely meting out unconscionably harsh sentences of ten, fifteen, and twenty years' imprisonment to individuals who did nothing more than distribute seditious leaflets or make "disloyal" speeches (recall that the most severe penalty authorized by the Sedition Act of 1798 was two years' imprisonment and that Lincoln "sentenced" Vallandigham only to exile in the Confederacy);[371] the state and local officials who failed to protect dissenters; the Congress that enacted the Sedition Act of 1918; and the Supreme Court justices, who strained to excuse the government's actions. Harry Kalven has rightly described the Court's performance in this era as "simply wretched."[372]

IN THE FALL OF 1919, Alfred Bettman, John Lord O'Brian's colleague in the Department of Justice, who was in charge of enforcement of the Espionage Act, corresponded briefly with Zechariah Chafee. Bettman privately conceded that the general "atmosphere of intolerance" had led to serious constitutional violations and that this "was one of the shadows in our conduct of the war."[373] He criticized some federal judges for having "lost their heads" in Espionage Act prosecutions,[374] and he expressed admiration for Chafee and others "who, instead of joining in the mob attacks on Socialism, Bolshevism, etc., or remaining supinely silent in the face of official lawlessness," courageously took "the field" to preserve civil liberties.[375]

The following January, at the height of the Red Scare, Bettman testified before the House Committee on Rules on the question whether the nation needed more sedition laws. He answered, resoundingly, no. Drawing on his own experience, Bettman warned that such laws are inevitably accompanied by other

were probably due both to the very different domestic situations in the Civil War and in World War I (where the war itself was geographically far removed from the United States) and to Wilson's awareness "of the political pitfalls of arbitrary action." The goal in the Civil War was largely one of temporary immobilization of potentially dangerous individuals; in World War I the goal was deterrence and punishment. Scheiber, *Wilson Administration* at 12–13 (cited in note 1).

Alfred Bettman

"sinister things," such as raids on peaceable assemblies and lawless mob action. He maintained that "the man who incites a riot . . . should be held guilty," but "if you try to reach the talk of violent things, then inevitably you will reach much talk that should be allowed." He advised the committee to restrict its "suppression to inciting a crime," for then it "will really reach everything that needs to be reached."[376] He added that we had learned that "the panic, the exaggeration of the facts, the seeing of danger in . . . corners where it does not exist . . . cannot just be cut off with the signing of an armistice."[377]

In his plea for no further restraints on free expression Bettman invoked Erskine May's description of the developments in England after the French Revolution:

> [The government] learned to treat people in the spirit of tyrants. Instead of relying upon the sober judgment of the country, they appealed to its fears; and in repressing seditious practices, they were prepared to sacrifice liberty of opinion. Their policy, dictated by the circumstances of a time of strange and untried danger, was approved by the prevailing sentiment of their contemporaries; but has not been justified . . . by the maturer judgment of posterity.[378]

THE GOVERNMENT'S EXTENSIVE REPRESSION of dissent during World War I and its conduct in the immediate aftermath of the war had a significant impact on American society. It was at this moment, in a reaction to the country's excesses, that the modern civil liberties movement truly began.[379] With the benefit of hindsight, many supporters of the Wilson administration were shocked by what the nation had done.

Before the war, the philosopher-educator John Dewey, one of the leading intellectuals of his day, argued that the government's suppression of dissent was justified on grounds of pragmatism.[380] After the war, however, he wrote in the *New Republic* that "the increase of intolerance of discussion to the point of religious bigotry" had led the nation to condemn as seditious "every opinion and belief which irritates the majority of loyal citizens."[381] Dewey regretted his earlier defense of these policies. He had underestimated the determination of the American people to "grovel in the sacrifice of their liberties" in order to prove their devotion to the cause. [382]

A decade later, Dewey's ideas about freedom of speech had developed still further. He observed that the attack on freedom is most likely to come from those who are entrenched in power and who fear that the general exercise of civil liberties "will disturb the existing order." He warned that those with power tend to label challenges to the status quo as dangerously radical and subversive and that those who are dedicated to preserving civil liberties must always steel themselves to be attacked as "enemies of the nation."[383] Like many of his contemporaries, Dewey came to understand as a result of his experiences during World War I that civil liberties "go into the discard when a nation is engaged in war."[384] In 1920, Dewey became an early and prominent supporter of the ACLU.

ON DECEMBER 13, 1920, Congress quietly repealed the Sedition Act of 1918 (but the Espionage Act of 1917 remains in effect to this day).[385] Shortly after becoming attorney general in 1924, Harlan Fiske Stone ordered an end to the Bureau of Investigation's surveillance of political radicals, explaining that "a secret police may become a menace to free government and free institutions because it carries with it the possibility of abuses of power which are not always quickly apprehended or understood." "It is important," he said, that the bureau's activities be "strictly limited to the performance of those functions for

Demanding Amnesty for "Political Prisoners"

which it was created," and this would no longer include investigations of the "political or other opinions of individuals."[386]

After the war, the question arose of amnesty for those who had been convicted under the Espionage and Sedition Acts.[387] An editorial in the *Washington Times* complained that the government "has not yet handed a prison cell to a single" wartime profiteer, wealthy draft-dodger, or capitalist who had defrauded the nation on wartime contracts, while those who are in jail "did nothing against the war except talk." The paper concluded that this disparity would erode public confidence in the fair-mindedness of their government.[388]

Before leaving office in March 1919, Attorney General Gregory, on the advice of O'Brian and Bettman, recommended to President Wilson the release or reduction in sentence of two hundred prisoners then in jail for Espionage or Sedition Act convictions.[389] Gregory explained that in many of these cases injustices had been done because of the "intense patriotism" of the jurors. In other instances, he said, the sentences had been clearly "out of proportion to the offense."[390] The president accepted these recommendations. On February 1, 1921, however, Wilson, without stating his reasons, rejected the recommendation of the Department of Justice that he commute Eugene Debs's sentence.[391]

Over the next several years, sustained efforts were made, both back-channel and in public demonstrations, to secure the release of Debs and the remaining "political prisoners."[392] On Christmas Day 1921, President Harding pardoned Debs and twenty-four others. In December 1923, President Coolidge ordered the release of the remaining prisoners.[393] Senator Borah, who had worked tirelessly to secure the pardons, stated, "I am delighted that a President of the United States has discovered the First Amendment to the Constitution and has had the courage to announce the discovery."[394] In 1931, Jane Addams received the Nobel Peace Prize. Shortly thereafter, President Franklin Delano Roosevelt granted amnesty to all individuals convicted under the Espionage and Sedition Acts, restoring their full political and civil rights.[395]

THE FIREBRAND

AFTER JUDGE CLAYTON SENTENCED the defendants in *Abrams*, Mollie Steimer and her codefendants were released on bail pending appeal to the Supreme Court. Steimer immediately resumed her political activities. She joined several other young anarchists in secretly publishing the *Anarchist Soviet Bulletin*, which urged workers to strike and to seize factories with the aim of replacing a society based on economic slavery with one based on individual freedom. By September 1919, J. Edgar Hoover had decided that the twenty-year-old firebrand was too dangerous to remain free. He ordered agents of the Bureau of Investigation to find and detain her for possible deportation.

Steimer was arrested, released, rearrested, imprisoned, threatened with deportation, held at Ellis Island (where she conducted a hunger strike), released, and then arrested and imprisoned again—this time for six months in the "Workhouse" on Blackwell's Island in the East River. Because she refused to acknowledge the authority of the prison officials, she was denied all privileges—no exercise, no visitors, no mail, no books. When the prison superintendent asked her why she had been sent to the Workhouse, she replied, "Because I am fighting for freedom." (In fact, she was there because she had been convicted of disorderly conduct for distributing the *Anarchist Soviet Bulletin*.) When she persisted in advocating anarchism to her fellow prisoners, she was locked in "the cooler"—a dark, isolated cell—and placed on a ration of bread and water.

On April 30, 1920, Steimer was transferred from the Workhouse to the penitentiary in Jefferson City, Missouri, to begin serving her fifteen-year sentence. Eighteen months later, the United States ordered her deported to Russia, with the understanding that she would never again set foot in the United States. When she was informed of this action, she refused to leave the penitentiary, because there was a threatened railroad strike and she would not ride on a train run by strikebreakers. After the strike was called off, Steimer, Abrams, and their codefendants were shipped back to their native Russia.

Steimer was not eager to return to Russia. By 1921, she understood that the Russian Revolution had taken a wrong turn and moved toward a highly centralized and authoritarian state, rather than toward the ideals of anarchism. Soon after her arrival, Steimer and Senya Fleshin, a fellow anarchist who became her lifelong companion, organized a group to aid the hundreds of anarchists who were then languishing in Russian jails. Steimer was repeatedly arrested for these activities. The conditions were so grim that she again declared a hunger strike. The authorities finally offered her a choice: three years in the infamous Solovetsky Islands concentration camp in Siberia, or deportation. On September 27, 1923, Russia deported Mollie Steimer to Germany. Few other people have the distinction of having been deported by *both* the United States *and* the Soviet Union.

In Berlin, Steimer renewed her relief work on behalf of fellow anarchist exiles from all over Europe. In 1933, when Hitler came to power, she fled to Paris. Her Jewish and anarchist identities caught up with her, however, and after the Nazis occupied France she and Fleshin escaped to Mexico.

When she was deported from the United States in 1921, Steimer vowed to remain true to her beliefs. During her years in Mexico, she maintained her correspondence with her anarchist comrades around the world. She died of a heart attack on July 23, 1980, at her home in Cuernavaca. Of the five defendants in *Abrams*, only Steimer died a committed anarchist; the others succumbed to disillusionment or pragmatism. She was eighty-two years old at her death. She had fought selflessly and courageously throughout her life for her principles and for what she believed to be a world of freedom, equality, and dignity.[396]

WORLD WAR II

"Nothing to Fear"?

German-American Bund Rally in 1939

*A*FTER THE EXCESSES of World War I, a more expansive view of free expression began to emerge. Between 1920 and 1940, Americans confronted a broad range of divisive issues, including Prohibition, contraception, evolution, labor reform, the Sacco and Vanzetti prosecution,* and the economic and social upheaval caused by the Great Depression. These conflicts gradually fostered a new social awareness and a heightened understanding of the earlier suppression of dissent.[1] Americans increasingly came to recognize that World War I era dissenters had not been as menacing as they had been led to believe, and they increasingly discussed the protection of civil liberties as a civic responsibility. This was reflected in new attitudes in government, the academy, the media, and the courts.[2]

---

* In May 1920, Nicola Sacco and Bartolomeo Vanzetti were accused of murdering two men during the course of a payroll robbery in South Braintree, Massachusetts. Neither Sacco nor Vanzetti had any prior criminal record, but they were well known to the authorities as anarchist militants who had been extensively involved in labor strikes, political agitation, and antiwar propaganda. The criminal trial focused on their political views and soon became an international cause célèbre. After a notorious trial, during which the themes of patriotism and radicalism were sharply contested, the jury found Sacco and Vanzetti guilty of robbery and murder in July 1921.

This marked only the beginning of a lengthy legal struggle to save the two men. There was evidence of perjury by prosecution witnesses and credible proof that others had committed the crime. Felix Frankfurter, then a law professor at Harvard, rallied "respectable" opinion behind the two men as a test of the rule of law itself. On the other side were those who were committed to defending the honor of the American justice system and to upholding "law and order." Finally, on August 23, 1927, Sacco and Vanzetti were put to death. By then, the dignity of the two men had turned them into powerful symbols of social justice for many throughout the world.

Nowhere was this shift more evident than in the Supreme Court. In two significant decisions in the 1920s, *Gitlow v. New York*[3] and *Whitney v. California*,[4] the Court considered the constitutionality of state laws making it a crime for any individual or organization to advocate the violent overthrow of government. Although the Court upheld these laws, it also, for the first time, seriously engaged the First Amendment. Echoing Judge Learned Hand's approach in *Masses*, the Court in *Gitlow* and *Whitney* emphasized that the challenged laws did not penalize "the advocacy of changes in the form of government by constitutional and lawful means," but only the express advocacy of "the overthrow of organized government by *unlawful* means."[5] The Court clearly implied that utterances that stopped short of express advocacy of criminal conduct would pose a different constitutional question.

Equally important, Justices Holmes and Brandeis continued to hammer away at the majority on the question of clear and present danger.[6] Brandeis's concurring opinion in *Whitney* in 1927 merits particular attention. In an eloquent passage, Brandeis set forth his view of the intentions and beliefs of the framers of the Constitution:

> Those who won our independence believed . . . liberty to be the secret of happiness and courage to be the secret of liberty. They believed that freedom to think as you will and to speak as you think are means indispensable to the discovery and spread of political truth; that without free speech and assembly discussion would be futile; that with them, discussion affords ordinarily adequate protection against the dissemination of noxious doctrine; that the greatest menace to freedom is an inert people; that public discussion is a political duty; and that this should be a fundamental principle of the American government.[7]

Brandeis then explained how these beliefs gave meaning to the First Amendment:

> Those who won our independence by revolution were not cowards. They did not fear political change. They did not exalt order at the cost of liberty. To courageous, self-reliant men, with confidence in the power of free and fearless reasoning applied through the processes of popular government, no danger flowing from speech can be deemed clear and present, unless the incidence of the evil apprehended is so imminent that it may befall before there is opportunity for full discussion. If there be time to expose through discussion the falsehood and fallacies, to avert the evil by the processes of education, the remedy to be applied is more speech, not enforced silence. Only an emergency can justify repression. . . .[8]

Unlike the speech at issue in *Schenck*, *Debs*, and *Masses*, the Communist Labor Party, at issue in *Whitney*, expressly advocated "unlawful acts of force [and] violence" as a "means of accomplishing . . . political change." Going beyond

Learned Hand, Brandeis argued that even advocacy of law "violation, however reprehensible morally, is not a justification for denying free speech where . . . there is nothing to indicate that the advocacy would be immediately acted on."[9]

Although Holmes and Brandeis still spoke only for themselves in these cases, their arguments began to take hold. From 1919 to 1927, a period bracketed by the decisions in *Schenck* and *Whitney*, the Court decided nine cases concerning the First Amendment, in all of which it rejected the constitutional argument.[10] Between 1927 and the beginning of World War II, however, the Court consistently sustained First Amendment claims.[11] Increasingly, it invoked the "clear and present danger" standard that had been so forcefully articulated by Holmes and Brandeis.[12]

In 1940, for example, the Court observed in *Cantwell v. Connecticut* that "sharp differences" often arise in the realm of political debate, for the "tenets of one man may seem the rankest error to his neighbor." Indeed, to "persuade others to his own point of view," a committed advocate may resort to "exaggeration, to vilification . . . and even to false statement." The Court explained that, despite such "excesses," the "people of this nation have ordained" that the freedom of speech is "essential to enlightened opinion" and that speech therefore may not be restricted in the absence of "a clear and present danger to a substantial interest of the State."[13] A year later, on the very eve of World War II, the Court made clear that it had established the principle that "before utterances can be punished" the "substantive evil must be extremely serious and the degree of imminence extremely high."[14] The Court had come a long way in the twenty years since *Schenck*, *Debs*, and *Abrams*.

PUBLIC DISCOURSE ABOUT FREE EXPRESSION also took a sharp turn from what it had been two decades earlier. In 1938, the *Wall Street Journal* published an editorial entitled "Liberty and Tolerance," which explained that "[i]t is for the citizen to keep unsleeping watch on civil liberty" and "to demand, most of all, Justice Holmes's 'tolerance for the thought we hate.'"[15]

The following year, the historian Henry Steele Commager, adverting to developments in Europe, warned of "ominous" times ahead. Seeking guidance in history, he asked whether any circumstance short of a threat to the very existence of the state could justify the suspension of civil liberties. Commager characterized the Sedition Act of 1798 as "political in character" and noted that its primary effect had been to inspire opposition and hasten "the triumph of Jeffersonian democracy." He described the Civil War as the one true emergency in the nation's history, the one "real threat" to our "national existence." But even in this crisis, he noted, Congress had not enacted a sedition law. Commager marveled that during the Civil War the government had permitted an "astonishing" freedom of criticism.

In contrast, Commager observed that during World War I the government had adopted laws under the pretext of "war necessity" that equated criticism of the war with disloyalty. He asserted that the enforcement of the Espionage Act had seriously undermined "the cause of democracy, for which the war was ostensibly fought," and added, "If there is any moral to be drawn from this historical review it is that suspension of the Bill of Rights, even in the face of emergency, is neither necessary nor wise." "The real danger," he explained, comes "from apathy, from a failure to comprehend the issues involved in any question of free inquiry, from misdirected patriotism which seeks to regiment thought." It "comes from those who believe that the way to fight anti-Americanism is to impose their own brand of Americanism on their fellow citizens." "Our task," he concluded, "is an educational one."[16]

That same year, Attorney General Frank Murphy explained that the "maintenance of civil liberties" is one of the "bulwarks of democracy." To make this more than mere rhetoric, he established a new Civil Liberties Unit in the Department of Justice to ensure that the rights of citizens, however unpopular, would be vigorously defended by the federal government.[17] Murphy pledged "the aggressive protection of the fundamental rights" of the American people.[18]

Shortly after Pearl Harbor, even as the perils of another world war faced the nation, Charles Seymour, the president of Yale University, published an influential essay in the *New York Times* reminding Americans that it is in periods of national emergency when free speech is most essential, for it is in precisely such moments "when the issues which confront government should be settled, for the sake of national safety, not by emotion or by force, but by reason."

Seymour acknowledged that government must be free to act with authority in a crisis and must not be unduly "hampered by the distractions of domestic agitators." But free speech, he warned, should be restricted only if it "actually threatens the security of the state." Pointing to the experience in World War I, he cautioned that the past held a "warning for the future." Echoing Commager, he concluded that the best way to avoid repeating the mistakes of the past was to foster a "public opinion which accords with the spirit of the First Amendment."[19]

Would this new attitude toward free speech hold in a wartime atmosphere? World War II presented a problem very different from that of World War I, when there had been no direct attack on the United States. Dissenters could, and did, argue that the nation did not *need* to go to war in 1917. After Pearl Harbor, however, Americans felt the United States had no choice but to declare war. They were therefore generally united in common cause. In terms of tolerance of what little dissent existed, this could cut in one of two ways. Either Americans could more comfortably tolerate dissent, which could readily be dismissed as misguided, but not dangerous; or they could bluntly crush dissent because war opponents were so marginal that their suppression would hardly be noticed. In this sense, World War II posed an issue quite distinct from those posed in 1798, 1861, or 1917.

TO AVOID THE MISTAKES OF THE PAST

ON JANUARY 4, 1940, Franklin Delano Roosevelt nominated Attorney General Frank Murphy as a justice of the Supreme Court, Solicitor General Robert H. Jackson as Murphy's successor as attorney general, and Assistant Attorney General Francis Biddle as Jackson's successor as solicitor general. It would fall largely to these three men to shape the nation's approach to civil liberties during World War II. Although Murphy, Jackson, and Biddle came from quite different backgrounds, each had learned the lessons of World War I, each was a committed civil libertarian, and each came into office determined to avoid the mistakes of the past.

BORN IN 1890 in Sand Beach, Michigan, Frank Murphy adored his mother and respected his father, a country lawyer who was active in local Democratic politics. In an effort to instill a Jeffersonian philosophy in his son, Murphy's father often read him the Declaration of Independence and the Constitution. Mary Murphy taught her children tolerance and infused in them a disdain for racial and religious prejudice. Years later, Murphy told Louis Brandeis that because of his upbringing he had decided as a child to "thrust [his] lance at intolerance."[20]

After graduating from the University of Michigan, Murphy embarked upon the practice of law, first in Sand Beach with his father and then with a small firm in Detroit. He soon developed a fascination for politics. In 1917, he noted, "It would not take much to make a socialist out of me."[21] With the outbreak of war in Europe, Murphy argued that the United States should maintain its neutrality and "avoid the horrible consequences of war." He was, he said, "dead set" against American intervention. Once President Wilson asked for a declaration of war, however, Murphy enlisted and served as a lieutenant in the infantry.[22]

After the war, Murphy returned to Detroit as an assistant U.S. attorney. In November 1919, as the Palmer raids struck Detroit with a fury, Justice Department officials swept up 450 suspected members of the Union of Russian Workers, an anarchist organization whose manifesto advocated revolution, but whose primary function in Detroit was as a social and educational club. At the time, Murphy supported the government's handling of these "radicals." He wrote his mother, "I sympathize deeply with down-trodden people," but "I have no sympathy with the foreigner who comes to this country and conspires to overthrow the government."[23] With time, however, his view began to change. Seven years later, at a meeting protesting the prosecution of Sacco and Vanzetti, Murphy warned of "the appetite for tyranny" and invoked the abuses of the Red Scare to illustrate the danger. He recalled that the Palmer raids had brutally flouted civil liberties.*[24]

Murphy was elected to Detroit's criminal court in 1923, a position he held for six years. As a judge, he was in the vanguard of progressive legal thought on such issues as bail reform and the "rehabilitative" goal of the criminal law. In 1925, he presided over a sensational murder trial that arose out of the effort of white mobs to prevent blacks from moving into a white neighborhood. Clarence Darrow represented the black defendants, charged with shooting whites who had attacked them. The prosecution resulted in a hung jury, and Murphy's conduct of the trial brought him national publicity. As one commentator noted, the "young judge" had succeeded in ensuring the fairest trial "ever accorded a Negro in this country."[25]

As the Depression crushed Detroit, Murphy was elected mayor in 1930. He made a solid record by supporting organized labor, civil liberties, and the city's responsibility to care for the poor. He joined the board of directors of the NAACP, even though this was politically perilous, and he insisted that Detroit be "notable" for its protection of free speech. His response to those who demanded that he jail Communists was that the best way to deal with communism was to give "better service to the people."[26] Although Detroit suffered several violent demonstrations during Murphy's tenure, he worked closely with Roger Baldwin and the American Civil Liberties Union to maintain a robust commitment to free expression.

In 1933, President Roosevelt appointed Murphy governor-general of the Philippines. He provided the Philippines with a comprehensive program of

---

* In the summer of 1923, after Murphy had returned to private practice, he represented a lawyer who had been sentenced to prison and disbarred for refusing to register for the draft during World War I. In arguing for the lawyer's readmission to the bar, Murphy argued that "the profession needs men who are willing to suffer for their conscience. Also ten years hence we may say he was right about the war." Letter from Frank Murphy to Hester Everard, July 14, 1923, excerpted in Fine, *Detroit Years* at 78 (cited in note 20).

health and social services, a modern criminal justice system, and a new commitment to civil liberties. In 1934, he issued executive orders prohibiting the police from interfering with "public assemblies" except "in extreme cases of grave public emergency."[27]

In 1936, Roosevelt asked Murphy to return to the United States to run for governor. Roosevelt believed that he would lose Michigan, a traditional Republican stronghold, unless Murphy agreed to head the state ticket. Eager to continue his climb in the Democratic Party, Murphy took the risk. Promising to provide Michigan with "the most progressive government of any state in the Union," he won a convincing victory and Roosevelt carried the state.[28]

In 1938, however, Murphy was defeated for reelection as Michigan returned to its more familiar Republican bent. In the course of this campaign, Murphy was endorsed by the Communist Party. As a result, he was tarred as a Communist by his Republican opponent and by the House Committee on Un-American Activities. He refused to disavow the endorsement, explaining that citizens had a right to endorse anyone they chose.[29] The following year, recognizing his debt to Murphy, Roosevelt appointed him attorney general of the United States.

ROBERT H. JACKSON WAS BORN in 1892 in a farmhouse in Spring Creek, Pennsylvania. Jackson's father was a rugged individualist and an outspoken Democrat in a Republican farming community. He passed on his determined independence to his son.[30] After graduating from high school, Jackson decided on a career in the law. Three years later, at the age of twenty-one, he was sworn in as a member of the New York bar. Jackson's formal education included no college and only one year of law school, but he was a voracious reader of history, biography, and the classics. He settled in Jamestown, New York, a town of 31,000.

Over the next twenty years, Jackson developed a flourishing small-town law practice. He represented a broad spectrum of clients, ranging, as he put it, from "railroads . . . to Negroes, to bankers to poor whites." He earned a reputation as the most gifted advocate in western New York and developed a profound sense of the role of the lawyer in American society. When rights "are threatened," he observed, they are worth only "what some lawyer makes them worth." "Civil liberties," he added, "are those which some lawyer, respected by his neighbors, will stand up to defend."[31]

During World War I, Jackson believed that the United States was wrong to "draft a conscript [army] to send to Europe," a position he openly advocated. This was a courageous and even dangerous stance in small-town America during the patriotic fervor of the Great War.[32] Francis Biddle later observed that "Jackson could not forget his experience" during World War I. He despised the German baiting, the vigilante groups, and the criminal prosecutions of individuals who had done nothing more than criticize the war. As a young lawyer, he stood tall "against the flood of hysteria."[33]

As governor of New York, Franklin Roosevelt had been much impressed with Jackson's legal ability and reputation for integrity. In 1934, to Jackson's surprise, President Roosevelt recruited him to Washington to serve as general counsel for the Bureau of Internal Revenue. Two years later, Roosevelt appointed him assistant attorney general in charge of the Tax Division. Jackson quickly became an effective advocate for the New Deal, a respected voice within the administration, and a valued adviser to the president. In 1938, Roosevelt appointed him solicitor general of the United States, the chief advocate for the nation before the Supreme Court. Justice Louis Brandeis so admired Jackson's skill as an advocate that he once quipped to Felix Frankfurter that "Jackson should be Solicitor General for life."[34] Roosevelt had different plans for him.

When Roosevelt appointed Attorney General Frank Murphy to the Supreme Court on January 4, 1940, he tapped Jackson to succeed Murphy as attorney general. Eighteen months later, Roosevelt appointed Jackson to the Supreme Court.

FRANCIS BIDDLE WAS A DIRECT DESCENDANT of Edmund Randolph, the first attorney general of the United States. Two of Biddle's other ancestors, Judge Charles J. Biddle and George W. Biddle, had made "bold, able and eloquent" speeches in support of Clement Vallandigham's constitutional rights during the Civil War.[35] Biddle was raised in the highest reaches of Philadelphia society. Born in Paris in 1886 during a family vacation, Biddle spent summers in Maine, traveled often in Europe, and was educated at Groton (where he came to know Franklin Roosevelt) and Harvard. After graduating from Harvard Law School in 1911, he was selected to serve as law clerk to Justice Oliver Wendell Holmes. During his year at Holmes's side, Biddle was first exposed to the Progressive movement. He became an ardent admirer of Theodore Roosevelt and fast friends with the young Felix Frankfurter.

After completing his heady year in Washington, Biddle returned to Philadelphia to practice law in the firm his father had founded. Although this was a decidedly upper-crust practice, Biddle insisted on devoting time both to legal aid and to the representation of criminal defendants. He was determined to enlarge the limits of his "background and education."[36] Over the next twenty years, he built a highly successful law practice, interrupted only by a brief enlistment in the Army during World War I and an uneventful term as an assistant U.S. attorney in Philadelphia.

In 1934, Biddle accepted appointment to a state commission to investigate the conduct of public and private police forces during coal strikes in western

Pennsylvania. He later reflected that this experience had had a profound effect on him. It gave him new insight into the "dismal conditions" under which the miners worked and a new awareness of "the shocking extent to which the law could be distorted by the authorities when the unlawful exercise of power was opposed."[37]

Later that year, President Roosevelt appointed Biddle chairman of the National Labor Relations Board. Five years later, Roosevelt named him to the U.S. Court of Appeals for the Third Circuit, a position Biddle did not want. Biddle complained that being a judge would be too much "like retiring." Roosevelt sympathized and told Biddle not to fret, because he had other things in mind for him. The following year, Roosevelt appointed him solicitor general of the United States, succeeding Robert Jackson in the post.

In 1940, when Roosevelt appointed Jackson to the Supreme Court, Jackson recommended to Roosevelt that he appoint Biddle to succeed him as attorney general. Roosevelt had reservations. Biddle was known to be an active civil libertarian. He had condemned, among other things, "the extravagant . . . prosecutions for sedition" as a "serious example of hysteria in the First World War."[38] Roosevelt feared that Biddle might not be sufficiently tough to cope with the demands of a wartime environment. After leaving Biddle dangling for several months as acting attorney general, Roosevelt finally relented and appointed him attorney general of the United States. Three months later, the Japanese bombed Pearl Harbor.

THE DIES COMMITTEE

WITH THE DEPRESSION, and the advent of fascism in Europe, new fringe movements came to challenge the central tenets of American society. On the left, the Communist Party of the United States, formed after World War I, gained significant support during the misery of the 1930s. On the right, a disparate array of fascist organizations, united by a fervent anti-Semitism and a fear of moral decline, sprang into being. The most visible of these fascist organizations was the German-American Bund, whose members sported Nazi-style uniforms and aped the Hitler salute. In 1935, a House committee proposed legislation to prohibit such groups from inciting disaffection with American institutions and values, but, reflecting the more open spirit of the times, this proposal was resoundingly defeated in Congress.[39]

With the rumblings of war in Europe, however, these organizations increasingly tested the depth of America's renewed commitment to tolerance. In the late 1930s, groups such as the Non-Sectarian Anti-Nazi League and Friends of

Democracy (whose advisory board included John Dewey, Thomas Mann, and Paul Douglas) came into existence with the goal of thwarting American-based fascism.

Members of these antifascist groups worried, as Sinclair Lewis had suggested in *It Can't Happen Here*, that Americans, who had grown accustomed to being duped by con men and ad artists, would be vulnerable to fascist propaganda.[40] Even traditional liberals, who had long championed civil liberties, were now calling for a halt to "anti-democratic propaganda."[41]

IN APRIL 1937, Representative Samuel Dickstein, who had made a name for himself campaigning against "Nazi rats, spies and agents," proposed that the House establish a new committee to investigate un-American propaganda. The House defeated his proposal by a vote of 184 to 38.[42] A year later, in May 1938, as the situation in Europe deteriorated, the House again considered this proposal. Opponents argued that such a committee would be a "fake side show" and do nothing but gain headlines for its members.[43] Supporters exhorted the House to save the country before it was too late.[44]

On May 26, the House voted to convene the House Un-American Activities Committee, by a vote of 191 to 41. Chaired by Representative Martin Dies of Texas, HUAC was charged with investigating "the extent, character and objects of un-American propaganda activities in the United States."[45] The *New Republic* described Dies as "physically a giant, very young, ambitious, and cocksure." He was in a hurry to make a national reputation. During the six years of its existence, the Dies Committee brought to light issues of legitimate public concern, but also proved that in reckless hands legislative investigating committees can do untold damage to innocent persons and national values.

The Dies Committee planned initially to focus on the German-American Bund, which had gained substantial membership from 1936 to 1938 under the leadership of Fritz Julius Kuhn. Born in Munich in 1895, Kuhn, a chemist, had fought in the German army and been an early member of the Nazi Party in the 1920s. Arriving in the United States in 1927, he became a citizen in 1933 and founded the Bund in 1936.[46] He wore black leather jackboots and insisted on being called the *Bundesleiter*.

Amid flowing swastikas and American flags, Kuhn proclaimed that the Bund was "a militant group of patriotic Americans" determined to stand fast against "[r]acial [i]ntermixture" and the "liberal-pacifist forces undermining" the traditional values of the United States.[47] Members of the Bund were required to pledge that they were "of Aryan descent, free of Jewish or colored racial traces."[48] Under Kuhn's leadership, the Bund grew to 25,000 members by 1938. Most Bund members had been born in Germany, and about half were still German citizens. The Bund published several newspapers, such as *Der Stürmer* and *Deutscher Weckruf und Beobachter*. Much of the material consisted of propaganda produced by the Nazi Party in Germany. The Bund also established youth camps to inculcate children in Nazi philosophy.[49]

Although it was widely suspected that the Bund was merely a front for Nazi Germany, its activities so alarmed some members of the American public that the German government on March 1, 1938, officially cut all ties to the Bund on the ground that it was "an unfortunate embarrassment."[50] Nonetheless, the Bund remained active, and in 1939 it drew 32,000 enthusiastic supporters to a rally in New York's Madison Square Garden.

As it turned out, however, the Dies Committee directed most of its attention not at the Nazis but at Communists. Dies was eager to expose alleged Communist "influences" in the New Deal. HUAC launched extensive investigations of liberal organizations whose activities it tarred as "un-American." Dies charged that Democratic candidates in Minnesota and California, who had been endorsed by the Communist Party, had "Communistic affiliations," that the American Civil Liberties Union was "a Communist-controlled organization that served the Party under the guise of preserving democracy," and that Eleanor Roosevelt was "one of the most valuable assets . . . the Communist Party possess[es]."[51]

The Dies Committee's proceedings were often wildly irresponsible and, as a consequence, were given spectacular coverage by the media. The first volume of the committee's hearings named 640 organizations, 483 newspapers, and 280 labor organizations as "Communistic," including the Boy Scouts, the ACLU, the Catholic Association for International Peace, and the Camp Fire Girls. The committee was especially concerned about Communist infiltration of Hollywood. "One witness . . . suggested that Shirley Temple . . . served communist interests."[52] Another charged that Frank Murphy, then the Democratic governor of Michigan, was "working hand in glove with the Communistic element in the unions."[53] Murphy denounced the committee for spreading "untruths" and labeled it "un-American and vicious."[54] Dies later accused Attorney General Robert Jackson of endorsing Communist organizations.[55] As the hearings progressed, the press reveled in these charges, although some newspapers labeled the proceedings "[p]oppycock" and "an orgy of . . . fantastic accusations."[56]

Anticipating the conduct of Joseph McCarthy a decade later, Dies repeatedly attacked members of the Roosevelt administration, especially Secretary of the Interior Harold Ickes and Secretary of Labor Frances Perkins, whom he accused of having "radical associates" (more specifically, he accused Ickes of membership in the ACLU). Dies demanded their resignation or dismissal, and in one particularly virulent speech included them in a list of "purveyors of class hatred," which he said was headed by Josef Stalin. Asked about these charges, President Roosevelt answered, "Ho-hum."[57]

HUAC aggressively used public disclosure as a political tactic. In October 1939, Dies announced that he had the names of "2,000 of the 4,700 Communists in the Chicago area."[58] Later that month, the committee publicly released the names of all government employees in Washington, D.C., who were members of the American League for Peace and Democracy, which the committee branded a "Communist front organization." This triggered an outraged response. Congressman John J. Dempsey of New Mexico declared that the committee's publication of this list was "un-American" and charged that Dies had "done a damnable thing." In defense of the committee's action, Congressman Jacob Thorkelson of Montana retorted that those who objected must be in sympathy with subversive activities.[59] President Roosevelt described the committee's conduct as "sordid."[60]

In 1941, Dies submitted to the attorney general a list of 1,121 federal employees who he claimed were "either communists or affiliates of subversive organizations."[61] He asserted that there were "six million Communist and Nazi sympathizers" in the United States and that they "constituted a real menace" to the national security.[62]

The FBI investigated the committee's charge of subversive infiltration of the

Congressman Martin Dies Attacks FDR on Radio

federal government and emphatically rejected HUAC's claims. Attorney General Biddle labeled the committee's charges "clearly unfounded" and declared that they should "never have been submitted for investigation" in the first place.[63] Dies responded by labeling the Department of Justice's investigation a farce. He accused Biddle of favoring the federal employment of subversives and vowed to continue his own service as the "one serious obstacle" to domestic subversion.[64]

Despite its excesses, the committee remained popular with the public.*[65] Although the press often criticized its use of "methods which offend against the very standards and traditions" it was designed to uphold, they also found many of its revelations helpful.[66] Walter Lippmann reflected on this dilemma in 1940, observing that the committee's conduct posed the "ancient moral question of whether the end justifies the means." Lippmann argued that although the committee was addressing a "formidable evil," its processes violated fundamental standards of American morality.[67] Franklin Roosevelt, who was also ambivalent about the Dies Committee, indulged in what one critic has labeled "the rhetoric of condemnation and the policies of appeasement."[68] It was precisely this sort of ambivalence that eventually gave rise to the unrestrained abuses of the Cold War and the era of McCarthyism.

THE SMITH ACT AND J. EDGAR HOOVER

As WE SAW IN CHAPTER 3, after the excesses of World War I Attorney General Harlan Fiske Stone warned of the dangers of allowing federal law enforcement officials to investigate political beliefs and associations. In August 1936, however, President Roosevelt, in disregard of this warning, secretly authorized J. Edgar Hoover to investigate suspected fascists and Communists in the United States. This assignment, which reflected Roosevelt's capacious view of his powers and his occasional indifference to civil liberties,[69] was welcomed by Hoover as an open invitation to reinitiate many of the tactics he had employed during the Red Scare.

Born in 1895, Hoover grew up on Capitol Hill, the son and grandson of government officials. After completing law school, Hoover asked his uncle, a friend

---

* In December of 1938, for example, 74 percent of the public supported the continuation of the investigation. *Dies Investigation Favored in Survey*, New York Times 62 (Dec 11, 1938). The committee's public support remained above 60 percent throughout its existence. In 1940, the House voted 344 to 21 to continue the committee. See Ogden, *Dies Committee* at 113, 183 (cited in note 45).

of John Lord O'Brian, to help secure him a position in the Department of Justice. Enthusiastic, straitlaced, and energetic, Hoover rose rapidly through the ranks. In less than a year, he was promoted to lead the Justice Department's new Enemy Alien Registration Section, giving him his first real taste of administrative power. In 1919, as the Red Scare exploded across the nation, Attorney General A. Mitchell Palmer appointed Hoover director of the new General Intelligence Division of the Bureau of Investigation and authorized him to lead the crusade against anti-American radicalism. Hoover, who had worked as a librarian at the Library of Congress for four years to pay for his education, immediately set up a complex filing system to collect and index information about every radical leader, organization, and publication in the nation.

After Attorney General Stone promoted him to head the Bureau of Investigation in 1924, Hoover continued his evolution into the consummate government bureaucrat. He was obsessively organized, moralistic, incorruptible, and brilliant at building alliances, protecting turf, and undermining his enemies. Adapting to the times, Hoover in the early 1930s refocused the bureau's activities away from political radicals and toward gangsters, as men like John Dillinger, "Pretty Boy" Floyd, and "Machine Gun" Kelly captured the public's imagination. A master publicist, Hoover used newspapers, magazines, books, and movies to glorify the "G-Man" and establish himself as a national celebrity. Increasingly, he viewed himself as the behind-the-scenes guardian of the nation's morals.[70]

Seizing the opening Roosevelt presented in 1936 to enable the bureau to return to its earlier ways, Hoover confidentially instructed his agents "to obtain from all possible sources information concerning subversive activities being conducted in the United States by Communists, Fascists and representatives" of other subversive organizations,[71] defining "subversive activities" as including, among other things, "the distribution of literature . . . opposed to the American way of life."[72]

The FBI promptly established an aggressive informer program and a massive system of classification. In effect, Hoover resumed his activities where Attorney General Stone had ordered them terminated twelve years earlier. In a 1938 memorandum, Hoover stressed the need to preserve the "utmost degree of secrecy in order to avoid criticisms." Conceding that undercover investigations of political beliefs were "repugnant to the American people," he explained that it would be unwise to seek special legislation that might focus attention on the government's plan to develop a program of such magnitude.[73] That same year, Hoover informed Roosevelt that the FBI had compiled an index of 2,500 probable subversives.[74]

The following year, Hoover sent a confidential memo to all FBI offices "informing [his] agents that the FBI was 'preparing a list of individuals, both aliens and citizens, . . . [whose] presence . . . in this country in time of war or national emergency would be dangerous to the public peace and the safety of the United

States government.'" These names had been obtained from subscription lists of German, Italian, and Communist newspapers, membership in various lawful organizations, and informant reports on attendance at public meetings and demonstrations.[75]

The outbreak of war in Europe in September 1939 forced the FBI's actions into the open, and in November 1939 Hoover revealed to a House subcommittee that the FBI had revived the General Intelligence Division.[76] Hoover disclosed that the division had "compiled extensive indices of individuals, groups and organizations engaged in . . . subversive" and other activities that might be "detrimental to the internal security of the United States."[77]

Upon learning of this development, Senator George Norris of Nebraska angrily responded that the FBI "exists only to investigate violations of law," not to gather information about potentially dangerous individuals. He warned that these activities "are going to bring into disrepute the methods of our entire system of jurisprudence."[78] Defending the Department of Justice against this accusation, Attorney General Jackson replied, "One of the first steps which I took upon assuming office was to review the activities and attitude of the Federal Bureau of Investigation" and to reaffirm "the principles which Attorney General Stone laid down in 1924." He naïvely assured Congress that Director Hoover agreed with those principles and that he and Hoover fully understood that the "usefulness of the Bureau depends upon a faithful adherence to those limitations."[*][79]

Several years later, Attorney General Biddle informed Hoover that there was no legal justification for keeping a "custodial detention" list of citizens, that the classification system used by the FBI was inherently flawed, and that Hoover's list should "not be used for any purpose whatsoever." Hoover, however, simply renamed the project and directed his agents to continue their work. He cautioned that this program "should at no time be mentioned or alluded to in investigative reports discussed with agencies or individuals outside the Bureau."[80]

THE SIGNING OF THE NAZI-SOVIET nonaggression pact on August 23, 1939, once again inflamed the nation against communism.[81] Following charges by the Dies Committee that the Federal Writers Project and the Fed-

---

[*] In May 1940, Roosevelt began sending Hoover hundreds of names and addresses of individuals who had written to him criticizing his foreign policy; in 1941, he directed Hoover to investigate individuals who opposed his Lend-Lease program. Goldstein, *Political Repression* at 250–51 (cited in note 42).

eral Theater Project were riddled with Communists,[82] Congress added a proviso to an appropriations bill prohibiting the disbursement of any funds to "any person who advocates, or who is a member of an organization that advocates the overthrow of the government . . . through force or violence." Later that year, in the Hatch Act,[83] Congress banned from federal employment any person who is a member of "any political party or organization" that advocates the "overthrow of our constitutional form of government."[84]

The shocking fall of France half a year later triggered a sense of alarm and vulnerability in the United States. Germany's stunning victory was attributed, especially by the humiliated French military, to the work of a "fifth column" of Nazi and Communist sympathizers within France. Congress promptly reenacted the Espionage Act of 1917, making its provisions applicable for the first time in peacetime,[85] and in a move reminiscent of John Adams and Woodrow Wilson, President Roosevelt quickly exploited the "treacherous use of the Fifth Column" in a 1940 message to Congress, in which he sought substantial increases in defense appropriations.[86]

As even civil libertarians began to rethink the role of civil liberties in an increasingly dangerous world,*[87] Congress passed the Alien Registration Act of 1940 (the Smith Act), which required all resident aliens to register with the government, streamlined the procedures for deportation, and forbade any person "knowingly or willfully" to "advocate, abet, advise, or teach the duty, necessity, desirability, or propriety of overthrowing or destroying any government in the United States by force or violence."[88] In practical effect, this was the sedition act Attorney General Palmer had failed to persuade Congress to pass in 1920.[89]

The act sailed through Congress without any serious opposition. The general view, in the words of Representative John J. Dempsey, was that opponents of the act, like Roger Baldwin of the ACLU, were "mealy-mouthed Americans."[90] Representative Emmanuel Celler of Brooklyn, who initially opposed the bill, eventually signed on, stating that "[i]n fear of a worse bill, we must accept" this one.[91]

Perhaps the most interesting statement in support of the Smith Act was made by its sponsor, Representative Howard W. Smith of Virginia: "We have heard a lot of talk here about abusing the poor alien. The gentlemen who have been talking

---

* Leading liberals, such as Walter Lippmann, and leading liberal journals, such as the *New Republic*, began giving the Dies Committee their support, and the American educational establishment began purging suspected Communist teachers. The National Education Association initiated a major campaign to expose subversive teachings, and in 1940 the ACLU decided to bar from its governing committees or staff any person "who is a member of any political organization which supports totalitarian dictatorship." See Steele, *Good War* at 74–75 (cited in note 1); Goldstein, *Political Repression* at 257–62 (cited in note 42).

that way cannot complain about this section. We have laws against aliens who advocate the overthrow of this Government by force, but do you know that there is nothing in the world to prevent a treasonable American citizen from doing so?"[92] The Smith Act "leveled" the playing field.

President Roosevelt declined to veto the Smith Act, insisting that its advocacy provisions could "hardly . . . constitute an improper encroachment on civil liberties in the light of present world conditions."[93] As we shall see, this was typical of Roosevelt's view of civil liberties. In general, he supported them in the abstract, but not when they got in his way.[94] Zechariah Chafee warned that the Smith Act was a "loaded revolver."[95] There were only two prosecutions under the Smith Act during World War II, largely because Attorneys General Murphy, Jackson, and Biddle opposed the law.[96] But, as Chafee had cautioned, the act would prove to be a weapon at the ready for the future.

"WHEN ARE YOU GOING TO INDICT THE SEDITIONISTS?"

THE OUTBREAK OF HOSTILITIES in Europe on September 1, 1939, created a mood of high anxiety in the United States. Attorney General Murphy declared that there would be no witch hunt for subversives, but he emphasized that there would be "no laxity" either. Pressured by the Dies Committee's incessant accusations that the Roosevelt administration was lax on radicals,[97] and "by clear signals" from the president, who insisted upon a "no-nonsense approach to un-Americanism," Murphy promised Roosevelt that he would demonstrate that "we are not a soft, pudgy democracy."[98]

As war engulfed the European theater, conservatives lost no time in pressing for harsher measures. Martin Dies publicly insisted that Murphy prosecute Communist and Bundist organizations and Congressman J. Parnell Thomas, a member of the Dies Committee, chastised Murphy for being "listless" in his prosecution of un-American activities. Dies warned Murphy that if he failed to act, the House Committee on Un-American Activities would act for him.

As if to underscore the point, in October 1939 Dies released the names of 563 government employees who were members of the American League for Peace and Democracy. He demanded that Murphy prosecute these individuals as agents of "the Communist International." Murphy refused to do so, reminding Dies that although it was his "duty and intention" to prosecute those who violated the law, it was also the duty of the Department of Justice to refrain from any actions that might violate "the fundamental rights and privileges of free assembly, free opinion, and free speech."[99]

Murphy was not always so stalwart, however. Under constant pressure from Roosevelt to placate Dies and to defuse criticisms that the administration was soft on Communists and Bundists, Murphy ordered the arrest in January 1940 of the leaders of the Christian Front, a virulently anti-Semitic group with several thousand members in the New York area. The government prosecuted seventeen members of this group on the theory that they had conspired to establish "by force of arms" a Nazi rule in the United States. J. Edgar Hoover charged that the defendants planned to "knock off about a dozen Congressmen" and "blow up the goddam Police Department." There was little evidence of guilt, however, and the jury refused to convict. After succeeding Murphy as attorney general, Robert Jackson observed that the charge was "a bit fantastic."[100]

Jackson also inherited from Murphy an indictment in Detroit against sixteen members of the Abraham Lincoln Brigade for conspiring to persuade Americans to fight against the fascists in the Spanish civil war.[*] Jackson regarded the prosecution as an embarrassment to the Department of Justice and promptly ordered the charges dismissed.[101] He was immediately attacked in the Senate by Republican Styles Bridges, who accused him of favoring Communists. Bridges snidely inquired whether with Jackson as attorney general it is to be "one rule for Communists, [and] another rule for those opposed to Communism?" Jackson replied that Senator Bridges "is to be forgiven for knowing nothing of the subject of which he talked."[102]

In April 1940, Jackson addressed the nation's federal prosecutors. He warned that "times of fear or hysteria" have often resulted in cries "for the scalps" of those with dissenting views. He exhorted his U.S. attorneys to steel themselves to be "dispassionate and courageous" in cases dealing with "so-called subversive activities." Such cases, he cautioned, pose a special threat to civil liberties because the prosecutor has "no definite standards" with which to determine what constitutes a subversive activity.

Jackson urged the nation's prosecutors to keep in mind that in times of

---

[*] The Abraham Lincoln Brigade consisted of individuals who were fighting alongside Communists against Franco and the fascists in Spain. Secretary of the Interior Harold Ickes speculated that Murphy had approved "this rotten thing" as the result of "Catholic church influence," although Murphy's biographer rejects that judgment. Rather, he concludes that Murphy initiated the prosecution because of the constant harping of the Dies Committee and his desire not to be charged with lax law enforcement. See Powers, *Secrecy and Power* at 235–36 (cited in note 70); Fine, *Washington Years* at 125–26 (cited in note 18).

Justice Robert Jackson

national crisis "[t]hose who are in office are apt to regard as 'subversive' the activities" of anyone who would bring about a significant change of policy or "a
change of administration." Reminding his audience that "[s]ome of our soundest
constitutional doctrines were once punished as subversive," he declared, "In the
enforcement of laws which protect our national integrity and existence, we
should prosecute any and every act of violation, but only overt acts, not the
expression of opinion."[103]

SHORTLY AFTER ROOSEVELT SIGNED the Smith Act in the
summer of 1940, he appointed Attorney General Jackson, like Frank Murphy
before him, to the Supreme Court. Francis Biddle was appointed acting attorney
general. Before this appointment, Biddle, a member of the ACLU,[104] had taken
a strong pro–free speech stand, cautioning against hysterical overreaction and
endorsing Justice Holmes's view that the appropriate response to un-American

speech was counterspeech, not suppression. Biddle had warned repeatedly against the dangers of public hysteria and excess. In the summer of 1941, he told the California bar, "We do not lose our right to condemn either measures or men because the country is at war."[105] In September of 1941, he promised "to see that civil liberties in this country are protected" and that we will "not again fall into the disgraceful hysteria of witch hunts . . . which were such a dark chapter in our record of the last world war."[106] This position did not sit well with Roosevelt, who questioned whether Biddle "was 'tough enough' to deal with the subversive element."[107]

After his appointment as acting attorney general, and largely at Roosevelt's insistence, Biddle reluctantly softened his stance. He urged civil libertarians to be more realistic and to recognize that limitations of civil liberties might be necessary. Although dubious about the constitutionality of the Smith Act, he nonetheless endorsed it. In the summer of 1940, he wrote Roosevelt that it would be difficult to obtain convictions under the act, but conceded that bringing some prosecutions might have a "salutary effect."[108]

Thereafter, the United States filed charges under the Smith Act against twenty-nine leaders of the Socialist Workers Party in Minneapolis, which had instigated several major work stoppages in the local defense industry. The SWP, a small Trotskyite sect, had argued that the United States should not get embroiled in another European war and opposed Roosevelt's armaments program.[109] The defendants were charged with conspiring to advocate the forceful overthrow of government. Eighteen of the defendants were convicted, and the Supreme Court denied review. Biddle later admitted that the defendants had been guilty of no more than rhetorical excess "in the time-honored Marxist lingo," and expressed regret for having authorized the prosecution.[110]

AFTER THE ATTACK ON PEARL HARBOR, Biddle was determined to avoid what he regarded as the grievous mistakes of World War I. On December 15, 1941, he attempted to help set the national tone in a speech commemorating the 152nd anniversary of the Bill of Rights. He reminded the nation that "although we had fought wars before, and our personal freedoms had survived, there had been periods of gross abuse, when hysteria and fear and hate ran high, and minorities were unlawfully and cruelly abused." He added, "Every man . . . who cares about freedom must fight [to protect it] for the *other* man with whom he disagrees."[111]

Two days later, Biddle instructed all U.S. attorneys that prosecutions for "alleged seditious utterances must not be undertaken unless consent is first obtained from the Department of Justice."[*][112] Shortly thereafter, several men were arrested in Los Angeles for allegedly praising Hitler, stating that Japan had done a "good job" in the Pacific, asserting that "the Japanese had a right to Hawaii" because there "are more of them there than there are Americans," and declaring that they would "rather be on the side of Germany than on the side of the British."[113] Another man was arrested for saying that "the President should be impeached for asking Congress to declare war."[114] They were charged with violating the Espionage Act of 1917. Biddle immediately dismissed the charges, stating that free speech ought not to be restricted unless public safety is "directly imperiled."[115] The nation had come a long way since World War I.

In fact, after Pearl Harbor, few people questioned America's participation in the war. Most of those who did had long been alienated from American society. They believed that national policy was set by an international conspiracy of Jews, Communists, bankers, and the British, that the attack on Pearl Harbor was due largely to our own unwise policies, that the war could serve no legitimate national purpose, and that the country should promptly extricate itself from the conflict through negotiation. The often vitriolic attacks of such critics began to grate on the nation's nerves. Even Biddle framed the central question as "whether the government should take steps to prevent a campaign seeking defeat, apparently well organized and springing from a central direction."[116] Although public pressure mounted on Biddle to punish these dissenters, he refrained from doing so, believing that critics of the war were protected by the First Amendment.[117]

Biddle's inaction led to a direct rebuke from the president.[118] Indeed, according to Biddle, it was Roosevelt who exerted the most pressure on him to prosecute dissent:

> The President began to send me brief memoranda to which were attached some of the scurrilous attacks on his leadership, with a notation: "What about this?" or "What are you doing to stop this?" I explained to him my view of the unwisdom of bringing indictment for sedition except where there was evidence that recruitment was substantially being interfered with, or there was some connection

---

[*] This action was applauded by the *New York Times*: "[I]t is reassuring to note that . . . there is an absence of hysteria in regard to this war that contrasts sharply with the feeling in the last war. To say this is not to discredit our predecessors but to thank them for having taught us. [During World War I], there were prosecutions and convictions that astonish us now. . . . We have reason to hope that that sort of thing is over; and just now when we have been commemorating the Bill of Rights we may be expected to have a deeper toleration of 'the thought we hate.'" *Civil Liberties*, New York Times E6 (Dec 21, 1941).

Attorney General Francis Biddle and J. Edgar Hoover

between the speech and propaganda centers in Germany. . . . He was not much interested in the theory of sedition, or in the constitutional right to criticize the government in wartime. He wanted this anti-war talk stopped. . . .

. . . After two weeks, during which F.D.R.'s manner when I saw him said as plainly as words that he considered me out of step, he began to go for me in the Cabinet. . . . When my turn came, as he went around the table, his habitual affability dropped. . . . "When are you going to indict the seditionists?" he would ask; and the next week, and every week after that, . . . he would repeat the same question.[119]

In January 1942, Roosevelt sent a note to J. Edgar Hoover asking "what was being done about William Dudley Pelley," an admirer of Hitler whose writing, Roosevelt observed, "comes pretty close to being seditious." "Now that we are in the war," he concluded, "it looks like a good chance to clean up a number of these vile publications." Unlike the situation during the Civil War, the prosecution of dissenters during World War II was not carried out "by irresponsible subordinates while the president occupied himself with high matters of state." Rather, Roosevelt "personally intervened to curtail far-right expressions that were only distantly dangerous or merely obnoxious."[120]

Over the next few months, the pro-Roosevelt press pressed the attack on fascists and former isolationists. The editor of the *Nation* complained that "[t]oler-ance, democratic safeguards, trust in public enlightenment" had all proved inadequate, and demanded that government "Curb the Fascist Press!" In April 1942, Roosevelt directly confronted Biddle, demanding to know what was being done about Pelley and pointedly asking him, yet again, "[W]hen are you going to indict the seditionists?"[121] Two months later, the arrests began.

"THE AMERICAN HITLER"

THE ONLY SON of an itinerant preacher, William Dudley Pelley was born in 1885 in Lynn, Massachusetts. His childhood was steeped in somber reflections about free will, salvation, infant damnation, and fire and brimstone.[122] In his early teens, he left school and began work in a toilet paper factory. An avid reader, Pelley was largely self-educated. At the age of eighteen, he signed on as a junior reporter for a local newspaper. Over the next decade, he worked as a police reporter for the *Boston Globe*, served as a writer and editor for several New England journals, and published more than a hundred feature articles and short stories in such national magazines as *Red Book*, *Collier's*, the *Saturday Evening Post*, and the *American Magazine*. One of his short stories, which focused on blood ties and Christian self-sacrifice, was included in *The Best Short Stories of 1918*.[123]

Pelley gradually worked his way to Hollywood, where he was hired as a screenwriter for MGM and Universal Studios. He wrote screenplays for Lon Chaney, Hoot Gibson, and Tom Mix, published several critically acclaimed novels about small-town America, and was listed in *Who's Who in America*. But he soon grew disillusioned with the "money-drunk" climate of the film industry. He suffered a string of business reverses, his wife deserted him, and he became enmeshed in a series of conflicts with editors and filmmakers. By 1925, he was on the verge of a nervous breakdown.[124]

Then, in the early morning hours of May 29, 1927, in his small cabin in the Sierra Madre, Pelley had an out-of-body experience. He later wrote that he had "died" for seven minutes. He left his physical body, "plunged down into a mystic depth of cool, blue space," bathed in a crystal clear Roman pool, and conversed with ethereal beings who inspired him to change his life by leading a national movement to reform society.[125] In 1929, Pelley published the story of this experience in the *American Magazine*. Some ten million people read "Seven Minutes in Eternity." He claimed that, wherever it is "humans go after being released," he went "there that night." Pelley had rediscovered his voice.

He moved to Asheville, North Carolina, established a printing press, and began publishing newspapers, religious tomes, and pamphlets advocating his increasingly bizarre theories. Typical titles included *That Great Migration of Souls to this Planet*, *Which Souls Make Up the Dark Forces?* and *Do Those Who Are Dead Meet God?* He claimed to possess a built-in "mental radio" through which he could tune in "the minds and voices of those in another dimension." He established Galahad College, which offered mail-order courses in such subjects as spiritual eugenics, cosmic mathematics, and ethical history.[126]

ON JANUARY 31, 1933, the day after Adolf Hitler was appointed chancellor of Germany, Pelley founded the Silver Legion of America, an organization dedicated to bringing fascism to the United States. His stated goal was to "preserve the form of constitutional government set up by the forefathers." Pelley revealed that he had been chosen to lead "the cream, the head, and the flower of our Protestant Christian manhood."[127]

Pelley stood five feet seven inches tall, had a long, narrow face, sharp features, piercing eyes, large wolfish teeth, and silver-gray slicked-back hair. He personally designed both the Silver Legion's flag (a square white banner emblazoned with a scarlet *L*) and its Nazi-like uniform (dark blue corduroy trousers and leggings, dark blue tie, silver shirt with a scarlet *L* on the breast).[128] The "Silver Shirts" were his version of Hitler's SS. Pelley traveled across the nation recruiting members, establishing training sites, speaking at rallies, and spreading his message that a cabal of Jews planned to take over the Christian nations of the world.

In his weekly newsletter, *Liberation*, Pelley blamed the Depression on a worldwide Jewish conspiracy and accused Roosevelt of being the dupe of an insidious Jewish and Communist plot. A 1934 Silver Shirt pamphlet warned that this "era of corruption" will culminate in the "greatest crime ever perpetrated on the American people" because this "Jewish-controlled administration is selling the people into bondage and leading them straight on to Communism."[129] Pelley vilified Franklin Roosevelt as the "Dutch Jew" who headed the "Great Kosher Administration."[130]

By 1934, there were 15,000 Silver Shirts[131] and *Liberation* had attained a circulation of 50,000. Pelley was the subject of articles in *Harper's Magazine* and the *New Republic*, which warned that he was dangerous and needed watching.[132] He explained his views about Hitler: "I know what those fellows [in Germany] were up against before Hitler took over. And if we have inflation here we'll be in the same boat. I believe that what Hitler is trying to do is set up a United States of Europe to do away with tariff barriers and racial prejudices." With respect to anti-Semitism, Pelley said that he "'absolutely and definitely would not' treat the 'Jewish problem' in this country as was done in Germany." "The happier solution," he explained, "would be to have one city in each State for Jews. Let them live there and run it and have their own culture."*[133]

"Chief Pelley," as he was addressed by his followers, generally counseled his Silver Shirts to obey the law. In some instances, however, his subordinates disregarded this advice. In 1933, a group of Silver Shirts in Salt Lake City kidnapped and severely beat a suspected Communist, leaving him for dead. In 1934, the San Diego branch of the Silver Legion began military training with arms and ammunition. On the whole, however, the Silver Shirts showed more bluster than bite.[134]

In 1935, Pelley announced his candidacy for president of the United States on the Christian Party ticket. His campaign slogan was "For Christ and Constitution." He proclaimed that "the time has come for an American Hitler."[135] He proposed "to disfranchise the Jews by Constitutional amendment" and to restrict "Jews in the professions, trades, and sciences" according to their "quota of representation in the population."[136] Only one state—Washington—permitted Pelley on the ballot, where he received 1,598 votes out of 700,000 cast.[137] He blamed his disappointing showing on Jewish sabotage of the voting machines.[138]

In 1940, the Dies Committee observed that a large number of organizations sympathetic to Nazi and fascist ideals had recently emerged in the United States.[139] It identified Pelley's Silver Shirts as "the largest, best financed, and certainly the best published" of these groups. It added that Pelley had anointed himself "the American Hitler," and characterized him as a "racketeer engaged in mulcting thousands of dollars annually from his fanatical and misled followers."[140]

FROM THE MID-1930s until December 7, 1941, a strong isolationist movement sprang up in the United States to oppose Roosevelt's shift away from a position of neutrality. The isolationists drew support from a wide range of business leaders, lawyers, educators, journalists, progressives, and pacifists. Such oth-

---

* In 1937, Pelley proposed sending the following Christmas card to Jews:

> Dear Shylock, in this season
>> When we're all bereft of reason,
> As upon my rent you gloat,
>> I would like to cut your throat.

Ribuffo, *Old Christian Right* at 60 (cited in note 40).

erwise diverse figures as Oswald Villard of the *Nation*, Colonel Robert McCormick of the *Chicago Tribune*, the news analyst Boake Carter, the aviator Charles Lindbergh, the novelist Kathleen Norris, General Hugh Johnson, the former Republican presidential candidate Alf M. Landon, the architect Frank Lloyd Wright, the former Illinois governor Frank Lowden, the redoubtable Alice Roosevelt Longworth, and the liberal journalist John Flynn all campaigned against America's participation in the war that raged in both Europe and the Far East.

A central theme of the isolationists was that the war was not a contest between right and wrong but a struggle between different conceptions of what is right. Thus, the United States could best serve its interests, and the interests of the world community, by attempting to broker a negotiated peace. Recalling the experience of World War I, the isolationists warned that if the United States entered the war to defend democracy abroad, it would risk losing democracy at home.

Roosevelt was especially concerned about the activities of America First, the most mainstream and most potent of the isolationist organizations. He viewed America First not only as defeatist but as treasonable. He called for a congressional investigation to determine whether America First was financed by Nazi Germany, but there was too much isolationist sentiment in Congress for his backers to muster sufficient support for such an investigation. Roosevelt also urged Attorney General Biddle to initiate a grand jury inquiry of America First, but Biddle concluded that there was no legal basis for such an investigation.[141]

For the most part, the positions advanced by America First were grounded in a sincere, if naïve, desire to protect America from the horrors of another foreign war. As the historian Charles Beard observed in *Harper's* in September 1939, "Those Americans who refuse to plunge blindly into the maelstrom of European and Asian politics are not defeatist or neurotic. They are giving evidence of sanity, not cowardice." But the isolationist movement was fatally tainted by strains of anti-Semitism, and the support of groups like the Silver Shirts and the German-American Bund helped poison the well of American isolationism.[*][142]

Defenders of the Roosevelt administration responded sharply to those who accused the president of attempting to drag the nation into war. The *New Repub-*

---

[*] In a speech on the floor of the House, Congressman John Rankin of Mississippi declared, "Wall Street and a little group of our international Jewish brethren are still attempting to harass the President . . . and the Congress . . . into plunging us into the European war unprepared." Although Lindbergh was not seen as an anti-Semite before his involvement in the isolationist movement, in September of 1941 he added fuel to the fire when he singled out "the British, the Jewish, and the Roosevelt administration" as the forces driving the nation to war. 77th Cong, 1st Sess, in 87 Cong Rec 4726 (June 4, 1941); *Assail Lindbergh for Iowa Speech*, New York Times 1 (Sept 13, 1941).

lic clamored for an investigation of America First and demanded that the National Association of Broadcasters ban Lindbergh from the radio. There were physical attacks on America First meetings in New York City, and prominent liberals accused America Firsters of being "Fifth Columnists" for the fascists. Roosevelt condemned members and supporters of America First as "those who unwittingly help" the "agents of Nazism."[143] Interior Secretary Harold Ickes, using language almost identical to that used by Federalists in 1798, charged that isolationists were eager to make terms with Hitler "at the expense of this country's welfare."[144] Advocates of isolationism were tarred as pro-Hitler, and in April 1941 the president characterized Charles Lindbergh as a modern "Vallandigham."[145]

Pelley was one of the most vitriolic supporters of American isolationism. His endorsement of the cause surely did it no good. In September 1939, Pelley warned in *Liberation* that patriotic citizens must join together to oppose a conspiracy, led by "Jewish internationalists" and the "New Deal Crackpot in Washington," designed to push the nation into a global war.[146] He even penned a song, "The Doughboy Blues," to be sung by American soldiers once Roosevelt had succeeded in pushing America into the war:

> O haven't you heard the news?
> We're at war to save the Jews;
> For a hundred years they pressed our pants,
> Now we must die for them in France!
> So we sing the Doughboy Blues—
> It's a helluva fate to choose,
> To die to save the Jews;
> But the New Deal busted and left us flat,
> So this war was hatched by the Democrat,
> To end our New Deal Blues.[147]

When the United States finally entered World War II, Pelley was distraught. He dissolved the Silver Legion because it was no longer advisable—or safe—to parade about in Nazi-style uniforms. After a few weeks of sulking, however, he launched two new magazines, *Roll Call* and the *Galilean*, to resume his attack. He aggressively criticized Roosevelt, asserting that he had imposed a prewar oil embargo on Japan in order to strangle its economy and force it into war, led the nation to the "verge of bankruptcy," and instigated the war in order to save his faltering New Deal economy.

In March 1942, Pelley wrote in the *Galilean* that Roosevelt had lied to the American people about Pearl Harbor when he assured them that the Pacific fleet was still intact. In fact, Pelley reported, the Japanese had completely destroyed the Pacific fleet. As he put it, "Japanese bombers made Pearl Harbor look like an abandoned W.P.A. project in Keokuk!"[148] It was this issue of the *Galilean* that

William Dudley Pelley

triggered Roosevelt's demand that Biddle "indict the seditionists."[*][149] (Pelley's characterization of the scope of American losses at Pearl Harbor was actually more accurate than the administration's misleading reports, which attempted to calm the public by minimizing the scale of the disaster.)[†][150]

---

[*] This was not the first time Roosevelt wanted to prosecute Pelley. In 1938, Pelley questioned Roosevelt's family claim to Hyde Park in *Liberation*. A furious Roosevelt asked J. Edgar Hoover whether it would be possible to prosecute Pelley "for a thing like this." Hoover suggested an indictment for criminal libel, but the matter went no further. The following year, Pelley accused Roosevelt of embezzling funds from the Warm Springs Foundation. Roosevelt again demanded action. Attorney General Frank Murphy said he was willing to prosecute Pelley for criminal libel, but warned the president that Pelley might subpoena him to testify. Again, the matter went no further. See Ribuffo, *Old Christian Right* at 74 (cited in note 40).

[†] See Blanchard, *Revolutionary Sparks* at 218 (cited in note 150):

> The first official communiqués from the islands indicated that only one old battleship and a destroyer had been sunk, that other ships had been damaged, and that American forces had inflicted heavy losses on the Japanese. . . . Shortly after the attack, Secretary of the Navy Knox visited Pearl Harbor, and in a press conference after his return, . . . announced that the battleship *Arizona* had been lost and that the battleship *Oklahoma* had capsized but could be righted; the rest of the Pacific fleet was fine. In reality, the *Arizona*, the *Oklahoma*, the *California*, the *Nevada*, and the *West Virginia* were all at the bottom of Pearl Harbor. . . . Full disclosure of the Pearl Harbor disaster awaited the end of the war.

THE FOLLOWING MONTH, the United States indicted Pelley under the Espionage Act of 1917 for making "false statements with intent to interfere with the operation or success of the military or naval forces of the United States or to promote the success of its enemies." The indictment included numerous counts based on statements Pelley had made in the *Galilean* between December 8, 1941, and February 23, 1942. The following are illustrative of these statements:

- "To rationalize that the United States got into the war because of an unprovoked attack on Pearl Harbor, is fiddle-faddle."
- "Mr. President . . . might, easily, by the turn of a phrase . . . have prevented the attack on Pearl Harbor."
- "Mr. President chose to surround himself with Zionists and a fearful war resulted from their counsels."
- "No realist in his senses would contend that there is unity in this country for the war's prosecution."
- "[T]he losses which Britain has taken in the Far East . . . may mean the end of the war."
- The United States is "bankrupt."[151]

At the time these statements were published, the *Galilean* had a national circulation of between 3,500 and 5,000. The trial began in Indianapolis on July 28, 1942. Charles Lindbergh appeared in the courtroom to support the defense. Although Lindbergh had never met Pelley, he said he was concerned that Pelley would not receive a fair trial and that freedom of expression would be sacrificed under the pressure of war hysteria.[152]

Pelley's lawyers proved profoundly inept. Not only did they fail to assert many possible objections, but at one point Pelley's own attorney inadvertently referred to him as "Mr. Hitler." In his closing argument to the jury, the federal prosecutor compared Pelley to Benedict Arnold, Aaron Burr, and Vidkun Quisling (the Nazi-appointed figurehead leader of Norway), proclaiming that no murderer ever "had a blacker heart than you, who tried to murder the coun-

---

See also Jackson, *That Man* at 104 (cited in note 94) (noting that the president did not inform even Robert Jackson of the full "extent of our losses" at Pearl Harbor until several weeks after the attack, and that Jackson had found the accurate report "shocking").

try that nurtured you." After seven days of testimony, the jury found Pelley guilty on eleven counts of seditious libel. Declaring that his "clever mind" made him especially dangerous, Judge Robert Baltzell sentenced Pelley to fifteen years in prison.[153]

The U.S. Court of Appeals for the Seventh Circuit affirmed the conviction. The court acknowledged that the very "nature" of these statements made their "refutation" difficult because many were mere "generalities with insidious connotations." Nonetheless, the court rejected Pelley's contention that his utterances were statements of "opinions, criticisms, arguments and loose talk" that could not properly be "proved" false. The court explained that readers of the *Galilean* had not been "candidly informed of the true character and value of the statements," which had been stated as "definite or inevitable facts" rather than as mere opinions or conclusions. Hence, Pelley's statements could reasonably be found to be false.

At Pelley's trial, the government resorted to some creative lawyering to establish the falsity of his statements. To prove that the nation was not "bankrupt," the prosecution called a banker to offer his expert opinion that this was not so. To prove that there was "national unity" behind the president, the prosecution called traveling salesmen to testify to what they had heard as they journeyed about the country.

To meet the requirements of the Espionage Act, the government had to prove "evil intent" as well as falsity. That is, it had to prove that Pelley had made false statements with the intent of hindering the war effort. To meet this burden, the prosecution presented evidence about the activities of the Silver Shirts in the mid-1930s, Pelley's 1936 campaign for the presidency, his expressions of admiration for Hitler, and his extensive personal library of German, Italian, and Japanese "originated propaganda." The prosecution also called an expert witness to testify that Pelley's utterances "were consistent and almost identical with the fourteen major themes of German propaganda."

Ultimately, however, the court of appeals concluded that the "argument that proof of intent is lacking hardly needs consideration." It explained that, "[i]n time of war, when success depends on unified national effort," an individual who falsely reports the country's "failure in battle," falsely asserts that the nation is "bankrupt," falsely claims that it has "incompetent leadership," and "extols the virtues" of the nation's enemies cannot plausibly deny that he had "a criminal intent to interfere with the operation or success of the military or naval forces." It is inconceivable, the court of appeals reasoned, that an individual would publish "such propaganda, at a time when his country was at war," other than in the hope of "weakening the patriotic resolve of his fellow citizens."[154]

The Supreme Court declined to review the case.* Pelley spent ten years behind bars at the Terre Haute penitentiary. He was paroled in 1952, on the condition that he not participate in any "political activities" in the future.[155]

THE PROSECUTION OF WILLIAM DUDLEY PELLEY AND THE SEDITION ACT OF 1798

HOW DOES THE PROSECUTION of Pelley in 1942 compare with the prosecutions of Republicans in 1798? The Sedition Act of 1798 declared it unlawful for any person to make "false, scandalous, and malicious" statements about the government, the president, or the Congress with the intent of bringing them into "contempt or disrepute" or of exciting against them the "hatred of the good people of the United States." Under this act, Congressman Matthew Lyon was convicted for "falsely" asserting that in the administration of President Adams "every consideration of the public welfare" was "swallowed up in a continual grasp for power," and the Republican journalist Thomas Cooper was convicted for "falsely" accusing Adams of undermining the nation's credit. These are illustrative of the assertions prosecuted under the 1798 act.[156]

WOULD PELLEY HAVE BEEN CONVICTED under the Sedition Act of 1798? The answer is surely yes. Pelley's statements were legally indistinguishable from those of Lyon and Cooper. The more interesting question is how far the nation had come from 1798 to 1942. As Justice Holmes rightly observed in his opinion in *Abrams*, "the United States through many years had shown its repentance for the Sedition Act of 1798."[157] Indeed, during the congressional debates on the Espionage Act of 1917, under which Pelley was convicted, even the most fervent proponents of the act fell all over themselves insisting that the Espionage Act of 1917 was a far cry from the Sedition Act of 1798.[158]

---

* Pelley attempted unsuccessfully to challenge his conviction on two other occasions. See *Pelley v. Matthews*, 163 F2d 700 (DC Cir 1947); *Pelley v. United States*, 214 F2d 597 (7th Cir 1954). In his 1954 challenge, Pelley argued that he had been denied a fair trial because his attorney at the 1942 trial had been warned by the prosecution that "if he did not 'pull his punches,'" and help put "Pelley away," his wife, a German alien, would be deported. A divided court of appeals denied him a hearing on this question. *Pelley*, 214 F2d at 601.

What was so bad about the Sedition Act of 1798? One problem was that it made truth a *defense*, rather than requiring the *government* to prove falsity. The Espionage Act of 1917 had been crafted with this flaw in mind, and as the court of appeals recognized in *Pelley*, in prosecutions under the "false statement" provision of the 1917 act the government had the burden of proving falsity. Thus, one objection to the Sedition Act of 1798 had been addressed.[159]

A second objection to the Sedition Act was that it covered statements of *opinion*, as well as statements of fact. Throughout the congressional debates in 1798, opponents of the act voiced this concern. Albert Gallatin and other Republicans argued that it would be impossible to prove statements of opinion "true" or "false," and that the proper response to "false" political opinions was public debate, not criminal prosecution for alleged "falsity." Indeed, the Republicans maintained that the very notion that political opinions could be deemed "false" was itself subversive of the Constitution.[160]

The court of appeals in *Pelley*, again acknowledging the lessons of history and the intent of the drafters of the Espionage Act of 1917, properly held that statements of political opinion could not be deemed "false" under the act. Thus, a second objection to the Sedition Act of 1798 had been addressed.*

But had it? The line between a statement of fact and a statement of opinion is often elusive. As the court of appeals conceded, the very "nature" of Pelley's assertions made their "refutation" difficult because they tended to be mere "generalities with insidious connotations." Rather than accepting Pelley's contention that his utterances consisted of "opinions, criticisms, arguments and loose talk," which could not constitutionally be declared false, the court argued that because Pelley had not "candidly informed" his audience of the "true character" of his statements—that is, because he had not informed his readers that these were statements of opinion rather than statements of fact—the jury could find them to be false.

What are we to make of this? Given this logic, the statements prosecuted under the Sedition Act of 1798 could also be deemed "false." Certainly, Lyon and Cooper, like Pelley, did not "candidly inform" their audiences that their utterances were mere statements of opinion.

---

* The Supreme Court has clearly held in the years since World War II that a statement cannot constitutionally be punished as "false" unless it contains "a provably false factual connotation." To illustrate the point, the Court has observed that the assertion that X "shows his abysmal ignorance by accepting the teachings of Marx and Lenin" cannot constitutionally be declared "false." Similarly, the Court has held that an individual cannot constitutionally be punished for "falsely" accusing another of "blackmail" or of being a "traitor," in circumstances where the accusation should reasonably be understood as mere hyperbole or metaphor. See *Milkovich v. Lorain Journal Co*, 497 US 1, 20 (1990); *Greenbelt Cooperative Publishing Association v. Bresler*, 398 US 7 (1970) ("blackmail"); *National Association of Letter Carriers v. Austin*, 418 US 264 (1974) ("traitor").

Moreover, if we cast our eyes over Pelley's assertions, it seems clear that most, if not all, cannot fairly be characterized as statements of "fact." His declarations that the president "chose to surround himself with Zionists," that it is "fiddle-faddle" to suggest that the attack on Pearl Harbor was "unprovoked," and that the "losses which Britain has taken in the Far East . . . may mean the end of the war" seem no different in this respect from the statements of the defendants in the Sedition Act prosecutions. As Gallatin warned in 1798, these are mixed statements that "contain not only facts but opinions." And even Pelley's arguably more factual statements, such as his claim that the United States was "bankrupt," should fairly be construed, in context, as mere political hyperbole.

The danger of allowing the government to treat Pelley's statements as falsifiable assertions is illustrated by the government's efforts to prove "falsity" by resort to the testimony of a banker, a traveling salesman, and an "expert" witness on German propaganda. This way of proceeding, though clever, does not provide much comfort about the deeper realities of the proceeding. As Gallatin presciently cautioned, what jury, in the face of war fervor and Pelley's odious rhetoric, would hesitate to declare his disloyal opinions "ungrounded, or, in other words, false?"[161]

Consider Pelley's statements that "to rationalize that the United States got into the war because of an unprovoked attack on Pearl Harbor, is fiddle-faddle" and that "we have by every act and deed performable aggressively solicited war with the Axis." The court of appeals considered these statements self-evidently and dangerously "false." But the judgment of history is more complex. Professor John Mearsheimer, a distinguished political scientist, has offered the following analysis of the events leading up to Pearl Harbor:

> Japan was anxious to avoid a fight with the United States, so it moved cautiously in Southeast Asia. . . . Unfortunately for Japan, . . . American policymakers were deeply worried that Japan would attack the Soviet Union from the east and help the Wehrmacht finish off the Red Army.
>
> [To prevent this], the United States employed massive coercive pressure against Japan to transform it into a second-rate power. . . . On July 26, 1941, with the situation going badly for the Red Army . . . and Japan having just occupied southern Indochina, the United States and its allies froze Japan's assets, which led to a devastating full-scale embargo against Japan. . . .
>
> The embargo left Japan with two terrible choices: cave in to American pressure and accept a significant diminution of its power, or go to war against the United States. . . . Japan's leaders tried to cut a deal with the United States in the late summer and fall of 1941. . . . But U.S. policymakers . . . refused to make any concessions to the increasingly desperate Japanese. . . . In effect, the Japanese would be defanged either peacefully or by force. . . . Japan opted to attack the United States, knowing full well that it would probably lose, but believing that it

might be able to hold the United States at bay in a long war and eventually force it to quit the conflict. . . . [The Japanese] were willing to take that incredibly risky gamble . . . because caving in to American demands seemed to be an even worse alternative.[162]

Pelley's accusations about the administration's foreign policy, like his charges about the magnitude of American naval losses at Pearl Harbor, were *not* "false" in any objectively verifiable sense. He may have been "right," and he may have been "wrong," but these were not assertions of fact to be resolved by a court of law. Yet it was on precisely that premise that the government outlawed them. Just as the accusations of Republicans in 1798, Copperheads in 1863, and antiwar dissenters in 1917 had some merit insofar as they questioned the government's motives and methods, so too were Pelley's accusations in 1942 a legitimate part of public debate about the war.

In the fervor of the moment, angry, ill-tempered criticism was transformed into criminal falsehood. Although Congress had clearly intended the "false statement" provision of the Espionage Act to apply only to false statements of *fact*, and although the court of appeals paid lip service to this principle, in practical effect the court accorded no more constitutional protection to Pelley's opinions in 1942 than the Federalist judges gave to Lyon's and Cooper's opinions in 1798.

THREE ADDITIONAL QUESTIONS merit discussion. First, even if Pelley's statements were not factually false, could he nonetheless have been punished for violating *other* provisions of the Espionage Act of 1917? Under the standards used during World War I, Pelley could certainly have been convicted of attempting to "cause insubordination" and "obstruct the recruiting or enlistment service." If Charles Schenck, Eugene Debs, and Mollie Steimer were guilty of violating those provisions, so too was Pelley. His statements in the *Galilean* surely had a "bad tendency" to hinder the war effort.

But, as we have seen, the World War I standard had been discredited by 1942, and the Supreme Court was already well on its way to embracing a variant of the Holmes/Brandeis "clear and present danger" test.[163] Whatever else one might say about Pelley's statements, there was certainly no clear and present danger that they would substantially and immediately impair the war effort. Indeed, that is why he was charged under the "false statement" provision and why the court of appeals emphasized that the falsity of Pelley's statements "was *sine qua non* to the existence of the offense."[164]

Second, could Pelley have been punished, consistent with the First Amendment, if he had actually made a *false* statement of fact? Suppose he had written in the *Galilean* that on December 8, 1941, American troops in Hawaii had massacred a thousand innocent individuals of Japanese ancestry? Assuming the government could prove falsity beyond a reasonable doubt, would this statement be punishable? At first blush, the answer would seem to be yes. But suppose Pelley had reasonably *believed* his statement was true? Suppose he had been told this by several people who had been present in Hawaii on December 8? Twenty years after the prosecution of Pelley, the Supreme Court observed in *New York Times v. Sullivan*[165] that because "erroneous statement is inevitable in free debate," even false statements of fact must sometimes be protected "if the freedoms of expression are to have the 'breathing space' that they 'need . . . to survive.'"[166] The Court therefore held that even factually false statements about the official actions of government officials cannot constitutionally be punished unless the speaker made the statement "with knowledge that it was false or with reckless disregard of whether it was false or not."*[167] In the prosecution of Pelley, however, as in the Sedition Act prosecutions, the government presented no evidence that Pelley knew his statements to be false or was reckless or even negligent in believing them to be true. In practical effect, the court of appeals held Pelley strictly liable for the "falsity" of his statements.

Third, Pelley argued that even if he had knowingly or recklessly made a false statement, the government could not constitutionally punish him unless it could prove that his statements had actually *harmed* the war effort. The court of appeals rejected this argument, holding that the Espionage Act did not require such proof. As precedent for this conclusion, the court cited the Supreme Court's World War I decisions in *Schenck* and *Debs*.[168] As we have seen, however, by 1942 the Court had eroded the precedential force of those decisions and had moved toward the "clear and present danger" test. The question, then, is whether this test, rather than the "bad tendency" standard, should govern when a defendant is prosecuted for making knowingly or recklessly *false* statements with the intent to hinder the war effort.[169]

Should false statements of fact receive the same constitutional protection as true statements and statements of opinion? The answer is no. As the Supreme Court recognized in *Chaplinsky v. New Hampshire*,[170] decided in the same year

---

* As Congressman Nicholas warned during the debates over the Sedition Act of 1798, in the absence of some such protection for false statements, printers would be "afraid of publishing the truth," for it might not always be possible "to establish the truth to the satisfaction of a court of justice," especially one that might be hostile to their views. Nicholas warned that the imposition of strict liability for false statements of fact would risk suppressing "every printing press . . . which is not obsequious to the will of Government." 8 *Annals of Congress* at 2141 (cited in note 160).

as *Pelley*, "[t]here are certain well-defined and narrowly limited classes of speech, the prevention and punishment of which have never been thought to raise any Constitutional problem." The Court offered as illustrations the obscene and the libelous, explaining that "such utterances are no essential part of any exposition of ideas, and are of such slight social value as a step to truth that any benefit that may be derived from them is clearly outweighed by the social interest in order and morality."[171]

In effect, then, the Court acknowledged that some types of speech are not fully within "the freedom of speech." Such "low"-value expression may be restricted in circumstances that would not justify the suppression of speech that merits full First Amendment protection.*[172] The paradigm of low-value speech is the false statement of fact. Whatever one might think about obscenity or commercial advertising, it is difficult to disagree with the proposition that false statements of fact are not the sort of expression the First Amendment was meant to promote. As the Supreme Court observed in 1974, "there is no constitutional value in false statements of fact."[173] Thus, although it may be appropriate to protect false statements of fact because "erroneous statement is inevitable in free debate," there is no reason to protect them because they are valuable in their own right.

One final twist should not pass unnoticed. Although civil and even criminal[174] liability for knowingly or recklessly false statements that defame a particular *individual* have been held consistent with the First Amendment, it does not necessarily follow that false statements that do *not* defame a particular individual pose the same constitutional question. When no identifiable individual is defamed, the harm caused by the false statement is more attenuated. Moreover, the very concept of defamation of the *government* is highly suspect. There is no

---

* Cass Sunstein has offered this account of how the Court determines whether a particular category of expression is of only "low" First Amendment value: "[I]n determining whether speech qualifies as low-value, the cases suggest that four factors are relevant. First, the speech must be far afield from the central concern of the first amendment, which broadly speaking, is effective popular control of public affairs." Second, "a distinction is drawn between cognitive and noncognitive aspects of speech." Third, "the purpose of the speaker is relevant: if the speaker is seeking to communicate a message, he will be treated more favorably than if he is not. Fourth, the various classes of low-value speech reflect judgments that in certain areas, government is unlikely to be acting for constitutionally impermissible reasons or producing constitutionally troublesome harms." Sunstein, 1986 Duke L J at 603–4 (cited in note 172).

A quarter of a century before *Chaplinsky*, Judge Learned Hand implicitly invoked such an analysis in his opinion in *Masses*, for one of the reasons Hand focused on express advocacy of law violation as a category of speech that may be restricted was that words "which have no purport but to counsel the violation of law cannot by any latitude of interpretation be a part of that public opinion which is the final source of government in a democratic state." *Masses Publishing Co. v. Patten*, 244 F 535, 540 (SD NY 1917).

deeply rooted historical tradition of criminal prosecutions for such statements (other than the discredited concept of seditious libel).

Moreover, it would be very dangerous to allow the government to pick and choose which false statements in public debate it will prosecute and which it will tolerate. The opportunities for selective prosecution and political abuse are obvious, and the prospect of using federal courts to decide on the truth or falsity of such statements in the absence of any concrete harm should give us pause. The very idea of using federal courts as "truth police" is surely problematic.

This suggests that when the government attempts to punish an individual for knowingly or recklessly making a false statement about the government itself, the prosecution should have to prove that the speech created a clear danger of substantial harm.[175] On this view, Pelley may have been right in arguing that even if he had knowingly or recklessly made a false statement of fact about the government, he still could not constitutionally be punished on the facts of his case.

As WE HAVE SEEN, under the standards used during World War I, Pelley could have been convicted of violating the provisions of the Espionage Act forbidding any person to "attempt to cause insubordination" or to "obstruct the recruiting or enlistment service of the United States." What is striking about Pelley's prosecution is that he was indicted and convicted *only* under the "false statement" provision of the act. As the court of appeals emphasized, "the gist of the substantive counts" against Pelley "is the publication and dissemination of 'false statements.'"[176]

This implies a clear recognition in 1942 that criminal prosecutions for expression of the sort that were commonplace during World War I were now of doubtful constitutionality, if not downright unthinkable. Although both the Department of Justice and the court of appeals in *Pelley* can be faulted for not working out the fine points of prosecutions for false statement, there is no question that the insistence on this *form* of prosecution marked an important leap forward. It was a clear acknowledgment that the prosecutions in *Schenck, Frohwerk, Debs,* and *Abrams* were no longer thought consonant with the constitution.

THE "GREAT SEDITION TRIAL" OF WORLD WAR II

IN JULY 1942, under continuing pressure from the public, the press, and the president, Attorney General Biddle announced the indictment of twenty-six American fascist leaders, charging them under both the Espionage Act of 1917 and the Smith Act of 1940 with conspiracy to undermine the morale of the armed forces. Although these defendants were vehemently anti-Roosevelt, anti-Communist (Communists were now America's allies), anti-Semitic, pro-German, and enthralled with Hitler, even lawyers in the Department of Justice were uneasy about how politics and public pressure had led to this sudden rash of indictments.

Zechariah Chafee condemned the indictment as "indefensible," Roger Baldwin described it as "monstrous," and Senator Robert Taft labeled it "witch hunting" that reminded him of the abuses of World War I.[177] Senator Burton K. Wheeler of Montana was outraged by the indictment and dared the administration to indict him as well. President Roosevelt, on the other hand, heartily congratulated Biddle on the attorney general's capitulation to his demands.[178]

Representative of the views of the defendants is the following passage from "The Political Genius of Hitler," published in the *Weckruf* on July 6, 1939:

> Unpalatable as it may be for us to accept the idea, it must be recognized that Hitler, when analyzed simply on the basis of historical fact, is not only the greatest political genius since Napoleon, but also the most rational. During five years, Hitler has not made one important mistake or suffered one serious setback. . . . He has transformed Germany from a vanquished nation . . . into the master of Europe. . . . A rational political genius who gets what he wants is incomprehensible to a people steeped in the irrational rationalism of men like Woodrow Wilson and Franklin D. Roosevelt who start things they cannot finish. . . .
>
> The Haves are on the defensive, but they must not expect to be able to solve their problem through a victorious war over the Have-nots. The Haves cannot afford to fight; the Have-nots can. However distasteful it may seem, the only policy for the survival of the Haves is one of appeasement. . . .[179]

Although the defendants had nothing in common except a shared hatred of Jews, communism, and Roosevelt, and a general faith in the principles of fascism, they were charged with conspiracy. The defendants were aptly described in the *New York Times* as "as queer a kettle of fish as was ever assembled by such means."[180] Another writer noted at the time, "Seldom have so many wild-eyed, jumpy lunatic fringe characters been assembled in one spot, within speaking, winking, and whispering distance of one another."[181]

The defendants included such characters as Lawrence Dennis, the "fascist philosopher"; Elizabeth Dilling, a Bible-thumping "child of God" who had given up her career as a concert harpist to enlist in the "cause"; Robert Noble, who preached that Germany had already won the war and that the United States should accept the "New Order"; Hans Diebel, a former Bund leader who ran the Aryan Bookstore in Los Angeles; and the anti-Semitic "prophet" Gerald L. K. Smith.

Newspapers across the political spectrum applauded the indictment, but the prosecution, in Francis Biddle's words, soon dissolved into a "dreary and degrading experience." "Nothing like [it]," he added mournfully, "had ever happened in an American court of law."[182] In April 1944, almost two years after they were indicted, and after several strained revisions of the indictment, the defendants finally went on trial.

The proceeding, popularly known as the "Great Sedition Trial" of World War II, was covered widely in the press by Walter Winchell, the *Washington Post*, the *New York Times*, and *Life* magazine. It was a legal and public relations nightmare for the government. Amid scenes of "uproar approaching the dimension of a riot," Judge Edward Eicher was determined to be fair. But the defendants were unruly and obstructionist. While the judge and the government attempted to follow conventional judicial procedures, the defendants wore Halloween masks, "moaned, groaned, laughed aloud, cheered and clamored." Throughout the trial, they "wailed" that it was all a "Jewish-Communist plot to curb their freedom of speech."[183]

The crux of the government's case was that the defendants had acted in concert with the enemy. But the government had no evidence to support its charge. The tenor of the trial was set by the prosecutor, O. John Rogge, who Robert Jackson had demoted because of his excessive zeal and ruthlessly antifascist views.[184] A brief excerpt from Rogge's opening statement offers a sense of the matter:

> As the Nazi war on the democratic world grew more intense, the evidence will show that the defendants increased their propaganda campaigns. They attacked . . . every step which our Government took to defend itself. When our country began to enlarge its army through the Selective Service Act, the defendants first fought against the enactment of the statute and then . . . preached to the soldiers that they were being trained, not because our country needed to be defended, but because our public officials and the Congress were betraying the American people. . . .
>
> While it is true that many Americans in good faith opposed our steps to prepare ourselves for the coming attack and to help fight the Nazis, the defendants cannot be identified with such persons . . . since the intent of the defendants was not a patriotic one, not an American one, but an intent . . . to promote the Nazi cause throughout the world.[185]

The trial quickly devolved into a circus that threatened to go on indefinitely. Even though the *Washington Post* had initially demanded the prosecution, by midtrial it was editorializing that the proceeding would "stand as a black mark against American justice for years to come" and urged the government to "end this sorry spectacle."[186] On November 30, 1944, before the case was submitted to the jury, an exhausted and miserable Judge Eicher suddenly died. As Biddle sadly observed, the "trial had killed him,"[187] and the result was a mistrial.

There the matter languished until December 1945, when the government finally dismissed the indictments—four months after the war had ended. Although the public had lost interest in the Great Sedition Trial well before it dragged to its pathetic conclusion, few people protested this attack on speech that was so "despised by the majority."[188]

The Great Sedition Trial left no legal precedent and put no one behind bars, but it did curtail right-wing propaganda during the war, compel thirty American fascists to defend themselves in court for four years, and set an important *political* precedent for the Smith Act prosecutions of Communists during the Cold War, which loomed just around the corner.*

"A DARK CHAPTER IN OUR RECORD OF THE LAST WORLD WAR"

BETWEEN 1926 AND 1936, Father Charles Coughlin rose from obscurity as a Roman Catholic parish priest to prominence as a national figure who was both worshiped and reviled. The secret of Father Coughlin's influence was his inimitable radio voice. Coughlin had a "rich, mellow, and musical" brogue that charmed and inspired. His "was a voice made for fervent hopes."[189]

He began his radio career in Royal Oak, Michigan, confronting the Ku Klux Klan. He soon turned his energies against communism, however, which he linked to divorce, birth control, and free love. Coughlin connected so effectively with the despair and discontent of the Depression that by the mid-1930s his weekly radio audience ran into the tens of millions and placed him ahead of even Gracie Allen and *Amos 'n' Andy*. He was "the radio star of his age."[190]

Within a few years, Coughlin became not only a powerful religious leader but a serious political force as well. He mailed out millions of copies of his sermons each week. Although initially enamored of Roosevelt, Coughlin changed his tune when the president declined to follow his advice about how to deal with the Depression (he counseled Roosevelt to print large amounts of unbacked paper money).

---

* These were not the only Espionage Act and Smith Act prosecutions during World War II, but they attracted the most attention. In total, some two hundred individuals were indicted under these acts over the course of the war. One series of prosecutions was directed against black nationalist leaders who identified with the Japanese. They saw the war as furthering the racist policies of the United States and maintained that the attack on Pearl Harbor was a blow for freedom because the Japanese would "redeem the Negroes from the white men in this country." See Steele, *Good War* at 182–85 (cited in note 1); Goldstein, *Political Repression* at 270 (cited in note 42); Washburn, *Question of Sedition* (cited in note 105).

Father Charles Coughlin

In 1934, Coughlin founded his own social movement, the National Union for Social Justice. He characterized Roosevelt as the "Great Betrayer" and adopted the battle cry "Roosevelt and Ruin!" In 1935, Roosevelt asked Frank Murphy to intercede with Coughlin, on the theory that as two Catholics from Detroit they could find common ground. After their meeting, Murphy thought he had made progress, but the reconciliation proved only momentary.[191]

By 1936, the National Union had more than five million members, and Coughlin's journal, *Social Justice*, had a circulation of more than a million. Coughlin's crusade offered a charismatic "father" figure to his legions of followers, who beseeched him, "[T]est us, try us, lead us!" After a disastrous effort to unseat Roosevelt in 1936, Coughlin moved even more sharply to the right.[192] By 1938, he was sounding more and more like a European fascist, as he praised the "social justice" of the Third Reich.

A month after *Kristallnacht*, Coughlin proclaimed that it was time for the American people to halt the international Jewish conspiracy's spread of communism. According to the *New York Times*, his radio sermons now made him the

German hero in America, and the Bund celebrated him as one of the few Americans who had the courage to withstand Jewish intimidation. Railing against "the problem of the American Jews,"[193] Coughlin frequently lifted entire passages of his sermons from Nazi propaganda.[194] His anti-Semitic outbursts horrified many Catholic leaders, but they diminished neither his appeal nor the size of his audience. Over the next year, *Social Justice* justified Hitler's seizure of Czechoslovakia and named the *Führer* "Man of the Week."[195]

Once the United States entered World War II, *Social Justice* castigated Roosevelt, belittled the American military, cited Allied setbacks as signs of impending collapse, and blamed the war on a British-Jewish-Roosevelt conspiracy. By the spring of 1942, Roosevelt had had enough. He directed Attorney General Biddle to deny mailing privileges to *Social Justice*, by then the most widely read of the virulently anti-administration publications.[196]

Noting the "striking similarity" between *Social Justice* and "Axis propaganda," Biddle argued that it had "made a substantial contribution to a systematic and unscrupulous attack upon the war effort of our nation."[197] In April, U.S. postal authorities invoked the Espionage Act of 1917 to ban *Social Justice* from the mails, pending a final determination. Biddle defended this action on the ground that Coughlin's journal had violated the "false statement" provision of the act.[198]

Coughlin responded with a letter to Biddle, which Coughlin released to the press, in which he offered to appear at any time before a grand jury to testify to the truth of the statements in *Social Justice*. Recognizing that Coughlin was attempting to play the role of martyr, and that a criminal prosecution would divide the nation, Biddle appealed to the church hierarchy. In May 1942, the Catholic Church assured the government that Father Coughlin would remain silent for the duration of the war (on pain of being defrocked), and *Social Justice* "voluntarily" surrendered its second-class mail permit.[*][199]

---

[*] The other major publication excluded from the mails during World War II was the *Militant*, the weekly journal of the Socialist Workers Party. According to Postmaster General Walker, the *Militant* was barred because it attempted "to embarrass and defeat the government in its effort to prosecute the war to a successful termination." Post Office Attorney William O'Brien explained, "It does not make any difference if everything *The Militant* [says] is true. We believe that anyone violates the Espionage Act who holds up and dwells on the horrors of war with the effect that enlistment is discouraged by readers." By mid-1942, the postal service had excluded some thirty publications from the mail. *Militant, Weekly, Barred from Mail*, New York Times 17 (Mar 8, 1943); *The Militant Case*, id at 22 (Apr 28, 1943). See Steele, *Good War* at 161–72 (cited in note 1); Blanchard, *Revolutionary Sparks* at 209–10 (cited in note 150).

As in World War I, state and local governments also addressed issues of loyalty and security. In 1940, New York enacted a law excluding from state employment all persons who advocated, or were members of organizations that advocated, the forceful overthrow of government. The next year, approximately thirty New York City teachers were dismissed or compelled to resign because of their alleged Communist Party affiliations. The Washington legislature refused to seat an elected state senator because he had once been a member of the Communist Party; the University of California declared that Communist Party membership was incompatible with appointment to the faculty; fifteen states banned the Communist Party from the ballot; and "Little Dies" committees sprang up in several states to investigate un-American activities.[200]

The German-American Bund was also the target of such actions. By September 1939, several states had outlawed the wearing of Bund uniforms. The Bund and its members were frequently harassed with charges of tax, financial, and zoning violations and investigated by state committees. In 1939, the Bund leader Fritz Kuhn was indicted in New York for alleged misuse of Bund funds. He was convicted and sentenced to two years in jail. "By the end of 1941, the Bund had been 'harassed out of existence.'"[201]

For the most part, however, the Roosevelt administration restrained state and local governments. As Biddle later recalled, he and Robert Jackson were anxious to avoid the kind of reckless state legislation that had sprung up during World War I.[202] In 1940, at a conference of governors, Roosevelt warned against the "cruel stupidities of the vigilante," and Attorney General Jackson cautioned that "mob efforts almost invariably seize upon people who are merely queer or who hold opinions of an unpopular tinge . . . or otherwise give offense."[203]

Various committees at the 1940 conference recommended that the "[u]se of private organizations and persons other than the constituted authorities" be "carefully restricted," that states not enact sedition laws, and that aliens "be spared from harassment and persecution."[204] State and local officials agreed to take seriously their responsibility to restrain vigilantes and to cede responsibility to combat disloyalty to the federal government.[205]

Throughout the war, the Roosevelt administration attempted to maintain clear lines of authority and to foster restraint at the state and local levels.[206] Attorneys General Jackson and Biddle campaigned actively against vigilantism and consistently spurned suggestions from private groups urging the revival of organizations like the American Protective League, which had played so destructive a role during World War I. Biddle pledged publicly that civil liberties would be protected and that we will "not again fall into the disgraceful series of witch hunts . . . which were such a dark chapter in our record of the last world war."[207]

FBI Director J. Edgar Hoover also played a positive role in this effort. His "primary goal" was to prevent the kind of mass hysteria that had infected the nation during World War I. He knew that such hysteria would lead to abuses of civil liberties and that this would eventually come back to haunt him. His message throughout the war was "leave it to the FBI." FBI bulletins advised state and local officials and private citizens, "[I]f you know of any un-American activities, report them to the FBI and then say nothing more." A 1942 FBI documentary, *The FBI Front*, hammered home the theme that citizens should not engage in "free-lance spy hunting" or vigilante action, and in speech after speech Hoover reiterated that "there is no place here for roving vigilantes."[208]

As a result of these efforts, no state passed a sedition act during World War II, there were very few state prosecutions for disloyalty, and incidents of vigilantism were rare. The most frequent targets of vigilantism were Jehovah's Witnesses, who opposed all war and refused to salute the flag. During the course of World War II, some five hundred Jehovah's Witnesses were beaten by mobs, tarred and feathered, tortured, castrated, or killed in more than forty states. In some of these incidents, local officials participated in the mob actions.[209] Violent persecution of Jehovah's Witnesses declined after May 1942, however, when the Civil Rights Division of the Department of Justice began to threaten local officials with federal prosecution if they failed to protect the constitutional rights of all American citizens. [210]

IN WORLD WAR I, the Wilson administration empowered George Creel's Committee on Public Information to promote war propaganda and whip up a spirit of patriotism and anti-German feeling. In World War II, there was less need for such propaganda, and the Roosevelt administration was less heavy-handed in its production and dissemination of such material. In 1942, Roosevelt established the Office of War Information (OWI) under the direction of Elmer Davis, a respected radio commentator, to distribute information about the progress of the war. In the early months of the conflict, Davis's greatest challenge was simply to obtain information from the military, which worked hard to keep the lid on bad news. After Pearl Harbor, Secretary of the Navy Knox gave a flagrantly misleading report of the extent of American losses, and as the Japanese swept through Singapore, Hong Kong, and Manila in the spring of 1942 the military did its best to cover up the magnitude of each defeat. Davis complained that military authorities seemed unaware "that a democracy fighting a total war will fight it more enthusiastically and effectively if it knows what is going on, and if it feels that its leaders trust it with as much information as it can possibly be given without giving aid and comfort to the enemy."[211] Only after the military began winning battles did it grow more forthcoming with its information.

As the war progressed, the OWI, following the example of the CPI in World War I, increasingly enlisted the media in the nation's propaganda effort. The OWI pressured the film industry, for example, to present an image of America "in which everyone was happy, brave, trustworthy, and loyal."[212] It pushed Hollywood to promote a similar image of America's allies. Ironically, as we shall see in chapter 5, some of the films presenting a positive image of the Soviet Union were later targeted by government investigating committees during the Cold War as unpatriotic and "pro-Communist."[213]

The experience of World War I left deep skepticism about the legitimacy of an official wartime propaganda agency in the United States, and there was constant tension within the OWI over whether its proper role was to tell Americans the truth or to shape the news to bolster morale. Republicans in Congress were particularly uneasy about the role of such an agency, fearing it would be used to deify the president and to further the administration's political ambitions. In light of these concerns, in the summer of 1943 Congress slashed the OWI's budget, rendering it essentially impotent to shape public opinion.[214]

"NO OFFICIAL, HIGH OR PETTY"

FOR THE MOST PART, the Supreme Court played a cautiously speech-protective role during the four years of World War II. In several narrowly drawn, but important, decisions the Court consistently upheld the rights of dissenters.

Schneiderman v. United States[215] involved the issue of denaturalization. For most purposes, citizenship acquired by naturalization is indistinguishable from citizenship acquired by birth. But federal law provides for the cancellation of naturalized citizenship if it was obtained by fraud.[216] Acting under such provisions, the government instituted a series of legal actions to cancel the naturalization of individuals who had "indicated by disloyal conduct that they were not at the time of naturalization 'attached to the principles of the Constitution.'"[217]

By the end of 1943, the United States had issued 146 "decrees of cancellation." Most of these involved former German nationals who had promoted "Nazi doctrines" in the United States or had been active in the German-American Bund. Illustrative of the statements that led to denaturalization proceedings were "No one can force us to give our souls to America" and "The term German is higher than German-American citizen."[218] Other denaturalizations involved members of the Communist Party, although these were relatively rare because of the Soviet-American wartime alliance. The effect of a decree of cancellation was to reinstate the individual's original nationality and, if that nationality was German, to render the individual subject to internment or deportation as an enemy alien. [219]

Schneiderman arrived in the United States from Russia in 1909 when he was three years old. In 1922, aged sixteen, he joined the Young Workers League. In 1927, he became a naturalized American citizen. Throughout this period, Schneiderman remained active in the Young Workers League and the Workers Party, which later became the Communist Party of the United States. In 1932, he was the Communist Party's candidate for governor of Minnesota. In 1939, the United States instituted denaturalization proceedings against him on the premise that in 1927, as a member of the Communist Party, he could not sincerely have accepted attachment to "the principles of the Constitution."

Writing for the Court, Justice Frank Murphy rejected this reasoning, holding that Schneiderman's professed belief in the "nationalization of the means of production" was not necessarily inconsistent with the "general political philosophy" of the Constitution and that his membership in the Communist Party did not in itself establish his opposition to the principles of the Constitution. Murphy distinguished sharply between radical political dissent, which is protected by the First Amendment, and "exhortation calling for present violent action which creates a clear and present danger," and held that the government could not constitutionally denaturalize an American citizen for membership in the Communist Party unless it could prove that the individual had personally endorsed the use of "present violent action which creates a clear and present danger." [220]

The following year, in *Baumgartner v. United States*,[221] the Court considered the case of a German-born individual who had become a naturalized citizen in 1932. Because Baumgartner later embraced Hitler and his doctrines of Aryan supremacy, the government canceled his naturalization on the theory that he had not been loyal to the United States at the time of his naturalization. Expanding on *Schneiderman*, the Court held that an individual could not be denaturalized for speaking "foolishly and without moderation," or for making even "sinister-sounding" statements "which native-born citizens utter with impunity."[222] *Baumgartner* effectively ended the government's program to denaturalize former members of the Bund.[223]

THE COURT ALSO DEALT during World War II with several prosecutions for "subversive" advocacy. In *Taylor v. Mississippi*, [224] the defendant was prosecuted for stating that "it was wrong for our President to send our boys . . . to be shot down for no purpose at all." The Court held that even in wartime "criminal sanctions cannot be imposed for such communication."[225] In *Hartzel v. United States*, [226] the defendant, a crude anti-Semite, was convicted for distributing pamphlets that depicted the war as a "gross betrayal of America," denounced "the Jews," and assailed the "patriotism of the President." Although the case was in many respects a rerun of *Schenck*, the Court reversed the conviction, noting that "an American citizen has the right to discuss these matters either by temperate reasoning or by immoderate and vicious invective, without running afoul of the Espionage Act."[227] *Hartzel* went a long way toward ending government efforts to prosecute antiwar dissent and demonstrated how far the Court had come since World War I.[228]

The Court also grappled with issues posed by Jehovah's Witnesses, especially the question of compulsory flag salute and pledge of allegiance. Before America's entry into the war, the Court held in *Minersville School District v. Gobitis*[229] that schoolchildren could constitutionally be expelled from public schools for refusing to salute the American flag. Three years later, however, in 1943, at the height of the war, the Court overruled *Gobitis* and in *West Virginia State Board of Education v. Barnette*[230] held unconstitutional a state law requiring all children in the public schools to salute and pledge allegiance to the flag. Justice Robert Jackson delivered the opinion of the Court:

> If there is any fixed star in our constitutional constellation, it is that no official, high or petty, can prescribe what shall be orthodox in politics, nationalism, religion, or other matters of opinion or force citizens to confess by word or act their faith therein. If there are any circumstances which permit an exception, they do not now occur to us.[231]

OVERALL, THEN, the nation's free speech record in World War II was mixed. On the one hand, the government clearly felt the tension between respect for constitutional values and the pressure to accommodate public opinion. The activities of the Dies Committee, the wide-ranging investigations of the FBI, the prosecution of Pelley, the Great Sedition Trial, and the government's aggressive denaturalization proceedings all reflected significant overreactions to the very real dangers of wartime.

Franklin Roosevelt, who enthusiastically supported free speech in principle, frequently exerted a negative influence, particularly when dissent conflicted with his political self-interest. Without his often aggressive insistence on "action," his attorneys general would have exercised even greater restraint than they did.

The community of lawyers and other citizens who came to a deeper appreciation of free expression in the wake of World War I too often fell back into a stance of passivity in the face of wartime anxiety.[232] As the experience of World War II demonstrates, it takes a good deal more fortitude to stand up for free speech for the opinions "we loathe" when a nation is at war than when it is at peace.

On the other hand, the widespread concern over the excesses of World War I, the rhetorical power of the Holmes/Brandeis dissents, the Supreme Court's increasingly speech-protective prewar decisions, the public's renewed commitment to free expression in the decade leading up to World War II, and the commitment of Attorneys General Murphy, Jackson, and Biddle not to repeat the mistakes of the past generated a powerful counterweight to the temptation to suppress dissident speech. Perhaps most important, the Supreme Court for the *first time* played a significant role in cabining the tendency of a government to punish those who dissent or otherwise voice "anti-American" values in wartime.[233]

ALIENS AND CITIZENS

AS ILLUSTRATED BY the Alien Acts of 1798 and the post–World War I Red Scare, war hysteria often translates into xenophobia. To some extent, this is understandable. In a war, citizens of an enemy nation who reside in the United States often have divided and uncertain loyalties. It is reasonable to suppose that they pose greater risks of espionage, sabotage, and subversion than either American citizens or other noncitizen residents. As Justice Jackson wrote for the Supreme Court in 1950, the "alien enemy is bound by an allegiance which commits him to . . . the cause of our enemy; hence the United States . . . regards him as part of the enemy resources" and may therefore take appropriate "measures to disable him from commission of hostile acts."[234]

Even resident aliens who are not citizens of an enemy nation may pose special risks because they do not have the same allegiance to the United States as American citizens. It is therefore predictable that a nation at war will keep especially close tabs on both "alien enemies" and "alien friends," to use the terminology of the Alien Acts of 1798. How we address these risks speaks volumes about our values, our sense of fairness, and our willingness to judge individuals as individuals.

THE ALIEN REGISTRATION ACT OF 1940 (the Smith Act) required all resident aliens to register with the Immigration and Naturalization Service (INS).[235] This was the first time the United States had ever made a "complete inventory" of noncitizens.[236] Attorney General Jackson warned that if the process was handled badly it would produce a profound sense of hostility among resident aliens. He cautioned Roosevelt that "there was . . . somewhat the same tendency in America to make goats of all aliens that in Germany had made goats of all Jews, and that it was going to be very difficult to maintain a decent administration" of the registration program. Although Jackson favored a somewhat "closer supervision of aliens," he opposed any "policy of persecuting or prosecuting aliens just because of their alienage."

At a press conference on May 23, 1940, Jackson attempted "to break the news of our policy as gently as possible." Because "aliens did not think they were criminals," they did not think the registration program should be handled by the FBI, which they rightly "regarded as an arm of the criminal" law. Jackson therefore announced that the registration process would be handled by "a separate bureau."[237] The government attempted to secure the voluntary cooperation of the aliens themselves and to persuade them of the legitimacy and importance of the measure. [238]

Jackson assigned Francis Biddle, then Jackson's solicitor general, the responsibility for overseeing the registration process. Biddle fully understood the sensitivity of the situation. As he later observed, "[t]he aliens, who had seen Hitler register the Jews as a preliminary to stripping them of their rights," were understandably anxious about the new registration requirement. Because the policy required *all* aliens to register, rather than only possible enemy aliens, it had the virtue of neutrality.

Biddle arranged for registration to take place at post offices, rather than at FBI or INS offices, thereby easing the sense of foreboding. He also orchestrated a comprehensive public relations campaign designed to reassure aliens that "no stigma" was attached to registration, that noncitizens were seen by the government as "future Americans," and that a significant goal of registration was to help protect "the personal liberties of law-abiding aliens."[239] Attorney General Jackson later concluded that, thanks to these efforts, the registration process was accomplished without serious difficulty.[240]

Of the almost 5 million aliens who registered under the 1940 act, approximately 600,000 were Italian nationals, 260,000 were German nationals, and 40,000 were Japanese nationals. Immediately after the attack on Pearl Harbor, the government classified all 900,000 of these individuals as "enemy aliens" under the Alien Enemies Act of 1798,[241] which authorized the government to apprehend, detain, and deport enemy nationals.

When Biddle asked Roosevelt to sign the proclamations necessary to authorize the attorney general to intern enemy aliens, Roosevelt suggested that it might be wise to intern all German nationals. Roosevelt commented that he wasn't much concerned about the Italians, because "[t]hey are a lot of opera singers," but the Germans, he said, were "different, they may be dangerous." Biddle was determined, however, to "avoid mass internment." Appalled by the British decision in 1940 to intern all 74,000 German and Austrian nationals, Biddle was convinced that the right approach was to consider enemy aliens as individuals.[242] The next question was which enemy aliens to detain.

In the years leading up to America's entry into World War II, the FBI had prepared a list of "potentially dangerous" Axis citizens in the United States. On September 6, 1939, less than a week after Germany invaded Poland, Roosevelt issued a statement requesting "all police officers, sheriffs, and other law enforcement officers in the United States promptly to turn over" to the FBI any information they had relating to espionage, sabotage, or subversive activities.[243]

Later that fall, J. Edgar Hoover informed Congress that the FBI's General Intelligence Division had "compiled extensive indices of individuals, groups, and organizations engaged in . . . subversive activities, in espionage activities, or in any activities that are possibly detrimental to the internal security of the United States." Hoover explained that these indices included the names of "known espionage agents, known saboteurs, leading members of the Communist Party, and the bund."[244] In June 1940, the FBI initiated its Custodial Detention Program, which compiled a list of individuals to be arrested in time of national emergency.[245]

On the night of December 7, 1941, the most dangerous of these individuals were immediately taken into custody. The first step was to arrest the 770 Japanese aliens who were on the FBI's Custodial Detention list.[246] Over the next several months, 9,121 enemy aliens were detained in this manner.[247] Approximately 5,100 (57 percent) were Japanese nationals, 3,250 (36 percent) were German nationals, and 650 (7 percent) were Italian nationals.[248] According to Attorney General Biddle, each of these detentions "was made on the basis of information concerning the specific alien taken into custody." Biddle authorized "no dragnet techniques."[249] In this program, the government seized approximately 1 of every 923 Italian nationals, 1 of every 80 German nationals, and 1 of every 8 Japanese nationals.

Although the Alien Enemies Act does not require a hearing before an enemy alien is detained, Biddle insisted that each individual taken into custody have a hearing. More than a hundred Enemy Alien Hearing Boards were established for this purpose.[250] As a result of these hearings, by June 30, 1943, 4,989 of the 9,121 detainees had either been paroled or released. Over the next six months, the government released or paroled an additional 730 enemy aliens, leaving 3,402 still in custody. By June 1944, the number of enemy aliens interned in this program had declined to 2,525. At that time, Attorney General Biddle observed that a substantial number of the remaining enemy internees would be held until the end

of the war, at which time the government would have to "face the difficult problem of differentiating between those persons who may properly be released" and
"those who should be repatriated to the country of their allegiance."[251]

IMMEDIATELY AFTER PEARL HARBOR, all enemy aliens who had not
been taken into custody—approximately 890,000—were subjected by presidential proclamation to restrictions on their freedom of movement and forbidden to
possess such items as radios, cameras, and weapons. Because most enemy aliens
posed no threat to U.S. national security, Biddle expressed hope that these restrictions could be eased amid growing confidence that all those who actually posed
a danger had been apprehended. In October 1942, Biddle lifted these restrictions
for all 600,000 Italian nationals (representing two-thirds of the enemy aliens in
the United States). He explained that "[o]fficial recognition of the loyalty of Italian aliens was an act of justice to the largest single group included in the original
alien enemy classification" and "an important weapon in the field of psychological warfare" in laying the foundation for military operations in Italy.[252]

German nationals did not fare as well as Italians, but they fared better than
they had during World War I. In 1917–18, anti-German sentiment ran rampant
and German citizens were subjected to widespread private and public harassment.
During World War II, the vast majority of German nationals managed to live relatively quiet lives without serious inconvenience. In part, this was due to the practical reality that by 1940 there were five million German Americans. This was a
significant voting bloc, and German Americans were economically important to
the nation. Any government policy that subjected German aliens to "dragnet techniques" or "indiscriminate" roundups would surely have alienated a critical component of American society.[253]

"A JAP'S A JAP"

JAPAN'S ATTACK ON PEARL HARBOR killed more than two
thousand people and destroyed much of the Pacific fleet. Within the next few
days, the United States declared war against Japan, Germany, and Italy. Two
months later, on February 19, 1942, President Roosevelt signed Executive Order
no. 9066, which authorized the Army to "designate . . . military areas" from
which "any or all persons may be excluded." Although the words "Japanese" or
"Japanese American" never appeared in the order, it was understood to apply
only to persons of Japanese ancestry.[254]

Over the next eight months, 120,000 individuals of Japanese descent were ordered to leave their homes in California, Washington, Oregon, and Arizona. Two-thirds were American citizens, representing almost 90 percent of all Japanese Americans. No charges were brought against these individuals; there were no hearings; they did not know where they were going, how long they would be detained, what conditions they would face, or what fate would await them. They were told to bring only what they could carry. Many families lost everything.

On the orders of military police, these persons were assigned to temporary "detention camps," which had been set up in converted racetracks and fairgrounds. Many families lived in crowded horse stalls, often in unsanitary conditions. Barbed wire fences and armed guard towers surrounded the compounds. From there, the internees were transported to one of ten permanent internment camps, which were located in isolated areas in wind-swept deserts or vast swamplands. Men, women, and children were placed in overcrowded rooms with no furniture other than cots. Although the internees had been led to believe that these would be "resettlement communities" rather than concentration camps, they once again found themselves surrounded by barbed wire and military police. There they remained for three years.

All this was done even though there was not a *single* documented act of espionage, sabotage, or treasonable activity committed by an American citizen of Japanese descent or by a Japanese national residing on the West Coast.[255]

WHY DID THIS HAPPEN? Certainly, the days following Pearl Harbor were dark days for the American spirit. Fear of possible Japanese sabotage and espionage was rampant, and an outraged public felt an understandable instinct to lash out at those who had attacked the nation. But this act was also very much an extension of more than a century of racial prejudice against the "yellow peril." Relations with Japan had been tense for several decades preceding Pearl Harbor. Much of this unease stemmed from Japan's protest of the discrimination experienced by individuals of Japanese ancestry in the United States. Laws passed in the early 1900s denied Japanese the right to become naturalized American citizens, to own land, and to marry outside of their race. In 1924, immigration from Japan was halted altogether.[256]

President Roosevelt, who was not exempt from the pervasive American prejudice against "Orientals,"[257] expressed concern long before 1941 that, in the event of war between the United States and Japan, individuals of Japanese descent could pose a dangerous source of "pro-Japanese fifth columnists." Indeed, anxiety about the loyalty of Hawaiians of Japanese ancestry can be traced as far back as the early

1920s, when the Army's War Plans Division produced a "Project for the Defense of Oahu." This plan, which was to be implemented in the event of conflict with Japan, included "contingency plans for imposing martial law in Hawaii, suspending the writ of habeas corpus, instituting registration of Japanese 'enemy aliens,' and selectively interning those believed to be dangerous." [258]

This plan remained in effect until the 1930s, when a new report was compiled—equally alarmist in its predictions of Japanese American disloyalty. After a further revision of these contingency plans, FDR received a final report in 1936, which apparently impressed him with its "description of subversive activity between Japanese sailors and the local population."[259] In 1936, Roosevelt initiated a program to investigate and neutralize possible disloyal activity among Japanese and Japanese American residents of Hawaii and the West Coast. His willingness to take such preventive measures against Japanese Americans was not matched by any similar effort to keep tabs on Americans of German or Italian ancestry, other than those engaged in fascist organizations or otherwise directly tied to Nazi propaganda activities.

Over the next few years, increasing tension between Japan and the United States, exacerbated by the Japanese assault on Nanking and other acts of overt territorial aggression, led the president to institute economic sanctions and diplomatic measures against Japan in an effort to make clear the seriousness of the situation. In 1940, Secretary of the Navy Knox wrote a memo to Roosevelt proposing fifteen steps to be taken "to impress the Japanese with the seriousness of our preparations" for war. These steps consisted mainly of military recommendations, but number 12 suggested that it was time to "[p]repare plans for concentration camps."[260]

During this period, the government stepped up its security efforts against Japanese aliens and Japanese Americans. Roosevelt directed the Army's G-2 unit and the Office of Naval Intelligence (ONI) to coordinate their anti-espionage and antisabotage activities with the FBI and gave the FBI full control over investigations of subversive activities. In November 1940, the FBI produced a detailed report on the situation in the territory of Hawaii, concluding that "the vast majority of local Japanese (except for a small, easily identifiable group which had not had time to assimilate) were American in their values and loyal to the United States."[261]

By December 1941, the FBI had compiled a list of some two thousand individuals of Japanese descent in Hawaii and on the West Coast whom it deemed "suspect." The master list, described as the "ABC list," divided individuals into three classes. Those on the "A" list were "immediately dangerous," those on the "B" list were "potentially dangerous," and those on the "C" list were suspected of harboring pro-Japan views. Among those on the ABC list "were leaders of Japanese-American civic groups, businessmen, language teachers, Buddhist priests, and martial arts instructors. This list constituted nearly the entire leadership of first-generation West Coast Japanese Americans."[262] It was from this list that the FBI identified the Japanese aliens it arrested in the days immediately after Pearl Harbor.

By December 1941, J. Edgar Hoover was confident that the FBI and the ONI had identified all persons of Japanese descent who could pose a threat to national security. He insisted that the risk posed by other individuals of Japanese descent was minimal.[263] In addition to the military and FBI investigations, Roosevelt commissioned an independent analysis of the issue. He asked the Chicago businessman Curtis Munson to travel to the West Coast to assess the "Japanese problem." Munson's final report found that the Issei, or first generation of Japanese immigrants, had "chosen to make this their home," had "brought up their children here," and "would take out American citizenship if they were allowed to do so." He estimated that the Nisei, or second generation, were "from 90 to 98% loyal to the United States" and "eager to show this loyalty." Munson added "that the Japanese are more in danger from the whites than the other way around." He concluded that Japanese in the United States would not "be any more disloyal than any other group in the United States with whom we went to war."[264]

On December 4, 1941, Eleanor Roosevelt announced that "no law-abiding aliens of any nationality would be discriminated against by the government." Two days later, Judge Jerome Frank, a distinguished federal judge, wrote that "if ever any Americans go to a concentration camp, American democracy will go with them." [265]

IN THE IMMEDIATE AFTERMATH of Pearl Harbor, there was no clamor for the mass internment of Japanese aliens or Japanese Americans. Shortly after the attack, Attorney General Biddle assured the nation that there would be "no indiscriminate, large-scale raids."[266] On December 8, Congressman John M. Coffee expressed his "fervent hope" that "residents of the United States of Japanese extraction will not be made the victim of pogroms directed by self-proclaimed patriots and by hysterical self-anointed heroes." He urged citizens to respect the Bill of Rights and to remember that "these folks" were also "the victims of a Japanese war machine, with . . . which they had nothing to do."[267]

In Hawaii, the military governor, General Delos Emmons, assured Japanese Americans that "there is no intention or desire on the part of the federal authorities to operate mass concentration camps" and that "[n]o person, be he citizen or alien, need worry, provided he is not connected with subversive elements." General Emmons added, "While we have been subjected to a serious attack by a ruthless and treacherous enemy, we must remember that this is America and we must do things the American Way. We must distinguish between loyalty and disloyalty among our people."[268] Indeed, the military never instituted a program of mass internment of Japanese Americans in Hawaii.

As already noted, in the days and weeks following the attack on Pearl Harbor the FBI arrested approximately two thousand Japanese aliens who were on its "ABC" custodial detention list. These individuals were accorded hearings under the procedures adopted by Attorney General Biddle and eventually either released, paroled, or interned along with German and Italian nationals who had been found dangerous to the national security. On December 10, FBI Director Hoover reported that almost all of the persons the FBI intended to arrest had already been taken into custody.[269] On that same day, the *Los Angeles Times* published an editorial urging restraint and warning against the dangers of vigilante activities by self-proclaimed "patriots." There was no outcry for mass internment.[270]

In the weeks that followed, however, a demand for the removal of all Japanese nationals and all American citizens of Japanese ancestry surged along the West Coast. The motivations for this sudden outburst of anxiety were many and complex. Certainly, this demand was fed by fears of a large-scale Japanese invasion of the mainland.[271] Conspiracy theories abounded, and neither government nor military officials did anything to allay these concerns. To the contrary, Mayor Fletcher Bowron of Los Angeles and other local officials were ready to believe and pass on to the public "even the wildest rumor of Oriental treachery." Bowron, for example, helped spread unsubstantiated stories that Japanese fishermen and farmers had been seen mysteriously waving lights along the shoreline. By January, California was awash in bizarre rumors of sabotage and espionage at Pearl Harbor.[272]

General John L. DeWitt, the top Army commander on the West Coast, was determined not to be caught up short like his counterpart in Hawaii. The son of an Army general who had been a decorated combat hero in World War I, DeWitt—short, myopic, bald, and highly excitable—was a career supply officer who suddenly found himself thrust into one of the most complex and unfortunate decisions in American history.

Several days after Pearl Harbor, DeWitt reported as true rumors that a squadron of enemy airplanes had passed over California. Naval investigators soon established that these rumors were unfounded. DeWitt then passed on as true a report of an imminent uprising of twenty thousand Japanese Americans in San Francisco. This report proved false. Then, in the second half of December, Japanese submarines sank several tankers along the West Coast, causing DeWitt to speculate, without foundation, that "Japanese Americans were aiding submarines by signaling them from the shore." The FBI and the Federal Communications Commission later discredited this speculation.[273]

Adding fuel to the fire, Navy Secretary Frank Knox personally inspected Pearl Harbor and reported back to the president that "there was a great deal of very active fifth column work going on both from the shore and from the sampans." Citing the danger of further espionage, Knox recommended to the president that the secretary of war "take all the aliens out of Hawaii and send them off to another island." Roosevelt "diplomatically praised Knox's handling" of the situation, but rejected his recommendation. He no doubt recognized that Knox was eager to deflect responsibility for the disaster at Pearl Harbor away from the navy and was therefore apt to embrace unsupported rumors of Japanese American treachery. Moreover, Roosevelt possessed contrary information from Charles Munson and J. Edgar Hoover, both of whom dismissed Knox's assertions as unwarranted.[274] Indeed, during the six weeks after Pearl Harbor, the president did not find it necessary to focus on this question. Throughout this period, Attorney General Biddle continued to assure the public that no one would be detained "on the score of nationality alone."[275]

AGITATION FOR A MASS EVACUATION of all persons of Japanese ancestry, rather than a more targeted program focusing only on enemy aliens found to be dangerous, was inflamed a month after Pearl Harbor. On January 2, the Joint Immigration Committee of the California legislature issued a manifesto purporting to connect the ethnic Japanese with alleged fifth-column activity in Hawaii. The manifesto charged that even ethnic Japanese born in the United States were "unassimilable," that American citizens of Japanese descent could "be called to bear arms for their Emperor," and that Japanese-language schools were teaching students that "every Japanese, wherever born, or residing," owed primary allegiance to "his Emperor and Japan."[276]

The Hearst newspaper columnist Damon Runyon erroneously reported two days later that a radio transmitter had been discovered in a rooming house that catered to Japanese residents. Who could "doubt," he asked, the "continued existence of enemy agents" among the Japanese population? On January 14, the Republican congressman Leland M. Ford insisted to both the Justice Department and the War Department that the United States must place "all Japanese, whether citizens or not," in "inland concentration camps." The American Legion demanded the internment of all 93,000 individuals of Japanese extraction then living in California.[277]

Such demands were further ignited by the report of the Commission on Pearl Harbor, which was released on January 25. Chaired by Supreme Court Justice Owen Roberts, the report, which was hastily researched and written, asserted that persons of Japanese ancestry living in Hawaii had facilitated Japan's attack on the United States. Although it was later determined that this charge was unfounded, the report played a key role in turning Americans against Americans.

Shortly after the release of the Roberts report, Henry McLemore wrote a column in the Hearst-owned *San Francisco Examiner*, calling for "the immediate removal of every Japanese on the West Coast." He added, "Personally, I hate the Japanese. And that goes for all of them."[278] On February 4, Governor Culbert Olson of California declared in a radio address that it was "much easier" to determine the loyalty of Italian and German aliens than of Japanese aliens and Japanese Americans. "All Japanese people, I believe, will recognize this fact," Olson added.[279]

General DeWitt initially resisted suggestions for the "wholesale internment" of the Japanese, insisting that "we can weed the disloyal out of the loyal and lock them up, if necessary." In early January, he condemned the idea of mass internment as "damned nonsense." But as political pressure began to mount, DeWitt changed his tune. California's governor, the mayor of Los Angeles, and most members of the West Coast congressional delegations now demanded that all persons of Japanese ancestry be removed from the West Coast.

Governor Olson declared that the public "feel that they are living in the midst" of their enemies, and California's attorney general, Earl Warren, argued that, whereas it was relatively easy to find out which Germans or Italian Americans were loyal, it was simply too difficult to determine which Americans of Japanese ancestry were loyal and which were not. Warren later added that "there is more potential danger among the group of Japanese who are born in this country than from the alien Japanese who were born in Japan."[280] DeWitt himself came to the rather astonishing view that "[t]he very fact that no sabotage has taken place to date is a disturbing and confirming indication" that the Japanese have carefully orchestrated their subversion so that when the sabotage comes it will be massive.[281]

Crudely racist statements permeated the debate over the "Japanese problem." In a meeting in January, General DeWitt stated, "The Japanese race is an enemy race and while many second and third generation Japanese born on United States soil, possessed of United States citizenship, have become 'Americanized,' the racial strains are undiluted." He later emphasized that "[i]t makes no difference whether he is an American citizen, he is still a Japanese." This was not true, however, of Germans and Italians. To the contrary, "[y]ou needn't worry about the Italians at all except in certain cases" and "the same for the Germans." "But we must worry about the Japanese all the time until he is wiped off the map." On another occasion, DeWitt famously proclaimed, "[A] Jap's a Jap."[282]

Similar sentiments, and worse, were expressed throughout the West Coast. The following statement by the manager of the Salinas Vegetable Grower-Shipper Association, a group that would gain financially from the roundup of Japanese Americans, captures the spirit of the moment:

We're charged with wanting to get rid of the Japs for selfish reasons. . . . We do. It's a question of whether the white man lives on the Pacific Coast or the brown men. They came into this valley to work, and they stayed to take over. . . . If all the Japs were removed tomorrow, we'd never miss them in two weeks, because the white farmers can take over and produce everything the Jap grows. And we don't want them back when the war ends, either.[283]

Throughout this period, Attorney General Biddle strongly opposed internment as "ill-advised, unnecessary, and unnecessarily cruel." In December, J. Edgar Hoover told Secretary of the Treasury Henry Morgenthau that the attorney general would not approve any "roundup" of Japanese aliens or Japanese Americans. He explained that the FBI had prepared individual cases on each of the alien enemies it had arrested and that each arrest had been approved by Biddle. Hoover emphasized that U.S. citizens of Japanese extraction "were not being included in any arrests," because the authority to "make arrests was limited to alien enemies." He added that Biddle had prohibited any arrests of American citizens "unless there were specific actions upon which criminal complaints could be filed."[284]

In late January, the California congressional delegation pressured Biddle to support internment. Biddle replied that "unless the writ of habeas corpus were suspended" he knew of no way in which "Japanese born in this country could be interned." On February 1, Biddle convened a meeting in his office with representatives of the War Department to discuss the question. He made clear that he would have "nothing to do with any interference with citizens," nor would he "recommend the suspension of the writ of habeas corpus."[285]

In the first two weeks of February, Biddle continued to argue the point. On February 7, over lunch with the president, he told Roosevelt that "mass evacuation" was inadvisable because "the F.B.I. was not staffed to perform it" and the army had offered "no reasons" that would justify it as a military measure.[286] Two days later, he wrote Secretary of War Henry Stimson that the Department of Justice would not "under any circumstances" participate in the evacuation of American citizens on the basis of race. On February 12, he again wrote Stimson that although "the Army could legally evacuate all persons in a specified territory if such action was deemed essential from a military point of view," it could not single out American citizens of Japanese origin.[287]

Biddle informed Stimson that J. Edgar Hoover had concluded that the demand for mass evacuation was based on "public hysteria" and that the FBI had already taken into custody all suspected Japanese agents. By early February, Hoover, the ONI, and military intelligence "all agreed that they had destroyed the Japanese espionage organization," and Hoover accused DeWitt of "getting a bit hysterical." Biddle explained to Stimson that "there is no evidence of any imminent Japanese attack" and "no evidence of any planned sabotage." He added that "a great many people distrust the Japanese, and various special interests would welcome their removal from good farm land and the elimination of their competition." Biddle reiterated that the Department of Justice "would have nothing to do" with any mass evacuation of Japanese Americans.[288]

Stimson himself had grave doubts about the constitutionality of a plan based on the "racial characteristics" of a particular minority group. He confided to his diary the absence of any persuasive "military necessity" for evacuation and his belief that the evacuation of all Japanese Americans from the West Coast would "make a tremendous hole in our constitutional system."[289]

The public clamor on the West Coast, however, continued to build. The American Legion, the Native Sons and Daughters of the Golden West, the Western Growers Protective Association, the California Farm Bureau Federation, the Chamber of Commerce of Los Angeles, and all the West Coast newspapers, including the liberal Los Angeles Daily News, cried out for a prompt evacuation of Japanese aliens and citizens alike. American "patriots" began to commit ugly acts of vigilantism and vandalism against Japanese Americans and their property.

In mid-February, national columnists like Walter Lippmann and Westbrook Pegler demanded stringent measures to deal with the ethnic Japanese. Lippmann dismissed the "fact that since the outbreak of the Japanese war there has been no important sabotage on the Pacific Coast" with the wholly unsubstantiated speculation that this proves "that the blow is well-organized and that it is held back until it can be struck with maximum effect."[290] Pegler shrieked, "[T]o hell with habeas corpus."[291] The attorney general of Idaho announced that all Japanese and Japanese Americans should "be put in concentration camps, for the remainder of the war," adding pointedly, "We want to keep this a white man's country." The attorney general of Washington chimed in that he favored the evacuation of all "citizens of Japanese extraction."[292]

On February 14, General DeWitt officially recommended that all persons of Japanese extraction be removed from "sensitive areas."[293] In a last-ditch effort to stave off mass internment, Biddle wrote the president on February 17. His letter blasted Lippmann and Pegler as "Armchair Strategists and Junior G-Men" for predicting a Japanese attack and sabotage on the West Coast "when the military authorities and the F.B.I. have indicated that this is not the fact." Biddle added that their columns came "close to shouting FIRE! in the theater."[294] Shortly thereafter, Biddle spoke with Roosevelt by phone. At the end of that conversation, a dejected Biddle agreed no longer to resist the mass incarceration of Japanese Americans. According to Biddle, the Justice Department lawyers were "devastated."[295]

On February 19, President Roosevelt signed Executive Order no. 9066. The matter was never discussed in the cabinet, "except in a desultory fashion,"[296] and the president did not consult General George Marshall or his primary military advisers, the Joint Chiefs of Staff.[297] The public rationale for the decision, laid out in General DeWitt's final report on the evacuation of the Japanese from the West Coast, was that time was of the essence and that the government had no reasonable way to distinguish loyal from disloyal persons of Japanese descent.

This report has rightly been condemned as a travesty.[298] It relies upon unsubstantiated and even fabricated assertions;* the government had already postponed action for more than two months after Pearl Harbor and did not actually initiate the internment until several months after February 19; the FBI had already taken into custody those individuals it suspected of potential subversion; two weeks before Roosevelt signed the executive order, General Mark Clark and Admiral Harold Stark testified before a House committee that the danger of a Japanese attack on the West Coast was "effectively nil"; and "[n]o proven instance of espionage after Pearl Harbor among the Japanese population in either Hawaii or the continental United States has ever been disclosed."[299] Moreover, the military did not intern the ethnic Japanese in Hawaii even though Hawaii had by far the greatest concentration of individuals of Japanese descent and even though it had been the site of the Japanese attack.[†300] The argument of military necessity was simply not credible.[301]

WHY, THEN, did the president sign the executive order? Robert Jackson described Roosevelt as a "strong skeptic of legal reasoning" and, despite his reputation, not a "strong champion of . . . civil rights." He "had a tendency to think in terms of right and wrong, instead of terms of legal and illegal. Because he thought that his motives were always good for the things that he wanted to do, he found difficulty in thinking that there could be legal limitations on them."[302] This was evident in Roosevelt's inclination to prosecute "the seditionists," his occasionally lawless approach to wiretapping, his eagerness to deport dissidents, and, of course, his willingness to intern almost 120,000 individuals of Japanese

---

* Much of the inaccurate and inflammatory material in the report asserting potential sabotage and espionage plots by Japanese Americans came from the files of the Dies Committee. See Irons, *Justice at War* at 212–18 (cited in note 256).

† At the outset of the war, Hawaii's population included 159,000 ethnic Japanese, representing 38 percent of Hawaii's population. This included 35,000 Japanese aliens. Whereas on the West Coast most persons of Japanese descent were taken into custody, in Hawaii only 1,466 were, and most were quickly released or paroled. Although martial law was declared in Hawaii almost immediately after Pearl Harbor, all those of Japanese descent who were detained received individualized loyalty hearings. See Scheiber and Scheiber, 3 Western Legal Hist at 344 (cited in note 300); Scheiber and Scheiber, 19 U Hawaii L Rev at 481–82 (cited in note 300).

extraction.[303] Francis Biddle speculated about why Roosevelt signed Executive Order no. 9066:

> I do not think he was much concerned with the gravity or implications of this step. He was never theoretical about things. What must be done to defend the country must be done. The decision was for his Secretary of War, not for the Attorney General, not even for J. Edgar Hoover, whose judgment as to the appropriateness of defense measures he greatly respected. The military might be wrong. But they were fighting the war. Public opinion was on their side, so that there was no question of any substantial opposition. . . . Nor do I think that the constitutional difficulty plagued him—the Constitution has never greatly bothered any wartime President. That was a question of law, which ultimately the Supreme Court must decide. And meanwhile—probably a long meanwhile—we must get on with the war.[304]

Undoubtedly, public opinion played a key role in the thinking of both the military and the president. Even Secretary of War Stimson thought internment a "tragedy," and it seems certain that the War Department yielded to political pressure. Indeed, there was almost no public protest of the president's decision. Only two West Coast public officials opposed internment—Senator Sheridan Downey of California and Mayor Harry P. Cain of Tacoma, Washington[305]—and even most civil liberties groups kept relatively quiet, presumably in the interest of national unity.*[306]

Although Roosevelt explained the order in terms of military necessity, there is little doubt that domestic politics played a role in his thinking, particularly since 1942 was an election year and Roosevelt was hardly immune to politics. Because of the attack on Pearl Harbor, public opinion strongly urged the president to focus American military force on the Pacific. Roosevelt preferred a Europe-first policy. The incarceration of 120,000 individuals of Japanese ancestry was, in part, a way to pacify the "Asia-Firsters." As the legal historian Peter Irons has observed, the internment decision "illustrates the dominance of politics over law in a setting of wartime concerns and divisions among beleaguered government officials."[307]

---

* The public hysteria on the West Coast in support of internment "stunned defenders of civil rights both inside and outside government circles, and they scrambled belatedly to organize pressure against evacuation." Religious organizations and "fair play" committees released statements opposing internment and a few liberal journals, such as the *Nation*, condemned the demand for evacuation. On the whole, however, public reaction against the Japanese internment was both "sporadic and ineffective." Robinson, *By Order of the President* at 102 (cited in note 257).

Internment

THE "UGLY ABYSS OF RACISM"

IN HIS SPECULATION about Roosevelt's thinking, Biddle noted that "ultimately the Supreme Court must decide." And so it did, in a series of decisions addressing the constitutionality of the military orders imposing a night-time curfew on Japanese Americans, excluding Japanese Americans from certain areas of the West Coast, and directing the internment of Japanese Americans in detention camps.[308]

The first case to reach the Court involved Gordon Hirabayashi, who was born in 1918 in Auburn, Washington. Hirabayashi's father ran a roadside fruit market. His parents were pacifists. He attended the University of Washington, where he assumed a leadership role in the YMCA and the Japanese Students Club. As a YMCA officer, he traveled in the summer of 1940 to New York City to attend the "President's School," held jointly at Columbia University and the Union Theological Seminary. While there he participated in passionate debates about pacifism and social activism.

On March 24, 1942, General DeWitt issued Public Proclamation no. 3—imposing a curfew on all enemy aliens, including Italians, Germans, and Japanese, and on American citizens of Japanese descent. With the assistance of a local legislator and the ACLU, Hirabayashi decided to challenge the curfew order by turning himself in to the FBI. He was prosecuted and convicted of violating a federal statute making it a crime for any person knowingly to disregard restrictions in a military area.[309]

In June 1943, the Supreme Court handed down its decision in *Hirabayashi v. United States*.[310] Chief Justice Stone (the same Harlan Fisk Stone who, as attorney general, had prohibited political surveillance by the FBI after the Red Scare) delivered the opinion of the Court. Although Stone observed in conference that he was shocked that "U.S. citizens were subjected to this treatment,"[311] he nonetheless upheld the constitutionality of the curfew:

> We cannot say that the war-making branches of the Government did not have ground for believing that in a critical hour such persons could not readily be isolated and separately dealt with, and constituted a menace to the national defense and safety, which demanded that prompt and adequate measures be taken to guard against it. . . . Distinctions between citizens solely because of their ancestry are by their very nature odious to a free people. . . . [But] it by no means follows that, in dealing with the perils of war, Congress and the Executive are wholly precluded from taking into account those facts and circumstances which are relevant to measures for our national defense . . . and which may in fact place citizens of one ancestry in a different category from others. . . .[312]

Justice Frank Murphy originally drafted a dissenting opinion, but Justice Frankfurter persuaded him that any disagreement within the Court would be disastrous for the nation. Murphy therefore reluctantly recast his draft as a concurring opinion, although it reads like a dissent:

> It is not to be doubted that the action taken by the military commander . . . was taken in complete good faith and in the firm conviction that it was required by considerations of public safety and military security. . . . It does not follow, however, that the broad guaranties of the Bill of Rights and other provisions of the Constitution protecting essential liberties are suspended by the mere existence of a state of war. It has been frequently stated and recognized by this Court that the war power, like the other great substantive powers of government, is subject to the limitations of the Constitution. See *Ex parte Milligan*. . . . [W]e can never forget that there are constitutional boundaries which it is our duty to uphold. . . .
>
> While this Court sits, it has the inescapable duty of seeing that the mandates of the Constitution are obeyed. That duty exists in time of war as well as in time

of peace, and in its performance we must not forget that few indeed have been the invasions upon essential liberties which have not been accompanied by pleas of urgent necessity. . . . "[313]

FRED KOREMATSU WAS BORN in 1919 in Oakland, California. After graduating from high school, he worked as a shipyard welder. In June 1941 he sought to enlist in the Navy, but was turned down because of gastric ulcers. On May 30, 1942, the police in San Leandro, California, stopped and questioned Korematsu, who was walking down the street with his girlfriend. He said his name was Clyde Sarah and claimed he was of Spanish Hawaiian origin. The police took him in for questioning, and he then admitted his real name and ethnicity. He explained that the rest of his family had been sent to the Tanforan assembly center, located in a converted racetrack, but that he had not reported, because he was trying to earn enough money to move to the Midwest with his girlfriend, who was Italian. He had even undergone plastic surgery in an effort to conceal his racial identity.

Korematsu was prosecuted for violating General DeWitt's May 9 Exclusion Order no. 34, which directed that all persons of Japanese ancestry must be excluded from the area under the supervision of the Western Command of the U.S. Army.[314] In 1944, in *Korematsu v. United States*,[315] the Supreme Court upheld Korematsu's conviction in a 6-to-3 decision. Justice Black delivered the opinion for the majority:

---

* In urging Murphy to change his opinion to a concurrence rather than a dissent, Frankfurter argued,

[D]o you really think it is conducive to the things you care about, including the great reputation of this Court, to suggest that everybody is out of step except Johnny, and more particularly that the Chief Justice and seven other Justices of this Court are behaving like the enemy and thereby playing into the hands of the enemy? . . . [C]an't you write your own views with such expressed tolerance that you won't make people think that when eight others disagree with you, you think their view means that they want to destroy the liberties of the United States?

Letter from Felix Frankfurter to Frank Murphy, June 10, 1943, excerpted in Fine, *Washington Years* at 443 (cited in note 18); Melvin I. Urofsky and Paul Finkelman, 2 *A March of History: A Constitutional History of the United States: From 1877 to the Present* 743 (Oxford 2d ed 2002). See also J. Woodford Howard Jr., *Mr. Justice Murphy: A Political Biography* 306 (Princeton 1968).

We cannot reject as unfounded the judgment of the military authorities . . . that there were disloyal members of [the Japanese American] population, whose number and strength could not be precisely and quickly ascertained. . . . Like curfew, exclusion of those of Japanese origin was deemed necessary because of the presence of an unascertained number of disloyal members of the group. . . .

[W]e are not unmindful of the hardships imposed . . . upon a large group of American citizens. But hardships are part of war, and war is an aggregation of hardships. All citizens alike, both in and out of uniform, feel the impact of war in greater or lesser measure. . . .

To cast this case into outlines of racial prejudice . . . confuses the issue. Korematsu was not excluded from the [West Coast] because of hostility to . . . his race . . . [but] because the . . . military authorities . . . decided that the . . . urgency of the situation demanded that all citizens of Japanese ancestry be segregated from the [area]. . . . We cannot—by availing ourselves of the calm perspective of hindsight—now say that at that time these actions were unjustified.[316]

The three dissenting justices were Owen Roberts, who had issued the report on Pearl Harbor, Frank Murphy, and Robert Jackson. Justice Roberts argued that it was patently unconstitutional for the government to insist that an individual submit "to imprisonment in a concentration camp" for no reason other than "his ancestry, without evidence or inquiry concerning his loyalty and good disposition towards the United States."[317] Justice Jackson's dissenting opinion took a somewhat different approach. Jackson argued, "My duties as a justice as I see them do not require me to make a military judgment as to whether General DeWitt's evacuation and detention program was a reasonable military necessity." Although the courts should not "interfere with the Army in carrying out its task," they may not "be asked to execute a military expedient that has no place in law under the Constitution." Jackson concluded, "I would . . . discharge the prisoner."[318]

Justice Murphy wrote a powerful dissent:

The judicial test of whether the Government, on a plea of military necessity, can validly deprive an individual of any of his constitutional rights is whether the deprivation is reasonably related to a public danger that is so "immediate, imminent, and impending" as not to admit of delay and not to permit the intervention of ordinary constitutional processes to alleviate the danger. Civilian Exclusion Order No. 34, banishing from a prescribed area of the Pacific Coast "all persons of Japanese ancestry," . . . does not meet that test. . . .

No adequate reason is given for the failure to treat these Japanese Americans on an individual basis by holding investigations and hearings to separate the loyal from the disloyal, as was done in the case of persons of German and Italian ancestry. . . . It is asserted merely that the loyalties of this group "were unknown and time was of the essence." Yet nearly four months elapsed after Pearl Harbor before the first exclusion order was issued; nearly eight months went by until the last order

Justice Frank Murphy

was issued; and the last of these "subversive" persons was not actually removed until almost eleven months had elapsed. Leisure and deliberation seem to have been more of the essence than speed. . . . Moreover, there was no adequate proof that the Federal Bureau of Investigation and the military and naval intelligence services did not have the espionage and sabotage situation well in hand during this long period. . . . I dissent, therefore, from this legalization of racism.[319]

THE THIRD CASE in the trilogy, *Ex parte Endo*,[320] decided on the same day as *Korematsu*, involved a petition for a writ of habeas corpus filed on behalf of Mitsuye Endo, a twenty-two-year-old clerical worker in the California Department of Motor Vehicles. Endo did not read or speak Japanese and had never visited Japan. Her brother was serving in the U.S. Army. Endo's petition alleged that she was a loyal citizen who had been unlawfully interned in a relocation center under armed guard. The government conceded that Endo was a loyal American citizen.

The Supreme Court held that Endo "should be given her liberty." The Court explained that Executive Order no. 9066 must be construed as "sensitive to and respectful of the liberties of the citizen." Because "[a] citizen who is concededly loyal presents no problem of espionage or sabotage," and because Executive Order no. 9066 had been designed to prevent such activities, the order could not be interpreted as authorizing the detention of a citizen whom the government conceded to be loyal. "Loyalty," the Court emphasized, "is a matter of the heart and mind, not of race, creed, or color." The Court therefore concluded that Endo was "entitled to an unconditional release."[321]

The Court issued this decision on December 18, 1944—one day after the Roosevelt administration had announced that it would release the internees. The timing was no accident. There is good reason to believe that the Court intentionally delayed its decision in *Endo* to allow the president rather than the Court to end the internment.[322] Indeed, there was a lengthy struggle within the Roosevelt administration about when to end the internment. In December 1943, Biddle and Secretary of the Interior Harold Ickes strenuously argued for the immediate release of all loyal Japanese Americans. In May 1944, Secretary of War Stimson made clear to Roosevelt that the internment could be ended "without danger to defense considerations." Nonetheless, the president chose to postpone any such decision, explaining that "the whole problem, for the sake of internal quiet, should be handled gradually." In plain truth, Roosevelt did not want to release the internees until after the 1944 presidential election because such a decision might upset voters on the West Coast. The president's "desire for partisan advantage in the 1944 elections provides the only explanation for the delay in ending internment."[323]

"WE NOW KNOW WHAT WE SHOULD HAVE KNOWN THEN"

IN THE YEARS immediately after World War II, attitudes about the Japanese internment began to shift. In the Evacuation Claims Act of 1948,[324] Congress authorized compensation for well-documented property losses suffered by the internees. Several factors spurred the enactment of this legislation, including a growing sense of guilt, a "moral obligation to make amends," gratitude to the Nisei fighting units that had served the nation during the war, and international condemnation. The process for obtaining compensation was agonizingly slow. By 1958, only 26,000 internees had received any compensation, at an average of $1,400 per internee. As one critic acidly observed, the goal of the program was not to offer reparations for the moral, constitutional, reputational, and economic wrongs done to Japanese Americans but to compensate them for lost "pots and pans." [325]

In a series of decisions shortly after the war, the Supreme Court embraced a new approach to the constitutionality of laws discriminating against aliens. Before World War II, the Court had routinely upheld such laws.[326] In *Takahashi v. Fish and Game Commission*,[327] however, the Court reversed course and held unconstitutional a California law that prohibited the issuance of a commercial fishing license to any "alien Japanese." The Court held that the state lacked constitutional authority "to single out and ban its lawful alien inhabitants, and particularly certain racial and color groups within this class of inhabitants, from following a vocation."[328] Shortly thereafter, in *Oyama v. California*,[329] the Court unanimously held unconstitutional California's Alien Land Law, declaring that discrimination between individuals "on the basis of their racial descent" is prohibited by the Constitution except in "the most exceptional circumstances."[330]

The following year, in *Duncan v. Kahanamoku*,[331] the Court considered the wartime situation in Hawaii. Immediately after the bombing of Pearl Harbor, the government had declared a state of martial law in Hawaii and set up military tribunals to take the place of ordinary courts of justice. In *Duncan*, the Court, reaffirming its 1866 decision in *Ex parte Milligan*, held that the invocation of martial law did not give military tribunals the power to supplant civil courts that were open and properly functioning.

MANY PARTICIPANTS IN the Japanese internment have reflected on the roles they played. Some knew at the time that internment was unconstitutional and immoral. In April 1942, Milton Eisenhower, the national director of the War Relocation Administration, which was responsible for running the detention camps, predicted sadly that "when this war is over . . . we, as Americans, are going to regret the . . . injustices" we have done. Two months later, he resigned his position.[332] Francis Biddle, who vigorously opposed internment, continued to deplore the government's action. In 1962, he wrote that internment had "subjected Americans to the shame of being classed as enemies of their native country without any evidence indicating disloyalty." Unlike citizens of German and Italian descent, Japanese Americans had been treated as "untouchables, a group who could not be trusted and had to be shut up only *because* they were of Japanese descent." Biddle concluded that this episode showed "the power of suggestion which a mystic cliché like 'military necessity' can exercise on human beings." Because of a "lack of independent courage and faith in American reality," the nation missed a unique opportunity to "assert the human decencies for which we were fighting."[333]

Justice Wiley Rutledge, who voted with the majority in *Hirabayashi*, *Korematsu*, and *Endo*, once told Chief Justice Stone that he had suffered "more anguish" over *Hirabayashi* than over any other case he had decided as a justice. Rutledge's biographer later observed that the Japanese internment cases "pushed Wiley Rutledge along the path to his premature grave."[334] Justice Hugo Black, on the other hand, the author of *Korematsu*, did not find these cases difficult. Years later, he volunteered that he would have done "precisely the same thing" again. Justifying his position, Black noted "We had a situation where we were at war. People were rightly fearful of the Japanese in Los Angeles, many loyal to the United States, many undoubtedly not." Black added that this was especially problematic because "they all look alike to a person not a Jap."[335]

Justice William O. Douglas, who also joined the majority in these cases, vacillated between regretting his vote to uphold the Japanese exclusion and defending, or at least explaining, the Court's action. In 1980, Douglas confessed, "I have always regretted that I bowed to my elders" in these cases, noting that these decisions were "ever on my conscience." On the other hand, Douglas explained that the Court "is not isolated from life. Its members are very much a part of the community and know the fears, anxieties, craving and wishes of their neighbors." Although this "does not mean that community attitudes are necessarily translated" into Supreme Court decisions, it does mean that "the state of public opinion will often make the Court cautious when it should be bold."[336]

In 1962, Chief Justice Earl Warren, who played a pivotal role as California

attorney general, reflected on *Korematsu*. Warren observed that war is "a pathological condition" for the nation, and that in such a condition "[m]ilitary judgments sometimes breed action that, in more stable times, would be regarded as
abhorrent." This places judges in a dilemma because the Court may conclude
that it is not in a very good position "to reject descriptions by the Executive of the
degree of military necessity." Moreover, judges cannot easily detach themselves
from the pathological condition of warfare, although with "hindsight, from the
vantage point of more tranquil times, they might conclude that some actions
advanced in the name of national survival" had in fact violated the Constitution.[337] In his 1974 memoirs, Warren conceded that Japanese internment was
"not in keeping with our American concept of freedom and the rights of citizens,"[338] and in later years he admitted privately that he regretted his own actions
in the matter.[339]

Years before he was appointed to the Supreme Court, Tom Clark had served
as an assistant attorney general under Francis Biddle. In that capacity, Clark had
acted as Biddle's liaison with General DeWitt's legal staff. Clark assigned lawyers
to assist the local U.S. attorneys in criminal prosecutions for violation of the military orders.[340] Upon retiring from the Supreme Court in 1967, Justice Clark stated,
"I have made a lot of mistakes in my life. . . . One is my part in the evacuation of
the Japanese from California. . . . [A]s I look back on it—although at the time I
argued the case—I am amazed that the Supreme Court ever approved it."[341]

THE MORALITY AND CONSTITUTIONALITY of the internment has continued to reverberate. As part of the celebration of the Bicentennial of the Constitution in 1976, President Gerald Ford issued Presidential Proclamation no.
4417, in which he acknowledged that we must recognize "our national mistakes
as well as our national achievements." "February 19th," he noted, "is the anniversary of a sad day in American history," for it was "on that date in 1942 . . . that
Executive Order 9066 was issued." Ford observed that "[w]e now know what we
should have known then"—that the evacuation and internment of loyal Japanese
American citizens was "wrong." Ford concluded by calling "upon the American
people to affirm with me this American Promise—that we have learned from the
tragedy of that long-ago experience" and "resolve that this kind of action shall
never again be repeated."[342]

Four years later, Congress established the Commission on Wartime Reloca-
tion and Internment of Civilians to review the implementation of Executive
Order no. 9066. The commission comprised former members of Congress, the
Supreme Court, and the cabinet, as well as several distinguished private citizens.
It heard testimony from more than seven hundred witnesses, including key gov-
ernment personnel who were involved in the issuance and implementation of

Executive Order no. 9066. It reviewed hundreds of documents that had not previously been available. In 1983, the commission unanimously concluded that the factors that shaped the internment decision "were race prejudice, war hysteria and a failure of political leadership," *not* military necessity. It recommended that "Congress pass a joint resolution, to be signed by the President, which recognizes that a grave injustice was done and offers the apologies of the nation for the acts of exclusion, removal and detention."[343]

That same year, Fred Korematsu and Gordon Hirabayashi filed petitions for writs of error *coram nobis* to have their convictions set aside for "manifest injustice."[344] The following year, Judge Marilyn Patel granted Korematsu's petition.[345] Judge Patel found that in its presentation of evidence to the federal courts in the course of Korematsu's prosecution and appeal, including in the U.S. Supreme Court, the government had *knowingly and intentionally* failed to disclose critical information that directly contradicted key statements in General DeWitt's final report, on which the government had asked the courts to rely.[346]

Judge Patel added that the Supreme Court's decision in *Korematsu* "stands as a constant caution that in times of war or declared military necessity our institutions must be vigilant in protecting constitutional guarantees," "that in times of distress the shield of military necessity and national security must not be used to protect governmental actions from close scrutiny and accountability," and "that in times of international hostility" the judiciary "must be prepared to exercise [its] authority to protect all citizens from the petty fears and prejudices that are so easily aroused."[347]

In 1987, the U.S. Court of Appeals for the Ninth Circuit granted Gordon Hirabayashi's petition for a writ of *coram nobis* and vacated his conviction. The court of appeals, in an opinion by Judge Mary Schroeder, found serious deceit in the United States's presentation of its case to the Supreme Court.[348] Judge Schroeder concluded that the original version of DeWitt's final report, designed to justify the military orders, did not "purport to rest on any military exigency, but instead declared that because of traits peculiar to citizens of Japanese ancestry it would be impossible to separate the loyal from the disloyal."

When officials of the War Department received the original report, they directed DeWitt to make substantial alterations to excise its racist overtones and add statements of military necessity. Copies of the original report were burned. When officials of the Justice Department were preparing to brief *Hirabayashi* in the Supreme Court, they sought all materials relevant to General DeWitt's decision making. The War Department did not disclose to the Justice Department the original version of the report.[349]

Judge Schroeder found that, given the importance the justices attached to the government's claims of military necessity in *Hirabayashi* and *Korematsu*, "the reasoning of the Supreme Court would probably have been profoundly and materially affected" had it been advised "of the suppression of evidence" that would have "established the . . . real reason for the exclusion order."[350]

In the last year of his presidency, Ronald Reagan signed the Civil Liberties Act of 1988,[351] which officially declared the Japanese internment a "grave injustice" that was "carried out without adequate security reasons" and without any documented acts of "espionage or sabotage." The act declared that the program of exclusion and internment had been "motivated largely by racial prejudice, wartime hysteria, and a failure of political leadership." The act offered an official presidential apology and reparations to each of the Japanese-American internees who had suffered discrimination, loss of liberty, loss of property, and personal humiliation at the hands of the U.S. government.[*][352]

The Court's decision in *Korematsu* was immediately condemned in the public and professional literature. Eugene Rostow, a professor at Yale Law School, termed the decision a "disaster." He chastised the Court for dealing with the facts as "Kiplingesque folklore" and for upholding a military policy that clearly had been based not on military necessity but on "ignorant race prejudice."[353] There is little doubt that even at the time of the decision the justices knew or should have known that the government's justifications for the internment were without merit, but they "chose to ignore" the facts.[354] Over the years, *Korematsu* has become a constitutional pariah. The Supreme Court has never cited it with approval of its result.[355]

MURPHY, JACKSON, AND BIDDLE

IT WAS NEVER ENTIRELY CLEAR why President Roosevelt nominated Attorney General Frank Murphy to replace Justice Pierce Butler. Murphy did not have the background or the intellectual depth ordinarily associated with a Supreme Court justice. Even Murphy doubted his capacity to handle the posi-

---

[*] The Civil Liberties Act of 1988 authorized a payment of $20,000 to each surviving internee. By 1998, the total payout was $1.6 billion, paid to 80,000 claimants. See Elazar Barkan, *The Guilt of Nations: Restitution and Negotiating Historical Injustices* 30–31 (Norton 2000).

tion. Robert Jackson, then Murphy's subordinate as solicitor general, strongly advised the president against the appointment, and Francis Biddle was certain Murphy was the wrong man for the job.[356] Nonetheless, suggesting that Murphy could grow into an "acceptable Justice" and that his colleagues on the Court would "keep him straight," Roosevelt nominated Murphy to the Court in 1939. Roosevelt's motives included a political need to replace Butler, a Catholic from the Midwest, with another midwestern Catholic; his confidence that Murphy would support the New Deal; and his desire to move Murphy, who was not a particularly deft administrator, out of the Department of Justice.[357] Murphy's appointment also enabled the president to promote Robert Jackson to attorney general and Francis Biddle to solicitor general.

Once on the Court, Justice Murphy staked out a position as a staunch defender of civil liberties. Although he did not score many points for judicial craftsmanship, he made a significant contribution as a voice for the downtrodden and the oppressed. He championed the rights of labor, the freedom of expression, and the interests of those caught up in the criminal justice system. He strongly supported the free speech rights of Jehovah's Witnesses and wrote the Court's critical opinion in *Schneiderman*, holding that the government could not constitutionally denaturalize an American citizen because of his membership in the Communist Party.[358] In his dissenting opinion in *Korematsu*, Murphy charged that the government had gone beyond "the very brink of constitutional power" and fallen into the "ugly abyss of racism." [359]

FRANKLIN ROOSEVELT APPOINTED Attorney General Robert Jackson to the Supreme Court in 1941. There was no question that Jackson was eminently qualified by intellect, experience, and disposition. He had a clear, elegant, and persuasive judicial style, punctuated by biting sarcasm and a sharp wit. As the Harvard professor Paul Freund once observed, Jackson "had style to delight, grace and power of expression to captivate."[360] His opinion for the Court in *Barnette*,[361] holding that even in wartime a school board could not compel students to salute the flag, is one of the most eloquent statements of constitutional freedom in the Court's history. His dissenting opinion in *Korematsu* expressed strong disapproval of the government's internment program, noting that "if any fundamental assumption underlies our system, it is that guilt is personal and not inheritable."[362] Throughout his tenure on the Court, Jackson supported individual rights and opposed arbitrary government action.[363] He criticized the Immigration Service's use of secret evidence and argued that President Truman's seizure of the steel industry during the Korean War was unconstitutional, noting that "the Constitution did not contemplate that the title Commander-in-Chief of the Army and Navy will constitute" the president "Commander-in-Chief of the country."[364]

In 1945, President Truman appointed Justice Jackson chief U.S. prosecutor at the war crimes trials at Nuremberg, a responsibility Jackson fulfilled with brilliance and dignity. In his opening statement, Jackson observed that "the wrongs which we seek to condemn and punish have been so calculated, so malignant, and so devastating, that civilization cannot tolerate their being ignored because it cannot survive their being repeated." Jackson helped set the tone for the proceedings when he added, "That four great nations, flushed with victory and stung with injury, stay the hands of vengeance and voluntarily submit their captive enemies to the judgment of the law is one of the most significant tributes that Power has ever paid to Reason." After completing his duties at Nuremberg, Jackson returned to the Supreme Court, where he continued to serve with distinction.

UNLIKE FRANK MURPHY and Robert Jackson, Francis Biddle was not appointed a justice of the U.S. Supreme Court. In 1942, when Justice Byrnes retired, President Roosevelt asked Biddle whether he was interested in the position. Biddle reminded the president that he had not enjoyed his brief stint on the court of appeals. He said that "being a judge was like being a priest," and that he preferred not to be so "cut off from the world." Biddle thus told Roosevelt that he was "happy" where he was and "did not wish to leave him during the war."[365]

In May 1945, six weeks after Roosevelt's death, President Truman, in a shake-up of the cabinet, asked for Biddle's resignation. Biddle was shocked and angry. A few months later, however, Truman appointed Biddle the American judge on the International Military Tribunal in Nuremberg. Over the next year, Biddle, along with judges from England, France, and the Soviet Union, heard evidence against twenty-one alleged Nazi war criminals, including Hermann Göring, Rudolf Hess, Albert Speer, and Julius Streicher. Biddle recalled, "There was no end to the horrors of the testimony." As he listened to Robert Jackson's grim presentation of evidence about Auschwitz, Dachau, Treblinka, and Mathausen, "Hitler's ghost haunted the courtroom." In the end, the tribunal sentenced eleven of the defendants to death by hanging. For Biddle, this was a profound experience, affirming that "the preservation of individual freedom, of personal integrity, alone can keep alive the human spirit."[366]

Like Judges Bourquin, Amidon, and Hand during World War I, Attorneys General Murphy, Jackson, and Biddle brought to public service a sense of integrity and a respect for constitutional values that helped guide the nation through one of its most perilous times. Although the Japanese American internment will forever be a stain on the nation's legal and constitutional history, Murphy, Jackson, and Biddle each opposed this policy in his own fashion. Moreover, because of their actions, the United States came through World War II with a stronger commitment to free speech than it had ever known before. Each of these men compromised at times, but on the whole they demonstrated the courage that Justice Brandeis characterized as the "secret of liberty."

THE COLD WAR

The First Amendment in Extremis

"McCarthyism"

*W*HEN WORLD WAR II DREW TO A CLOSE, the United States slipped almost seamlessly into the Cold War. The Berlin blockade, the fall of China, and the Korean War were not independent events but part of "a slow-motion hot war, conducted on the periphery of rival empires."[1] During this era, the United States demonized current and former members of the Communist Party and their "fellow travelers," and a host of political opportunists fed—and fed upon—the image of the Communist as insidious, malignant, and dangerous to American values. It was a period marked by the bare-knuckled exploitation of anticommunism. Fearful of domestic subversion and nuclear annihilation, Americans turned against one another in what would prove to be one of the most repressive periods in American history.[2]

When Harry Truman became president in 1945, the federal and state statute books were already laced with anti-Communist legislation. As America's wartime alliance with the Soviet Union fragmented, Truman came under increasing attack from a coalition of southern Democrats and anti–New Deal Republicans who sought to manipulate fears of Communist aggression. In the 1946 congressional elections, a young Richard Nixon charged that his opponent voted the "Moscow" line; an obscure Senate candidate in Wisconsin, Joseph R. McCarthy, accused his opponent of being "Communistically inclined"; and Senator Hugh Butler, a Republican of Nebraska, charged that "if the New Deal is still in control of Congress after the election, it will owe that control to the Communist party." B. Carroll Reece, the chairman of the Republican National Committee, maintained that "Democratic party policy . . . bears a made-in-Moscow label." The "choice which confronts Americans," he warned, is "between Communism and Republicanism."[3] The Republican Party won a sweeping victory, picking up fifty-four seats in the House and eleven in the Senate. Red-baiting had proved an effective political strategy.

Thereafter, the issue of "loyalty" became a shuttlecock of party politics, as Democrats scrambled to defuse this new Republican strategy. In 1947, Truman's secretary of labor demanded that the Communist Party be outlawed. "Why," he asked, "should they be able to elect people to public office?" Attorney General Tom Clark suggested that "those who do not believe in the ideology of the United States" should not be "allowed to stay in the United States." By 1948, Truman was boasting on the stump that he had imposed on the federal civil service the most extreme loyalty program in the "Free World." Leaving no doubt of the matter, Truman proclaimed, "I want you to get this straight now. I hate Communism."[4]

There were limits, however, to Truman's anticommunism. In 1950, he vetoed the McCarran Internal Security Act, which called for the registration of all Communists. Truman explained that the act was the product of public hysteria and would lead to "Gestapo witch hunts." Congress passed the act over Truman's veto.[5]

Red-baiting reached unprecedented levels in the 1950 election. John Foster Dulles, challenging Herbert Lehman for the Senate in New York, said of Lehman, "I know he is no Communist, but I know also that the Communists are in his corner." In California, Congressman Richard Nixon secured election to the Senate by circulating a pink sheet accusing his Democratic opponent, Helen Gahagan Douglas, of voting the Communist line. And in Florida, Congressman George Smathers defeated Claude Pepper by describing him as "Red Pepper" and tarring him as an "apologist for Stalin."[6]

The long shadow of the House Un-American Activities Committee fell across the American culture and campuses. Robert Hutchins observed, "The question is not how many teachers have been fired [for their beliefs], but how many think they *might* be. . . . The entire teaching profession of the U.S. is now intimidated."[7] In hearings before HUAC, a rash of prominent actors and movie producers testified that Hollywood had been infected by un-American propaganda. Red hunters demanded, and got, the blacklisting of such writers as Dorothy Parker, Lillian Hellman, James Thurber, and Arthur Miller.

In the Communist Control Act of 1954, Congress stripped the Communist Party of all rights, privileges, and immunities.[8] Only one senator, Estes Kefauver, dared vote against it. Irving Howe lamented "this Congressional stampede to . . . trample the concept of liberty in the name of destroying its Enemy."[9] Loyalty programs, emergency detention plans, undercover surveillance, legislative investigations, and criminal prosecutions of Communists swept the nation.[10]

In an era of rampant McCarthyism, government at all levels hunted down "disloyal" individuals and denounced them for past or present beliefs or associations. Anyone stigmatized as a "Red" was instantly damned as one who would betray his country. He became a menace to his friends and an outcast to society. It became hazardous to sign a petition, join a political organization, or express a nonconforming opinion.[11] As John Lord O'Brian observed in 1948, in this atmosphere of suspicion and mistrust, a mere charge of "disloyalty" could result in "lasting disgrace."*[12]

The struggle over Communist "subversion" would implicate many themes and values. At its core, it was about protecting the national security, preventing espionage, and preserving military and scientific secrets. But it was about much more than that. The very ideals of communism threatened the established order. Communism was "godless." If it infected the nation, it would endanger religious beliefs and values. Communism opposed private property. If it crept into labor unions and legislatures, it would foster industrial strife and the redistribution of capital. Communism was insidious. If it infiltrated schools, newspapers, and motion pictures, it would poison national values and destroy the will to resist. Communism was immoral. If it tainted political discourse, it would lead to a loss of liberty, justice, and spiritual goodness. Communism was cancerous. If it corrupted public employees, it would subvert American government from within. As Bishop Fulton J. Sheen put the point, "the basic struggle" was not only over military security but also over whether "man shall exist for the state, or the state for man."[13]

"BOY WONDER"

"BRILLIANT," "ACERBIC," "DARING," "MAGNETIC"— all words used to describe Robert Maynard Hutchins. Born in Brooklyn in 1899, Hutchins was greatly influenced by his father, a distinguished Presbyterian minister who taught that knowledge and truth were what mattered most in life. In 1907, the Reverend Hutchins moved his family to Ohio, where he accepted a position as professor of homiletics at Oberlin College.

---

* By the mid-1950s, 13.5 million Americans—more than 20 percent of the national workforce—were employed under the shadow of a loyalty program. Some 11,000 Americans had been fired for suspected "disloyalty," more than 100 had been prosecuted under the Smith Act, and more than 130 had been jailed for contempt of HUAC for refusing to cooperate with their interrogators. See Brown, *Loyalty and Security* at 181, 487–88 (cited in note 10); Goldstein, *Political Repression* at 374–75 (cited in note 3).

Growing up in an academic community under the influence of a strong and highly respected father, Robert Hutchins developed a keen sense of leadership and a taste for social responsibility. He learned the values of intellectual rigor and independent thought and came to believe that open debate and rational discussion would lead people to sound decisions.

After attending Oberlin College for two years, Hutchins volunteered for the ambulance corps during World War I. He despised the regimentation of military life, however, and the patriotic fervor of the Great War repelled him. When a professor of history almost lost his position because of his German heritage, both Hutchins and his father defended him to the Oberlin community. Woodrow Wilson's characterization of World War I as a "moral crusade" and the government's frenzied repression of dissent left Hutchins with a lifelong "revulsion" for wartime excess.[14]

After returning from the war, Hutchins completed his undergraduate education at Yale, where he grew enamored of the law. In 1922, James Rowland Angell, the new president of Yale, invited Hutchins to serve as secretary of the university, a position that placed him at the center of one of the nation's great institutions of higher learning. Although this was more than a full-time position, Hutchins still found time to resume his legal studies. In 1925, he was appointed instructor of law, in 1927 associate professor, and in 1928 professor and dean of the Yale Law School. He was twenty-nine years old.

John Wigmore, the conservative dean of the Northwestern University Law School, and a Yale alumnus, criticized Hutchins's appointment on the ground that he would "create unrest among his colleagues" and "unsettle the minds" of his students.[15] And so he did. Hutchins publicly challenged the convictions of Sacco and Vanzetti, condemning the trial court's "gross mishandling" of the prosecution by allowing hatred of the defendants' anarchist views to corrupt their trial.[16] Yale alumni, including Supreme Court Justice William Howard Taft, chastised the university for allowing Hutchins to take such a position. A year later, Hutchins was appointed president of the University of Chicago.

Founded in 1892 by John D. Rockefeller, the University of Chicago was designed to combine an American-style undergraduate college with a German-style graduate research university. Its creation was one of those events that "brought into focus the spirit of an age."[17] The university was bold, ambitious, and breathtaking in its rapid rise to prominence. The early faculty included such extraordinary scholars as John Dewey, Ernst Freund, Thorstein Veblen, and America's first three Nobel laureates—Albert Michelson, Robert Millikan, and Arthur Compton. When Hutchins arrived in 1929, the faculty was said to be "the best to be found in any institution in the country."[18]

The trustees of the university wanted a president who would break the mold. They wanted someone dynamic, creative, and charismatic. Hutchins was their man. He made an immediate impression when he arrived on campus in the summer of 1929. He was tall, dark, and striking in appearance. When he walked into a room, "he commanded instant attention."[19] Edward Shils once described him as "handsome beyond my descriptive powers."[20] The press dubbed him the "boy wonder."[21]

Hutchins could charm and delight an audience. He had a clear, resonant voice and an ironic, sometimes biting sense of humor. He was a master of the self-deprecating witticism and the withering wisecrack. On one occasion, when he was still at Yale, a visiting Supreme Court justice observed, "I understand you teach your students that the nine old men down in Washington are all senile, ignorant of the law, and indifferent to the public welfare." Hutchins quipped, "Oh, no, Mr. Justice, we don't teach them anything like that. We let them find it out for themselves."[22] As *Time* magazine observed, Hutchins was sometimes "entirely too . . . smart alecky."[23]

Hutchins was also a champion of academic freedom. In a 1931 address to the American Association of University Professors, he declared, "We have got to make ourselves clear. The only [question] that can properly be raised about a professor . . . is his competence in his field. His . . . political views . . . are not the concern of his university."[24] Over time, Hutchins's commitment to this ideal would be sorely tested.

In at least one respect, Hutchins's timing was dreadful. He arrived at the University of Chicago only a few months before the Depression, which had a devastating impact on higher education. One of its less obvious consequences was its effect on political and intellectual thought. By the early 1930s, students at the university began to turn to Marxism in their search for explanations for the Depression and remedies for the suffering it caused. Heated debates about the merits of free enterprise exploded on campus. No other campus rivaled the intellectual cauldron of the University of Chicago of the 1930s in its open and often fierce discourse about communism and capitalism.

In 1932, a student organization invited William Z. Foster, the Communist Party's candidate for president, to lecture on campus. This triggered a storm of protest from some alumni and local business leaders. Hutchins explained that "our students . . . should have freedom to discuss any problem that presents itself." He rejected the call for "censorship," arguing that the "cure" for bad ideas "lies through open discussion rather than through inhibition and taboo."[25] This did not sit well with some of the university's benefactors, but Hutchins stood his ground.

In 1935, the Hearst newspapers launched a nationwide attack on Communist propaganda in American universities, focusing on the University of Chicago. The president of the National Association of Manufacturers decried Hutchins as a "parlor red" who had allowed his university to devolve into "a hot bed of radicalism."[26] At a speech in Chicago, Hutchins responded to his critics. "The answer to such charges," he declared, is "not denial, nor evasion, nor apology." Rather, it is "the assertion that free inquiry is indispensable to the good life, that universities exist for the sake of such inquiry, that without it they cease to be universities, and that such inquiry and hence universities are more necessary now than ever."[27]

Two months later, on April 13, 1935, Charles R. Walgreen, the drugstore magnate, wrote Hutchins that he was withdrawing his niece, Lucille Norton, from the University of Chicago, explaining, "I am unwilling to have her absorb the Communistic influences to which she is assiduously exposed." Walgreen charged that, as a student in a social sciences course, Norton had been required to read Marx's *Communist Manifesto*. He could not fathom why "one of our country's leading universities . . . should permit, even to a limited degree, seditious propaganda under the guise of academic freedom." Walgreen released his letter to the press, which immediately broke the story as front-page news.[28]

Less than a week later, the Illinois Senate established a special committee to investigate "subversive communistic teachings" in "certain tax exempt colleges and universities in the State of Illinois." The committee made the University of Chicago its first and only target of investigation. On April 18, Hutchins addressed the nation on an NBC radio program. "Americans," he said, "must decide whether they will . . . tolerate the search for the truth." He cautioned that "if they will not, then . . . we can blow out the light and fight it out in the dark, for when the voice of reason is silenced, the rattle of machine guns begins."[29]

The Walgreen hearings commenced on May 14. Charles Walgreen, the first witness, testified to a dinner conversation with his eighteen-year-old niece:

> We were discussing Communism and capitalism, and . . . I said to Lucille, "you are getting to be a Communist." And she said, "I am not the only one, there are a lot more on the campus."
>
> I said to Lucille, "Do you realize that this means the abolition of the family, the abolition of the Church, and especially . . . the overthrow of our government?" And she said, "Yes, I think I do, but don't the ends ever justify the means?"
>
> "Don't you realize that this means bloodshed?" Again, she said, "Yes, but how did we get our independence, wasn't it by revolution?"
>
> "Well, Lucille, are they really teaching you these things over at the University?" And she said, "No, I don't think they are teaching it to us. . . . [but] we have a lot of reading on Communism."[30]

Walgreen accused several professors, including the English professor Robert Morss Lovett, of being Communist sympathizers. Lovett, a member of the Chicago faculty since 1893, was a venerable teacher with a penchant for left-wing causes. He was a member of several organizations associated with the Communist Party (so-called Communist-front organizations).

By the end of the hearings, four of the five committee members voted to terminate the proceedings. They "exonerated" the university on the charge of teaching communism, but recommended that it dismiss Professor Lovett because of his outside activities. Hutchins refused. Indeed, when a faculty member confronted Hutchins with the threat "[I]f the trustees fire Lovett you'll receive the resignations of twenty full professors," Hutchins replied, "Oh no I won't. My successor will."[31]

Hutchins landed on the cover of *Time* magazine, which lauded his "courage" and "vision."[32] Charles Walgreen eventually recanted. When the University of Chicago vice president (and future adversary of Joseph McCarthy) William Benton reproached Walgreen for his conduct in this affair, Walgreen donated $550,000 to the university to establish the Walgreen Foundation for the Study of American Institutions.* Walgreen died in 1938. At his family's request, Hutchins spoke at his funeral.

━━━━━━━━━━━━
━━━━━━━━━━━━

REDS

WHO WERE THESE "REDS" who inspired such fear and loathing? Alan Barth, a longtime editorial writer for the *Washington Post*, explained in 1952 that the Communist Party of the United States (CPUSA) was not a "political party in the accepted American sense of the term," but an organization that was effectively controlled by the Kremlin. He added that there had been nothing in the prior experience of the United States "quite like this organization, which consistently serves a foreign power" and is "made up of men and women who wish to transform America in the image . . . of the Soviet Union" and believe that "nondemocratic means will be justified and necessary to effect that change." At the same time, Barth wisely cautioned that to recognize that Communists opposed American institutions was not a reason for concluding that "they gravely imperiled the nation."[33]

Founded in 1919, the CPUSA was immediately forced underground in the post–World War I Red Scare. The party never attained any appreciable size. At the peak of its membership, in 1940, it had barely 100,000 dues-paying members. From an electoral standpoint, the party was essentially irrelevant. Whereas Eugene

---

* Legend has it that on the first day of the Walgreen hearings, as Hutchins walked past the complainant's table, he leaned over and affably said, "Mr. Walgreen, this is going to cost you half a million dollars." Ashmore, *Unreasonable Truths* at 131 (cited in note 16).

Robert Maynard Hutchins

Debs had received almost a million votes in 1912 and 1920 as the Socialist Party candidate for president, the Communist Party candidate for president never scraped together more than 100,000 votes, and rarely exceeded 50,000. No member of the Communist Party was ever elected to Congress. The circulation of the *Daily Worker* from 1945 to 1950 was roughly 20,000, hardly a major force in American journalism.[34]

The CPUSA did have a hard core of dedicated members, but they could never bring much coherence to the party because of its extraordinarily high turnover in membership. From the mid-1920s to the mid-1950s, turnover was as high as 33 percent *annually*. As a consequence, by the 1950s, when the party's active membership was less than 10,000, there were as many as 250,000 *former* members of the CPUSA in the United States, a fact that would prove critical.[35]

WHO JOINED THE COMMUNIST PARTY or became a fellow traveler? A small cadre of American Communists—estimated at between 200 and

400 in the late 1940s—were active agents of the Soviet Union. Fervently hostile to capitalism, religion, and American-style democracy, they participated in a highly secretive and sometimes effective conspiracy of espionage and subversion on behalf of the Soviet Union.[36]

But they represented only a *tiny* fraction of those who were characterized as Reds, and for obvious reasons they were never public about their associations or activities. The vast majority of American Reds were drawn to communism in the 1930s, not to serve the Soviet Union, but because communism seemed the best hope in the struggle for justice at home and against fascism abroad. Most first turned to communism as a result of the Depression, which brought with it a profound sense of desperation and dislocation. With a third of all Americans unemployed and the earnings of those with jobs cut by two-thirds, the Depression triggered a severe loss of confidence in America's business and political leaders, a widespread demand for economic and social reform, and a desperate search for answers.

After 1929, people listened more attentively to arguments for a planned, classless society, in which each individual would contribute according to his ability. On urban breadlines and devastated farms, Americans questioned the cruel consequences of capitalism. As Eugene Lyons later noted, "In a time of head-splitting questions, the Communists offered answers."[37] Socialist ideals appealed not only to the downtrodden but also to many idealists, liberals, and intellectuals. With President Roosevelt's recognition of the Soviet Union in 1933, Americans were more open than ever to learning about communism. Such progressive voices as the *New Republic* and the *Nation* acknowledged that New Deal liberalism and communism shared many of the same ideals.[38]

The CPUSA advocated public housing to replace slums and public works to provide jobs; it championed racial equality and the rights of labor; it embraced a broad range of progressive social and economic reforms; it played a key role in the efforts to save Sacco and Vanzetti and the Scottsboro Boys.* In this era of intense social turbulence and exuberant political energy, hundreds of clubs, associations, committees, and alliances sprang into being to fight for economic,

---

* On March 25, 1931, nine black youths, who came to be known as the Scottsboro Boys, were accused of raping two white women on a Southern Railroad freight train. The defendants were promptly tried with inadequate counsel before an all-white jury. Eight of the nine were sentenced to death. The case became a cause célèbre. The CPUSA, the NAACP, and the ACLU all participated at various time sin the many appeals and retrials of the case. Twice the Supreme Court overturned the convictions. See *Powell v. Alabama*, 287 US 45 (1932) (defendants had been denied due process of law because of the incompetence of counsel); *Norris v. Alabama*, 294 US 587 (1935) (holding unconstitutional the systematic exclusion of blacks from the jury). Four of the nine defendants were released from prison in 1937; the last was not released until 1950. See Dan T. Carter, *Scottsboro: A Tragedy of the American South* (LSU 1979).

social, political, racial, and international justice. Most members of these groups were not Communists, or even Communist "sympathizers," but they and the Communists shared many of the same goals. Hundreds of thousands—perhaps millions—of Americans joined such organizations in the 1930s, not because they wanted to "overthrow the government" but because they wanted to help in good causes as a civic responsibility.*[39]

Of course, most of these people, including many of America's leading intellectuals, were at least generally aware of the grim realities of life in the Soviet Union. But information about the Soviet Union was often muddled, and Americans desperate for change tended—mistakenly—to discount the horror stories about Stalinist Russia, especially when they could be dismissed as the exaggerations of the more capitalist-minded elements of the press. Moreover, publication in 1936 of the new Soviet constitution, which purported to embrace democratic values, encouraged the hope that freedom could flourish in a Communist society.

Equally important, the Soviet Union, in contrast to England, France, and the United States, took an early and firm stand against the rise of fascism. Of all the major powers, only the Soviet Union urged the League of Nations to impose sanctions on Mussolini when he attacked Ethiopia in 1935, and only the Soviet Union offered equipment and supplies to the Spanish Republic when it was assaulted by Nazi planes and Italian troops. American Communists organized the League against War and Fascism and the League for Peace and Democracy, which drew broad and enthusiastic support from Americans who shared an aversion to fascism.[40]

There can be no doubt, however, that many of the actions of the Communist Party of the United States in this era, often under the direction of the Soviet Union, were cynically manipulative of American public opinion. Individuals who should have known better and who should have questioned more carefully turned a blind eye to the mass brutalities visited upon the Russian people.[†]

---

* As the future Supreme Court justice Abe Fortas observed, "in the thirties and part of the forties, thousands of fine, thoroughly non-Communist people contributed to Spanish relief organizations, attended anti-Fascist meetings, participated in rallies against Hitler, joined in organizations to promote friendship with the Soviet Union when it was our wartime ally, and even took out memberships in book clubs to get books and phonograph records at a discount." Abe Fortas, *Outside the Law*, Atlantic Monthly 42, 44–45 (Aug 1953).

† Arthur Herman argues that although membership in the Communist Party or Communist-front organizations in 1930s and 1940s may not have been proof of disloyalty to the United States, it was certainly proof "of an intellectual fecklessness, if not actual dishonesty." He contends that Americans who became Communists or fellow travelers in this era demonstrated that they lacked the "rational and moral" qualities that are essential to American society. In his view, those who

After the United States entered World War II as an ally of the Soviet Union, Americans viewed both the Soviet Union and the Communist Party more favorably than at any time since the Russian Revolution. President Roosevelt worked hard during the war to persuade the American people that the Soviet Union was a trustworthy and appropriate ally in the battle against fascism. Americans greatly admired the courage of the Russian people in withstanding the Nazi onslaught and came to view the Soviet Union as a "beleaguered democratic state allied with the United States in its conflict with fascism."[41] Roosevelt confidently assured the nation that "we are going to get along very well with . . . the Russian people—very well indeed."[42] Most Americans considered the Soviet Union a great power with legitimate security aims that sometimes conflicted with those of the United States, but they were hopeful that the United States and the Soviet Union could work together to preserve the peace.[43]

With the end of World War II, and the abrogation of the Yalta accord, the international situation deteriorated rapidly, and most Americans who still had ties to the Communist Party or to organizations or causes with connections to the Communist Party quickly severed them.* But, by then, it was too late. The most infamous question of the next two decades—"Are you now or *have you ever been* . . . ?"—encompassed the past.

---

denied "the brutal reality of the Soviet Union" were analogous to those who deny "the reality of the Holocaust today." This is overdrawn. Certainly, ideology and a naïve wishful thinking contributed to the "progressive" view of the Soviet Union in the 1930s and 1940s. But more apt analogies might be between those who did not accept reports of Soviet atrocities in the 1930s and 1940s and those who did not accept reports of the Holocaust *during* World War II or to those who believed there were weapons of mass destruction in Iraq in 2003. Herman, *Joseph McCarthy* at 69–70 (cited in note 3).

* After August 23, 1939, when the Soviet Union and Nazi Germany signed a nonaggression pact, the CPUSA lost most of its members. During World War II, the CPUSA, under the leadership of General Secretary Earl Browder, worked closely with the United States to support the war effort. In anticipation of continued cooperation between the United States and the Soviet Union, the party even softened its opposition to capitalism. As the war drew to a close, however, and Soviet-American relations began to deteriorate, Browder was replaced by leaders who reflected a more hard-line approach. Under William Z. Foster, Eugene Dennis, and Robert Thompson, the CPUSA embraced a more confrontational attitude. But even in the darkest days of the Cold War, the party did not seriously entertain any revolutionary schemes, and there was no credible evidence that it ever drew up any plans for sabotage or espionage, even in the event of war with the Soviet Union. Caute, *Great Fear* at 186–87 (cited in note 3).

THE RED MENACE, 1945–1950

THIS SECTION AND THE NEXT will trace the events from 1945 to 1954 that made up the nation's second Red Scare. To understand this period, it is essential to have a sense of the rapid deterioration of the international situation and the pervasive sense of fear that gripped the American people. As we will see, some of this fear was justified, but much of it was whipped up by politicians, journalists, religious leaders, and businessmen eager to serve their own ends. After this overview, we will then examine more closely the federal loyalty program, the activities of the House Un-American Activities Committee, the phenomenon of Joseph McCarthy, and the role of the Supreme Court.

AS WORLD WAR II drew to a close, and the Japanese American internment camps were dismantled, the prospects for civil liberties seemed bright. Recent Supreme Court decisions had bolstered First Amendment protections, and in July 1945 the ACLU issued a report that looked optimistically to the future. The United States had emerged from World War II with a sense of great achievement. This was a time to enjoy the fruits of national sacrifice. The United States now had half the world's gross national product and the most powerful military the world had ever known. But instead of entering an era of peace and prosperity, the economy was in a shambles and the world seemed more dangerous than ever.

As at the end of World War I, the postwar era brought severe economic dislocations. In 1946, living costs rose sharply and shortages and strikes racked the nation. In May, President Truman seized the railroads to prevent a nationwide strike; in November, he obtained a court order enjoining a mine workers strike. Business blamed this labor unrest on Communist agitation. *Nation's Business* warned that anyone who "stirs up needless strife in American trade unions advances the cause of Communism." In 1947, Congress, over Truman's veto, passed the Taft-Hartley Act, which attempted to eliminate Communist influence in the labor movement by denying essential privileges to any union whose officers did not swear that they were not members "of the Communist Party, or affiliated with such party."[44]

The collapse of the Soviet-American alliance further poisoned the national mood. Roosevelt had promised an era of collaboration, but U.S.-Soviet relations began to disintegrate even before VJ Day. President Truman bitterly assailed the Soviet Union for violating the Yalta agreement and blocking free elections in Eastern Europe.[45]

Although the power of the American military (including exclusive possession of the atom bomb) should have guaranteed the nation's security, Americans soon came to realize that there was no longer any safety in the traditional American safeguard of geographic isolation. As the United States had demonstrated in World War II, long-range bombers and aircraft carriers—and the prospect of intercontinental ballistic missiles—made the United States more vulnerable than ever to enemy attack. Americans had to confront the perplexing paradox of "unmatched American strength and unprecedented American vulnerability."[46]

President Truman cast the growing tensions between the United States and the Soviet Union in moralistic terms. He argued that the greatest obstacle to international peace derived from a "modern tyranny led by a small group who have abandoned their faith in God."[47] The president's trumpeting of such themes strengthened the American perception that the Soviets were duplicitous by nature and fostered an atmosphere in which American security was seen as imminently in peril.[48]

Truman warned Americans that the Russians understood only one language—the language of force, "and that is the language they are going to get."[49] In a St. Patrick's Day address, he exhorted his audience, "We must not fall victim to the insidious propaganda that peace can be obtained solely by wanting peace. This theory is advanced in the hope that it will deceive our people and that we will permit our strength to dwindle." Communism, he added, "denies the very existence of God." "This threat to our liberty and to our faith must be faced by each one of us."[50]

The more Truman gave vent to such themes, the more Americans saw the world as divided into good and bad, light and dark, with the United States defending freedom against an evil empire, and the more Americans became susceptible to those who called for "an anticommunist program at home to match the anticommunist program abroad."[51]

The national anxiety was further heightened when two major spy scares erupted in 1945–46. The first involved the disclosure of secret documents about China to *Amerasia*, a leftist journal concerned with Far Eastern affairs; the second involved Canadian charges that during the war twenty-two individuals had conspired to steal information about the atom bomb for Russia. J. Edgar Hoover informed Truman that, in light of these events, the FBI would "intensify its investigation of Communist Party activities" and take " 'steps to list all members of the Communist Party and others who would be dangerous in the event' of a 'serious crisis' with the Soviet Union." Truman directed Hoover to give top priority to investigating possible Communist espionage, especially within the federal government.[52]

In July 1946, the House Civil Service Committee appointed a subcommittee to investigate the effectiveness of the government's loyalty program. After two weeks of hearings, the subcommittee concluded that there was an "immediate necessity" for action and recommended the creation of a "complete and unified program" to protect the U.S. government "against individuals whose primary loyalty is to governments other than our own."[53]

In October, the U.S. Chamber of Commerce issued a highly publicized report charging that Communists had infiltrated government agencies, including the State Department, and nongovernmental organizations, especially unions, schools, radio, movies, television, newspapers, and libraries. The report called for concerted action to drive "subversives" out of these and other influential positions.[54]

Similar cries for a crackdown on domestic Communists came from the Catholic Church. Francis Cardinal Spellman published an article entitled "Communism Is Un-American." He warned that Communists are "digging deep inroads into our nation" and "trying to grind into dust the blessed freedoms for which our sons have fought, sacrificed, and died." Bishop Fulton J. Sheen, one of the Catholic Church's most prolific writers and speakers, assailed communism in a torrent of books, articles, lectures, and sermons and condemned "fellow travelers" and others "whose hearts bleed for Red fascism." The 600,000-member Knights of Columbus demanded an all-out war against the "infiltration of atheistic Communism into our American life."[55]

After the Republican triumph in the 1946 congressional elections, the new Republican-controlled Congress promptly made clear its intention to play the "Red card." In January 1947, the House Un-American Activities Committee announced a new program to expose Communists and Communist sympathizers in the federal government. J. Parnell Thomas, the new chairman of HUAC, pledged that the new Congress would "ferret out" all those who seek to destroy the American "way of life."* After sixteen years out of power, the Republicans seized the opportunity to investigate every facet of the Roosevelt and Truman administrations.[56]

---

* J. Edgar Hoover played a key role in unleashing HUAC's investigation of Communists. In March 1947, he warned the committee that although only a small number of Communists were in the United States, a similarly small number in Russia had precipitated the Bolshevik Revolution. Hoover stated that he feared "for the liberal and progressive who has been hoodwinked and duped into joining hands with the Communists." *Menace of Communism*, Statement by J. Edgar Hoover, Director of the FBI, before the House Committee on Un-American Activities, S Doc 26, 80th Cong, 2d Sess 11 (Mar 26, 1947).

Truman found himself caught in a vise of conflicting pressures. The Republicans charged he was soft on communism, whereas the Progressive wing of the Democratic Party accused him of being too rigid in his dealings with the Soviet Union. The intraparty conflict exploded in the fall of 1946 when Truman fired Secretary of Commerce and former Vice President Henry Wallace for giving a speech Truman thought too conciliatory to Russia. Wallace's view—that the Truman administration's escalation of tensions with the Soviet Union was unnecessary and would endanger American values—was shared by such figures as Walter Lippmann, Albert Einstein, Fiorello La Guardia, Elliott Roosevelt, and Henry Morgenthau Jr. Indeed, a significant part of the Democratic Party had begun to coalesce around Wallace as a likely anti-Truman candidate for the 1948 Democratic presidential nomination.[57]

Facing pressure on two fronts, Truman devised a two-prong strategy designed to defuse the political right by co-opting its internal security program and to undermine the political left by tarring it as disloyal. Critical to this strategy was the "Truman Doctrine," which the president announced on March 12, 1947. In a declaration of almost religious fervor, Truman pledged that the United States would assume the role of defender of freedom and commit all of its might to contain and confront the Soviets with indomitable counterforce whenever and wherever they threatened the "Free World."[58]

With the Progressives clearly in mind, Truman proclaimed that any opposition to this policy would threaten the national security of the United States.[59] Noting the enormity of this commitment (including the Marshall Plan, the deployment of American forces throughout the world, and the development of a new generation of nuclear weapons), Senator Arthur Vandenberg counseled Truman that if he wanted the American people to support these initiatives he would have to "scare the hell" out of them.[60] Truman agreed.

The second prong of Truman's strategy was to preempt the loyalty issue.[61] Only weeks after the 1946 elections, Truman appointed a temporary commission to study the government's loyalty program. In its report to Truman in February 1947, this commission concluded that the presence of even a single disloyal person within the federal government "presents a problem of such importance that it must be dealt with vigorously and effectively."[62]

Following the advice of the temporary commission, Truman on March 21 established by executive order a new loyalty program for all civilian government employees. Under this program, *every* present and prospective federal employee would be subjected to an extensive loyalty investigation. The executive order provided that no individual may work for the federal government if "reasonable grounds exist for belief" that he is "disloyal to the Government of the United States." Among the activities that could be deemed "disloyal" was any "[m]embership in, affiliation with or sympathetic association with any foreign or domestic organization . . . designated by the Attorney General as totalitarian, fascist, Communist, or subversive."[63]

It was this program, more than any other single action, that laid the foundation for the anti-Communist hysteria that gripped the nation over the next decade. The historian Henry Steele Commager described the Truman loyalty program as "an invitation to precisely that kind of witch-hunting which is repugnant to our constitutional system."[64]

Truman himself was of two minds about the loyalty program. On the one hand, he needed to protect his right flank politically. On the other, he was worried about the impact on civil liberties. In his memoirs, he reflected on the "periods of mass hysteria in this country which led to witch hunts." He was quite conscious of that history and wary of the fact that "demagogues . . . have always seized upon crises to incite emotional and irrational fears."

Thus, in his executive order establishing the program, Truman emphasized the need to protect government employees from "unfounded" charges of disloyalty. He naïvely believed that his program would protect individuals against accusations based on mere "rumors or unsubstantiated gossip." When an open letter from Zechariah Chafee, Erwin Griswold, and other law professors charged that the program failed to provide due process to those accused of disloyalty, Truman promised that there would be no "witch hunt" and that no charges of disloyalty would be based upon mere hearsay or innuendo. He would later acknowledge—and regret—how wrong he had been.[65]

In December 1947, the Truman administration published its first attorney general's list of subversive organizations, which quickly became the official national "blacklist."[66] Inclusion of an organization on the attorney general's list was tantamount to public branding, without a hearing. Contributions to listed organizations quickly dried up, membership dwindled, and available meeting places became scarce. The most profound impact, however, was not on the listed organizations but on the freedom of Americans to dissent from official orthodoxy.[67]

The revived House Un-American Activities Committee, now under Republican control, made headlines throughout 1947. In its most highly publicized hearings, it launched an extensive investigation of the motion picture industry. After a succession of "friendly" witnesses accused screenwriters, directors, and actors of smuggling Communistic propaganda into their movies, ten "unfriendly" witnesses, including Dalton Trumbo and Ring Lardner Jr., were imprisoned for contempt of Congress when they refused to cooperate with HUAC. The "Hollywood Ten" stood on the principle that the committee's investigation of their activities and beliefs violated the First Amendment.[68]

Not to be outdone, the Truman administration made more than a hundred highly publicized deportation arrests in early 1948 targeting prominent aliens who led left-wing unions, opposed administration foreign policy, or supported Henry

Wallace's Progressive Party. The arrests sent a chill warning to noncitizens that they should avoid "dubious" political activities and associations.[69] Several months later, the administration announced the indictment of Eugene Dennis and eleven other leaders of the Communist Party on charges of violating the Smith Act by conspiring to advocate the overthrow of the government.[*][70]

Shortly thereafter, Whittaker Chambers, a senior editor of *Time*, dropped a bombshell. A short, pudgy, and intensely self-conscious man, Chambers testified before HUAC in July 1948 that Alger Hiss, the "embodiment of the liberal elite,"[71] had been a member of a Communist cell with him in the 1930s, when Hiss was working for the State Department. The tall, handsome, and elegant Hiss, a graduate of Johns Hopkins University and the Harvard Law School, had studied under Professor Felix Frankfurter, was a law clerk to Justice Oliver Wendell Holmes, worked at a prestigious law firm, and served the Roosevelt administration in a series of positions. He was a man of impeccable credentials.

When Hiss learned of Chambers's accusation, he instantly issued a formal denial and dared Chambers to repeat his calumny outside the privileged sanctuary of a congressional hearing. When Chambers did exactly that, Hiss sued him for libel. This seemed the end of the matter, especially after Secretary of State Dean Acheson vouched for Hiss's integrity and President Truman contemptuously dismissed the investigation as a "red herring," a groundless fishing expedition in which unscrupulous legislators were seeking publicity by "slandering a lot of people that don't deserve it."[72]

Despite his attack on HUAC, Truman continued his assault on the left. As Wallace's Progressive Party began to demonstrate real drawing power in early 1948, Truman and his supporters charged that the Progressives were controlled by Communists. Truman personally castigated "Henry Wallace and his Communists" and suggested that Wallace go to Russia and "help them against his own country." Democratic Senator J. Howard McGrath of Rhode Island, later Truman's attorney general, added that "a vote for Wallace . . . is a vote for the things for which Stalin, Molotov and Vishinsky stand."[73] By late May, Alistair Cooke could note that "the Democrats and the Republicans are now racing each other for the anti-Communist stakes."[74]

The administration's campaign against the Progressives was devastating. Progressive Party spokesmen were harassed by local officials, pelted with fruit, heck-

---

[*] Later in 1948, the Justice Department and the FBI agreed on a plan providing for the "detention of dangerous individuals at the time of an emergency." The plan called for the suspension of the writ of habeas corpus and the arrest under one master warrant issued by the attorney general of all subjects listed on the FBI's security index, which J. Edgar Hoover had been compiling since 1939. Goldstein, *Political Repression* at 311–12 (cited in note 3).

led into silence, assaulted, and even stabbed and kidnapped. In Illinois, a Progressive Party candidate for the Senate was stoned by a mob and told by local police to "get out of town." Wallace and his vice-presidential running mate, Senator Glen Taylor, were prohibited from speaking at universities in Ohio, Iowa, California, Missouri, and Michigan. When the votes were counted in the 1948 election, the Progressive Party received only one-fifth of the support projected just a year earlier. The lesson was clear. Any challenge to America's anti-Soviet policy of containment could be effectively damned as "un-American."[75]

THE REPUBLICANS FULLY EXPECTED to sweep the 1948 elections. After sixteen years of Democratic control of the White House, the time seemed ripe for a change. Republicans were certain that, building upon their success in 1946, Dewey would defeat Truman and they would finally be in position to dismantle the New Deal and restore the pre-Roosevelt economic and social order. To achieve this end, they aggressively used HUAC and other investigating committees to suggest that the programs of the Roosevelt-Truman administrations were the product of Communist influence. Their central argument was that Communists had subverted American institutions by infiltrating the highest positions in Democratic administrations.[76] Truman responded by accusing Republicans of "recklessly" casting "a cloud of suspicion over the most loyal civil service in the world."[77]

Truman won a startling and decisive victory over both Dewey and Wallace. In the flush of victory, one of the first steps he intended to take was to put an end to HUAC. In postelection press conferences, Truman repeatedly referred to HUAC as "defunct," "obsolete," and "unnecessary." He directed the attorney general to draft a resolution that the newly elected Democratic Congress could use to terminate the committee.[78]

But before Truman could execute his plan, Whittaker Chambers charged in December 1948 that Alger Hiss had not only been a Communist but had been part of an espionage ring that channeled secret government documents to the Soviet Union. Working closely with Congressman Richard Nixon, Chambers took HUAC investigators to his Maryland farm, where he dramatically removed from a hollowed-out pumpkin a microfilm of classified State Department documents he claimed Hiss had given the conspirators a decade earlier.[79] The Hiss case exploded once again into the national headlines.[80] Three months later, the FBI arrested Judith Coplon, a Justice Department employee who had been secretly copying FBI reports and turning them over to the Soviets.[81] The Hiss and Coplon cases seemed to confirm Republican charges that the Roosevelt and Truman administrations had been lax in protecting the nation's security.[82] Truman abandoned his plan to ax HUAC.

That summer, international events rocked the nation. In August, China fell to the Communists. Americans had been convinced that Chiang Kai-shek's alleged popularity, bolstered by $3 billion of American aid, would stave off a Communist revolution. Now, suddenly, a quarter of the world's population was "lost" to the Reds. The following month, the Soviet Union exploded its first atomic bomb. Americans—stunned and frightened—were wholly unprepared for this news. Many communities issued dog tags to schoolchildren so their bodies could be identified after a nuclear attack; ads appeared in newspapers offering to sell property at exorbitant prices because it was "out beyond the atomic blast"; and editorials advocated an immediate preemptive war against Russia "before it is too late." Everywhere the same questions arose: How had we lost China? How had Russia gotten the bomb?[83]

Republicans quickly linked these questions to their charges of Communist infiltration. Republican senators claimed that the Truman State Department had betrayed Chiang Kai-shek and turned China over to the Communists.[84] Such claims fit well with the postwar view that the United States was so dominant militarily that only incompetence or perfidy could have caused such disasters. Americans were certain that Soviet scientists could never have developed the bomb on their own. Thus, the "secret" must have been purloined by Soviet spies. Americans increasingly came to believe that the greatest threat to national security was betrayal by disloyal Americans.[85]

By the end of 1949, the ACLU, which had been so optimistic only four years earlier, titled its annual report *In the Shadow of Fear*, which warned that "the imagined insecurity of the strongest democracy in the world . . . has created an atmosphere in which fear makes the maintenance of civil liberties precarious."[86]

THE RED MENACE, 1950–1954

THE DECADE OF THE 1950S began inauspiciously. Alger Hiss was convicted of perjury and sentenced to five years in prison.*[87] The following day, Secretary of State Acheson described the Hiss case as a "tragedy" and said, "I

---

* This was his second trial. His first had ended in a hung jury.

do not intend to turn my back on Alger Hiss." Although Acheson was being loyal to a friend in a time of trouble, conservatives were aghast at his expression of continuing "loyalty" to a man who had just been convicted of lying under oath about having once been a Communist, especially when there were still unresolved allegations that he had been not only a secret Communist but a Soviet spy. Richard Nixon called Acheson's remark "disgusting," and others saw it as a perfect illustration of the failure of New Deal Democrats to take seriously the problem of Communist subversion.[88]

Ten days later, on January 31, President Truman announced that the United States intended to develop a hydrogen bomb, despite Albert Einstein's warning that such a weapon could destroy all life on Earth. Americans began to discuss bomb shelters and the need for mass graves in the event of a nuclear attack. Four days later, Klaus Fuchs, a British physicist who had been involved in the Manhattan Project, confessed to having passed atomic secrets to the Soviet Union between 1943 and 1947. Fuchs's testimony led to the arrest of several alleged conspirators, including Harry Gold, David Greenglass, Morton Sobel, and Julius and Ethel Rosenberg.

Republican Senator Homer Capehart fumed, "How much more are we going to have to take? . . . In the name of heaven, is this the best America can do?" On February 6, the Republican National Committee issued a statement deploring the Truman administration's "soft attitude" toward Communists in the federal government. On February 7, J. Edgar Hoover announced that there could be as many as half a million Communists and fellow travelers in the United States.[89]

Then, on February 9, a little-known first-term Republican senator from Wisconsin delivered a Lincoln Day radio address at a dinner sponsored by a Republican Women's Club in Wheeling, West Virginia. Senator Joseph McCarthy's speech incorporated the usual conservative bombast about Alger Hiss and traitors in the federal government. But McCarthy then departed from his script and asserted, in now infamous words, that he was privy to inside information:

> And ladies and gentlemen, while I cannot take the time to name all the men in the State Department who have been named as active members of the Communist Party and members of a spy ring, I have here in my hand a list of 205 — a list of names that were made known to the Secretary of State as being members of the Communist Party and who nevertheless are still working on and shaping policy in the State Department.[90]

This was a complete fabrication. McCarthy had no such list.[91] The State Department immediately issued a vehement denial. Over the next few days, as the story gathered steam, McCarthy found himself in the eye of a storm. He altered his numbers, but was unwavering in his claim to possess inside information. President Truman issued a furious statement declaring that there was not a word of truth in McCarthy's charges. Audaciously, McCarthy replied that "President Truman should refresh his memory." On February 19, McCarthy promised to give the Senate "detailed information" about the Communists in the State Department.[92]

Senator Millard Tydings of Maryland was appointed to chair the Senate committee that would receive McCarthy's information. Tydings assured reporters that his committee's investigation would be "neither a witch hunt . . . nor a whitewash." A conservative Democrat, Tydings promised to "let the chips fall where they may."[93] On March 8, the Tydings Committee convened in the Senate caucus room. In a blatant lie, Senator McCarthy stated that he had gathered his information "over painstaking months of work." He reluctantly agreed to disclose at least some of the names to the committee.

After lengthy machinations and feverish digging through old files, McCarthy finally named his first State Department subversive—Dorothy Kenyon, a sixty-two-year-old New York attorney, former judge, and former U.S. delegate to the United Nations Commission on the Status of Women. McCarthy claimed that Kenyon belonged to at least twenty-eight subversive organizations. That afternoon, Kenyon told reporters, "Senator McCarthy is a liar." She demanded an opportunity to appear before the committee. On March 14, Kenyon testified to the committee, "I am, and always have been, an independent, liberal, Rooseveltian Democrat, devoted to and actively working for such causes as the improvement of the living and working conditions of labor and the preservation of civil liberties." She "admitted" to having been a member of the Americans for Democratic Action, the American Civil Liberties Union, the American Association of University Women, the Association for the Aid of Crippled Children, and similar organizations. She flatly denied that she had ever been a Communist or a fellow traveler and stated that she had never joined or assisted any organization *known by her* to be "even slightly subversive." Kenyon was typical of the individuals named by Senator McCarthy, and his accusations against her were emblematic of his often breathtaking recklessness.[94]

On June 1, the Tydings Committee announced, "We have seen the character of private citizens and of Government employees virtually destroyed by public condemnation on the basis of gossip, distortion, hearsay and deliberate untruths." It found that the "methods employed" to give McCarthy's charges of disloyalty in the State Department "ostensible validity . . . are a fraud and a hoax perpetrated on the Senate . . . and the American people."[95]

Although McCarthy's charges had been proved both spurious and damaging to innocent persons, many Republicans had come to see McCarthy as "their

"I HAVE HERE IN MY HAND—"

"I Have a List!"

ticket to political power."* Republican leaders and conservative commentators were bolstered by opinion polls showing burgeoning public support for his crusade to stamp out Communist subversion. Joe McCarthy had become a national phenomenon. A morose, reckless demagogue, McCarthy received thousands of letters each day, many of which included accusations of "disloyal" neighbors, co-workers, relatives, and friends. He received a flood of financial contributions and became the most sought-after speaker in the United States.

In speeches across America, McCarthy stormed that there was a "plot" at the highest reaches of the government "to reduce security and intelligence protection to a nullity." He smeared innocent individuals and waved fictitious "lists." He roared that "no one can be for the Administration Democrat Party and at the

---

* Not all Republicans supported McCarthy. On the same day that the Tydings Committee released its report, the freshman Republican senator Margaret Chase Smith of Maine read on the Senate floor a "Declaration of Conscience," which she and six other Republicans had signed. It was a direct attack on McCarthy and the right wing of the Republican Party: "[C]ertain elements of the Republican party have materially added to this confusion in the hopes of riding the Republican Party to victory through the selfish political exploitation of fear, bigotry, ignorance and intolerance." William S. White, *Seven G.O.P. Senators Decry "Smear" Tactics of McCarthy*, New York Times 1 (June 2, 1950).

same time against Communism." Audiences were enthralled. They were swept away by his absolute certitude and impassioned patriotism. A popular slogan declared, "America loves [McCarthy] for the enemies he has made." And he was only just beginning. [96]

EARLY ON SUNDAY MORNING, June 25, 1950, North Korean artillery opened fire on South Korean army positions south of the thirty-eighth parallel, the line dividing Communist North Korea from the Republic of South Korea. The opening barrage was followed by intense tank and infantry attacks at all points along the parallel. Within days, the UN Security Council called upon member nations to give military aid to South Korea and President Truman authorized General Douglas MacArthur to invade North Korea.

Coming close on the heels of the convictions under the Smith Act of the leaders of the Communist Party, the Hiss and Coplon prosecutions, the arrests of the Rosenbergs, and Senator McCarthy's charges of Communist infiltration, the outbreak of the Korean War unleashed a frenzy of anti-Red hysteria. Republican rhetoric, reminiscent of Federalist charges in 1798, reached fever pitch. The Senate Republican leader, Kenneth Wherry, railed that Secretary of State Dean Acheson was stained with "the blood of our boys in Korea." Senator William Jenner called Secretary of Defense George Marshall a "front man for traitors" and "either an unsuspecting stooge or an actual co-conspirator with the most treasonable array of political cutthroats ever turned loose in the Executive Branch." Senator Robert Taft of Ohio seethed that the "greatest Kremlin asset" is the "pro-Communist group in the State Department," which promotes the Communist cause "at every opportunity."[97]

By late summer, anti-Communist agitation was out of control. Many cities rushed to adopt their own loyalty programs for public employees; others began to remove "Communistic" books from school and public libraries. Congress hastily enacted the notorious McCarran Internal Security Act of 1950,*[98] which required all "Communist-action" and "Communist-front" organizations to register with the attorney general. A Communist-action organization was defined as one substantially controlled by the Soviet Union or any other foreign government

---

* The McCarran Act had originated in legislation proposed in 1947 by Republicans Karl Mundt and Richard Nixon. The Mundt-Nixon bill sputtered in Congress for several years, but in 1950, with American troops fighting and dying in Korea, the Senate overwhelmingly approved the legislation. It sailed through the House on a bipartisan vote of 354 to 20.

that directed the "world Communist movement." A Communist-front organization was defined as one substantially controlled by a Communist-action organization. The act required all such organizations to disclose to the attorney general the names of their officers, the sources of their funds, and (in the case of Communist-action organizations) a list of all of their members.

The act established the Subversive Activities Control Board (SACB) and empowered it to declare organizations to be Communist-front or Communist-action organizations if they failed to register voluntarily. The act barred all members of registered organizations from government employment or employment in any private industry engaged in government defense work. It denied registered organizations all tax exemptions and required them to label all of their publications and broadcasts "Communist organization." Finally, the act authorized the president, in the event of war or insurrection, to detain all persons he reasonably believed might participate "in acts of espionage or sabotage," with no provision for judicial review and no right to confront adverse witnesses (although the act did provide for limited administrative hearings).

The McCarran Act has aptly been described as one of the most grievous assaults on freedom of speech and association "ever launched in American history." It was "designed to make it impossible" for left-wing organizations "to function, simply by . . . designating them" subversive, without requiring proof of any unlawful conduct by anyone.[99]

Harry Truman opposed the act from its very inception. He promised to "veto any legislation . . . which adopt[s] police-state tactics and unduly encroache[s] on individual rights," and he assured lawmakers that he "would do so regardless of how politically unpopular it was—election year or no election year." Although the vice president and the Democratic leaders of both the House and the Senate urged him to sign the bill, Truman vetoed it, declaring that "no considerations of expediency can justify the enactment of such a bill as this, a bill which would greatly weaken our liberties and give aid and comfort to those who would destroy us."

Truman insisted that "instead of striking blows at Communism," the provisions of this act "would strike blows at our own liberties." He argued that "we need not fear the expression of ideas, we do need to fear their suppression." Truman invoked the experience of the Alien and Sedition Acts, noting that the lesson of history was that "extreme and arbitrary security measures strike at the very heart of our free society, and that we must be eternally vigilant against those who would undermine freedom in the name of security."

Truman's decision to veto the McCarran Act was surely courageous, and reflected an honest desire to protect civil liberties. But by 1950 his credibility on these issues had been demolished by his own rampant anticommunism and the positions he had taken in order to protect himself against right-wing attacks.

Swelled by the loss of China, the Soviet detonation of the atomic bomb, the outbreak of the Korean War, and the charges of McCarthy and others, a rising tide of fear swamped Truman's plea for moderation.[100] His veto was swiftly overridden in the House by a vote of 286 to 48 and in the Senate by a vote of 57 to 10. Truman could not persuade even a majority of his own party to stand with him.[101]

AS THE 1950 ELECTIONS APPROACHED, Republicans continued to decry the alleged "Communist conspiracy" within the Democratic administration. Senator Robert Taft announced that a Republican victory would finally remove from power those who had demonstrated "continued sympathy for communism." The central thesis of the Republican National Committee's election handbook for candidates was that a "dark conspiracy" was at the very heart of America's international troubles. Republican candidates accused their opponents of flirting with communism, courting the "pinks," having "strong Communist sympathies," "appeasing Russia," and "coddling Communists." [102]

Senator Joe McCarthy was now a national celebrity whose face graced the covers of both *Time* and *Newsweek*. He received more invitations to speak than all other Republican spokesmen combined. He criss-crossed the country campaigning vigorously in support of his favored candidates and against those he personally opposed. He attacked Democrats as "parlor pinks and parlor punks" and exhorted Americans to roust from office the "prisoners of a bureaucratic Frankenstein."

McCarthy reserved for Senator Millard Tydings a special vengeance, labeling him a "Commiecrat" and accusing him of "protecting Communists for political reasons." McCarthy's staff worked hand in glove with Tydings's opponent in Maryland in an effort to bring Tydings to his knees. Leaving no enemy untouched, McCarthy also campaigned aggressively against others who had crossed him.[103]

The Democrats attempted desperately to fend off these assaults. Truman argued that the "internal security of the United States is not seriously menaced by the Communists in this country," whom he termed a "noisy but small and universally despised group." He charged that those who claimed that the nation was in peril from domestic subversion had "lost all proportion, all sense of restraint, all sense of patriotic decency." Vice President Alben Barkley condemned those who would "abridge our freedoms and sow rumors and suspicions among us." Fed up with the incessant attacks, Truman wrote that "all this howl about organizations a fellow belongs to gives me a pain in the neck."[104]

Pain in the neck or not, the Republicans' Red-baiting reaped a political windfall. In what turned out to be the most "bitter and factious" midterm election of the twentieth century,[105] the Republicans gained five seats in the Senate and twenty-eight in the House. Even more important, they won every election in which they aggressively pinned the "soft on communism" label on their opponents. Everett Dirksen whipped the Democratic Senate leader, Scott Lucas, in Illinois; Richard Nixon crushed Helen Gahagan Douglas in California; and, most satisfying of all to Joseph McCarthy, his nemesis—Senator Millard Tydings—was swept from office in Maryland.

In the wake of the 1950 elections, Truman attempted to put a stop to the witch-hunting by establishing a distinguished, bipartisan committee to investigate alleged Communist infiltration of the government. He appointed a World War II hero, Admiral Chester Nimitz, to chair the committee. Truman announced that although "we are . . . concerned by the threat to our government and our national life arising from the activities of the forces of communist imperialism," we are also "concerned lest the measures taken to protect us from these dangers infringe the liberties guaranteed by our Constitution."[106] Anti-Truman senators quickly rendered the committee ineffective.[107]

Again showing his ambivalence over this issue, Truman then switched gears and sought to defuse the anti-administration firestorm by toughening the federal loyalty program he had first put in place in 1947. Under the original program, an individual could be dismissed or denied federal employment if the government had "reasonable grounds" to believe he was "disloyal." In early 1951, Truman amended the program so that an individual could be discharged or denied employment if the government had "a reasonable doubt" of his "loyalty." Under this more aggressive standard, 2,756 of the 9,300 employees who had already been cleared under the loyalty program found themselves once again under scrutiny.[108]

As these domestic developments played out, the world situation deteriorated even further. The media focused obsessively on the "arms race," reporting that Soviet military strength now vastly exceeded that of the United States. According to Life magazine, the Soviet army was four times larger than the American. A Life headline warned, "War Can Come; Will We Be Ready?" Calling to mind accounts of the mood in Philadelphia in 1798, Herblock, the Washington Post's extraordinary political cartoonist, later recalled that the air in Washington "was so charged with fear" that it would take "only a small spark to ignite it."[109]

The baleful news from Korea contributed to a heightened sense of national distress and anxiety. The Chinese entered the conflict with 300,000 troops in November 1950. Americans, expecting victory by Christmas, now learned of bitter defeats. As the death toll of American soldiers mounted, eventually exceeding 30,000, the question "Who lost China?" took on ever greater resonance. By December 1950, the murderous retreat of the American army led to talk of evacuating all American troops from Korea—of an "American Dunkirk." Truman noted in his diary that "it looks like World War III is here." General Douglas MacArthur and the Joint Chiefs of Staff advised Truman to recognize a formal "state of war" with China and to consider dropping atom bombs on Chinese cities. Although Truman refused to "go down that trail," he did declare a national emergency, quadrupling the defense budget, imposing wage and price controls, and calling on every American "to put aside his personal interests for the good of the country."[110]

On June 14, 1951, as public fear and frustration intensified, Joseph McCarthy addressed the Senate. In a three-hour harangue, McCarthy attacked General George C. Marshall, former chief of staff of the American military, former secretary of state, and founder of the Marshall Plan, as a tool of the Communists. McCarthy asked how Americans could "account for our present situation unless we believe that men high in this Government are concerting to deliver us to disaster. This must be the product of a great conspiracy, a conspiracy on a scale so immense as to dwarf any previous such venture in the history of man." McCarthy charged that Marshall was the central figure in this "conspiracy of infamy," this "strategy of defeat."[111]

Governor Adlai Stevenson of Illinois called this attack "hysterical," while Senator William Benton of Connecticut characterized McCarthy's performance as the product of an "unsound mind."[112] In August, Truman directly challenged McCarthy, referring to this "scurrilous work" of smear and accusation. He deplored McCarthy's resort to character assassination and charged him with leading a campaign against the Bill of Rights. He warned that "scaremongers and hatemongers" had "created such a wave of fear and uncertainty that their attacks upon our liberties go almost unchallenged. Many people are growing frightened—and frightened people don't protest." He explained that all Americans were in peril "when even one American—who had done nothing wrong—is forced by fear to shut his mind and close his mouth."[113]

Senator Robert Taft called the president "hysterical" and McCarthy responded, "If Truman wants to make the fight against Communism . . . an issue in the campaign, I will welcome it. It will give the people a chance to choose between Americanism or a combination of Trumanism and Communism." Mainstream Republicans were drawn ever closer to McCarthy. At the 1952 Republican National Convention, McCarthy was invited to deliver a major address. He roused the convention, thundering to a cheering audience, "My good friends, I say one Communist in a defense plant is one Communist too many. One Communist on the faculty of one university is one Communist too many. One Communist among the American advisers at Yalta was one Communist too many. And even if there were only one Communist in the State Department, that would still be one Communist too many."[114]

The Republican Party platform charged the Democrats with shielding "traitors" and undermining the very "foundations of our Republic." The Republican nominee for president, General Dwight D. Eisenhower, selected as his running mate Richard Nixon, one of the nation's most infamous Red-baiters. During the 1952 campaign, Eisenhower invoked the issue of Communist infiltration on more than thirty occasions.[115]

Throughout the campaign, Republicans, cheered on by Nixon, hammered away at the theme of anticommunism. In West Virginia, the Republican Senate candidate charged that his opponent had a record of "continuous sympathy to the Communist thinkers"; in Maryland, the Republican candidate J. Glenn Beall avowed, "We have got to slug it out, toe to toe, with the parlor pinks"; in Indiana, Republican Senator William Jenner alleged that if his opponent was elected "the Red network will continue to work secretly and safely for the destruction of the United States"; and in Washington, the Republican senator accused his Democratic opponent, Henry "Scoop" Jackson, of "Communist mollycoddling." Joseph McCarthy charged that the Democratic nominee for president, Adlai Stevenson, had "given aid to the Communist cause" and repeatedly referred to him as "Adlie" and "Alger" Stevenson. Nixon labeled the Democrats the "party of Communism" and referred to Truman and Stevenson as "traitors."[116]

THE REPUBLICANS SWEPT the 1952 elections, winning not only the House and Senate but the White House as well. Joe McCarthy, reelected to the Senate, was perceived to be invincible. As William S. White wrote in the *New York Times*, Senator McCarthy "is now in a position of extraordinary power." He "is a very bad man to cross politically."[117] With the Senate firmly in Republican hands, McCarthy became chairman of the Senate's Permanent Subcommittee on Investigations. With this "impregnable political base," McCarthy planned to investigate Communist infiltration of the State Department, the Federal Communications Commission, and the nation's colleges and universities. He pursued his targets in a marble caucus room that, in the words of one witness, often "stank with the odor of fear."[118]

By mid-1953, both *Newsweek* and the *New York Times Magazine* were speculating that McCarthy was aiming for the presidency in 1956. Fearing for the nation, former President Truman made a nationally televised speech in which he accused the Republican National Committee of "shameful demagoguery" and defined McCarthyism as "the corruption of truth, the abandonment of our historical devotion to fair play, . . . and the unfounded accusation against any citizen in the name of Americanism or security." It is, he said, a "horrible cancer that is eating at the vitals of America."

Even Republicans finally began to worry that McCarthy was a loose cannon. The president's brother publicly described McCarthy as "the most dangerous menace to America."[119] But the president vacillated. Eisenhower's strategy was to steer clear of McCarthy. Although confiding to friends that the whole McCarthy business "is a sorry mess; at times one feels almost like hanging his head in shame when he reads some of the unreasoned, vicious outbursts of demagoguery," he refused to act, saying that he would not "get into the gutter with that guy."[120] For the moment, he either passively supported or actively appeased McCarthy's tactics.[121]

At the same time, the Eisenhower administration was busily ratcheting up the government's anti-Communist campaign. By 1953, the federal government was investigating 10,000 citizens for possible denaturalization and 12,000 aliens for possible deportation—triple the number of two years earlier. Building on Truman's example, the new administration indicted an additional forty-two Communists under the Smith Act. In the spring of 1953, Attorney General Herbert Brownell petitioned the SACB to direct twelve more organizations to register under the McCarren Act as "communist-fronts."[122] In December 1953, Americans regarded Communists in government as the nation's "number one problem."[123] The following year, Eisenhower signed the Communist Control Act of 1954, which "outlawed" the Communist Party and declared that it was "not entitled to any . . . rights, privileges and immunities."[124]

As in World War I, the campaign to expose and punish un-Americanism was pursued not only by the federal government but by state and local governments as well. By 1955, forty-four states had enacted legislation making it a crime to advocate the overthrow of government. Some states went even further. Connecticut made it a crime for any person to distribute "disloyal, scurrilous or abusive matter concerning the form of government of the United States." An Indiana statute declared that its express purpose was to "exterminate Communism and Communists." Texas authorized a twenty-year prison sentence for members of the Communist Party. Michigan authorized life imprisonment. Tennessee authorized the death penalty. Several states directly outlawed the Communist Party. Massachusetts made it a crime for any person to allow any meeting of the party on his premises.[125]

Many states also excluded members of the Communist Party from the political process. By 1954, thirty-five states barred the Communist Party's candidates from the ballot. Following the lead of HUAC, many states established investigating committees to expose subversive individuals. In New Hampshire, the legislature authorized the attorney general to hunt down Communists and fellow travelers, even though the FBI had reported that there were only forty-three Communists in the state. Thirteen states set up their own legislative investigating committees. These committees hounded schoolteachers, labor leaders, actors, lawyers, state employees, and judges. They publicly listed thousands of individuals they found to be "subversive." As California's Tenney committee noted, the goal was to "quarantine" such people as though they "were infected with smallpox."[126]

A plague of loyalty oaths spread across the nation. By 1956, forty-two states and more than two thousand county or city governments required loyalty oaths for public employees. Some states and municipalities went on from there. Ohio denied unemployment compensation to those who refused to swear that they did not belong to an organization that advocated the forceful overthrow of government; California denied public housing to those who refused to take such an oath; Washington required an oath of all insurance salesmen, Texas of all pharmacists, and New York of all persons who sought a license to fish; all states precluded Communists and fellow travelers from becoming members of the bar.[127] States and cities were caught in a frantic contest to enact the most repressive anti-Communist legislation possible. As Truman had warned, a "cancer" of fear now afflicted the nation.

"ABSOLUTE" LOYALTY

A CRITICAL FEATURE OF THIS ERA was the loyalty investigation. Why did the federal government feel the need to screen out potentially disloyal employees? Certainly, disloyal employees pose certain risks. They might disclose confidential scientific, military, or diplomatic information; destroy government files; falsify information; make decisions or give advice intended to harm the national interest; foster distrust and suspicion within the government; recruit other employees to collaborate in their subversive activities; and so on. Given these risks, it seems sensible for the government to screen employees for possible disloyalty.[128]

But before 1939 the United States did not investigate its employees in this manner. Federal employees were required take an oath to support and defend the Constitution, but beyond that the government assumed American citizens would be loyal. Indeed, Civil Service Rule I, adopted in 1884, expressly forbade the government to inquire into the "political . . . opinions or affiliations of any applicant" for the federal civil service. Of course, if a federal employee committed an unlawful act in the course of her employment, or otherwise acted improperly, she could be disciplined, discharged, or prosecuted. But the government did not screen individual citizens in an effort to ferret out possible disloyalty in advance.[129]

In 1939, however, Congress adopted a provision of the Hatch Act that pro-hibited any person employed by the federal government from holding "member-ship in any political party or organization which advocates the overthrow of our constitutional form of government." This was construed to exclude from federal employment active members of the German-American Bund and the CPUSA.[130]

After Pearl Harbor, the government established a limited loyalty program under which federal civil service employees could be dismissed if there was a "reasonable doubt" of their loyalty to the United States. The program was not rig-orously enforced, however, and the Roosevelt administration generally prohib-ited open-ended inquiries into the political beliefs and associations of individual citizens. For the most part, public employees were dismissed only for overt acts of disloyalty.[131]

As WE HAVE SEEN, in 1946 the House Civil Service Committee recommended the appointment of a commission to establish a "complete and unified program" to protect the government "against individuals whose primary loyalty is to governments other than our own."[132] For several months, President Truman dragged his feet on this recommendation. But, alarmed by his party's defeat in the 1946 elections, he finally decided to adopt a tighter federal security program.[133]

At this moment, by elevating political expediency above his concern for indi-vidual liberties, Truman failed both himself and his nation. Unfortunately, from 1945 to 1948 no strong advocate of civil liberties was in the White House. No one in Truman's inner circle of advisers insisted that the administration look more closely at this question, think more rigorously about the implications of such a program, or explore other avenues of responding to the political pressure.[134] There is an important lesson here, for Truman's decision to appoint the Tempo-rary Commission on Employee Loyalty proved one of the great blunders of his presidency, and what followed over the next decade testifies to the peril of failing to include within the councils of government a broad range of independent-minded advisers representing diverse political, constitutional, and policy per-spectives. Had Truman heard such a voice in November 1946, he might never have had to regret what happened later.

The chair of the temporary commission, A. Devitt Vanech, announced at the outset of the inquiry that the presence of "even one disloyal" employee in the fed-eral civil service would constitute a "serious threat . . . to the security of the United States." Reflecting the spirit of the times, a representative of military intel-ligence explained to the commission, "A liberal is only a hop, skip, and a jump from a Communist. A Communist starts as a liberal." Following Vanech's lead, the commission concluded that "the presence within the government of any disloyal" individual "presents a problem of such importance that it must be dealt with vigorously."[135]

On March 25, 1947, Truman issued Executive Order no. 9835, which adopted most of the temporary commission's recommendations. The goal of this order was to provide "maximum protection" against the "infiltration of disloyal persons into the ranks" of government service.[136] Every federal civilian employee and every applicant for federal civilian employment would henceforth undergo a loyalty investigation, without regard to whether the job in question had anything to do with national security. No person would be eligible for federal employment if "reasonable grounds exist for belief" that he "is disloyal to the Government of the United States."[137] The goal was "absolute" security.[138]

Those who framed this program failed to anticipate the excessive costs of achieving this goal, both to the individuals investigated and to the society as a whole. Executive Order no. 9835 set forth a detailed procedure for loyalty investigations. The investigation of each employee or applicant was to be overseen by the relevant agency or department head and would include a careful review of the individual's high school and college records and the files of local law-enforcement agencies, the FBI, HUAC, the Civil Service Commission, and military and naval intelligence.

If any "derogatory" information was uncovered in this investigation, the FBI would conduct a "full field investigation" of the individual—a thorough FBI probe of his present and past relationships, sympathies, associations, beliefs, writings, motives, and intentions. FBI agents would interview his current and former friends, neighbors, teachers, co-workers, associates, employers, and employees in an effort to learn what these people thought about his loyalty, what organizations he had joined, what journals and books he had read, and what sentiments he had expressed.[139]

All of this information would then be consolidated in the person's FBI file, which would be transmitted, along with an FBI report, to the relevant loyalty board. Under the executive order, every federal agency was required to create one or more loyalty boards for this purpose. (At the peak of the program, there were two hundred such boards in the federal government.) If, after reviewing the FBI report, the loyalty board found "reasonable grounds" to doubt the individual's loyalty, it would convene a hearing.

The employee could appear before the loyalty board, consult with counsel, and present witnesses and affidavits in his "defense." But he had no right to confront the witnesses against him or even learn their identity. The executive order provided that the identity of informants must be kept confidential (even from the individual under investigation) whenever the FBI certified that concealment was necessary to protect its sources. The FBI insisted on nondisclosure in 90 percent of the hearings.[140] If, after the hearing, the departmental loyalty board reached a decision adverse to the individual, he could appeal to a Civil Service Commission Loyalty Review Board.

Although Executive Order no. 9835 did not define "disloyalty," it authorized the attorney general to list those organizations that he considered "totalitarian, fascist, communist, or subversive." Past or present membership in, or "sympathetic association" with, a listed organization could warrant a finding of disloyalty.[141] In March 1948, the Justice Department published its first list of subversive organizations.* The initial list included 78 organizations. In May, the administration listed 32 additional organizations. By 1950, the list had grown to 197; by 1953, to 254.†[142]

Under Executive Order no. 9835, an organization had no right to a hearing, no right to contest the attorney general's finding that it was "subversive," and no right to judicial review.‡[143] The power granted to the attorney general to list an organization may well have been "the most arbitrary and far-reaching power ever exercised by a single public official in the history of the United States."[144] Moreover, because the criteria for listing were vague and undisclosed, and because new groups were constantly being added to the list, citizens had to be wary about joining *any* organization. The only "safe" course was not to join anything.[145]

---

* Illustrative of these Communist "front" organizations were the International Workers Order, a fraternal benefit society that specialized in low-cost insurance; the Jewish People's Fraternal Order, an offshoot of the IWO; the Jefferson School of Social Science, which was run by the Communist Party and enrolled more than 45,000 adult students between 1944 and 1948; the American Russian Institute; the National Council for American-Soviet Friendship; the Joint Anti-Fascist Refugee Committee, which was initiated in 1942 to provide relief for refugees of the Spanish civil war; and the American Peace Crusade. Almost all of these and other "front" organizations were put out of commission by their inclusion on the attorney general's list. See Caute, *Great Fear* at 172–78 (cited in note 3).

† Over time, it became apparent that the attorney general's list was being used by the Truman administration not only to pillory organizations connected in some way to communism but also to bludgeon organizations that opposed its Cold War policies. When the Connecticut State Youth Conference protested American intervention in Greece in the spring of 1947, it was listed. When the American Council for a Democratic Greece criticized the administration's foreign policy in May 1948, it was listed. When the American Committee for the Protection of Foreign Policy opposed the government's deportation policy, it was listed. See Caute, *Great Fear* at 169–70 (cited in note 3).

‡ In *Joint Anti-Fascist Refugee Committee v. McGrath*, 341 US 123 (1951), the Supreme Court held the lack of a hearing unconstitutional. Although this "ruling virtually declared the list illegal," the executive took no notice until 1953, when Attorney General Herbert Brownell finally issued new regulations "providing listed organizations with a chance to protest *after* they had been listed." But even then the Justice Department dragged its feet, and it was not until July 1955 that the first hearing was granted and not until 1958 that an organization was actually removed from the list. Caute, *Great Fear* at 170 (cited in note 3).

Truman's decision to establish a rigorous employee loyalty program magnified popular fears about the seriousness of the threat to national security. Although Truman hoped that the procedures spelled out in his 1947 executive order would protect individuals against "unfounded accusations of disloyalty," the program failed dismally in this respect.[146]

The assignment to department and agency heads of primary responsibility to administer the program proved problematic. Predictably, a chief concern of these bureaucrats was to demonstrate their zeal in ferreting out possible subversives. As a consequence, the practices and procedures of the departmental loyalty boards often left much to be desired.[147]

More important, in passing judgment on a person's loyalty—or disloyalty—the loyalty boards were almost completely dependent upon the FBI investigative reports. But in undertaking "full field" investigations, the FBI did not attempt to gauge the reliability of the information it gathered. Its reports included all charges against an individual, digested and undigested, "solicited and unsolicited, verified and unverified." Much of the information was unsubstantiated hearsay—mere gossip, rumor, and slander. In the view of the FBI, its charge was not to *evaluate* accusations but to gather and report as much raw information as possible.*

The FBI made no pretense that its files contained only reliable information. To the contrary, J. Edgar Hoover readily conceded that the files included unchecked and "unevaluated" information and that individuals named in the files could well be innocent of any wrongdoing. The sources of information were, in fact, often suspect. Persons accused of disloyalty commonly implicated as many other people as possible in order to prove their "contrition." Other informers were paid for their services, providing a clear incentive to embellish the facts to boost their income.[148] Because the FBI usually insisted its sources remain confidential, it was often impossible for loyalty boards to know whether any particular informant was a "paragon of veracity, a knave, or the village idiot."[149]

Loyalty hearings often took on the character of a "medieval inquisition."[150] The charges tended to be vague and almost impossible to rebut: "You have sympathetically associated with members of an organization known to be subversive." But with whom? Which organization? Where? When? Because the accusers

---

* From the FBI's perspective, it was useful to retain all information because one could never know what tidbit might someday prove helpful.

were anonymous, the accused could only guess. Consider the following charges that were actually leveled against specific individuals in these hearings: "You have associated for a considerable time with persons who are known communists." "You have during most of your life been under the influence of your father, who . . . was an active member of the Communist Party." "Communist literature was observed in the book shelves and Communist art was seen on the walls of your residence." One man was charged with disloyalty because he had written a Ph.D. dissertation that relied on material obtained from the Institute of Pacific Relations, which HUAC had "cited as a Communistic Front organization."

Individuals accused of disloyalty were often fiercely interrogated. They were asked such questions as "How many times did you vote for Henry Wallace?" "Have you provided any sort of religious training for your children?" "Do you think that workers in the capitalist system get a relatively fair deal?" Do you know people who have expressed "an ideology that differs from American philosophy?" What are your feelings "concerning racial equality?" Loyalty boards asked individuals whether they had read "suspicious" books (such as Edgar Snow's *The Pattern of Soviet Power* or the novels of Howard Fast), whether they had seen "foreign films," and whether they had listened to the records of Paul Robeson.[151]

Only a quarter of the hearings involved allegations of past or present membership in the Communist Party. In less than 10 percent of the cases was such membership actually proved. After 1948, none of the hearings involved current members of the CPUSA. Rather, they focused on charges of past membership in the CPUSA, past or present membership in other "listed" organizations, or, most often, more remote forms of "guilt by association." A signature on a petition, a small donation, a name on a mailing list, presence at a public meeting, a conversation with a passing acquaintance—all could generate suspicion of "sympathetic" association. Two-thirds of the cases that reached the hearing stage included a charge that the individual had in some way associated with *others* who might be subversive.[*]

Consider the following description of the not very "agreeable" experience of an individual called to account before a loyalty board on suspicion of disloyalty:

---

[*] One employee, for example, was charged with disloyalty in 1952 for writing a letter to the Berkeley Board of Education congratulating it on allowing Paul Robeson to make a speech in a public high school. In another case, a thirty-year-old divorced mother of two was charged with disloyalty because of her "close and continuing association" with her brother, who was allegedly sympathetic to communism. At her hearing, a loyalty board member asked whether she would inform her supervisor if she learned that her brother was involved with an organization on the attorney general's list. The board recommended her discharge. See Bontecou, *Federal Loyalty-Security Program* at 108–9, 141–42 (cited in note 65). See generally Caute, *Great Fear* at 282–83 (cited in note 3).

It involves . . . an accusation of a sort that injures in a most intimate way anyone who has a love of country and a sense of having served it faithfully. It involves . . . the humiliation of having to appeal for testimonials to friends, to former employers, to acquaintances prominent in public life, whose willingness to offer an endorsement may make the difference between survival and ruin; and this appeal for help means naturally the painful admission that the supplicant is under suspicion of disloyalty. . . . It involves a long and sometimes costly process . . . in which the individual is obliged to grope blindly in a desperate attempt to discover what part of his past has brought him under suspicion.[152]

The plight of Dorothy Bailey is revealing. A graduate of the University of Minnesota, Bailey pursued graduate studies in labor relations at Bryn Mawr and then took a job in 1933 as a clerk-typist in the U.S. Employment Service in Washington, D.C. She worked for this agency for the next fourteen years, rising to the position of supervisor. In 1947, she was laid off because of a reduction in force, but was rehired by the Employment Service the following year. At that time, as a rehire, she was subjected to the federal loyalty program. The regional loyalty board informed her, "[We have] received information to the effect that you are or have been a member of the Communist Party, . . . that you have attended meetings of the Communist Party [and that you are or were] a member of the American League for Peace and Democracy."

Bailey denied that she had ever been a member of the Communist Party or had ever attended a meeting of the Communist Party, except as part of a graduate seminar at Bryn Mawr in 1932. She admitted that she had belonged to the American League for Peace and Democracy and had attended two of its meetings in 1938 or 1939. At her hearing before the regional loyalty board, Bailey, an African American, was asked whether she had ever written a letter to the American Red Cross protesting the segregation of blood.[*] Most of the hearing focused on her activities as president of Local 10 of the United Public Workers of America. The UPWA was referred to as "Communist-dominated," although it was not on the attorney general's list.

Bailey suspected that she had been "fingered" as a Communist by her opponents in a recent and very bitter intra-union fight. But the loyalty board refused to disclose the names of her accusers. During the proceedings, Seth Richardson, the chairman of the loyalty review board, noted that the FBI had provided reports

---

[*] The loyalty board member who asked this question justified his inquiry by explaining that "objection to blood segregation is a recognized 'party line' technique." Brown, *Loyalty and Security* at 43 (cited in note 10).

from several people who had accused Bailey of disloyalty, although he confessed, "I haven't the slightest knowledge as to who they were or how active they have been in anything."

Bailey presented evidence of a variety of positions she had taken over the years that were directly inconsistent with the Communist line. She also presented the testimony or affidavits of seventy-five reputable individuals who knew her well either professionally or socially, each of whom affirmed that Dorothy Bailey was not disloyal. Nonetheless, the regional board found her ineligible for government employment because of "doubts about her loyalty."[*][153]

H OW MANY GOVERNMENT EMPLOYEES were affected by the federal loyalty program? During the Truman era (1947–53), more than 4.7 million individuals were investigated. Approximately 1 percent of these investigations unearthed enough "derogatory" information to trigger full-field investigations by the FBI, which conducted roughly 40,000 such investigations. Approximately 8,000 (or 20 percent) of these investigations led to the filing of formal charges before a departmental or agency loyalty board. These boards cleared more than 90 percent of the individuals investigated, finding no reasonable basis to doubt their loyalty. They thus ordered the discharge of approximately 500 individuals. On appeal, the Civil Service Commission's Loyalty Review Board overturned about a third of these findings of disloyalty.

Thus, from 1947 to 1953, roughly 350 federal employees were discharged because of doubts about their loyalty.[†] In addition, approximately 2,200 federal employees, upon learning they were under investigation, "voluntarily" resigned rather than allow the process to continue.[154]

At first glance, one might muse that these numbers don't look so bad. After

---

[*] The U.S. Court of Appeals for the District of Columbia Circuit observed that Bailey had been subjected to procedural "rules which run counter to every known precept of fairness," but nonetheless held this justified in light of the world situation. See *Bailey v. Richardson*, 182 F2d 46, 53–54 (DC Cir 1950). The Supreme Court divided 4 to 4 on the case and thus allowed Bailey's dismissal to stand. See *Bailey v. Richardson*, 341 US 918 (1951). In a different case, Justice Douglas, with Dorothy Bailey in mind, protested that to condemn an individual for disloyalty "without meticulous regard for the decencies of a fair trial is abhorrent to fundamental justice." *Joint Anti-Fascist Refugee Committee v. McGrath*, 341 US 123, 180 (1951) (Douglas concurring).

[†] This is a conservative figure. See Brown, *Loyalty and Security* at 55 (cited in note 10) (estimating 560 findings of disloyalty during the Truman era); Bontecou, *Federal Loyalty-Security Program* at 145 (cited in note 65) (estimating 378 findings of disloyalty by March 1952).

all, the FBI cleared 80 percent of the individuals on whom it conducted full-field investigations, the agency and departmental loyalty boards exonerated 90 percent of those who were formally accused of disloyalty, and the Civil Service Commission's Loyalty Review Board reversed a third of these findings on appeal. In the end, only about .00007 of all federal civilian employees (roughly one in 13,000) who were subjected to investigation in the Truman era were discharged for disloyalty.

But this misses the point. Even setting aside the question whether these individuals actually posed a threat to the United States or "deserved" to be discharged, we need to step back to grasp the true impact of this program. Suppose more than 90 percent of all criminal defendants were found "not guilty" at trial. We would know immediately that something was terribly amiss in our criminal justice system. Although a loyalty hearing is not a criminal trial, the experience of an individual subjected to such a proceeding was often terrifying, humiliating, and grievously harmful to his reputation, even if he was ultimately "cleared" by the tribunal. Even those exonerated of disloyalty suffered severe and long-lasting hardship.[*155]

Moreover, the harm was not limited to those dragged before a loyalty board. Because of the ambiguity of the very concept of "disloyalty," and the highly secretive nature of the process, no federal employee—or *prospective* federal employee—could consider herself exempt from the danger of investigation. Any slip of the tongue, any unguarded statement, any criticism of official policy, any "suspicious" friendship, or any "questionable" reading matter could lead to her undoing.[†]

---

[*] One reason for the incredibly high rate at which loyalty boards dismissed charges of disloyalty was that government investigators did not even interview the accused until the hearing itself, at which point, after weeks or often months of torment, the accused could finally explain himself. See Bontecou, *Federal Loyalty-Security Program* at 89–90 (cited in note 65).

[†] A manual for civilian employees of the U.S. Navy captures the feel of the times:

A number of our citizens unwittingly expose themselves to unfavorable or suspicious appraisal which they can and should avoid. This may take the form of an indiscreet remark; an unwise selection of friends or associates; membership in an organization whose true objectives are concealed behind a popular and innocuous title; attendance at and participation in the meetings and functions of such organizations even though not an official member; or numerous other clever means designed to attract support under false colors. . . .

It is advisable to study and seek wise counsel prior to association with persons or organizations of any political or civil nature, no matter what their apparent motives may be. . . .

Appendix to Navy Civilian Personnel Instructions, excerpted in Brown, *Loyalty and Security* at 191 (cited in note 10).

The loyalty program created a pervasive sense of being "watched." It was as if a noxious cloud had engulfed the nation, and numbers alone cannot capture how corrosive the policy had become. Almost every federal agency employed its own "security officers," whose job it was to unearth information about agency employees. These officers scrutinized and recorded the conduct, sentiments, associations, relationships, conversations, and personal lives of employees. They compiled secret dossiers on "suspect" individuals and shared them with the FBI, the Civil Service Commission, and HUAC. They rewarded "tips" and encouraged employees to report on one another. To keep things simple, they often proposed "deals" to employees against whom they harbored "suspicions"—if the employee would resign, the security officer would suspend the inquiry. The pressure on honest, law-abiding, loyal employees to yield to the whims, prejudices, and abuse of security officers was often insurmountable.[156]

The FBI's insistence on shielding the identity of informers exacerbated the danger. In only 6 percent of the loyalty hearings did the accused learn the identity of her accuser. In those few cases in which the informer's identity came to light, the stupidity or venality of the accusation was often shocking, adding to the sense of vulnerability. In one case, for instance, the informer testified that she had reported the accused because he had a mustache and never wore his tie home at the end of the day. The informer explained that she had "heard people say that . . . those are indications that he is not a capitalist." In another case, the informer revealed at the hearing that he had accused the employee of disloyalty because the employee "thought the colored should be entitled to as much as anybody else," a view the informer associated with communism. The anonymity of informers left every federal employee open to the vagaries of crackpots, schemers, scandalmongers, and personal enemies.[157]

As John Lord O'Brian observed at the time, secret investigations foster "suspicion, distrust . . . and a general undermining of morale."[158] It was *essential* to avoid suspicion. The cost of being ensnared in a loyalty investigation was fearsome. As one lawyer commented, those dismissed from government employment "cannot find jobs; the FBI hounds them; their social standing in the community is ruined; they receive crank mail; their friends desert them." Abe Fortas, who represented many individuals before loyalty boards, noted that even those cleared of disloyalty suffered "heartaches and personal disasters."[159]

The only sensible approach was to keep one's head down. Prudence was the order of the day. One government employee remarked, "If Communists like apple pie and I do, I see no reason why I should stop eating it. But I would." It was dangerous to be seen speaking with the wrong person or reading the wrong journal. One federal employee discovered a collection of the *New Masses* when he moved into a house. To avoid the risk that someone might think he read such material, he burned it. It was always safer not to join an organization. One could never know who else might be a member. In this era, the fragility of free expression—the capacity to frighten individuals into remaining silent rather than risk harm to themselves and their families—was powerfully demonstrated and exploited.[160]

THE LOYALTY PROGRAM first promulgated in 1947 evolved over time. As we have seen, in 1951 President Truman amended the program to *expand* the standard of "disloyalty."[161] In May 1953, President Eisenhower announced a further revision. Executive Order no. 10450 established a new and even more expansive standard of disloyalty—"any behavior, activities or associations which *tend to show* that the individual is not reliable or trustworthy" would henceforth be sufficient for dismissal.[162] In October, Eisenhower amended Executive Order no. 10450 to add a new basis for automatic dismissal—invocation of the Fifth Amendment privilege against compelled self-incrimination before a congressional committee in an inquiry involving alleged disloyalty.[163]

The Eisenhower administration boasted in late 1953 that 1,456 employees had left the government under its new loyalty program. Shortly before the 1954 congressional elections, Vice President Nixon trumpeted that seven thousand federal employees had been dismissed or resigned as a result of the Eisenhower program and that the administration was "kicking the communists and fellow travelers . . . out of government . . . by the thousands."[164] Between 1947 and 1956, approximately 2,700 federal civil service employees were dismissed and another 12,000 "voluntarily" resigned as a result of the government's loyalty program.[165]

It was never quite clear precisely what this program was intended to accomplish.[166] It was certainly not well calculated to catch spies. No spy would have been so naïve as to join a "listed" organization or so clumsy as to be discovered by the largely unprofessional federal security officers. Rather, the program was intended, at best, to identify and exclude from federal employment those American citizens who might be tempted to assist foreign agents or otherwise fail to perform their responsibilities faithfully. In theory, of course, this goal is perfectly legitimate. In practice, however, it was a train wreck. In their investigations of more than four million federal civilian employees, the government's two hundred loyalty boards did not uncover a *single* instance of actual espionage or subversive malfeasance.[167]

Most critics of the federal loyalty program have focused on the procedural unfairness of the hearings. The lack of specificity in the charges, the anonymity and unreliability of informers, the inability to confront and cross-examine one's accusers, the wide discretion of the loyalty boards, and the absence of factual findings combined to create a sense that these were "star-chamber" proceedings devoid of the most fundamental guarantees of due process.[168]

But there was an even deeper difficulty. The government's inability to define "disloyalty," its focus on beliefs and associations rather than overt acts, and its effort to predict future criminal behavior on the basis of an individual's past or present disagreement with government policy doomed the program from the start. The very concept of "loyalty" is painfully elusive. It is defined entirely by a state of mind. Does it mean "my country, right or wrong"? Can a citizen oppose government policies—including a war—and still be "loyal"?[169]

The negative impact on "loyal" Americans—those who were wrongfully discharged, those who resigned rather than submit to the process, those who were chilled in their political expression and activities, those who were degraded and humiliated in their everyday lives—far outweighed any *legitimate* benefit the government derived from the program. The loyalty program stifled meaningful debate, demanded conformity, and discouraged Americans from thinking, reading, talking, or acting in any way that was out of the "mainstream" of contemporary political, cultural, or social thought.

Perhaps most important, it reversed the essential relationship between the citizen and the state in a democratic society. As Madison, Gallatin, Jefferson, and others came to understand during the controversy over the Sedition Act of 1798, the citizens of a self-governing society must be free to think and talk openly and critically about issues of governance. Under the loyalty program, however, it was the *government* that defined which thoughts and ideas would be permitted. Dissenting views, nonconforming opinions, were deemed "disloyal." This reflected an utter lack of confidence in the American people. Nothing "so dangerously corrupts" the integrity of a democracy "as a loss of faith" in its own citizens.[170]

HUAC: "THE OTHER SIDE OF THE BARRICADES"

THE FEDERAL LOYALTY PROGRAM was just one weapon in the nation's "war on subversion." Another was the congressional investigation, which was deployed in this era with unprecedented intensity and viciousness. Unlike the federal loyalty program, congressional investigations were not limited to federal employees. Rather, they intruded into every sphere of American life, including labor, education, entertainment, religion, journalism, business, and philanthropy.

For the most part, these hearings served as a means to expose and publicly humiliate individuals without according them the traditional protections of due process. Most of these investigations had no legislative purpose. They were designed to generate publicity, enhance the power of the inquisitors, and blacken the reputations of victims. As the federal loyalty program spread fear throughout the civil service, the congressional investigation chilled the whole of American society.

Hearings into "un-American" activities were undertaken by a host of committees eager to get in on the action, including House Committees on Military Affairs, Education, Labor, Public Works, Foreign Affairs, and Veterans Affairs, and Senate Committees on Government Operations, Interstate and Foreign Commerce, Labor, and the Judiciary. The most infamous of these hearings, the ones that snared the spotlight, were those of the House Un-American Activities Committee.[171]

In 1948, HUAC explained its mission as follows:

> [T]he House Committee on Un-American Activities has . . . a very special responsibility. It functions to permit the greatest court in the world—the court of American public opinion—to have an undirected, uncensored, and unprejudiced opportunity to render a continuing verdict on all of its public officials and to evaluate the merit of many in private life who either openly associate and assist disloyal groups or covertly operate as members or fellow travelers of such organizations.[172]

No other congressional committee has ever claimed for itself so capacious a jurisdiction.

THE FIRST CONGRESSIONAL INVESTIGATION was initiated in 1792 when the House of Representatives appointed a committee to investigate a disastrous expedition against the Indians. Since then, both the House and the Senate have regularly used the power of investigation to gather information to enable Congress to enact legislation, oversee the work of administrative agencies, and inform the public.[173]

Until 1881, the power of congressional investigation was exercised without judicial oversight.[174] Then, in *Kilbourn v. Thompson*,[175] the Supreme Court held that the House could not constitutionally authorize an investigation without clearly defining a legitimate legislative goal. Half a century later, the Court made clear in *McGrain v. Daugherty*[176] that "a witness rightfully may refuse to answer where the bounds of the [investigatory] power are exceeded or the questions are not pertinent to the matter under inquiry."[177] It was against this slender legal and constitutional background that HUAC came into being.

As WE SAW IN CHAPTER 4, the House initially established HUAC in 1938 when it adopted the Dies resolution, which called for a special committee to investigate "the extent, character, and objects of un-American propaganda" and "all other questions in relation thereto."[178]

From its inception, the committee acknowledged that "Congress does not have the power to deny to citizens the right to believe in, teach, or advocate communism, fascism, and nazism." But, under the chairmanship of Martin Dies, it insisted that Congress "does have the right to focus the spotlight of publicity upon their activities."[179] More emphatically, the committee proclaimed in 1940 that its primary purpose was to protect "constitutional democracy by . . . pitiless publicity."[180]

In its campaign to punish by exposure, the committee pursued its own conception of what beliefs and associations were "un-American." Its central target in the late 1930s and early 1940s was the New Deal. As Martin Dies explained, "If democratic government assumes the responsibility for abolishing all poverty and unemployment, it is simply preparing the way for dictatorship. . . . The Fifth Column and the Trojan Horse organizations can never be properly dealt with so long as we retain in the government service . . . hundreds of left-wingers and radicals who do not believe in our system of private enterprise."[181]

With World War II, and particularly with the Soviet-American alliance, the Dies committee gradually became moribund. When Martin Dies decided not to seek reelection in 1944, the committee, which had devolved into Dies's own one-man circus, seemed on the verge of extinction. But in January 1945, in a remarkable feat of legislative legerdemain, Congressman John Rankin of Mississippi maneuvered the House into creating for the first time a *standing* committee on un-American activities.*[182]

Rankin despised Communists, socialists, liberals, New Dealers, civil libertarians, intellectuals, blacks, aliens, and Jews. On the floor of the House, he once proclaimed, "[I]t is not a disgrace to be a real Negro . . . [I]f I were a Negro, I would want to be as black as the ace of Spades. I would then go out with Negroes and have a real good time." On another occasion, he described Walter Winchell,

---

* Whereas the Dies Committee was a special committee that had to be renewed every year, Rankin managed to establish HUAC in 1945 as a permanent committee that would continue in existence until it was affirmatively abolished.

a Jewish radio commentator, as "a little slime-mongering kike." Rankin's views on communism bordered on the insane. He explained that "alien-minded" communism "hounded and persecuted the Savior during his earthly ministry, inspired his crucifixion, derided him in his dying agony."[183]

Despite Rankin's incendiary views, the new standing committee muddled along under his chairmanship with no serious agenda and no noticeable impact. The Republican victory in the 1946 midterm elections, however, changed everything. The committee's new chairman, J. Parnell Thomas, was, if anything, even more odious than Rankin. Elected to the House in 1936 after an uneventful career as a small-businessman, Thomas hated the New Deal and New Deal liberals "with every fiber of his being." He was arrogant, petty, vain, and narrow-minded. Riddled with prejudices and insecurities, Thomas had no sense of propriety and no regard for the truth. As Robert Carr has observed, "seldom has an important Congressional agency been so handicapped by the vulgarity of its leader."[184]

A key figure during Thomas's chairmanship was Robert Stripling, who served as HUAC's chief investigator from its founding in 1938 until 1948. Stripling was a tall, thin young man, with slicked-down black hair, a sallow complexion, dark rings under his eyes, and a disconcerting habit of "constantly pursing his thin lips together, as if continually revolted at something." He was generally seen as sinister, dedicated, and fanatical.[185]

Upon assuming the chairmanship, Thomas and the new Republican majority lost no time in announcing HUAC's bold new aims. The committee declared that it would "expose and ferret out . . . Communists and Communist sympathizers" in the federal government; expose Communists who had infiltrated the labor movement, education, and Hollywood; institute "a counter-educational program" against un-American propaganda; and develop comprehensive files on subversive and potentially subversive organizations and individuals.[186]

HUAC made good on this agenda. In 1947 and 1948, it compiled dossiers on 25,591 individuals and 1,786 organizations and created a list of 363,119 persons who at some time in the past had signed a Communist Party election petition. By the end of 1948, the committee could boast that "each day brings a huge amount of valuable new material to Committee files," materials that it then "classified, indexed, and added to the growing specialized collection." Within a few years, Stripling would proudly announce that HUAC's files contained "more than one million names, records, dossiers, and data pertaining to subversion."[187]

The committee also sought to educate the public. During the Eightieth Congress, HUAC published a series of pamphlets addressing the "100 Things You Should Know about Communism." More than a million copies were distributed. These pamphlets included the following kernels of wisdom:

Q: What is Communism?

A: A System by which one small group seeks to rule the world.

Q: Why do people become Communists?

A: Basically, because they seek power and recognize the opportunities that Communism offers the unscrupulous. . . .

Q: Where can a Communist be found in everyday American life?

A: Look for him in your school, your labor union, your church, or your civic club.

Q: Is everybody a Communist who defends Russia?

A: Oh, no. Some of the loudest Russia lovers are only fellow-travelers and members of Communist fronts.[188]

IT WAS IN ITS HEARINGS that HUAC shined. In 1947, it began by questioning several individuals suspected of clandestine Communist activities. These hearings began after Louis Budenz, a reformed Communist and former editor of the *Daily Worker*, stated on a radio interview that "a shadowy figure," unknown even to Budenz, was the "real head of Communism in America." Within a few days, two enterprising New York reporters disclosed that Budenz's "shadowy figure" was Gerhart Eisler. On February 6, 1947, Eisler was summoned before HUAC.

The primary witness against Eisler was his estranged sister, Ruth Fischer, who had not seen him in twenty years. Fischer testified that her brother was "the head of a network of agents of the secret Russian state police" and a "dangerous terrorist."[189] Eisler refused to take the oath unless he was first permitted to make a three-minute statement to the committee. Chairman Thomas ruled the statement out of order. This led to an impasse, as a result of which HUAC cited Eisler for contempt. While out on bond, he skipped the country by stowing away on a Polish liner, never to return to the United States.[190]

The inquiry into Gerhart Eisler led HUAC to Gerhart's brother, Hanns Eisler, who was born in Austria, served in the Austrian army in World War I, and then turned to music. He studied with Arnold Schoenberg and taught at the Music Conservatory of Vienna. After arriving in the United States in 1940, under the sponsorship of Eleanor Roosevelt, he served as a professor of music at the New School for Social Research in New York and received a grant from the Rockefeller Foundation. As a freelance composer, he produced symphonies, chamber music, and scores for several Hollywood movies. He testified, accurately, if immodestly, that he was a composer "of international reputation."[191]

Hanns Eisler's interrogation is suggestive of the Alice-in-Wonderland quality of many of HUAC's interrogations. Early in Eisler's testimony, Robert Stripling asked, "Mr. Eisler, are you now, or have you ever been, a Communist?" Eisler replied that in 1926 he had "made application" to the Communist Party in Germany, but had never followed up on the application or participated in any Communist Party activities. He explained, "I found out very quick that I couldn't combine my artistic activities with the demand of any political party, so I dropped out." He insisted throughout his testimony, "I am not now a Communist."[192] The committee was relentless in pursuing his relationship with the Communist Party in Germany twenty years earlier. The following exchange between Chairman Thomas and Eisler is illustrative:

THOMAS: For how many years were you a member of the Communist Party?
EISLER: I was not really a member. I didn't pay the membership dues. I was not active in the political organization of the Communist Party. . . .
THOMAS: I want to know how long you were a member.
EISLER: Mr. Chairman, since I went immediately to Paris and came back in the fall, to Berlin—
THOMAS: That is all right. How many years?
EISLER: No years.
THOMAS: How many months were you a member?
EISLER: Technically, maybe for a couple of months.
THOMAS: Two months?
EISLER: Look, Mr. Chairman, if you join a union and don't pay union dues and don't participate in union activities—I am automatically suspended if I do that. . . .
THOMAS: How did you withdraw [from the Party], by the way?
EISLER: The very simple thing is that I didn't join, really . . . I didn't pay my membership dues, and I was automatically suspended. . . .
THOMAS: Automatically. When was that?
EISLER: That must be the end of 1926.
THOMAS: You joined when?
EISLER: January 1926. . . .
THOMAS: You have . . . admitted that you were a Communist for almost a year.[193]

HUAC's ultimate interest, of course, was not in Eisler's conduct twenty years earlier in Berlin but in his activities since. Its goal, in Stripling's words, was "to show that Mr. Eisler is the Karl Marx of Communism in the musical field" and that the International Music Bureau, which Eisler had helped conceive in 1935, "was a major program of the Soviet Union in their effort to bring about a world revolution and establish a proletarian dictatorship."[194] Eisler maintained that this was all nonsense.

To establish its claims, the committee questioned Eisler about several lauda-tory news stories in the CPUSA's newspaper, the *Daily Worker*. One story, from January 15, 1935, described Eisler as a "revolutionary musician and composer" and noted that his international tour of Leningrad, Moscow, Copenhagen, Brus-sels, Paris, London, and the United States had been supported in the United States by "the Workers Music League, John Reed Club, League of Workers Theaters, Anti-Nazi Federation . . . and other groups." Stripling implied that because the Workers Music League was "a Communist organization," it was reasonable to infer that Eisler had been a Communist in 1935.[195]

Another article in the *Daily Worker*, from February 18, 1935, depicted Eisler as "one of the leading spirits in music for the worker." Eisler explained, "[T]hey want to show that in Germany I wrote a lot of music, especially in the last years before Hitler came to power, and that I did my best as an artist to help with my music in this very difficult struggle." Eisler added that when he came up with the idea for the International Music Bureau, his aim had been to bring together "anti-Fascist artists [and] composers" in the interest of exchanging "cultural experiences." "Don't forget," he reminded the committee, "this is music, and nothing else."[196]

Later in the hearing, Stripling read into the record an article Eisler had writ-ten and published in July 1935 in a Russian newspaper. The title of the article was "The Destruction of Art." In it, Eisler stated, "The dark epoch of fascism makes it clear to each honest artist that close cooperation with the working masses is the only way leading to creative art. . . . It would not be long before there would not be left a single great artist on the other side of the barricades."[197] Stripling demanded that Eisler explain what he meant by "on the other side of the barricades." Eisler replied that at the time he was referring to Germany, to the "fight against Hitler."[198]

Stripling inquired about many of Eisler's compositions, especially those with such provocative titles as "Fifty Thousand Strong," "The Barricades," "Com-rades," "Solidarity," and "The Scottsboro Boys." Eisler explained that he wrote the music, not the words, but that the pieces reflected important social and polit-ical movements.

Stripling was particularly intrigued by the song "In Praise of Learning," which included the verse "Fear not, be not downhearted, / Begin, you must learn the lesson / You must be ready to take over." Stripling asked Eisler what he had meant by "You must be ready to take over." Eisler explained that the song had appeared in a play for which he had written the music in 1929. (The words had been writ-ten by Bertolt Brecht.) Eisler noted that the play, based on a novel by Maxim Gorky, was about "the struggle of the Russians from 1905 to 1917." This led to the following exchange:

THOMAS: You didn't mean that you must be ready to take over now, did you?

EISLER: I can't understand your question.

THOMAS: You said that it applied to Germany.

EISLER: Not only to Germany. It was a show, a musical song in a show. It applied to the situation on the stage.

THOMAS: Would it also apply here to the United States? . . .

EISLER: It is from a quotation by Maxim Gorky, the famous writer. The song is based on the ideas of Maxim Gorky. This song applies to the historical [struggle] of the Russian people from 1905 until 1917.

THOMAS: Would you write the same song here now?

EISLER: If I had to write a historical play about Russia, I would write it—and the poet would let me have the words.

THOMAS: Would you write the same song here in the United States now about "you must take over" here in the United States?

EISLER: No.

THOMAS: You have changed your opinion, then?[199]

And so it continued. In 1948, Hanns Eisler and his wife were deported.

HUAC: "ON THE TRAIL OF THE TARANTULA"

THE MOST SENSATIONAL OF HUAC's 1947 hearings arose out of its investigation of Hollywood. The committee first became interested in Hollywood in the days of Martin Dies. Soon after saving the Committee from extinction in 1945, Congressman Rankin announced that he had received information that "one of the most dangerous plots ever instigated for the overthrow of this government has its headquarters in Hollywood." He noted, excitedly, "[W]e're on the trail of the tarantula now."[200] A few days later, Rankin proclaimed, "[W]e are out to expose those elements that are insidiously trying to spread subversive propaganda, poison the minds of your children, distort the history of our country, and discredit Christianity." More specifically, he spoke of "the loathsome, filthy, insinuating un-American undercurrents that are running through various [motion] pictures."[201]

Although the committee did not pursue these claims under Rankin's leadership, it did so quickly once the Republicans gained control. Gerhard Eisler was the bridge between HUAC's earlier investigations and its investigation of Hollywood. In early 1947, a subcommittee chaired by J. Parnell Thomas journeyed to Hollywood to get the lay of the land from "friendly" witnesses, including the actors Robert Taylor and Adolphe Menjou and the producer Jack Warner. The subcommittee made headlines when it concluded that "scores of screen writers who are Communists have infiltrated into the various studios and it has been through this medium that most of the Communist propaganda has been injected into the movies." Communists "have employed subtle techniques in pictures, in glorifying the Communist system and degrading our own system." Thomas announced to an eager press that the subcommittee had been "furnished with a complete list of all the pictures which have been produced in Hollywood in the past eight years which contain Communist propaganda."[202]

Before the full committee in the fall, Thomas promised to prove that Communists had infiltrated the motion picture industry; that prominent scriptwriters were Communists; that Communists had introduced Communist propaganda into motion pictures; and that the Roosevelt administration had pressured the industry to produce pro-Communist films.[203] In a room crowded with klieg lights, cameras, and microphones, HUAC trotted out a galaxy of Hollywood stars and moguls. Politically naïve actors, actresses, and producers were invited to attest publicly to their deepest suspicions, jealousies, and resentments about their colleagues and competitors.[204]

The committee began by calling a series of "friendly" witnesses, including the producers Jack Warner, Louis B. Mayer, and Walt Disney; the directors Leo McCarey and Sam Wood; the writers Rupert Hughes and Morrie Ryskind; and the actors Robert Taylor, Gary Cooper, Ronald Reagan, and Adolphe Menjou. Lela Rogers, the mother and agent of Ginger Rogers, and Ayn Rand, the novelist, also appeared as "friendly" witnesses. The testimony of these individuals ranged from the perceptive "to the strange, the bitter, and the stupid."[205] Asked whether she and her daughter had ever turned down scripts because they "were un-American or Communist propaganda," Lela Rogers cited Theodore Dreiser's *Sister Carrie* as a compelling example.[206]

No one doubted that there were Communists and fellow travelers in Hollywood, as in most sectors of American life at this time. The question was whether such individuals had smuggled "Communist propaganda into films." During the first week of hearings, four movies were mentioned: *Mission to Moscow*, a 1943 Warner Brothers film based on the autobiography of the American ambassador to the Soviet Union from 1936 to 1938; *Song of Russia*, a 1943 MGM film starring Robert Taylor, which told the tale of an American orchestra leader who traveled to the Soviet Union and fell in love with a Russian pianist; *North Star*, a 1943 Samuel Goldwyn production, based on an original story by Lillian Hellman depicting the Nazi invasion of Russia in 1941; and *None but the Lonely Heart*, a 1944 RKO film, directed by Clifford Odets and starring Cary Grant and Ethel Barrymore, which portrayed life among the poor in London.[207]

Jack Warner, a "friendly" witness, who even offered to establish "a fund to ship to Russia the people who . . . prefer the communistic system to ours," vehe-mently denied that *Mission to Moscow* had been in any way improper. He explained that "if making *Mission to Moscow* in 1942 was a subversive activity, then the American Liberty ships which carried food and guns to Russian allies . . . were likewise engaged in subversive activities. The picture was made only to help a desperate war effort. . . ."[208]

Louis B. Mayer, the head of MGM, responded to the objections to *Song of Russia*: "Mention has been made of the picture, *Song of Russia*, as being friendly to Russia at the time it was made. Of course it was. It was made to be friendly. . . . It was in April of 1942 [and it] seemed a good medium of entertainment and . . . offered an opportunity for a pat on the back for our then ally, Russia."[209]

AMONG THE "FRIENDLY" WITNESSES, Ayn Rand, Adolphe Menjou, Gary Cooper, and Ronald Reagan were especially interesting. Born in St. Peters-burg, Rand emigrated to the United States in 1926. She had published two nov-els, including *The Fountainhead*, an international best seller. Rand's testimony focused on *Song of Russia*, which she characterized as Communist propaganda because it gave "a good impression of communism as a way of life."

According to Rand, at the very beginning of the film an American conductor, played by Robert Taylor, is seen giving a concert in America for Russian war relief. He starts playing the national anthem, which then "dissolves into a Russ-ian mob, with the sickle and hammer on a red flag very prominent above their heads." Rand testified that this made her "sick." It "was a terrible touch of propa-ganda."[210] Rand then went through the movie scene by scene to identify other facets of the film that were "Communist propaganda." For example, when the American conductor visits Russia, he meets a Russian girl from a village. But, Rand pointed out, this was impossible because the Russian state police would never have allowed the girl to come to the city without permission. Later, in a park, the lovers encounter "happy little children in white blouses running around." But, Rand complained, the movie had no scenes of "food lines" or of "homeless children in rags," such as she had seen in Russia.[211]

Adolphe Menjou, who had been a Hollywood star for more than three decades, also fancied himself an expert on "Marxism, Fabian socialism, commu-nism, Stalinism, and its probable effects on the American people." Although con-ceding that he had seen nothing he would define as "Communist propaganda" in American movies, he hastened to add that he had seen a lot that was against "good Americanism."

Robert Stripling asked Menjou whether he thought John Cromwell, who was politically active in the Screen Directors Guild, was a Communist. Menjou replied that "he acts an awful lot like one," noting that Cromwell had once said to him that "capitalism in America was through." Menjou offered to provide the committee with "a list of names" he had gathered. He boasted, "I am a witch-hunter if the witches are Communists. I am a Red-baiter. I make no bones about it whatsoever. I would like to see them all back in Russia."[212]

Gary Cooper's hit films included *Unconquered, Pride of the Yankees,* and *Mr. Deeds Goes to Town.* Cooper testified that he had heard "Communistic influences" voiced in the motion picture industry. For example, he had "heard tossed around such statements as, 'Don't you think the Constitution of the United States is about a hundred and fifty years out of date?' and—oh, I don't know,—I have heard people mention that, well, 'Perhaps this would be a more efficient Government without a Congress'—which statements are very un-American." When asked about outlawing the Communist Party, Cooper said, "[I]t would be a good idea, although I have never read Karl Marx and I don't know the basis of Communism, beyond what I have picked up from hearsay. From what I hear, I don't like it because it isn't on the level."[213]

Ronald Reagan was president of the Screen Actors Guild at the time of his testimony before HUAC. He disappointed the committee. Asked whether any members of the guild were also members of the Communist Party, Reagan replied that he had heard this was so but had no personal knowledge of the matter. Asked whether Communists had tried to dominate the guild, Reagan stated that some members had attempted "to put over their own particular views on various issues," but he added, "I guess . . . you would have to say that our side was attempting to dominate, too, because we were fighting just as hard to put over our views." Asked "what steps should be taken to rid the motion-picture industry of any Communist influences," Reagan responded, "Sir . . . I detest, I abhor their philosophy, but . . . I never as a citizen want to see our country become urged, by either fear or resentment of this group, that we ever compromise with any of our democratic principles. . . . I still think that democracy can do it."*[214]

---

* Reagan's later conduct was less admirable. On July 30, 1951, Reagan wrote a guest column, "Reds Beaten in Hollywood," for the *Citizen News,* in which he described the Communists' "bold plot to seize control of the talent guilds . . . through which the subversive brethren hoped eventually to control contents of films and thus influence the minds of 80,000,000 movie goers." He gave great credit to HUAC for having helped foil this plot and boasted, "Today, even the fellow traveller has disappeared from the Hollywood scene." Reprinted in Bentley, ed, *Thirty Years of Treason* at 293–94 (cited in note 68).

THE SECOND WEEK of the Hollywood hearings was dedicated to HUAC's interrogation of actors, writers, and directors it suspected of poisoning America's film industry. The committee's strategy was to subpoena them in order to ask, "Are you now or have you ever been a member of the Communist Party?" The committee called eleven witnesses to testify at this stage of the hearings.[215]

The most famous was Bertolt Brecht, the German playwright and poet who had collaborated with Hanns Eisler. Brecht emphatically denied that he was or had ever been a Communist. The other ten witnesses refused to answer the committee's question concerning past or present membership in the Communist Party. All asserted that their political beliefs and affiliations were entitled to the same privilege of secrecy as the ballot box. Their plea fell on deaf ears.[216]

Typical of the committee's exchanges was its interrogation of John Howard Lawson, a well-known screenwriter, associated with such movies as *Sahara*, *Algiers*, *Action in the North Atlantic*, and *Blockade*. Lawson, the first president of the Screen Writers Guild, had worked with almost every major Hollywood studio, including MGM, Columbia, and 20th Century Fox:

LAWSON: You have spent 1 week vilifying me before the American public—

THOMAS: Just a minute—

LAWSON: And you refuse to allow me to make a statement on my rights as an American citizen.

THOMAS: I refuse you to make the statement because of the first sentence . . . That statement is not pertinent to the inquiry . . . *[Note: The first sentence of Lawson's written statement was: "For a week, this Committee has conducted an illegal and indecent trial of American citizens, whom the Committee has selected to be publicly pilloried and smeared."]*

LAWSON: The rights of American citizens are important in this room here, and I intend to stand up for those rights, Congressman Thomas.
. . .

THOMAS: . . . You know what has happened to a lot of people that have been in contempt of this committee this year, don't you?

LAWSON: I am glad you have made it perfectly clear that you are going to threaten and intimidate the witnesses, Mr. Chairman. *[The Chairman repeatedly pounds the gavel.]* I am an American citizen and I am not at all easy to intimidate. . . .

STRIPLING: Mr. Lawson, are you now or have you ever been a member of the Communist Party of the United States? . . .

LAWSON: You are using the old technique, which was used in Hitler Germany in order to create a scare here—*[The Chairman repeatedly pounds the gavel.]*—In order that you can then smear the motion-picture industry, and you can then proceed to the press, to any form of communication in this country. . . . The Bill of Rights was established precisely to prevent the operation of any committee which could invade the basic rights of Americans. Now, if you want to know—

THOMAS: *[Pounding the gavel.]* We are going to get the answer to that question if we have to stay here for a week. Are you a member of the Communist Party, or have you ever been a member of the Communist Party?

LAWSON: It is unfortunate and tragic that I have to teach this committee the basic principles of American—

THOMAS: *[Pounding the gavel.]* That is not the question. That is not the question. The question is: Have you ever been a member of the Communist Party?

LAWSON: I am framing my answer in the only way in which any American citizen can frame his answer to a question which absolutely invades his rights . . .

THOMAS: *[Pounding the gavel.]* Excuse the witness. . . .[217]

The other "unfriendly" witnesses who followed Lawson to the stand were Alvah Bessie, Herbert Biberman, Lester Cole, Edward Dmytryk, Ring Lardner Jr., Albert Maltz, Samuel Ornitz, Adrian Scott, and Dalton Trumbo. Like Lawson, each refused to answer any questions about past or present Communist membership. After each one's testimony, a committee investigator read into the record whatever evidence the committee had compiled about his alleged Communist affiliations. At the conclusion of the hearings, each of the "Hollywood Ten" was charged with contempt of Congress.[218]

A group of actors, writers, and directors, hurriedly assembled under the leadership of John Huston, sent a delegation to Washington to protest the committee's actions, but to no avail. All of the Hollywood Ten were convicted and sentenced to prison for contempt of Congress. Chairman Thomas explained that the constitutional claims of the witnesses were nothing other than "a concerted effort on the part of the Communists, their fellow travelers, their dupes, and paid apologists to create a fog about constitutional rights, the first amendment, and so forth."[219]

In the end, HUAC failed to demonstrate that Hollywood was a hotbed of Communist activity. The only claim it could prove was that some Communists, near-Communists, former Communists, and former near-Communists worked in the film industry, particularly as writers. The only evidence of pro-Soviet propaganda concerned films that had been made during the World War II alliance of the United States and the Soviet Union against Nazi Germany. HUAC nonetheless concluded that "Hollywood was in the grip of a Red terror."[220]

The movie studios, concerned about profits and export licenses, surrendered without a peep. They promptly issued a statement declaring, "We will forthwith discharge or suspend without compensation those in our employ, and we will not re-employ any of the [Hollywood Ten] until such time as he is acquitted, or has purged himself of contempt, and declared under oath that he is not a Communist."[221] They pledged not to employ any person who refused to answer the question "Are you now or have you ever been a member of the Communist Party?"[*]

Over the next several years, some 250 writers, directors, and actors were blacklisted in Hollywood, including Howard Da Silva, Will Geer, Dashiell Hammett, Lillian Hellman, Zero Mostel, Dorothy Parker, Lionel Stander, and Dalton Trumbo. Many of their colleagues, such as Humphrey Bogart, Lucille Ball, Kirk Douglas, Gene Kelly, Katharine Hepburn, John Huston, Gregory Peck, Frank Sinatra, Orson Welles, and William Wyler, came to their aid. Unfortunately, this often backfired. Of the 204 members of the Hollywood community who signed an amicus brief in the Supreme Court supporting the Hollywood Ten, 84 were later blacklisted themselves. Some who tried to defend those who had been blacklisted ended up naming names in order to avoid a similar fate.[†]

For a glimpse into the ugliness of the accusations, and the manner in which they were conveyed in the press, consider this excerpt from the columnist Jimmie Tarantino's regular feature in *Hollywood Life*:

> LENA HORNE, SINGER-ACTRESS . . . Horne is a supporter of the commie party in many ways. Her name has been used in countless cases bringing in support and money . . . The Daily Worker has had her help . . . In 1945, Lena received an award from the NEW MASSES, a commie publication . . . She was a fund raiser for the PEOPLE'S DAILY WORKER . . . She once acted as a speaker for the Civil Rights Congress, a red front . . . Lena gave free entertainment to the

---

[*] In a statement of almost breathtaking hypocrisy, the studio heads proclaimed that their goal was to protect the industry from the danger that "fear" would inhibit the creative process. Their argument was that by eliminating "subversives" from the industry they would "safeguard free speech" for the "innocent." Waldorf Statement, Dec 3, 1947, excerpted in Larry Ceplair and Steven Englund, *The Inquisition in Hollywood: Politics and the Film Community, 1930–1960* 455 (California 1983).

[†] HUAC was particularly incensed at Arthur Miller for his play *The Crucible*, which used the Salem witch trials to dramatize the contemporary Red hunt. When a furious committee counsel Arens asked Miller whether he was aware that the Communist press had drawn parallels between *The Crucible* and the activities of HUAC, Miller calmly replied, "The comparison is inevitable, sir." See Caute, *Great Fear* at 100 (cited in note 3).

Communist Party State Committee of N.Y. . . . in an affair honoring . . . a noted Communist . . . La Horne was a performer who aided in a radio program, "FIGHTERS FOR FREEDOM," a known commie red front. . . .[222]

In the face of similar attacks, José Ferrer took out paid advertisements in a desperate effort to rehabilitate himself;[223] Charlie Chaplin left the country; after Edward G. Robinson sent a check to help Dalton Trumbo's family while he was in prison for contempt, he was harassed and denied work; Elia Kazan, who had been a member of the Communist Party in the early 1930s, refused initially to name names, but then caved before HUAC and turned in Clifford Odets, among others;* Odets, an accomplished radical playwright, also caved before HUAC and pleaded that he had been duped by the Communists. In order to continue working, Jerome Robbins, the choreographer of *West Side Story*, Lee J. Cobb, a star of *On the Waterfront*, and Sterling Hayden, a decorated war hero, all repented their "sins" under the glare of HUAC's klieg lights.†[224]

Shortly before his HUAC testimony, Ring Lardner Jr. received the Academy Award for writing *Woman of the Year*, starring Katharine Hepburn and Spencer Tracey. Sentenced to a year in prison, Lardner later explained why he had refused to answer HUAC's questions:

> [I]f I am a member of the Communist Party I would be exposing myself to the bigotry and inspired hysteria which is forcing not only Communists but all Left-of-Center political groups into semi-secret status. . . . If I am not a member, I would be exposing other men to the same bigotry and blacklist by contributing to the precedent that all non-Communists must so declare themselves in order to isolate the actual offenders. Further, it would be clear to everyone, including me, that I had purged myself in order to please my past and prospective employers.‡[225]

---

* Kazan was shunned as a result of his conduct for decades thereafter, a legacy that followed him to his death in 2003.

† Radio, television, and theater were also subject to the blacklist. The *New York Times* reported that 1,500 individuals in radio and television had been affected by the blacklist. Alfred E. Clark, *TV "Blacklist" Cited by Susskind in Faulk's Suit*, New York Times 12 (Apr 28, 1962). Among those blacklisted in radio and television were Leonard Bernstein, Joseph Cotton, John Garfield, Judy Holliday, Kim Hunter, Burl Ives, Gypsy Rose Lee, Arthur Miller, and Pete Seeger, to name just a few. See Miller, *Judges and the Judged* (cited in note 224).

‡ Years later, Lardner admitted in an article in the *Saturday Evening Post*, "I was at that time a member of the Communist Party, in whose ranks I had found some of the most thoughtful, witty and generally stimulating men and women of Hollywood. I also encountered a number of bores and unstable characters, which seemed to bear out Bernard Shaw's observation that revolutionary movements tend to attract the best and worst elements in a . . . society." Ring Lardner Jr., *My Life on the Black List*, Saturday Evening Post 38 (Oct 14, 1961).

THE "BLOND SPY QUEEN" AND THE *TIME* EDITOR

IN THE SPRING OF 1947, a federal grand jury in New York—the same grand jury that later indicted the leaders of the Communist Party—subpoenaed dozens of witnesses in an investigation of possible Soviet espionage. Most of these witnesses had been named either by Elizabeth T. Bentley or by Whittaker Chambers. Bentley and Chambers had both been couriers for the Soviet Union. In all, Bentley and Chambers named more than fifty persons as members of Communist "cells." The grand jury did not indict a single one of them.

In the summer of 1948, the action shifted to HUAC, which lacked even the procedural safeguards of a grand jury.[226] On July 31, Bentley, the "blond spy queen," testified before HUAC that some thirty federal employees had disclosed confidential information to Soviet agents. Bentley's testimony generated headlines for months.

Having graduated from Vassar in 1930, Bentley then studied in Italy for several years and earned a master's degree from Columbia University.[227] She explained how she had first become interested in the Communist Party in the early thirties: "I was haunted by the problems of our maladjusted economic system. Although I was only in my mid-twenties, I had already seen two depressions. . . . Each had left in its wake suffering, starvation, and broken lives." Moreover, "I was quite infuriated with what I had learned about fascism in Italy, and the only people who would listen to me were the people in the American League Against War and Fascism, and . . . I gradually got into that, and gradually there I met Communists, both in Columbia and downtown." As Bentley came to know these young Communists, she was "impressed" by their "intense energy" and "optimism." They were "continually engaged . . . in humanitarian projects, such as better housing for the poor, more relief for the underprivileged, and higher wages for the workers. It is they, I thought, who are the modern Good Samaritans."[228]

Three years after Bentley joined the Communist Party in 1935, she met and fell in love with Jacob Golos, a party functionary. After Germany attacked the Soviet Union in 1941, Bentley, under Golos's direction, became an underground courier between Communist cells in Washington, D.C., and Golos in New York. According to Bentley, the material she passed to Golos included "[m]ilitary information, particularly from the Air Corps, on production of airplanes, their destinations to the various theaters of war and to various countries, new types of planes being put out, information as to when D-day would be, all sorts of inside military information."[229]

Golos died in 1943. Although Bentley continued as a courier for a while longer, she gradually became disillusioned with the party because she found it to be increasingly under the thumb of Moscow. By July 1944, she was caught between "the merciless Russian machine" and the "tyrannical American government" in a "strange little no-man's land" all her own. She concluded that the Russians treated "human beings as if they were little more than pawns on a chessboard." Her friends in the party "had become, in the hands of the Communist movement, no longer individuals but robots."

After months of anxiety, Bentley decided that the American system was the "one bulwark against the growing power of Communism." If she turned in her former colleagues, "they would no longer be useful to the Soviet machine." Returned to "a normal life again, perhaps they, too, could find their way back to that integrity which they had lost." One day, almost "without knowing" what she was doing, she wandered into a church and found herself "trying to pray." A "strange peace came over me," she later wrote, and the "voice of my conscience" rang out: "You know now that the way of life you have followed these last ten years was wrong; you have come back to where you belong. But first you must make amends!"[230]

Soon thereafter, in August 1945, Bentley brought her story to the New Haven branch of the FBI. The federal agents encouraged her to maintain her contacts with the Communist Party. She finally "broke cover" in 1947 when the FBI directed her to testify before the federal grand jury. Bentley also made eight appearances before four different congressional committees. In her testimony before HUAC, she named thirty current or former government employees as members of the Communist Party. Seventeen of these individuals were never subpoenaed and did not appear before the committee. Six were subpoenaed but declined to answer questions, invoking the Fifth Amendment. Seven answered all the committee's questions and categorically denied Communist Party membership or the disclosure of any confidential information.[231]

One of the most prominent individuals named by Bentley was Harry Dexter White, who had served as Henry Morgenthau's assistant secretary of the treasury. A bold thinker, White was the principal architect of the International Monetary Fund. When he learned of Bentley's accusation, he insisted on appearing personally before HUAC. In August 1948, he told the committee that although he knew many of the people named by Bentley, he did not know that any of them was a Communist, if in fact any was. Suffering from a weak heart, and "emotionally outraged" by the humiliation of his experience, White died three days after his testimony.*[232]

---

* According to some researchers, White was indeed a spy, and President Truman "had known this since the end of 1945 and had done nothing about it." Herman, *Joseph McCarthy* at 243 (cited in note 3). See Sam Tannenhaus, *Whittaker Chambers: A Biography* 479–80 (Random House 1997).

Elizabeth Bentley

Perhaps the most dramatic case to emerge out of Bentley's testimony involved William Remington. Bentley described Remington as "the typical clean-cut American lad" and nicknamed him the "infant prodigy." Remington, a graduate of Dartmouth and Columbia, had worked for both the War Production Board and the Commerce Department. After Bentley named him to the grand jury as a member of the Communist Party who had provided her with classified government documents, the grand jury subpoenaed him. Remington denied that he had ever given Bentley confidential information and that he had ever been a member of the Communist Party. No charges were brought against him, and he was thereafter cleared by a Commerce Department loyalty board.[233]

Bentley then repeated her accusations against Remington on a radio show. He promptly sued her and the show's sponsors for libel. In early 1950, he agreed to a settlement, which was paid by the sponsors. In April, however, HUAC learned that when Remington was nineteen years old he had joined the Communist Party. It turned the matter over to the Department of Justice. A federal grand jury then indicted him for perjury because he had testified to the earlier grand jury that he had never joined the party. Remington was convicted, but his conviction was overturned on appeal. He was then prosecuted and convicted again. This time the court of appeals upheld his conviction, over a scathing dissent by Judge Learned Hand. Remington was sentenced to three years in prison. In 1954, he was murdered by a fellow prisoner.[234]

There were always doubts about Bentley's credibility. Nonetheless, as a result of her testimony, four individuals were imprisoned for perjury (none for espionage) and countless others had their reputations, careers, and personal lives savaged.[235] For Bentley, the "worst ordeal of all was sitting in the Committee hearing and watching [her] old comrades as they testified." Those who were still committed "Communists stood firmly on their constitutional grounds and refused to talk." The others, Bentley recalled, "slid and slithered around the questions, trying to exculpate themselves," while "insinuating that I was a 'neurotic' and 'drank too much.'" As she listened to their testimony, she understood that they were "spiritually dead," and she "felt sick."[236]

FOUR DAYS AFTER BENTLEY completed her testimony before HUAC, Whittaker Chambers appeared as a witness. Chambers testified that he had joined the Communist Party in 1924:

> I had become convinced that the society in which we live, western civilization, had reached a crisis, of which the First World War was the military expression, and that it was doomed to collapse or revert to barbarism. . . . In the writings of Karl Marx I thought that I had found the explanation of the historical and economic causes. In the writings of Lenin I thought I had found the answer to the question, What to do?

Over the next decade, Chambers "served in the underground." He explained that the primary purpose of his cell was not espionage but "the Communist infiltration of the American government." By 1937, he had "repudiated Marx's doctrines and Lenin's tactics" and had come to understand communism as "a form of totalitarianism." He therefore broke with the party in 1939. He testified that in the ten years since leaving the party he had "sought to live an industrious and God-fearing life," fighting "communism constantly by act and written word."[237]

As we have seen, in the course of his testimony Chambers alleged that Alger Hiss had been a member of the Communist Party and an active participant in a Washington cell. At the time Chambers claimed to have known him, Hiss was merely an assistant to the assistant secretary of state. But over the next decade he moved up rapidly to serve as executive secretary of the Dumbarton Oaks conference, secretary-general of the United Nations Charter conference, and as a member of the U.S. delegation to the Yalta conference. At the time of Chambers's testimony before HUAC, Hiss was president of the Carnegie Endowment for

Alger Hiss and Robert Stripling

International Peace. He was the perfect target for those who wanted to discredit the New Deal and the Democratic Party in the upcoming 1948 election.[238]

Hiss emphatically denied Chambers's charge and declared that he had "never laid eyes on him." Two days later, he appeared before the committee as a voluntary witness. He stated unequivocally, "I am not and never have been a member of the Communist Party. . . . I have never followed the Communist Party line, directly or indirectly. To the best of my knowledge, none of my friends is a Communist." He testified, "[T]he statements made about me by Mr. Chambers are complete fabrications."[239]

By the end of his testimony, Hiss had made a favorable impression on the committee members, who were inclined to believe him. Richard Nixon, however, was skeptical. In a series of executive sessions in which he cross-examined both men, Nixon became convinced that Hiss was lying. Under pressure from Nixon, Hiss grudgingly admitted that he might once have known Chambers under another name—George Crosley.* But Hiss still indignantly insisted that

---

* A contemporary evaluation of Nixon's performance as a member of HUAC is interesting: "It is hard not to overpraise Nixon, for he brought to the committee enthusiasm, a willingness to work

Chambers's key allegations about him were false and challenged him to "make those same statements out of the presence of this committee without their being privileged for suit for libel." He added, "I challenge you to do it, and I hope you will do it damned quickly."[240] This challenge led directly to Hiss's downfall: Chambers repeated the charge on a radio program; Hiss sued for libel; Chambers produced the infamous Pumpkin Papers; Hiss was eventually prosecuted and convicted of perjury; and, through tough lawyering, Richard Nixon firmly established his place in the national spotlight.[241]

THE DEMOCRATS REGAINED control of HUAC after the 1948 election. Although the committee remained active, none of its subsequent investigations achieved the level of abuse that had marked its hearings under J. Parnell Thomas, who eventually landed in prison himself.*[242]

From 1945 to 1957, HUAC heard testimony from more than 3,000 witnesses and cited 135 individuals for contempt—more than the entire Congress had cited for contempt in the entire history of the United States to that point. It amassed dossiers on hundreds of thousands of Americans who had done nothing illegal, or even wrong. Its published reports, which often included lists of alleged "subversives" and "subversive" organizations, were marred by the reckless use of evidence and the repetition of unfounded accusations. It shamelessly threatened and browbeat those who questioned its authority. Its hearings left behind a trail of tarnished reputations and ruined careers. As Francis Walter, HUAC's chairman from 1955 to 1963, explained, the committee's goal was to expose Communists and fellow travelers "before their neighbors and fellow workers," with the "confidence" that loyal Americans "will do the rest of the job." In this, HUAC was successful. Thousands of "exposed" individuals were fired, many were blacklisted, and some were even beaten by local vigilantes. In the end, however, HUAC's hearings resulted in the convictions of only *two* federal employees—Alger Hiss and William Remington, both of whom were convicted only of perjury.[243]

Moreover, during all the years of its existence, HUAC proposed only two

---

hard, ability as a lawyer, and a reasonable detachment and sense of fairness, qualities that have been rare among the committee's members. Nonetheless, at several points he was guilty of bad errors of judgment and as time went on he showed increasing signs of partisanship and personal ambition." Carr, *House Committee* at 229 (cited in note 56).

* Thomas was convicted for accepting kickbacks from persons on his staff. Ironically, he served time in federal prison with some of the very individuals he had held in contempt of HUAC. See Ring Lardner Jr., *My Life on the Black List*, Saturday Evening Post 38 (Oct 14, 1961).

pieces of legislation that were actually enacted by Congress. In 1943, Martin Dies managed to attach a rider to a deficiency appropriations act, forbidding the payment of salaries to three named federal employees whom Dies had attacked as disloyal. The Supreme Court held the rider unconstitutional as a bill of attainder.[244] And in 1948, Congressmen Karl Mundt and Richard Nixon drafted the Mundt-Nixon Bill, which eventually became the registration component of the McCarren Internal Security Act of 1950. Between 1951 and 1958, HUAC held legislative hearings on *none* of the twelve bills that were referred to it.[245]

But HUAC mastered the art of "guilt by association." Imagine being subjected to the following sequence of inquiries:

Are you now or have you ever been a member of the Communist Party?

Are you now or have you ever been a member of any Communist-front organization?

Have you ever attended a meeting of the Communist Party or of any Communist-front organization?

Have you ever signed a petition or received any mail from the Communist Party or any Communist-front organization?

Are any of your work associates, neighbors, or friends involved with the Communist Party or any Communist-front organization?

Do you own or have you ever read any books or articles by Lillian Hellman, John Fast, Ring Lardner Jr., Dalton Trumbo, Karl Marx, Dorothy Parker, or any other un-American writer?

Do you know X [a work associate, neighbor, or friend]?

Did you know that X has made financial contributions to a Communist-front organization?

Are you a member of your local chess club?

Did you know that Y, a member of your local chess club, has in the past supported a Communist-front organization?

In this manner, an organization would be contaminated by the presence of any allegedly subversive person, and every member of the organization could then be contaminated by the mere fact of membership in an organization containing a tainted member. HUAC aggressively fostered the mind-set of the witch hunt. As in the witch trials of Salem, what the committee wanted was "public denunciation, public purgation, a purification of the convert by means of his public humiliation as he betrayed his old friends and comrades."[246]

In both the public and the private spheres, HUAC helped create a status of virtual outlawry in which citizens could be cruelly "stigmatized though never convicted of any offense." The operative principle of HUAC was repentance, confession, betrayal. The lesson was clear. To avoid being tainted, an individual "had better not join anything, or lend his name to anything, or say anything, or do anything" that might now or *later* be construed as "disloyal."[247]

It is surely true that at the height of the Cold War a small, highly disciplined cohort of dedicated Communists, working in secret with agents of the Soviet Union, sought to harm the United States, and many well-meaning Americans misjudged both Stalin and the domestic Communist movement. But the danger that hard-core Communists presented to the United States was not the "subversion" of the American people. It was the danger of espionage and sabotage. The appropriate way for a democratic government to address that danger is not to stifle open debate or to foster a climate of fear and timidity. It is, rather, to focus precisely on the criminal conduct and to use appropriate *law enforcement* tools to identify, punish, and deter dangerous lawbreakers.[248] This is the essential line between a police state and a free society.

TAIL GUNNER JOE

HERB BLOCK, the brilliant *Washington Post* political cartoonist, coined the word "McCarthyism" on March 29, 1950, when he used it as a label on a tar barrel.[249] McCarthy, who was born near Appleton, Wisconsin, on November 15, 1908, was the fifth of seven children. The McCarthys were a close, happy family—hardworking, religious, and proud of their Irish heritage. McCarthy attended school in a one-room schoolhouse. He was a boisterous, socially awkward youth who loved to roughhouse.

After finishing elementary school, McCarthy worked on the family farm for several years and then opened his own business raising chickens and selling eggs. At the age of nineteen, he returned to school and completed the equivalent of four years of high school in nine months. In 1930, he enrolled at Marquette University, where he boxed and cultivated the image of a tough guy. With rugged features and thick arms, he was a formidable young man. In his third year at Marquette, he entered law school.

McCarthy struggled through several difficult years as a small-town lawyer before deciding in 1939 to run for a circuit judgeship. At thirty years of age, he was the youngest judge ever elected in the county. Even then, though, his campaign tactics were perceived as thoroughly dishonest, ferocious, and effective.

In early 1941, McCarthy stunned his friends by confiding his intention to run for the U.S. Senate in 1944. Pearl Harbor, however, threw a wrench into his plans. He enlisted in the Marines and was sent as an intelligence officer to the South Pacific, where he connived to get as much publicity as possible. He issued his own press releases, labeled himself "Tail Gunner Joe" (though he was not a tail gunner), and launched his campaign for the Senate from the Solomon Islands. After fracturing his foot during a prank, McCarthy fabricated a military citation, claiming he had been injured in combat. Returning home in July 1944, he campaigned energetically, but failed to win the Republican nomination.[250]

He immediately set to work to win election to the Senate in 1946. He campaigned for the next two years, criss-crossing the state in an effort to wrest the Republican nomination away from Senator Robert M. La Follette Jr., the son of the legendary Progressive leader. On August 8, 1946, McCarthy played the "Communist card" for the first time, charging that La Follette had "paved the way" for the Communists in Eastern Europe. After defeating La Follette, McCarthy turned his Red-baiting on his Democratic opponent, whom he accused of being a "megaphone" for the Communists. McCarthy learned quickly that such attacks roused his audiences and left his opponents off-balance. As the election neared, he promised to remove the "Communists from the public payroll" and accused President Truman of attempting to "Sovietize our farms." He won handily.[251]

At the age of thirty-eight, Joe McCarthy arrived in the Senate with an impressive head of steam, but like many newcomers to Washington, he soon floundered. He became known as an uncouth outsider devoid of personal charm or legislative ability. He was given the degrading nickname the "Pepsi-Cola Kid" because of his work for the soft-drink lobby. McCarthy badly needed a new direction. By the end of 1949, he "had largely lost the confidence of even his fellow party members." Then, in January 1950, at a dinner in the Colony Restaurant in Washington, D.C., Father Edmund A. Walsh, dean of the Georgetown School of Foreign Service, suggested that he exploit the "Communism in government" issue.[252]

On February 9, 1950, Senator Joseph McCarthy became a household name. With his fraudulent claim that he possessed a list of 205 employees of the State Department who were card-carrying Communists, McCarthy burst into the national headlines.[253] When called on his lie, he bluffed. On February 10, he offered to show his "list" to a reporter, but then "discovered" he had left it in another suit. As the story grew, and the Truman administration bristled, McCarthy insisted that he wanted "to be sure they aren't hiding these Communists any more." On February 19, he promised to give the Senate "detailed information" about the Communists in the State Department.[254]

The Democratic Senate majority leader, Scott Lucas, declared on the floor of the Senate that McCarthy should be "ashamed" of his conduct and demanded that he prove his accusations. McCarthy, however, refused to reveal the names, explaining that it would be inappropriate for him to make the names public until a Senate committee had reviewed them in closed session.

Still bluffing, he pulled stacks of photographs and papers from his bulging briefcase, suggesting this was his proof. He rambled on for some five hours, rattling off fabricated statements about the allegedly subversive activities and associations of unnamed State Department employees. He equivocated, distorted, manipulated, and lied. Throughout his tirade, McCarthy was interrupted by other senators, "who expressed frustration, anger, and even disbelief at what they were hearing on the floor of the United States Senate."[255]

Although some critics denounced McCarthy's "campaign of indiscriminate character-assassination,"[256] most Americans believed he had uncovered scores of Soviet spies. McCarthy's deceit was made possible, both in this instance and later, by a combination of factors.

McCarthy possessed a truly unique character. He had the "gifts" of unparalleled audacity, unyielding stubbornness, and a street fighter's instinct for the jugular. He also had a knack for slicing invective and a natural talent for self-promotion.

McCarthy was the "right" man for the "right" moment. He struck a powerful, if dangerous, chord in American society. In 1950, Americans were deeply fearful for their nation's future. Communism was a daunting enemy. As events in Eastern Europe, China, and Korea had demonstrated, the nation faced a violent, aggressive, and insidious adversary. Moreover, this was not an adversary that would leave Americans in peace. Like the French at the end of the eighteenth century, the Soviets in the middle of the twentieth century worked indefatigably to subvert other nations from within, and America was no exception. The enemy was not only a soldier on a battlefield but also, quite possibly, a neighbor, co-worker, teacher, reporter, union member, or passing acquaintance. Americans were fearful not only about their military security but also about the security of their religious, moral, and national values, their free enterprise system, their labor movement, their media, and their educational system. The enemy was not just the Russians and the Chinese but "un-Americanism." And Joe McCarthy knew it.

Moreover, McCarthy had the unwavering support and protection of a powerful coterie of right-wing journalists, publishers, religious leaders, businessmen, and politicians. With such publishers as William Randolph Hearst Jr. and Colonel Robert R. McCormick, such influential columnists and broadcasters as Westbrook Pegler and Fulton Lewis Jr., such religious leaders as Francis Cardinal Spellman and Bishop Fulton J. Sheen, and such powerful Republican senators as Kenneth Wherry, Karl Mundt, Homer Ferguson, and William Jenner all in his corner, McCarthy could flourish in even the most contentious political environment.

Finally, McCarthy was embraced not only by the far right but by the vast majority of the Republican Party, including most moderate Republicans, who saw him as the instrument through which they could finally unravel the New Deal and regain control of the national government.[257]

BUT THE DEMOCRATS still controlled Congress in February 1950, and on February 22 the Senate adopted a resolution authorizing "a full and complete study and investigation" of McCarthy's claims.[258] As we have seen, the Democratic leadership appointed Millard E. Tydings of Maryland to chair the investigating committee. Conservative Republicans, fearful that the investigation would halt their political momentum, came to McCarthy's aid as he prepared for the hearings. Even with this assistance, however, he could not defend his accusations.[259]

McCarthy's most celebrated charge involved Professor Owen Lattimore, the director of the Page School of International Relations at Johns Hopkins University. After the embarrassment of his false charges against Dorothy Kenyon, McCarthy, in an effort to recoup his losses, suddenly announced that he would reveal to the nation the name of "the top Russian espionage agent in America." As the press and the nation waited with bated breath, he added that he was "willing to stand or fall on this one." Richard Rovere, then covering the story for the *New Yorker*, surmised that at that moment McCarthy had not the faintest notion whose name he was about to offer up. It was Lattimore's that won the honor.

A prolific Asia scholar and former editor of the left-wing *Pacific Affairs*, Lattimore had once been a fellow traveler and was widely known to be sympathetic to the Communist cause in China. Beyond that, however, McCarthy's accusation was baseless. On April 6, Lattimore, represented by Abe Fortas, appeared before the Tydings Committee. A bespectacled, slightly balding man with a professorial air, Lattimore denounced McCarthy's charges as "base and contemptible lies" and accused him of instituting a "reign of terror" in the United States. A series of witnesses demolished McCarthy's charge that Lattimore had been disloyal to the United States.*[260]

The Kenyon and Lattimore cases illustrate the intractability of these sorts of inquiries. Was Lattimore the top Soviet spy in the United States? Certainly not. Was either Kenyon or Lattimore a Communist? No. Had Kenyon once been a member of organizations that had some connection to Communist influences? Yes. Had Lattimore given advice to the U.S. government that conservatives

---

* The government's persecution of Lattimore continued with a "lengthy grilling" by the Senate Internal Security Subcommittee in 1954. He was then indicted for perjury. It was not until 1955, when a federal judge dismissed the perjury prosecution, that Lattimore's ordeal finally drew to a close. Bennett *Party of Fear* at 468 n 25 (cited in note 45). See generally Owen Lattimore, *Ordeal by Slander* (Little, Brown 1950).

viewed as helpful to the Soviet Union and the Chinese Communists? Yes. Did Lattimore know individuals who were themselves Communist agents? Probably.[261] Were Kenyon and Lattimore "security risks"? Perhaps.

Both Kenyon and Lattimore *could* have been influenced by acquaintances or colleagues whose purpose was to further the cause of communism. Both Kenyon and Lattimore had held positions in which they could have influenced the formulation or implementation of American policy. Both were thus more likely to have been "security risks" than individuals who had had *none* of their experiences, associations, or acquaintances. But what are we to make of this? Should the United States have refused to employ or consult people like Kenyon and Lattimore because of their past and present associations? How should one draw the line?

Whatever the answer to that question, McCarthy's charges were not so fine-tuned. As the Tydings Committee worked on its report, McCarthy lashed out with increasing virulence. He decried the "egg-sucking liberals" whose "pitiful squealing . . . would hold sacrosanct those Communists and queers" who had sold China into "atheistic slavery." With no apparent sense of irony, he charged that his critics had resorted to a "screaming, squealing, and whining smear." He accused Secretary of State Dean Acheson of furnishing the Communists "with bullets to keep a Christian population under Soviet discipline" and sneered that Acheson opposed communism "with a lace handkerchief, a silk glove, and . . . a Harvard accent." He warned that "the time has come to pinpoint . . . the most dangerous Communists, and if lumberjack tactics are the only kind they understand, then we shall use those tactics."[262]

On July 14, the Tydings Committee issued a 313-page report. It was signed by the three Democratic committe members; one Republican member wrote a brief minority report, and the other wrote nothing. The report denounced McCarthy. His charges, it said, represented "perhaps the most nefarious campaign of half-truths and untruth in the history of this Republic." The report added that "for the first time in our history, we have seen the totalitarian technique of the 'big lie' employed on a sustained basis." It examined each of McCarthy's claims and rebutted the charges against each of the individuals he had named. It concluded further that McCarthy's fabrication and distortion "seriously impaire[d] the efforts of . . . [the] Government to combat . . . subversion."[263]

McCarthy immediately went on the attack, labeling the report "a green light to the Red fifth column in the United States." He described it as a clear "signal to the traitors, Communists, and fellow travelers in our Government that they need have no fear of exposure from this Administration." He added that the "most loyal stooges of the Kremlin could not have done a better job of giving a clean bill of health to Stalin's Fifth Column in this country."[264] Although most Republicans understood that McCarthy's allegations were fraudulent, they nonetheless rallied to his cause. Senator William Jenner, for example, alleged that Tydings had "conducted the most scandalous and brazen whitewash of treasonable conspiracy in our history."[*][265]

In a tone reminiscent of the 1790s, Democrats and Republicans railed at one another. Republican Senator Homer Ferguson charged that the Committee had embraced the "techniques of Goebbels." At one point, Senator Tydings stormed across the Senate chamber and shook his fist at another senator, shouting, "I do not start fights, but I do not run away from them!" The Tydings report was adopted on a straight-party-line vote. The columnists Joseph and Stewart Alsop observed that "something has gone wrong, very wrong, in the capital of the United States." A "miasma of neurotic fear and internal suspicion is seeping in over the nation's capital, like some noxious effluvium from the marshy Potomac." In a speech in late July, McCarthy called the authors of the Tydings report "men without the mental or moral capacity to rise above politics in this hour of the nation's gravest danger." An audience of four thousand people "roared its approval."[266]

Over the next three years, McCarthy not only weathered the Tydings report but grew in popularity and power. He campaigned aggressively—and successfully—to defeat Senators Millard Tydings and Scott Lucas; won reelection in Wisconsin; enjoyed a featured role at the 1952 Republican National Convention; and attained even greater influence with his blistering attacks on the Truman administration and General George C. Marshall.

As McCarthy's arrogance soared, he decided to take on Drew Pearson, one of the nation's most powerful journalists. Pearson had criticized McCarthy. McCarthy replied by charging that Pearson was "one of the voices of international Communism." He exhorted the public to boycott the Adam Hat Company, Pearson's radio sponsor. Within ten days, the company dropped its sponsorship of Pearson's program. The *Washington Post* warned that what McCarthy "is trying to do is not new. It worked well in Germany and in Russia." It reminded its readers that dissent had been "silenced in those lands by intimidation."[267]

Following Tydings's defeat in the 1950 election, a Senate committee con-

---

[*] One notable exception to the Republican support of McCarthy was Senator Margaret Chase Smith, who denounced fellow senators for "abusing our individual powers and privileges" and who observed, "Those of us who shout the loudest about Americanism in making character assassinations are all too frequently those who, by our own words and acts, ignore some of the basic principles of Americanism—The right to criticize. The right to hold unpopular beliefs. The right to protest. The right of independent thought." Blanchard, *Revolutionary Sparks* at 247 (cited in note 44).

demned the "back street" measures that had been used to "destroy the public faith" in Tydings's loyalty. It described the practices of his opponents as "destructive of fundamental American principles." Among other things, his opponents, anticipating the "dirty tricks" of 1972, distributed a fabricated photograph that purported to show Tydings huddling in intimate conversation with Earl Browder, the leader of the Communist Party. The committee observed that, in employing such tactics, Tydings's opponents had acted with flagrant disregard for "the very fabric of American life." The report noted the obvious: "Senator McCarthy was a leading and potent force in the campaign against Senator Tydings."[268]

In light of these findings, Democratic Senator William Benton of Connecticut boldly argued that the Senate should demand McCarthy's resignation, and that if he failed to resign, the Senate should expel him. A warm, ebullient, and brilliant man, Benton had had a remarkable career. In 1929, he and Chester Bowles founded the New York advertising agency of Benton and Bowles; he then served as vice president of the University of Chicago, working closely with Robert Maynard Hutchins; became chairman of the board of the *Encyclopaedia Britannica*; and then served as assistant secretary of state, before entering the Senate.

McCarthy immediately denounced Benton as a "mental midget." Not a single senator rose to defend Benton against McCarthy's wrath. *Newsweek* and the *Christian Science Monitor* both observed that McCarthy had cowed the Senate into silence.[269] In September 1951, the Senate reluctantly appointed a committee to consider Benton's motion for McCarthy's expulsion.

McCarthy refused to appear before the committee, but he went after Benton with a vengeance. He attacked Benton on television; sued him for libel, claiming $2 million in damages; ordered an investigation of his taxes; and called for his expulsion from the Senate, charging that Benton employed "Communists, fellow travelers, or dupes of the Kremlin" and owned "lewd" and "Communist-produced art works."[270] Although McCarthy knew he couldn't win his libel suit, he told friends that he wanted Benton "to wake up every morning with the awful possibility that one day he might have to pay Joe McCarthy $2 million." That, he chortled, will make him "sweat."[271] Benton ruefully observed to friends, "[T]here couldn't be a better example . . . to illustrate why experienced politicians don't get mixed up with fellows like McCarthy. Instead of pursuing McCarthy—I am the fellow who is being pursued."[272]

Finally, in July, McCarthy agreed to testify before the committee. He ranted for five hours against Benton, charging that the Connecticut senator moved in a "motley Red-tinted crowd" and had befriended numerous Communists and fellow travelers, including the Harvard law professor Zechariah Chafee.[273] Over the next several months, Senate Republicans stalled the work of the committee, and the investigation lost steam. Then, on election day 1952, while the matter was still pend-

Millard Tydings and William Benton

ing, Senator William Benton was defeated for reelection. McCarthy sneeringly asked an interviewer, "How do you like what happened to my friend Benton?"[*][274]

In the waning days of the Eighty-second Congress, the committee finally issued a report implying that McCarthy had engaged in misconduct, but stopping short of recommending expulsion or censure.[275] By this time, McCarthy was the most feared man in America. Democrats were thoroughly intimidated. As one Democratic senator observed, "[Y]ou may get a lot of moral support for fighting Joe, but if you lose your seat in the Senate—as Millard Tydings or Bill Benton did—that's no good." Reflecting the realities of the situation, Senator Lyndon Johnson observed that McCarthy will have to be "a Republican problem." But even the newly elected Republican president did not want to cross him.[276]

---

[*] After the election, Benton complained about the "scurrilous" attacks directed at him by a recent Yale graduate, William F. Buckley Jr., who attempted to prove that Benton was "Communistic." Benton warned that Buckley is a "dangerous young man." Reeves, *Joe McCarthy* at 451 (cited in note 3).

"SO RECKLESS AND SO CRUEL"

ONE OF MCCARTHY'S first steps upon assuming the chairmanship of the Senate's Permanent Subcommittee on Investigations in 1953 was to recruit a staff of young, tough-minded investigators. He hired Roy Cohn, Robert Kennedy, and David Schine, among others. McCarthy appointed the twenty-five-year-old Cohn as his chief counsel. Brilliant, ambitious, and ruthless, Cohn had graduated from Columbia Law School at the age of nineteen and quickly developed an interest in subversive activities. As an assistant U.S. attorney, he helped prosecute several leaders of the Communist Party, Julius and Ethel Rosenberg, William Remington, and others accused of perjury before congressional committees. Cohn had a dark complexion, sleepy eyes, and a prominent scar on his nose. Like McCarthy, the fiercely arrogant, vulpine, and supercilious Cohn craved publicity.

Robert Kennedy was the twenty-seven-year-old son of Joseph Kennedy, who both admired and supported McCarthy. Bobby Kennedy had recently graduated from the University of Virginia Law School, where he had earned a reputation for being hot-tempered and vindictive. Cohn hired G. David Schine as the subcommittee's unpaid chief consultant. Schine was tall, slim, blond, and good-looking. The scion of a wealthy family, he attended Harvard and then became president of Schine Hotels, Inc. He first came to Cohn's attention when he wrote an amateurish pamphlet titled "Definition of Communism," which he placed in every room in his family's hotel chain.[277]

With his staff in place, McCarthy continued his hunt for Reds. In February 1953, he launched an investigation of Voice of America, an agency established during World War II to promote a positive view of the United States by publishing magazines, distributing newsreels, operating libraries, and broadcasting radio programs around the world. McCarthy charged that VOA was riddled with Communists and fellow travelers. In televised hearings, he asserted that VOA libraries contained books by "Soviet-endorsed" authors. When his staff examined VOA catalogs, they rooted out more than thirty thousand volumes written by "un-American" authors, including the likes of Lillian Hellman, Jean-Paul Sartre, Dashiell Hammett, Theodore H. White, Arthur M. Schlesinger Jr., John Dewey, Robert M. Hutchins, W. H. Auden, Edna Ferber, and Stephen Vincent Benét.

The State Department, which oversaw VOA, immediately banned all books, music, and paintings by "Communists, fellow-travelers, et cetera" from all VOA facilities and programs. Terrified VOA librarians hurriedly discarded and even burned books that had been placed on what appeared to be an official State

Roy Cohn and Senator Joseph McCarthy

Department blacklist. In succeeding weeks, McCarthy continued to badger and intimidate VOA witnesses. A few resigned in protest, and several hundred were fired. One committed suicide because, as he wrote his wife in a farewell note, "once the dogs are set on you everything you have done since the beginning of time is suspect." Ultimately, the hearings uncovered no evidence of any unlawful conduct.[278]

In the summer of 1953, having cut his teeth on VOA, McCarthy turned on the Eisenhower administration. On August 3, he criticized the administration for allowing trade with Communist countries. In the fall, after Eisenhower had attempted to ease the nation's hysteria by predicting that by 1954 anticommunism would no longer be a national issue, McCarthy directly contradicted the president. He declared on a radio show that "practically every issue we face today . . . is inextricably interwoven with the Communist issue" and that "the raw, harsh unpleasant fact is that Communism . . . will be an issue in 1954." White House staffers saw this as a "declaration of war against the President."[279]

Meanwhile, sitting as a one-man subcommittee (the other members had stopped participating), McCarthy began televised hearings into alleged Communist infiltration of several government agencies, including the Government Printing Office, the American delegation to the United Nations, the CIA, and the Army. These investigations, which directly challenged the Eisenhower administration, grew increasingly extreme. In one instance, McCarthy learned that seven years earlier a guard in the Army Signal Corps had signed a nominating petition for a Communist candidate. McCarthy hauled high-ranking Army officers before his subcommittee and insisted they fire the person who had certified the guard's loyalty. That person, he charged, must be either "incompetent beyond words, or in sympathy with Communism." When the officers refused to submit to this demand, McCarthy threatened to call Secretary of the Army Robert T. Stevens as a witness to explain the Army's conduct.[280]

In mid-October, McCarthy held a series of closed-door hearings to investigate Communist infiltration of the Army. He informed the press that he had uncovered a dangerous spy ring. As a result of his accusations, thirty-three civilian employees were suspended pending further investigation. Roy Cohn announced that McCarthy intended to subpoena all members of the Army loyalty boards who had failed to catch the allegedly disloyal employees. On November 13, Secretary of the Army Stevens reported that the Army had completed a full investigation of all thirty-three individuals and found no evidence of disloyalty.

Over the next four months, McCarthy continued his hearings in an effort to embarrass the Army. He accused another fifty civilian employees of disloyalty. He slandered witnesses and ridiculed, debased, and humiliated dozens of innocent individuals, many of whom had to litigate for years to regain their positions. Some never recovered their reputations.[281]

During these hearings, McCarthy interrogated General Ralph W. Zwicker about a former Army dentist who had had ties to the Communist Party. McCarthy accused Zwicker, a battlefield hero of World War II, of "hedging and hemming" and of being unfit "to wear that uniform." He told Zwicker he did not have "the brains of a five-year-old child."[282] A few days later, Secretary of the Army Stevens issued an order forbidding any Army officer to appear before McCarthy's subcommittee. Stevens explained that he would not "permit the loyal officers of our armed services to be subjected to such unwarranted treatment."[283] Enraged, McCarthy threatened Stevens in a telephone call: "Just go ahead and try it," McCarthy warned. "I am going to kick the brains out of anyone who protects Communism. . . . You just go ahead and do it. I will guarantee you that you will live to regret it."[284]

When a transcript of McCarthy's interrogation of General Zwicker was made public, newspapers across the nation expressed outrage. The New York Times described McCarthy's treatment of Zwicker as "arrogant, narrow-minded and reckless."[285] Edward R. Murrow devoted his entire See It Now television show to a "chillingly effective" attack on McCarthy. Murrow let the film clips speak for themselves, inviting viewers to witness firsthand McCarthy's overbearing demeanor, ugly sneer, and incessant, high-pitched giggle. Murrow concluded that "this is no time for men who oppose Senator McCarthy's methods to keep silent."[286]

Members of the Eisenhower administration, concerned about possible divisions within the Republican Party, instructed Stevens to withdraw his directive. Reluctantly, he did so. McCarthy gloated that Stevens could not have surrendered "more abjectly than if he had got down on his knees." The administration's capitulation triggered a firestorm among the nation's press, and the momentum seemed to shift. The *New York Herald Tribune*, the *Milwaukee Journal*, the *Chicago Sun-Times*, and the *Detroit Free Press* all charged that the Army had "surrendered" to McCarthy.[287] Walter Lippmann attacked McCarthy's "cold, calculated, sustained and ruthless effort to make himself feared." He warned that the junior senator from Wisconsin was attempting to intimidate the president. The columnists Joseph and Stewart Alsop cautioned that if Eisenhower "permits just one more appeasement of Senator McCarthy, he can say goodbye to his own authority."[288]

While the furor boiled, McCarthy directly challenged the president, writing that "far too much wind has been blowing from high places" in defense of Communists in the Army. James Reston observed, "President Eisenhower turned the other cheek today, and Sen. Joseph McCarthy . . . struck him about as hard as the position of the President will allow."[289]

MCCARTHY HAD AT LAST exhausted Eisenhower's patience. When McCarthy attacked George Marshall in 1951, Eisenhower, who personally owed much to Marshall, was furious, but bit his tongue. During the 1952 campaign, Eisenhower tried to avoid McCarthy, but they finally came face to face in Wisconsin in early October. Sharing the same podium with McCarthy, Eisenhower planned to say,

> I know that charges of disloyalty have, in the past, been leveled against General George C. Marshall. I have been privileged for thirty-five years to know General Marshall personally. I know him, as a man and as a soldier, to be dedicated with singular selflessness and the profoundest patriotism to the service of America. And this episode is a sobering lesson in the way freedom must not defend itself.[290]

But the day before the scheduled address, McCarthy and Eisenhower met in private. Eisenhower scolded McCarthy for his "un-American methods in combating Communism" and told him, "I'm going to say that I disagree with you." McCarthy warned, "If you say that, you'll be booed." Eisenhower replied that he had been booed before and that being booed didn't bother him. Eisenhower's advisers begged him to delete his comments about Marshall. Moments before the speech, a frustrated Eisenhower snapped, "Take it out."[291] Harry Truman and Mrs. Marshall never forgave Eisenhower for dropping this passage from his speech.[292]

After McCarthy attacked Eisenhower's Army, the president finally acted. Ironically, the instruments of McCarthy's destruction were his own lieutenants, David Schine and Roy Cohn. Schine had been drafted into the Army in November 1953 and assigned to Fort Dix, in New Jersey. Acting both in his own name and in that of McCarthy, Cohn persistently exhorted Fort Dix's commander and others in the military chain of command to accord Schine privileged treatment, such as relieving him of guard duty and granting him extra leaves and special equipment. Whenever he met resistance, Cohn threatened to take action against the protesting officer.[293]

The Army made public a report on the matter, detailing McCarthy's and Cohn's efforts to intimidate Army officers on Schine's behalf.[294] McCarthy and Cohn claimed that the military was trying to frame them in retaliation for their revelations of disloyalty in the Army.[295]

On March 15, Vice President Nixon delivered a televised speech in which he charged that "men who have in the past done effective work exposing Communists in this country have, by reckless talk and questionable methods, made themselves the issue rather than the cause they believe in so deeply." McCarthy charged back that the American people were "sick and tired" of the "constant yack-yacking" that he was not nice to Communists. In private conversation, he now referred to "that prick Nixon." On March 16, McCarthy boldly announced that his own subcommittee would conduct a full, impartial, and public inquiry into the Army-McCarthy dispute.[296]

In the weeks leading up to the Army-McCarthy hearings, public support for McCarthy began to erode. Corporate, religious, and academic leaders criticized his conduct. McCarthy fumed that his enemies were going all out to rally support from the usual bleeding hearts and chameleon politicians. Although the issue in the hearings was technically whether Cohn and McCarthy had sought improper privileges for Schine, no one had any doubt that the real question was whether the hearings would bring down McCarthy.

The Senate Caucus Room was blindingly bright from the glare of television lights.* From the first moment, McCarthy interrupted the hearings with a refrain

---

*Lyndon Johnson intentionally arranged to have the Army-McCarthy hearings televised so the American people could see firsthand "what the bastard was up to." Johnson was confident that if he gave McCarthy enough rope, he would hang himself. Dallek, *Unfinished Life* at 188–89 (cited in note 123). See Herman, *Joseph McCarthy* at 256 (cited in note 3).

he was to make famous: "Point of order, Mr. Chairman!" McCarthy made a spectacle of himself. As Roy Cohn later recalled, "with his easily erupting temper, his menacing monotone, his unsmiling mien, his perpetual 5 o'clock shadow," McCarthy was "the perfect stock villain."[297]

Sitting across from McCarthy was Joseph Welch, a sixty-three-year-old lawyer with the prestigious Boston law firm of Hale & Dorr. Welch had been retained to represent the Army. Short, paunchy, and balding, Welch had a folksy manner, a keen mind, and incisive instincts. He had originally intended to bring with him to Washington two young associates, James St. Clair, who twenty years later would represent President Richard Nixon in the Watergate investigation, and Frederick G. Fisher. But Fisher informed Welch that as a law student at Harvard he had belonged to the National Lawyers Guild, a left-wing legal organization. Welch sent him back to Boston because he did not want anything to divert attention from the task at hand.[298]

Predictably, the hearings began on a sour note. After Secretary of the Army Stevens testified that the Schine case involved a clear "perversion of power," McCarthy accused him of "flagrant dishonesty."[299] The most dramatic moment of the hearings occurred on June 9. During Welch's cross-examination of Roy Cohn, McCarthy interrupted and in a malevolent tone of voice announced to the world that Welch "has in his law firm a young man named Fisher . . . who has been for a number of years a member of an organization which was named, oh, years and years ago, as the legal bulwark of the Communist party." Welch's response, seen live by millions on television, was withering:

> Until this moment, Senator, I think I never really gauged your cruelty or your recklessness. . . . Little did I dream you could be so reckless and so cruel as to do an injury to that lad. . . . If it were in my power to forgive you for your reckless cruelty, I [would] do so. I like to think I am a gentleman, but your forgiveness will have to come from some one other than me. . . . Let us not assassinate this lad further, Senator. You have done enough. Have you no sense of decency, sir, at long last? Have you left no sense of decency?[300]

Welch then rose and walked from the hearing room, which exploded into applause. It was the moment that indelibly exposed McCarthy as the ruthless demagogue that he was.*

---

* McCarthy's decision to raise this issue about Fischer violated an agreement Cohn had made two days earlier with Welch. They had agreed that McCarthy would not mention Fisher's involvement with the National Lawyers Guild and Welch would not mention Cohn's military record (he had flunked the physical). Cohn was horrified when McCarthy acted in blatant disregard of this

Joseph Welch at Army-McCarthy Hearings

The Army-McCarthy hearings ended on June 17, 1954, after thirty-six days of testimony and 187 hours of live television coverage. On September 1, the sub-committee released its report, which found, among other things, that Cohn had exceeded his authority and McCarthy had inappropriately permitted Cohn to intercede with the Army on Schine's behalf.[301]

In the weeks after the hearings, McCarthy's popularity plummeted. From January through August 1954, his "unfavorable" rating rose from 29 percent to 51 percent. The *Christian Science Monitor* observed tellingly that McCarthy's investigations had failed to produce the conviction of a single spy or to uncover a single Communist working in a classified defense position. Prominent figures, including Paul Hoffman of the Ford Foundation, Dean Erwin Griswold of the Harvard Law School, and the theologian Reinhold Niebuhr called upon the Senate to censure McCarthy.[302]

---

understanding. It has been suggested that Welch had plotted out this entire scene in advance. Fisher went on to have a very successful career. In 1973, he was elected president of the Massachusetts Bar Association. See Reeves, *Joe McCarthy* at 628–29 (cited in note 3); Bennett, *Party of Fear* at 309 (cited in note 45); Griffith, *Politics of Fear* at 259–60 n 46 (cited in note 3); Herman, *Joseph McCarthy* at 275–76 (cited in note 3).

On June 11, 1954, a seventy-four-year-old Republican senator, Ralph Flanders of Vermont, acting in direct defiance of the Republican leadership, introduced a formal resolution to censure Joseph McCarthy. Before doing so, however, Flanders personally handed McCarthy a written invitation to attend the Senate session at which he would present the resolution. Flanders's resolution charged that McCarthy had engaged in conduct unbecoming a member of the U.S. Senate.[*303]

Even Democrats were uneasy about Flanders's resolution, which risked upsetting the Senate's long-standing tradition of "live and let live." Moreover, as James Reston noted at the time, although McCarthy's public support had dwindled, it is a precept of most politicians that "you never antagonize any group . . . if you can avoid it," and if "you have to choose between two groups, you always choose to antagonize the one that is less vindictive." In this instance, that was "certainly not the pro-McCarthy crowd."[304]

Over the next several months, the matter percolated slowly, almost grudgingly, through the Senate process. Finally, on September 27, 1954, a six-member bipartisan Senate select committee unanimously recommended that McCarthy be condemned (the word "condemned" had been substituted for "censured") for "contemptuous, contumacious, and denunciatory" conduct. The report concluded that McCarthy's behavior had dishonored "the entire Senate."[305]

A succession of senators took the floor to call for McCarthy's condemnation. The Democrat John Stennis of Mississippi accused McCarthy of pouring "slush" and "slime" upon the Senate; the Republican Arthur Watkins of Utah denounced McCarthy for "abuse heaped upon abuse"; the Democrat Sam Ervin of North Carolina, who would later chair the Watergate hearings, urged the Senate to go beyond censure and to expel McCarthy; the Republican Prescott Bush, the father of one president and grandfather of another, denounced McCarthy for creating "dangerous divisions among the American people"; Lyndon Johnson, the Democratic Senate minority leader, declared that McCarthy's language toward his fellow senators did not belong in the *Congressional Record*, but was "more fittingly inscribed on the wall of a men's room."[306]

McCarthy charged that he was "the victim of a Communist campaign" and that the Communist Party "has now extended its tentacles to . . . the United States Senate." He denounced the select committee for having "imitated Communist methods" and allowed itself to be the "unwitting handmaiden" of the Commu-

---

[*] In the preceding 165 years, the Senate had only twice censured a member: in 1902, for a fistfight on the floor of the Senate; in 1929, for having improperly brought an outsider into an executive session of a Senate committee.

nist conspiracy. After two weeks of harsh and often bitter debate, the Senate adopted the resolution by a vote of 67 to 22. Every Democrat present supported the motion; the Republicans were evenly divided.[*307]

In the 1954 elections, the Democratic Party regained control of both Houses of Congress. Pro-McCarthy candidates were handily defeated in Illinois, Michigan, Montana, Oregon, Wisconsin, and Wyoming. McCarthy had at last been humiliated.

McCARTHY'S RISE AND FALL had taken almost five years. Throughout all this time, during which hundreds, if not thousands, of innocent individuals had had their reputations destroyed, Democrats dithered over whether and how to take him on. Even Lyndon Johnson, the masterful leader of the Senate Democrats, was wary. Although he eventually played a pivotal role in orchestrating the vote of condemnation, for years he counseled patience. McCarthy, he warned colleagues, "will go that extra mile to destroy you." Johnson described McCarthy as "the sorriest senator up here," but cautioned that "he's riding high now, he's got people scared to death some Communist will strangle 'em in their sleep, and anybody who takes him on before the fevers cool—well, you don't get in a pissin' contest with a polecat."[308]

The extent to which McCarthy had intimidated the Senate was evident as early as 1951. During a speech on the floor in which he presented "proof" of Communist infiltration, McCarthy piled hundreds of documents in front of him, supposedly substantiating his charges. He defied any senator to inspect them. Senator Herbert Lehman of New York, a distinguished and dignified public servant, walked courageously to McCarthy's desk and held out his hand for the documents. There was silence. Then, according to the *Washington Post* columnist

---

[*] One Democratic senator did not vote on the matter—John F. Kennedy, who was in the hospital. This omission came back to haunt Kennedy later in his career. See Dallek, *Unfinished Life* at 189–92 (cited in note 123). Among those who defended McCarthy, perhaps the best statement was made by the freshman senator Barry Goldwater: "All the discredited and embittered figures of the Hiss-Yalta period . . . have crawled out from under their logs to join the efforts to get even. . . . I suggest that Senator McCarthy is facing a censure vote in this body because he has put his finger fearlessly upon the men in high places who, through stupidity or muddled ideology, have stood in the way of an all-out fight against communism, both in America and abroad." 83rd Cong, 2d Sess, in 100 Cong Rec S 16001–6002 (Nov 12, 1954).

Stewart Alsop, "McCarthy giggled his strange, rather terrifying little giggle." As Lehman looked around the Senate chamber for support, "not a man rose." His fellow senators lowered their eyes or looked away. McCarthy growled under his breath, "Go back to your seat, old man."[309]

Two years after his condemnation, McCarthy sat slumped in a chair, staring vacantly ahead. Snubbed by his colleagues in the Senate, ignored by the press, he bemoaned his fate. "I can't take it," he sighed. "They're after me. They're out to destroy me. I'm trying, I'm trying. I'm doing everything I can to ferret out these rats, these people who want to destroy our country. . . . No matter where I go, they look on me with contempt. I can't take it any more." A chronic alcoholic, McCarthy died of cirrhosis of the liver on May 2, 1957.[310]

FOR FIFTY YEARS, Joseph McCarthy's name has evoked associations of terror, meanness, irresponsibility, and cruelty. These associations relate both to Joe McCarthy and to the era of McCarthyism, of which he was merely a part. It is important to think hard about McCarthy not only because this was a critical period in American history but also because McCarthy's legacy continues even now to be contested. Recently, in light of disclosures from KGB and other previously secret or inaccessible files, an effort has been made to rehabilitate McCarthy as a loyal American who "was making a good point badly."[311] This version of history runs essentially as follows:

In the 1930s and 1940s, many Americans turned to communism out of desperation. Some bought wholeheartedly into the Communist agenda. Others were mere dupes. The latter were those who joined Communist-front organizations—organizations set up and secretly controlled by the Communist Party in order to gain resources, contacts, and adherents for the Communist movement. These organizations purported to serve a range of "liberal" causes—save Sacco and Vanzetti, promote the labor movement, oppose fascism, end racism—but their ultimate, more insidious goal was to lay the groundwork for communism in the United States. Individuals who became active in these organizations knowingly or recklessly turned a blind eye to the mass executions and gulags of the Soviet Union, thus demonstrating their own moral weakness, a defect that in itself marked them as potentially dangerous to America.

These two decades also saw a dramatic expansion in the size of the federal government, especially in the executive branch, caused by the need to implement expansionist New Deal policies and to fight a world war. With this extraordinary increase in the number of federal employees, which occurred at a time when the

Soviet Union was America's ally, the government inevitably hired many people who were in varying degrees sympathetic to communism. Some were actively committed to the Communist cause; others were mere fellow travelers.

With the onset of the Cold War, it was suddenly imperative for the nation to look more closely at persons who could influence government action. Once the United States and the Soviet Union had become mortal enemies, those who might once have seemed reasonable security risks could no longer be trusted. But the officials in charge of the federal government—men like Dean Acheson and George Marshall—had no stomach for investigating their liberal friends and supporters to determine whether they might be closet Communists or Communist sympathizers or dupes. Put simply, the Truman administration "knew there were employees who were security risks working in its own State Department, and it had done little about it." If the Democrats refused to protect the nation, then HUAC and Joe McCarthy had to do it for them.

Conservatives were particularly galled by the accusation of liberals that McCarthy and other Red hunters were engaged in repressive "witch hunts" that threatened American democracy and violated the First Amendment. It was evident to conservatives that it was the Communists, not the anti-Communists, who posed the more serious threat to these values, especially in light of the failure of liberals to see clearly the evils of Stalinist Russia. No government, they felt, could long survive if it could not, or would not, deal with those who would destroy it from within.

Even more galling was the hypocrisy conservatives saw in the liberals' passionate invocation of the First Amendment. After all, less than a decade earlier Franklin Roosevelt and his crew had harassed America Firsters, denounced isolationists as appeasers and anti-Semites, investigated antiwar congressmen, silenced Father Coughlin, prosecuted "the seditionists," and imprisoned William Dudley Pelley. Why was the investigation and condemnation of American Communists in the late 1940s and early 1950s any "worse" than the investigation and condemnation of American Nazis in the late 1930s and early 1940s?

To be sure, even revisionist historians concede that McCarthy was over the top in his conduct. He lied, he bullied, and he humiliated many innocent individuals. None of that, they concede, was excusable. But it was merely a matter of degree— an overexuberant excess. What McCarthy contributed, they argue, was a fearless insistence on keeping alive a profoundly important inquiry in the face of Democratic and liberal opposition. On this view, McCarthy's stubbornness enabled him to be "undeterred by attacks or even refutation." Confronted by a concerted liberal effort to sweep under the carpet the Democratic failure to protect the nation's security at a time of great peril, McCarthy was a "lightning rod in the face of Democratic criticism." Even if he was wrong in his details, "he was right in the big things," and his persistence "heartened his allies and infuriated his opponents."[312]

The difficulty with this analysis is that it blurs the critical distinction between means and ends. Certainly, the goal of preserving the nation's security from unlawful espionage, sabotage, and foreign influence is legitimate. Certainly, there were well-justified concerns about these matters during the Cold War. But a democracy is about means as well as ends. It is not enough to say that Joe McCarthy meant well, but went about it the wrong way. McCarthy violated the fundamental norms and the essential values of the American constitutional system. There is simply no excusing, defending, or mitigating that reality.

FRANCIS BIDDLE AND JOHN LORD O'BRIAN REVISITED

WHAT DID THOSE who were involved in the controversies over free speech during World War I and World War II think of the Cold War? What did they learn from their own experiences? Francis Biddle and John Lord O'Brian both shared their thoughts on these matters, and it is enlightening to consider their reflections on the loyalty program, McCarthy, and the stresses of the Cold War.

When Biddle returned to the United States from Nuremberg, the nation was already in the early years of this era. Distressed by the emerging political atmosphere, he began work on *The Fear of Freedom*, published in 1951.[313] Biddle warned that "in times of panic" we tend to believe that "our freedom to think as we please is endangered by the expression of opposing views," and that to protect our own point of view, "others must be stifled." This is what Biddle meant by the "fear of freedom." He perceptively explained that power in America now rests on public opinion and that the struggle for freedom is "no longer against an oppressive tyrant," but against "the people themselves, who, in fear of an imagined peril" may demand the repression of others.

He cautioned that "Americans are not often aware of the . . . lessons of their own history." An understanding of our past, he argued, proves that "fear is an infection that spreads quickly" and that "intolerance is dangerously contagious." In Biddle's view, the most disturbing thing about McCarthy's rise to power was that a large part of the American public, and many of their elected representatives, supported him. Fear, "fanned by politicians," had left the public deeply distrustful of their fellow citizens. Our political leaders, he warned, had resorted to the "hallowed practice" of inciting the public to confuse "panic with patriotism."

The challenge was easily stated: "How can we protect our nation from acts . . . that may endanger our national security, and at the same time preserve our traditions of freedom?" The legitimate need to prevent sabotage and espionage had been twisted into "attempts to control and punish the spread of ideas." The primary error, Biddle observed, was the nation's departure from its fundamental constitutional commitment that individuals should be "penalized for their conduct, not for their beliefs, and not for the acts of those with whom they associate."

Biddle concluded that any broad-based effort to sort out security risks by inquiring into loyalty will inevitably turn into "a crusade to enforce conformity." Because the means readily get confused with the ends, anyone who criticizes the means will wind up being tarred as unpatriotic. It will "take courage," he said, "as it has always taken courage, to resist."[314]

JOHN LORD O'BRIAN, who had played so central a role in the Department of Justice during World War I, published *National Security and Individual Freedom* in 1955.[315] Reflecting on his experience, O'Brian observed that one of the principal dangers to democracy is the "craving for security at any price." Although conceding that the dangers that faced the nation during the Cold War were "serious," he explained that the challenge for democracy is to carefully "appraise the extent of these dangers" and then to undertake the difficult task of "balancing" the *real* threat to national security against the "rights of the free citizen."[316]

A review of the programs and policies adopted during the Cold War led O'Brian to conclude that the United States had established a system of "preventive law" that deviated sharply from traditional American values. He charged that government had resorted to punishing dissent and unorthodoxy on the theory that this was necessary to prevent ideas from leading people to commit "acts which are wrongful." The experience under the loyalty programs, the legislative investigations, and the Smith Act, he observed, proved yet again that "once the power is given to government officials to inquire into the associations and opinions of . . . individuals, there is literally no limit to the expansion of inquisitions . . . which must inevitably result."[317]

O'Brian noted that one of the lessons of history is that government officials always attempt to justify broad restraints on civil liberties "as necessary to prevent sabotage and espionage," even though there is usually little evidence to support their claims:

> In World War I, after America entered the war, there were no instances in which sabotage was proven. The same is true of World War II, and after three years' administration of the . . . Loyalty Order, . . . not a single instance of sabotage or espionage had been shown. . . . As far as espionage is concerned, it is obvious that

none of the programs or regulations would have prevented the treachery of Fuchs, the Rosenbergs, or real Communists of that ilk.[318]

O'Brian observed that what seemed to frighten people most was not the fear of spies and saboteurs but the fear that other Americans might be "converted to the cause of Communism." To him, this reflected an appalling "lack of confidence in the integrity of their fellow Americans" and a devastating failure of confidence in the American system.

In O'Brian's view, the violations of civil liberties in this era had been made possible by the creation of an "atmosphere of unreasoning fear," an atmosphere generated, nurtured, and "seized upon by unscrupulous politicians" for partisan ends. The nation's leaders had confused and misled the people about the "real issues," thus "threatening our democratic traditions." Like Biddle, O'Brian lamented the dearth of leaders "courageous and outspoken in the cause of individual freedom."[319]

O'Brian cautioned that although the "emotional excitement engendered in the name of patriotism during a war" may originate in legitimate concerns, it too often ends in overblown and dangerous efforts to suppress dissent. Lamenting the tendency of each generation of national leaders to claim that the dangers they face in wartime are more grave than those their predecessors faced, he criticized those who argued during the Cold War that the nation confronted dangers "without precedent" and then used that self-serving claim to justify "new limitations upon the freedoms guaranteed by the First Amendment."

Finally, O'Brian wondered whether "the greatest danger to our institutions" might rest not in the threat of subversion but "in our own weaknesses in yielding" to fear and our willingness to "disregard the fundamental rights" of others. He expressed the hope that "our judges will in the end establish principles reaffirming" the nation's commitment to civil liberties.[320]

It is thus to "our judges" that we now turn.

DENNIS V. UNITED STATES

THE COLD WAR generated unprecedented First Amendment activity for the Supreme Court. As a consequence of World War I, the Court handed down six decisions involving the First Amendment. As a result of the Cold War, it handed down *sixty* such decisions. For roughly a decade, this was the dominant issue on the Court's docket. During this period, the Court's approach evolved. At the outset, the Court strongly endorsed efforts to combat domestic subversion. Later, it played a critical role in helping bring this era to a close. This shift was due to several factors, including a change in the makeup of the Court, a deepening understanding of the issues, and a greater appreciation of the Court's responsibility to protect civil liberties—even in wartime. The key decision, the one that shaped the debate, was *Dennis v. United States*.[321]

ON JULY 28, 1948, a federal grand jury in New York indicted under the Smith Act twelve members of the national board of the Communist Party for conspiring to advocate the duty and necessity of overthrowing the government of the United States by force and violence. The trial began on January 17, 1949, in the Foley Square courthouse in lower Manhattan and continued until October 21. It was the longest criminal trial in American legal history. Like the trials of Eugene Debs during World War I and of the American fascists during World War II, it was the subject of incessant headlines. And like the trial in *Abrams*, the Great Sedition Trial of World War II, and later the Chicago Conspiracy trial, the proceedings were circuslike from the opening bell. Indeed, on the first day of trial, four hundred policemen and plainclothes detectives surrounded the courthouse.[322]

It is important to note two preliminary points. First, it was unclear at the time precisely what the First Amendment required. During World War I, the Supreme Court gave scant protection to speakers who criticized the government. Certainly, under the standards applied in *Schenck*, *Debs*, and *Abrams*, the advocacy of the Communist Party in the late 1940s could be punished. In the years between 1920 and 1950, however, the Court had increasingly moved toward the Holmes-Brandeis "clear and present danger" test. Under this test as enunciated by Justices Holmes and Brandeis, the advocacy of the Communist Party in the late 1940s could not be punished. But what, precisely, were the *controlling* precedents and doctrines in 1950?

Second, the precise charge in *Dennis* posed a bit of a puzzle. The defendants were charged, not with attempting to overthrow the government, not with conspiring to overthrow the government, not with advocating the overthrow of government, but with *conspiring to advocate* the overthrow of government. How does one make sense of "clear and present danger" when the "danger" is so far removed from the defendants' acts?[323]

During the Justice Department's deliberations over whether to indict the leaders of the CPUSA, there was considerable uncertainty among the government's lawyers about whether they could prove that the defendants had advocated "revolution by violence."[324] Despite this uncertainty, the local U.S.

attorney, strongly encouraged by J. Edgar Hoover, indicted the defendants. The timing was hardly accidental. The prosecution was clearly intended to bolster the Truman administration's anti-Communist credibility in anticipation of the 1950 election. The *Washington Post* acidly observed that the goal of the prosecution was not to protect the "security of the state" but to exploit "justice for the purpose of propaganda."[325]

In the trial, the government presented evidence that a central tenet of Marxism-Leninism, set forth in many pamphlets and other writings of the CPUSA, was that capitalism rests upon the oppression of those who do not own the means of production (the "proletariat"); that no entrenched faction (the "bourgeoisie") would ever voluntarily permit itself to be displaced by peaceful change; and that the transition to a more just and classless society (the "dictatorship of the proletariat") would therefore *require* the forceful overthrow of the existing government at some time in the future, when circumstances were propitious.[326]

More specifically, the prosecution maintained that the CPUSA recruited and indoctrinated members by highlighting minority grievances, insisting that capitalism was dying, depicting the government as an arm of Wall Street, encouraging admiration for the Russian Revolution, and arguing that any American war against the Soviet Union would be imperialistic and unjust. The government called to the stand thirteen FBI undercover agents who had infiltrated the CPUSA. They testified that the party believed that the right moment for violence would be during a time of war or depression, that it would use sabotage against the United States in the event of a war with the Soviet Union, and that it taught its members that they would eventually have to help overthrow the U.S. government.[327]

The defendants responded that this completely misconceived the CPUSA. They maintained that under Marxism-Leninism the use of force was justified only if the ruling class actively prevented a peaceful transition to socialism. The defense pointed to the CPUSA constitution, which expressly repudiated the use of force and violence. According to the defendant John Gates, the editor in chief of the *Daily Worker*, all of this was irrelevant in the United States because the majority of Americans had not yet been persuaded of the merits of socialism.

Eugene Dennis, the general secretary of the party, argued that the demands of Marxism-Leninism were contingent upon historical circumstance. He testified that "you cannot find out what to do in 1949 by reading what Lenin said the Russian workers should do under quite different circumstances in 1917." William Z. Foster, the former head of the CPUSA, explained that the party sought to convert Americans to socialism not by force or violence but by educating the masses and persuading a majority of citizens that socialism was in their best interests. He underscored Dennis's point that the violent passages from the Communist "classics" that the prosecution had read to the jury had been torn out of context and had no bearing on the actual goals or activities of the Communist Party of the United States. The prosecution dismissed all this as mere window dressing and cover-up.

At the end of the trial, Judge Harold Medina set forth what he saw as the central issue in the case. In his view, the Smith Act did not prohibit advocacy of "the abstract doctrine" that it was moral or principled to overthrow "organized government by unlawful means," but it did prohibit the "advocacy of *action* for the accomplishment of that purpose . . . as speedily as circumstances would permit." Applying this view of the law to the evidence, Medina held that "there is sufficient danger . . . to justify the application of the statute under the First Amendment." With this as a given, the jury found the defendants guilty. A week later, Judge Medina sentenced them to the maximum penalty of five years in prison.*328

The defendants appealed to the U.S. Court of Appeals for the Second Circuit. The opinion of the court of appeals was written by Chief Judge Learned Hand, who was then seventy-nine years old. Although Hand had been denied appointment to the court of appeals in 1917 because of his opinion in *Masses*, he was promoted to the appellate bench in 1924 by President Coolidge. At the time of this promotion, Walter Lippmann wrote that Hand was "one of the great figures of the American courts, recognized wherever law is expounded . . . as a mind of extraordinary richness and distinction." Another admirer noted that Hand was the only American judge who deserved to be "bracketed" with Holmes and Brandeis.329 Over the next three decades, Hand distinguished himself as one of the truly great judges in American history. Now, more than thirty years after his opinion in *Masses*, he found himself once again at the center of a First Amendment firestorm.

LIKE MOST AMERICANS, Learned Hand was uneasy. He viewed international communism with "trepidation" and never doubted that the United States would have to stand firm against Stalin's aggressive foreign policy. But, as early as 1947, recalling the nation's experience during World War I, he worried that

---

* At the end of the trial, which was at times disorderly, Medina held all five of the defense attorneys in contempt of court and sentenced them to prison terms ranging from thirty days to six months. The Supreme Court upheld Judge Medina's action in *Sacher v. United States*, 343 US 1 (1952). Various state and federal bar associations then barred these lawyers from practicing law in the future. These actions were subsequently upheld by the Supreme Court, including the decision of the Supreme Court bar to exclude one of the lawyers, Isserman, from ever practicing again before the Supreme Court itself. See *In re Isserman*, 345 US 286 (1953); *Isserman v. Ethics Committee*, 345 US 927 (1953). But see *Sacher v. Association of Bar of New York*, 347 US 388 (1954). For an account of the trial, see Belknap, *Cold War in the Courtroom* at 208 (cited in note 324).

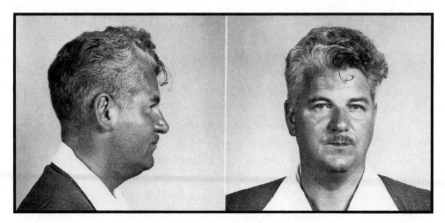

Eugene Dennis

"witch hunters" were once again being given free "rein to set up a sort of Inquisition, detecting heresy wherever non-conformity appears."

Shortly before Joseph McCarthy's speech in Wheeling, Hand wrote a friend that the "hysteria in this country has now reached such a peak that there are few who would dare to acknowledge any Communist inclinations, if they had them." He charged Republicans with outright "indecency" in their willingness "to do anything to get back into power." In a public address, Hand affirmed that, "risk for risk," he would rather take the "chance that some traitors will escape detection" than risk spreading across the land "a spirit of general suspicion and distrust." He warned that a nation is in peril "where each man begins to eye his neighbor as a possible enemy; where non-conformity with the accepted creed . . . is a mark of disaffection; where denunciation . . . takes the place of evidence; where orthodoxy chokes off freedom of dissent." He added that the "mutual confidence on which all else depends" can be preserved only by an "open mind and a brave reliance upon free discussion." Hand confided to Felix Frankfurter that his deepest fear for the nation was of "McCarthy and the Cartesian Crew."*[330]

In his opinion for the court of appeals, Hand *upheld* the convictions of the leaders of the Communist Party. How could the hero of *Masses* act in a manner so clearly reflective of the spirit of McCarthyism? It has been said that Hand him-

---

* By "Cartesian," Hand was alluding to the attempt of the philosopher René Descartes to unify all knowledge as the product of clear reasoning from self-evident premises. For Hand, a lifelong skeptic, an attribute of McCarthyism he found particularly unnerving was its absolute and unquestioning embrace of certain fundamental beliefs as simply unchallengeable.

self had fallen prey to the very forces he had warned against.[331] There may be some truth in this criticism, but before leaping to that conclusion, we should review his analysis in *Dennis*.

At the outset, Hand made clear that the evidence presented by the government at trial supported Judge Medina's finding that the defendants had "engaged in an extensive concerted action to teach . . . the doctrines of Marxism-Leninism," including the necessity and legitimacy of resort to force and violence to overthrow the government "when a propitious occasion will arise." He then affirmed what he had said in *Masses*: the First Amendment presupposes that "official opinion may be wrong," and rests upon a "skepticism as to all political orthodoxy" and a belief that "there are no impregnable political absolutes."[332]

But, Hand added, the First Amendment "concerns beliefs alone, not actions." Thus, "nobody doubts that, when the leader of a mob already ripe for riot gives the word to start, his utterance is not protected by the Amendment." Harking back to *Masses*, Hand observed that the First Amendment could reasonably be interpreted as not protecting speech that is part of the "provocation to unlawful conduct," whether that conduct "be remote or immediate."

Hand then asked how *Dennis* would be decided "had this view of the Amendment" — *his* view of the Amendment — "been taken." He reasoned that, as applied to *Dennis*, this approach would mean that although the effort of the defendants "to persuade others of the aims of Communism would have been protected," that protection would be lost insofar as the defendants' speech was "coupled," as it was, "with the advocacy of unlawful means."[333]

Of course, Hand's view of the First Amendment was not the view of the Supreme Court, and it thus fell to Hand to make sense of then prevailing Supreme Court doctrine. Noting that the Court had "evinced a tenderness towards political utterances since the First World War," he embarked upon an exhaustive and "wearisome" analysis of its decisions from 1919 to 1950. He concluded that the test in all cases is "clear and present danger," which "has come to be used as a shorthand statement" for a complex and multifaced judgment. The rule he extracted from thirty years of jurisprudence was that "in each case" the court "must ask whether the gravity of the 'evil,' discounted by its improbability, justifies such invasion of free speech as is necessary to avoid the danger." In other words, as the gravity of the feared harm increases (e.g., violent overthrow of government is more grave than rioting; rioting is more grave than littering), the degree of likelihood and imminence necessary to justify a restriction of speech decreases accordingly.[334]

Applying this test to *Dennis*, Hand noted that although the First Amendment might require society to allow even its most "bitter" critics to vent their "venom" to the public, the situation in *Dennis* was "very different":

The American Communist Party . . . is a highly articulated, well contrived . . . organization, numbering thousands of adherents, rigidly and ruthlessly disciplined, many of whom are infused with a passionate Utopian faith that is to redeem mankind. . . . The violent capture of all existing governments is one article of the creed of that faith, which abjures the possibility of success by lawful means. . . . Our democracy . . . must meet that faith . . . on the merits, or it will perish; we must not flinch at the challenge. . . .

The question before us . . . is how long a government, having discovered such a conspiracy, must wait. When does the conspiracy become a "present danger?" The jury has found that the conspirators will strike "as soon as success seems possible," and obviously, no one in his senses would strike sooner. . . . We do not understand how one could ask for a more probable danger, unless we must wait till the actual eve of hostilities. . . . We hold that it is a danger "clear and present."[335]

So, what explains Chief Judge Hand's opinion in *Dennis*? First, it is worth noting that Hand still preferred his approach in *Masses* to the "clear and present danger" test. This was evident not only in his opinion in *Dennis* but also in his private correspondence. In 1951, he wrote Frankfurter that Justice Holmes had "slipped his trolley on 'clear and present danger.'" Hand added that he had "never felt satisfied" that the "clear and present danger" standard embodied "an adequate qualitative distinction," and remained certain that it would continue to be "baffling . . . in application." In another letter, he declared to his former law clerk Elliot Richardson, "I dissent from the whole approach to the problem of Free Speech which the Supreme Court has adopted during the last thirty-five . . . years."[336]

Nonetheless, as a judge on the court of appeals, Hand was bound to follow the decisions of the Supreme Court. As he later explained, as a responsible jurist he "had no alternative." Personally, Hand confessed that he would "never have prosecuted those birds." In his view, the prosecution would do nothing but "encourage the faithful and maybe help the Committee on Propaganda." But, he added, this "has nothing to do with my job."[337] His job was faithfully to apply the law.

Finally, it is interesting to note how Hand applied *Masses* to *Dennis*. Although many commentators who applauded his opinion in *Masses* have criticized him for "caving in" in *Dennis*, Hand makes clear that, in his view, *Masses* required affirmance of the convictions in *Dennis*. As we saw in chapter 3, Hand held in *Masses* that if a speaker "stops short of urging" others to violate the law, he "should not be held to have attempted to cause its violation." Hand explained that, "if that be not the test," then "every political agitation which can be shown to be apt to create a seditious temper" could be declared illegal.[338]

But *Dennis*, unlike *Masses*, involved speakers who *did* urge others to violate the law. Indeed, as Hand noted, the defendants in *Dennis* had "engaged in an extensive concerted action to teach . . . the doctrines of Marxism-Leninism," including the necessity and legitimacy of resort to force and violence to overthrow the government "when a propitious occasion will arise." And, as Hand interpreted *Masses*, it meant that express "provocation to unlawful conduct" is unprotected by the First Amendment, whether the unlawful conduct "be remote or immediate." In his view, "the advocacy of violence may, or may not, fail; but in neither case can there be any 'right' to use it."[339]

Hand underscored this view in his letters. In June 1951, he wrote Frankfurter, "[S]o far as the constitution goes, I cannot see why it should protect any speech which contains 'aid[ing], abetting, counsel[ing]' etc., to *violate* any law." Six months later he wrote that if a speaker seeks to "bring about a violation of existing law," he saw "no reason why the constitution should protect him, however remote the chance may be of success." He explained that "every society which promulgates a law means that it shall be obeyed until it is changed, and any society which lays down means by which its laws can be changed makes those means exclusive. . . . If [this is] so, how in God's name can an incitement to do what will be unlawful if done, be itself lawful?"[340]

In this sense, then, not only was Learned Hand faithfully following Supreme Court precedents rather than his own inclinations in *Dennis*, but his own inclinations would have led him to the very same outcome, though for quite different reasons.

UNLIKE LEARNED HAND, the Supreme Court was not bound slavishly to follow its own precedents. Moreover, as Hand acknowledged for the court of appeals, the Court's precedents in this area were hardly crystalline. To the contrary, in the thirty years since World War I, the Court had moved decidedly toward the Holmes-Brandeis approach, under which the convictions in *Dennis* would clearly have to be reversed. The critical question for the justices in *Dennis* was how far down that path the Court had moved, or was prepared to move.

As Harry Kalven once observed, everything about *Dennis* "conspired" to make it "a great moment" in Supreme Court history. It was high drama. It involved the direct criminal prosecution of the leaders of the Communist Party at the height of the nation's anxiety over Communist subversion. And the Court treated it as a "great case." The justices produced five separate opinions totaling one hundred pages. But despite all the hoopla and the golden opportunity to clarify the law, the Court could produce no majority opinion.[341]

The plurality opinion, joined by only four justices, was written by Chief Justice Fred Vinson. Vinson, a lifelong pragmatist, brought no strong ideological or philosophical predilections to his work. He believed that careful thought and harmonious debate would produce sound answers to difficult questions. He had served in all three branches of the federal government before his appointment as chief justice in 1946.

President Truman nominated Vinson in part because they were good friends and in part because Vinson was known as a conciliator.[342] In recent years, squabbling within the Court, especially between Justices Hugo Black and Robert Jackson, had gotten out of hand. It had grown personally ugly and institutionally destructive. Truman decided that the Court needed a peacemaker as chief justice. But things didn't go as planned. Before long, Vinson and Frankfurter were enmeshed in a bitter feud of their own, exacerbating the already tense relations among the justices. Vinson, a Kentucky mountaineer, simply could not abide Frankfurter, whose lofty professorial airs irritated him beyond fury. For his part, Frankfurter viewed Vinson as "shallow."[343] On one occasion, during a conference among the justices, Vinson and Frankfurter almost came to blows. Justices Minton and Clark had to restrain Vinson until he could regain his composure.[344]

Court watchers were especially concerned about the closeness of the Truman-Vinson friendship. Between 1946 and 1950, Truman appointed four justices: Fred Vinson, Harold Burton, Sherman Minton, and Tom Clark. Truman invariably sought out appointees who thought as he did. From this perspective, he did quite well. All four of his appointees tended to vote alike, and they almost always supported Truman. Vinson and Truman were particularly tight. Vinson was one of Truman's poker buddies and one of his most intimate confidants. Against this background, there was plenty of reason to doubt Vinson's independence.[345]

In a 6-to-2 decision, the Court in *Dennis* upheld the convictions.[346] Vinson's plurality opinion, joined only by Minton, Burton, and Stanley Reed, contained four critical steps. First, Vinson held that the Smith Act did not prohibit "academic discussion of the merits of Marxism-Leninism." By its own terms, Vinson explained, the act "is directed at advocacy, not discussion." It did not restrict debate or discussion "in the realm of ideas." This is noteworthy because it invokes the "express advocacy" theme first articulated by Judge Hand in *Masses*.[347]

Second, Vinson turned to the daunting challenge of defining the circumstances in which speakers could be punished for their speech. Although conceding that the Court had never "expressly overruled the majority opinions" in such earlier decisions as *Schenck*, *Debs*, *Gitlow*, and *Whitney*, Vinson nonetheless declared that "there is little doubt that subsequent opinions have inclined toward the Holmes-Brandeis rationale."[348] In other words, by 1951 the underground tradition of Justices Holmes and Brandeis had become more powerful precedent than the opinions from which they had dissented. This is a stunning and seemingly unequivocal victory for "clear and present danger."

Third, Vinson "must decide what that phrase imports." That is, "what has been meant by the use of the phrase 'clear and present danger'"? At this point, Vinson's vaunted pragmatism took hold:

> Obviously, the words cannot mean that before the Government may act, it must wait until the putsch is about to be executed, the plans have been laid and the signal is awaited. If Government is aware that a group aiming at its overthrow is attempting to indoctrinate its members and to commit them to a course whereby they will strike when the leaders feel the circumstances permit, action by the Government is required.[349]

In effect, Vinson reasoned *backward* from his putsch example in order to give meaning to the phrase "clear and present danger." The phrase cannot mean that the danger must be "clear and present," for that would lead to nonsensical results if the danger, such as a putsch, is very grave. It must therefore mean something else.

Here, Vinson turned gratefully to Chief Judge Hand, whose restatement of the test in the court of appeals "is as succinct and inclusive as any . . . we might devise." Thus, the true meaning of "clear and present danger" is that in each case the court "must ask whether the gravity of the 'evil,' discounted by its improbability, justifies such invasion of free speech as is necessary to avoid the danger." This is hardly what Holmes and Brandeis had in mind. Although Hand was stuck as a court of appeals judge with the responsibility to interpret and apply the morass of existing Supreme Court precedents, the Supreme Court itself had the authority and opportunity in *Dennis* both to clarify the law and to ratify what Vinson said it had done—recognize that a long series of Supreme Court opinions had embraced the Holmes-Brandeis standard. Instead, by lifting Hand's analysis in the court of appeals, Vinson managed to snatch defeat from the jaws of victory.

Finally, Vinson applied the newly minted "discounted" "clear and present danger" test to *Dennis*. Not surprisingly, he found the danger to be both "clear" and "present," even though it was neither. As Vinson explained, the formation by the defendants of a "highly organized conspiracy, with rigidly disciplined members subject to call when the leaders . . . felt that the time had come for action, coupled with the inflammable nature of world conditions, similar uprisings in other countries, . . . convince us that their convictions were justified." So much for "clear and present danger."[350]

Justices Frankfurter and Jackson each filed a concurring opinion. After canvassing the entire corpus of First Amendment jurisprudence up to 1951, Justice Frankfurter set forth three conclusions. First, free speech cases "are not an exception to the principle" that judges "are not legislators, that direct policy-making is not our province." This is, in effect, a call for judicial restraint. Second, the Court's prior decisions cannot be reconciled by any single formula, "clear and present danger" or otherwise, but represent the results of a "careful weighing of conflicting interests" in each case. In other words, Frankfurter rejected the acceptance of any single "test" for resolving these cases, preferring instead a more open-ended and explicit form of ad hoc judicial balancing. Third, "not every type of speech occupies the same position on the scale of values," and "on any scale of values" speech expressly advocating the overthrow of government by force or violence "ranks low." Indeed, "throughout our decisions there has recurred a distinction between the statement of an idea which may prompt its hearers to take unlawful action, and advocacy that such action be taken." Thus, once again we see the invocation of a principle similar to the line first drawn by Judge Hand in *Masses*.[351]

Frankfurter then frankly acknowledged that there are dangers in suppressing even express advocacy of violence. He therefore implicitly answered Hand's question: How can express advocacy "to do what will be unlawful if done, be itself lawful?" In Hand's view, expressed in a letter to Frankfurter, not only is speech that expressly urges others to violate the law undeserving of First Amendment protection, but it is reasonable for the government "to require the utterer to separate the wheat from the chaff."[352] In other words, it is reasonable for the government to punish a speaker who expressly advocates the violent overthrow of government even if his speech also includes valuable contributions to public discourse. To avoid criminal liability, the speaker should drop the former and retain the latter.

Frankfurter saw more clearly than Hand the complexities of this issue. Frankfurter observed that, "as the evidence in this case abundantly illustrates," the advocacy of overthrow is typically "coupled" with "criticism of defects in our society." Frankfurter was concerned that silencing the advocacy of overthrow may also silence the criticism. Whereas Hand thought the speaker should separate the wheat from the chaff, Frankfurter more realistically recognized that sometimes the rhetoric of revolution is so deeply imbedded in the discourse of dissent that, as a practical matter, the separation will not happen. In such circumstances, if we punish the chaff, we lose the wheat. Frankfurter therefore recognized that there is a "public interest . . . in granting freedom to speak their minds even to those who advocate the overthrow of the Government by force."[353]

Taking the point a step further, Frankfurter noted that suppressing "advocates of overthrow inevitably will also silence critics who do not advocate overthrow but fear that their criticism may be so construed." Indeed, "it is self-delusion to think that we can punish [the defendants] for their advocacy without adding to the risks run by loyal citizens who honestly believe in some of the reforms these defendants advance." Frankfurter perceptively noted that it "is a sobering fact that in sustaining the convictions before us we can hardly escape restriction on the interchange of ideas."[354]

In light of the climate of the times, this was a powerful and trenchant insight. Although Frankfurter characterized express advocacy of violence as "low" on the First Amendment "scale of values," he nonetheless recognized the dangers in its suppression. Unlike Hand, he would not uphold the suppression of express advocacy unless "the danger created by advocacy of overthrow justifies the . . . restriction on freedom of speech." Ultimately, however, Frankfurter resorted to his deferential approach to judicial review and voted to uphold the convictions because, in his view, the "primary responsibility" for adjusting these conflicting interests rests with Congress, rather than with the courts.[355]

Justice Jackson also filed a concurring opinion. He said that he would reserve the "clear and present danger" test, "unmodified, for application . . . in the kind of case for which it was devised." The Holmes-Brandeis approach was appropriate "when the issue is criminality of a hot-headed speech on a street corner, or circulation of a few incendiary pamphlets," for in such circumstances it "is not beyond the capacity of the judicial process" to decide whether a clear and present danger exists. But, he reasoned, the "problem of a well-organized, nationwide conspiracy" of the sort posed by the Communist Party was an entirely different matter. Moreover, echoing *Masses*, Jackson maintained that, even in the more simple type of case, express advocacy of unlawful conduct "can be made a crime," even if the government cannot prove "that the odds favored its success by 99 to 1, or some other extremely high ratio."[356]

Justices Black and Douglas dissented. Douglas conceded that there were circumstances in which the government could punish someone for teaching the techniques of sabotage or the assassination of the president. But, he noted, there was no evidence in this case that the defendants had done any such things. To the contrary, the real charge against the defendants was that they had conspired to teach and to organize other people to teach Marxist-Leninist doctrine from four books that were readily available on library shelves all over America. Douglas declared that once we make such conduct criminal "we enter territory dangerous to the liberties of every citizen."[*]

Douglas also objected to the casual way in which Vinson, Frankfurter, and Jackson took "judicial notice" of the threat of communism. He argued that if the Court was going to take judicial notice of the realities of the situation, it should reach a very different set of conclusions:

---

[*] According to Douglas, the four books were Stalin, *Foundations of Leninism* (1924); Marx and Engels, *Manifesto of the Communist Party* (1848); Lenin, *The State and Revolution* (1917); and *History of the Communist Party of the Soviet Union (B.)* (1939). See *Dennis*, 341 US at 582 (Douglas dissenting).

Communism in the world scene is no bogeyman; but Communism as a political faction or party in this country plainly is. Communism has been so thoroughly exposed in this country that it has been crippled as a political force. Free speech has destroyed it. . . . How it can be said that there is a clear and present danger that this advocacy will succeed is, therefore, a mystery. . . . In America, [the Communists] are miserable merchants of unwanted ideas; their wares remain unsold. The fact that their ideas are abhorrent does not make them powerful.[357]

Douglas therefore concluded, "[I]f we are to proceed on the basis of judicial notice, it is impossible for me to say that the Communists in this country are so potent . . . that they must be suppressed for their speech."[358]

Justice Black was appalled by the way in which Vinson, Frankfurter, and Jackson had distorted the "established" "clear and present danger" test in order to affirm these convictions. Indeed, when Vinson first circulated his draft opinion to the other justices for comment, Black lashed out in anger, noting in his marginal comments that the proposed new "clear and present danger" standard "permits courts to sustain anything"; that, "in other words, courts can approve suppression of free speech at will"; and that Vinson "puts 'speech' and 'armed internal attack' in the same category." Incredulous at Vinson's description of the threat of worldwide communism, Black scribbled, "The goblin'll get you." Next to Vinson's putsch point, Black scrawled, "Good semantic emotionalism and ghost conjuring!" At another point, Black wrote, "Emergency, crisis, always the plea of those who would give dictatorial powers to rulers." Summing up his own philosophy of the First Amendment, Black wrote on the draft of Jackson's concurring opinion, "1st Amendment presumes that free speech will *preserve*, not destroy, the nation."[359]

Striking a note of despair in his dissenting opinion, Black offered a prescient observation: "Public opinion being what it now is, few will protest the conviction of these [Communists]. There is hope, however, that in calmer times, when present pressures, passions and fears subside, this or some later Court will restore the First Amendment liberties to the . . . place where they belong in a free society."[360]

THE OPINIONS IN *DENNIS* posed several fundamental questions. First, is express advocacy of unlawful conduct deserving of First Amendment protection? Clarifying his opinion in *Masses*, Learned Hand argued in *Dennis* that such speech is not protected by the First Amendment, because it is a constitutionally illegitimate method of bringing about political change. In the Supreme Court, however, seven of the eight justices (all but Jackson) held that such advocacy is entitled to at least *some* constitutional protection. On the other hand, six of the eight justices (all but Black and Douglas) agreed with Hand that express advocacy of unlawful conduct is entitled to *less* constitutional protection than other modes of political discourse.

Second, is there any way to answer Chief Justice Vinson's point about the putsch? Surely, Vinson is right that it would be absurd to argue that the government must stay its hand until there is a clear and present danger of violent revolution. But does this prove, as he argued, that a strict "clear and present danger" test makes no sense? No. The ultimate "danger" here is not speech but action. It is the danger of strikes, boycotts, riots, bombings, sabotage, and assassinations. Nothing in the "clear and present danger" test—which applies only to speech— suggests that the government may not take a broad range of aggressive law enforcement steps to prevent those dangers. What the test does say, however, is that the government must direct its efforts along all those other dimensions *first*, before it can resort to the too convenient and politically charged expedient of suppressing dissident speech.

The notion that the government would be helpless to combat a truly dangerous conspiracy if it could not suppress its public *expression* is absurd, and the Court should simply have said so. It is at this point that the peculiarity of the charge in *Dennis* becomes especially resonant. Recall that the defendants were prosecuted not for conspiring to overthrow the government but for conspiring to *advocate* overthrow of the government. One cannot help thinking that the Department of Justice framed the charge as it did because it knew it could not prove an actual conspiracy to overthrow the government, let alone a serious danger of overthrow, or even attempted overthrow. Ironically, the defendants were prosecuted for their speech because they could not have been successfully prosecuted for their actions, or for any danger they actually presented to the United States.[361]

Third, what are we to make of Justice Jackson's argument that the "unmodified" Holmes-Brandeis version of the "clear and present danger" test should be inapplicable to a case like *Dennis* because it is "beyond the capacity of the judicial process" to decide whether a clear and present danger exists in such a case, which involves "a well-organized, nation-wide conspiracy" with international links and implications? This argument carries no weight. Certainly, there are situations in the law, and in constitutional law, where it is "beyond the capacity of the judicial process" to deal well with some factual questions. Certainly, if a court were called upon to assess with precision the danger posed by the CPUSA at some indefinite point in the future, in light of developing world events, it would stretch judicial resources to, and perhaps beyond, their limits.

But under the "unmodified" Holmes-Brandeis standard, the question was whether the advocacy of the CPUSA posed a clear and present danger to the United States on July 28, 1948, the day the defendants were indicted. This is not at all a hard question. No one believed this to be so. Thus, Jackson's real objection is not to the *difficulty* of applying the "unmodified" "clear and present danger" test, but to the *result* it required. That is a different matter entirely.

Fourth, why isn't Chief Justice Vinson's modified version of the "clear and present danger" test the "new and improved" version? After all, if the government can constitutionally restrict speech that creates an immediate 90 percent chance of a relatively modest evil (for example, persuading a few people to refuse induction into the army), shouldn't it be able to restrict speech that creates a less immediate 20 percent chance of a more serious evil (for example, causing a riot) or a very remote 1 percent chance of a very grave evil (for example, attempting to overthrow the government)? This seems logical.[362]

But it is a very bad idea. It is difficult to predict future events. As a general rule, the farther out in the future the event, the less confident we can be of our predictions. Insisting on a close temporal connection between speech and harm increases our confidence that the prediction has some validity. Moreover, in a free society the suppression of speech should be a last, not a first, resort. Unless the feared harm is imminent, and there is *no alternative* to restricting speech, the government should use other methods to prevent the harm. The temptation to suppress dissident speech on the pretext or the honest, but mistaken, belief that it is dangerous is both natural and pervasive. Insisting on a close temporal connection and a high likelihood of serious harm assures us that it is the *danger* and not abhorrence of the ideas that is driving the government's action.[363]

As evident in *Dennis*, the "discounted" version of clear and present danger is nothing more than open-ended balancing. Does the danger to society outweigh the harm to First Amendment interests? Such an unstructured inquiry invariably lends itself to ideological manipulation and provides no useful guidance to lower-court judges, legislators, police officers, or speakers. The very ambiguity of the standard creates an intolerable uncertainty of application and a potent chilling effect on free expression. Holmes and Brandeis had it right.

Fifth, how dangerous was the Communist Party of the United States in the late 1940s and early 1950s? Was it, as Justice Douglas observed, a mere "bogeyman"? Douglas was certainly correct that communism was of no consequence as a "political" force in the United States. But the prosecution under the Smith Act was not about the Communist Party as a "political" force. No one feared that the party was about to "overthrow" the U.S. government by winning elections. The fear was that the party, as an agent of the Soviet Union, would subvert American government through espionage and sabotage and by instigating labor, class, and racial conflict and discontent.

After the collapse of the Soviet Union, newly available information confirmed that the Soviets exercised considerable control over the CPUSA. Moreover, these files disclosed that Communists in sensitive government positions posed a real security risk. In short, the information revealed in the 1990s suggests that the fears of the majority of the justices in *Dennis* were not unfounded.[364] There was a conspiracy, it did involve leaders of the CPUSA, it did have links with international communism, and it did involve espionage against the government of the United States. But to the extent there was criminal conduct, the individuals who engaged in such conduct should have been investigated and prosecuted for their crimes. That is quite different from prosecuting *other* people—the defendants in *Dennis*—for their advocacy of Marxist-Leninist doctrine.

ULTIMATELY, OF COURSE, Justice Black's prediction proved right. Over time, the Court and the nation came to regard *Dennis* as an embarrassment, or worse. Although in the short run it opened the door to a rash of repressive programs designed to stigmatize and punish individuals suspected of being Communists or fellow travelers, in the long run it was shunted aside and, eventually, overruled. We must ask, though, why six of the eight justices bent over so far backward in *Dennis* to affirm the convictions. Whereas in World War I the Court had no prior experience with the First Amendment, by 1951 the Court had built an increasingly strong record of protecting free expression. It had invoked the Holmes-Brandeis "clear and present danger" test in a broad range of First Amendment decisions, including the World War II cases involving both fascists and Communists.

One explanation for this sudden collapse of confidence turns on the makeup of the Court. Justices Frankfurter and Jackson had long embraced a highly deferential view of the Court's role, particularly in matters concerning national security. Their opinions in *Dennis* were therefore more or less in line with their general judicial philosophies. Add to Frankfurter and Jackson the four Truman appointees, all of whom shared Truman's worldview, and there was a ready-made majority in *Dennis*.[365]

Beyond that, however, as Justice Douglas observed about *Korematsu*, we see once again that the justices of the Supreme Court are "not exempt from the fears and beliefs of other Americans." Indeed, it was quite natural for them to adopt the prevailing anti-Communist assumptions as a way to make sense of the legal issues in *Dennis*.[366] The drumbeat of anti-Red hysteria shaped the perceptions of most Americans, including most of the justices.

In the face of overwrought legislative findings,[367] the frenzied investigations of HUAC, the federal loyalty program, the disclosures of Bentley and Chambers, the frantic accusations of Joseph McCarthy, the increasing anxiety of the public following Stalin's domination of Eastern Europe, the Soviet atomic bomb, the fall of China, and the outbreak of the Korean War, it is no wonder that the Court succumbed to what Justice Black described as "present pressures, passions and fears." Even such sophisticated and experienced judges as Hand, Frankfurter, and Jackson were captured by the image of the domestic Communist as treacherous, malignant, and powerful. As Professor William Wiecek has noted, for the justices to have resisted "the ideological and emotional pressures of the Cold War era would have required superhuman wisdom and equanimity," qualities that were lacking in a majority of the justices in *Dennis*.[368]

JUNE 17, 1957

THE PUBLIC REACTION to *Dennis* was mixed. The *New York Times* applauded the Court for affirming that "liberty shall not be abused to its own destruction." The *Washington Post* praised it for reconciling "liberty and security in our time" and assured the public that, contrary to Justice Black's belief, *Dennis* would stand the test of time. On the other hand, the *St. Louis Post-Dispatch* described the opinion as "narrow, timid and confused," the *New Republic* accused the Court of paying "tyranny the tribute of imitation," and the *New York Post* charged that the justices had exhibited the "timidity of scared politicians."[369]

The Court's decision in *Dennis* provided a green light to Red hunters. On June 20, 1951, only two weeks after decision, the FBI arrested 17 second-tier Communist Party leaders in New York. Over the next three months, it arrested an additional 24 leaders in cities across the nation. Between 1951 and 1957, the government arrested and prosecuted under the Smith Act 145 members and leaders of the Communists Party. Of these defendants, 108 were convicted, 10 were acquitted, and the rest were still awaiting trial on June 17, 1957.

Typically, the charges involved such matters as teaching the writings of Lenin ("the proletarian revolution is impossible without the forcible destruction of the bourgeois state machine") and Stalin ("the law of violent proletarian revolution . . . is an inevitable law of the revolutionary movement"); attending or participating in meetings at which such ideas were taught; participating in the publication or circulation of pamphlets advocating such ideas; attending a class on the "History of the Communist Party of the Soviet Union"; and so on. In none of these prosecutions was there any evidence of any concrete plans to use force or violence to overthrow the government.[370]

But this was only part of the picture. As we have seen, the effort to suppress Communists and fellow travelers took many forms. Criminal prosecution was far from the most common. More often, such individuals were denied government employment, publicly exposed and humiliated, deprived of government benefits, and blacklisted. To what extent, if any, did these other actions violate the First Amendment?

In light of *Dennis*, one would expect the government to have carte blanche to expose an individual's Communist affiliations, deny him the opportunity to run for political office, and exclude him from public employment. After all, if it is constitutional to put Communists in jail, these less severe sanctions must be constitutional as well. And that, indeed, is what the Court held.

In *Garner v. Board of Public Works*,[371] decided on the same day as *Dennis*, the Court upheld a law requiring every employee of the city of Los Angeles, from sanitation workers to firefighters, to take an oath swearing that at no time since 1943 had he belonged to any organization that advocated the unlawful overthrow of government. The Court explained that this was "a reasonable regulation to protect the municipal service."[372]

The following year, in *Adler v. Board of Education*,[373] the Court upheld New York's Feinberg law, which prohibited any member of any organization that advocated the overthrow of government from serving in any position in any public school. The Court reasoned that public employment is a privilege, not a right, and that government may therefore deny that privilege to Communists and fellow travelers because teachers shape "the attitude of young minds towards the society in which they live." [374]

In *Harisiades v. Shaughnessy*,[375] also decided in 1952, the Court upheld the deportation of three noncitizens, each of whom had come to the United States prior to 1920, married, raised a family, and lived his entire adult life in America. Because each of these men had at some point joined the Communist Party, the Court held that they could lawfully be deported—even though each had ended his membership in the party at least a dozen years earlier.[376] Justice Black told the Court's law clerks that the country was in more "desperate trouble on the First Amendment than it has ever been in, much worse than during the Palmer Raids" or during the period of the Alien and Sedition Acts.*[377]

---

* A year later, in *Shaughnessy v. United States ex rel Mezei*, 345 US 206 (1953), the Court upheld the authority of the attorney general to imprison an alien, with no formal accusation of crime and no trial, on the basis of an anonymous allegation that he posed a danger to the national security. Justice Jackson protested that simple procedural justice could hardly imperil the national security. He added, "[N]o one can make me believe that we are that far gone." Id at 228 (Jackson dissenting). See David Cole, *Enemy Aliens: Double Standards and Constitutional Freedom in the War on Terrorism* 136–39 (New 2003). See also *Barsky v. Board of Regents*, 347 US 442 (1954) (upholding the suspension of a doctor's license to practice medicine because he refused to turn over documents to HUAC).

In sum, in the years after *Dennis* the Court placed the full weight of its authority behind the aggressive anti-Communist prosecutions, programs, policies, investigations, and exclusions that marked the first decade of the Cold War.[378] As Justice Douglas later put it, the Court had decided to run "with the hounds."[379]

JUNE 17, 1957 marked the end of the Cold War in the Supreme Court.[380] On that day, the Court handed down four decisions that reversed the course of constitutional history. The most important of these decisions was *Yates v. United States*.[381] Before turning to *Yates*, however, we must note the changes that had taken place between 1951 and 1957: Stalin died in 1953; an armistice was declared in Korea; the Senate condemned Joseph McCarthy; and the public attitude toward the Red menace began to relax. Although the pursuit of Communists and fellow travelers continued, the hysteria that had so fixated the nation had begun to abate.

Moreover, between 1951 and 1957 there were four changes in the makeup of the Court: Chief Justice Earl Warren replaced Fred Vinson, and Justices Brennan, Whittaker, and Harlan replaced Justices Reed, Minton, and Jackson. Thus, four justices who had taken a deferential approach to anti-Communist programs and policies were succeeded by four who brought a fresh perspective to the problem. The difference was palpable.

ON JULY 26, 1951, the FBI arrested Oleta Yates and eleven other leaders of the Communist Party in California. The trial was standard fare. The prosecution proved that the defendants had advocated Marxist-Leninist principles, the jury convicted, and the judge sentenced the defendants to five years in prison. The defendants claimed that their convictions violated the First Amendment.[382]

The Supreme Court agreed to hear the case, which seemed a routine rerun of *Dennis*. But this time, in a 6-to-1 decision, the Court overturned the convictions.[383] Justice John Marshall Harlan's opinion for the Court has aptly been described as "a sort of *Finnegans Wake* of impossibly nice distinctions."[384] Harlan's opinion effectuated an exquisitely subtle revolution. The revolution was subtle both because the distinction between *Dennis* and *Yates* was ephemeral and because Harlan purported merely to be interpreting the Smith Act, rather than ruling on its constitutionality. The revolution was successful because Harlan added a clear constitutional overlay to his opinion. Like Judge Hand in *Masses*, Harlan interpreted the statute narrowly to avoid having to hold it unconstitutional, thus implying that a broader construction would have violated the First Amendment.

At the outset, Harlan held that the Smith Act did not prohibit advocacy of "forcible overthrow as an abstract principle, divorced from any effort to instigate *action* to that end." He explained that the "distinction between advocacy of abstract doctrine and advocacy directed at promoting unlawful action is one that has been consistently recognized in the opinions of this Court." Thus, the Court "should not assume that Congress chose to disregard a constitutional danger zone so clearly marked." To respect this "danger zone," Harlan held that "mere doctrinal justification of forcible overthrow," even "if engaged in with the intent to accomplish overthrow," was not punishable under the act. Such advocacy was simply "too remote from concrete action." He underscored that the "essential distinction is that those to whom the advocacy is addressed must be urged to *do* something, now or in the future, rather than merely to *believe* in something."[385]

Justice Harlan thus alchemized this area of the law. He did not insist that the danger must be imminent, but he did insist that, to be punishable, the advocacy of unlawful conduct must include a call for specific, concrete action, whether "now or in the future." A speaker who teaches the general principles and doctrines of Marxism-Lenism, even with the intent to promote a revolution, will not cross the line drawn in *Yates*.

Yates embodied a delicate judicial effort to enable the government to prohibit the most dangerous forms of advocacy, while at the same time acknowledging, as Frankfurter had acknowledged in *Dennis*, the risk to robust public discourse of broadly restricting even the advocacy of violence. *Yates* did not go as far as the Holmes-Brandeis version of clear and present danger in protecting speech that poses a harm only in the future, but it went far enough to put an end to the prosecution of Communists under the Smith Act.

In reviewing the record in *Yates*, Harlan found a dearth of statements that could fairly be construed as "advocacy of action." Such statements were "completely overshadowed by the hundreds of instances in the record in which overthrow, if mentioned at all, occurs in the course of doctrinal disputation" that is "remote from action." Indeed, after reviewing the record, Harlan took the extraordinary step of not only reversing the convictions but of "foreclos[ing] further proceedings against those of the [defendants] as to whom the evidence . . . would be palpably insufficient upon a new trial." Thus, with respect to five of the defendants in *Yates*, the Court directed orders of acquittal.[386]

Yates sounded the death knell for the Smith Act as a weapon in the campaign against American Communists. On remand, the government dropped the charges against the remaining defendants in *Yates*. It then dismissed its pending charges against Communist leaders in Boston, Cleveland, Connecticut, Detroit, Philadelphia, Pittsburgh, Puerto Rico, and St. Louis. The Justice Department reluctantly conceded that it could not "satisfy the evidentiary requirements laid down by the Supreme Court." After June 17, 1957, the government filed no further prosecutions under the Smith Act.[387]

AN ISSUE CLOSELY TIED to the prosecutions in *Dennis* and *Yates* involved the question of membership. Most of the Cold War prosecutions were directed against leaders of the Communist Party, either nationally or locally. These defendants were engaged in the activities of the party. But what about individuals who were only members of the Communist Party? In what circumstances, if any, could they be criminally punished for their membership? In cases like *Garner*, *Adler*, and *Harisiades*, the Court had held that members of the party could be deported or denied public employment, as long as they had *known* of the party's advocacy of unlawful conduct when they were members. Could such "knowing" members be punished criminally as well? Certainly, in the years between *Dennis* and *Yates*, the assumed answer was yes.

Four years after *Yates*, however, the Court observed in *Scales v. United States*[388] that a "blanket" prohibition of knowing membership in organizations having "both legal and illegal aims" could pose "a real danger that legitimate political expression or association might be impaired." The Court therefore held that even if an organization engaged in advocacy of action that could be punished under the Smith Act, an individual member could not be punished unless he not only knew of the organization's illegal advocacy but was an "active" member with the "specific intent" to further the organization's illegal ends. *Scales* thus sharply limited the circumstances in which current or former members of the Communist Party could be criminally prosecuted for their membership.[389]

A central question after *Yates* and *Scales* concerned the continuing vitality of decisions like *Adler* and *Garner*. Even if the government cannot criminally *punish* an individual for membership in the Communist Party, can it deny Communists the "privilege" of public employment? In *Elfbrandt v. Russell*,[390] the Court effectively overruled its earlier decisions and held unconstitutional an Arizona statute requiring every state employee to swear that he was not a member of an organization that advocated the violent overthrow of government. Echoing *Scales*, the Court held that such a law, which disadvantages membership without regard to whether the individual has "the 'specific intent' to further the illegal aims of the organization," violates the freedoms of speech and association.*[391]

Thereafter, the Court eviscerated virtually all of the anti-Communist loyalty programs that had been instituted in the 1940s and 1950s. In a series of decisions, it held unconstitutional a law denying Communists passports, invalidated denaturalization orders based on membership in the Communist Party, held unconstitutional a statute denying Communists property tax exemptions, and set aside a federal law making it difficult for individuals to receive foreign "Communist propaganda."[392]

ANOTHER CRITICAL ISSUE, which gave the Court more difficulty, was that of disclosure. As we have seen, government agencies during the Cold War frequently used public exposure to harass and humiliate individuals for their "un-American" beliefs and associations. This poses an issue different from that of a criminal prosecution or even the denial of a privilege, for the government in this situation is not directly *penalizing* an individual for constitutionally protected activity. Any negative impact the individual may suffer can arguably be seen as merely "incidental" to the government's inquiry.

Nonetheless, in some circumstances the Court held the compelled disclosure of one's beliefs and associations unconstitutional. In *NAACP v. Alabama*,[393] for example, the Court invalidated, as applied to the NAACP, an Alabama statute requiring every out-of-state association to disclose its membership list to the state. The Court observed that such disclosure could constitute a serious "restraint on freedom of association," particularly "where a group espouses dissident beliefs." Because revelation of the identity of NAACP members in Alabama had in the

---

* The following year, the Court held unconstitutional the Feinberg law it had previously upheld in *Adler*. See *Keyishian v. Board of Regents*, 385 US 589 (1967). It went even further in *United States v. Robel*, 389 US 258 (1967), holding unconstitutional a provision of the Subversive Activities Control Act that prohibited any member of any Communist organization from working in a defense facility. The Court explained that even in the context of defense facilities the government must achieve its goals with narrowly drawn regulations and a due regard for "First Amendment freedoms." Id at 268.

past clearly exposed these individuals "to economic reprisal, loss of employment, threat of physical coercion, and other manifestations of public hostility," the Court held that the state could not constitutionally compel the NAACP to turn over its membership list unless it could demonstrate a "compelling" interest in the information.[394]

In the Cold War context, the issue of public exposure arose most often in the realm of legislative investigations. To some extent, this was dealt with through the privilege against compelled self-incrimination. In a series of decisions in the mid-1950s, the Court held that a witness before a legislative committee could plead the Fifth Amendment and refuse to answer questions if his answers might tend to incriminate him.[395]

Although this offered protection against possible future criminal prosecutions, it left these witnesses vulnerable to serious abuse. Legislative investigators in this era commonly vilified witnesses who invoked the privilege as "Fifth Amendment Communists," thus accomplishing their goal of public exposure and humiliation. Because invocation of the privilege was viewed as tantamount to an admission of "guilt"—whether or not the individual had actually committed a crime—"Fifth Amendment Communists" were routinely stigmatized and subjected to severe discrimination, not unlike members of the NAACP in Alabama. Moreover, and wholly apart from the issue of self-incrimination, many witnesses had sound reasons to keep private their beliefs and associations and, perhaps even more important, not to name others who may have shared them.

The question, then, was whether the Constitution places any restraint on these investigating committees, beyond the witness's right to "plead the Fifth." The Court first considered this question in *Watkins v. United States*,[396] decided on the same day as *Yates*. Watkins, a labor leader, refused to answer HUAC's questions about the political activities of individuals he believed no longer to be members of the Communist Party. He was convicted of contempt of Congress. In an opinion by Chief Justice Warren, the Court, anticipating *NAACP v. Alabama*, observed that "the mere summoning of a witness and compelling him to testify . . . about his beliefs, expressions and associations" may seriously interfere with First Amendment freedoms. "And where those forced revelations concern matters that are . . . unpopular, or even hateful to the general public, the reaction in the life of the witness may be disastrous." The Court reversed Watkins's conviction on technical grounds, but made clear that there is no legitimate "congressional power to expose for the sake of exposure."[397]

The Court directly addressed the question two years later in *Barenblatt v. United States*.[398] Barenblatt, an instructor at Vassar College, was subpoenaed to testify before HUAC during an inquiry into alleged Communist infiltration into the field of education. After answering a few preliminary questions, he refused to answer questions concerning his past and present membership in the Communist Party. Like many witnesses, Barenblatt declined to assert the Fifth Amendment, but instead invoked a First Amendment right not to answer such questions. He was convicted of contempt of Congress.

The Court, in a 5-to-4 decision, upheld Barenblatt's conviction. It rejected his contention that HUAC could ask only about *unlawful* speech or association. Justice Harlan explained that because "the investigatory process must proceed step by step" it was reasonable for HUAC to explore these broader questions of Communist Party membership, as long as it did not attempt to "pillory" the witness, use "indiscriminate dragnet procedures," or ask questions that were not relevant to a legitimate subject of inquiry.[399]

Justice Black, in dissent, chastised the majority for ignoring "the real interest in Barenblatt's silence" — "the interest of the people as a whole in being able to join organizations, advocate causes and make political 'mistakes' without later being subjected to governmental penalties for having dared to think for themselves." Stripping bare the fiction of HUAC's purportedly "legitimate" goals, Black charged that "the chief aim, purpose and practice" of HUAC is "to try witnesses and punish" them by exposure, "humiliation and public shame."[400]

Although *Barenblatt* upheld the constitutionality of congressional inquiries into Communist activities and affiliations, the Court sharply narrowed the precedential force of *Barenblatt* several years later. In *Gibson v. Florida Legislative Investigating Committee*,[401] a Florida legislative committee investigating the alleged infiltration of Communists into various organizations, ordered Gibson, the president of the Miami branch of the NAACP, to disclose to the committee whether several individuals who had been identified as Communists were members of the NAACP. Gibson refused and was held in contempt.

The Court held that Gibson's conviction violated the First Amendment because the committee had failed to show "a substantial connection between the Miami branch of the NAACP and Communist *activities*." The Court explained that, in the absence of such a showing, there was insufficient justification to intrude "into the area of constitutionally protected rights of speech, press, association and petition."[402]

Thus, although the Supreme Court limped weakly into this era, it later embraced a more independent stance and played a pivotal role in helping bring this sorrowful period to a close.[403] The nation's anti-Communist fever had begun to break even before the Court's decision in *Yates*, but *Yates* and its progeny hastened this process and injected a much needed voice of reason into America's public discourse. Moreover, these decisions continued the gradual evolution of First Amendment doctrine. As we shall see, they laid the foundation for the more mature and more principled First Amendment jurisprudence that would take root a decade later, during the Vietnam War.

"PARALYSIS RATHER THAN PROTEST"

THE LESSONS OF THE COLD WAR for a robust system of self-government are both sobering and essential. By the mid-1950s, a decade of political repression had created a pervasive sense of apprehension among Americans that they could suffer serious consequences if they openly expressed their opinions.[404] As Harry Truman had warned, "scaremongers" had generated such a wave of fear that their attacks on civil liberties went "almost unchallenged."[405]

On July 4, 1951, a reporter in Madison, Wisconsin, circulated a petition asking people to support the preamble to the Declaration of Independence. Ninety-nine percent refused to sign. Drew Pearson diagnosed this as "a disease of fear—unreasoning fear, mortal fear, fear of ideas, fear of books, fear of the good old American right to sign a petition." Pearson lamented that this disease was "marching like a monster through the minds of its victims."[406] As Justice Black ruefully observed, "constitutional liberties have a pretty hard time when people get . . . frightened."[407]

The "Silent Generation" of the 1950s was a legacy of this national anxiety. According to Henry Steele Commager, the political repression of this era bred a stifling "conformity" that was manifested in "an uncritical and unquestioning acceptance of America as . . . a finished product, perfect and complete."[408] Norman Mailer described the 1950s as "the years of conformity and depression." He added that "we suffer[ed] from a collective failure of nerve."[409]

From 1946 to 1954, there was a steady erosion in the support of civil liberties among those individuals and institutions we rely upon most to preserve and protect the freedom of expression—the press, intellectuals, liberal politicians, lawyers, courts, and educators.

Some elements of the press, such as the *Washington Post*, the *New York Times*, the *New York Post*, and the *St. Louis Post-Dispatch*, and some commentators, such as Drew Pearson, Edward R. Murrow, Herb Block, and James Reston, challenged the repression of civil liberties, but most of the media focused narrowly on specific issues and failed to present the full picture. For the most part, the press, intimidated by the very real threat of economic boycott, wavered in its support of civil liberties.[410]

Many liberal intellectuals and politicians also failed to follow their own long-held and often well-articulated principles. Some were too slow to acknowledge the evils of Stalinism; others defensively overreacted to those evils and developed an almost obsessive anti-Sovietism. Max Ascoli, for instance, wrote approvingly of *Dennis* because we "cannot take chances with the ringleaders of a conspiracy that, if successful, would pervert and destroy our institutions." Sidney Hook argued that HUAC did more good than harm because it educated the public about the dangers of Soviet infiltration. And Diana Trilling declared in 1952 that "the idea that America is a terror-stricken country in the grip of hysteria is a Communist-inspired idea."[411]

Perhaps most important, many liberal politicians, lifelong champions of political freedom, simply collapsed in the face of the anti-Communist onslaught. The *New York Times* aptly described the Senate when it enacted the McCarran Act of 1950 over President Truman's veto as a realm of "hysteria and frantic, unthinking fear." Senator Herbert Lehman, one of the few liberal Democrats who opposed the act, observed, "[T]he fever of fear was on my colleagues." And, as we have seen, only one senator—Estes Kefauver—had the courage to oppose the Communist Control Act of 1954. Of course, the fear was not unwarranted. Elected officials knew all too well what had happened to Millard Tydings, Scott Lucas, William Benton, and others who had opposed the furies of their age.[412]

Lawyers, in particular, had every reason to resist the machinery of repression. The absence of even minimal standards of due process in loyalty programs and legislative inquisitions was open, flagrant, and notorious. The specter of loyalty boards discharging individuals for their suspected beliefs on the basis of anonymous reports should have enraged lawyers, whose profession is, if nothing else, about guaranteeing fair procedure. In fact, however, large segments of the profession evidenced little concern for the protection of civil liberties.

Moved by Attorney General Tom Clark's warning that lawyers should be careful about representing those who "act like Communists," and by the harsh punishments for criminal contempt imposed by Judge Harold Medina on the attorneys who had represented the defendants in *Dennis*, the bar's response was one of "paralysis rather than protest." John Frank observed in 1951 that it is "now . . . almost impossible to obtain 'respectable counsel'" in loyalty cases. Frank added that "public opinion has risen to such a point that many lawyers believe they will be professionally ruined" if they appear to be soft on communism and "take such cases."[413]

Sadly, the American Bar Association called in 1951 for the expulsion of all members of the Communist Party and urged all state and local bar associations to disbar such individuals. Many state and local bar associations adopted loyalty tests and denied admission to the bar to would-be lawyers who refused to answer questions about their political beliefs and affiliations. Even organizations expressly dedicated to the protection of civil liberties faltered. The Americans for

Democratic Action embraced an anti-Communist stance, and the ACLU rejected for its governing boards or staff any person whose "devotion to civil liberties" was "qualified by adherence to . . . totalitarian doctrine."[414]

Although most lawyers who should have known better chose to remain silent, not all stayed on the sidelines. Abe Fortas is a good example of a successful and prominent lawyer who chose to represent individuals who were dragged before the loyalty boards or HUAC, proceedings he viewed as fundamentally "lawless." By the late 1940s, loyalty cases consumed between 20 and 50 percent of Arnold, Fortas & Porter's working hours.

This was difficult and often painful work. After representing his first client before a loyalty board, one lawyer observed that the "degradation" of the entire process had literally made him ill. Fortas represented a broad spectrum of people, including Owen Lattimore, Dorothy Bailey, a Berkeley engineer, a physicist employed by the National Bureau of Standards, a Yale professor, the child of an old friend, and the wife of a neighbor. He was touched by the "Kafkaesque plight of those suspected of disloyalty."[415]

But even Fortas would not represent a current or former member of the Communist Party. Although he struggled with the wisdom of this policy, he ultimately defended it on the ground that his reputation for not defending Communists was invaluable to him in his representation of those who had only been fellow travelers. As one member of Fortas's firm noted at the time, in proceedings before the loyalty boards, if you've ever been "a member of the Communist party, you're dead." Fortas was interested in saving those who could be saved. Other lawyers and law professors, such as Thomas Emerson and Joseph Rauh, courageously represented even those who had been members of the party. Those who accepted the burdens and challenges of this responsibility fulfilled the highest ideals of the legal profession and served their nation well, indeed.[416]

AN AREA OF SPECIAL FOCUS for the Red hunters was education. As the Supreme Court observed in *Adler*, teachers warranted particular attention because they shape "the attitudes of young minds towards the society in which they live." According to J. Edgar Hoover, the stakes in this realm were especially high because "every Communist uprooted from our educational system is one more assurance that it will not degenerate into a medium of propaganda for Marxism." The pervasive use of loyalty tests at all levels of education led to the dismissal of hundreds of teachers and the intimidation of many thousands of others.

Professor Robert Bolwell, a professor of American literature at George Washington University, observed, "[A]fter finishing a lecture, I sometimes wonder if somebody is going to take it to Papa or to some reporter." Even "one lecture," he said, "could damn anybody." In March 1954, the *Christian Science Monitor* reported that a "subtle, creeping paralysis of freedom of thought and speech" was "attacking college campuses." Colleges and universities experienced an increased pressure for conformity, a lessening of tolerance for dissident ideas, and a reluctance on the part of both faculty and students to express novel or controversial opinions. It was the most frightening strain of "political correctness" ever to infect American campuses.

Deans at several institutions reported that students had become frightened to voice liberal views, or to become identified with peace or free speech, because such views had "become associated with Communism." Any criticism of the nation was likely to be decried as unpatriotic. Carl Ackerman, the dean of the Columbia Graduate School of Journalism, noted that "the vast majority of teachers . . . have learned that promotion and security depend upon conformity."[417]

The hunt for "subversive" ideas in the educational process inhibits debate where it most needs to be uninhibited. When Professor Owen Lattimore was dragged before a Senate subcommittee after he was accused by Joe McCarthy of disloyalty, he pleaded with the subcommittee not to "permit a psychology of fear to paralyze the scholars and writers of this nation." Lattimore explained that "the danger of suppressing freedom of scholarship and opinion is . . . not merely a threat to the scholars" but "a direct and immediate danger to the national interest."[418] To no avail.

In the late 1940s, the University of Washington was accused of being a "hotbed" of communism. The state's Canwell committee launched a full-scale investigation of subversion on campus. Ten tenured faculty members were "named" as members of the Communist Party. Several had never been members; others had once been members but had since withdrawn; and three were apparently current members. The Faculty Committee on Tenure and Academic Freedom recommended retaining all ten professors because "the mere fact of membership in the Communist Party" should not subject a faculty member to "removal" if his performance as a teacher and scholar is acceptable.

Overriding this conclusion, the president of the university, Raymond Allen, recommended to the board of regents that the three professors who were still members of the party be dismissed, a recommendation the regents accepted. Allen explained that "men in academic life . . . are engaged in . . . the pursuit of truth wherever it may lead." But a professor who is "sincere in his belief in Communism" cannot "be a sincere seeker after truth."[419]

What happened at the University of Washington was repeated throughout the nation. Scores of colleges and universities fired hundreds of professors because of their actual or suspected, past or present, membership in the Communist Party.

The University of California discharged twenty-five faculty members because they refused to sign a loyalty oath. One college fired a faculty member because he had once served as chairman of a local Citizens for Henry Wallace Committee. Much of the educational establishment foundered in its defense of academic freedom. The National Education Association opposed the employment of Communist Party members as teachers. Even the Association of American Universities resolved that Communist Party membership "extinguishes the right to a university position."[420] It was, in David Caute's words, the era of "The Great Fear."[421]

"HOW WOULD THEY EVER LEARN BETTER?"

IN 1949, A LITTLE-KNOWN STATE SENATOR from Mt. Vernon, Illinois, introduced the "Broyles bills" in the Illinois legislature. These bills declared ineligible for any public office or any position as an instructor, teacher, or professor in any school, college, or university in Illinois any person who was directly or indirectly affiliated with any Communist or Communist-related organization.[422] To protest these bills, 106 University of Chicago students traveled to Springfield and, in a sometimes indecorous manner, paraded through the streets of the state capital chanting their opposition.[423]

Illinois legislators were livid. One proclaimed that he would not send his "pet dog to the University of Chicago." Another asserted that "the students looked so dirty and greasy on the outside that they couldn't possibly be clean American on the inside." A few days later, Senator Broyles declared that it "appears that these students are being indoctrinated with Communistic and other subversive theories contrary to our free system of representative government," and launched another investigation of the University of Chicago to determine whether it harbored professors who taught "un-American" ideas.[424]

Almost fifteen years after the Walgreen affair, the first witness to testify before the committee was Robert Maynard Hutchins. He began by emphasizing that the University of Chicago guaranteed its professors "absolute and complete academic freedom." Although conceding that some members of the faculty might belong to Communist-related organizations, he insisted that this was none of the university's business. The University of Chicago, he explained, "does not believe in the un-American doctrine of guilt by association." Hutchins also acknowledged that there was a student Communist Club on campus, which included some students who were "sympathetic to Communism." He emphatically rejected the proposition that it would serve the public interest to exclude such students from higher education, for if "we did, how would they ever learn better?"[425]

Hutchins then turned to the relationship between education and free expression:

> The American way has been to encourage thought and discussion. . . . The whole educational system . . . is a reflection of the American faith in thought and discussion as the path to peaceful change and improvement. The danger to our institutions is not from the tiny minority who do not believe in them. It is from those who would mistakenly repress the free spirit upon which those institutions are built. . . .[426]

Hutchins was cross-examined by the committee's counsel, J. B. Matthews, a professional Red hunter who had once worked for HUAC. At one point, Matthews asked Hutchins about Maud Slye, a retired professor who had had a distinguished career in cancer research and who was known to be affiliated with several "Communist-front" organizations:

MATTHEWS: You are acquainted, I take it, . . . with the recent action of the Board of Regents of the University of Washington at Seattle, are you not?

HUTCHINS: Yes. . . .

MATTHEWS: Would you be willing to have administrators of the University of Chicago use the University of Washington action as a precedent? . . .

HUTCHINS: The answer is "No." . . .

MATTHEWS: The records . . . show . . . that some 69 odd persons listed in the latest available directory of the University of Chicago as professor . . . have been affiliated with 135 Communist front organizations, in 465 separate affiliations. Now I should like to know if that is not something for which the University might well be alarmed.

HUTCHINS: I don't see why. . . .

MATTHEWS: You don't think that that is indicative of the fact that the University of Chicago is allowing its prestige to be used in the Communist Front movement?

HUTCHINS: I don't think so, especially when you consider the alternative. . . . Suppose . . . you have a Nobel Prize winner, undoubtedly competent in his field, and he joins an organization of which the Attorney General at the moment happens to disapprove. Is it suggested that I am to interfere with his freedom of association, freedom of speech and freedom of thought? I hope not. . . .

MATTHEWS: Do you recall the manner in which President Truman charac-
terized Communist Party members when he was asked about it?
HUTCHINS: I do.
MATTHEWS: His statement was that they are all traitors.
HUTCHINS: I recall his statement.
MATTHEWS: Do you concur with the President?
HUTCHINS: Am I required to?[427]

At the conclusion of the hearings, a petition bearing the names of three thousand University of Chicago students was submitted to the investigative committee. The petition read,

> As students of the University of Chicago, we believe that the position of our Uni-
> versity, which encourages and maintains the free examination of all ideas, is the
> strongest possible safeguard against indoctrination. Because we believe this pol-
> icy of academic freedom for both students and teachers is the best preparation for
> effective citizenship in the American tradition, we are confident that the people
> in the State and nation will join with us to encourage the freedom of the Univer-
> sity of Chicago and to support it against attack.

Upon receiving this petition, Senator Broyles demanded "to know . . . something about the signers, of the type of students" they are. "We shouldn't accept
just anything."[428]

As in the Walgreen affair, the Broyles investigation collapsed.* The Broyles
bills languished in the Illinois House and eventually died a quiet death without
ever being called up for a final vote.[429]

AS PRESIDENT OF the University of Chicago, Hutchins believed
that, in a world cursed with Nazism and Stalinism, the preservation of democracy

---

* The conventional wisdom is that had other academic leaders been as outspoken as Hutchins
in opposing such investigations, they might have mitigated the damage. One commentator noted
that Hutchins's testimony before the committee was "perhaps the most signal deliverance on the
principles of academic freedom" made to any political investigating committee in this era. Francis
Biddle contrasted Hutchins's bold defense of academic freedom with that of James Conant, the
president of Harvard, who sought "to find a middle ground." Robert M. MacIver, *Academic Freedom in Our Time* 186 (Columbia 1955); Biddle, *Fear of Freedom* at 156 (cited in note 127). See also
Ellen W. Schrecker, *No Ivory Tower: McCarthyism and the Universities* 21 (Oxford 1986).

required the cultivation of free minds, disciplined by reason. The responsibility of higher education, he wrote, was to provide Americans with the "moral courage" and the "intellectual clarity" that were necessary in times of great crisis. The university must instill in citizens "candid and intrepid thinking about fundamental issues" to enable them to "formulate, to clarify, to vitalize the ideals which should animate mankind."[430]

In 1950, after serving for more than two decades as university president, Hutchins accepted a position with the Ford Foundation, where he encouraged the development of educational television and international cultural exchange. From 1954 until his death in 1977, he was president of the Fund for the Republic and the Center for the Study of Democratic Institutions, a residential facility for the study, discussion, and clarification of democratic ideas and institutions. In these years, Hutchins focused on projects documenting violations of civil liberties by congressional investigating committees, promoting public understanding of the Bill of Rights, fostering community education programs about race relations, and investigating the mistreatment of Mexican migrant workers.

At the center, Hutchins gathered together such luminaries as Reinhold Niebuhr, Harry Kalven, Alexander Meiklejohn, J. William Fulbright, Walter Lippmann, William Benton, William O. Douglas, Robert F. Kennedy, Gunnar Myrdal, Kenneth B. Clark, Jacques Barzun, Walter Reuther, and Thurgood Marshall in an effort to help clarify their thinking—and the thinking of citizens generally—on issues of law, politics, peace, poverty, civil liberties, and education. Hutchins himself was never satisfied that he had achieved his goals. But, as Edward Shils has written, Hutchins was a man of honor who tried to live up to his convictions.[431] Certainly, his most lasting legacy was that at a time when other university presidents, and most national leaders, retreated in the defense of freedom, he was fearless.[432]

THE VIETNAM WAR

The Supreme Court's First Amendment

Anti–Vietnam War Demonstration at U.S. Capitol

*T*HE VIETNAM WAR RAISED OLD—and new—questions about the nature and depth of the American commitment to free speech in wartime. Opposition to the war came from many quarters, and antiwar protesters employed a broad range of tactics to challenge the war, including prayer vigils, petitions, teach-ins, mass public demonstrations, civil disobedience, draft card burning, street violence, and bombings.[1]

Over more than a decade of conflict, the war in Vietnam provoked increasingly bitter dissent and increasingly furious repression. It turned daughter against father, student against teacher, citizen against government. It was an era marked by the Chicago Democratic Convention, the Kent State killings, the Pentagon Papers, and the Days of Rage. Many Americans came to believe that the nation was, quite literally, "coming apart."[2]

To understand the free speech issues that arose in this period, it is necessary to have some sense of how and why the United States found itself mired in a conflict halfway around the world. After struggling for centuries to free themselves from Chinese domination, the people of Vietnam came under French rule in the mid-nineteenth century. At the end of World War II, a resurgent nationalistic Vietnamese movement gained strength. From 1946 to 1954, the Communist Vietminh, led by Ho Chi Minh, waged a fierce guerilla war against the French, culminating in the climactic French defeat at Dienbienphu. The 1954 Geneva Accords divided Vietnam. The Democratic Republic of Vietnam, in the North, was led by Ho Chi Minh. The government the French had installed in the South was controlled by Ngo Dinh Diem. Although the Geneva Accords mandated a Vietnam-wide unification referendum in 1956, Diem scuttled this plan.

The United States supported Diem as part of a global effort to contain the spread of communism. The Vietcong, made up of remnants of the Vietminh in the South, continued its fight to overthrow Diem and unify Vietnam. By the time John F. Kennedy became president in 1961, Vietnam was a shambles.* Kennedy had long been aware of the pitfalls of Southeast Asia. As early as 1954, he had warned on *Meet the Press* that it would be a grievous "mistake" for the United States to get involved militarily in Vietnam, because "[n]o amount of American military assistance" can "conquer an enemy which is everywhere and at the same time nowhere" and "which has the sympathy and covert support of the people."[3]

Early in his presidency, Kennedy received conflicting advice. General Maxwell Taylor and White House aide Walt Rostow recommended that the United States substantially increase its military aid to South Vietnam in order to stabilize the situation; Ambassador Averell Harriman and Undersecretary of State Chester Bowles opposed any additional U.S. involvement. Others cautioned that even if the United States won militarily in Vietnam, it was destined to lose the political struggle.[4]

But with Cuba and Laos already lost and Berlin a stalemate, Kennedy decided that both the nation and his administration needed to demonstrate strength and that Vietnam seemed a "good place to make a stand."[5] Thus, with misgivings,[6] in 1961 Kennedy ordered four hundred Special Forces troops and other military advisers to Vietnam in order to prop up the failing South Vietnamese army. Kennedy continued to be anxious, however. He told Arthur Krock that "United States troops should not be involved in combat on the Asian mainland," and expressed his concern to Arthur Schlesinger that "the troops will march in; the bands will play; the crowds will cheer; and in four days . . . we will be told we have to send in more troops. It's like taking a drink. The effect wears off, and you have to take another." He predicted that if we made a serious military commitment in Vietnam, "we would lose" just the way "the French had lost."[7]

Nonetheless, by December 1961, the number of American troops in Vietnam had increased to 3,164. A year later, that number had more than tripled. But the administration was still unclear about its goals and strategies for Vietnam. Military leaders assured the president that success was imminent, but the situation continued to deteriorate. The Pentagon refused to admit publicly that troop levels were steadily rising or that Americans were now actively engaged in combat.

---

* As early as 1954, President Eisenhower pledged U.S. support to Diem in resisting "aggression or subversion" through military means, on the condition that South Vietnam undertake needed reforms. Manchester, *Glory and Dream* at 917 (cited in note 6).

Under intense pressure from Vietcong guerrillas, the Diem regime ever more ruthlessly suppressed dissent. In the spring of 1963, mass anti-Diem demonstrations erupted in Hué. In a tragedy that foreshadowed what was to come in the United States, South Vietnamese troops fired on the protesters, killing nine. In condemnation of this act, Buddhist monks began to immolate themselves in public. Madame Nhu, Diem's sister-in-law, cruelly ridiculed the suicides as "monk barbecue shows." Diem's forces rounded up more than 1,400 monks, which only intensified opposition to his regime. On November 1, 1963, Diem was assassinated. By the end of the year the United States had over 16,000 soldiers in Vietnam.[8]

Over the next several years, under President Lyndon Johnson, the United States poured ever more armaments and men into South Vietnam. By the end of 1965, the number of American troops had increased to 184,000; by the end of 1966, to 385,000; by the end of 1967, to more than 500,000.[9] By the time the United States finally withdrew from Vietnam in 1973, more than 50,000 Americans had died there.[10]

THE PACIFIST

WHEN VIETNAM ENTERED America's consciousness, David Dellinger was already in his fifties. A husky man of average height, he had a ruddy complexion and a face creased with laugh lines. He was gregarious, easily approachable, and almost always cheery. Born into a socially prominent Massachusetts family, he was the son of a distinguished Boston lawyer who was chairman of the Town Republican Committee, a friend of Calvin Coolidge, and, in Dellinger's words, "the best grown-up I knew at being friends with everyone, rich or poor, milkmen and company presidents."

As a boy, Dellinger closely followed the Sacco and Vanzetti prosecution. When he was twelve, and Sacco and Vanzetti were about to be executed, he pleaded with his father either to ask the governor to pardon them or to take him to the governor so he could plead on their behalf. His father, who got along with everyone, "rich or poor," did not like atheists, labor leaders, or anarchists and refused his request.[11]

When Dellinger was a student at Yale in the early 1930s, his first love was philosophy, but he grew disillusioned with the lifeless way it was taught. Years later, he recalled that he had felt in college what the German philosopher Ludwig Wittgenstein had said about the subject: "What is the use of studying philosophy if all that it does for you is to enable you to talk?" Dellinger switched to economics.

Building upon the values he had demonstrated as a youth, Dellinger helped organize a union of university employees. Yale then being a conservative bastion for the sons of the elite, this did not sit well with the university. His dean called him into his office and warned that the union campaign was backed by Communists and that he should steer clear of the situation. Dellinger had never met a Communist, but the dean's warning made him "curious to find out what Communists were like." Over time, he noticed that almost every cause he supported was called "Communist."[12]

After graduating from Yale, Dellinger was awarded a fellowship to study economics at Oxford. Upon returning to the United States, he accepted a position at Yale's Dwight Hall (the University Christian Association) as a freshman counselor. He briefly flirted with communism, but decided against joining the CPUSA because of its manipulative tactics and his distrust of the Soviet Union.

Over the next three years, in a continuing quest for understanding, Dellinger joined the "hobo" world of the Depression, riding freight trains, staying in "hobo jungles," standing in breadlines, begging for food. Inspired by the example of Francis of Assisi, Dellinger learned through this experience that he had to fashion "a way of life that would not accept either the spiritual poverty of the rich or the material poverty of the poor."[13]

He then enrolled at Union Theological Seminary in New York, the home of such luminary theologians as Reinhold Niebuhr and Paul Tillich. When the draft law was passed in 1940, Dellinger was exempt from military service because of his status as a divinity student. But because he viewed conscription as immoral, and did not believe he should be entitled to a special exemption, he refused either to register for the draft or to accept his exemption. Along with seven other students from Union Seminary, he was prosecuted, convicted, and sentenced to federal prison. Dellinger defiantly sat in the segregated black section of the prison theater, for which he was promptly placed in solitary confinement. When he continued to disobey prison regulations, he was placed in the "hole," with "no light, no bed, shivering in the midst of summer in a cell that was damper and darker" than any place he had ever imagined. It was there that he began to understand the meaning of nonviolent resistance.[14]

After Dellinger was released from prison, he was again arrested, prosecuted, and convicted in 1943 for refusing to report for an army physical, having forfeited his exemption. He was sentenced to two years in the federal penitentiary at Lewisburg, Pennsylvania, where he remained until 1945.[15]

Living in the obscurity of a collective community in New Jersey, Dellinger established *Direct Action*, a small journal that supported democratic socialism

David Dellinger

and abjured violent revolution. In 1955, with the help of several socialists, anarchists, and radical pacifists, including A. J. Muste and Bayard Rustin, he established a new journal, *Liberation*. Utopian and eclectic, *Liberation* "was designed
to be a forum for ideas and reports on the 'political fundamentalism' of nonviolent revolutionary politics and active individual resistance." Its contributing
authors included Michael Harrington, Norman Mailer, Martin Luther King Jr.,
James Baldwin, Jules Feiffer, Dorothy Day, and Lewis Mumford. *Liberation*
objected to both the "political slavery" of Soviet-style Marxism and the social
inequity of American-style capitalism. It argued that whatever differences might
exist between the Soviet Union and the United States, both posed a threat to the
"survival of civilization."[16]

As the antiwar movement was beginning, Dellinger was scheduled to speak
at a "peace and disarmament" rally in New York City in the spring of 1963. The
event was sponsored by a broad coalition of groups whose leaders had agreed to
focus the rally only on nuclear testing. Just before he was to speak, several students
raised signs calling for the withdrawal of U.S. forces from Vietnam. As Dellinger
recalled, "At the time most Americans hardly knew that there was a place called
Vietnam, let alone that the United States had . . . a militarily active mission there."
The director of the rally ordered the signs removed. When Dellinger finally got
the microphone, he "felt it necessary to say more" about Vietnam than he had

originally intended. He linked Vietnam to nuclear disarmament, explaining that both issues arose out of the nation's drive for "global dominance and the . . . profits that go with it." When he finished, the leaders of the protest angrily told him that he would never again be allowed to speak at such an event.

That was not to be. As the senior "statesman" of what later would become the radical antiwar movement, Dellinger would play a critical role in shaping the mood and style of protest in the United States during one of the most tumultuous periods in the nation's history.[17]

THE ROOTS OF THE ANTIWAR MOVEMENT

THE VIETNAM ERA ANTIWAR MOVEMENT traced its origins to the nuclear disarmament protests of the 1950s. By 1955, with the first signs of a possible easing of tensions in Soviet-American relations, some Americans began to call for arms control and a negotiated end to the Cold War. Among the more prominent of them were Norman Cousins, I. F. Stone, Linus Pauling, Albert Einstein, and Norman Thomas. They differed from one another on many issues but were united in their belief that, in the long run, the arms race could benefit neither the United States nor the rest of the world. As Norman Thomas wrote in 1955, "Never was I surer than now that . . . lovers of peace must concentrate on their drive for controlled disarmament."[18]

A group of students at the University of Chicago, following in the footsteps of their Hutchins era predecessors, established the Student Peace Union in an effort to open the disarmament movement to students. The founders of the SPU hoped that a "new era" could be built on the awareness that what had happened in Hiroshima could happen in New York or Moscow or London. Inspired by the civil rights movement, the SPU argued that nonviolent protest could be used in support of the peace movement as well. By 1962, SPU had more than two thousand members and chapters on campuses across the nation.[19]

That year, the Women's Strike for Peace, a group of "middle-aged, middle-class, white women," organized protests by more than 25,000 women across the country to demonstrate their deep concern about "the question of human survival,"[20] a group of doctors formed Physicians for Social Responsibility and issued a report in the *New England Journal of Medicine* detailing the medical consequences of a nuclear war, and Dr. Benjamin Spock, author of the most widely used child care book in the nation, joined the Committee for a Sane Nuclear Policy (SANE) because of the potential harms that nuclear testing posed to children.[21]

Then, in a major address at American University in June 1963, President

Kennedy called for a reexamination of the Cold War, noting that the United States and the Soviet Union had "a mutually deep interest in a just and genuine peace."[22] Kennedy explained that he sought not "a *Pax Americana* enforced on the world by American weapons of war" but a peace for all nations "for all time." As a step in this direction, he proposed a halt to the arms race. This speech, "one of the great state papers of any twentieth-century" president, led to the signing of a treaty in September banning atmospheric nuclear testing.[23] The *Bulletin of Atomic Scientists* proclaimed that the "old order of priorities is being revised in America."[24]

WITH THIS ACHIEVEMENT, the energy for defusing the Cold War began to dissipate, and the political left increasingly turned its attention to civil rights. Sit-ins, freedom rides, the March on Washington, and Dr. King's "I Have a Dream" speech captured public attention and support for the blossoming civil rights movement, which over time would offer both inspiration and guidance to antiwar protesters. Indeed, the civil rights movement would teach "the Vietnam generation that nonviolent public protest was a responsible, heroic, and effective way" to express its dissent.[25]

As the "New Left" began to focus on issues of racial equality, it began to fashion a more overarching perspective that called for fundamental reform of the "system" in order to eliminate racism, unemployment, militarism, and poverty. A leading voice in this transition was Students for a Democratic Society (SDS), which was founded at the University of Michigan in 1960 by Al Haber and a small circle of friends, including Tom Hayden, the talented editor of the University of Michigan student newspaper, and Rennie Davis, an anti–nuclear testing activist at Oberlin College.*[26]

Hayden and other members of SDS gathered in June 1962 at Port Huron, Michigan, to draft a new "manifesto." The Port Huron Statement made clear that what haunted this generation of leftists was not the specter of Communism but the "mood of McCarthyism."[27] The Port Huron Statement, a complex distillation of then current social criticism, argued that the ills of society were interrelated. Racism and nuclear proliferation were both consequences of the pervasive disparity between "liberal" ideals and the realities of contemporary society. The

---

* SDS was originally established as the student branch of the League for Industrial Democracy, which traced its own roots back to the Intercollegiate Socialist Society of 1905, whose members included Jack London, Upton Sinclair, John Reed, and Walter Lippmann. In 1966, SDS and LID split apart over ideological differences. See Jacobs and Landau, *New Radicals* at 28–29 (cited in note 39).

SDS statement insisted that "the evils manifest in American society—unemployment, economic insecurity, segregation, the threat of nuclear war—cannot be attacked piecemeal, because they are symptoms of one disease, not separate and distinct maladies." [28] What was needed was a social revolution that would transform the underlying culture.[29] The young leaders of SDS believed, in David Dellinger's words, that people must choose "between being liberals who . . . minimize personal risk . . . and being radicals who concentrate on historical exigency rather than on personal safety."[30]

Three "themes" framed the nascent peace movement of the early 1960s.[31] First, its participants believed that twentieth century life had degenerated into a state of "unreason and insanity."[32] In Allen Ginsberg's words, "I saw the best minds of my generation destroyed by madness."[33] The cruelty of World War I battlefields, the incomprehensible evil of the Holocaust, the nightmarish tragedies of Hiroshima and Nagasaki, the excesses of McCarthyism, and the very concept of mutually assured destruction ("MAD") as a strategic policy suggested a world torn loose from any rational or moral social order.*

Second, they believed that the Cold War had generated a deadening conformity and "numbness" in the American people. Preoccupied with the need for security, Americans had become morally paralyzed and seemed locked into a course on which they would willingly betray their own most fundamental values in order to preserve them.[34]

Third, they yearned to act boldly on the basis of personal idealism and moral courage. The theologian Thomas Merton posited that the Cold War represented "a crisis of man's spirit."[35] These young idealists sought meaning and authenticity. They embraced an ethic of personal commitment, risk, and direct action. They shared a sense that they were participating in a social movement that would awaken the nation's conscience and "change America for the better."[36]

Having come of age in the "sanitized" years after World War II, the relatively privileged members of this generation were both surprised and disaffected by what they now saw as the status quo, and they were determined to change it.[37] They arrived at these issues from a social and economic background completely different from that of the anarchists and socialists of World War I or the American Communists of the 1930s and 1940s. But as the forces of their generation played out in their lives, classes, experiences, and conversations, they responded first with "a sense of loss," then with a "youthful moral outrage, and finally with an outburst of protest."[38]

---

* The 1964 movie *Dr. Strangelove* captured this mood.

"I DON'T WANT US TO GET INTO THAT DANGEROUS SITUATION"

THE TURBULENT EVENTS of the mid-1960s made this era a mine-field for those seeking social and political change. In 1964 alone, Lyndon Johnson introduced his plan for the Great Society,* black and white volunteers led dangerous voter registration drives in Mississippi, race riots raged in Harlem, the Free Speech Movement burst on the scene at Berkeley,[39] and the Republican Party nominated Barry Goldwater for president.[40] Goldwater attacked Johnson for failing to stand up to communism and proposed the use of nuclear weapons to defoliate South Vietnam. He argued that "the Good Lord raised up this mighty Republic to be a home for the brave . . . not to cringe before the bullying of Communism." Johnson, a master politician, seized the political center. He pledged to save South Vietnam from the Communists, but rejected Goldwater's demands as irresponsible. He insisted that a political solution was both essential and possible and that the United States "is not engaged in the war and does not intend to be."[41]

On the left, those already uneasy with the situation in Vietnam argued that the United States had neither sufficient national interest nor sufficient moral justification to be involved militarily. Walter Lippmann maintained that the "price

---

* In an address in Ann Arbor on May 22, 1964, President Johnson described his aspirations for the future:

> The Great Society rests on abundance and liberty for all. It demands an end to poverty and racial injustice, to which we are totally committed in our time. But that is just the beginning. The Great Society is a place where every child can find knowledge to enrich his mind and to enlarge his talents. It is a place where leisure is a welcome chance to build and reflect, not a feared cause of boredom and restlessness. It is a place where the city of man serves not only the needs of the body and the demands of commerce, but the desire for beauty and the hunger for community. It is a place where man can renew contact with nature. It is a place which honors creation for its own sake and for what it adds to the understanding of the race. It is a place where men are more concerned with the quality of their goals than the quantity of their goods.

Johnson's ambitious agenda was to end poverty, promote equality, improve education, rejuvenate cities, and protect the environment. *President's Michigan Speech on "Great Society,"* 20 Congressional Quarterly Almanac 874 (1965).

of a military victory" in Vietnam would be higher than America's "vital interests can justify."[42] Senator Wayne Morse of Oregon declared that further U.S. military action in Vietnam would be "outlawry" and warned that "outlaws have a way of coming to a bad end."[43] Democratic Senator Ernest Gruening of Alaska announced that Johnson's policy eventually would be "denounced as a crime."[44]

For the most part, though, there was still little public opposition to the war. The SDS and others on the far left were focused more on the civil rights struggle. They did not yet see Vietnam as a priority and, in any event, had no practical alternative to supporting Johnson in the 1964 election.[45] This left Johnson a free hand. In August 1964, he reported that American naval vessels had been subjected to an "unprovoked" attack by North Vietnamese torpedo boats in the Gulf of Tonkin.[46] He responded with an air strike on North Vietnam and won quick congressional approval for the Gulf of Tonkin Resolution, which authorized "all necessary measures" to repel any attack on U.S. forces and to "prevent further aggression."[47] This became the legal basis for further escalation of the war. Johnson went on to score an overwhelming victory in the 1964 presidential election.[48]

Half a year later, Johnson escalated the war another step by launching a massive bombing campaign—Rolling Thunder—against North Vietnam. The goal was to force the enemy to negotiate and thus avoid the need for the United States to engage in mass ground combat, which would surely be costly. Over the next ten weeks, B-52s devastated the North, but American leaders had underestimated the resilience of the enemy.[49]

In the spring of 1965, SDS called an Easter march demanding that the United States withdraw its troops from Vietnam. The conflict, it proclaimed, is "causing untold harm to the people of Vietnam and is also damaging American democracy."[50] At this time, the central challenge faced by the nascent antiwar movement[51] was to persuade the American people that the United States had made a mistake and that it was better to admit the mistake than to pursue indefinitely a war that was at once futile and unjust.[52]

War critics began to pose fundamental questions about America's political, military, and strategic aims in Vietnam, and whether they were attainable. They asked whether the United States should pursue unilateral military action in Vietnam, or whether it should stay its hand in the absence of multinational cooperation. And they questioned whether it was moral for the United States to inflict such suffering on the Vietnamese people in order to achieve its own military and strategic goals.

These were legitimate and important issues, but there was no real public debate over them. The administration did not regard its policy in Vietnam as open to question, and the president did not want debate on the war to deflect energy from his Great Society, the core priority of his administration. Johnson particularly feared, as he later put it, that a congressional debate on "that bitch of a war" would destroy "the woman [he] really loved—the Great Society."[53]

As a practical matter, Johnson became president without having any notion of a foreign policy. Early in his presidency, an aide remarked, "He wishes the rest of the world would go away and we could get ahead with the real needs of Americans."[54] In the fall of 1963, John Kennedy had sent Henry Cabot Lodge to Vietnam with instructions to bring back a frank assessment of the situation. Lodge grimly concluded that the government of South Vietnam was in dire straits. Because Kennedy was assassinated before Lodge could deliver his report, Lodge reported to Johnson instead. The new president, unsure of himself and of his relationship with the American people, responded, "I am not going to be the President who saw Southeast Asia go the way China went." And, on that note, Lodge's candid assessment was dismissed out of hand.[55]

Like John Adams, Abraham Lincoln, Woodrow Wilson, Franklin Roosevelt, and Harry Truman, Lyndon Johnson feared that war opponents in the United States were harming American interests by raising false hopes among the enemy that the United States would weaken and eventually disengage from the conflict. Johnson refused to criticize—let alone *prosecute*—his detractors, however, because most of his fiercest opponents on the war issue, like Senators George McGovern, Frank Church, and Mike Mansfield, were among the strongest supporters of his domestic program. Administration officials therefore did not respond to criticisms of the war, other than to suggest that critics did not understand the full complexity of the situation.[56]

The Johnson administration's guarded response to its critics also reflected a fundamental change in America's constitutional culture. In 1798, the Federalists successfully prosecuted Congressman Matthew Lyon for criticizing the nation's war policies, and during World War I the United States successfully prosecuted the leader of the Socialist Party, Eugene Debs, who had received a million votes for the presidency in 1912, sentencing him to ten years in prison. It is impossible, however, to imagine the president of the United States in 1963 initiating—or even *contemplating*—a criminal prosecution of George McGovern or Frank Church for his opposition to the war in Vietnam. Gradually, over 165 years and several wars, America's understanding of free speech and its commitment to open public debate, even in wartime, had changed profoundly.

On the other hand, like his predecessors, particularly Adams, Wilson, and Truman, Johnson portrayed the war to the American people as a straightforward moral contest between ruthless enemy aggression and the just cause of liberty. It was a simple matter of right and wrong. If direct censorship was no longer available to silence critics, secrecy, deceit, and half-truths still remained effective weapons in the government's propaganda arsenal. By maintaining tight control over information, being less than forthright in its reports, and constantly overstating its achievements and downplaying its failures, the administration avoided alarming the public over the increasing likelihood that "a major war was in the offing."[57]

As always, though, there was a limit to how long the government could mislead the people. Despite the relentless pounding of enemy targets, the military situation continued to deteriorate, and in April 1965 the president announced that he would have to send an additional forty thousand troops to Vietnam.[58] As skepticism mounted and criticism intensified, the administration found itself increasingly unable to sustain its fictions. In June, it admitted for the first time that American soldiers were directly involved in the ground war.

Johnson then made a pivotal decision. On July 23, at a meeting at Camp David, he received what turned out to be prescient advice from Clark Clifford, one of his closest advisers: "I don't believe we can win in South Vietnam. If we send in 100,000 men, the North Vietnamese will meet us. If North Vietnam runs out of men, the Chinese will send in volunteers. Russia and China don't intend for us to win the war. I can't see anything but catastrophe for my country."[59]

Johnson dismissed Clifford's advice, as he had earlier disregarded Lodge's. As any observer of Johnson knew, he did not respond well to such challenges, and with his hackles up he announced later that month that American forces in Vietnam would be augmented by another 50,000 troops, bringing the total to 125,000.[60] He added that, to meet this demand, draft calls would be increased. He explained to the American people that this increase was necessary in order "to convince the Communists that we cannot be defeated by force of arms."[61]

Johnson asked for the public's support, and he received it, much as Americans had responded patriotically to similar calls in 1798, 1861, 1917, 1941, and 1950. In 1965, some 67 percent of all Americans supported the president's policy in Vietnam.[62] But the mood was one of resignation rather than enthusiasm, and there were the first rumblings about a "credibility gap."[63] Johnson, who at his best could be remarkably open, optimistic, and accessible, began to see doubters as critics and critics as traitors. Increasingly, there was "no way to reach him . . . other than to pledge total loyalty." Cornered by circumstances, knowing "what he was in for," unable to admit he had made a mistake, Johnson would desperately plunge ahead, with no plan and no strategy, other than not to "lose."[64]

WITH THE CONTINUING ESCALATION of the war, the opposition grew more intense. In March 1965, professors at the University of Michigan initiated a new form of protest—the teach-in. More than three thousand students and faculty members participated in lectures, debates, and discussions about the war. Within a week, similar events took place on 35 campuses; by the end of the academic year, the idea had spread to more than 120 colleges and universities across the nation.[65]

On April 17, an SDS-sponsored event in Washington drew 20,000 demonstrators. Joan Baez, Phil Ochs, and Judy Collins sang; I. F. Stone, Staughton Lynd, and Senator Ernest Gruening addressed the crowd; and marchers presented proposals at the Capitol calling for an end to the war.[66] In May, more than 20,000 people participated in a marathon teach-in at the University of California at Berkeley. The following month, 18,000 people attended an antiwar rally in Madison Square Garden.[67] An interfaith delegation of Christian and Jewish clergy visited Washington to appeal for peace, and other religious leaders called for a new Geneva conference to bring about an end to the conflict.[68]

At the same time, sharp divisions were already cleaving the antiwar movement. The larger, "liberal" group, represented by Wayne Morse, Benjamin Spock, and Walter Lippmann, advocated a gradual withdrawal of American troops and a negotiated peace. To them, the central problem was the war, which they questioned by conventional means. The much smaller, but more vocal, "radical" group, represented by SDS, demanded an immediate and full withdrawal of American troops. Its spokespersons held that the American action in Vietnam was merely symptomatic of more serious ills, and they continued to argue that fundamental change was essential if the nation was honestly to address the broader issues of race, class, poverty, power, wealth, and injustice.[69]

A major challenge for those who opposed the war, especially those in the liberal faction, was how to criticize the nation's policy without providing, or seeming to provide, "aid and comfort to the enemy." Like their predecessors, opponents of the war in Vietnam were vilified as traitors or dupes who were (intentionally or unintentionally) encouraging the enemy.*[70] Senator Thomas Dodd of Connecticut castigated antiwar demonstrations as "tantamount to open insurrection,"[71] and Senator Richard Russell of Georgia charged dissenters with

---

* The danger that the antiwar movement would be tarred as "Communist" played a major role in the debates over whether antiwar activities should include Communists. Longtime activists like A. J. Muste, who had seen countless lives destroyed by anti-Communist witch hunts, worried that if the antiwar movement were smeared as Communist it would quickly be discredited and squelched. This question bitterly divided the "old guard," who were inclined to exclude Communists, and the New Left, who favored a "non-exclusionary" policy. Until 1965, SDS excluded Communists, but that summer it decided to take a more open approach and eliminated its anti-Communist exclusion clause. See Zaroulis and Sullivan, *Who Spoke Up?* at 39–40 (cited in note 11); Sale, *SDS* at 210–11 (cited in note 26).

disloyalty because "[e]very protest will cause the Communists to believe they can win if they hold on a little longer."[72]

In the face of such accusations, the historian Henry Steele Commager argued that the charge of aiding the enemy was "a form of blackmail" intended to smother all debate over the war. Another war critic cleverly turned the argument around, explaining that dissenters protested the government's war policy, "not because we are 'anti-American,' but because the government is."[73]

Because Lyndon Johnson did not want to risk dividing the Democratic Party, he and his administration continued publicly to tolerate dissent. Privately, though, Johnson wondered, "How can an American Senator or an American newspaperman or an American student tie the hands of our fellow American military men? Are they duped; are they sucked in?"[74]

Johnson's view of dissent was very much shaped by his own experience in the Senate. On matters of foreign policy, he had come to believe that the president needed to be virtually "unassailable." He insisted that, when the safety of the nation was at stake, the people and their elected representatives should support the president and not publicly question or criticize his decisions. During the years when Johnson led the Democrats in the Senate, he took "great pride" in following this position even during Eisenhower's presidency. Recalling those years, Johnson later observed, "People said to me, 'Why don't you get up and criticize?' I replied, 'We ought not to do anything that might be misunderstood by foreign countries. He is the only President we have, and I am going to support that President, because if I make him weaker I make America weaker.'"[75]

As the Vietnam War wore on, Johnson's discomfort with public criticism of his policies became increasingly evident. He believed in the *right* to dissent, but he "did not believe that it should be exercised."[76] He was also acutely aware, however, of the risks of suppression. At a cabinet meeting, he expressed his deeply felt concerns about the danger of triggering another witch hunt: "We are confronted with a dilemma . . . as a result of the extremes of McCarthyism. . . . You immediately become a dangerous character or suspect if you express strong feelings about our system. . . . I don't want us to get into that dangerous situation. I love this system. . . ."[77]

SOME ELEMENTS OF THE PUBLIC were less tolerant. As in the Civil War, when individuals could literally buy their way out of the draft, the issue of military service generated sharp class distinctions, which predictably spilled over into divisions over questions of loyalty and dissent. During the Vietnam War, most sons of the affluent and the middle class, taking advantage of a broad range of educational and occupational deferments, managed to avoid being drafted or, at the least, being assigned to ground combat. The sons of blue-collar families, on the other hand, were much more likely to serve in the military and die in Vietnam.

Perhaps ironically, then, it was the children of the affluent and the middle class who most vehemently opposed the war, and the blue-collar community that most actively supported it. One might assume that those whose lives were most directly at risk would be the first to oppose a war, but the opposite is often the case. At least in the early stages of a conflict, those whose sons and daughters, friends and neighbors, are most in peril are most likely to support the military mission, for that is the only way to comprehend and to justify the potential sacrifice.

These class tensions were evident as early as 1965, when antiwar protests provoked hostile, sometimes violent responses. Peace marchers in New York were pelted with fists, eggs, and red paint; antiwar demonstrators in Cleveland were challenged by counterdemonstrators who provoked fights and burned an antiwar banner; and David Miller, the first person publicly to burn his draft card in protest against a new federal statute making draft card burning a criminal offense, was attacked by an angry mob. Hostility to the antiwar movement was so intense that in 1965 one-third of Americans believed that citizens had no right to protest the war. The *Nation* warned, "Let the hysteria expand, and it will be surprising if they do not regard all opposition as traitorous."[78]

The government began to take a more active role in promoting such divisions. On the eve of a planned nationwide protest scheduled for October 15–16, 1965, the staff of the Senate Internal Security Committee issued a report alleging that the antiwar movement was controlled by "communist and extremist elements who are openly sympathetic to the Vietcong and openly hostile to the United States."[79] After the event, which attracted 100,000 demonstrators, Johnson's press secretary publicly expressed the president's concern that "even well-meaning demonstrators can become the victims of communist" manipulation and his surprise that any "citizen would feel toward his country in a way that is not consistent with the national interest."[80]

As the year wore on, Johnson grew more and more convinced that "opponents of his Vietnam policy were part of an international Communist conspiracy."[81] He was sure that one of the "gut reasons" for the liberal opposition to his Vietnam policy was that they had "just plain been taken in." By 1966, he was openly speculating that the Russians were feeding information and questions to antiwar senators. As a consequence, he encouraged the CIA to expand its domestic intelligence operation in an attempt to uncover major connections between foreign agents and domestic dissenters.[82]

"A MOVEMENT CANNOT GROW WITHOUT REPRESSION"

TELEVISION INFLUENCED PUBLIC OPINION in a way that had never previously been encountered. Daily coverage brought home to Americans vivid images of the devastating effects of American bombing and, especially, of napalm, which horribly burned Vietnamese civilians. War critics denounced the administration for its indifference to the plight of innocent victims. Moreover, the daily images of wounded American soldiers and rows of American body bags began to take their toll. On August 5, 1966, CBS televised one of the first truly graphic documentaries on the war. The next morning, a furious Lyndon Johnson called the CBS president, Frank Stanton: "Frank, are you trying to fuck me? Frank, this is your president and yesterday your boys shat on the American flag."[83]

By mid-1966, public approval of the president's handling of the war had fallen below 50 percent, and one in three Americans felt that U.S. intervention in Vietnam had been a mistake. Polls showed that most Americans wanted "to honor" the nation's commitment to the South Vietnamese, but also wanted "to see the war come to an honorable end as rapidly as possible."[84] During 1966, the number of American soldiers in Vietnam rose from 200,000 to almost 400,000. Predictions of imminent victory continued to flow from the administration, but they increasingly lacked credibility.[85] The *New Republic* observed, "[T]he public is tired and sick of Vietnam, and we feel the thing is approaching some kind of a showdown."[86]

AS IN THE CIVIL WAR and World War I, the ever growing draft calls added to the public's concern. Young men and their families began to question why they should put their lives on the line for a war whose purposes were unclear. Opposition to the draft among African Americans became particularly acute as they asked why they should die for a nation that refused to recognize their civil rights. In 1966, the Student Nonviolent Coordinating Committee (SNCC), an organization dedicated to protecting the civil rights of African Americans, became the first significant group outside the antiwar movement to express its sympathy for draft resistance. SNCC explained, as the military reluctantly conceded, that the draft and the war had had an especially severe impact on blacks, who were being killed in Vietnam disproportionately to other Americans. A poem circulating in the black community in Mississippi ended with the lines "Maybe the people in Vietnam / can't register to vote / Just like us."[87]

Anti-LBJ Demonstration

The refrain "We won't go" began to echo across college campuses, and for the first time resistance to the draft became a significant strategy in opposing the war.[*] Recognizing that this was a natural issue for an organization of *students*, SDS pledged in December 1966 to oppose conscription and support draft resistance.[88]

David Dellinger, Tom Hayden, Staughton Lynd, and other antiwar dissidents visited Vietnam. They came back convinced of the horrifying impact of the war on the Vietnamese people and of the growing hatred of the Vietnamese for the United States. When they reported these observations, they, as well as more neu-

---

[*] An event that heightened student awareness of the war was the government's decision in the spring of 1966 to consider academic achievement in deciding who to draft. The goal was to "rank students according to scholastic ability so that the least successful might be drafted." Faculty members and students at many colleges and universities protested this policy, in part because it distorted and corrupted the academic mission. To circumvent the policy, some faculty members threatened to give A's to all of their students (or all of their *men* students). The Selective Service created an even greater uproar when it announced that it planned to give all draft-eligible college students a standardized test and to revoke the college deferment of all students who did not pass. Ferber and Lynd, *Resistance* at 38–41 (cited in note 14). See also Zaroulis and Sullivan, *Who Spoke Up?* at 85–86 (cited in note 11).

tral observers, such as *New York Times* editor Harrison Salisbury, were condemned as dupes of Hanoi.[89] The House Un-American Activities Committee issued a report charging that the antiwar movement was sustained by Communist influence.[90] In response, Senator William Fulbright of Arkansas warned that Johnson's policy in Vietnam was generating a new "war fever." Senator Goldwater denounced Fulbright for giving "aid and comfort" to the enemy. A Mississippi church was burned to the ground after it hosted an antiwar prayer vigil, and the headquarters of an antiwar group in Berkeley was bombed.[91]

SOUTH VIETNAMESE *CIVILIAN* CASUALTIES were averaging two thousand per week by early 1967. The journalist Jonathan Schell wrote in the *New Yorker*, "We are destroying, seemingly by inadvertence, the very country we are supposedly protecting." Although most Americans still supported the war, and were prepared to see it go on for some time, popular approval of the president's handling of the war fell to a new low of 43 percent.[92]

In February 1967, Martin Luther King Jr. came out publicly against the war, calling upon dissenters to bring to the antiwar movement "the fervor of the civil rights movement." In a speech in New York's Riverside Church on April 4, King described the U.S. government as "the greatest purveyor of violence in the world today" and urged "every man of humane convictions" to protest this war.[93] Within the White House, there was talk that King had "thrown in with the commies."[94]

On April 15, 1967, antiwar demonstrators participated in the long-anticipated Spring Mobilization to End the War in Vietnam.[95] Hundreds of thousands of people marched peacefully against the war in cities across the nation. As many as 200,000 demonstrated in New York; more than 50,000, in San Francisco. The protests were much larger than even the planners had hoped.[96] The government, however, had decided to undermine the event even before it began. Shortly before April 15, HUAC issued a report warning that the Spring Mobilization had been planned "primarily by communists," the president made public the fact that the FBI was "keeping an eye" on antiwar activities, and Secretary of State Dean Rusk asserted that the "world-wide communist apparatus is working very hard" to instigate and plan the antiwar demonstrations.*[97]

---

* The following months saw even more questionable actions. Postmaster General Lawrence O'Brien banned a magazine from the mail on the ground that it encouraged black soldiers to "sabotage operations" in Vietnam. In June 1970, a federal court declared this action illegal. See Goldstein, *Political Repression* at 438 (cited in note 30). Los Angeles police attacked peaceful

IN THE FALL OF 1967, a group of forty peace activists met in Bratislava, Czechoslovakia, with representatives of the North Vietnamese and the National Liberation Front. The Vietnamese showed graphic photographs of the suffering of the Vietnamese people and told moving stories of courageous resistance to overwhelming American firepower. The American activists, including Tom Hayden and Rennie Davis, came back parroting what they had heard, without appreciating the extent to which they had been manipulated.[98] These contacts with the enemy infuriated the American government, angered most of the American public, and fragmented the antiwar movement, which now divided sharply into radicals, who endorsed the North Vietnamese position that the United States must unilaterally withdraw from Vietnam, and liberals, who advocated a measured withdrawal combined with negotiations.[99]

The greatest challenge to the antiwar movement in 1967, however, was neither internal division nor repression by the administration, but the seeming apathy of the political center. Although popular support for the president's handling of the war continued to fall, and 75 percent of Americans thought the nation had "bumbled" into a bigger war than anyone had imagined possible, most Americans still had no idea what to do about their concerns. They did not want a prolonged war, but nor did they want to desert the South Vietnamese. Increasingly, they were attracted to the idea of a gradual withdrawal, tied to a strengthening of the South Vietnamese army so it could continue the war on its own.[100]

The New Left, however, had begun to lose patience with efforts to change the government's position by building public opinion. As Tom Hayden noted, "the establishment does not listen to public opinion."[101] The more radical elements of the antiwar movement shifted toward resistance and confrontation. In

---

demonstrators, clubbing protesters and bystanders alike, sending at least forty people to the hospital. See Cray, *Enemy in the Streets* at 228–33 (cited in note 121); Skolnick, *Politics of Protest* at 247 (cited in note 112); Zaroulis and Sullivan, *Who Spoke Up?* at 119 (cited in note 11). When the Women's Strike for Peace announced its intent to rally in front of the White House, the Department of the Interior declared that no more than one hundred persons could picket the gate of the White House at one time. The WSP defiantly picketed the White House en masse and went head to head with the police, pushing the police line, crawling between officers' legs and trampling the fence. See Swerdlow, *"Not My Son"* at 168 (cited in note 20). A few hours before another antiwar protest, President Johnson signed a law banning protests on Capitol Hill, leading to the arrest of demonstrators who attempted peacefully to read the names of American soldiers who had died in Vietnam. The law was subsequently held unconstitutional. See Goldstein, *Political Repression* at 439 (cited in note 30).

the spring of 1967, SDS members popularized the phrase "From Protest to Resistance" in order to capture the growing view that "they had moved into a deeper and riskier commitment" to ending the war.[102] They had learned from the civil rights movement that there was power in polarization. Jerry Rubin argued, "[A] movement cannot grow without repression. The Left needs an attack from the Right and the Center. Life is theater, and we are the guerillas attacking the shrines of authority."[103]

One way to enlist moral courage, create "theater," and provoke repression was to resist the draft. In 1967, support gathered for a national "We won't go!" initiative. Students at Yale, Stanford, Princeton, Brown, Chicago, Cornell, Wisconsin, and more than twenty other campuses began organizing draft resistance as an expression of opposition to the "immorality" of the war. Proponents of this tactic forcefully advocated their position:

> The armies of the United States have, through conscription, already oppressed or destroyed the lives and consciences of millions of Americans and Vietnamese. We have argued and demonstrated to stop this destruction. We have not succeeded. Murderers do not respond to reason. Powerful resistance is now demanded: radical, illegal, unpleasant, sustained. . . . We are ready to put ourselves on the line for this position. . . .[104]

The students were supported in this initiative by a number of leading writers and intellectuals, including Mary McCarthy, Arthur Miller, and Norman Mailer, who argued that public apathy could be addressed only by decisive and dramatic action. Recalling the failure of intellectuals to oppose World War I, they urged academic leaders to expose the government's deceptions and resist illegitimate authority.[105]

Beginning in 1967, some 5,000 young men turned in their draft cards in public demonstrations. Over the next several years, more than 25,000 men were indicted for draft offenses, of whom 8,750 were convicted and 3,250 were sentenced to prison.[106]

IN THE SPRING OF 1967, the leaders of the Spring Mobilization began to plan a new series of events for October—the National Mobilization to End the War in Vietnam, or Mobe. SDS, which had grown disillusioned with such protests, opposed the Mobe because "these large demonstrations . . . have no significant effect on American policy" and, even worse, delude citizens into "thinking that the 'democratic' process in America functions in a meaningful way."[107]

As plans for the Mobe moved forward, the summer of 1967 saw increasing racial violence in America's cities. There were constant clashes between urban blacks and local police, many involving fire bombings, lootings, and sniper fire. In July, 4,700 U.S. paratroopers were called into Detroit to help national guardsmen quell a riot that resulted in forty-three deaths. The Black Panther leader H. Rap Brown warned that what had happened in Detroit would "look like a picnic" compared with what was coming later, and Stokely Carmichael urged black Americans on to "total revolution."[108] The United States was in the midst of the worst civil violence in fifty years.[109]

Anguished by the race riots and fearful that his Great Society was collapsing around him, Lyndon Johnson announced that another 55,000 men would be sent to Vietnam, bringing the total to 525,000. By October, Johnson's approval rating on his handling of the war had fallen to 28 percent.[110] More Democratic Party leaders came out against the war, and twenty-six prominent Catholic intellectuals proclaimed that Christians were "morally obliged to . . . oppose this war."[111] The calls for civil disobedience, especially refusal of induction, gained steam. On October 16, some 1,100 young men destroyed or turned in their draft cards. The following day, 3,500 protesters attempted to shut down an Army induction center in Oakland, California, triggering a police response that sent 20 protesters to the hospital.[112]

In planning for the October Mobe, David Dellinger enlisted Jerry Rubin to head up the event. Not yet thirty years of age, Rubin had studied at Oberlin, started a promising career in journalism, moved to Jerusalem to study sociology at Hebrew University, participated in the Berkeley Free Speech Movement, traveled unlawfully to Cuba, interviewed Che Guevara, organized major antiwar demonstrations in California, and mocked American capitalism by entering the balcony of the New York Stock Exchange with Abbie Hoffman and throwing money onto the floor of the exchange, leading stockbrokers to scramble wildly (in front of television cameras) to gather the falling dollar bills.

Dellinger's goal in recruiting Rubin was to reinvigorate the antiwar movement and infuse it with the more radical (and sometimes zany) politics of the younger activists. He saw in Rubin a creative tactician who could appeal to young people's imaginations. Dellinger understood that this was a gamble. He was attempting to meld deeply committed and intensely political antiwar protesters with counterculture types who were more inclined to "Turn On, Tune In, Drop Out." The committed activists viewed "hippies" as self-centered and self-indulgent, whereas the hippies viewed traditional forms of protest as pathetic and futile. Juggling these two often antagonistic forces posed a constant challenge to those who sought to energize and expand the antiwar movement.

By bringing these two communities into alignment, Dellinger helped forge the unique combination of ideological awakening, political responsibility, and cultural creativity that helped give the late 1960s and early 1970s their distinctive place in American history. Ironically, it was a relatively staid, middle-aged pacifist who accomplished this feat.[113]

The first thing Jerry Rubin did after being tapped by Dellinger was recruit his friend Abbie Hoffman. After graduating from Brandeis, Hoffman had become active in the civil rights movement. He was arrested in Mississippi during Freedom Summer, and two years later founded Liberty House in New York, which sold the products of poor people's co-ops in Mississippi. Hoffman maintained that "the first duty of a revolutionary is to get away with it." He and Rubin made a remarkable, if sometimes bizarre, duo. Together, they began to give the Mobe "a counterculture twist." Determined to "exorcise" the military, Hoffman promised that demonstrators would levitate the Pentagon. Their goal was to turn the war itself into a "theater of the absurd" in order to pierce the apathy of the American people.[114]

On October 21, 1967, some 6,000 federal marshals and troops gathered in Washington in anticipation of the event.* More than 100,000 antiwar demonstrators convened at the Lincoln Memorial to hear speeches and sing protest songs with Phil Ochs and Peter, Paul, and Mary. Dellinger then took the microphone and declared, "[T]his is the beginning of a new stage in the American peace movement in which the cutting edge becomes active resistance."[115] Whether he knew what was about to happen next has never been clear.

That afternoon, roughly 50,000 protesters crossed Arlington Memorial Bridge and headed to the Pentagon. They marched under a banner reading "Support Our GIs, Bring Them Home Now!" When they reached the Pentagon, several thousand demonstrators broke through lines set up by federal troops and then refused to leave the Pentagon grounds. The face-off between demonstrators and soldiers was stark, tense, and emotional:

> It is safe to say that the beginning of this confrontation has not been without terror on each side. The demonstrators, all too conscious of what they consider the profound turpitude of the American military . . . are prepared (or altogether unprepared) for any conceivable brutality. . . . On their side, the troops have listened for years to small-town legends about the venality, criminality, filth, corruption, perversion, addiction, and unbridled appetites of that mysterious group of city Americans referred to . . . as hippies; now . . . the troops do not know whether to expect a hairy kiss on their lips or a bomb between their knees. Each side is coming face to face with its own conception of the devil![116]

---

* Once the government announced it was sending in federal marshals and paratroopers to protect the Pentagon, SDS realized that the Mobe might turn into something more than just another mass demonstration. At the last moment, it therefore changed its position and urged its members to participate. See Ferber and Lynd, *Resistance* at 135–36 (cited in note 14).

Some protesters called upon the troops to join them; one young woman "brought her two fingers to her mouth, kissed them and touched [a] soldier's lips"; some demonstrators put flowers in the soldiers' rifle barrels; others urinated on the Pentagon, threw rocks at first-floor windows, and taunted, insulted, and spat upon the soldiers, who stood fixed at attention. Neither side budged. Some time after midnight, new columns of troops—paratroopers—replaced the first group.

The paratroopers carried M-14 rifles, bayonets, and clubs. Paddy wagons pulled up. Suddenly, the soldiers formed a wedge and sliced through the demonstrators, who were sitting, arm-in-arm, in rows. Although the only physical damage caused by the protesters had been a few broken windows, the troops used tear gas, rifle butts, and cudgels to scatter and beat the protesters. By the end of the night, 647 demonstrators had been arrested and 47 hospitalized. The Pentagon remained unlevitated.[*][117]

Five days later, Selective Service Director Lewis Hershey sent a letter to all local draft boards stating that registrants who participated in "illegal demonstrations," interfered with recruiting, or otherwise violated Selective Service regulations would be subject to immediate reclassification and induction. Hershey explained, "Deferments are only given when they serve the national interest. It is obvious that any action that violates the Military Selective Service Act or the Regulations or the related processes cannot be in the national interest."[†][118]

---

[*] Norman Mailer's description is priceless:

Now [I] recognized that this was the beginning of the exorcism of the Pentagon, yes the papers had made much of the permit requested by a hippie leader named Abbie Hoffman to encircle the Pentagon with twelve hundred men in order to form a ring of exorcism sufficiently powerful to raise the Pentagon three hundred feet. In the air the Pentagon would then, went the presumption, turn orange and vibrate until all evil emissions had fled this levitation. At that point the war in Vietnam would end.

Norman Mailer et al, *Reporting Vietnam: American Journalism, 1959–1969* 510 (Library of America 1998).

[†] From December 1, 1967, to December 1, 1968, 537 students who turned in their draft cards lost their student deferments and were deemed eligible for induction as a result of this directive. In one case, an Oklahoma SDS member was reclassified because his draft board determined that it did not feel that his "activity as a member of SDS is to the best interest of the U.S. government." *National Student Association v. Hershey*, 412 F2d 1103, 1118 n 44 (DC Cir 1969). The use of punitive reclassification as a weapon to intimidate war protesters who otherwise qualified for draft exemptions was declared unconstitutional by the Supreme Court in a series of decisions. See, for example, *Oestereich v. Selective Service System*, 393 US 233 (1968); *Gutknecht v. United States*, 396 US 295 (1970); *Breen v. Selective Service System*, 396 US 460 (1970). See also Bannan and Bannan, *Law Morality and Vietnam* at 88 (cited in note 236); Goldstein, *Political Repression* at 439 (cited in note 30); Sale, *SDS* at 406–7 (cited in note 26).

The public reaction to the Mobe was largely critical. NBC nightly news commentator David Brinkley characterized the demonstrators as "coarse" and "vulgar." Barry Goldwater described the demonstration as "hate-filled, anti-American, pro-Communist and violent." Although most Americans were unhappy with the president's handling of the war, they still viewed antiwar demonstrations as "acts of disloyalty against the boys in Vietnam."[119]

But the protests continued. On October 27, Father Philip Berrigan and three other protesters were arrested for pouring blood over draft files in Baltimore as an act of civil disobedience. "Stop the Draft" protests occurred in thirty cities, leading to the arrest of some six hundred people.[120] More and more, the police used nightsticks and blackjacks on demonstrators and onlookers alike. Although protesters often provoked the police by blocking access to buildings and taunting officers, the police response was increasingly angry, indiscriminate, and excessive.[121]

Lyndon Johnson was in anguish. He swore that he was "not going to let the Communists take this government," publicly referred to protesters as "storm troopers," leaked accusations that the CIA had proof that the antiwar movement was directly linked to Communist subversion, and ordered the FBI and CIA to step up their surveillance of dissidents.[122] On November 15, CIA Director Richard Helms submitted a preliminary report to the president on the extent of Communist influence. The report concluded, "On the basis of what we now know, we see no significant evidence that would prove Communist control or direction of the U.S. peace movement or its leaders." Moreover, "[m]ost of the Vietnam protest activity would be there with or without the Communist element." Johnson suppressed the report, and the administration continued to claim publicly that the antiwar movement was Communist directed.[123] The *Christian Century* observed that it was "difficult to think of a moment since the Civil War" when the words "crisis" and "doom" were more appropriate.[124]

THE 1968 CHICAGO DEMOCRATIC NATIONAL CONVENTION: "A SCENE FROM THE RUSSIAN REVOLUTION"

NO SINGLE EVENT OF THE 1960S better dramatized the divisions and anguish of the American people in this era than the 1968 Democratic National Convention. It brought together all the elements of party politics, peaceful dissent, war fever, violent confrontation, police repression, and the unprecedented power of television to draw an entire nation into a moment of breathtaking emotion. No American who watched the remarkable events of that August fails to recall where she was when all hell broke loose in Chicago.

Lyndon Baines Johnson

———————

BEFORE THE END OF 1967, dissent from the war had occurred largely outside the political process. Toward the end of the year, however, Allard Lowenstein and Curtis Gans attempted to recruit a candidate to lead a "Dump Johnson" movement. Senators Frank Church, Robert Kennedy, and George McGovern were reluctant to challenge an incumbent president of their own party, but the "Dump Johnson" group persuaded Senator Eugene McCarthy of Minnesota to mount the challenge. On November 30, 1967, McCarthy, a witty, genteel poet, who had been passed over by Johnson for the 1964 vice-presidential nomination, announced his candidacy for the Democratic presidential nomination, promising a negotiated end to the conflict in Vietnam.[125]

McCarthy was given no chance to unseat the president. But on January 30, 1968, on the eve of Tet, the Vietnamese lunar New Year, Communist forces launched a massive assault throughout South Vietnam that shocked both American military experts and the American public. Until Tet, the Vietcong and the North Vietnamese army had fought in the jungles and paddies. Now, for the first time, they attacked in the cities. By the end of February, more than 1,100 Americans and 2,300 South Vietnamese soldiers had been killed, along with some 12,000 South Vietnamese civilians.

Although the Tet offensive eventually was repulsed, and was not viewed as a military success by the enemy, the ferocity of the attack undermined the credibility of Johnson administration claims that U.S. forces were in control of the country, that the North Vietnamese and the Vietcong no longer had the capacity to wage anything but a hit-and-run war, and that the war was drawing to a close. Ever more disturbing images filtered into American living rooms, including the horrifying photograph of a Saigon police officer casually shooting in the head a hand-tied young man who had been identified as a member of the Vietcong. James Reston of the *New York Times* pointedly asked, "What is the end that justifies this slaughter?"[126] Reflecting the nation's growing sense of despair, Walter Cronkite wondered, "What the hell is going on? I thought we were winning the war."[127]

By late February, Eugene McCarthy's campaign in the New Hampshire primary had begun to gain momentum. Thousands of young volunteers helped distribute literature and man phone banks. On March 12, McCarthy received 42 percent of the Democratic vote, a result that stunned most Americans. McCarthy had proved that Johnson was vulnerable. Several days later, Senator Robert Kennedy of New York, who had long privately criticized Johnson's policy in Vietnam, announced that he, too, would seek the Democratic presidential nomination.

In the White House, Johnson sank into a depression, commenting plaintively to friends, "[T]he only difference between the Kennedy assassination and mine is that I am alive and it has been more torturous."[128] Secretary of Defense Clark Clifford, an old Washington hand who had just replaced Robert McNamara, added to the president's woes. Clifford informed Johnson that there had been "a tremendous erosion of support" for the war among national opinion leaders, who had concluded that "we are in a hopeless bog."[129] These leaders had reluctantly reached the conclusion that when it came to Vietnam the nation's military commanders simply do not "know what they're talking about."[130]

Clifford persuaded Johnson to sit down on March 28 with a group of "wise men," experienced advisers who had played key roles in the Truman, Eisenhower, Kennedy, and Johnson administrations, to hear their diagnoses. These men, including Dean Acheson, Cyrus Vance, General Maxwell Taylor, Henry Cabot Lodge, Abe Fortas, and George Ball, counseled the president that the war was "threatening to tear the United States apart."[131] The consensus was that "this thing is hopeless," that the president had "better begin to de-escalate and get out."[132]

Johnson was shocked, but he took their judgment to heart. Three days later, on March 31, 1968, he informed the nation that he had sharply restricted American bombing in North Vietnam and turned down the Pentagon's request for an additional 206,000 American troops. He then stunned millions glued to their televisions by announcing, "I shall not seek, and I will not accept, the nomination of my party for another term as your President." Creating a sense that the American involvement in Vietnam was finally drawing to a close, Johnson promised to devote his remaining nine months in office to the search for peace.[133]

ONLY DAYS AFTER Johnson's announcement, Martin Luther King Jr. was assassinated in Memphis, Tennessee, on April 4. The nation suffered a convulsion of violence, with riots in more than a hundred cities, leading to forty-six deaths and more than 200,000 arrests. Chicago's Mayor Richard Daley ordered police to "shoot to kill" arsonists on the city's burning West Side.[134]

On April 23 came the mass student occupation of buildings at Columbia University to protest the university's war-related research and its treatment of the surrounding black community. This event marked a turning point in the nature of student protest. For the first time, students fully occupied a university building; for the first time, they passed the bounds of civility, using profanity, smoking the president's cigars, and destroying university files; and for the first time, police were called in to evict and arrest student demonstrators with the use of force.[135]

Moreover, for the first time, universities themselves came to be seen by antiwar protesters as part of the nation's power structure and thus part of the problem. Richard Nixon, a candidate for the Republican presidential nomination, decried the Columbia event as "a national disgrace" and condemned "those professors who fawn on student violence."[136] Columbia became the model of what was to come.[137]

By then, the Vietnam War was already the longest war in American history. American combat deaths now numbered more than thirty thousand.[138] During the week of the Columbia protest, Vice President Hubert Humphrey announced his candidacy for the Democratic presidential nomination, calling for an end of the war without "humiliation or defeat."[139] The candidates battled through a series of bitter primary contests in search of delegates for the upcoming Democratic National Convention in Chicago. Then, on June 6, after winning the California primary, Robert Kennedy was assassinated. The nation "sagged in ghastly stillness, as though the last lines of reason had been breached."[140]

MEANWHILE, THE LEFT WING of the antiwar movement shattered. SDS had grown from 10,000 members in 1965 to more than 80,000 in 1968, but it was torn apart by internal factionalism.[141] Angry and impatient after years of seemingly futile protest, the more radical elements of the New Left fell into a spasm of nihilism and embraced tactics that were increasingly ugly, violent, and counterproductive. They began sporting buttons proclaiming, "Victory to the National Liberation Front," waving the NLF flag, and shouting, "Ho, Ho, Ho Chi Minh / The NLF is gonna win."[142] As the SDS member Todd Gitlin recalled, "It no longer felt sufficient—sufficiently estranged, sufficiently furious—to say no to aggressive war; we felt driven to say yes to revolt." Although the radicals represented only a small fraction of the antiwar movement, they garnered a highly disproportionate share of media attention and infuriated mainstream America.[143]

By this time, the only ally SDS had left in the traditional antiwar leadership was David Dellinger, who continued to try to shepherd SDS, the counterculture forces, and the more moderate faction of the movement in the same direction. Dellinger later recalled this as "one of the most uphill fights" he had ever had to make.[144] The fractiousness of the antiwar movement led to the founding of the Youth International Party by Jerry Rubin and Abbie Hoffman in early 1968. The "yippies" promised the "politics of ecstasy."

Although the "mainstream" leaders of SDS, such as Dellinger, Tom Hayden, and Rennie Davis, hoped to organize a peaceful demonstration in Chicago,

Rubin and Hoffman were determined to "overcome war madness with comic relief" and to disrupt the Democratic National Convention with a "Political Circus"—replete with dancing bears and a 150-pound pig named Pigasus that would be nominated for the presidency and then devoured."[145] Their goal was to entice thousands of young people to Chicago in August to hold a "Festival of Life" in opposition to the "Convention of Death."[146] They would blend "pot and politics" and "burn Chicago to the ground." Rubin and Hoffman captured the imagination of the media, who took them more seriously than they deserved.[147]

Hoping to keep protesters out of Chicago, Mayor Richard M. Daley refused to grant any parade or park permits to demonstrators and armed the city to the teeth. The Chicago Amphitheatre, the site of the Democratic National Convention, was surrounded with barbed wire, all twelve thousand Chicago police officers were placed on twelve-hour shifts, more than five thousand national guardsman were mobilized, a thousand FBI agents were dispersed throughout the city, and six thousand U.S. Army troops, equipped with flamethrowers, bazookas, and bayonets, were stationed in the suburbs.

Daley's intimidation worked. Most people who had planned to come to Chicago to protest the war stayed away. The threat of violence was too great for most citizens who wanted only to express their views, not to get beaten or gassed. Only three or four thousand demonstrators showed up on the day the convention opened. But those who came were determined to have their say, even if it meant a confrontation.[148]

Hayden, Dellinger, and Davis reassured the media that their goal was not to interfere with the Convention, but they acknowledged that, if attacked by Daley's police, the demonstrators would defend themselves.[149] The yippies, on the other hand, baited the media and the mayor with absurd threats and fantastic predictions. They said they would set off smoke bombs in the convention hall, release greased pigs, paint cars to make them look like taxis in order to kidnap delegates, have yippie women pose as prostitutes to entrap delegates, and burn draft cards in a huge display that would read "Beat Army." When Abbie Hoffman and Jerry

---

* On Wednesday, August 18, in Grant Park, Jerry Rubin formally nominated Pigasus:

The Republican Party has nominated a pig for President and a pig for Vice-President. The Democratic Party is going to nominate a pig for President and a pig for Vice-President. And our campaign slogan is 'Why take half a hog when you can have the whole hog.' And so we're nominating a pig for President. We're requesting Secret Service protection. Our pig promises to run on the following principles, the same principle this country has always been governed on—garbage.

Dellinger, *From Yale to Jail* at 333 (cited in note 11).

Rubin announced they would slip LSD into the city's water supply, Mayor Daley ordered twenty-four-hour-a-day police protection of the city's reservoirs. When Hoffman mockingly suggested that he would call off the yippie protests for $100,000, the *Chicago Tribune* headlined, "Yippies Demand Cash from City."[150]

The "Battle of Chicago" began on the night of Sunday, August 25, when 150 police officers dispersed a demonstrators' encampment in Lincoln Park with nightsticks, mace, and tear gas. The justification for the police action was that the demonstrators lacked a park permit, which had been denied by the city. On Monday night, the protesters returned and challenged the police with taunts, rocks, verbal abuse (calling the police "pigs," "fascists," and "fuckers"), and a hit-and-run retreat through the streets along Lincoln Park. On Tuesday night, when anti-war demonstrators held an "unbirthday party" for Lyndon Johnson, Chicago police officers removed their badges and attacked protesters, reporters, and onlookers with clubs and mace.[151]

Meanwhile, four miles to the south, the convention met under tight security in an atmosphere that felt to Allard Lowenstein like that of "a police state."[152] Norman Mailer described it as one of "the bitterest, the most violent, the most disorderly, most painful" political conventions in American history.[153] On Wednesday night, August 28, the convention rejected a peace plank proposing a bombing halt, mutual withdrawal, and efforts to encourage the South Vietnamese to negotiate with the Vietcong.

Frustrated and furious, a crowd of between five and ten thousand gathered in Grant Park, across Michigan Avenue from the Chicago Hilton, where many of the delegates were staying. Police officers formed a wedge and marched into the crowd, clubbing. Some demonstrators fought back; most tried to find some way to escape. Dellinger attempted to rally the protesters to participate in a nonviolent march toward the Amphitheatre, but the police and National Guard blocked the way. A distraught Hayden grabbed a microphone and shouted, "This city and the military machinery it has aimed at us won't permit us to protest in an organized fashion. Therefore, we must move out of this park . . . and turn this overheated military machine against itself. Let us make sure that if blood flows, it flows all over the city. If they use gas against us, let us make sure they use gas against their own citizens."[154]

The crowd, sealed off on three sides, tried to escape to the north, but the National Guard blocked the way, beat panic-stricken demonstrators with rifle butts, and sprayed vast clouds of tear gas. In front of the Hilton, two phalanxes of police officers scythed into the crowd, smashing heads, yelling, "Kill, kill, kill." The terrified crowd crashed through the front windows of the hotel and scampered over the broken glass to try to escape the police, who chased them into the Hilton to club and beat them.

Theodore White's description of the scene is worth quoting at length:

Dusk has now closed and in the dark [there is a] triple-ranked police formation, lined up quietly in varying shades of blue, their billy-clubs held at rest across their thighs . . . [The demonstrators] yell to the cops "Hey, Hey, Go Away." . . .

[Then, like] a fist jolting, like a piston exploding from its chamber, comes a hurtling column of police. . . . And as the scene clears, there are . . . police clubbing youngsters, police dragging youngsters, police rushing them by the elbows, their heels dragging, to patrol wagons. . . . It is a scene from . . . the Russian Revolution. . . . There are splotches of blood. . . . [Demonstrators] in the front . . . rank kneel, with arms folded across their breasts. They take up a song, "America the Beautiful." . . . A commotion explodes in the front rank; one sees the clubs coming down. . . . There is much blood now. . . . The chants change . . . to "The Whole World is Watching."[155]

Norman Mailer later recalled that it was a "murderous paradigm of Vietnam."[156] The entire "Kafkaesque" scene was televised live to a shocked nation. More than 1,000 people, including 192 policemen and 65 newsmen, were injured and 662 were arrested.*[157]

Several months later, the official Walker report concluded that the "violence was made all the more shocking by the fact that it was often inflicted upon persons who had broken no law, disobeyed no order, made no threat. These included peaceful demonstrators, onlookers, and large numbers of residents who were simply passing through, or happened to live in, the areas where confrontations were occurring."[158] I. F. Stone observed, "The war is destroying our country as we are destroying Vietnam."[159] Dellinger later recalled that the conduct of the police in Chicago "helped convince millions of people that the society was falling apart and would not return to normal until the war was ended."[160]

Most Americans, however, accepted the official line that the police had had no choice. Even those who supported withdrawal in Vietnam tended to blame the demonstrators.[161] For the SDS leadership, "Chicago proved once and for all . . . that the country could not be educated or reformed out of its pernicious system." They were now certain that it was time for them to jettison their "fears of being 'too radical' " and to take a "new commitment to revolution directly to the youth of America."[162]

In the meantime, the Democrats nominated Hubert Humphrey and the nation elected Richard Nixon president of the United States.[163]

---

* Inside the convention, Governor Abraham Ribicoff of Connecticut deplored the "Gestapo tactics in the streets of Chicago." Mayor Daley, literally shaking with rage, screamed on national television that Ribicoff should go "fuck" himself. With an air of dignity, Ribicoff "leaned down from the podium and said in his most patrician voice, 'How hard it is to accept the truth.'" Mailer, *Siege of Chicago* at 180–81 (cited in note 153). See also Zaroulis and Sullivan, *Who Spoke Up?* at 195–96 (cited in note 11).

1968 Democratic National Convention

Days of Rage, Kent State, and May Day

In his victory statement the morning after the election, Richard Nixon declared that "a great objective" of his administration would be "to bring the American people together." Throughout the 1968 campaign, Nixon had pledged to "end the war," and shortly after assuming office he declared his intention to withdraw American combat forces from Vietnam. He was confident this would defuse dissent at home and soften Ho Chi Minh's intransigence at the negotiating table.[164]

In May 1969, Nixon announced the withdrawal of 25,000 American troops and, at the same time, embraced a policy of "Vietnamization," under which the United States would gradually turn ground combat over to the South Vietnamese. He projected that by the end of 1970 the number of American soldiers in Vietnam would be less than 300,000, down from a high of 543,000 in 1968, and that with these troop reductions he would gradually phase out the draft. Although this strategy was designed to placate the antiwar movement, the proposed pace of American extrication was seen by war opponents as much too slow. Indeed, as it turned out, during the period in which the war actually "wound down," more than 20,000 more Americans and hundreds of thousands of Vietnamese died in Vietnam, and the United States pulverized Indochina with several times the bomb tonnage it had dropped in all of World War II.[165]

With the events surrounding the Chicago Democratic National Convention and the election of Richard Nixon, frustration and anger swelled within the antiwar movement. After years of protest, it had succeeded in replacing Lyndon Johnson, the champion of the Great Society, with Richard Nixon, the quintessential Red baiter of the 1940s and 1950s who exemplified everything the antiwar movement despised. The man who had savaged Helen Gahagan Douglas, conspired with Whittaker Chambers, and defended Joseph McCarthy was now president of the United States.

Not surprisingly, in one of the first major statements of his presidency, Nixon announced a hard-line approach toward dissent, condemning unruly antiwar protests: "It is not too strong a statement to declare that this is the way civilizations begin to die. The process is altogether too familiar to those who would survey the wreckage of history." In a series of graduation speeches, Nixon threatened that it "has not been a lack of civil power, but the reluctance of a free people to employ it, that . . . has stayed the hand of authorities faced with confrontation."[166]

Despite this warning, demonstrations turned more violent. Bombings of ROTC and other campus buildings rose from ten in the spring of 1968 to eighty-four in the spring of 1969. Three hundred colleges and universities experienced seriously disruptive antiwar demonstrations in the spring of 1969, many involving student strikes, building takeovers, and the destruction of property.[167]

A new group at the radical fringe of the antiwar movement now burst upon the scene. Building upon the "romantic" radicalism and image of the Black Panthers, the Weathermen, who split off from SDS in June 1969, declared war not just on the war in Vietnam but on the entire "imperialist system that made war a necessity."* They announced that "sustained armed struggle against the state [was] the best means of creating revolutionary consciousness among the mass of American people."[168] The Weathermen were hip, attractive, and confident. Carl Oglesby described them as having a "Butch Cassidy and Sundance attitude — they were blessed, they were hexed, they would die young, they would live forever." They "made revolution look like fun." At the "core of the Weathermen mystique" was Bernardine Dohrn, who "combined lawyerly articulateness with a sexual charisma."†[169]

---

* The Weathermen took their name from Bob Dylan's line "You don't need a weatherman to know which way the wind blows."

† After graduating from the University of Chicago Law School in 1967, Dohrn became assistant executive secretary of the National Lawyers Guild. At NLG, she was soon involved in the defense of Dr. Spock and the Reverend Coffin in the draft-counseling conspiracy prosecution. She traveled around the country speaking at law schools and encouraging students to support draft resistance. In

The Weathermen condemned the antiwar movement for having "made a secret, unspoken agreement with the ruling class not to struggle beyond certain limits." They were confident they had freed their minds for "a life-or-death revolutionary struggle for power."[170] They issued a call for four "Days of Rage" in Chicago in October 1969 to demonstrate their disdain for the system. Although they expected thousands to join them, only two or three hundred protesters showed up. They were dressed to the hilt, with helmets, goggles, medical kits, chains, and clubs. As Tom Hayden sardonically observed, "[t]hey looked exactly like the people" he and other SDS leaders had been "accused of being."[171]

After preparing themselves with chants of "Ho, Ho, Ho Chi Minh," the Weathermen charged into Chicago's most exclusive neighborhoods waving NLF flags, trashing cars, and breaking windows. By the time the dust and tear gas had settled, the police had shot six Weathermen and arrested 250.[172] Most of the antiwar movement was appalled by these antics, but with their outlaw daring, the Weathermen captivated the imagination of some elements of SDS. "'They're crazy,' one heard, 'but you've got to admit they've got guts.'"[173]

Only a week after the Days of Rage came the immense October 15, 1969, Moratorium. Envisioned as a series of nationwide events in which "predominately moderate and even apolitical types" could participate in expressing their opposition to the war, the idea was "to pause, to hold vigils, to gather quietly in town squares, to have meetings on campuses." Several million Americans took part, without serious incident.[174] Another massive demonstration was planned for mid-November in Washington, D.C.

On November 3, the president addressed the nation. Although this was an opportunity to soothe dissent by focusing on his continuing policy of troop withdrawal, Nixon, following the advice of Attorney General John Mitchell, instead appealed to those Americans who would *not* be demonstrating on November 15. He addressed his remarks to what he termed the "Silent Majority," promising he would not allow "the policy of this nation to be dictated by the minority who . . . try to impose [their view] on the nation by mounting demonstrations in the streets." He added, "North Vietnam cannot defeat or humiliate the United States. Only Americans can do that." This marked a pivotal shift in the president's

---

1968, she became involved in SDS and led an SDS workshop on women's liberation. Her transition from radicalism to militancy was triggered by the assassination of Martin Luther King. Shortly after his murder, she was at the barricades at Columbia. When SDS began to split apart at its June 1968 convention, Dohrn was elected interorganizational secretary of the faction that eventually became the Weathermen. See Sale, SDS at 404–51 (cited in note 26); Garfinkle, *Telltale Hearts* at 167–68 (cited in note 6).

approach. Echoing the worst moments of Adams and Wilson, Nixon now claimed that a foe within the United States was even more dangerous to the national interest than the enemy in Vietnam.[*]

Moreover, instead of reaffirming his program of withdrawal, Nixon directly threatened Hanoi. He warned that if the enemy took any action that "jeopardizes our remaining forces in Vietnam, I shall not hesitate to take strong and effective measures to deal with that situation." Although the speech was a "smash hit" with the Silent Majority, it deeply angered antiwar advocates, who now questioned Nixon's determination to end the war.[†175]

A month later, three-quarters of a million people participated in the November Moratorium in Washington, D.C.—the largest antiwar demonstration in American history. Leading up to the event, Alexander Butterfield, a deputy assistant to the president, sent a memorandum to Nixon setting forth the administra-

---

[*] The extent to which the administration was now prepared to demonize its opponents was made even clearer by Vice President Spiro Agnew. Shortly after the October Moratorium, Agnew castigated those who opposed the war:

A spirit of national masochism prevails, encouraged by an effete corps of impudent snobs who characterize themselves as intellectuals. . . . The recent Vietnam Moratorium is a reflection of the confusion that exists in America today. Thousands of . . . young people . . . saw fit to demonstrate for peace [without stopping] to consider that the leaders of the Moratorium had billed it as a massive public outpouring of sentiment against the foreign policy of the President of the United States. . . .

Several days later, responding to criticism of his remarks, Agnew elaborated,

Small cadres of professional protesters are allowed to jeopardize the peace efforts of the President of the United States. It is time to question the credentials of their leaders. . . . If, in challenging, we polarize the American people, I say it is time for a positive polarization. . . . The mature and sensitive people of this country must realize that their freedom of protest is being exploited by avowed anarchists and communists who detest everything about this country and want to destroy it.

Witcover, *White Knight* at 305, 308–9 (cited in note 187).

[†] It was at this time that the Nixon administration ramped up its attack on the press. After Nixon's speech, many television and newspaper commentators were critical. Vice President Agnew responded to the critics on November 13 in a speech demanding that the television networks, which enjoy "a monopoly sanctioned and licensed by the government," be "made more responsive to the views of the nation." The president's communications director, Herbert Klein, warned that if the media did not eliminate their "bias" against the president, then they will "invite the government to come in." Schell, *Time of Illusion* at 53–56, 67–69 (cited in note 164); Witcover, *White Knight* at 313–14 (cited in note 187). The Nixon administration's effort to intimidate the press escalated throughout this era. See Goldstein, *Political Repression* at 494–97 (cited in note 30).

Richard M. Nixon

tion's plans to counter the Moratorium. The memorandum called for an orchestrated "barrage of wires and letters to the President" supporting his policies; a publicity campaign describing the "undesirable" character of the groups planning to participate in the November event; and an organized effort to persuade Americans that dissenters were giving "aid and comfort to the other side."[176]

Increasingly reflecting the Nixon of the McCarthy era, the administration spread rumors that the November Moratorium had been planned by Communists and was designed to be violent. To scare away protesters, it announced that more than forty thousand federal troops and police officers would be on hand. Justice Department officials resisted the grant of parade and park permits, and the FBI discouraged bus companies from chartering buses to those planning to attend.

On November 13, the first day of the Moratorium, 186 individuals were arrested for "disorderly conduct" while praying peacefully on the Pentagon's public concourse.*[177] Two days later, a massive crowd gathered at the Washington

---

* These convictions were later overturned by a federal court, which held that the government had discriminatorily enforced the regulation prohibiting "disorderly" conduct on government property. See Goldstein, *Political Repression* at 498 (cited in note 30).

Monument. Senators George McGovern of South Dakota and Charles Goodell of New York addressed the audience, Arlo Guthrie and Pete Seeger performed, and a sea of humanity sang "Give Peace a Chance."

Then a group of about two thousand militants, led by Jerry Rubin and Abbie Hoffman, broke away from the larger group to march on the Justice Department. Weathermen, yippies, and other self-proclaimed radicals dispersed throughout the city, carrying NLF flags, throwing rocks, bottles, red paint bombs, and smoke bombs, constructing barricades, and starting fires. Someone raised a Vietcong flag at the Justice Department. Downtown Washington was filled with tear gas.[178] Attorney General Mitchell, viewing the scene from his office, said it "looked like a Russian Revolution." The White House was delighted.[179]

Antiwar protests intensified in violence as the decade drew to a fractious end. From the fall of 1969 to the spring of 1970, at least 250 bombings, about one per day, were directed at ROTC buildings, draft boards, induction centers, other federal offices, and the headquarters of multinational corporations. The goal of these bombings was to "bring the war home."[*] In February 1970, students burned a bank in Santa Barbara, California. One student was killed and two others were wounded by police. In March, twelve students were shot by police in Buffalo during an antiwar demonstration. That same month, three young radicals were killed when their "bomb factory" blew up in a New York City town house. In April, twenty students were wounded during a clash with national guardsmen at Ohio State University. In California, Governor Ronald Reagan, asked about campus militants, said, "If it takes a bloodbath, let's get it over with."[†][180]

---

[*] The Weatherman Bill Ayers described his understanding of this phrase: "We're not just saying bring the troops home . . . we're saying bring the *war* home. We're saying you're going to pay a price because . . . this country is going to be torn down. . . ." Bill Ayers, *A Strategy to Win*, in Jacobs, ed, *Weatherman* at 187–88 (cited in note 168). See also Zaroulis and Sullivan, *Who Spoke Up?* at 301 (cited in note 11).

[†] Reagan's comment followed a "People's Park" disorder at Berkeley during which police banned peaceful marches, made mass arrests, and used tear gas, shotguns, clubs, and bayonets to control demonstrators (who were armed with rocks and bottles), killing one protester, blinding another, and injuring more than two hundred. *Newsweek* wondered "what has happened to America? What has happened to our sense of perspective, our tradition of tolerance, our view of armed force as a last—never a first—resort?" Goldstein, *Political Repression* at 511 (cited in note 30); Harris, *Justice* at 186–87 (cited in note 150).

IN HIS FIRST YEAR IN OFFICE, Richard Nixon had made progress. He could boast that the Communists had lost momentum, the South Vietnamese had moved toward Vietnamization, and he had reduced the number of American forces in Vietnam by 100,000. But in the spring of 1970, he initiated measures in Southeast Asia that put at risk—indeed, shattered—everything he had achieved.[181]

He announced on April 30 that he had ordered American forces to invade Cambodia in order to cut North Vietnamese and Vietcong supply lines. Nixon's speech revealing this decision made even some of his closest advisers "cringe." It was defensive, pugnacious, and strident. He declared that the United States "will not be humiliated" and will not act "like a pitiful helpless giant" when "the forces of totalitarianism and anarchy . . . threaten free nations." He lashed out at Hanoi for ignoring "our warnings," rejecting "every effort to win a just peace," and trampling "on solemn agreements." He attacked the antiwar movement, warning that "here in America great universities are being systematically destroyed." By so polarizing the nation, Nixon not only failed "to bring us together" but crystallized and animated his opposition.[182]

The *New York Times* labeled the Cambodian incursion a "virtual renunciation" of Nixon's pledge to end the war, and the *Wall Street Journal* warned against even "deeper entrapment" in Southeast Asia. More than two hundred State Department employees signed a public petition protesting the bombing of Cambodia.

The president's speech triggered immediate protests that Nixon had *widened* the war. The reaction on Capitol Hill was sharply critical. During a meeting on May 3, Nixon coached his aides to accuse his critics of "giving aid and comfort to the enemy," emphasizing that they should use that precise phrase. He told his staff to "stick it in hard. . . . Hit 'em in the gut."[183] Henry Kissinger later recalled that Nixon was "somewhat overwrought."[184]

Antiwar forces called for a major demonstration in Washington. In the meantime, protests exploded on campuses across the nation. At Kent State University in Ohio, students burned down the ROTC building. Nixon denounced "these bums."[185] Governor James Rhodes condemned the students as "Nazi Storm Troopers." He declared martial law and dispatched units of the National Guard to the Kent State campus. On Monday, May 4, these national guardsmen, without warning, responded to taunts and rock throwing by firing their M-1 rifles into a crowd of students, killing four, wounding thirteen.[186] Vice President Spiro Agnew described the tragedy as "predictable" and warned that "grave dangers . . . accompany the new politics of violence and confrontation."[187]

Student protests erupted on more than half the nation's campuses. Within a few days, 1.5 million students walked out of classes, shutting down a fifth of the nation's colleges and universities. It was the "most massive and shattering protest in the history of American higher education."[*][188] Thirty ROTC buildings were burned or bombed in the first week of May. National Guard units were mobilized in sixteen states. At the University of California at San Diego, a young man, wearing a placard saying, "In the name of God, end the war," doused himself with gasoline and lit a match, burning himself to death.[189]

As the Presidential Commission on Campus Unrest later concluded, this conflict on American campuses had "no parallel in the history of the nation." Reflecting divisions "as deep as any since the Civil War," the enmity between opposing groups had reached alarming proportions. Events surged out of control. It was a "frightening moment." Americans were confronted with television images of hurled rocks, jeering crowds, savage police, and streaming blood. The Pentagon was on alert. Bayonets and tear gas were everywhere. Even businessmen panicked. The stock market suffered its worst week in forty years, sinking to an eight-year low. More violence, more deaths, seemed inevitable.[190]

Thousands of students stormed the nation's capital to lobby for an end to the war. They were joined by more than a thousand lawyers, a hundred corporate leaders, thirty-three university presidents, and a host of professional and civic leaders. Enough, they told Congress, was enough. Henry Kissinger later observed that "the very fabric of government was falling apart. The Executive Branch was shell-shocked. After all, their children and their friends' children took part in the demonstrations."[191]

On short notice, more than 100,000 people gathered in the nation's capital on May 9 to protest the Cambodian "incursion" and the violence at Kent State. In the early morning hours, President Nixon visited a group of protesters at the Lincoln Memorial. Nixon told them, "I know you think we are a bunch of sons-

---

[*] The mood on college campuses was one of increasingly bitter animosity. Congress exacerbated the situation by enacting a series of provisions cutting off federal financial aid to any students who disrupted school activities. Thirty-two states passed laws in 1969 and 1970 requiring the withdrawal of state financial aid from students violating campus rules or the criminal prosecution of persons involved in sit-ins in campus buildings. More than 1,800 campus protesters were arrested in the first two weeks of May 1970. At least ten public universities banned the SDS and many more banned or censored a variety of underground and student newspapers. Some public universities fired or refused to hire faculty members who strongly opposed the war. See Mona G. Jacqueny, *Radicalism on Campus, 1969–1971: Backlash in Law Enforcement and in the Universities* 71–72 (Philosophical Library 1972); Goldstein, *Political Repression* at 442, 519–23 (cited in note 30); Sale, SDS at 443–44, 547, 551, 645 (cited in note 26); Andrew H. Malcolm, *Judges Bar a Curb in U.S. Aid to Student Who Protested War*, New York Times 32 (Dec 29, 1972).

Kent State

of-bitches." He urged them to keep their demonstrations peaceful, noting, "I feel just as deeply as you do" about achieving peace. He then talked ramblingly about football, his travels, and the lessons of history, to the bewilderment and resentment of demonstrators.[192]

Angry at the invasion of Cambodia, many national leaders who had not previously spoken against the war now made themselves heard. Father Theodore Hesburgh, the president of Notre Dame, and Robert Goheen, the president of Princeton, called for an announced end date for American action in Vietnam. Newly formed groups of Nobel laureates, publishers, lawyers, architects, and civic leaders called for an end to the war. The Senate Foreign Relations Committee accused Nixon of usurping Congress's war-making power and denounced the "constitutionally unauthorized, Presidential war in Indochina."[193] Several senators, including the Republicans John Sherman Cooper of Kentucky and Mark Hatfield of Oregon and the Democrats Frank Church of Idaho and George McGovern of South Dakota, introduced resolutions to cut off funds for U.S. military operations in Southeast Asia.

In late June, the Senate voted to repeal the Gulf of Tonkin Resolution to demonstrate its displeasure with the president's unilateral actions.[194] Opinion polls showed that 58 percent of Americans opposed sending American troops into

Cambodia and a clear majority wanted the United States to pull out of Vietnam as soon as possible.[195]

The summer of 1970 brought a flood of demonstrations, some violent, including the bombing of several military recruitment centers and the Army Mathematics Research Center at the University of Wisconsin, which killed a thirty-three-year-old researcher.[196] Earl Warren observed that there had been "no crisis within the memory of living Americans" comparable to the one then enveloping the nation.[197]

Nixon was shocked by the depth of anger at the events of early May 1970. For the first time since he took office, "a sense of panic enveloped Richard Nixon and the men around him." Kissinger recalled that "the fear of another round of demonstrations permeated all the thinking about Vietnam in the Executive Branch that summer." The president, he said, was on the edge of "psychological exhaustion" and his "mood oscillated wildly." Vice President Agnew lashed out at critics as "charlatans of peace." William Safire recalled that Nixon decided that summer that his critics should now be used by the administration "as the villain, the object against which all of our supporters . . . could be rallied."*[198]

The explosion of antiwar activity after Nixon's announcement of the invasion of Cambodia precipitated counterdemonstrations. Twenty thousand people marched in St. Louis in support of the war, and 200 hard-hatted construction workers chanting, "Kill the Commie bastards," beat up 70 students participating in an antiwar rally on Wall Street. Vice President Agnew called for separating the "impudent" dissenters "from our society—with no more regret than we should feel over discarding rotten apples from a barrel."[199] A parade of 100,000 Nixon supporters marched through New York City, and construction workers in a dozen cities demonstrated in support of the president and attacked peace protesters. The president donned a hard hat imprinted with the words "commander-in-chief."[200]

Nixon took to the campaign trail in October 1970 in an effort to spur support from the Silent Majority, who were committed to "a just peace in Vietnam." He castigated the "thugs and hoodlums that have always plagued the good people,"

---

* Throughout this period, the administration continued its efforts to control the media. The White House aide Jeb Stuart Magruder was encouraged to do "some creative thinking" about how to undermine a co-anchor of the NBC evening news, and H. R. Haldeman sought to discredit the Harris poll, explaining, "There is a lot of dirty work that could be done here." Another White House aide, Charles Colson, initiated "off-the-record" meetings with the chief executives of the major networks in an effort to pressure them. He reported to Haldeman, "[T]hey are damned nervous and scared and we should continue to take a very tough line." Schell, *Time of Illusion* at 108–9, 126–27 (cited in note 164).

and wanted to show them "how little respect [he] had for their . . . mindless rant-ing."[201] Upon seeing a group of antiwar protesters in San Jose, Nixon leaped onto the hood of his car and waved his arms over his head while flashing the "V" for victory sign with both hands. The protesters, enraged, threw stones at the car. As Nixon sped off, he told his aides with a cackle, "That's what they hate to see!"[202]

In Ohio, a grand jury absolved the Ohio National Guard of any responsibil-ity for the deaths of the four students, but indicted twenty-five Kent State students for various crimes of disorder arising out of the May 4 tragedy. The Internal Secu-rity Division of the Department of Justice initiated a new campaign to crush rad-ical dissent, and the Senate and House Internal Security Committees escalated their investigations of left-wing "subversion."[203]

BY THE END OF 1970, the energy of the antiwar movement had begun to wane. Suffering from a sense of futility and fatigue, dissenters were exhausted. They had used "nearly every manner of protest—from self-immolations to bombings and from petitions to demonstrations—but the fighting continued.[*] More Americans than ever called the war a mistake, and yet it droned on." Many activists gave up and moved on to other causes, such as the environment or women's liberation.[204] Although public opposition to the war was at an all-time high, the number and scale of antiwar demonstrations dwindled. As the political commentator James Wechsler wrote in early 1971, Richard Nixon had "broken the spirit of the vast numbers of his countrymen who loathe the war but now feel help-less to do anything about it."[205]

Then, in late January, the president faced a critical decision—whether to order South Vietnamese troops, with American air support, to invade Laos. The justifications for this action were similar to those that had led to the Cam-bodian incursion in 1970. This time, though, the president fretted over the

---

[*] Another form of protest was adopted by Vietnam veterans who conducted "war crimes hear-ings" in December 1970 and January–February 1971. Spurred by the revelation of the My Lai mas-sacre in 1969, 142 veterans testified at these "hearings" to having witnessed or participated in a broad range of atrocities, including rape, cutting off ears, cutting off heads, torture, shooting civil-ians, poisoning food stocks, and razing entire villages. See John Kerry, Testimony before the Sen-ate Foreign Relations Committee, Apr 22, 1971, excerpted in Alex Barnett, ed, Words That Changed America: Great Speeches That Inspired, Challenged, Healed, and Enlightened 296–99 (Lyons 2003); Elliott L. Meyrowitz and Kenneth J. Campbell, Vietnam Veterans and War Crimes Hearings, in Small and Hoover, eds, Give Peace a Chance at 129–40, 135 (cited in note 20); Cran-dell, They Moved the Town at 145–47 (cited in note 208).

danger of reenergizing dissent. He even considered forgoing the invasion to preserve the peace at home. As it turned out, his anxiety over the public's response was well founded.

From the very beginning, the operation was a disaster. Initially, the administration ordered a complete news embargo on the progress of the attack, infuriating political leaders and arousing press and public suspicion. Then, as the images of combat filtered back to the United States, the public was appalled. Night after night, Americans saw panicked South Vietnamese troops fleeing in the face of fire and clinging to the skids of American helicopters to escape the enemy. "Vietnamization" seemed hopeless.

Responding to what it saw as biased reporting, the administration launched an aggressive public relations campaign that included highly exaggerated claims of success, exacerbating the growing sense of distrust. Even when the president and administration officials offered accurate reports, the public no longer believed them. Johnson's credibility gap had become Nixon's. By the end of March, the president's approval rating had fallen to an all-time low.[206] Nixon later recalled that this was "the lowest point of my first term as President," noting, "[I]t seemed possible that I might not even be nominated for re-election in 1972." It was this doubt that planted the seeds of Watergate.[207]

Even worse, as Nixon had feared, the invasion of Laos reignited antiwar protest. In April, three thousand members of Vietnam Veterans against the War tossed their medals into a pile in front of the U.S. Capitol. It was a powerful and moving experience for the nation and for the veterans, who now saw their medals as symbols of "shame" for service in an immoral war.[208] Leaders of VVAW were invited to testify before the Senate Foreign Relations Committee. Trying to explain America's role in Vietnam, one witness, paraphrasing the comic strip character Pogo, acidly noted that we have "identified the enemy. He is us."[209]

On April 24, 1971, as many as half a million people gathered in Washington to demand America's immediate withdrawal from Vietnam. The overall mood was pessimistic. Despite the continuing reduction in the number of American ground troops, it seemed the war would go on indefinitely, with the United States bombing North Vietnam until nothing remained but dust.

A week later, several thousand protesters assembled in the nation's capital with the plan to use massive nonviolence to paralyze the city. Their goal was to block bridges and intersections in an effort to convey the message that if the government did not end the war, it would face "social chaos."[210] On May 3, before the demonstrators had a chance to act, police and the military swept the downtown area, spraying tear gas and indiscriminately arresting seven thousand people, who were incarcerated in RFK Stadium. Newsweek commented that the military attack on the protesters "seemed more appropriate to Saigon in wartime than Washington."[211]

Although some commentators challenged the government's response, the president was pleased. At one point, he suggested to aides that they should hire some teamsters to beat up the demonstrators. A few days later he told his aide Charles Colson, "One day we will get them—we'll get them on the ground where we want them. And we'll stick our heels in, step on them hard and twist— right, Chuck, right?"*[212]

As this comment suggests, the White House was becoming "gripped by a 'siege' mentality."[213] By July 1971, a record high 65 percent of Americans agreed that the United States should withdraw, "even if the government of South Vietnam collapsed."[214] Over the next several months, there was growing concern that the government's war on dissent was corroding national values. Allegations of extensive government spying began to appear in the media. Then, in March 1972, the publication of documents stolen from an FBI office in Pennsylvania suggested that the government had indeed been engaged in unprecedented surveillance and harassment of dissenters. By April, almost half of all Americans believed that the crisis was causing a fundamental "breakdown" of American institutions.[215] As citizens were only just beginning to learn, the Nixon administration had grown ever "more hostile to basic concepts of civil liberty."[216]

"A Call to Resist Illegitimate Authority" and the Law of Conspiracy

By 1965, the act of publicly burning one's draft card had become a potent means of protest.† This was more than just a clever way to

---

* Police abandoned all normal arrest procedures, and hundreds of bystanders and journalists were swept up in the police dragnet. In subsequent days, another 6,200 persons were arrested, including 1,200 who were peacefully listening to a speech on the Capitol steps. Out of 13,400 people who were arrested, only 745 were convicted of any offense. In January 1975, a federal jury awarded $12 million to those arrested on the Capitol grounds for violations of their First and Fourth Amendment rights. Six months later, a federal judge ruled that there had been massive civil liberties violations and unnecessary police violence during every major demonstration in Washington, D.C., between 1969 and 1975 and ordered *all* arrest records arising out of those demonstrations erased. See Goldstein, *Political Repression* at 497–99 (cited in note 30); Schell, *Time of Illusion* at 149–51 (cited in note 164); Hopkins, *"May Day"* at 80–88 (cited in note 212).

† The idea of destroying a draft card as a form of symbolic protest did not originate during the Vietnam War. Draft resisters of the 1940s and 1950s also used this device. See Ferber and Lynd, *Resistance* at 3–4 (cited in note 14).

express one's opposition to the war. Burning a copy of the Constitution is also a clever way to express opposition, but burning a copy of the Constitution (as distinct from burning the original) was not a crime. Burning a draft card was. Thus, this act represented not only symbolic dissent but direct *resistance*. Those who publicly burned their draft cards placed themselves at immediate risk of criminal prosecution. This act therefore took genuine commitment. It crossed the line between protest and civil disobedience.

The draft card, which young men were required by law to carry at all times, became "the symbol *par excellence*" of the nation's military force in Vietnam. One antiwar activist declared that, because of what they represented, draft cards "deserved to be burned." Not surprisingly, those young men who publicly burned their draft cards in 1965, when others were dying in the jungles of Vietnam, aroused outrage among elements of the American public. It was a simple act, but it "resonated with defiance."[217]

On July 29, 1965, some four hundred antiwar protesters picketed a military induction center in New York City. Up to that point, no one had been prosecuted for burning a draft card. But after the July 29 event, *Life* magazine featured a photograph of a young man burning his draft card at the demonstration, and some congressmen took notice. Congressman Mendel Rivers of South Carolina introduced a bill to make the willful destruction or mutilation of a draft card a criminal offense.

In the debate over this bill, Rivers attacked a "vocal minority in this country [who] thumb their noses at their own Government." He described the legislation as a "clear answer to those who would make a mockery of our efforts in South Vietnam by engaging in the mass destruction of draft cards." Congressman William Bray of Indiana added, "Beatniks and so-called 'campus cults' have been publicly burning their draft cards to demonstrate their contempt for the United States." Senator Strom Thurmond of South Carolina described draft card burning as "treason" and announced that such conduct "must not be tolerated by a society whose sons, brothers and husbands are giving their lives in defense of freedom."[218]

The legislation was quickly enacted by overwhelming votes in both chambers of Congress. The New York *Daily News* published a cartoon depicting draft card burners as rats and demanded that the government immediately prosecute such "Communist-incited beatniks, pacifists and damned idiots."[219]

OVER THE NEXT SEVERAL MONTHS, the government began to prosecute individuals who burned their draft cards, thus posing the question, Is

David Paul O'Brien Burns His Draft Card

the public burning of a draft card as a symbolic expression of opposition to the war protected *speech* within the meaning of the First Amendment?

Of course, the "act" of burning a draft card is not "speech" in the conventional sense. It does not use words. And surely one can express opposition to the war without burning a draft card. Moreover, if burning a draft card is "speech," is publicly urinating on an induction center "speech"? Is blowing up an induction center "speech"? Such acts also symbolically express one's opposition to the war. If these acts are "speech," must they be given the same constitutional protection as a public speech or a leaflet criticizing the draft?

Prior to the Vietnam War, the Supreme Court had recognized that some nonlinguistic acts could qualify as protected speech under the First Amendment. For example, the Court had held that the display of a red flag, as a symbol of opposition to organized government, was constitutionally protected speech.[220] Indeed, in the *Barnette* case, in which the Court held unconstitutional the compelled pledge of allegiance during World War II, Justice Robert Jackson explained that "symbolism is a primitive but effective way of communicating ideas" because it "is a short cut from mind to mind."[221]

But can it possibly be that an individual has a First Amendment right to violate a law, so long as his purpose in doing so is to express his opposition to the law? Does one have a constitutional right to speed on the highway to protest speed limits? To smoke marijuana in a public demonstration to protest drug laws? To run naked down a public street to protest antinudity laws?

In 1968, the Supreme Court addressed this puzzle in *United States v O'Brien*.[222] On the morning of March 31, 1966, David Paul O'Brien and three other young men burned their draft cards on the steps of the South Boston courthouse. A sizable crowd, including several FBI agents, witnessed the event. O'Brien was arrested, tried, and convicted of knowingly destroying his draft card in violation of the 1965 law. He testified at trial that he had burned his draft card in the hope of inspiring others to "reevaluate their positions" with respect to the draft and "the armed forces."[223]

The Court, in an opinion by Chief Justice Earl Warren, upheld O'Brien's conviction. At the outset, Warren observed that, on its face, the 1965 law "deals with conduct having no connection with speech." Indeed, a "law prohibiting destruction of Selective Service certificates no more abridges free speech on its face than a motor vehicle law prohibiting the destruction of drivers' licenses, or a tax law prohibiting the destruction of books and records." Because such laws do not *expressly* regulate speech, they are quite different, from a First Amendment perspective, from laws that expressly forbid any person to criticize the draft or distribute antiwar leaflets.[224]

Thus, the question in *O'Brien* was whether a law of general application—a law not directed at speech on its face—can violate the First Amendment because it has an *incidental* effect on free expression. Put differently, in what circumstances, if any, does an individual have a First Amendment right to violate a law of general application in order to enable him to speak more effectively? Chief Justice Warren concluded that such a law can constitutionally be applied to speech so long as it furthers a "substantial governmental interest." He then held that because the government has a "substantial" interest in requiring individuals to be in possession of their draft cards at all times, it could constitutionally punish their intentional and "wanton" destruction.*[225]

The decision in *O'Brien* was criticized on several grounds. Some objected that the Court did not give adequate weight to draft card burning as a valuable means of expression. On this view, burning a draft card was a particularly effective "way of attracting the attention of the national news media," and for the gov-

---

* The Court suggested that the registrant's possession of his draft card is important to enable him to prove upon demand that he was registered for the draft, to remind him of his responsibility regularly to inform his draft board of any change of address, and to enable him immediately to contact his draft board in case of national emergency.

ernment to prohibit "such an effective form of propagating one's views" was to "greatly diminish" the ability of the individual to "make his dissent known."[226] As Justice John Harlan observed in his concurring opinion, however, "O'Brien manifestly could have conveyed his message in many ways other than by burning his draft card."[227] Moreover, "much of the effectiveness of O'Brien's communication . . . derived precisely from the fact that it was illegal." Ironically, then, "[h]ad there been no law prohibiting draft card burning . . . he might have attracted no more attention than he would have by swallowing a goldfish."[228] Thus, had O'Brien won his case, he would have largely destroyed the power of draft card burning as a form of symbolic protest.

O'Brien was also criticized on the ground that the Court overstated the "substantiality" of the government's interest. On this view, the requirement that an individual must at all times possess his draft card served only "functions of dispensable convenience rather than urgent necessity." Thus, the Court should have weighed whether "the conduct in question [was] likely to cause a harm greater than the abridgment of freedom of expression," and then invalidated the application of the law to O'Brien's symbolic expression.[229]

The Court, however, clearly sought to avoid having to balance on a case-by-case basis the "value" of the violation of the law as symbolic speech against the "importance" of the government's interest in enforcing the law. In this judgment, the Court was on firm ground. If O'Brien had a First Amendment right to violate the 1965 law by burning his draft card, how would the Court then decide the case of urination on a public building, or speeding, or smoking marijuana, or running naked through the streets?

Even putting aside the obvious problem of deciding whether any particular criminal defendant was really "speaking," rather than just urinating, speeding, getting high, or exposing himself in public, this sort of ad hoc inquiry would mire the courts in endless disputes about the relative costs and benefits of whether people must be permitted to violate laws of general application for speech purposes. Although the outcome in *O'Brien* seemed "repressive" at the time, it was in fact the right decision based on a sound understanding of core First Amendment principles—except in extraordinary circumstances, there is no First Amendment right to violate otherwise valid laws that have only an *incidental* effect on free expression.[230]

A third prong of the attack on *O'Brien* was that the 1965 law was not an *incidental* restriction of speech. There was, after all, clear evidence in the legislative record that congressmen like Mendel Rivers and William Bray had proposed and supported this legislation precisely *because* it would put draft card burners in prison. On this view, although the law had been drafted to *appear* to be neutral and to apply "on its face" to *any* destruction of a draft card, whether in public or private, whether to express a political position or to light a barbecue, its real *pur-

pose was not to facilitate the smooth functioning of the Selective Service by requiring registrants to possess a draft card at all times, but to punish those "traitors" who "thumb their noses at their own government."

This posed a serious challenge for the Court. If the 1965 law had expressly declared it unlawful for any person to "burn a draft card as a symbolic expression of opposition to the draft," it would clearly have been unconstitutional. Such a law would not have been "unrelated" to free expression, but would have aimed directly at speech. The Court would have analyzed it just like a law making it a crime for any person to give a speech against the draft. As the Court unanimously recognized in *O'Brien*, symbolic acts can constitute protected expression, and if the government attempts directly to regulate the *message* communicated, rather than the underlying act, it will run smack into the First Amendment.

But this was not the case in *O'Brien*. The 1965 law prohibited not "draft card burning as a form of speech intended to criticize the government" but *any* intentional destruction of a draft card. And the government defended the law not on the ground that draft card burning was un-American or seditious but on the ground that the law served legitimate interests wholly "unrelated" to whether any particular draft card was destroyed as a form of speech, or otherwise. The Court thus had to decide how to deal with the legislative record. Was this a neutral law that had only an "incidental" effect on speech, or was it a fraud, designed to achieve through duplicity what Congress could not do openly?

The Court declined the invitation to invalidate the 1965 law on the ground that the true congressional purpose was "to suppress the freedom of speech." In reaching this result, Chief Justice Warren invoked the "familiar principle of constitutional law" that a court should "not strike down an otherwise constitutional statute on the basis of an alleged illicit legislative motive." He explained that "[i]nquiries into congressional motives" are "hazardous" because what "motivates one legislator to make a speech about a statute is not necessarily what motivates scores of others to enact it." Moreover, to invalidate a law on the basis of judicial "guesswork" based on what a "handful" of legislators said about it would mean that the same law might be constitutional in one jurisdiction but not in another, and that the same legislation "could be reenacted in its exact form if the same or another legislator made a 'wiser' speech about it." In this instance, the Court concluded that there was sufficient ambiguity about the various motives of different legislators to give Congress the benefit of the doubt.[231]

This was the most awkward element of the Court's opinion. As one commentator noted at the time, "[w]hat emerges with indisputable clarity" from a review of the legislative history of the 1965 law is that "the intent of its framers was purely and simply to put a stop to this particular form of anti-war protest, which they deemed extraordinarily contemptible and vicious—even treasonous—at a time when American troops were engaged in combat."[232] Although only three members of Congress commented directly on the law, it is difficult to conceive that Congress would have enacted this legislation at this particular moment in time except for the storm over draft card burning. In this sense, the Court's suggestion that the actual motive for the legislation was unascertainable or ambiguous simply blinked reality. On the other hand, the Court was right that direct judicial inquiry into actual legislative motivation as a justification for voiding legislation is an extremely indelicate and clumsy tool, and even in the circumstances of *O'Brien* the better part of wisdom, if not valor, counseled in favor of the Court's resolution.[233]

O'BRIEN HELD THAT an individual could constitutionally be punished for destroying his draft card. But what of those who *advocated* draft resistance by others? On January 5, 1968, the United States indicted the "Boston Five"—Dr. Benjamin Spock, the Reverend William Sloane Coffin Jr., Mitchell Goodman, Michael Ferber, and Marcus Raskin—for conspiring to aid, abet, and counsel violations of the draft law.* Coffin was the nationally renowned chaplain of Yale University; Spock, the best-known pediatrician in the United States; Goodman, a New York writer; Ferber, a Ph.D. student at Harvard; and Raskin, codirector of the Institute for Policy Studies in Washington, D.C. Although all of the defendants actively opposed the war, they barely knew one another.

Because of Dr. Spock's celebrity status, news of the indictment splashed across the nation's headlines. The *Washington Post*, the *New York Times*, and *Life* magazine heralded it as a "landmark case of conscience and the law."[234]

The indictment charged that in August 1967 Coffin and Spock had distributed a document entitled "A Call to Resist Illegitimate Authority"; that on October 2 Coffin, Goodman, Raskin, and Spock had participated in an antiwar press conference at the New York Hilton; that on October 16 Coffin and Ferber had addressed a meeting in Boston at which Coffin accepted draft cards turned in by registrants for the draft; and that on October 20 Coffin had given a speech during a demonstration at the Justice Department, after which he, Raskin, Spock, and Goodman deposited 185 draft cards and 172 notices of classification at the Department of Justice.

---

* For the same reasons that the Court held in *O'Brien* that the punishment of draft card burning did not violate the First Amendment, the punishment for refusing induction, even if intended as a form of symbolic protest against the war, also did not violate the First Amendment.

"A Call to Resist Illegitimate Authority" was an 800-word statement signed by more than 150 individuals. It asserted that the war in Vietnam violated the U.S. Constitution, the Geneva Accords of 1954, and the United Nations Charter because it had neither been declared by Congress nor authorized by the UN; that the conduct of the war violated the Geneva Conventions of 1949 insofar as it involved "the burning and bulldozing of entire villages" and the "summary executions of civilians"; and that "resistance against illegitimate authority," including by "refusing to be inducted" and "refusing to obey specific illegal and immoral orders," is courageous and "justified."[235]

Those who signed the "Call" pledged to continue to lend their "support to those who undertake resistance to this war . . . in whatever ways may seem appropriate." Signers included the novelists Philip Roth and George Elliott, poets Robert Lowell and Lawrence Ferlinghetti, journalists Nat Hentoff and Jack Newfield, drama critic Robert Brustein, sculptor Alexander Calder, essayist Susan Sontag, historian Christopher Lasch, philosopher Herbert Marcuse, theologian Thomas Merton, and chemist Linus Pauling, to name just a few. Eventually, the "Call" was signed by 23,000 people.[236]

In his October 16 speech in Boston, Coffin reminded his audience that "men at times will feel constrained to disobey the law out of a sense of obedience to a higher allegiance." Coffin declared, "[T]o us the war in Vietnam is a crime. And if we are correct, if the war is a crime, then is it criminal to refuse to have anything to do with it?"[237] Four days later, Coffin declared, "We hereby publicly counsel these young men to continue in their refusal to serve in the armed forces as long as the war in Vietnam continues, and we pledge ourselves to aid and abet them in all the ways we can."[238]

COULD COFFIN CONSTITUTIONALLY be punished for counseling refusal of induction? Recall Lincoln's "poor soldier boy" hypothetical during the Civil War. Lincoln reasoned that if the government could punish the "poor soldier boy" who had been encouraged to desert, surely it could punish the individual who had encouraged him to do so. Certainly, Coffin's case would have been open-and-shut during World War I. Under then prevailing precedents, both the "Call" and Coffin's speeches would have sufficed for conviction. If Charles Schenck and Eugene Debs were guilty of attempting to obstruct the draft, Coffin was guilty as well. Indeed, even Judge Learned Hand had made clear in *Masses* that the government could constitutionally punish an individual for *expressly* advocating draft resistance, and there could be no clearer illustration of "express advocacy" than Coffin's remarks on October 20.

But by 1968 the Supreme Court's decisions in cases like *Schenck* and *Debs* were no longer "good law." As we have seen, during World War II and the Cold War the Court rejected the reasoning and results of those earlier precedents. By 1968, the governing test was not "bad tendency" but the *Dennis-Yates* version of "clear and present danger."

Moreover, although Coffin had unambiguously counseled "young men to continue in their refusal to serve in the armed forces," and therefore satisfied Hand's "express advocacy" standard, the Supreme Court had made clear in a long line of cases, including *Dennis* and *Yates*, that express advocacy of unlawful conduct is not unprotected by the First Amendment. Rather, even a speaker who expressly counseled others to act unlawfully could be punished *only* if his speech had created a "clear and present danger" of serious harm.

Although the Court in *Dennis* had played fast and loose with the meaning of "clear and present danger" when the feared harm was the violent overthrow of government, the danger posed by Coffin's speech was more akin to—indeed, exactly like—the danger posed in the World War I cases, which the Court had scrupulously distinguished in *Dennis*. As the Court made clear in *Dennis*, in circumstances like those posed in *Schenck* and *Debs*, the "proper" approach was that set forth by Justices Holmes and Brandeis in their separate opinions in *Abrams*, *Gitlow*, and *Whitney*.

Under that standard, there could be no question that Coffin did not create an "emergency,"[239] or a danger of "present conflagration"[240] or "immediate serious violence."[241] As Brandeis had argued in *Whitney*, "even advocacy of violation, however reprehensible morally, is not a justification for denying free speech where . . . there is nothing to indicate that the advocacy would be immediately acted on."[242] General Lewis Hershey, the director of the Selective Service, admitted that there was no evidence that Coffin had actually *caused* anyone to resist the draft.[243] Thus, had the government charged Coffin (and the 150 other individuals who initially signed the "Call") with counseling resistance to the draft, it could *not* constitutionally have obtained a conviction.

In the actual prosecution of the Boston Five, however, the government argued that it did not need to prove clear and present danger, because the defendants had been indicted not for *counseling* resistance to the draft but for *conspiring* to counsel resistance.

AS WE SHALL SEE, the government used many weapons in its effort to discredit and debilitate antiwar dissent in the 1960s and 1970s. One of the most important was the charge of "conspiracy." Conspiracy is a complex and troubling concept in the criminal law, even without a First Amendment overlay. Conventional prosecutions for conspiracy to murder or to embezzle can tie judges, jurors, lawyers, and defendants into knots.[244] Justice Robert Jackson once described conspiracy law as "that elastic, sprawling and pervasive offense . . . so vague that it almost defies definition."[245] When conspiracy law intersects with the values of free speech, the obstacles to clear thinking, and the potential for abuse, are almost insurmountable.

Before we return to the Boston Five prosecution, a few simple examples may help illustrate the problem. Suppose five individuals have a conversation in which they agree to give a series of public speeches urging blacks to vote in Montgomery, Alabama, during the civil rights movement. Here the individuals may be said to have entered into a "conspiracy," but it is a conspiracy to encourage people to exercise their constitutional right to vote. There are three elements in this situation—the conspiracy (which consists of the agreement to give the public speeches); the speeches (which are themselves clearly protected by the First Amendment), and the acts (that is, the voting, which is clearly legal activity).

It seems evident that if Alabama attempted to punish this conspiracy it would violate the First Amendment. As the Supreme Court has long recognized, individuals have a First Amendment right to associate with one another to further constitutionally protected objectives. Thus, a "conspiracy" to form the NAACP, the Libertarian Party, or the Green Party could not constitutionally be punished. The same holds true for a "conspiracy" to advocate voting.

A trickier situation arises when people conspire to commit unlawful acts in an effort to encourage or enable others to exercise their constitutional rights. For example, suppose five people agree to kidnap the police chief of Montgomery, Alabama, on election day because he has been the primary obstacle to blacks' voting. The problem here is that although the ultimate goal—to enable people to exercise their right to vote—may be admirable, the *means* they plan to use to achieve that goal are unlawful.

Do the conspirators have a constitutional right to kidnap the police chief? The answer, surely, is no. As we have already seen in the context of draft card burning, a basic rule of thumb is that the First Amendment ordinarily does not accord an individual a constitutional right to violate a law of otherwise general application. The law prohibiting kidnapping, like the 1965 law on draft cards, does not, on its face, stifle anyone's speech. It is unrelated to the suppression of expression. Thus, a conspiracy to engage in an unlawful kidnapping is not protected by the First Amendment, even though the conspirators intend to undertake the kidnapping for a "good" reason.

Another variation—the Boston Five variation—arises when individuals "conspire" to *advocate* unlawful conduct by others. Suppose, for example, five people agree to make speeches urging others to refuse induction or blow up induction centers. If an individual's advocacy cannot constitutionally be punished, what of a *conspiracy* to advocate? One might think that if it cannot be a crime to do an act (such as making speeches counseling draft resistance), then it cannot be a crime to conspire to do that act. But it is not so simple.

Modern conspiracy law, like the law of seditious libel, originated in the Star Chamber, and it still bears some of the repressive character of that era. In 1611, the Star Chamber explained that the essence of the crime of conspiracy rests in the *agreement*, rather than in the crime that is being planned. Thus, conspiracy law "relieves the prosecutor of the necessity of proving any actual wrongdoing by the defendant."[246]As Clarence Darrow explained, a boy who steals candy is guilty of the misdemeanor of petty larceny; two boys who agree to steal candy, but *don't do it*, are guilty of the *felony* of conspiracy. For this reason, Darrow deemed it "a serious reflection on America that this worn-out piece of tyranny, this drag-net for compassing the imprisonment . . . of men whom the ruling class does not like, should find a home in our country."[247] Indeed, the crime of conspiracy has routinely been used by prosecutors to "get" union organizers, political dissenters, radicals, and other "dangerous" individuals who could not otherwise be convicted of an offense.

Thus, in the Boston Five conspiracy trial, the government argued that it did not need to prove that the "Call" satisfied the "clear and present danger" standard. It was sufficient to prove that the defendants had *conspired* to counsel resistance to the draft.*

But even that proved a challenge for the prosecution. Although the defendants all actively opposed the draft and the war, they barely knew one another before the indictment. It is thus unlikely that they had actually "conspired" to do anything, except in the loosest sense of the word. At one point during the trial, to make out the conspiracy, the prosecutor asked the defendant Marcus Raskin whether on October 20, 1967, during Coffin's speech at the Justice Department, he remembered "Dr. Spock next to Mr. Coffin applauding for a long time." Spock's attorney,

---

* Recall that *Dennis* involved a similar problem. That is, in *Dennis* the leaders of the Communist Party were prosecuted not for advocating the violent overthrow of government but for *conspiring* to advocate such overthrow. It was unclear in *Dennis*, however, whether the Court would have treated the prosecution for advocacy of violent overthrow any differently from a prosecution for conspiracy to advocate. Of course, the very fact of a conspiracy may be relevant in assessing the degree of danger posed by the speech, and the Court did take that into account in *Dennis*. But the Court did not suggest in *Dennis* that the burden on the government to demonstrate "clear and present danger" was any less merely because the charge was conspiracy.

Leonard Boudin, furiously objected that applause is not a crime and that "it's improper to use this as an indication of conspiracy." The prosecution was permitted, over Boudin's objection, to present this "evidence" of conspiracy.

Four of the five defendants were convicted; only Marcus Raskin was found "not guilty" of participating in the "conspiracy." Several weeks later, federal Judge Francis J. W. Ford, who had presided over the trial, pronounced sentence. Ford, an eight-five-year-old jurist, who reminded Jessica Mitford of "Charles Laughton commanding his *Bounty*," had been tough on the defendants throughout the trial. At sentencing, he "outdid" himself, thundering that the defendants had been found guilty of "rebellion against the law," an act "in the nature of treason." "It would be preposterous," he added, to allow those who had "conspired to incite Selective Service registrants to violate the law to escape under the guise of free speech." Ford then sentenced each of the four defendants to two years in prison. William Coffin observed that the trial had been "dismal, dreary, and above all, demeaning." It was, he said, "unworthy of the best of America."[248]

A federal appeals court later reversed all of the convictions on technical grounds, and the government did not attempt to reprosecute.[249]

RADICALISM ON TRIAL: THE CONSPIRACY TRIAL

THE BOSTON FIVE TRIAL was the only such conspiracy prosecution brought under the Johnson administration. The Nixon administration, however, used conspiracy law extensively to prosecute radical antiwar leaders. These included prosecutions of the "Catonsville Nine," the "Kansas City Four," the "Evanston Four," the "Gainsville Eight," and so on. In all of these cases, as in the Boston Five prosecution, the charges either collapsed during trial, were dismissed because of unlawful government surveillance, or were reversed on appeal.

The Catonsville prosecution involved charges against Daniel and Philip Berrigan and seven others for stealing 278 files from a draft board and then publicly burning them with homemade napalm (a mixture of gasoline and Ivory Snow flakes). As they did so, in front of television cameras, they recited the Lord's Prayer and calmly awaited arrest. They handed a statement to the press declaring, "We confront the Catholic Church, other Christian bodies, and the synagogues of America with their silence . . . in the face of our country's crimes."[250]

Philip Berrigan, a strapping Josephite priest, had served as an Army officer in World War II. His brother Daniel, a Jesuit priest and poet, later wrote about this protest, "Our apologies, good friends, for the fracture of good order, the burning of paper instead of children. . . . The time is past when good men can remain silent, when obedience can segregate men from public risk." The four-day trial was an international media event. It drew thousands of supporters, who marched through the streets and jammed the courtroom. The Berrigans and their co-conspirators were all convicted and sentenced to prison.[251]

In the Gainsville prosecution, the government charged eight members and supporters of Vietnam Veterans against the War with conspiring to disrupt the Republican National Convention in Miami in 1972 by using devices ranging from "fried" marbles, ball bearings, and cherry bombs to automatic weapons and incendiary devices. At trial, however, the only evidence the government could produce of any weapons concerned sling shots, and the jury acquitted the defendants of all charges.

Another major conspiracy case involved charges in 1971 against the Reverend Philip Berrigan and seven other members of the Catholic antiwar movement on charges of conspiracy to raid draft boards, destroy draft records, blow up heating tunnels in Washington, D.C., and kidnap Henry Kissinger. The government's evidence was weak, and the jury deadlocked, 10 to 2, in favor of acquittal.[*252]

On the whole, these prosecutions had two contradictory effects: they intimidated, harassed, and distracted some elements of the antiwar movement, and they gave invaluable publicity and moral authority to those who were prosecuted. The most visible of the conspiracy trials, the one that generated the most headlines and the most national attention, the one that best captured their circus-like atmosphere, was *the* conspiracy trial, which arose out of the 1968 Democratic National Convention in Chicago.

AFTER THE URBAN RIOTS that followed the assassination of Martin Luther King, many authorities accused black militants, like Stokely Carmichael and H. Rap Brown, of traveling around the nation inciting riots. Congress responded by passing a new antiriot act, making it unlawful for any person to cross state lines "with the intent to incite, organize, promote, encourage, participate in or carry on a riot."[253]

In the wake of the Chicago Democratic Convention, Lyndon Johnson's

---

[*] After the trial, one of the jurors said, "I thought the whole thing was kind of funny, the idea of a bunch of priests and nuns zipping off with Henry Kissinger." Berrigan later went to prison for having a letter smuggled out of jail. He was the only person in the history of the United States ever prosecuted on such a charge. Zaroulis and Sullivan, *Who Spoke Up?* at 378–79 (cited in note 11). See also Goldstein, *Political Repression* at 488–89 (cited in note 30).

Attorney General, Ramsey Clark, refused to prosecute any of the demonstrators under this legislation. After Richard Nixon assumed the presidency, however, Attorney General John Mitchell directed a federal grand jury to proceed against demonstration leaders. In a revealing comment that captured the difference between the two administrations, Will Wilson, Mitchell's assistant attorney general, opined that Ramsey Clark's "trouble was that he was philosophically concerned with the rights of the individual."[254]

On March 20, 1969, the grand jury returned indictments against eight demonstrators—David Dellinger, the SDS leaders Tom Hayden and Rennie Davis, the yippie leaders Jerry Rubin and Abbie Hoffman, the Black Panther chairman, Bobby Seale, and two professors active in the antiwar movement, John Froines and Lee Weiner. They were charged with conspiracy to cross state lines with the intent to incite a riot and with crossing state lines to incite a riot.[255]

The defendants in the "conspiracy trial" were a disparate group. Seale had not known any of his fellow defendants before he arrived in Chicago on August 27 and had had nothing to do with planning the protests. Indeed, the Black Panthers scorned such demonstrations as weak and futile gestures. But the Nixon Justice Department was eager to prosecute Black Panthers, whom it despised as "a bunch of hoodlums." The other seven defendants shared an opposition to the war, but as often as not were at each other's throats. As Abbie Hoffman wrote on the eve of trial, the "Chicago Eight are probably the most non-conspiring conspiracy ever hatched." (Presumably, he was unaware of the "Great Sedition Trial of World War II.") On another occasion, he observed that this group "couldn't agree on lunch." The government, he concluded, had "decided to put radicalism on trial."[256]

It has never been clear whether the leaders of the National Mobilization Committee to End the War in Vietnam intended to promote violence in Chicago. Well before the convention, Hayden and Davis issued a statement on behalf of SDS declaring that the protests in Chicago should not involve "violence and disruption," but should "be nonviolent and legal." Similarly, Dellinger declared that "We are not going to storm the convention with tanks or mace. But we are going to storm the hearts and minds of the American people." Two years later, Dellinger reaffirmed that it was never the intention of the mobilization to "invade the Amphitheatre or disrupt the convention."[257]

The federal judge assigned to preside over the trial was Julius J. Hoffman, a diminutive, stern seventy-three-year-old with a long history of siding with the government.[258] In the pretrial proceedings, Hoffman consistently ruled against the defendants, denying defense motions to suppress evidence obtained in allegedly unlawful wiretaps and to delay the trial so Seale's attorney could recover from surgery. Seale objected bitterly to being tried without his lawyer of choice. As the trial proceeded, he grew furious with Hoffman and the prosecutors, calling them "fascists," "racists," and "pigs." Enraged, Judge Hoffman ordered Seale gagged and bound to a chair in the courtroom. William Kunstler, one of the defense attorneys, objected to "this medieval torture" and "this unholy disgrace to the law." As the trial became ever more chaotic, Hoffman declared a mistrial for Seale and summarily sentenced him to an unprecedented four-year prison term for contempt of court.[259]

The government's evidence against the other defendants consisted largely of the testimony of undercover agents who claimed they had heard the defendants discuss disruption, the destruction of property, and plans to break windows, set fires, and ignite smoke bombs. The defendants mocked these witnesses and accused them of lying.[*] They insisted that they had planned a peaceful protest and that events had turned violent because of the actions of the Daley administration and the police.

A parade of witnesses testified on their behalf, including Jesse Jackson, Arlo Guthrie, Pete Seeger, and Julian Bond. Throughout the trial, the defendants displayed contempt for Judge Hoffman and for the entire proceeding. It was, for them, an opportunity for guerrilla theater and an invitation to ridicule the system. At various times, they refused to rise when the judge entered the courtroom, hooted and scoffed at prosecutors and government witnesses, waved a Vietcong flag from the defense table, and came into court wearing judicial robes in derisive imitation of Judge Hoffman.

After four and a half tumultuous months of trial, the jury found the seven remaining defendants not guilty on the conspiracy charge, but found Dellinger, Davis, Hayden, Hoffman, and Rubin guilty of crossing state lines with intent to incite a riot. Before sentencing the defendants, Judge Hoffman offered them an opportunity to speak to the court. Dellinger told the judge, "All the way through this, I have been ambivalent in my attitude toward you, because there is something spunky about you that one has to admire, however misguided and intolerant I believe you are." Dellinger added that throughout the trial he had been comparing Julius Hoffman "to George III of England . . . because you are trying to hold back the tide of history, although you will not succeed." In a more yippie-like vein, Rubin said "Julius, you radicalized more young people than we ever could." He congratulated Judge Hoffman on being "the country's top Yippie."[260]

Judge Hoffman, barely disguising his disgust for the defendants, sentenced each of them to the maximum term of five years in prison. Hoffman then piled on 175 contempt sentences ranging from two and a half months to more than

---

[*] One undercover informer had penetrated so deeply into the antiwar movement that in October 1969 his name was on the letterhead of the New Mobilization as a member of the steering committee "at the very moment he was appearing as a government witness/informer in the Conspiracy trial in Chicago." Zaroulis and Sullivan, *Who Spoke Up?* at 221 (cited in note 11).

Make a New Year's Revolution
Join the Conspiracy

Abbie   Rennie   John   Lee

Tom   Dave   Jerry

we get by with a little help from our friends:
COMMITTEE TO DEFEND THE CONSPIRACY: 28 E. Jackson Blvd., Chicago, Ill. 60604

Season's Greetings from the Conspiracy Seven

four years against the seven defendants and their lawyers. Shortly thereafter, Richard Nixon invited Judge Hoffman to breakfast with him at the White House.

On appeal, all of the contempt and substantive convictions were overturned by the court of appeals, which noted, among other things, that the defendants had been denied a fair trial because of the "deprecatory and often antagonistic attitude" of Judge Hoffman. Thereafter, the government abandoned the substantive charges, but retried the defendants and their lawyers on 38 of the 175 contempt charges. In the retrial, three of the defendants and one of their lawyers were found guilty on a total of 13 charges of contempt, but the judge refused to impose any sentence on them because they had been so goaded by Judge Hoffman's improper, provocative, and "condemnatious conduct."[261]

As one commentator has observed, the Chicago conspiracy trial "was not one of the august moments in American jurisprudence."[262] Although the defendants may or may not have been guilty of encouraging disruption, Attorney General Ramsey Clark's decision not to pursue the matter was surely the wiser course. The prosecution was launched in part because of Mayor Daley's continuing rage at the defendants for embarrassing his city, and in part because of the Nixon administration's determination to incapacitate the leaders of the antiwar movement and to make perfectly clear that the new Republican administration would not stand for such conduct in the future. The net effect, however, was to give greater visibility to the defendants, who were transformed into national celebrities, and to embarrass the American system of justice.[*]

"EXPOSE, DISRUPT AND OTHERWISE NEUTRALIZE"

DURING THE RED SCARE after World War I, in the years leading up to World War II, during World War II, and throughout the Cold War, J. Edgar Hoover and his Federal Bureau of Investigation played a major role in investigating dissident political activity. In some instances, the FBI's actions were clearly authorized; in others, Hoover disobeyed direct orders to terminate his activities. Over a period of at least twenty-five years, he disregarded or "misconstrued" instructions from Attorneys General Harlan Fiske Stone, Robert Jackson,

---

[*] Tom Hayden estimated that during the trial the defendants, who were out on bail the entire time, made at least five hundred campus appearances, allowing them to attain "a celebrity status equivalent to the leading rock music groups of the day." Hayden, *Justice in Streets* at 296, 300 (cited in note 171).

and Francis Biddle and hid his activities from the executive, judicial and legislative branches. He was the single, unifying figure in a half century of political surveillance of Americans.

In the 1950s, the FBI initiated an even more aggresive counterintelligence program (COINTELPRO) against the Communist Party of the United States. Hoover instituted this program without the knowledge or authorization of either the attorney general or the president.[263] The goal of this operation was to go beyond surveillance to active political harassment and disruption.

Under its initial COINTELPRO, the FBI attempted to undermine the CPUSA. It actively encouraged the media to publish information that would embarrass or humiliate members of the party, fostered animosity and division among party members by fabricating rumors of disloyalty and betrayal, secretly arranged for meeting places to be denied the party, set organized crime against the CPUSA by sending forged letters, and undermined the political campaigns of candidates who challenged or criticized HUAC.[264]

In 1961, the FBI extended COINTELPRO to the Socialist Workers Party; in 1964, to "white hate" groups, such as the Ku Klux Klan; and in 1965, on the premise that Communists had infiltrated the civil rights movement, to civil rights organizations and leaders, including the NAACP and Dr. Martin Luther King.[265]

As antiwar protests escalated in the mid-1960s, the FBI, with prodding from the Johnson administration, expanded its domestic intelligence activities. At the 1964 Democratic National Convention, the FBI kept tabs on all "dissident" groups within the Democratic Party and kept the president informed of their plans. In early 1965, the government installed wiretaps on both SDS and SNCC.[266] In April, President Johnson personally asked Hoover to investigate alleged Communist infiltration of the antiwar movement.[267]

Hoover leapt at the opportunity. He was confident that the investigation would prove that the Communist Party had played an "ever-increasing role in generating opposition to the United States position in Vietnam" and that Communists were "participating in the activities" of SDS.[268] The ensuing FBI report found Johnson's and Hoover's suspicions unfounded. It concluded that the CPUSA "*wanted* to influence" the antiwar movement, but that its actual influence "was quite negligible."[269]

Undaunted, the FBI expanded its surveillance to "teach-ins" and other campus antiwar activities. A teach-in in Philadelphia, for example, resulted in a forty-one-page FBI intelligence report, incorporating remarks by ministers, professors, and other participants. The report, compiled by undercover informants, was distributed widely to military intelligence, the State Department, and the Internal Security Division of the Justice Department.[270]

Lyndon Johnson also requested and received FBI reports on antiwar senators, congressmen, journalists, and academics. At his instructions, the FBI investigated the philosopher Hannah Arendt, newsman David Brinkley, and columnist Joseph Kraft, among others. As his anxiety about dissent grew, Johnson directed Hoover to investigate citizens who had sent antiwar letters or telegrams to the White House.[271]

In 1966, the FBI began to turn its COINTELPRO against the New Left.[*] Special agents in the Boston field office solicited a local editorial cartoonist to prepare a cartoon ridiculing antiwar protesters as "traitors."[†272] In 1968, after the student protests at Columbia University, the Bureau formally launched a new COINTELPRO in order to hasten the collapse of the New Left. The key directive stated that the goal was to "expose, disrupt and otherwise neutralize the activities of the various New Left organizations, their leadership and adherents." FBI agents were instructed to frustrate "every effort of these groups . . . to recruit new . . . members," to disrupt the activities of these groups, to spread misinformation about meeting places and times, to exploit "organizational and personal conflicts," and to promote suspicion, distrust, and dissension within the leadership. Hoover exhorted his agents to approach these new responsibilities with "imagination and enthusiasm."[273]

The Philadelphia field office responded with particular verve, suggesting fraudulent news leaks and sending anonymous letters to the parents of antiwar protesters, accusing them of homosexuality or other "weaknesses and deficiencies."[274] Agents in other cities fabricated anonymous letters attacking local colleges for tolerating student radicals,[275] sent fraudulent letters to universities and public officials from "parents" of students complaining that the university had allowed "an atmosphere to build up on campus that will be fertile" for radical activities, and disseminated phony leaflets deriding SDS activists.[276] Agents in Detroit proposed spraying a left-wing publishing organization with the scent of "foul smelling feces," and FBI agents in Hollywood sent anonymous letters to a prominent gossip columnist attacking antiwar supporters in the film industry.[277]

---

[*] One complication that frustrated the FBI in dealing with the New Left is that it was so disorganized and unstructured. The FBI was unable to use the traditional "membership" model it had used in its investigation of Communists (including members of officially "listed" organizations) to ascertain who should be investigated. See Theoharis, *Spying on Americans* at 57 (cited in note 263).

[†] In early 1968, J. Edgar Hoover characterized SDS as dangerously "anarchistic and nihilistic," and reported that a workshop at an SDS convention had trained individuals in sabotage and explosives. Ironically, this workshop had been scheduled by SDS precisely to draw FBI undercover agents to it so they would not infiltrate the more substantive parts of the convention. Goldstein, *Political Repression* at 438 (cited in note 30). See also Sale, *SDS* at 456 (cited in note 26).

In its effort to destabilize and incapacitate the left, FBI agents wrote letters to employers to cause the firing of antiwar activists; distributed fraudulent college newspapers defaming peace activists; sent anonymous letters to campaign contributors and other supporters of antiwar candidates to sabotage their campaigns; mailed anonymous letters to the spouses of antiwar activists, suggesting that their partners were having extramarital affairs; and spread false rumors that individuals were embezzling funds or secretly cooperating with the FBI.*

FBI agents infiltrated New Left organizations in order to disrupt their activities; caused antiwar activists to be evicted from their homes; disabled their cars; intercepted their mail; wiretapped and bugged their conversations; planted derogatory information about them in the press; prevented them from renting facilities for meetings; incited police to harass them for minor offenses;† sabotaged and disrupted peaceful demonstrations; and instigated physical assaults against them.‡278

---

* An example of these fabricated letters was one written in a "sympathetic" tone by an anonymous "Concerned Friend" to the father of a student at Georgetown University, warning the father that his son had become involved with "radical anti-war and anti-democratic groups." According to the "friend," the son "manages to be actively present at any and every wild type of demonstration going on in Washington" and "tries to stir up people and to attack the Government, the war and just about any other issue that his organization can seize upon." The anonymous "friend" then expresses "concern" that this fine young man "is making a mess of what started out to be a promising future," states that he had tried without success to explain to the son the "dangerous situation in which he is involving himself," and winds up urging the father to "try to straighten him out before he messes himself up completely." FBI Memorandum from Washington, D.C., Field Office to Headquarters, Jan 6, 1969, and FBI Memorandum from Headquarters to Washington, D.C., Field Office, Jan 22, 1969, both excerpted in Davis, *Assault on Left* at 126 (cited in note 269).

† A memo from Hoover to the special agent in charge of the Albany field office noted, "Since the use of marijuana . . . is widespread among members of the New Left, you should be alert to opportunities to have them arrested by local authorities on drug charges. Any information concerning the fact that individuals have marijuana or are engaging in a narcotics party should be immediately furnished to local authorities and they should be encouraged to take action." FBI Memorandum from J. Edgar Hoover to SAC, Albany, July 5, 1968, reprinted in Churchill and Vander Wall, *COINTELPRO Papers* at 183–84 (cited in note 265).

‡ A few illustrations: a state undercover agent served as cochair of the SDS chapter in Columbia, South Carolina; another state undercover agent worked his way up to chairman of the SDS chapter at the University of Texas; members of the city of Chicago "Red squad" infiltrated the SDS chapter at Northwestern University, led a sit-in in 1968, and then actively participated in a highly disruptive 1969 Weathermen action; other Chicago undercover operatives provided explosives to the Weathermen, encouraged them to shoot police, and led an assault upon a uniformed police sergeant during a demonstration, which was widely publicized as "proving the violence" of the New Left. See Churchill and Vander Wall, *COINTELPRO Papers* at 225 (cited in note 265); Wise, *American Police State* at 311, 319 (cited in note 277).

THE FBI's COINTELPRO was not the only government program directed against the antiwar movement. As we saw in chapter 4, in the years leading up to World War II, the FBI created a security index list of individuals to be detained in case of war or national emergency. In 1967, the FBI began compiling a new agitator index, which included leaders of the anti-war movement.[279]

The Central Intelligence Agency also entered the picture. In 1956, the CIA began opening international mail in order to pursue foreign intelligence. In 1966, it expanded this program to include mail sent to or from individuals involved in the antiwar movement, even where the inquiry was directed toward domestic rather than foreign intelligence. Over the next few years, the CIA turned over to the FBI information resulting from more than twenty thousand mail openings, including material—often of a highly personal nature—about individuals involved in antiwar demonstrations, teach-ins, and similar activities.[280]

The CIA also engaged directly in wholly domestic spying. In 1967, it initiated Project MERRIMAC, which was designed to protect CIA facilities and personnel against anti-war protests by infiltrating and monitoring an array of antiwar organizations, such as SDS and the Women's Strike for Peace. That same year, the CIA created Project RESISTANCE, an aggressive effort to gather information about radical activities in the United States. This program compiled material on more than twelve thousand individuals, particularly those active on college campuses.

The most drastic domestic CIA program was Operation CHAOS, which was initiated in 1967 as a result of pressure from President Johnson. Its purpose, in clear violation of the CIA's legislative charter, which expressly prohibited the CIA from undertaking any "internal security" role, was to investigate possible Communist or other "subversive" involvement in the antiwar movement. Although the CIA consistently reported that foreign involvement was minimal, Presidents Johnson and Nixon continued to insist on further investigation.[281] As the Rockefeller Commission on the CIA later reported, Operation CHAOS "became a repository for large quantities of information on the domestic activities of American citizens," much of which was routinely shared with the FBI and the White House.[282]

At roughly the same time that the CIA established CHAOS, Army intelligence began its own large-scale domestic spying operation. The purported goal was to enable the Army to plan effectively for domestic disorders. Directed initially at possible race riots, CHAOS expanded quickly. By October 1967, some 130 Army intelligence agents were actively infiltrating, photographing, and reporting on an antiwar march at the Pentagon. The following year, the Army expressly directed its domestic intelligence program at the antiwar movement.

Army intelligence assigned fifteen hundred undercover agents to collect information about virtually every group seeking significant change in the United States.[283] The Army gathered information on more than 100,000 opponents of the Vietnam War, including Senator Adlai Stevenson of Illinois, Congressman Abner Mikva, Georgia State Senator Julian Bond, Martin Luther King Jr., and Joan Baez. Among the organizations the Army investigated were the ACLU, Americans for Democratic Action, the Anti-Defamation League, the American Friends Service Committee, and *Ramparts* magazine. Army intelligence agents monitored private communications, infiltrated antiwar organizations, participated in antiwar protests and demonstrations, and posed as press representatives. The Army disseminated the material it gathered, including information about the private political, financial and sex lives of tens of thousands of individuals, to a broad range of government agencies, among them local police, the FBI, the CIA, and the National Security Agency (NSA).[284]

At the behest of the White House, the NSA in 1967 began to intercept telephone communications involving the antiwar movement. Because this program was directed at American citizens, it was clearly illegal. To ensure security, NSA devised separate filing systems for these intercepts and classified the records "Top Secret." On July 1, 1969, it formalized this program under the code name MINARET, and directed the program "to restrict the knowledge that such information is being collected."[285]

WHEN RICHARD NIXON assumed the presidency in January 1969, he already had in place a "formidable apparatus to effect a program of political repression." His administration took full advantage of this apparatus. From the outset, Nixon pressed the FBI to expand its domestic surveillance activities. In 1969, the Justice Department directed the FBI to gather information about individuals who participated in campus antiwar protests, and J. Edgar Hoover instructed his agents to record all "inflammatory" speeches.[286] Over the next two years, the Justice Department asked the FBI for information on the "income sources of revolutionary groups," the FBI instructed its agents to investigate all individuals who belonged to SDS or other "militant New Left campus organizations," and Hoover directed his agents to report the "identities of speakers" at antiwar demonstrations. FBI reports on these matters were disseminated to the White House, the CIA, the State Department, the military intelligence agencies, the Secret Service, and the Department of Justice.[287]

The administration prodded the FBI to expand its New Left COINTELPRO and pushed the CIA to intensify its domestic surveillance activities. During the

Nixon administration, the CIA furnished the FBI with more than one thousand domestic intelligence reports per month. This information was gathered by undercover agents, break-ins, wiretapping, and mail openings. Eventually, 300,000 names were indexed in the CIA's computers. The CIA was fully aware of the illegality of these activities. In passing one report on to the White House, CIA Director Richard Helms noted, "[T]his is an area not within the charter of this Agency, so I need not emphasize how extremely sensitive this makes the paper."[288]

Army intelligence developed a new plan in April 1969, calling for the identification of all individuals "involved, or expected to become involved, in protest activities."[289] Attorney General John Mitchell went so far as to claim that the president had the authority to authorize electronic domestic intelligence surveillance *without court order.*[290]

The Nixon administration enlisted the Internal Revenue Service on a massive scale. In 1969, it informed the IRS of the president's concern that "tax-exempt funds may be supporting activist groups." Eight days later, the IRS established the Activist Organizations Committee to "collect relevant information on organizations predominantly dissident or extremist in nature and on people prominently identified with these organizations." This committee was later renamed the Special Services Staff (SSS) to disguise its real purpose.[291]

By 1974, the SSS had compiled files on 8,585 individuals. The IRS routinely furnished this information, including lists of contributors to SDS and other antiwar organizations, to the FBI, the Secret Service, Army intelligence, and the White House. The goal was to "deal a blow to dissident elements" through the use of targeted tax audits and tax investigations. The SSS investigated such individuals as the columnist Joseph Alsop, folk singer Joan Baez, journalist Jimmy Breslin, New York City Mayor John Lindsay, actress Shirley MacLaine, and U.S. Senator Charles Goodell. The organizations it investigated included the ACLU, the American Jewish Committee, the National Organization of Women, the National Council of Churches, and the Americans for Democratic Action. This program was kept strictly secret because of its "political sensitivity."[292]

In 1970, the White House began compiling an "enemies list" under the direction of Charles Colson, special assistant to the president. Some two hundred individuals and eighteen organizations were targeted for "special" government attention. Among those on the list were former Attorney General Ramsey Clark, Congresswomen Bella Abzug and Shirley Chisholm, Senators Edward Kennedy, Edmund Muskie, and Walter Mondale, the presidents of Harvard, Yale, the Ford Foundation and the Rand Corporation, actors Gregory Peck and Carol Channing, and journalists James Reston, Marvin Kalb, Daniel Schorr, and Joseph Kraft.[293]

A month after the Kent State killings, Nixon moved to centralize domestic intelligence in the Oval Office. At his request, White House assistant Tom Charles Huston proposed a new White House unit to oversee the investigation of political dissent. A "right-wing ideologue" with "a messianic view of America's Cold War mission," Huston was convinced the nation was "worm-eaten with domestic enemies and subversives." Even Nixon thought him "inflammatory." On one occasion, Nixon admiringly described him as "a son of a bitch . . . who will work his butt off and do it dishonorably."[294]

In July 1970, Huston prepared a memorandum, which came to be known as the Huston Plan, recommending intensified electronic surveillance, monitoring of international communications, and "mail coverage" (that is, opening and reading mail); expanded use of undercover informants and "surreptitious entry"; and the creation of a central agency on domestic intelligence with representatives from the White House, FBI, CIA, NSA, and the military. The Huston Plan has fairly been characterized as a "blueprint for a police state in America."[295]

Although the president initially approved the plan, J. Edgar Hoover objected, partly because he saw the Huston Plan as a threat to the FBI's independence, and partly because he feared public exposure. Rather than buck Hoover, Nixon withdrew his support.[*296] Although the Huston Plan was never formally adopted, many of its recommendations were later "implemented piecemeal."[297] By the mid-1970s, Henry Steele Commager could aptly observe that if "repression is not yet as blatant or as flamboyant as it was during the McCarthy years, it is in many respects more pervasive and more formidable."[298]

THE GOVERNMENT'S SECRET MACHINATIONS "to expose, disrupt and otherwise neutralize" the New Left were not known to the public until March 8, 1971, when an antiwar group—the Citizens' Commission to Investigate the FBI—broke into an FBI office in Media, Pennsylvania, and stole

---

[*] Several years later, on the eve of the Watergate hearings, the White House counsel Fred Buzhardt warned the president that the public was about to learn for the first time about the Huston Plan. Buzhardt suggested that Nixon emphasize the "perilous times" the nation faced in 1970 and justify the plan as a necessary step "to combat domestic subversion." Kutler, ed, *Abuse of Power* at 507 (cited in note 294). Nixon mistakenly dismissed the matter as unimportant, noting, "I don't think the country is going to get excited about a damn plan that was drawn up . . . to control the Goddamn riots." Conversation in the Oval Office between Richard Nixon, Fred Buzhardt, and Alexander Haig, May 16, 1973, id at 515.

approximately one thousand confidential documents. The group released excerpts to members of Congress, journalists, and organizations who were named in files. One of the documents, dated September 16, 1970, was mysteriously captioned "COINTELPRO-New Left." This document, the first public intimation of the existence of this covert program, recommended intensified FBI interviewing of dissidents to "enhance the paranoia" and to underscore the fear that "there is an FBI agent behind every mailbox."[299]

The administration's response to these disclosures was to warn that any further disclosures "could endanger the lives or cause other serious harm to persons engaged in investigation activities on behalf of the United States."[300] The *Washington Post* countered that these revelations showed that the FBI had been implementing a form "of internal security appropriate for the Secret Police of the Soviet Union." The *Post* argued that "the American public needs to know what the FBI is doing" and "needs to think long and hard about whether internal security rests . . . upon official surveillance and the suppression of dissent or upon the traditional freedom of every citizen to speak his mind on any subject, whether others consider what he says wise or foolish, patriotic or subversive, conservative or radical."[301]

Over the next several weeks, as more of the FBI's COINTELPRO activities came to light, several major newspapers and congressmen called for J. Edgar Hoover's resignation. Under intense public pressure, Hoover announced on April 28, 1971, that he had officially terminated COINTELPRO. At that time, the FBI had some 2,000 agents engaged in domestic intelligence activities, and they were supervising an additional 1,700 domestic intelligence informants and 1,400 "confidential" sources. By April 1971, the antiwar movement had been the target of several hundred seriously "disruptive" FBI actions intended to prevent citizens from "speaking, teaching, writing or publishing."[*302]

After the public disclosure of these activities, Congress authorized investigating committees to probe more deeply. The Senate Select Committee to Study

---

* Similar activities were taking place at the state and local levels. According to one estimate, by January 1972 more than five hundred cities had political intelligence divisions, generally known as Red squads, attached to their local police operations. In addition, many states had their own intelligence operations. Most of the state and local agencies compiled massive intelligence files, engaged in overt surveillance and photographing of political demonstrations, and infiltrated dissident groups with informers and provocateurs. The New York City intelligence operation had files on 1.2 million persons. In many instances, the CIA directly supported these state and local activities. See Nick Egleson, *The Surveillance Apparatus*, in Paul Cowan, Nick Egelson, and Nat Hentoff, eds, *State Secrets: Police Surveillance in America* 3–85 (Holt, Rinehart and Winston 1974); Goldstein, *Political Repression* at 504–8 (cited in note 30); Harris, *Justice* at 126–27 (cited in note 150); Schell, *Time of Illusion* at 61–62 (cited in note 164).

Governmental Operations with Respect to Intelligence Activities made the following findings:

> The Government has often undertaken the secret surveillance of citizens on the
> basis of their political beliefs, even when those beliefs posed no threat of violence
> or illegal acts. . . . The Government, operating primarily through secret inform-
> ants . . . has swept in vast amounts of information about the personal lives, views,
> and associations of American citizens. Investigations of groups deemed poten-
> tially dangerous—and even of groups suspected of associating with potentially
> dangerous organizations—have continued for decades, despite the fact that those
> groups did not engage in unlawful activity. . . . FBI headquarters alone has devel-
> oped over 500,000 domestic intelligence files. . . .[303]

In March 1971, the Army announced that it was banning any further collection of information about individuals and organizations "unaffiliated" with
the military, except where "essential" to the military mission, and that it was
destroying all material it had previously gathered. The Senate Judiciary Subcommittee on Constitutional Rights, which conducted hearings into the Army's
surveillance program, concluded that it had served no legitimate governmental
purpose, but had seriously infringed "the rights of the citizens it was supposed to
be safeguarding."*[304]

In 1976, President Gerald Ford formally prohibited the CIA from using electronic or physical surveillance to collect information on domestic activities of
Americans and banned the NSA from intercepting any communication made
within, from or to the United States. The new FBI director, Clarence Kelly, publicly apologized for FBI abuses under J. Edgar Hoover, conceding that the
bureau had engaged in activities that "were clearly wrong and quite indefensible"
and that must "never" be repeated.[305]

That same year, Attorney General Edward Levi, following the example of Attorney General Harlan Fiske Stone after the 1919–20 Red Scare, imposed stringent
limitations on the investigative authority and activities of the FBI. In these "guide-

---

* MINARET was terminated in 1972. As in other instances, the termination was driven less by
concerns about illegality than by fear of public exposure and adverse political consequences. In the
government's prosecution of several Weathermen, the defendants moved for disclosure of all federal
surveillance directed at them. The government objected on grounds of "national security." A federal
court granted the defendants' motion, and the Supreme Court affirmed. See *United States v. United
States District Court*, 407 US 297 (1972). Thereafter, the government terminated MINARET and
moved to dismiss the prosecution *(United States v. Ayres)* so that it would not have to disclose the
unlawful wiretaps. See Theoharis, *Spying on Americans* at 122–25 (cited in note 263).

lines," Levi expressly prohibited the FBI from investigating, discrediting, or disrupting any group or individual on the basis of protected First Amendment activity. The guidelines declared that the FBI could investigate only *criminal* conduct and that it would no longer be permitted to monitor protected First Amendment activity, except in a legitimate and narrowly tailored effort to enforce the criminal law. The guidelines provided further that the FBI could not initiate an investigation of any organization engaged in protected First Amendment activity in the absence of "specific and articulable facts" justifying a criminal investigation. Finally, the guidelines adopted a series of procedural requirements to implement these restrictions. The Levi guidelines were hailed as a major advance in law enforcement and a critical step forward in protecting the rights of American citizens against overzealous and misguided government officials.*[306]

Like Attorney General Stone's policy in 1924, the Levi guidelines represented good government at its best. Without regard to whether these limitations were required by the Constitution, and without waiting for legislative action, Levi imposed these regulations on the FBI as a matter of sound public policy. The protection of civil liberties demands not only compliance with the Constitution, but also thoughtful, restrained use of government power.

But that still leaves the question whether the activities implicated in COINTELPRO, the Huston Plan, and the Army, CIA, and NSA domestic intelligence programs of the late 1960s and early 1970s were constitutional. Some plainly were not. For example, it is settled that, as a general rule, the government cannot constitutionally break into a person's home, open her mail, bug her office, or tap her telephone without probable cause and a warrant. Such activities clearly violate the Fourth Amendment, which forbids "unreasonable searches and seizures." Even Huston recognized that the black-bag jobs he proposed were unconstitutional.

The constitutionality of other activities is less certain. Consider government surveillance of public meetings and demonstrations. Suppose an antiwar group sponsors a public event at which speakers will attack the wisdom and morality of a war. May the FBI or a local Red squad send a government agent to attend the meeting in order to photograph participants and record the names of those in attendance? Under current law, this surveillance would not violate the Fourth

---

* Shortly after promulgating these guidelines, Attorney General Levi terminated the FBI's thirty-eight-year-old investigation of the Socialist Workers Party, which had involved more than thirty FBI informers and had accumulated eight million file entries from 1960 to 1976. Despite this massive investigation, the federal government had not succeeded in filing a single criminal prosecution of the SWP or its members in more than thirty-five years. Levi explained that under the new guidelines there was no legitimate basis for continuing this investigation. See Goldstein, *Political Repression* at 540 (cited in note 30).

Amendment, because the Court has held that individuals have no "reasonable expectation of privacy" in not being observed when they are voluntarily in a public place, so there is no "search" within the meaning of the Constitution.[307]

On the other hand, this practice would clearly violate the Levi guidelines. Would it violate the First Amendment? The First and Fourth Amendments protect different values. The former protects free expression, association, and religion; the latter, one's general sense of privacy. The argument that this practice violates the First Amendment, even though it does not violate the Fourth, finds support in the Supreme Court's "compelled disclosure" cases of the late 1950s and early 1960s. As we saw in chapter 5, the Court has held in cases like *NAACP v. Alabama* and *Gibson v. Florida Investigating Committee* that for the government to invade the privacy of protected First Amendment activities may violate the Constitution. This is so because the freedoms of speech, association, and religion are protected "not only against heavy-handed frontal attack, but also from being stifled by more subtle governmental interference."[308]

In the situation of the public meeting, knowledge that government agents (whether undercover or in uniform) are, or may be, taking names and photographs would undoubtedly chill the willingness of some people to attend the event. The fear of ending up on a government "list" or in a Red squad, FBI, or HUAC file merely for participating in a public rally or attending a public lecture will inevitably cause some, perhaps many, people to stay away. We have seen this throughout our history. Thus, unless the government has a clear, articulable, legitimate, and evenhanded justification for engaging in such surveillance, this practice should be held to violate the First Amendment.*

What of the use of informers and secret agents? The Court has held that the government's use of undercover agents to deceive individuals into revealing information about themselves or inadvertently granting informers access to nonpublic meetings, places, and conversations is not a "search" within the meaning of the Fourth Amendment. The Court's rationale is that in day-to-day life individuals must "assume the risk" that those with whom they deal are not who they purport to be. Thus, if your friendly neighborhood drug dealer turns out to be a snitch or

---

* If the government has a clear, legitimate, and evenhanded justification for being present at the public event, its conduct may be warranted. For example, the government has a responsibility to provide reasonable police protection at mass public demonstrations. The presence of the police for that purpose is constitutionally permissible. But this would not justify "taking names" or photographs of individuals engaged in constitutionally protected First Amendment activity. On the other hand, if the government has reasonable grounds to believe that criminal activity is afoot, it may engage in surveillance, including "taking names," as long as its purpose is to investigate criminal activity and its investigation is narrowly tailored to that end.

your inquisitive meterman is snooping in your basement for the government, you have no basis for complaining that this is an "unreasonable search."[309]

Whatever the merits of this doctrine in the Fourth Amendment context (I think it misguided), it should *not* govern the use of such deceit to infiltrate a political or religious organization. For the government to put such organizations in a position where they have to suspect every member of secretly being a government spy would empower the government to undermine the mutual trust that is essential to effective political or religious association. As Harlan Fiske Stone noted after the post–World War I Red Scare, "a secret police may become a menace to free government and free institutions."[310] This practice should be held to violate the First Amendment unless the government has reasonable grounds to believe that the political or religious organization is involved in *criminal* activity and the investigation is narrowly tailored to that end.[*] And for the government to plant an agent in such an organization with the express *purpose* of disrupting its protected First Amendment activities should be deemed a blatant violation of the Constitution.

Although the Supreme Court has not had occasion to rule on the constitutionality of these activities,[311] it is striking how the government's efforts to control dissent have shifted over the years. In 1798, 1861, 1917, 1941, and 1951 the government criminally prosecuted Jacobins, Copperheads, anarchists, fascists, and Communists for their dissent. During the Vietnam War, however, there was no systematic effort to *prosecute* individuals for their opposition to the war. In saying this, I do not mean to dismiss or belittle the prosecutions of O'Brien, Spock, Coffin, the Berrigans, or the Chicago Seven. In varying degrees, they were problematic, or worse. But whatever the legitimacy of those prosecutions, they did not represent a wholesale effort to stifle dissent through criminal prosecution. Throughout this era, the government relied much more than in the past on indirect, surreptitious, and less effective means of quelling opposition. Indeed, when all was said and done, the ferocity and persistence of the antiwar protests in this era drove two presidents from office. As Todd Gitlin has rightly observed, in com-

---

[*] It is easier to state this principle than to implement it. Suppose, for example, a member of an organization, like Elizabeth Bentley with the Communist Party in the 1950s, decides voluntarily to cooperate with the government. Does it violate the First Amendment for the government to use the information she provides? Does it violate the First Amendment for the government to ask her to continue to participate in the organization and to report back what she learns? At what point does she become a "government agent"? Another issue concerns a political organization that expressly advocates unlawful conduct to effect political change. Is mere *advocacy* a sufficient basis to infiltrate the organization? Does it matter whether it is advocacy of future rather than immediate unlawful conduct? What bearing does the Court's 1957 decision in *Yates* have on this question? See *Alliance to End Repression v. City of Chicago*, 742 F2d 1007 (7th Cir 1984) (interpreting a consent decree so as not to prohibit investigation based on express advocacy of violence).

parison with past episodes, "the repression of the late Sixties and early Seventies was mild."[312]

There are many reasons for this, including the unpopularity of the Vietnam War, which made direct criminal prosecution more difficult, and the compelling fact that most antiwar protesters were the sons and daughters of the middle class, who could not so easily be targeted as the "Other." But the courts, and especially the Supreme Court, played a critical role as well.

THE PENTAGON PAPERS

ON THE MORNING OF Sunday, June 13, 1971, several people noticed a smiling Daniel Ellsberg walking across Harvard Square in Cambridge, Massachusetts, carrying a large stack of New York Timeses. After a tortuous journey, the Pentagon Papers had finally begun to see the light of day.

Four years earlier, on June 17, 1967, Secretary of Defense Robert McNamara had commissioned the compilation of a "History of U.S. Decision-Making Process on Vietnam Policy, 1945–1967." For almost seven years, McNamara had been a key architect of the nation's policy in Vietnam. By 1967, he had begun to have doubts. He later explained that his objective in ordering the report "was to bequeath to scholars the raw material from which they could reexamine the events of the time."[313] It took two years for those working on the secret project to complete the study—a work of 7,000 pages in forty-seven volumes. When McNamara later read the report, he commented, "[Y]ou know, they could hang people for what's in there."[314]

Although most of what was in the study was common knowledge, it shed important light on key aspects of America's involvement in Vietnam. It documented, for example, that at the end of World War II President Truman had rejected urgent appeals from Ho Chi Minh for American assistance; that while the 1954 Geneva conference was still in session, the United States was actively planning paramilitary operations in Saigon against the North; that President Kennedy's "advisers" in Vietnam had not merely advised the South Vietnamese but had participated directly in military operations; that the U.S. government had knowingly publicized false South Vietnamese intelligence reports about the extent of Communist infiltration; that the Gulf of Tonkin Resolution had been rammed through Congress under blatantly false pretenses; and that the U.S. government had concealed from the American public the fact that extensive bombing of North Vietnam had done little to impair the Communists' military capacity, but had killed tens of thousands of Vietnamese civilians.[315]

As Senator Mike Gravel of Alaska observed, the study revealed "the purposeful withholding and distortion of facts" from the American people and the utter disregard "for the impact of our actions upon the Vietnamese people." Gravel added that the Pentagon Papers showed, ironically, "that the enemy knew what we were not permitted to know."[*][316]

BORN IN CHICAGO IN 1931, Daniel Ellsberg attended Harvard, served as president of the undergraduate literary magazine, and wrote a brilliant senior thesis on the emerging field of economic game theory. He received a Woodrow Wilson fellowship to study advanced economics at Cambridge University and, after completing his studies in England, volunteered for a hitch in the Marines.

Following a stint in the Middle East, he returned to Harvard as a prestigious "junior fellow" to study decision theory. After earning his Ph.D., he accepted a position with the Rand Corporation, one of the nation's most high-powered defense research centers, where he specialized in developing strategies to deter a Soviet nuclear attack. Ellsberg was frequently called in to consult with high government officials on national security matters. During the Kennedy years, he accepted a position in the Defense Department under Secretary of Defense McNamara. A committed hawk, Ellsberg was dedicated to the American policy in Vietnam.[317]

In mid-1965, he volunteered to serve in Vietnam as a State Department representative. As he came to know the Vietnamese people, his understanding of the war began to change. For the first time, he questioned what the United States was doing there. He came to appreciate not only the suffering caused by the war, but also that the information reported back to the United States was dangerously inaccurate.[†]

---

[*] Leslie Gelb, the primary author of the Pentagon Papers, explained that he had classified the study as "top secret" simply as a matter of routine because the Defense Department required that any compilation of documents "bear the highest classification of any of its parts." Ungar, *Papers* at 41 (cited in note 313).

[†] On one occasion, in October 1966, Ellsberg was flying back to the United States with Secretary of Defense McNamara. Near the end of the flight, McNamara said, "We've put more than a hundred thousand more troops into the country over the last year, and there's been no improvement." Indeed, he added, "the underlying situation is really *worse!*" Ten minutes later, after the plane landed in Washington, D.C., McNamara told reporters, "Gentlemen, I've just come back from Vietnam, and I'm glad to be able to tell you that we're showing great progress in every dimension of our effort." Ellsberg, *Secrets* at 141–42 (cited in note 317).

He later observed that "a major 'lesson of Vietnam' was the impact on policy" of persistent "lying to superiors," which resulted in a disastrous "failure at the presidential level to recognize realities."[318]

After returning to the United States and his position at Rand in 1967, Ellsberg continued to consult with top-level officials in the government and even played a role in compiling the Pentagon Papers. At the same time, however, he now pursued his own review of the war. He began reading the entire Pentagon Papers, a copy of which had been given to Rand. He concluded that Vietnam had never been a war of "aggression from the North," as the government had claimed, or even a "civil war." Rather, it was "a war of foreign aggression, American aggression." He came "to see as morally wrong our prolongation of the war against the wishes of most of Vietnam's inhabitants, who would gladly have accepted terms to end it that we refused to consider."[319]

Ellsberg later explained that his reading of the Pentagon Papers finally convinced him that the only appropriate course was withdrawal. Increasingly, he felt a sense of personal responsibility for his role in justifying the war. At an antiwar conference in August 1969, he came to a stark realization: "I had risked my life . . . a thousand times driving the roads [in Vietnam]. . . . If I could do that when I believed in the war, and even after I didn't, it followed . . . that I was capable of going to prison to help end it."[320] In the fall of 1969, working secretly, Ellsberg and Anthony Russo, a former Rand associate, began to make copies of the entire 7,000-page study.

As Ellsberg grew more outspoken in his views, he no longer fit in at Rand. He moved back to Massachusetts in 1970, accepting a position at MIT's Center for International Studies. In the meantime, he quietly explored ways to make the Pentagon Papers public. By March 1971, Ellsberg had decided that the only way to do this was through the press. When he learned that Neil Sheehan, a former UPI correspondent he had known in Vietnam, had moved to the *New York Times*, Ellsberg decided to give Sheehan a redacted copy of the "top secret" study.[*][321]

UPON RECEIVING THE PENTAGON PAPERS, the leaders of the *New York Times* had to wonder what they had gotten themselves into. Were the Papers for real? Was it worth the effort to review thousands of pages of material

---

[*] Ellsberg did not disclose those portions of the Pentagon Papers that he thought might endanger the national security.

that might have nothing new in them? Was it "right" for the *Times* to publish material that had been "stolen" from the government?

As they read the Papers, they realized it was much more than a rehash of what was already known. Moreover, the study had ended in 1968, so what it disclosed was history, rather than current military plans. A fierce debate developed within the *Times* about whether and how to proceed.

To review the massive quantity of material, the *Times* assigned Sheehan, three other reporters, and a swarm of support personnel to work in a closely guarded suite of rooms in the New York Hilton. For three months, they read, sorted, and analyzed the Pentagon Papers and struggled to grasp the significance of what they had read.[322] On June 11, the *Times* finally decided to proceed with a ten-part series, to begin two days later.

Because the *Times* did not sensationalize the story, it took several days for the Nixon administration to realize what was happening. No one in the Department of Justice had ever heard of the Pentagon Papers, but by the end of the second day opinions within the government began to crystallize. The Defense Department demanded a strong response. Some Republican leaders, however, like Senator Robert Dole, the chairman of the Republican National Committee, argued against any effort to interfere with publication. They maintained that because the study ended in 1968, its primary focus would be on the Kennedy and Johnson administrations, and its publication would therefore work to the advantage of Republicans. The president shared this view.[*]

There were complications, however. In June 1971, the administration was engaged in secret negotiations with China about a possible Nixon visit, and National Security Advisor Henry Kissinger was concerned that China would balk if it learned that America could not keep its secrets. Moreover, by mid-1971 the administration had been secretly bombing Cambodia for almost two years, and denying reports to the contrary. If the administration looked the other way in this instance, it would be an open invitation to reporters to publish confidential material that might directly damage the administration.[323]

A further complexity was the administration's already antagonistic relationship with the media. Angry at what they perceived as a "liberal bias" among journalists, Nixon and others in his administration had sharply attacked the press. The central figure in these attacks, Vice President Spiro Agnew, had castigated the media as "self-appointed guardians of our destiny" and purveyors of "editorial

---

[*] Inspired by the leak of the Pentagon Papers, Nixon decided it would be expedient to leak even more documents to reveal the shortcomings of his Democratic predecessors. He observed that "if we do this correctly," the Democratic Party will be "gone without a trace." Kutler, ed, *Abuse of Power* at 45 (cited in note 294).

doublethink" who abused their influence over public opinion. He had gone so far as to suggest that the press should no longer be permitted to "wield a free hand in selecting, presenting, and interpreting the great issues of the nation."[324] Against this backdrop, any effort by the administration to enjoin or criminally punish the *New York Times* for its publication of the Pentagon Papers would unleash a firestorm of criticism from the press.

In the end, Kissinger's concerns won out. On Monday, June 14, Attorney General Mitchell sent a telegram to Arthur Sulzberger, publisher of the *Times*, stating that the June 13 and 14 issues of the *Times* contained information bearing "a top-secret classification." Mitchell added that "publication of this information" was "directly prohibited" by the Espionage Act of 1917 and that further publication would "cause irreparable injury to the defense interests of the United States." He therefore requested that the *Times* "publish no further information of this character and advise" him that it had "made arrangements for the return of these documents to the Department of Defense."[325]

Two hours later, the *Times* transmitted a response, which it released publicly: "The *Times* must respectfully decline the request of the Attorney General, believing that it is in the interest of the people of this country to be informed of the material contained in this series of articles." The *Times* added that if the government sought to enjoin any further publication of the material, it would contest the government's position, but would "of course abide by the final decision of the court."

The next morning's edition included not only the third installment in the series but also a front-page story headlined, "Mitchell Seeks to Halt Series on Vietnam But *Times* Refuses."[326] Months later, the *Times* managing editor, A. M. Rosenthal, pondered what "it would have meant in our history and in the history of the newspaper business if the headline had been 'Justice Department Asks End to Vietnam Series and *Times* Concedes.' "[327]

EVENTS ESCALATED QUICKLY. On Tuesday, June 15, the U.S. government filed a complaint for injunction against the *New York Times* in the federal district court in Manhattan—the same Foley Square courthouse that had seen the trial of the *Masses* case in 1917, the prosecution of Jacob Abrams and Mollie Steimer in 1919, and the prosecution of Eugene Dennis and the other leaders of the Communist Party in 1949.

The case was assigned to Judge Murray Gurfein, a Nixon appointee who had served in Army intelligence during World War II. Gurfein had been sworn in only days earlier. This was his first case as a judge. After a brief hearing, Gurfein granted the government's request for a temporary restraining order on the ground that "any temporary harm that may result from not publishing during the pendency of the application for a preliminary injunction is far outweighed by the irreparable harm that could be done to the interests of the United States government if it should ultimately prevail" in the case.[328] This was the *first* time in the almost 200-year history of the United States that a federal judge had restrained a newspaper from publishing specific information. Judge Gurfein ordered both sides to submit legal briefs by Friday, June 18.

AT THIS POINT, a brief digression into the law of prior restraint seems warranted. As we have seen, in the debates over the Sedition Act of 1798, Federalists argued that the meaning of the First Amendment was fixed in Blackstone's 1769 commentary that under the common law "liberty of the press . . . consists in laying no *previous* restraints upon publications, and not in freedom from censure for criminal matter when published."[329] James Madison and other Republicans rejected this view. Madison argued that it would be "a mockery to say that no law should be passed preventing publications from being made, but that laws might be passed for punishing them in case they should be made." In other words, why prohibit the government from denying a license to speech because it is "seditious," if the government can punish it "once it is uttered?"[330]

In theory, at least, this remained an open question until the end of World War I. In the late nineteenth and early twentieth centuries, many courts still adhered to the view that if the government eschewed previous restraints, it was free to punish speech that could "be adjudged of a pernicious tendency."[331] On the other hand, most scholarly commentators echoed Madison and sharply criticized this approach.[332] The matter was finally resolved, for all intents and purposes, by Justice Oliver Wendell Holmes in *Schenck*, when he observed in passing, "It well may be that the prohibition of laws abridging the freedom of speech is not confined to previous restraints, although to prevent them may have been the main purpose."[333] This rather offhand dictum has forever since settled the question. The First Amendment is not limited to previous restraints.

But that left at least two questions: Does the First Amendment impose an especially high burden on prior restraints? What exactly is a prior restraint? With respect to the first question, the Court made clear in 1931 in *Near v. Minnesota*[334] that "for approximately one hundred and fifty years there has been almost an entire absence of attempts to impose previous restraints upon publications" and that this reflects "the deep-seated conviction that such restraints would violate constitutional right."[335] *Near* unequivocally affirmed that prior restraints are *especially* disfavored under the First Amendment.

With respect to the second question, the historical model of a prior restraint was licensing. Licensing posed unique problems. As Blackstone observed, "[t]o subject the press to the restrictive power of a licenser . . . is to subject all freedom of sentiment to the prejudices of one man, and make him the arbitrary and infallible judge of all controverted points in learning, religion, and government."[336] Under a licensing scheme, the licenser, rather than a court and jury, determines which publications are permitted.

Moreover, if a publisher fails to request a license, or disregards its denial, he is automatically guilty of a crime, whether or not a license would or should have been granted. This is quite different from the situation in which an individual decides to speak in violation of a criminal statute. In that situation, the individual is free to assert the unconstitutionality of the statute in his defense. In the licensing context, however, the crime is publishing without a license, and the speaker is punishable *even if the license could not lawfully have been denied.*

The Court held in *Near* that injunctions pose the same difficulty. Most significantly, the "collateral bar" rule governs injunctions. Under this rule, an individual may challenge an injunction that bars him from publishing *only* by appealing the grant of the injunction to a higher court. He may not violate the injunction and then assert its unconstitutionality in his defense. That is, as with a traditional licensing scheme, the publisher may not "collaterally" attack the constitutionality of the injunction. If he violates an injunction not to publish, he may be punished for violating the injunction even if the injunction would have been overturned on appeal as unconstitutional. It has thus been said that although a criminal statute "chills," an injunction "freezes."[337]

WHEN DANIEL ELLSBERG SAW that the June 16 issue of the *New York Times* did not include the next installment in the series, but instead reported the *Times's* decision to obey Judge Gurfein's injunction, he was livid. Given the importance of the material, and what he had risked to make it pubic, he felt that the *Times* should have disobeyed the injunction. He began to consider other outlets for the Papers. An obvious possibility was the *Washington Post*, which was miserable at having been scooped by the *Times*. He contacted Ben Bagdikian, an assistant managing editor at the *Post* he had known at Rand. On Wednesday, June 16, Ellsberg offered Bagdikian a copy of the Pentagon Papers.

That evening, another journalist reported that Ellsberg had been the source of the leak. Ellsberg immediately went into hiding so he could continue to monitor publication of the Papers before he was taken into custody. For almost two weeks, he was subject to what the press described as "the largest FBI manhunt since the Lindbergh kidnapping."[338]

During his days as a fugitive, Ellsberg was interviewed from secret places by a variety of journalists. In one instance, Walter Cronkite asked him what he considered "the most important revelations to date from the Pentagon documents." Ellsberg replied,

> I think the lesson is that the people of this country can't afford to let the President run the country by himself, . . . without the help of the Congress, without the help of the public. . . . What these studies tell me is we must remember this is a self-governing country. We are the government. . . . [W]e cannot let the officials of the Executive Branch determine for us what it is that the public needs to know about how well and how they are discharging their functions. . . .[339]

In the meantime, the editors of the *Post* found themselves with both an opportunity and a dilemma. The *Times* had had three months to review the Papers and prepare their articles. The *Post* editors recognized that if they were going to use the Papers, they would have to do so immediately. Gathered in the home of Ben Bradlee, the *Post's* managing editor, a group of reporters, lawyers and editors began working feverishly both to decide what to do and to do it, simultaneously. The *Post's* lawyers argued that it would be irresponsible to publish excerpts from the Papers in haste; the editors and reporters were adamant that they could do so responsibly. Finally, on Thursday, June 17, the *Washington Post's* publisher, Katharine Graham, gave the directive: "go ahead."[340]

The following morning, while the *Times* was still under a restraining order, the *Post* published its first article disclosing previously secret contents of the Pentagon Papers. Within hours, Assistant Attorney General William Rehnquist was on the phone with Ben Bradlee, reading him essentially the same message Attorney General Mitchell had telegraphed to the *Times* four days earlier. Bradlee replied, "I'm sure you will understand that I must respectfully decline."[341] Rehnquist then contacted the *Post's* lawyers and asked them to meet representatives of the Department of Justice at the federal courthouse in Washington, D.C.

That afternoon, the government filed suit for an injunction, alleging that the *Post*, in violation of the Espionage Act of 1917, had willfully communicated information it "knew or had reason to believe . . . could be used to the injury of the United States . . . to persons not entitled to receive such information."

At this point, it is instructive to recall the debates in Congress over the Espionage Act of 1917. As originally proposed by the Wilson administration, the act contained a provision—the "press censorship" provision—that would have made it unlawful for any person in time of war to publish any information that the president, in his judgment, had declared to be "of such character that it is or might be useful to the enemy." This provision, however, was resoundingly rejected by Congress as a "glaring attempt . . . to muzzle the press."[342] Thus, in accusing the *Times* and the *Post* of violating the Espionage Act, the government had to argue that they had violated the provisions of the act dealing with actual "espionage." In light of Congress's explicit rejection of the press censorship provision, the government's effort fifty years later to extend the "espionage" prohibition to the publications of the *Times* and the *Post* was clearly a stretch. This was almost precisely what Congress had rejected in 1917.

The government's suit against the *Post* was assigned to Judge Gerhard Gesell, a "liberal" judge who had had considerable experience both with the press, as a former reporter, and with national security, as a former government official. After hearing arguments on the government's request for a temporary restraining order, Gesell, unlike Judge Gurfein in New York, ruled immediately against the government. Gesell reasoned that the government was misusing the Espionage Act of 1917, which had never been intended to authorize "censorship of the press." Moreover, Gesell explained that an injunction was in any event unwarranted because the government had failed to specify any particular material in the Pentagon Papers whose publication would directly "injure the United States."[*343]

The next day, Judge Gurfein, after hearing further arguments, lifted his temporary restraining order against the *Times*. Gurfein observed that the Espionage Act had never been intended to interfere with the right of a newspaper "to vindicate the right of the public to know." The government had failed, he said, to present evidence of a serious danger to the nation. What is protected by the First Amendment, he added, "is not merely the opinion of the editorial writer" but "the free flow of information so that the public will be informed about the government and its actions." This, he noted, "has been the genius of our institutions throughout our history."[344]

Over the next few days, the two cases rapidly worked their way up to the Supreme Court of the United States.[†] During the pendency of the appeals, how-

---

[*] Later in the proceedings, the Justice Department wanted to present to Judge Gesell some of the more damaging materials in the Papers, but it insisted that it be a secret hearing, excluding even the defendants (that is, the *Washington Post*). Gesell responded, "We don't do things that way," adding, "If that's the way it's going to go, I'll dismiss the case." Graham, *Personal History* at 452 (cited in note 340).

[†] The U.S. Court of Appeals for the Second Circuit ordered a remand to Judge Gurfein for further fact-finding; the U.S. Court of Appeals for the District of Columbia Circuit upheld Judge Gesell's order denying the government's request for an injunction. Thus, both the *Times* and the United States sought review in the Supreme Court. See *United States v. New York Times Co*, 444 F2d 544 (2d Cir 1971); *United States v. Washington Post Co*, 466 F2d 1327 (DC Cir 1971). As these cases proceeded, the leaks continued and some twenty other newspapers published additional material from the Pentagon Papers, including the *Boston Globe*, the *Chicago Sun-Times*, the *St. Louis Post Dispatch*, and the *Christian Science Monitor*. See Ungar, *Papers* at 175–92 (cited in note 313). Most of these newspapers received the material from Ellsberg, who was now leaking like a sieve in order to ensure that the government could not control the situation.

ever, both the *Times* and the *Post* were temporarily restrained from publishing any additional material from the Papers. Thus, although they had won stunning victories in both New York and Washington, they were still under the dark cloud of prior restraint.

ON FRIDAY, JUNE 25, the Supreme Court agreed to review the *New York Times* and *Washington Post* cases together and to hold an unprecedented Saturday morning session on June 26 in order to hear oral arguments. It is important to note that this was not the "Warren Court" that had so revolutionized constitutional law in the 1950s and 1960s. Chief Justice Earl Warren had retired in 1969, and Richard Nixon had filled two vacancies on the Court. With his appointments of Warren Burger and Harry Blackmun, already dubbed the Minnesota Twins because of their tendency to vote together for conservative positions, Nixon had realigned the makeup of the Court in an effort to change its direction. It was unclear just what the "Burger Court" would do.

On Wednesday, June 30, the Court announced its decision.[345] Reflecting both the unprecedented nature of the case and the immediacy of the issue, each justice wrote an opinion. Six justices held that the government had not met its "heavy burden of showing justification" for a prior restraint on the press.[346] The Court therefore ordered that the *Times* and the *Post* were free to resume publication of the Pentagon Papers.

Justice Hugo Black, the unrepentant author of *Korematsu*, but a fierce "absolutist" on the First Amendment, had issued an eloquent dissent twenty years earlier in *Dennis*. It was thus not surprising that Black concluded that "every moment's continuance of the injunctions against these newspapers amounts to a flagrant, indefensible, and continuing violation of the First Amendment." He emphasized that the First Amendment protected the press "so that it could bare the secrets of government and inform the people," and he rejected the claim of national security as a legitimate ground for limiting this right, because the "word 'security' is a broad, vague generality whose contours should not be invoked to abrogate the fundamental law embodied in the First Amendment."[347]

Justice William O. Douglas, also a consistently strong proponent of free speech who had dissented in *Dennis*, conceded, "These disclosures may have a serious impact." Even so, he argued, "that is no basis for sanctioning a previous restraint on the press." Because "[o]pen debate and discussion of public issues are vital to our national health," any such restraint on the press necessarily flouts "the principles of the First Amendment."[348]

Justice William J. Brennan Jr., an Eisenhower appointee whose confirmation to the Supreme Court had been opposed only by Senator Joseph McCarthy, had surprised just about everyone in his fifteen years on the Court by becoming the chief architect of the Warren Court's First Amendment jurisprudence. Brennan insisted in the *Pentagon Papers* case that even in wartime a prior restraint on the press could be constitutional *only* if the government proved that "publication must inevitably, directly, and immediately cause the occurrence of an event kindred to imperiling the safety of a transport already at sea." Brennan held that the government had failed to present such evidence. The most it had offered was vague "surmise or conjecture that untoward consequences may result." He therefore concluded that "every restraint issued in this case . . . has violated the First Amendment."[349]

Justice Thurgood Marshall, the Court's first African American justice, had been appointed in 1967 by Lyndon Johnson after making an enduring mark on American legal history as lead counsel for the NAACP in *Brown v. Board of Education*.[350] Marshall agreed with Black, Douglas, and Brennan that the injunction was unconstitutional, adding that although the executive branch may have authority in some circumstances to invoke the jurisdiction of the courts to protect the national security, it may not do so in an effort to prevent conduct that Congress "has specifically declined to prohibit." Because Congress had rejected the "press censorship" provision in 1917, and had not enacted such legislation in the half century since, there was no legal basis for the president to make the "activity of the newspapers unlawful."[351]

Justice Potter Stewart, a political conservative and judicial centrist, tended to support an expansive view of the First Amendment, an orientation shaped by his experience as editor of a student newspaper at Yale. Stewart acknowledged that the president has "enormous power in the . . . areas of national defense and international relations," but then argued that, because this is so, the most "effective restraint" upon executive power in these areas rests in "an informed and critical public opinion." He concluded, "We are asked . . . to prevent the publication by two newspapers of material that the Executive Branch insists should not, in the national interest, be published. I am convinced that the Executive is correct with respect to some of the documents involved. But I cannot say that disclosure of any of them will surely result in direct, immediate, and irreparable damage to our Nation or its people."[352]

Justice Byron White, a former All-American football star and a Rhodes scholar, had been appointed by John Kennedy in 1962. Just as Brennan had disappointed conservatives with his liberal inclinations, White had disappointed liberals. He was generally a cautious jurist who usually sided with the Court's more conservative justices, except in cases involving racial equality. White's position in the *Pentagon Papers* case was surprising. He agreed with the government that disclosure of the information would "do substantial damage to public interests," but nonetheless held that the government had failed to meet "the very heavy burden that it must meet to warrant an injunction against publication." He added, in passing, that this did not mean that a criminal prosecution for the publication of information endangering the national security would necessarily also be unconstitutional."[353]

Chief Justice Burger and Justices Harlan and Blackmun dissented. Burger, who had been appointed chief justice two years earlier by Nixon, sided with the government. Burger protested that the Court had acted with "unseemly haste." He noted that the *Times* had "had unauthorized possession of the document for three to four months, during which . . . its expert analysts [studied them and prepared] the material for publication. During all of this time, the *Times*, presumably in its capacity as trustee of the public's 'right to know,' [held] up publication for purposes it considered proper and thus public knowledge was delayed." Why, then, he asked, should the U.S. government, "from whom this information was illegally acquired, . . . be placed under needless pressure?" He protested that the Court's rush to judgment had produced "a parody of the judicial function."[354]

Justice John Marshall Harlan was the Court's master craftsman. A superb lawyer with conservative instincts, he had frequently dissented during the era of the Warren Court. Occasionally, though, he could see his way to a more civil libertarian understanding of the First Amendment. Perhaps the best example was his landmark opinion for the Court in NAACP v. *Alabama*, which protected the NAACP from the compelled disclosure of its membership lists. The *Pentagon Papers* controversy, however, was not, for Harlan, such a case; he accused the Court of being "irresponsibly feverish." In his view, the primary responsibility for decisions about national security rests with the executive, and courts should interfere in such matters only in "exceedingly narrow" circumstances. Because national security issues involve considerations for which courts have "'neither aptitude, facilities nor responsibility,' " they should accord the executive considerable "deference."[355]

Finally, Justice Harry Blackmun, a conservative Nixon appointee who would evolve into one of the Court's most liberal justices by the 1980s, added a word of warning:

---

* This suggestion caused some consternation among the press. Indeed, after the Supreme Court decision, the Justice Department threatened Katharine Graham, the publisher of the *Washington Post*, with possible prosecution if the *Post* published any portions of the Papers the government "felt endangered national security." A representative of the administration warned the *Post* that many in the administration "hate the *Post* like poison" and that Nixon "wants to tear out the guts" of the *Times* and the *Post*. Graham, *Personal History* at 455–56 (cited in note 340).

I strongly urge, and sincerely hope, that these two newspapers will be fully aware of their ultimate responsibilities to the United States of America. . . . I hope that damage has not already been done. If, however, damage has been done, and if, with the Court's action today, these newspapers proceed to publish [information that results in] "the death of soldiers, the destruction of alliances, the greatly increased difficulty of negotiation with our enemies, the inability of our diplomats to negotiate," . . . [the] prolongation of the war and of further delay in the freeing of United States prisoners, then the Nation's people will know where the responsibility for these sad consequences rests."[356]

THE PUBLICATION OF THE PENTAGON PAPERS was a major event in the history of American journalism. A voluminous, "top secret" study of the Vietnam War, prepared within the recesses of the Department of Defense, had been made available to the public "through an unprecedented breach of security—a study that brought together more than twenty years of decision-making and revealed that the American people had been systematically misled by their elected and appointed leaders." Even an old Washington hand like Secretary of Defense Clark Clifford commented that he had "never seen anything like it."[357]

Every day for a month, the story dominated the nation's headlines. After reviewing the Pentagon Papers, the *New York Times* reporter Neil Sheehan came to the sobering judgment that the government of the United States was not what he had thought it was. It was as if there were a secret government within the government, "far more powerful than anything else," that had "survived and perpetuated itself . . . using the issue of anti-Communism as a weapon against the other branches of government and the press." This inner government did "not function necessarily for the benefit of the Republic but rather for its own ends," using secrecy as a way of protecting itself, not so much from threats by foreign governments, but from "detection from its own population on charges of its own competences and wisdom."[358]

---

* Fifteen years later, former Solicitor General Erwin Griswold, who had argued the government's case in the Supreme Court, wrote that there was "massive overclassification" by the government and that "the principal concern of the classifiers is not with national security, but rather with governmental embarrassment of one sort or another." He added that "there is very rarely any real risk to current national security from the publication of facts relating to transactions in the past, even the fairly recent past." This, he said, "is the lesson of the Pentagon Papers experience." Erwin Griswold, *Secrets Not Worth Keeping*, Washington Post A25 (Feb 15, 1989).

Daniel Ellsberg

AND WHAT OF DANIEL ELLSBERG? On Monday, June 28, after he had distributed all of his remaining copies, Ellsberg voluntarily turned himself in to the FBI. He was promptly indicted on three felony charges, later increased to a dozen, carrying a possible total sentence of 125 years in prison.

The White House saw this as an opportunity. Three days before Ellsberg surrendered to the authorities, Charles Colson wrote a memo to H. R. Haldeman suggesting that a prosecution of Ellsberg would "arouse the heartland" because he "is a natural villain." Moreover, Ellsberg's prosecution would both "discredit the peace movement" and "taint the press." On June 29, the president told Colson to find a way to tie Ellsberg "in with some communist groups." Nixon later added that this could be a great moment for HUAC: "[W]hat a marvelous opportunity for the committee. They can really take this and go. . . . [Y]ou know what's going to charge up an audience. Jesus Christ, they'll be hanging from the rafters. . . . Going after all these Jews."[359]

The president also recognized that there was a need to manage leaks better in the future—both to prevent those that could damage his administration and to orchestrate those that could damage his critics. On July 1, he explained to Haldeman and Colson, "[W]e have to develop . . . a program for leaking information." He emphasized that this program had to be "[r]un from the White House without being caught." Within a few weeks, this led to the creation of the "plumbers," whose initial charge was to leak information damaging to the Democrats, gather information about Ellsberg, and plug leaks that might damage the administration.[360]

In the meantime, the prosecution of Ellsberg and Anthony Russo proceeded apace. The indictment charged that they had conspired to deprive the government of its "lawful function of withholding classified information from the public," to steal or convert to private use the lawful property of the United States (that is, the Pentagon Papers), and to give documents related to the national defense to persons not authorized to receive them (that is, the *Times*, the *Post*, and the American public), in violation of the Espionage Act of 1917.[361]

Although the Supreme Court had held that the press could not constitutionally be enjoined from publishing the Pentagon Papers, this did not resolve the question whether Ellsberg and Russo could constitutionally be punished for "stealing" them. The basic problem is familiar. Suppose an individual steals a camera in order to make a movie. Can he be punished for theft? The answer is surely yes. As we saw in the context of draft card burning, there is generally no First Amendment right to violate a law of general application because it has an incidental effect on free expression. The law against theft can constitutionally be applied to the person who steals a camera to make a movie. If the would-be moviemaker can be punished, shouldn't Ellsberg and Russo be punishable as well?*

As events turned out, the courts never had to resolve this question in the Ellsberg/Russo prosecution. On September 3, 1971, the plumbers, acting under orders from the White House, burglarized the offices of Daniel Ellsberg's psychiatrist, Dr. Lewis Fielding. The purpose of the break-in was to obtain information that could be used to create a "negative press image" of Ellsberg. As Charles Colson said in a telephone conversation with Howard Hunt, one of the plumbers, the goal is to "put this bastard into one hell of a situation and discredit the New Left."

In the spring of 1973, after Judge Matthew Byrne, who was presiding over the prosecution, learned of this burglary—and other unlawful surveillance activities—he dismissed all charges against the defendants because the "unprecedented" government misconduct offended the "sense of justice" and "incurably infected the prosecution of this case."† In the Oval Office, President Nixon complained to his former chief of staff, H. R. Haldeman, that "the sonofabitching thief is made a national hero and is going to get off on a mistrial. And the *New York Times* gets a Pulitzer Prize for stealing documents. . . . *What in the name of God have we come to?*"[362]

DID PUBLICATION OF the Pentagon Papers have any discernible impact on the Vietnam War? Interestingly, neither Nixon nor Ellsberg thought so. Nixon thought the primary effect of the Papers was to embarrass prior Democratic administrations, and he was eager to maintain that focus. As he said in September 1971, the "main thing" is "to keep it stuck into the Democrats." Apart from the immediate political ramifications, Nixon told his advisers, "I don't give a damn" about the Pentagon Papers, and "I don't think people care."[363]

---

* One might offer at least two arguments to distinguish these situations: first, that the law prohibiting public employees from disclosing classified information is a direct, rather than an incidental, regulation of speech; second, that the information disclosed in the Pentagon Papers was of such extraordinary importance to public discourse that the First Amendment protects the "whistle-blowing."

† In burglarizing Fielding's office, the plumbers hoped to find information about Ellsberg's political and psychological motivations and perhaps learn the identities of his accomplices. The break-in, conducted under the guidance of Hunt and G. Gordon Liddy, did not turn up anything useful. Eventually, John Erlichman, Egil Krogh Jr., Colson, and Liddy were all convicted of conspiracy to violate the psychiatrist's civil rights and/or to obstruct justice.

In December 1972, when asked to assess the immediate impact of the Papers, Ellsberg said "Nothing." The American people, he explained, "have no control of American foreign policy." Ellsberg later elaborated on this answer:

> Most Americans . . . had wanted out of the war long before the papers were published; a majority had even come to regard it as immoral. Perhaps the majorities in both cases were larger now, after the publicity and the headlines about the papers. . . . But to what effect? In the face of that majority sentiment, the president . . . kept the war going by reducing ground troops, while he increased the bombing, and by recurrently convincing the public that he was on the verge of a settlement. He did that [repeatedly]. . . .[364]

This is too pessimistic a view. Although the war labored on for two dreary years after publication of the Pentagon Papers, the disclosures helped shape American public opinion about the war, the nation's use of military force to direct world events, and the appropriate authority of presidents relative to Congress in such matters. Even more important, the Pentagon Papers fostered a greater public awareness of the dangers of government secrecy and a deeper and more probing skepticism about the candor of national leaders. By 1971, the public had come to understand that many of the government's actions during the McCarthy era had been arrogant, duplicitous, and cynical. But, in the context of their own time, they were reluctant to believe that it had happened again. The Pentagon Papers proved otherwise. In the long run, this will stand us in good stead. We may learn slowly, and only in fits and starts, but we do learn. (Post 9/11, we have returned again to many of these same questions.)

Moreover, in the perverse way history sometimes unfolds, by triggering the creation of the plumbers, who later broke into the offices of the Democratic National Committee in the Watergate, publication of the Pentagon Papers ultimately led to the resignation of Richard Nixon. Most important of all, though, the Pentagon Papers controversy changed the nation's understanding of the First Amendment and the Supreme Court's conception of its responsibilities under the Constitution. The decision was a bold, confident, and courageous assertion of judicial independence and authority in the face of emphatic and disingenuous executive claims of national security. It showed the nation what an *independent* federal judiciary can and should do.

THE SUPREME COURT AND VIETNAM:
"THE PERFECT ENDING TO A LONG STORY"?

HOLMES WROTE THAT "the best test of truth is the power of the thought to get itself accepted in the competition of the market." Perhaps the best evidence of that proposition is the evolution of both national attitudes about the freedom of speech and Supreme Court doctrines interpreting the First Amendment. By allowing the meaning of free expression to remain an open question, subject to continuing deliberation, experience, and insight, the United States had come a long way from the views of Federalist Congressman Harrison Gray Otis and Supreme Court Justice Samuel Chase.

Think how far the nation had come even during the twentieth century. During World War I, the Supreme Court upheld the convictions of socialists and anarchists who distributed leaflets criticizing the war. This, the Court said, created a "clear and present danger." A half century later, during the Vietnam War, the Court held that the U.S. government could not even *delay* the publication of confidential, classified, stolen Defense Department documents, despite government claims that publication would undermine American alliances, cause the deaths of American soldiers, delay the release of American prisoners of war, and impair the nation's security.

During oral argument in the *Pentagon Papers* case, Justice Stewart posed a hypothetical to Alexander Bickel, who was representing the *New York Times*: "Let us assume that when the members of the Court go back and open up this sealed record, we find something there that absolutely convinces us that its disclosure would result in the sentencing to death of a hundred young men whose only offense" was that they were American soldiers who had been captured by the Vietcong. "What should we do?" Bickel assured Justice Stewart that this was not such a case, but then conceded, when pressed, "I am afraid that my inclinations to humanity overcome the somewhat more abstract devotion to the First Amendment in a case of that sort."[365]

This may have been the "right" answer from a tactical standpoint at oral argument, but it was *not* the right answer under the First Amendment. The Pentagon Papers involved information at the very heart of our democracy. It revealed that the American government had systematically lied to the American people about the nature, purpose, conduct, and consequences of an ongoing war. What could more perfectly capture the essence of the First Amendment? What would it mean to say that citizens are "self-governing" if their government can constitutionally censor publications in order to hide from them its own deceit about matters of fundamental national importance?

Of course, *Pentagon Papers* was *not* the hardest possible case. By the time the Papers were published, they were three years old. They divulged no secret invasion plans, but only diplomatic and political decisions reached by administrations no longer in office. Although profoundly embarrassing, they did not pose a "clear and present danger" to vital national security interests.

But what about Justice Stewart's hypothetical? Suppose the government had proved that disclosure of the Papers would lead to the death of a hundred American prisoners of war. Suppose, for example, the Papers had revealed for the first time that the U.S. military had brutally executed a hundred North Vietnamese prisoners of war, and the government persuaded the Court that if the *Times* and the *Post* published this fact the North Vietnamese would retaliate in kind. In such circumstances, should the justices, as Bickel suggested, allow their "inclinations to humanity overcome the somewhat more abstract devotion to the First Amendment"?

The answer, though painful, must be no. It is misleading to cast this as a trade-off between "real" lives and "abstract" principle. This information is fundamental to public debate and understanding. Should we replace our military leaders? Change our policies? Prosecute those responsible? Impeach the president? If publication of this information would lead the nation to greater wisdom and, perhaps, to negotiate an end to the war, how many American soldiers would be *spared*? How many Vietnamese lives would be saved?

Moreover, if we accept Bickel's concession, we must then ask how many American lives must be at risk in order to justify the suppression of such information. If a hundred lives is sufficient for censorship, what about fifty? What about ten? In what circumstances should we be willing to nullify the capacity for informed public deliberation? Note, too, that in wartime we often sacrifice the lives of soldiers to gain a hill or a village. Is the gain of that hill or village more important to the national interest than the right of the American people to know that their leaders have deceived them for two decades or (in my hypothetical) ruthlessly executed a hundred prisoners of war? Consider also the recent disclosures of American abuses of prisoners of war in Iraq. Should the Bush administration have been able to suppress the public revelation of these atrocities and hide them from the American people because of claims that they would embarrass the nation and trigger possible retaliation?

This brings us back to Judge Learned Hand's 1917 opinion in *Masses*. Hand rejected arguments about relative harm as reasons for censoring important public debate. He did not want to hear about "clear and present danger." In his view, if a speaker contributed to public debate (which did not include *express* advocacy of law violation), the government could not punish him because his speech might "cause" others to do bad things. On that score, Judge Hand had it right.

ALTHOUGH THE PENTAGON PAPERS case did not involve concrete proof that publication would cause the death of one hundred American soldiers, the justices conceded that publication would "do substantial damage to public interests." This was a critical development in constitutional law, for the *realistically* potential harm to the United States from publication of the Pentagon Papers dwarfed the realistically potential harm to the nation in any other First Amendment controversy ever decided by the Supreme Court. Compared with the Pentagon Papers, the leaflets in *Abrams*, the manifesto in *Gitlow*—even the advocacy in *Dennis*—were trivial. At the very least, the government's demonstrated inability to preserve secrets would almost certainly inhibit other nations from making secret diplomatic or military "deals" with the United States. In the *Pentagon Papers* decision, the Supreme Court, for the first time in American history, stood tall—in wartime—for the First Amendment.

But *Pentagon Papers* was only one of a long series of decisions during the Vietnam War in which the Court emphatically protected the right to dissent. Although these decisions cut across many different facets of First Amendment jurisprudence, they reflected an impressive commitment to protecting free expression—even in wartime.

Tinker v. Des Moines Independent Community School District[366] involved dissent in a public school. Three high school students wore black armbands in order to protest the Vietnam War. School officials directed the students to remove the armbands. When they refused to do so, the officials suspended them, claiming that the armbands might upset other students and disturb school activities. The Supreme Court held this unconstitutional, stressing that "in our system, undifferentiated fear or apprehension of a disturbance is not enough to overcome the right to freedom of expression."*[367]

In *Schacht v. United States*,[368] the Court held unconstitutional a federal law declaring it unlawful for any person to wear an American military uniform in a the-

---

* Because the school authorities had not prohibited "the wearing of *all* symbols of political or controversial significance," but only "a particular symbol—black armbands worn to exhibit opposition to this Nation's involvement in Vietnam," this case was distinguishable from *O'Brien*, the draft card decision. In *Tinker*, the punishment was triggered by the *content* of the students' message.

atrical production that tends to "discredit" the armed forces. Once again, the Court insisted on evenhandedness of regulation, holding that because the statute "leaves Americans free to praise the war in Vietnam but can send persons . . . to prison for opposing it, [it] cannot survive in a country which has the First Amendment."[369]

In a string of decisions building on *Schacht*, the Court invalidated laws prohibiting individuals from treating the American flag with contempt. During this era, a favorite tactic of state and local officials was to arrest and prosecute antiwar activists for "desecration" of the flag. By May 1971, the ACLU was defending at least a hundred of these cases.[370] In *Smith v. Goguen*,[371] for example, the defendant wore a small cloth replica of the American flag sewn to the seat of his trousers. For this act, he was convicted of violating a Massachusetts statute prohibiting any person to publicly mutilate, trample upon, deface, or treat contemptuously the flag of the United States. The Court held this law unconstitutional, explaining that "casual treatment of the flag in many contexts has become a widespread contemporary phenomenon" and that the ambiguity of the law would invite discriminatory application.[*][372]

In *Spence v. Washington*,[373] in protest of the invasion of Cambodia and the killings at Kent State, Spence displayed a U.S. flag out of the window of his apartment. Affixed to the flag was a large peace symbol. He was convicted of violating Washington's "flag misuse" statute, which made it a crime for any person to exhibit an American flag to which is attached or superimposed "any word, figure, mark, picture, design, drawing, or advertisement." The Court held that, as applied to Spence's activity, which the Court described as "a pointed expression of anguish . . . about the . . . affairs of his government," the statute "impermissibly infringed protected expression."[†][374]

---

* Like *Tinker* and *Schacht*, the flag desecration issue turned on the lack of evenhandedness in the government's regulation of speech. Although individuals were allowed to use the flag (like the uniform in *Schacht*) to convey "patriotic" messages, they were forbidden to use it to convey "unpatriotic" messages. Indeed, government officials seized upon the flag as a means of emphasizing *their* patriotism. The president and his supporters even took to wearing American flag pins and cufflinks. No one suggested, of course, that these were "improper" or disrespectful uses of the flag. War opponents objected that the flag was being used not to unite but to divide Americans. See DeBenedetti, *American Ordeal* at 288–89 (cited in note 1). In the years since the Vietnam War, the Court has strengthened still further the use of the flag as an important means of political dissent. See *Texas v. Johnson*, 491 US 397 (1989); *United States v. Eichman*, 496 US 310 (1990) (both holding unconstitutional a prosecution for burning the American flag)

† State and local governments also frequently used "offensive speech" laws to harass antiwar demonstrators and stifle antiwar protests. The Court consistently invalidated such prosecutions. See, for example, *Cohen v. California*, 403 US 15 (1971) (invalidating a breach-of-the-peace conviction for wearing a jacket bearing the words "Fuck the Draft"); *Papish v. Board of Curators of Uni-*

Tinker, *Schacht*, *Smith*, and *Spence* would all have come out differently in 1798 or 1917. These speakers all engaged in dissent that would certainly have been held to have violated the Sedition Act of 1798 or the Espionage Act of 1917. By World War II, the Court had begun to move in a direction that would have cast doubt on these prosecutions, but it is far from clear that the Court in that era would have accorded much protection to flag desecration or using the uniform of the U.S. military to satirize the war. By the time of the Vietnam War, however, the Court had worked through these issues and come to a clearer appreciation of the First Amendment.

The Court had come to understand that free expression is fragile, that dissent is easily chilled, that government often acts out of intolerance when it suppresses dissent, and that it is essential to protect speech at the margin. If flag desecration can be prohibited, why not burning the Constitution? Why not burning the president in effigy? Why not speaking contemptuously of the president? Before long, we are back to 1798. As Learned Hand insisted, the First Amendment demands a line that is "difficult to evade."[375]

DURING THE VIETNAM WAR, the Court dealt with cases even closer to the core issue of subversive advocacy—closer, that is, to *Schenck*, *Abrams*, and *Dennis*. In *Bond v. Floyd*,[376] for example, decided in 1966, the Court held that the Georgia House of Representatives could not constitutionally refuse to seat Julian Bond, a duly elected representative, because he had endorsed statements criticizing the war and the draft. Four days before Bond was scheduled to be sworn in, the Student Nonviolent Coordinating Committee, of which he was the communications director, issued a statement declaring its "sympathy" and "support" for the men "who are unwilling to respond to a military draft."

In a unanimous opinion, the Court held that Bond "could not have been constitutionally convicted" for violating the federal statute punishing any person who "counsels, aids, or abets another to refuse or evade registration," because the SNCC statement could not "be interpreted as a call to unlawful refusal to be drafted." Citing *Yates*, the Court declared that "Bond could not have been convicted for these

---

versity of Missouri, 410 US 667 (1973) (invalidating the expulsion of a student for distributing a newspaper on campus containing a political cartoon depicting a policeman raping the Statue of Liberty and using the phrase "Mother-fucker").

statements consistently with the First Amendment."[377] In this decision, the Court, building on *Yates*, firmly embraced the position Judge Hand had stated so eloquently in *Masses*. Although SNCC's statement unambiguously opposed the draft and "supported" those who refused to serve, it could not "constitutionally" be punished, because it stopped short of *express advocacy* of law violation.

Three years later, the Court handed down its landmark decision in *Brandenburg v. Ohio*.[378] Although *Brandenburg* did not involve dissent from the war, but arose out of the prosecution of a Klansman for threatening racial violence, the Court took the opportunity to revisit *all* of its prior decisions about subversive advocacy. The case involved the constitutionality of an Ohio statute almost identical to the statute the Court had upheld in 1927, over the objections of Justices Brandeis and Holmes, in *Whitney v. California*.[379] The Ohio statute made it unlawful for any person to advocate "the duty, necessity, or propriety of crime, sabotage, violence, or unlawful methods of terrorism as a means of accomplishing industrial or political reform." Thus, the question posed in *Brandenburg* was not whether a person could be punished if his speech stopped short of express advocacy of unlawful conduct (the question answered in the negative in *Bond*), but whether and in what circumstances a person could constitutionally be punished for *expressly advocating* unlawful conduct.

The Court noted that in *Whitney* it had upheld the California law because "'advocating' violent means to effect political and economic change involves such danger to the security of the State that the State may outlaw it." But, the Court observed, "*Whitney* has been thoroughly discredited by later decisions." Citing *Dennis* and *Yates*, it held, "These later decisions have fashioned the principle that the constitutional guarantees of free speech and free press do not permit a State to forbid or proscribe advocacy of the use of force or of law violation except where such advocacy is directed to inciting or producing imminent lawless action and is likely to incite or produce such action."*[380] Thus, not only did the Court invalidate the Ohio law, but exactly fifty years after *Schenck*, the Supreme Court finally and unambiguously embraced the Holmes-Brandeis version of clear and present danger!

Moreover, as the Stanford law professor Gerald Gunther observed at the time, if we read *Brandenburg* together with *Bond*, it is apparent that in these two decisions the Court combined the most speech "protective ingredients of the *Masses* incitement emphasis with the most useful element of the clear and pres-

---

* Although *Yates* may support this proposition, the Court's citation of *Dennis* seems rather casual. In *Dennis*, the Court adopted a "discounted" version of clear and present danger. The Court suggested in *Brandenburg* that *Yates* had already construed *Dennis* in this manner. Sometimes, such disingenuousness is helpful to the evolution of a legal principle.

ent danger heritage" to produce "the most speech-protective standard yet evolved by the Supreme Court."[381] Indeed, after *Bond* and *Brandenburg*, the Court's approach would seem to permit the punishment of subversive advocacy *only* if three conditions are satisfied: there must be *express* advocacy of law violation; the advocacy must call for *immediate* law violation; and the immediate law violation must be *likely* to occur.[382] With this development, the Court effectively overruled in one fell swoop *Schenck, Frohwerk, Debs, Gilbert, Schaefer, Abrams, Gitlow, Whitney*, and *Dennis*.*[383] In subsequent decisions, the Court has adhered to this view.[384]

As THE CONSTITUTIONAL SCHOLAR Lee Bollinger has suggested, only time will tell "whether the scope of First Amendment rights articulated in the *Brandenburg* era reflects the distilled wisdom of historical experience, which makes it more likely to survive in future periods of social upheaval, or whether the *Brandenburg* era will turn out to be just one era among many, in which the freedom of speech varies widely and more or less according to the sense of security and tolerance prevailing in the nation at the time." He cautions that although it has been more than thirty years since *Brandenburg*, it is also true that "just about every time the country has felt seriously threatened the First Amendment has retreated."[385]

Indeed, a cynic about the evolution of First Amendment doctrine might note that during World War I the Court enunciated the "clear and present danger" test, but then construed it in such a way as to uphold the convictions of those who protested the war. Then, in the 1920s, it looked back on the World War I cases with regret and embraced a more speech-protective approach that would have protected the speech of Charles Schenck, Eugene Debs, and Mollie Steimer, but that enabled the Court to uphold the convictions of Benjamin Gitlow and Anita Whitney. Then, in the 1950s, the Court looked back with regret on its decisions

---

* The Supreme Court's willingness to stand up to overblown claims of national security during the Vietnam War was evident not only in the First Amendment context but in other areas as well. In 1969, for example, Attorney General John Mitchell asserted that the president had the constitutional authority to authorize electronic surveillance without court order "concerning domestic organizations which seek to attack and subvert the government by unlawful means." *Dellinger v. Mitchell*, 442 F2d 782, 784 (DC Cir 1971). Mitchell's position was unanimously rejected by the Supreme Court in *United States v. United States District Court*, 407 US 297 (1972), in which the Court held that the government must obtain a court order when seeking electronic surveillance of "domestic" radicals.

in the 1920s and revised its approach in a way that would have protected the speech of Gitlow and Whitney, but that enabled it to uphold the conviction of Eugene Dennis. On this view, one might conclude that the Court repeatedly learns just enough to scold the mistakes of the past, but never quite enough to avoid the mistakes of the present.

The cynic would be wrong. In my view, the Court has learned over time that it is impossible to excise from public debate only those views that are thought to be "dangerous," without undermining free speech more generally. The Court has learned from its own experience that although each generation's effort to suppress *its* idea of "dangerous" speech seemed justified at the time, each proved with the benefit of hindsight to be an exaggerated response to a particular political or social conflict. The Court has thus come to appreciate that there is a natural tendency of even well-intentioned citizens, legislators, presidents, and judges to suppress ideas they find offensive or misguided, to inflate the potential dangers of such expression, and to undervalue the dangers of suppression. As Judge Hand explained in *Masses*, these insights are no "scholastic subterfuge," but "hard bought acquisition[s] in the fight for freedom."

Brandenburg represents the (contemporary) culmination of this process. By combining the best of Hand and the best of Holmes, *Brandenburg* has built a "fortress" around core political speech. The Court has attempted to tie its *own* hands and to make it difficult, if not impossible, for the government to suppress seditious criticism in the next era of fear and hysteria. In this sense, *Brandenburg* reflects the Court's conviction that "debate on public issues should be uninhibited, robust, and wide-open, and that it may well include vehement, caustic, and sometimes unpleasantly sharp attacks on government and public officials." This is "the central meaning of the First Amendment."[386] As Harry Kalven has said, *Brandenburg* is "the perfect ending to a long story!"[387]

Of course, whether *Brandenburg* is really "the perfect ending" remains to be seen. Judge Richard Posner chides that "when the country feels very safe the Justices . . . can . . . plume themselves on their fearless devotion to freedom of speech," but "they are likely to change their tune when next the country feels endangered."[388] That remains the challenge for the future. Have we learned the lessons of our past, or will we again fall victim to overblown fears, partisan manipulation, and exaggerated claims of national emergency?

Whether Posner is right or wrong, *Brandenburg* is *not* the "end" of the story. In a society that adheres to the most fundamental principles of the First Amendment, there can be no "end" to this story. No truths are sacred; no decisions are inviolable. Like *Schenck*, *Gitlow*, and *Dennis*, all of which once seemed the "end" of the story, *Brandenburg* will rightly be subject to continuing question, debate, and deliberation.

Moreover, no single decision can ever "end" this story, because government officials have proved insistently creative in pursuing their ends. As we have seen, when the government "loses" one means of controlling dissent, it quickly finds others to replace it. When direct criminal prosecution of dissidents became more difficult after World War II, the government promptly turned to loyalty tests and legislative investigations to deny dissenters employment and expose them to public harassment and humiliation. When those means of suppressing dissent came into question, the government expanded its use of surveillance and disruption to intimidate and silence its critics. When those techniques of managing dissent were challenged, the government moved more aggressively to control information and to deny citizens access to knowledge about the activities of their own government.[*]

And so it will continue. There is no "end" to this story. As Holmes observed in *Abrams*, and as history so plainly teaches, to preserve our liberties for ourselves and our children, we must be "eternally vigilant." This is the responsibility of each succeeding generation.

"THE GOVERNMENT HAS MISREAD THE TIMES"

DURING THE 1968 Democratic National Convention, David Dellinger and Tom Hayden had a sharp disagreement. On Wednesday, August 18, the police attacked the protesters who had gathered in Grant Park. Dellinger, on the speakers' platform, urged the demonstrators to "please sit down" and "stay where you

---

[*] As David Halberstam has observed, during the Vietnam era the leaders of a democracy had not even

> bothered to involve the people of their country in the course they had chosen; they knew the right path and they knew how much could be revealed, step by step along the way. They had manipulated the public, the Congress and the press from the start, told half-truths, about why we were going in, how deeply we were going in, how much we were spending, and how long we were in for. When their predictions turned out to be hopelessly inaccurate, and when the public and the Congress, annoyed at being manipulated, soured on the war, then the architects had been aggrieved. They had turned on those very symbols of the democratic society they had once manipulated, criticizing them for their lack of fiber, stamina and lack of belief. . . . So they lost it all.

Halberstam, *Best and Brightest* at 655–56 (cited in note 48).

are." He said, "This is being done for the whole world to see. Let them see who is committing the violence here." A distraught Hayden then took the microphone and shouted, "Rennie Davis is in the hospital with a split head. He's going to be all right, but he would want you to do for him what he is unable to do . . . and that is make sure that if blood is going to flow, it will flow all over the city. . . . If we are going to be disrupted and violated, let this whole stinking city be disrupted and violated."

To Dellinger's "amazement," the protesters responded to police violence with nonviolent resistance—holding their ground, absorbing the brutality, carrying injured friends to safety, and determinedly chanting, "The whole world is watching!" It was Dellinger's moment.[389]

At the end of the conspiracy trial, when Dellinger was about to be sentenced to prison for crossing state lines to incite a riot, he told Judge Julius Hoffman:

> The Government has misread the times in which we live. . . .
>
> [T]here is the beginning of an awakening in this country . . . and it is an awakening that will not be denied . . . because however falsely applied the American ideal was from the beginning, when it excluded Black people and Indians and people without property, nonetheless there was a dream of justice and equality and freedom. . . . And I think that dream is much closer to fulfillment today than it has been at any time in the history of this country. . . .
>
> I think I shall sleep better and happier and with a greater sense of fulfillment in whatever jails I am in for however many years than if I had compromised, if I had pretended the problems were any less real than they are. . . .[390]

Throughout his life, David Dellinger, remained a committed pacifist, an outspoken activist for conscientious objection, nonviolent resistance, prison reform, and Native American rights, and an arch-opponent of free trade, nuclear testing, and the Iraq War. In 1998, at the age of eighty-three, he was arrested for protesting at the site of a nuclear reactor. Until his death in June 2004, he continued whenever possible to visit college campuses both to preach the virtues of nonviolent protest and to learn from the young, who, he said, "have insights we do not."[391]

THE SECRET OF
LIBERTY

War on Terrorism

As Justice Robert Jackson observed more than half a century ago, "It is easy, by giving way to the passion, intolerance and suspicions of wartime, to reduce our liberties to a shadow, often in answer to exaggerated claims of security."[1] Indeed, the United States has a long and unfortunate history of overreacting to the dangers of wartime. Again and again, Americans have allowed fear to get the better of them. Some measure of fear, of course, is inevitable—even healthy—in time of war. Otherwise, it would be impossible for a nation to make the great sacrifices war demands. An essential challenge to democracy is to find a way to channel this fear so that it plays a constructive rather than a destructive role.

Although each of the six episodes we have examined presented a distinct challenge, in every instance the nation went too far in restricting civil liberties. To be sure, this cannot be proved with the exactitude of mathematics. Nor can one prove it merely by looking back and blithely inferring that because each of these wars ended well, the restrictions of civil liberties were unwarranted. As with any counterfactual, we cannot know for certain what would have happened if Lincoln had not suspended the writ of habeas corpus, if Wilson had not prosecuted those who protested World War I, or if Truman had not imposed a federal loyalty program during the Cold War. Perhaps the Confederate States of America would still be with us; perhaps we would have lost World War I; perhaps the Berlin Wall would still be standing. Perhaps. But with the benefit of hindsight[2] and a deeper understanding of the nature of these events than existed at the time, it is difficult to believe that any of these results would have followed.

Because it is impossible to know the counterfactual for certain, we have to rely to some degree on reasoning by inference. Certainly, we know that in every one of these episodes the nation came after the fact to regret its actions and to understand them, in part, as excessive responses to war fever and/or government manipulation. The Sedition Act of 1798 has been condemned in the "court of history," Lincoln's suspensions of habeas corpus were declared unconstitutional by the Supreme Court in *Ex parte Milligan*, the Court's own decisions upholding the World War I prosecutions of dissenters were all later effectively overruled, and the internment of Japanese Americans during World War II has been the subject of repeated government apologies and reparations. Likewise, the Court's decision in *Dennis* upholding the convictions of the leaders of the Communist Party has been discredited, the loyalty programs and legislative investigations of that era have all been condemned, and the efforts of the U.S. government to "expose, disrupt and otherwise neutralize" antiwar activities during the Vietnam War have been denounced by Congress and the Department of Justice.

These after-the-fact judgments should not be controversial. They are sound conclusions based on comprehensive information about the actions and motives of the government in each of these episodes. Moreover, it should hardly surprise us that a nation swept up in war fever would lose all sense of proportion and lash out at those deemed "disloyal." Fear, anger, and fervent patriotism naturally overwhelm the capacity of individuals and institutions to make clearheaded judgments about risk, fairness, and danger. We all know this as a matter of personal experience. It is difficult to make calm, thoughtful decisions in a state of passion.[3]

The challenge of remaining levelheaded may be even greater at the collective level than at the individual level, for as the powerful emotions triggered by war cascade through the nation, they grow ever more intense.[4] Suspicion feeds suspicion; fear breeds fear. People see spies and saboteurs around every corner, and rumors run rampant. As the distinguished political scientist John Keane has observed, "Fear eats the soul of democracy."[5] After World War I, Judge Charles Fremont Amidon recalled that in Espionage Act prosecutions otherwise "sober, intelligent" men acted "with the savagery of wild animals."[6] Terms like "contagion" aptly capture the phenomenon.

When citizens grow fearful, they demand that their leaders protect them, and public officials quickly respond.[7] It is natural to seek safety in the face of danger, especially when it appears we can lessen the risk to ourselves by disadvantaging "others"—whether they be Jacobins, secessionists, anarchists, Japanese Americans, Communists, or hippies.[8] This response enables us both to secure our own safety and to vent our fury at those we already view with suspicion or contempt. If we have to put some aliens or radicals in jail to increase our sense of security, so be it. Indeed, all the better. This is not theory. It is the unimpeachable lesson of history.

In each of our six episodes, the United States *excessively* sacrificed the freedom of speech. In light of the inevitable pressures of wartime, is there anything we can do to prevent this in the future? Are we doomed to repeat this pattern over and over again?

CAN WE DO BETTER?

BEFORE ADDRESSING THAT QUESTION, we should consider two preliminary issues. First, does the fear produced by wartime in fact cause people to *overreact*? Certainly, fear is an appropriate response to danger.[9] Fear can sharpen our focus, draw attention to prior misjudgments (perhaps we failed to protect ourselves adequately against the risk of terrorist attacks before September 11), and enable us to protect ourselves better in the future.

But here we are concerned not with fear in that limited sense but with fear that runs out of control, fear that impairs rather than informs sound decision making. Even in its most instinctive form, fear is risk averse. We are more likely to flee from a shadow we think to be an attacker than to move closer to determine whether it is an attacker.[10] This is a natural and sensible response. The risk of being "wrong" if we flee is much less than the risk of being "wrong" if we inspect. What concerns us here, however, is *excessive* fear—fear that is pathological and leads to irrational decisions—decisions that would *not* be made by individuals with equal knowledge, in a state of calm. Faced with the dilemma of the shadow, we would all endorse the decision to flee, even if we were evaluating that dilemma at leisure. The decisions to adopt the Sedition Act of 1918 or the McCarran Internal Security Act of 1950, however, were *not* decisions we would ratify in a state of calm. They were severe *overreactions* based on excessive and ill-informed fear.

Second, how seriously should we take these wartime suppressions of dissent? Even if the nation overreacted, were these important errors, or merely incidental consequences of the inevitably perilous course of war? Civil libertarians often argue that once constitutional rights are compromised, they are lost forever. If that were true, it would surely be essential to avoid *any* unnecessary limitation of free speech, regardless of circumstance. If rights, once lost, could not later be regained, then civil liberties would be in a permanent downward spiral. But that is not the case. In fact, after each of our six episodes, the nation's commitment to free speech rebounded, usually rather quickly, sometimes more robustly than before.

Of course, it was not inevitable that this would be so, but it has been our historical experience. In that sense, then, the worst-case scenario—that rights once lost are not regained—has not yet come to pass.* As long as wars are of reasonably limited duration, this is an important consideration in assessing the long-term dangers of suppressing dissent in wartime.

But this does not mean that wartime repression is unimportant. For government unjustifiably to deny an individual her freedom—whether freedom of speech, freedom of religion, or freedom from detention—for a year, or several years, is a matter of moment to both the individual and the nation. For government to tell an individual that she may not state her opposition to the war, pray to her god, or leave an internment camp until a war is over is a drastic assault on individual liberty.

It is often argued, however, that given the sacrifices we ask citizens, especially soldiers, to make in time of war, it is a small price to ask others to surrender some part of their peacetime liberties to help win the war. As members of Congress argued in defense of the Sedition Act of 1918,[11] surely people can restrain their criticism of the war in order to maintain the national unity that is essential to the war effort. And as the Court argued in *Korematsu*, "hardships are part of war, and war is an aggregation of hardships."[12]

This is a seductive, but dangerous, argument. To fight a war successfully, it is necessary for soldiers to risk their lives. But it is not necessarily necessary for others to surrender their freedoms. That necessity must be demonstrated, not merely presumed. And this is especially true when, as almost always happens, the individuals whose rights are sacrificed are not those who make the laws, but minorities, dissidents, and noncitizens. In those circumstances, "we" are making a decision to sacrifice "their" rights—not a very prudent way to balance the competing interests.

This argument is particularly misguided when the freedom of speech is at issue. A critical function of free speech in wartime is to help the nation make wise decisions about how to conduct the war, whether its leaders are leading well, whether to end the war, and so on. If free speech is essential to self-governance in ordinary times, it is even more critical when citizens must decide whether to let the Southern states secede, withdraw our troops from Vietnam, or launch a

---

* The clearest judicial warning about a possible ratchet-down effect was offered by Justice Jackson in *Korematsu*, where he observed, "[O]nce a judicial opinion rationalizes [an emergency in] order to show that it conforms to the Constitution or rather rationalizes the Constitution to show that the Constitution sanctions such [a response to the emergency], the Court for all time has validated . . . [a] principle [that] lies about like a loaded weapon ready for the hand of any authority that can bring forward a plausible claim of an urgent need." *Korematsu v. United States*, 323 US 214, 246 (1944) (Jackson dissenting). For a rebuttal, see Posner and Vermeule, 56 Stan L Rev at 605 (cited in note 9).

regime change in Iraq. Those questions *cannot* be put in suspension during a war, much as some political leaders might want to do so.

The commitment to free speech is not only about the personal rights of those who are silenced; it is about the functioning of democracy itself. Insofar as government silences dissent, in wartime or otherwise, it warps the thinking process of the community and undermines the very essence of self-government. Free and open debate can help save the nation from tragic blunders. Indeed, democracies generally fare better than dictatorships in long wars precisely because "of the greater ability of citizens in democracies" to dissent and help shape "proposed courses of action."[13] Thus, although wartime restraints of free speech may be time bound, and may not carry over once peace is restored, they have profound implications *during* the war both for the individual and for the nation.

SO, CAN WE DO BETTER? Surely, yes. Despite the fears that swept the nation in the periods we have examined, *some* individuals maintained a sense of perspective and recognized that the demands for suppression were unwarranted. Examples include, among many others, Congressmen Albert Gallatin and Edward Livingston in 1798; Professors Zechariah Chafee and Emily Balch, Senator Joseph France of Maryland, and Judges Bourquin, Amidon, and Hand during World War I; Justices Holmes and Brandeis during the Red Scare; Attorneys General Murphy, Jackson, and Biddle during World War II; Robert Maynard Hutchins, Joseph Welch, and Senators Kefauver and Lehman during the Cold War; Justices Black and Douglas in *Dennis*; and so on. If they could understand the realities they faced, others can as well.

Moreover, the nation did not always succumb to wartime hysteria. Many proposals for the suppression of speech were rejected in these periods because individuals in positions of authority understood them to be unwise. For example, oppressive as the Sedition Act of 1798 may have been, it was appreciably less severe than other proposals Congress rejected at the time.* Similarly, Con-

---

* One of these proposals, for example, did not recognize truth as a defense. Another would have defined as "seditious" any expression that stated or implied that officers of the government had enacted laws because of motives that were hostile to the liberties of the people. See James Morton Smith, *Freedom's Fetters: The Alien and Sedition Laws and American Civil Liberties* 107–10 (Cornell 1956); Michael Kent Curtis, *Free Speech, "The People's Darling Privilege": Struggles for Freedom of Expression in American History* 63 (Duke 2000).

gress in 1917 enacted a version of the Espionage Act much less repressive than the one proposed by the Wilson administration. And although Wilson was prepared to go quite far in suppressing dissent, he rejected calls to suspend the writ of habeas corpus. It is, ultimately, a matter of degree. For the nation to "do better" in the future means not that it will strike the "perfect" balance between liberty and security but that it will err more often on the side of liberty than it has in the past.

Over time, we *have* made progress. Like the assertion that we have "excessively" restricted speech in the past, this judgment is impossible to prove with certainty. Each situation is distinct, and no one can predict definitively that the United States will never reenact the Sedition Act of 1798 or undergo another era of McCarthyism. Indeed, if the United States had been struck within a single month with six terrorist attacks on the scale of those of September 11, who knows what measures the nation would have adopted?

Nonetheless, the major restrictions of civil liberties of the past would be *less* thinkable today than they were in 1798, 1861, 1917, 1942, 1950, or 1969. In terms of both the evolution of constitutional doctrine and the development of a national culture more attuned to civil liberties, the United States has made substantial progress. This is a profound and hard-bought achievement. We should neither take it for granted nor underestimate its significance. It is a testament to the strength of American democracy.[14]

IN READING THE LESSONS OF HISTORY, we can divide the six episodes into two distinct groups in terms of the intensity of the suppression of dissent. In 1798, World War I, and the Cold War, public hysteria and intolerance were especially severe; in the Civil War, World War II, and the Vietnam War, the clamor to squelch dissent was more restrained. Although these are differences only of degree, they are nonetheless revealing.

The most salient explanation of these differences focuses on the extent to which national political leaders *intentionally* inflamed public fear. In the three more restrained eras, a variety of factors account for the government's relative restraint. During the Civil War, Lincoln desperately needed to retain the allegiance of the border states and the more tenuous states of the Northwest. This imposed a limit on how severely his administration could punish dissent. For the most part, Lincoln had to tolerate dissent in order to maintain what was left of national unity, and, for the most part, he did.

In World War II, there was a broad consensus in support of the war, and dissent never threatened to demoralize or divide the people. It never rose to the level of serious concern after Pearl Harbor. Thus, although Roosevelt's personal tolerance of criticism never matched Lincoln's, he felt no need to incite a nationwide attack on dissenters. It was sufficient to target those relatively few persons, like William Dudley Pelley, who insisted on goose-stepping their way into jail. At least with respect to seditious speech, there was no hysteria to be controlled or promoted.

During the Vietnam War, the government exercised relative restraint in punishing dissent both because courts would likely have rebuffed as unconstitutional any widespread effort to prosecute individuals merely for protesting the war and because most dissenters in this era were the children of the middle class, and thus could not so easily be demonized. Although the government resorted to less blatant, more surreptitious means to disrupt dissent, it could not launch a broad program of direct criminal prosecution. Moreover, as we saw in chapter 6, Lyndon Johnson was reluctant to savage his antiwar critics because they supported his domestic agenda. Richard Nixon was more willing to attack his critics, and often did. But by the time he assumed office, the nation was already so weary and so ambivalent about the war that he could never muster the kind of widespread fury that real hysteria demands. Thus, in each of the relatively "restrained" episodes, national political leaders either did not feel the need to inflame popular fear and passion against dissenters or were constrained in their willingness or ability to do so.

In the three eras in which the nation most aggressively silenced dissent, by contrast, national leaders went out of their way to exacerbate anger against those who challenged their motives or policies. This contributed significantly both to the degree of public hysteria and to the repression of dissent. In enacting and enforcing the Sedition Act of 1798, for example, the Federalists cynically manipulated the nation's apprehensions in a partisan effort to destroy the Republicans. They accused Republicans of treason and inflamed the public with vivid and exaggerated predictions of imminent terror. Federalist congressmen warned of "bloodshed, slaughter, pillage, and a complete subjection to France," sounded the alarm that there was "an army of spies and incendiaries scattered through the Continent," and charged that Republicans would watch "our dwellings burning" with "the calmness of indifference."[15]

During World War I, Woodrow Wilson faced the challenge of rallying a nation to fight a war even though it had neither been attacked nor threatened with attack. To create an "outraged public" and inspire citizens to make the sacrifices war demands, Wilson, with the assistance of George Creel and the Committee on Public Information, fostered a public mood of fear, anger, and rabid patriotism. From the very outset, he made clear that "disloyalty" would be "dealt with with a firm hand of stern repression." In seeking a declaration of war, he charged that Germany had "filled our unsuspecting communities . . . with spies and set criminal intrigues everywhere afoot."[16] To underscore the point, after Congress adopted the Espionage Act of 1917, Attorney General Gregory warned possible dissenters that they could expect no mercy from "an avenging Government."[17] In less than a year, the United States, whipped into a state of frenzy, enacted the Sedition Act of 1918, which exceeded even the Sedition Act of 1798 in outlawing "any language intended to bring the form of government of the United States, or the Constitution of the United States . . . into contempt, scorn, contumely or disrepute."[18]

Similarly, during the Cold War, Republicans ruthlessly fed the public's fear of communism for partisan political gain, and Harry Truman, in an effort to fend off his political enemies, cynically exploited the nation's anxieties. Republicans warned that Reds were working secretly "for the destruction of the United States," slandered civil libertarians as "parlor pinks," and charged Democrats with shielding "traitors" and intentionally undermining the very "foundations of our Republic."[19] Joseph McCarthy outdid even the most scurrilous of his fellow Republicans, accusing Democrats of giving "a green light to the Red fifth column" and attacking them as "stooges of the Kremlin."[20]

Although the pressures of wartime inevitably create a mood of fear and anxiety that can readily explode into intolerance and vigilantism, in these three episodes national political leaders went out of their way to inflame these responses by promoting a climate conducive to repression. As 1798, World War I, and the Cold War illustrate, public officials not only *respond* to the demands of a fearful public but sometimes deliberately *manipulate* the public in order to create national hysteria. History teaches that it is the *interaction* of "ordinary" war fever with cynical efforts by opportunistic political leaders that is most likely to result in what Jefferson called "the reign of witches."[21]

HOW, THEN, DO WE GET IT RIGHT in the future? The most daunting obstacle to a more measured response is the practical reality that by the time citizens and public officials realize they are in the midst of a crisis, it may already be too late.[22] In this realm, as in many others, the time to prepare for a crisis is *before* rather than after it strikes.

A critical determinant of how the nation responds to wartime is the attitude of the public itself. Citizens in a self-governing society are responsible for their own actions and those of their government. They cannot expect public officials to act calmly and judiciously without regard to the nature of their own response.* As Judge Learned Hand reflected in 1944,

> I often wonder whether we do not rest our hopes too much upon constitutions, upon laws and upon courts. These are false hopes; believe me, these are false hopes. Liberty lies in the hearts of men and women; when it dies there, no constitution, no law, no court can save it.[23]

In some of the six episodes, the public responded remarkably well. In 1800, for example, Americans voted the Federalists out of power. The election of Jefferson and the demise of the Federalist Party were, in no small part, a direct rebuke to the Federalists for the Sedition Act of 1798. Similarly, during the Civil War, although some Republicans demanded that the government suppress "disloyal" speech, many Republican newspapers, political leaders, and party members raised their voices against the more egregious efforts of military commanders to suppress Copperhead opposition. Indeed, one of the most impressive features of the controversy over Clement Vallandigham's arrest and banishment was that Republicans as well as Democrats condemned the government's actions.

More often, however, the public has either failed to protest the suppression of dissent or vociferously demanded and supported it. In World War I and the Cold War, for example, most members of the public were either swept up in the frenzy or, at the very least, cowed into submission. With few exceptions, even the traditional bulwarks of civil liberties—the legal profession, higher education, the press, "liberal" politicians and intellectuals, and committed civil libertarians—were unwilling to confront the storm of public accusation and condemnation. Fearful of losing clients, contributions, subscribers, votes, status, respect, and employment, even those who should have known better bowed to the fierce pressures to conform.

Because the protection of liberty ultimately "lies in the hearts of men and women," citizens must understand and internalize the value of civil liberties and the need—indeed, the duty—to tolerate and even to *consider* dissenting views. They must appreciate why civil liberties matter and why *they* have a responsibility to protect them. They must understand that even well-meaning individuals are tempted to do things under the influence of mob mentality that "they would be entirely ashamed to do on their own."[24]

Of course, it is not easy to abide dissent. As Justice Holmes commented in

---

* Reflecting upon such issues, Robert Jackson once noted that there are circumstances in which "fear and anxiety create public demands" for assurances of security "which may not be justified by necessity but which any popular government finds irresistible." Jackson, 1 Buff L Rev at 107 (cited in note 1).

Abrams, "Persecution for the expression of opinions seems . . . perfectly logical."[25] If we are certain we are right, and those who disagree with us are wrong, the most "logical" course is for *us* to silence *them*. But as Holmes explained, "time has upset many fighting faiths," and if we listen to critics, rather than silence them, we may learn something and even change our minds.

To withstand the perils of war fever, a nation needs not only *legal* protection of civil liberties but a *culture* of civil liberties. Educational institutions, government agencies, political leaders, foundations, the media, the legal profession, and civil liberties organizations all can help cultivate an environment in which citizens are more informed, open-minded, skeptical, critical of their political leaders, tolerant of dissent, and protective of the freedoms of *all* individuals. Above all, as Judge Hand observed, the "spirit of liberty is the spirit which is not too sure that it is right."[26] These are values and capacities that can be learned, ingrained, and exercised over time. We see this clearly today in the effort to build democracy in Iraq. This is not a onetime event but a *continuing* process of reaffirmation and education.[27]

To the extent the United States has made progress over time, it is largely because Americans have come increasingly to celebrate and take pride in the nation's commitment to civil liberties. Inspired by such events as America's role in World War II, the Supreme Court's 1954 decision holding racial segregation unconstitutional, and the achievements of the civil rights movement, Americans have embraced an almost romantic vision of what makes this nation unique. Although there are continuing disagreements over such issues as abortion, pornography, and same-sex marriage, the *aspiration* of Americans to be fair, tolerant of others, and respectful of constitutional liberties may be more deeply embedded in American culture today than at any time in the nation's history. It is largely for that reason that government efforts to suppress dissent have increasingly been called into question, and why such measures when disclosed to the public are often perceived as dangerous abuses of official power. As Cornell law professor Steven Shiffrin has noted, the First Amendment in particular "speaks to the kind of people we are and the kind of people we aspire to be." It plays a central "role in the construction of an appealing story, a story about a nation that promotes independent people" and that "respects, tolerates, and even sponsors dissent.[27] "Of course, this progress is conditional, and can readily be lost in the right (or the wrong) circumstances. But it is real progress, and it should be acknowledged, nurtured, and celebrated as an essential part of the American character.

The media play a key role in this process. In addition to their general educative capacity, the media have a more immediate impact on the public's response to a crisis. By sensationalizing "newsworthy," but low-risk, dangers, they can generate a sense of panic that quickly cascades through society. People routinely overreact to vivid depictions of frightening, but low-probability, dangers. Lurid reports of sniper shootings, for example, send ripples of fear through communities, triggering excessively cautious responses. This can have a devastating effect on society when the precipitating event is a terrorist attack or a fear of espionage in wartime. In such circumstances, the "excessively cautious" response may not be merely to avoid the sniper's haunts but to insist that government detain and deport aliens, anarchists, Japanese Americans, or Muslims because of an exaggerated sense of the danger they actually pose to the nation.*28

ALTHOUGH THE PERSPECTIVE and disposition of the public are critical in determining the nation's response to wartime, it eventually falls to the federal government to enact and enforce the laws, implement policies, and interpret the Constitution. How well have the three branches of the federal government fulfilled these responsibilities, and how can they do better in the future?

Over the years, Congress has enacted the Sedition Act of 1798, the Sedition Act of 1918, and the McCarran Internal Security Act of 1950. This is a dreary record of legislative achievement. On the other hand, as we have seen, Congress has not reflexively adopted every repressive law ever proposed. To the contrary, Congress has demonstrated that it is quite capable of acting with restraint. Too often, however, it has either failed to exercise a check on public hysteria or, in some instances, moved far beyond anything the public demanded.

This is understandable. Congressmen are susceptible to stampeding fear. Even apart from their own anxieties, elected officials are naturally responsive to the wants of voters. They are likely to act quickly and decisively when citizens are in a state of panic.† Indeed, once fear overwhelms the public, there is no sure way

---

* Like the media, civil liberties organizations can play both an educational role and an ameliorative one even after a crisis arises. Although such organizations have not always had the courage of their convictions, they have made invaluable contributions. Organizations like the Free Speech League in World War I and the ACLU today ensure that perspectives that might otherwise be disregarded are well presented in legal and political discourse. They articulate often unpopular positions to judges, legislators, and others so that *they* can make better-informed and more thoughtful decisions. Particularly in times of national emergency, when many others are silenced by fear, such organizations deserve and need the nation's support.

† John Stuart Mill insisted that protection "against the tyranny of the magistrate is not enough," and that constitutional government also requires protection "against the tyranny of the prevailing opinion and feeling; against the tendency of society to impose . . . its own ideas and practices . . . on those who dissent from them." Mill, *On Liberty*, in John Stuart Mill, *Utilitarianism, On Liberty, Considerations on Representative Government* 73 (Everyman's Library 1972). See Sunstein, *Why*

to defuse it. Even conscientious efforts to reassure people by explaining that they are "overreacting" tend only to exacerbate their anxiety.[29] In such circumstances, the best way to alleviate public fear may be to demonstrate that the government is taking action, whether or not such action is likely otherwise to be effective. This may calm the public, but the very fact that the government takes drastic action also affirms the legitimacy of the fear. And, of course, the precise *nature* of the "drastic" action is critical. It is one thing to announce a tripling of the defense budget and quite another to jail or deport hundreds or even thousands of people in order to salve the public's fears.

Some members of Congress have courageously stood fast and insisted that the nation do the right thing, rather than what the public demands or what seems expedient or opportunistic at the moment. But such individuals have been the exception. More often, Congress responds to war fever with draconian legislation.

There are several steps Congress could take to break, or at least alleviate, this pattern. It could adopt standing "rules" or protocols, for example, to guide it whenever it considers wartime legislation that would limit civil liberties.* An obvious peril in wartime is that Congress will act rashly in response to public hysteria. To prevent this, Congress could enact a rule prohibiting it from enacting wartime legislation that limits dissent *without full and fair deliberation.* A recent illustration of unwarranted expedition was Congress's adoption of the USA PATRIOT Act of 2001. In its rush to act decisively in response to the attacks of September 11, Congress ignored its established procedures, abandoning both the committee process and the requirement of full floor debate. Moreover, it did this in the face of serious and well-articulated concerns about the act's impact on civil liberties.[30] A clear rule against such action, a mandatory "cooling off" period, would have afforded Congress a fuller opportunity to consider the more problematic features of the legislation. The debates over the Espionage Act of 1917 provide a useful illustration of an instance in which full deliberation led to more thoughtful and more carefully crafted legislation.

Societies Need Dissent at 23 (cited in note 4) (legislators, "like everyone else, ought to be expected in some cases to abandon their otherwise clear assessment of policy and law if people are united against them").

   * Such protocols should apply not only to wartime legislation directed at dissent but to any wartime legislation that restricts the civil liberties of any particular group. Whenever such legislation is directed at a specific group, it is likely to be problematic, for it is too easy for members of the "majority" to sacrifice the rights of "others" in order to secure their own safety. This is why there is a strong constitutional preference for laws that apply neutrally to all persons. See Gross, 112 Yale L J at 1037 (cited in note 30); Blasi, 85 Colum L Rev at 457 (cited in note 54); Sunstein, 151 U Pa L Rev at 1011 (cited in note 7); William J. Stuntz, *Local Policing after the Terror*, 111 Yale L J 2137, 2165 (2002).

Another such protocol might require any wartime legislation limiting civil liberties to contain a "sunset" provision. Because such legislation will often be warped by the effects of the crisis, it should automatically be reconsidered within a relatively short time. Interestingly, both the Sedition Act of 1798 and the PATRIOT Act of 2001 incorporated this device. The former was by its own terms to expire on March 3, 1801, the date of the next presidential inauguration. The latter included a sunset requirement for at least some of its provisions of December 31, 2005. This was a sound idea, poorly executed. Four years is too long. Most wars do not last that long; in any event, enormous damage can be done by misguided legislation in four years. To be effective, such provisions should require reconsideration no less than annually.

There are obvious objections to such rules. For one thing, it is not easy to define the precise circumstances in which such protocols should kick in.[31] What is "wartime" legislation? Moreover, legislators in a state of high emotion can always find ways to circumvent such rules by arguing that they are inapplicable to the *particular* crisis they face. And the same hysteria that might lead Congress to enact unwise or unconstitutional legislation in the first place might also lead it simply to override any protocols that are intended to restrain precipitate action. These are all reasonable objections, but they suggest only that such rules are imperfect, not that they cannot help at the margin. Anything that slows the process, allows for greater deliberation, and limits the potential scope and impact of hastily enacted legislation limiting civil liberties is salutary.[32]

Congress could also respond better in the future by taking the Constitution more seriously. Just as a deeper understanding of civil liberties might enable the public to react more calmly to the exigencies of wartime, so too a deeper appreciation of constitutional rights might help their elected representatives better meet their responsibilities. This may seem naïve. A cynic would argue that Congress won't care one whit about the Constitution in times of real or perceived crisis. The cynic would be wrong.

How well has Congress fulfilled its responsibilities in the past? There are two elements to this question: How seriously has Congress taken its independent obligation to act in accord with the Constitution? How seriously has it taken the decisions of the Supreme Court?

In dealing with free speech in wartime, Congress has *never* directly defied a decision of the Supreme Court regarding the meaning of the First Amendment. When Congress enacted the Sedition Act of 1798, the Espionage Act of 1917, and the Sedition Act of 1918, the Court had not yet had occasion to construe the First Amendment, so Congress was essentially on its own. In 1798, it fully debated the constitutionality of the proposed legislation, although the positions on both sides of the debate were largely colored by partisan interest. But in their reliance on Blackstone and their amelioration of the most extreme elements of the common law of seditious libel, the Federalists made a perfectly plausible case for the constitutionality of the Sedition Act. Whatever the judgment of the "court of history," in 1798 the Federalist position was certainly credible. Likewise, Congress took quite seriously its constitutional responsibilities in debating the Espionage Act of 1917 and, as in 1798, clearly rejected provisions it believed unconstitutional.

Even in the nation's most extreme antispeech legislation, the Sedition Act of 1918, Congress seriously addressed its constitutional responsibilities. As we saw in chapter 3, during the debate Senator France of Maryland proposed an amendment to limit the scope of the legislation.[33] The Senate voted unanimously to adopt this amendment. It was only after the Justice Department vehemently opposed the France amendment that the Senate acquiesced.

Thus, in each of these instances, Congress—proceeding without any Supreme Court guidance—took seriously its constitutional responsibilities. (This is not to suggest that these acts were, or should have been thought to be, constitutional. It is only to suggest that even in these extreme instances Congress addressed the First Amendment issues and reached results that were not at the time implausible.)

By the time Congress enacted the Smith Act of 1940, the McCarran Internal Security Act of 1950, and the Communist Control Act of 1954, the Supreme Court had begun to develop its own interpretation of the First Amendment. None of these laws defied those decisions. In the mid-1920s, the Court held in Gitlow[34] and Whitney[35] that the government could constitutionally prohibit the express advocacy of violent overthrow of government. The Court did not cast serious doubt on those precedents until its 1957 decision in Yates.[36] Thus, whatever we might think today of the constitutionality of the Cold War era legislation, those laws were consistent with prevailing judicial precedent at the time they were enacted. Indeed, as evidenced by his opinion for the court of appeals in Dennis, even Judge Learned Hand would have upheld them at the time.

Moreover, Congress has enacted no legislation directly prohibiting dissent (other than express advocacy of violent overthrow of the government) since the Sedition Act of 1918, and it has enacted no legislation directly prohibiting even express advocacy of violent overthrow since Yates. All this clearly suggests that Congress *does* attempt to act within the confines of the Constitution, particularly when it has guidance from the Supreme Court, and even in time of war.*[37]

---

* This also suggests, by the way, that congressional protocols requiring the use of ordinary legislative processes to ensure adequate deliberation and sunset provisions might have a positive impact. If Congress can discipline itself to act within the constitutional parameters set out by the Court, there is no reason to believe it cannot discipline itself to act within the legislative parameters it sets out for itself.

A similar evaluation applies to the executive. For the most part, wartime presidents have not gone out of their way to celebrate dissent. Adams, Wilson, and Roosevelt could hardly be deemed champions of free speech in 1798, 1917, or 1942. Lincoln and Truman did better. In the Vallandigham controversy, Lincoln offered a thoughtful analysis of free speech in wartime, and throughout the Civil War he tolerated a storm of criticism without *once* calling for its suppression. Truman's record was more mixed. At his worst, Truman surrendered completely to public pressure and political self-interest when he promulgated the federal loyalty program in 1947. At his best, however, when he vetoed the McCarran Internal Security Act of 1950 and boldly challenged Joseph McCarthy, he was the most courageous presidential defender of wartime dissent the nation has ever known.

Perhaps the single most important step presidents can take to improve the response of the executive branch in future crises is to ensure that every administration has within its highest councils individuals who will ardently and credibly defend civil liberties. Public servants like John Lord O'Brian, Alfred Bettman, Frank Murphy, Robert Jackson, Francis Biddle, and Clark Clifford all played significant roles in helping to temper the government's response to wartime hysteria. As Cass Sunstein has explained, when like-minded members of a group deliberate among themselves, they usually "end up taking a more extreme position in line with their predeliberation tendencies." This is especially likely, and especially dangerous, when people are angry or frightened. In such circumstances, even a lone dissenter can play a critical role.[38]

It was no coincidence that Harry Truman adopted the federal loyalty program at a time when his inner council lacked such a voice, and one of the most serious concerns about the administration of President George W. Bush is the absence of any senior official representing civil libertarian views. Individuals presenting a dissenting view may lose the policy debate, but an administration *without* such a voice is much more likely to embrace extreme positions than one that fosters genuine internal deliberation. This is critical.

WHAT IS THE APPROPRIATE ROLE of courts in wartime? To what extent can the First Amendment, as interpreted and applied by the judiciary, restrain the pressures for wartime suppression of dissent? Justice Jackson described the form in which these questions usually reach the Supreme Court: "Measures [ordinarily] violative of constitutional rights are claimed to be necessary to security, in the judgment of officials who are best in a position to know, but the necessity is not provable by ordinary evidence and the court is in no position to determine the necessity for itself. What does it do then?"[39]

After two centuries of wrestling with this question, we seem to have reached consensus on two key propositions: the Constitution applies in time of war, but the special demands of war may affect the application of the Constitution. This was essentially the position Lincoln advanced during the Civil War, and it is the position Chief Justice Rehnquist supports today.[40] We have thus wisely rejected the more extreme positions—that the Constitution is irrelevant in wartime, and that wartime is irrelevant to the application of the Constitution.

This means that in applying the governing constitutional standard in any particular area of the law—whether clear and present danger, compelling governmental interest, "unreasonable" searches and seizures, or whatever—it is appropriate for courts to take the special circumstances of wartime into account in determining whether the government has sufficient justification to limit the constitutional right at issue. It does *not* mean, however, that courts should abdicate their responsibilities in the face of assertions of national security or military necessity.

Some scholars contend that this stance accords courts excessive authority in time of war. In their view, because war presents the nation with unique challenges and dangers, the ordinary standards of judicial review should be suspended entirely. Under this view, whereas the Court's 1969 decision in *Brandenburg*[41] states the proper First Amendment test for reviewing restrictions of dissent in normal times, courts should defer to the executive in wartime and resort in such circumstances to something more like the World War I era "bad tendency" test. After all, when national security is at stake, the potential harm to the nation is particularly grave. If judges err in their assessment of the possible dangers of dissent and prohibit the government from acting when action is necessary, the consequences could be dire. Moreover, judges are not particularly well suited to make critical judgments about issues of national security, for such judgments often involve matters of great complexity and secrecy. Courts are therefore more likely to flounder in dealing with such matters than in addressing more run-of-the-mill constitutional disputes. When grave issues of national security are at stake, we should be more willing to tolerate the risks of unconstrained executive power—including the risk that such power will be abused for political gain. Or so the argument goes.[42]

There is some merit in these concerns, but not much. The comparative advantages of courts over the executive and legislative branches in interpreting and enforcing constitutional rights are striking. Responsiveness to the electorate is essential to the day-to-day workings of democracy, but as the framers of the Constitution well understood, that responsiveness can also lead elected officials too readily to sacrifice the rights of a despised or feared minority. In the realm of free speech, judges with life tenure and a more focused attention to the preservation of constitutional liberties are much more likely to protect First Amendment rights than the elected branches of government. As Anthony Lewis has observed, "the distinctive American contribution to the philosophy of government has been the role of judges as protectors of freedom."[*][43]

The central question, of course, is not how to protect constitutional rights in wartime but how to protect those rights *while still allowing the government to respond effectively to a crisis.* If courts are irresponsibly aggressive in protecting civil liberties in wartime, if they are inclined to cripple the nation's capacity to wage war effectively, if they regard the Constitution as "a suicide pact,"[44] it would certainly make sense to empower the elected branches to override their judgments. But nothing could be further from the truth. Throughout our history, judges have erred on the side of deference in times of crisis. Like other citizens, judges do not want the nation to lose a war, and they certainly do not want to be responsible for a mass tragedy. As Chief Justice Rehnquist has observed, "judges, like other citizens, do not wish to hinder a nation's 'war effort.' "[45] Moreover, as we have seen, judges, like other citizens, are not immune to the fears and anxieties of the moment. This makes them even more prone—indeed, perhaps too prone—to err on the side of deference.[46]

Not surprisingly, then, in *Schenck, Korematsu, Dennis,* and a host of other wartime decisions, the Supreme Court has applied constitutional standards in a way that strongly accords the president and Congress the benefit of the doubt. Although Congress and the president have often *underprotected* free speech in wartime, there is not a single instance in which the Supreme Court has *overprotected* wartime dissent in a way that caused *any* demonstrable harm to the national security. The argument that courts cannot be trusted because they will recklessly shackle the nation's ability to fight is simply unfounded.

Of course, there will be occasions when the judiciary gives greater protection to civil liberties than the legislature or the executive. This is appropriate. The elected branches tend to give inadequate weight to civil liberties in wartime, and it is the responsibility of courts in our constitutional system to act as a corrective.

---

[*] The framers were aware of this:

This independence of the judges is equally requisite to guard the Constitution and the rights of individuals from the effects of those ill humors which the arts of designing men, or the influence of particular conjunctures, sometimes disseminate among the people themselves, and which, though they speedily give place to better information and more deliberate reflection, have a tendency, in the meantime, to occasion dangerous innovations in the government, and serious oppressions of the minor party in the community.

Federalist no. 78, in Garry Wills, ed, *The Federalist Papers by Alexander Hamilton, James Madison, & John Jay* 397 (Bantam 1982).

But there is no reason in logic or national experience to believe that courts give *excessive* protection to those rights in a way that jeopardizes the national security.

On the other hand, as we have seen, history is replete with instances in which the nation has excessively suppressed dissent without any compelling or even reasonable justification. The problem is not too much judicial enforcement of the First Amendment in wartime, but too *little*. Although some judges, like George Bourquin, Charles Amidon, and Learned Hand, proved themselves courageous, independent, and confident in their faith in civil liberties, too many others have been too timid, too much "company men," and too easily cowed by the clamor around them. And although the Supreme Court has occasionally taken a strong stance in defense of civil liberties in wartime, as in *Yates* and *Pentagon Papers*, in most other instances, like *Schenck*, *Dennis*, and *Korematsu*, the justices have yielded too readily to their own fears or to executive and legislative demands that they not stand in the way.

Moreover, even if judges and justices were much more insistent in their protection of civil liberties in wartime, the potential "dangers" would not be so dire. There are many ways to achieve a desired level of security. If one measure is unavailable, others can be pursued. Suppose, for example, the Supreme Court had invalidated the Sedition Act of 1798, the Espionage Act of 1917, or the Smith Act of 1940, preventing the government from prosecuting critics of John Adams, opponents of the draft in World War I, or members of the Communist Party in the 1950s. Even in the unlikely event that this would have hampered the protection of national security, the government could easily have attained the same overall *level* of safety by, for instance, increasing the penalties for particular crimes, such as draft evasion or espionage, or by committing greater resources to ferreting out spies and saboteurs.

In a world of limited resources, the government must always choose between different means of achieving its objectives. Should it expand the number of FBI agents? Spend more on training? Invest in more advanced technology? The First Amendment takes off the table the suppression of dissent as "convenient" means of achieving the government's goals. It does this for compelling reasons. Laws punishing dissent are especially appealing to public officials in wartime because they are relatively inexpensive, cater to the public's witch-hunt mentality, create the illusion of decisive action, burden only those who already are viewed with contempt, and enable public officials to silence their critics in the *guise* of serving the national interest. Thus, as the Constitution commands, such measures should be a last, not a first, resort.°

° It might be argued that judicial decisions denying the government the ability to use its first-choice response—stifling dissent—force it to be "inefficient" in protecting national security. But if

Assertive judicial review of government claims that the president should be given a free hand in dealing with issues of "national security" and "military necessity" serves another critical function. Accountability is essential to good government. Officials who can mask their decisions behind a screen of self-invoked secrecy are sure to abuse their authority. A highly deferential stance to government restrictions of civil liberties in wartime invites such abuse. Officials who know they will have to explain and defend their actions before an independent branch of government are more likely to tread carefully when the pressures of the moment make the temptation to cut corners difficult to resist. As history teaches, exacting judicial review cannot guarantee respect for constitutional rights in wartime, but deferential judicial review virtually guarantees that such rights will be unnecessarily sacrificed.

Judge Richard Posner has recently presented a contrary analysis, and it is worth considering. In celebration of something he calls "pragmatic constitutional reasoning," Posner criticizes civil libertarians for embracing an "unsound" approach "to the balance between liberty and security." He argues that what judges do in interpreting and applying the Constitution is to weigh "the competing interests at stake—call them public safety and liberty." He charges that civil libertarians give undue weight to constitutional rights. In his view, "[n]either interest should enjoy priority over the other in the balancing process," and because the relative importance of liberty and security will vary "from time to time," the law "should be flexible."[47]

To the extent Posner rejects the extreme position that the *outcomes* of constitutional analysis should never vary with the circumstances, I agree. Constitutional analysis does entail a balancing of interests, whether reflected in the "clear and present danger" test or the "bad tendency" standard. A particular speech may create a clear and present danger in one setting, but not in another, and the circumstances of wartime are relevant in making such determinations.

Posner errs, though, when he insists that courts should weigh liberty and security "equally." He bases this judgment on two assumptions—security is as

---

stifling dissent seems an efficient means of protecting national security, it is most likely because the government does not fairly take account of the interests of those Jacobins, anarchists, and Communists whose speech is punished or chilled in order to achieve greater security (or greater apparent security) for the majority of citizens who are not inconvenienced. Nor does it give any weight to the deleterious impact on government decision making when dissident perspectives are excised from public discourse. If those interests were properly weighed, the suppression of dissent would seem much less "efficient." That, in any event, is the theory of the First Amendment. I should add that I do not for a moment suggest that protecting free speech is "costless." The point, rather, is that the protection of free speech is worth some cost to society, and that in the past we have tended to miscalculate both the costs and the benefits.

important as liberty, and the nation is as likely to underprotect security as it is to underprotect liberty. I do not take issue with the first assumption. For these purposes, I concede that security is as "important" as liberty, though I am not quite sure what that means. But even accepting that premise, I disagree with the second assumption. Posner acknowledges that on occasion the United States has excessively restricted civil liberties in wartime. But the real lesson of history, he argues, is the opposite. In his view, "[o]fficialdom has repeatedly and disastrously underestimated" dangers to the nation's security; he offers as examples its underestimation of the risk of secession leading up to the Civil War, the danger of a Japanese attack on the United States in 1941, the threat of Soviet espionage in the 1940s, the possibility of the Tet offensive during the Vietnam War, and, of course, the risk of terrorist attacks before September 11.[48]

No doubt, some of this is right. But it is irrelevant. That the government may underestimate these other dangers is no reason to shut our eyes to the fact that it *also* underestimates the dangers of silencing dissent. The proper response to Posner's insight is for the government to take those other dangers more seriously. The right way to do that, however, is not by stifling free speech or otherwise restricting civil liberties. There is no evidence that it was the nation's overprotection of constitutional rights that *caused* these misjudgments. "Pragmatic constitutional reasoning" should make some effort to connect cause and effect.

Moreover, and more fundamentally, nothing Posner says addresses the fact that there are systemic, pathological reasons why public officials leap too quickly to restrict dissent in wartime. Pragmatic constitutional reasoning must consider those systemic factors if it is to strike the right "balance" between liberty and security. Otherwise, as we have seen repeatedly in our history, we *unnecessarily* lose liberty without any corresponding gain in security.

Judge Posner argues that this is all futile because it "is only with the benefit of hindsight that a reaction can be separated into its proper and excess layers. In hindsight, we know that interning the Japanese-American residents of the West Coast did not shorten World War II. But was that known at the time? If not, should not the government have erred on the side of caution, as it did?"[49] Again, this misses the point. Because we know from "hindsight" that there is a repeated *pattern* of excessive restriction of civil liberties in wartime, the goal is not only to recognize this pathology when it occurs, which may indeed be difficult, but to create *safeguards* that will make it less likely to happen in the future.

The law is rife with presumptions designed to improve decision making. We exclude certain types of evidence in criminal trials, for example, because we presume it will unduly prejudice or inflame the jury. We presume people to be innocent until proven guilty beyond a reasonable doubt in part because we know that once an individual stands accused by the state the jury is likely to begin its deliberations with a strong bias toward guilt. We require a warrant for searches and seizures because we don't trust law enforcement officers to decide for themselves whether there is probable cause. In terms of free speech in wartime, the nation needs to erect similar presumptions to guard against overreaction. Indeed, much of the evolution of First Amendment doctrine from *Schenck* to *Brandenburg* reflects precisely this process of building a fortress of doctrinal presumptions in order to withstand the undue pressures to stifle dissent in the worst of times.

All that said, there remains the question whether anything courts do in these periods really matters. It is often said that, as a practical matter, presidents do what they please in wartime. Attorney General Biddle once observed that "the Constitution has never greatly bothered any wartime President,"[50] and Chief Justice Rehnquist has suggested, "There is no reason to think that future wartime presidents will act differently from Lincoln, Wilson, or Roosevelt."[51]

The record, however, is more complex. Although presidents may think of themselves as bound more by political than by constitutional constraints in time of war, the two are often linked. Lincoln did not propose a sedition act, Wilson rejected calls to suspend the writ of habeas corpus, and Bush has not advocated a federal loyalty program for Muslim Americans, much less confined them in internment camps. Even in wartime, presidents have not attempted to restrict civil liberties in the face of *settled* Supreme Court precedent. Although presidents often push the envelope where the law is unclear, they do not defy established constitutional doctrine.

Perhaps this is because they respect the law or perhaps it is because they do not want to pick a fight with the Supreme Court in the midst of a war. Whatever the explanation, the phenomenon is unmistakable, and it is important. The Supreme Court is not powerless to influence these matters. As Chief Justice Rehnquist has noted, a decision "in favor of civil liberty will stand as a precedent to regulate future actions of Congress and the Executive branch in future wars."[52] The record bears this out.

This suggests that in periods of relative calm the Court should consciously construct constitutional doctrines that will provide firm and unequivocal guidance for later periods of stress. Perhaps the best example of this in modern constitutional law is the Court's 1969 decision in *Brandenburg*, in which the Court redefined fifty years of jurisprudence in order to articulate a clear and unambiguous standard to deal in the future with issues like those raised by the Sedition Act of 1798, the Espionage Act of 1917, and the Smith Act of 1940—issues at the very heart of the First Amendment.[53]

As the Court has learned by experience and sustained reflection, if the nation is to preserve civil liberties in the face of war fever, the Court must define clear constitutional rules that are not easily circumvented or manipulated by prosecutors, jurors, presidents, or even future Supreme Court justices. Malleable princi- ples, open-ended balances, and vague standards may serve well in periods of tran- quillity, but they will fail us just at the point when we most need the Constitution. As the law professor Vincent Blasi has argued, the Court must establish firm principles in ordinary times in order to ensure that the nation does not under- protect dissent in times of crisis.[54]

This raises a further problem. Even if the Court does articulate clear doc- trines that firmly protect the freedom of speech, and even if the president and the Congress abide by such decisions in wartime, we have repeatedly seen that as soon as the Court closes off one avenue of repression, others appear. The legal scholar Mark Tushnet has noted this phenomenon:

> Judges . . . develop doctrines and approaches that preclude the repetition of
> the last generation's mistakes. Unfortunately, each new threat generates new pol-
> icy responses, which are—almost by definition—not precluded by the doctrines
> designed to make it impossible to adopt the policies used last time. And yet, the
> next generation again concludes that the new policy responses were mistaken.
> We learn from our mistakes to the extent that we do not repeat precisely the same
> errors, but it seems that we do not learn enough to keep us from making new and
> different mistakes.[55]

As we have seen, after the Supreme Court made it difficult in the 1940s for the United States to criminalize "disloyal" speech, public officials shifted to loy- alty programs that denied "disloyal" individuals the "privilege" of public employ- ment. After the Court held this unconstitutional, the government shifted to public exposure to harass political dissidents. After the Court held this unconstitutional, the government moved to undercover infiltration, disruption, and monitoring in order to undermine wartime dissent. As long as government officials persist in devis- ing inventive new ways to weaken dissent, courts must stay in the chase.

But this is not a lesson in futility. Over the decades, and in the face of ever more speech-protective constitutional standards, the efforts of government to suppress dissent have become both more subtle and less effective. Mollie Steimer was sentenced to fifteen years in prison, and then deported. That is a far cry from an FBI agent harassing an antiwar protester fifty years later by mailing an anony- mous letter to her parents reporting her "radical" activities. Both actions are unconstitutional and indefensible, but if the Supreme Court has moved the nation from the former to the latter, we have indeed come a long way.

Finally, it is often repeated as a form of conventional wisdom that the Supreme Court will not decide a case against the government on an issue of mil- itary security during a period of national emergency. The decisions most often cited in support of this proposition are *Korematsu* and *Dennis*. Clinton Rossiter once observed that "the government of the United States, in the case of military necessity," can be "just as much a dictatorship, after its own fashion, as any other government on earth." The Supreme Court, he added, "will not, and cannot be expected to, get in the way of this power."[56]

This does not give the Court its due. There are many counterexamples. As we have seen, during World War II the Court consistently upheld the First Amendment rights of American fascists and Communists in a series of criminal prosecutions and denaturalization proceedings,[57] effectively putting an end to the government's efforts to punish such individuals for their speech. In 1943, at the very height of the war, the Court boldly held in *Barnette*[58] that the government could not constitutionally compel children in West Virginia public schools to pledge allegiance to the American flag, a decision that triggered a furious public response. Less than a year after the attack on Pearl Harbor, the Court held that civilians in Hawaii could not be tried by military tribunals,[59] and in 1944 the Court held that Executive Order no. 9066 did not authorize the detention of individuals of Japanese ancestry who had been found to be loyal American citizens, effectively marking the end of the Japanese American internment.[60] During the Cold War, the Court rejected President Truman's attempt to seize the steel industry[61] and, in a series of decisions beginning with *Yates*,[62] helped usher out the era of McCarthyism. During the Vietnam War, in a rash of decisions illustrated most dramatically by *Pentagon Papers*,[63] the Court confidently rejected national security claims by the executive and vigorously enforced First Amendment freedoms.

So, although it is true that the Court tends to be careful not to overstep its bounds in wartime, it is also true that the Court has a long, if uneven, record of fulfilling its constitutional responsibility to protect civil liberties—even in time of war.[64] And because the Congress and the president have consistently deferred to the Supreme Court's interpretation of the First Amendment, these decisions have had a major impact on how the United States responds to the exigencies of wartime.[65]

THE WAR ON TERRORISM

THE TERRORIST ATTACKS OF September 11, 2001, horrified the American people, perhaps even more than the Japanese bombing of Pearl Harbor. Images of the collapsing towers of the World Trade Center left the nation in a profound state of shock, grief, and uncertainty. Afraid that September 11 brought merely the first of a wave of terrorist attacks, Americans expected and, indeed, demanded that their government take immediate and decisive steps to protect the nation.

In the aftermath of September 11, the government's response, with history as a guage, has been both positive and negative. President Bush deserves credit for his response to the risk of hostile public reactions against Muslims and Muslim Americans. The contrast with Wilson's rhetoric about German Americans and with Roosevelt's treatment of Japanese Americans is striking. This is a good example of lessons learned.

Moreover, as of this writing there have been no federal criminal prosecutions of any individuals for criticizing the administration's policies against terrorism.* The federal government has jailed no one for antiwar dissent. This is a far cry from the nation's experience in 1798, the Civil War, World War I, World War II, and the Cold War, and again shows how far we have progressed. American values, politics, and law have reached a point where such prosecutions seem almost unthinkable. A reasonable analogy to the prosecution of Eugene Debs during World War I would have been the prosecution of Howard Dean in 2004 for his opposition to the war in Iraq. The very implausibility of this prospect is testament to the nation's advance.

Of course, no cultural or legal change is irrevocable. There is no guarantee that government will not again prosecute wartime dissenters or that courts will not find ways to circumvent *Brandenburg*. But the cultural, political, and constitutional barriers the United States has erected to protect antiwar speech from outright suppression are higher than they have ever been, and thus far they have held.

On the other hand, like previous wartime leaders, members of the Bush administration have used fear to their political advantage and tarred their opponents as "disloyal." Shortly after September 11, President Bush warned, in terms strikingly reminiscent of language used by Adams, Wilson, and Nixon, "You are either with us or with the terrorists." Although the president was referring specifically to other nations, Attorney General John Ashcroft went even further, castigating American citizens who challenged the government's restrictions of civil liberties: "To those who scare peace-loving people with phantoms of lost liberty,

---

* There have been several state prosecutions, however. Shortly after September 11, New York officials arrested and charged two individuals for engaging in highly offensive expression arising out of the World Trade Center tragedy. In one case, a man who stood on Forty-second Street in Manhattan and screamed at passersby that more firefighters and others should have been killed in the terrorist attacks was prosecuted for inciting a riot. See *People v. Upshaw*, 741 NYS2d 664 (2002). In the second case, state officials filed, but later dismissed, charges against a man who displayed a picture of Osama Bin Laden at the site of the former World Trade Center buildings. See *No Charges against Bin Laden Supporter*, NY L J 6 (Apr 26, 2002). In a federal matter, the United States has prosecuted an anti-Bush protester, Brett Bursey, who refused to leave a restricted-access area in an airport where the president's plane was scheduled to land. Bursey refused to obey a Secret Service order that he move to a designated "free speech zone" that was a considerable distance from the president's location. He was convicted and sentenced to a fine of $500. The case is on appeal. See Economist.com (July 8, 2004).

my message is this: Your tactics only aid terrorists, for they erode our national unity and diminish our resolve. They give ammunition to America's enemies."[*66]

In the wake of September 11, the United States faced grave and uncertain dangers, and the administration immediately claimed far-reaching powers to address the crisis. In principle, this is sensible. The executive can act more quickly and more effectively in an emergency than either Congress or the judiciary, and every president who has faced such a crisis—including Lincoln, Wilson, and Roosevelt—has asserted and aggressively exercised extraordinary executive authority. This is a necessary and proper response to a crisis, but one that must be tempered with due regard for the nation's commitment to civil liberties.

Immediately after September 11, Americans were more than willing to accept significant encroachments on their freedoms in order to forestall further attacks. To reinforce this willingness, the Bush administration repeatedly declared that the terrorists had taken "advantage of the vulnerability of an open society" and that the government therefore needed to impose new restrictions on civil liberties.[67] Some of these restrictions were modest in scope and addressed serious deficiencies in the nation's intelligence apparatus. Others, however, were far more problematic.

The more questionable restrictions included indefinite detention, with no access to judicial review, of more than a thousand *noncitizens* who were lawfully in the United States and had not been charged with any crime; blanket secrecy concerning the identity of these detainees;[68] refusal to permit many of these detainees to communicate with an attorney; an unprecedented assertion of authority to eavesdrop on constitutionally protected attorney-client communications;[69] secret deportation proceedings; the incarceration for more than two years of an American citizen, arrested on American soil, incommunicado, with no access to a lawyer, solely on the basis of an executive determination that he was an "enemy combatant";[70] significant new limitations on the scope of the Freedom of Information Act;[71] expanded authority to conduct undercover infiltration and surveillance of political and religious groups; increased power to wiretap, engage in electronic eavesdropping, and covertly review Internet and e-mail communications; new power secretly to review banking, brokerage, and other financial records; and expanded authority to conduct clandestine physical searches.[72]

The centerpiece of the Bush administration's antiterrorism strategy was the USA PATRIOT Act,[73] an exceedingly complex statute drafted by the Justice

---

* On March 10, 2004, after Senator John Kerry of Massachusetts "clinched" the Democratic presidential nomination, Jim Gilmore, the former chairman of the Republican National Committee, accused Kerry of "a long pattern of trying to diminish national security." *Patriot Acts*, Nightline (ABC News Mar 10, 2004).

Department and rammed through a grief-stricken Congress only six weeks after September 11. Attorney General Ashcroft and other federal officials accused anyone who questioned the necessity or constitutionality of the proposed legislation of being "soft on terrorism," and Congress passed the act in an atmosphere of urgency and alarm that precluded serious deliberation. Indeed, no more than a handful of congressmen had even read the legislation before it was rushed into law. Although civil liberties organizations had identified serious flaws in the PATRIOT Act, even members of Congress known as "strong voices in favor of civil liberties" failed to object.[74]

The result was a statute that has fairly been characterized as opportunistic and excessive. The PATRIOT Act smuggled into law several investigative practices that have nothing to do with fighting terrorism, but that law enforcement officials had for years tried unsuccessfully to persuade Congress to authorize. It failed to require reasonable executive branch accountability, undermined traditional—and essential—checks and balances, and disregarded the fundamental principle that government intrusions on civil liberties should be narrowly tailored to avoid unnecessary invasions of constitutional rights.[*][75]

Although Congress readily acquiesced in the administration's demand for the PATRIOT Act, it soon grew more skeptical about further calls to limit civil liberties. When Attorney General Ashcroft announced his intention to institute a new Terrorism Information and Prevent System (TIPS), which would have exhorted citizens to monitor and report on other citizens in a manner reminiscent of the World War I program George Creel described as a "thing of screams and extremes," Congress objected, forcing Ashcroft to withdraw the proposal.[76]

Congress also blocked funding for the administration's Total Information Awareness program, which was designed to develop a vast surveillance system and database of personal and commercial information in order to detect "suspicious" behavior patterns among American citizens. Even leading Republicans balked at this proposal. Senator Charles Grassley of Iowa, for example, rightly objected that TIA posed a "chilling threat to civil liberties."[77]

In January 2003, the Justice Department floated plans for PATRIOT Act II, entitled the Domestic Security Enhancement Act of 2003. This legislation would have reduced judicial oversight over surveillance, created a DNA database resting on unchecked executive "suspicion," lifted existing judicial restraints on local police spying on religious and political organizations,[78] authorized the fed-

---

[*] A key moment will come at the end of 2005, when the federal government decides whether to renew those provisions of the PATRIOT Act that are subject to the "sunset" requirement. In his 2004 state of the union address, President Bush called upon Congress to renew "this vital legislation." *State of the Union*, New York Times A18 (Jan 21, 2004).

eral government to obtain library and credit card records without a judicial warrant, and permitted the federal government to keep secret the identity of *anyone* detained in a terror investigation—including American citizens. PATRIOT Act II met with howls of public, press, and bipartisan congressional opposition, and the administration buried the proposal.

Thus, although the initial response of Congress and the public was to support the administration's demands for additional powers, once fears had settled, the response was more clear-eyed and more resistant to further expansions of executive authority.[79] As journalist Jeffrey Rosen wrote in May 2003, "a principled, bipartisan libertarian constituency" emerged that was willing to defend civil liberties "even in the face of popular fears" and aggressive executive plans to expand its power.[80]

THE BUSH ADMINISTRATION went out of its way after September 11 to excite rather than calm public fears. The attacks of September 11 were the most shocking ever suffered on American soil. A terrified public reasonably feared more attacks. The administration immediately characterized the event as the first stage of a "war," rather than as a heinous crime. Declaring a "war" on terrorism was more than a rhetorical device to rally the public, for it enabled the administration to assert the extraordinary powers traditionally reserved to the executive in wartime.

Moreover, just as the assault on communism during the Cold War gave new purpose and direction to a foundering Republican Party, the "war" on terrorism gave new purpose to a presidency that was drifting before September 11. The president's declaration that the threat of international terrorism was not merely a "war" but a war that would last *indefinitely* added to the sense of gravity and public anxiety. Bush's claim that "the war against terrorism will never end" is misleading and dangerous. As Richard Posner has rightly observed, it is simply "impossible to say at this time whether there will be a substantial threat of international terrorism" five, ten, or twenty years from now.[81]

On the other hand, if the administration is correct that the war on terrorism will grind on indefinitely, that is all the more reason to be scrupulous in scrutinizing proposed restrictions of civil liberties. Although the claim of perpetual war may appear to be a compelling reason to steel the nation to the long task ahead by stripping away all "unnecessary" civil liberties, the opposite is true. As we have seen, a saving "grace" of America's past excesses is that they were of "short" duration and that, once the crisis passed, the nation returned to equilibrium. A war of indefinite duration, however, compounds the dangers both by extending the period during which civil liberties are "suspended" and by increasing the risk that "emergency" restrictions will become a permanent fixture of American life.

Another striking feature of this period is that, as in past episodes, the Bush administration may have seriously misled the American people in order to heighten the public's insecurity and build support for escalating the war. Just as the Federalists exaggerated the risk of a French invasion in 1798 to justify a military buildup, and Lyndon Johnson exaggerated the events surrounding the Tonkin Gulf incident in order to justify a more aggressive strategy in Vietnam, George Bush exaggerated the evidence that Saddam Hussein had weapons of mass destruction in order to justify his invasion of Iraq. As the former ambassador James Goodby has written, in the Bush administration fear has too often "become the underlying theme of domestic and foreign policy." The "bottom line has been . . . 'You are scared—trust us.'"[82]

AFTER THE FBI's COINTELPROs came to light in the 1970s, Attorney General Edward Levi promulgated stringent guidelines restricting the FBI's authority to investigate political and religious activities. The 1976 guidelines prohibited the bureau from investigating any group or individual on the basis of protected First Amendment activity, from monitoring any such activity except in a narrowly tailored effort to enforce the criminal law, and from investigating any organization engaged in protected First Amendment activity in the absence of "specific and articulable facts" justifying a criminal investigation.

The Levi guidelines embodied values similar to those affirmed by Attorney General Harlan Fiske Stone in 1924 when he ordered the FBI to terminate its surveillance of political activities after the abuses of the 1919–20 Red Scare. As Stone explained at the time, "a secret police may become a menace to free government and free institutions because it carries with it the possibility of abuses of power which are not always quickly apprehended or understood." It is imperative, he proclaimed, that the FBI no longer investigate the "political or other opinions of individuals."[83]

In the quarter century after Levi formulated his guidelines, two of his successors, William French Smith and Richard Thornburgh, attorneys general under Presidents Reagan and George H. W. Bush, weakened the guidelines, but left their essential core intact.[84] On May 30, 2002, however, Attorney General Ashcroft effectively dismantled the Levi guidelines.[85] Ashcroft expressly authorized the FBI to enter any place or attend any event that is open to the public in order to gather information that may be relevant to criminal activity, thus enabling the FBI once again to monitor a wide range of constitutionally protected political and religious activities without any showing that unlawful conduct might be afoot. According to the *New York Times*, the FBI has been busy collecting "extensive information on the tactics, training and organization of antiwar demonstrators." In a familiar refrain, the FBI has explained that its goal is to identify "anarchists and 'extremist elements' " and not to monitor "the political speech of law-abiding protesters."[86]

Now, it may seem only sensible, as Ashcroft argued in defense of his change in the guidelines, that FBI agents should be able to monitor public events in the same manner as other members of the public. But it is not so simple. An individual planning to attend a political meeting or a rally protesting the war in Iraq, for example, will be much more hesitant to attend if he knows FBI agents may be taking names. Such surveillance, whether open or surreptitious, can have a significant chilling effect on First Amendment freedoms.

The Ashcroft guidelines also eliminated the long-standing requirement that FBI investigations affecting political and religious activities be undertaken with special care. The new rules authorize the FBI, in investigating political and religious organizations, to "use the same investigative techniques they would use when investigating any other type of organization," such as organized crime or a terrorist cell.[87] The effect is to expose religious and political organizations to *extensive* FBI monitoring without *any* objective grounds for suspicion and with much *reduced* supervisory control.[*88]

An even more troubling free speech issue arising out of the "war" on terrorism concerns the Bush administration's obsession with secrecy. Overbroad assertions of secrecy cripple informed public discourse. It is impossible for citizens to engage in responsible political debate if they are denied access to critical information about the actions of elected officials. As Senator Daniel Patrick Moynihan once observed, "secrecy is the ultimate form of regulation because people don't even know they are being regulated."[89]

---

[*] An excellent example of the Bush administration's insensitivity to First Amendment concerns in this respect was its effort to require Drake University to turn over to federal prosecutors all of its records relating to a November 15, 2003, conference against the war in Iraq and all records relating to the Drake chapter of the National Lawyers Guild, which had sponsored the forum. The government served subpoenas not only on Drake University but also on the leader of the Catholic Peace Ministry, the former coordinator of the Iowa Peace Network, and a member of the Catholic Worker House. The justification for the subpoena was that the day after the conference several protesters were arrested during an antiwar demonstration at the Iowa National Guard Headquarters. Among other things, the government demanded information about all persons who had attended the November 15 meeting. After vehement protests from civil liberties organizations across the nation, the Justice Department withdrew the subpoena. See *Subpoenas on Antiwar Protest Are Dropped*, New York Times A18 (Feb 11, 2004); *University Records on Antiwar Meeting Sought*, Washington Post A10 (Feb 8, 2004).

Excessive secrecy has been a consistent feature of the Bush administration, ranging from its refusal to disclose the names of those it detained after September 11 and its narrowing of the Freedom of Information Act, to its unprecedented closure of deportation proceedings and its redaction of "sensitive" information from tens of thousands of government documents and Web sites.[90]

Some degree of secrecy in the interest of national security is, of course, essential, especially in wartime. But the Bush administration's obsessive secrecy effectively constrains oversight by both the press and the public and directly undermines the vitality of democratic governance. As the legal scholar Stephen Schulhofer has noted, one cannot escape the inference that the cloak of secrecy imposed by the Bush administration has "less to do with the war on terrorism" than with its desire "to insulate executive action from public scrutiny."[91] This policy will weaken our democratic institutions and "leave the country less secure in the long run."[92]

IT IS, OF COURSE, much easier to look back on past crises and find our predecessors wanting than to make wise judgments when we ourselves are in the eye of the storm. But that challenge now falls to this generation of Americans.* Freedom can endanger security, but it is also the fundamental source of American strength. As Justice Louis Brandeis explained in 1927, "Those who won our independence . . . knew that . . . fear breeds repression" and that "courage is the secret of liberty."[93] Those are the two most central lessons for Americans to bear in mind.

---

* In two recent decisions, the Supreme Court rejected two very broad assertions of the Bush administration with respect to the war on terrorism. In *Rasul v. Bush* (2004), the Court held, by a vote of 6 to 3, that federal courts have habeas corpus jurisdiction to consider challenges to the legality of the detention of foreign nationals captured abroad in connection with hostilities in Afghanistan and incarcerated by the military at the Guantánamo Bay, Cuba. Noting that "[a]t its historical core, the writ of habeas corpus has served as a means of reviewing the legality of Executive detention," the Court decisively repudiated the administration's argument that the legality of these detentions were beyond the scope of judicial review.

In *Hamdi v. Rumsfeld* (2004), the Court, by a vote of 8 to 1, turned aside the administration's claim that the president of the United States could constitutionally order the indefinite detention of American citizens as "enemy combatants" without even according such individuals the right to "contest the factual basis for that detention" in a fair hearing before an independent tribunal. In a plurality opinion, Justice O'Connor observed, "In so holding, we necessarily reject the Government's assertion that separation of powers principles mandate a heavily circumscribed role for the courts

To strike the right balance, this nation needs political leaders who know right from wrong; federal judges who will stand fast against the furies of their age; members of the bar and the academy who will help Americans see themselves clearly; a thoughtful and responsible press; informed and tolerant citizens who will value not only their own liberties, but the liberties of others; and justices of the Supreme Court with the wisdom to know excess when they see it and the courage to preserve liberty when it is imperiled. And, so, we shall see.

---

in such circumstances. . . . We have long . . . made clear that a state of war is not a blank check for the President, when it comes to the rights of the Nation's citizens." Indeed, it "is during our most challenging and uncertain moments that our Nation's commitment to [civil liberties] is most severely tested; and it is in those times that we must preserve our commitment at home to the principles for which we fight abroad."

Upon learning of the Supreme Court's decisions in the Guantánamo Bay and *Hamdi* decisions, Fred Korematsu, now eighty-five years old, told me he was "delighted" by the Court's decision: "By recognizing the overriding importance of civil liberties even in wartime, the Supreme Court has taken a critical step away from some of its more regrettable decisions in the past. . . . Perhaps more importantly, it has learned the lesson of our own history—that especially in wartime, the nation depends on independent federal courts to guard the liberties of all and to be skeptical of claims of military necessity."

NOTES

INTRODUCTION

[1] Alexander Meiklejohn, *Free Speech and Its Relation to Self-Government* 15–16 (Harper 1948).

[2] Vincent Blasi, *Free Speech and Good Character: From Milton to Brandeis to the Present*, in Lee C. Bollinger and Geoffrey R. Stone, eds, *Eternally Vigilant: Free Speech in the Modern Era* 61, 62, 84–85 (Chicago 2002). See Lee C. Bollinger, *The Tolerant Society: Freedom of Speech and Extremist Speech in America* (Oxford 1986).

[3] See Fredrick Schauer, *Free Speech: A Philosophical Inquiry* (Cambridge 1982); Vincent Blasi, *The Checking Value in First Amendment Theory*, Am B Found Res J 521 (1977).

[4] Thomas Emerson, *The System of Freedom of Expression* 7 (Random House 1970).

[5] *Abrams v. United States*, 250 US 616, 630–31 (1919) (Holmes, J, dissenting).

[6] David Richards, *Free Speech and Obscenity Law: Toward a Moral Theory of the First Amendment* 123 U Pa L Rev 45, 62 (1974).

[7] William H. Rehnquist, *All the Laws But One: Civil Liberties in Wartime* 222 (Random House 1998).

[8] *Chaplinsky v. New Hampshire*, 315 US 568, 571–72 (1942).

[9] See Larry B. Kramer, *The People Themselves: Popular Constitutionalism and Judicial Review* (Oxford 2004).

CHAPTER I

[1] Richard H. Kohn, *Eagle and Sword: The Federalists and the Creation of the Military Establishment in America, 1783–1802* 195 (Free 1975); James Rogers Sharp, *American Politics in the Early Republic: The New Nation in Crisis* 5 (Yale 1993).

[2] Farmers' Library 3 (Oct 28, 1794).

[3] *Twelve Reasons against a Free People's Employing Practitioners in the Law, as Legislators*, Farmers' Library 1 (Aug 19, 1794).

[4] M. Lyon, *Letter for the Vermont Gazette and the Political Registrar*, Farmers' Library 1 (June 10, 1793); *Letter from the Vermont Gazette to Matthew Lyon*, Farmers' Library 2 (May 13, 1793).

[5] Letter from Matthew Lyon to Armisted Mason, Jan 16, 1817, excerpted in Aleine Austin, *Matthew Lyon: "New Man" of the Democratic Revolution, 1749–1822* 76 (Pennsylvania State 1981).

[6] Jeffrey L. Pasley, *"The Tyranny of Printers": Newspaper Politics in the Early American Republic* 110 (Virginia 2001).

[7] 7 *Annals of Congress* 234–35 (Gales and Seaton 1851).

[8] William Cobbett, 6 *Porcupine's Works* 16 (Gosnell 1801).

[9] See Austin, *Matthew Lyon* at 17–18, 95–100 (cited in note 5).

[10] 7 *Annals of Congress* at 979 (cited in note 7). See generally id at 1047–58.

[11] See generally Austin, *Matthew Lyon* at 97–98 (cited in note 5); John C. Miller, *Crisis in Freedom: The Alien and Sedition Acts* 104–6 (Little, Brown 1951).

[12] 7 *Annals of Congress* at 985 (cited in note 7); *The Spitting Irish Lyon*, Porcupine's Gazette 3 (Feb 13, 1798).

[13] Letter from Roger Griswold to an unnamed correspondent, Feb 25, 1798, excerpted in Austin, *Matthew Lyon* at 100 (cited in note 5). See Richard N. Rosenfeld, *American Aurora* 11–13 (St Martin's 1997).

[14] Letter from James Madison to Thomas Jefferson, Feb 18, 1798, in David B. Mattern et al, eds, 17 *The Papers of James Madison* 82 (Virginia 1991); 7 *Annals of Congress* at 1002 (cited in note 7).

[15] *From the Aurora*, Carey's United States Recorder 3 (July 12, 1798).

[16] Austin, *Matthew Lyon* at 108 (cited in note 5). See James Morton Smith, *Freedom's Fetters: The Alien and Sedition Laws and American Civil Liberties* 177 (Cornell 1956).

[17] Francis Wharton, *State Trials of the United States* 333 (Carey and Hart 1849).

[18] George Washington, *Proclamation of Neutrality*, in John C. Fitzpatrick, ed, 32 *The Writings of George Washington* 430–31 (Government Printing Office 1939).

[19] Foreshadowing events to come, Washington's effort to preserve American neutrality in the war between England and France by making concessions to the English irritated the pro-French faction in the United States. See Page Smith, *Election of 1796*, in Arthur M. Schlesinger Jr. and Fred L. Israel, eds, 1 *History of American Presidential Elections, 1789–2001* 62–63 (Chelsea House 2002).

[20] These divisions appeared along fault lines similar to ones already established between the Federalists and the Anti-Federalists during the debates over ratification of the Constitution. See Saul Cornell, *The Other Founders: Anti-Federalism and the Dissenting Tradition in America, 1788–1828* 7 (North Carolina 1999).

[21] Marcus Cunliffe, *Elections of 1789 and 1792*, in Schlesinger and Israel, eds, 1 *History of American Presidential Elections* at 13–14 (cited in note 19).

[22] Smith, *Election of 1796* at 65 (cited in note 19); Cunliffe, *Elections of 1789 and 1792* at 13 (cited in note 21).

[23] Letter from Uriah Tracy to Alexander Hamilton, Apr 6, 1797, in Harold C. Syrett, ed, 21 *The Papers of Alexander Hamilton* 24–26 (Columbia 1974); Letter from Senator Oliver Wolcott to Secretary Oliver Wolcott, Mar 20, 1797, in George Gibbs, ed, 1 *Memoirs of the Administrations of Washington and John Adams* 476 (Van Norden 1846); Letter from Thomas Jefferson to John Taylor, June 1, 1798, in Paul L. Ford, ed, 8 *The Works of Thomas Jefferson* 430 (Putnam 1904) (the quotation is Jefferson's paraphrase of a prior letter written by Taylor). Jefferson responded negatively to this suggestion. See Sharp, *American Politics in the Early Republic* at 188–90 (cited in note 1). On the other hand, Adams's inaugural address was intended to be conciliatory, and some Republicans were even more satisfied with the speech than the members of Adams's own party. Needless to say, this made the Federalists increasingly anxious. See Smith, *Election of 1796* at 74–75 (cited in note 19).

[24] Letter from Thomas Jefferson to James Madison, May 10, 1798, in Ford, ed, 8 *The Works of Thomas Jefferson* at 418–19 (cited in note 23). See Sharp, *American Politics in the Early Republic* at 175 (cited in note 1).

[25] Address of John Adams to Special Session of Congress, May 16, 1797, in 2 *Journal of the Senate* 358–60 (Gales and Seaton 1820).

[26] Stanley Elkins and Eric McKitrick, *The Age of Federalism* 573, 583–84 (Oxford 1993).

[27] John Adams, *Notes for Message to Congress*, excerpted in Elkins and McKitrick, *Age of Federalism* at 585 (cited in note 26); id at 586; John Adams, *Message from the President of the United States to Both Houses of Congress, Delivered on March 19, 1798*, in *American State Papers* 4 (Wright and Richardson 1798).

[28] See Smith, *Freedom's Fetters* at 7 (cited in note 16); Elkins and McKitrick, *Age of Federalism* at 587–88 (cited in note 26).

[29] Smith, *Freedom's Fetters* at 8 (cited in note 16).

[30] Jefferson (not a "framer") observed in 1789 that if he "could not go to heaven but with a [political] party," he would rather not go there at all. Letter from Thomas Jefferson to Francis Hopkinson, Mar 13, 1789, in Julian P. Boyd, ed, 14 *The Papers of Thomas Jefferson* 650 (Princeton 1958).

[31] The "demon of partisanship" was first let loose in the newspaper war of 1792, in which the formation of political parties was brought fully into the open. Elkins and McKitrick, *Age of Federalism* at 282 (cited in note 26). In his farewell address, Washington warned against "the baneful effects of the spirit of party." George Washington, *Farewell Address, Sept 19, 1796*, in John C. Fitzpatrick, 35 *The Writings of George Washington* 226 (Government Printing Office 1940). But to no avail. During the election of 1792, Adams expressed astonishment "at the blind spirit of party which has seized on the whole soul" of Jefferson, and he argued that the Federalists must fight the enemy with every means at their disposal. Cunliffe, *Elections of 1789 and 1792* at 27 (cited in note 21). In Jefferson's view, however, once Washington was gone, "these energumeni of royalism, kept in check hitherto by the dread of his honesty, his firmness, his patriotism . . . now mounted the car of State and free from his control . . . drove headlong and wild, looking neither to right nor left, nor regarding anything but the objects they were driving at." David P. Currie, *The Constitution in Congress: The Federalist Period 1789–1801* 125 (Chicago 1997).

[32] See Alexander Addison, *Reports of Cases in the County Courts of the Fifth Circuit* 211–12 (Colerick 1800) (Addison, a leading Federalist judge, conceded that the people had a right to elect their leaders, but maintained that they were "too apt to confound right with capacity, and power with skill." He asserted that they did not understand that the "art of government" is a "science" that "requires knowledge, study and reflection." The great danger, he warned, was that the people could not "judge rightly" the "conduct of administration"); James P. Martin, *When Representation Is Democratic and Constitutional: The Federalist Theory of Representation and the Sedition Act of 1798*, 66 U Chi L Rev 117, 133–52 (1999).

[33] Seth Ames, ed, 2 *The Works of Fisher Ames* 81 (Little, Brown 1854); Miller, *Crisis in Freedom* at 14–17 (cited in note 11).

[34] See Cornell, *Other Founders* at 199 (cited in note 20).

[35] See Smith, *Freedom's Fetters* at 10–11 (cited in note 16); Elizabeth Lawson, *The Reign of Witches: The Struggle against the Alien and Sedition Laws* 13–14 (Civil Rights Congress 1952).

[36] See 8 *Annals of Congress* 1354–55 (Gales and Seaton 1851).

[37] See Smith, *Freedom's Fetters* at 11–12 (cited in note 16).

[38] Larry D. Kramer, *The People Themselves: Popular Constitutionalism and Judicial Review* 182 (unpublished manuscript).

[39] Letter from Thomas Jefferson to Edward Rutledge, June 24, 1797, in Andrew A. Lipscomb and Albert Ellery Bergh, eds, 9 *The Writings of Thomas Jefferson* 411 (Thomas Jefferson Memorial Association 1905); Deborah Norris Logan, *Memoir of Dr George Logan of Stenton* 54 (Hist Soc of Pa 1899), in Rosenfeld, *American Aurora* (cited in note 13); Aurora (May 10, 1798).

[40] See Elkins and McKitrick, *Age of Federalism* at 588 (cited in note 26).

[41] 8 *Annals of Congress* at 1518 (cited in note 36); id at 1693–94; id at 1518; id at 1633; id at 1641.

[42] Id at 1691; id at 1484.

[43] Id at 1495; id at 1498; id at 2073–74.

[44] Id at 1483.

[45] Id at 1342.

[46] Id at 2071; id at 1503; id at 1824.

[47] Id at 1577; id at 1961.

[48] Id at 1482; id at 2071–72; id at 1531; id at 1342.

[49] Id at 1677.

[50] Id at 1498; id at 1345; id at 1482; id at 2077; id at 1507.

[51] Id at 1680; id at 1509; id at 1500.

[52] John Adams, *Answer of the President, to the Inhabitants of the Town of Wells, in the State of Massachusetts*, Gazette of the United States 2 (June 27, 1798); Letter from John Adams to the Inhabitants of Arlington and Bandate, Vermont, June 25, 1798, in Charles Francis Adams, ed, 9 *The Works of John Adams* 202 (Little, Brown 1854); *To the Inhabitants of Chester County, in the South of Pennsylvania*, Claypoole's American Daily Advertiser 1 (May 29, 1798).

[53] Alexander Hamilton, *The Stand No. 1, Mar 30, 1798*, in Syrett, ed, 21 *Papers of Alexan-*

der Hamilton at 384 (cited in note 23).

[54] See Sharp, *American Politics in the Early Republic* at 12 (cited in note 1); Manning J. Dauer, *The Adams Federalists* 198–211 (Johns Hopkins 1953); Stephen G. Kurtz, *The Presidency of John Adams: The Collapse of Federalism* 310–13 (Pennsylvania 1957); Kohn, *Eagle and Sword* at 195 (cited in note 1).

[55] Miller, *Crisis in Freedom* at 41 (cited in note 11); Samuel Eliot Morison, 1 *The Life and Letters of Harrison Gray Otis* 108 (Houghton Mifflin 1913); Charles R. King, ed, 2 *The Life and Correspondence of Rufus King* 426 (Putnam 1904); 8 *Annals of Congress* at 1567 (cited in note 36) (emphasis added). Congressman Craik also argued that "no foreigner coming into this country" should ever be permitted to become a citizen. Id at 1779.

[56] On the Naturalization Act, see Smith, *Freedom's Fetters* at 22–34 (cited in note 16); Miller, *Crisis in Freedom* at 47–48 (cited in note 11).

[57] The act authorized the president "to order all such aliens as he shall judge dangerous to the peace and safety of the United States, or shall have reasonable grounds to suspect are concerned in any treasonable or secret machinations against the government thereof, to depart out of the territory of the United States, within such time as shall be expressed in such order. . . ." An Act Respecting Alien Enemies, 5th Cong, 2d Sess, in 1 *Public Statutes at Large* 577–78 (Little, Brown 1845).

[58] 8 *Annals of Congress* at 1995 (cited in note 36).

[59] Id at 1980–82.

[60] Id at 2006–11.

[61] Id at 1989; id at 2017; id at 1992.

[62] Id at 1984–85; id at 2018. Federalists argued further that because a deportation proceeding is not a criminal prosecution, the rights attendant to criminal proceedings are irrelevant. See id at 2019–20; id at 1958–59; id at 1984. Republican Congressman Livingston replied, "Good Heaven! To what absurdities does an over-zealous attachment" to the goals of this measure lead its supporters to argue that "plotting against our Government is no offence!" He described the supporters of drawing a "fine hypothesis" in arguing that this is not the punishment of a crime but an act of prevention. Id at 2011. Livingston also noted that if the Federalists are right in saying that the rights do not apply, because these are not crimes, then the same would be true if such a law were applied to citizens. See id at 2013, 2020–21.

[63] Id at 2012–14; Letter from James Madison to Thomas Jefferson, May 20, 1798, in Rosenfeld, *American Aurora* at 128 (cited in note 13); Letter from Thomas Jefferson to James Madison, May 31, 1798, id at 136; 8 *Annals of Congress* at 2012–14 (cited in note 36).

[64] Id at 2014.

[65] Id at 2022; id at 2016; id at 2017–18.

[66] Kenneth Roberts and Anna M. Roberts, eds, *Moreau de St. Méry's American Journey, 1793–1798* 252 (Doubleday 1947). See Sharp, *American Politics in the Early Republic* at 177 (cited in note 1); Lawson, *Reign of Witches* at 30–31 (cited in note 35). For recent commentary on the rights of aliens, see David Cole, *Enemy Aliens* (New Press 2003); Gerald L. Neuman, *Strangers to the Constitution: Immigrants, Borders, and*

Fundamental Law (Princeton 1996).

[67] Richmond Examiner (June 21, 1798), excerpted in Miller, *Crisis in Freedom* at 32–33 (cited in note 11); Joseph Hopkinson, *What Is Our Situation? And What Our Prospects? A Few Pages for Americans, by an American* 29 (1798).

[68] 8 *Annals of Congress* at 2098 (cited in note 36).

[69] Alexander Addison, *Liberty of Speech, and of the Press*, in *A Charge to the Grand Juries of the County Courts of the Fifth Circuit of the State of Pennsylvania* 12 (1799); Pennsylvania Gazette (Oct 18, 1797), excerpted in Miller, *Crisis in Freedom* at 32 (cited in note 11).

[70] Letter from Abigail Adams to Thomas B. Adams, Nov 8, 1796, in 2 *Letters of Mrs. Adams, the Wife of John Adams* 231 (Little, Brown 2d ed 1840); Miller, *Crisis in Freedom* at 79 (cited in note 11). See also Albany Centinel 3 (Nov 2, 1798): "From a Jacobin print, nothing is to be gathered but misinformation and falsehood."

[71] Henry Cabot Lodge, ed, 7 *The Works of Alexander Hamilton* 377 (Putnam 1904).

[72] Addison, *Liberty of Speech, and of the Press* at 14 (cited in note 69); Letter from John Adams to the Mayor, Aldermen, and Citizens of Philadelphia, in Adams, ed, 9 *Works of John Adams* at 182 (cited in note 52); John Adams, *Answer: To the Citizens of Newark, in the State of New Jersey*, Gazette of the United States 2 (May 2, 1798).

[73] Miller, *Crisis in Freedom* at 29 (cited in note 11).

[74] Smith, *Election of 1796* at 64, 70 (cited in note 19); Aurora (Feb 16, 1793); Aurora (Dec 7, 1792); Aurora (Sept 11, 1795); Letter from George Washington to Benjamin Walker, Jan 12, 1797, in Rosenfeld, *American Aurora* at 30 (cited in note 13). Washington was thin-skinned. In 1792, he expressed his desire not to seek a second term, because of the newspaper "attacks upon almost every measure of government." Washington feared that such abuse of public officers and measures would rend "the Union asunder." Although most of these criticisms were not aimed at him personally, Washington took them personally. Letter from George Washington to Edmund Randolph, Aug 26, 1792, in Schlesinger and Israel, eds, 1 *History of American Presidential Elections* at 53 (cited in note 19). In 1796, he told his vice president, John Adams, that he would not seek a third term, because of his "disinclination to be longer buffeted in the public prints by a set of infamous scribblers." Letter from George Washington to Alexander Hamilton, June 26, 1796, in Rosenfeld, *American Aurora* at 31 (cited in note 13).

[75] See Pasley, *"Tyranny of Printers"* at 79–97 (cited in note 6).

[76] See id at 97–102; Miller, *Crisis in Freedom* at 64–66 (cited in note 11); Rosenfeld, *American Aurora* at 56–58, 110–17 (cited in note 13).

[77] Gazette of the United States 3 (May 14, 1800).

[78] Pasley, *"Tyranny of Printers"* at 72 (cited in note 6); *Original Communications*, Gazette of the United States 3 (May 26, 1792).

[79] William Cobbett, 1 *Porcupine's Works* 374 (Gosnell 1801); Cobbett, 6 *Porcupine's Works* at 52–53 (cited in note 8); William Cobbett, 7 *Porcupine's Works* 294–95 (Gosnell 1801); Porcupine's Gazette 2 (Mar 17, 1798).

[80] An Act for the Punishment of Certain Crimes against the United States, 5th Cong, 2d Sess, ch 74 (1798). The Sedition Law did not mark the first attempt by the Federalists

to attack their political opponents. In May 1797, less than three months after Adams's inauguration, a federal grand jury at Richmond, Virginia, handed down a presentment denouncing Republican Congressman Cabell for criticizing the Adams administration in letters to his constituents. Although Cabell was never brought to trial, his indictment was a sign of things to come. See Sharp, *American Politics in the Early Republic* at 169–71 (cited in note 1); Smith, *Freedom's Fetters* at 95 (cited in note 16). See Michael Kent Curtis, *Free Speech, "The People's Darling Privilege": Struggles for Freedom of Expression in American History* 63 (Duke 2000).

[81] 8 *Annals of Congress* at 2110 (cited in note 36); id at 2164. This was not the first time that Gallatin had spoken out against the Federalists in favor of freedom of speech. In addressing the Whiskey Rebellion, Gallatin drew a sharp distinction between "publication of sentiments and acting." He insisted that "we must distinguish between an opinion merely that this or that measure is wrong" and a declaration that the speaker intends to act in an unlawful manner "or advice to others to act." Henry Adams, ed, 3 *The Writings of Albert Gallatin* 5–6 (Lippincott 1879).

[82] 8 *Annals of Congress* at 2161 (cited in note 36); id at 2107.

[83] 2 *Abridgement of the Debates of Congress* 257 (Appleton 1857); *Communications*, Massachusetts Mercury 2 (June 12, 1798); 8 *Annals of Congress* at 2093–94 (cited in note 36).

[84] Id at 2096–101.

[85] Id at 2096–98.

[86] Id at 2109.

[87] Id at 2110.

[88] Id at 2140, 2145; id at 2105–6. Another serious objection to the act was the source of federal authority to enact such legislation at all. See Currie, *Constitution in Congress* at 260–61 (cited in note 31).

[89] 8 *Annals* of Congress at 2145, 2112, 2167–68 (cited in note 36).

[90] Id at 2162.

[91] Id at 2140–41.

[92] Id at 2146.

[93] Id at 2147–48.

[94] William M. Blackstone, 4 *Commentaries* *151–52.

[95] 8 *Annals of Congress* at 2145, 2148–49, 2151 (cited in note 36).

[96] Id at 2160; id at 2142.

[97] Leonard W. Levy, *Emergence of a Free Press* xv (Oxford 1985).

[98] Zechariah Chafee, *Free Speech in the United States* 18–20 (Harvard 1941). The system of prior restraint remained in effect in England until 1694, when the authorizing legislation expired and was not renewed. See generally, Levy, *Emergence of a Free Press* at 3–15 (cited in note 97); Fredrick Seaton Siebert, *Freedom of the Press in England, 1476–1776* 41–104, 127–263 (Illinois 1952). A special concern with prior restraint remains an important part of contemporary First Amendment doctrine.

[99] See, e.g., David M. Rabban, *The Ahistorical Historian: Leonard Levy on Freedom of Expression in Early American History*, 37 Stan L Rev 795 (1985); William T. Mayton, *From a Legacy of Suppression to the "Metaphor of the Fourth Estate,"* 39 Stan L Rev

139 (1986); Curtis, *Free Speech*, at 94–116 (cited in note 80); Smith, *Freedom's Fetters* at 418–33 (cited in note 16). For a view more supportive of the Federalist interpretation, see William Winslow Crosskey, 2 *Politics and the Constitution in the History of the United States* 767–68 (Chicago 1953); Thomas F. Carroll, *Freedom of Speech and of the Press in the Federalist Period: The Sedition Act*, 18 U Mich L Rev 615 (1919–20).

100 Benjamin Franklin, *An Account of the Supremest Court of Judicature in Pennsylvania, viz. The Court of the Press* (Sept 12, 1789), in Albert Henry Smyth, ed, 10 *The Writings of Benjamin Franklin* 37 (Macmillan 1907).

101 Indeed, to the Anti-Federalists, nothing seemed more threatening to liberty than the prospect that the new national government might use the law of libel as a political weapon to suppress dissent. See Cornell, *The Other Founders* at 128–34 (cited in note 20).

102 Geoffrey R. Stone, Louis M. Seidman, Cass R. Sunstein, Mark V. Tushnet, Pamela S. Karlan, *The First Amendment* at 3–5 (Aspen 2d ed 2003); T. B. Howell, ed, 14 *State Trials* 1128 (Hansard 1816).

103 James F. Stephen, 2 *A History of the Criminal Law of England* 350 (Macmillan 1883).

104 Siebert, *Freedom of the Press in England* at 269 (cited in note 98). See Philip Hamburger, *The Development of the Law of Seditious Libel and the Control of the Press*, 37 Stan L Rev 661 (1985).

105 William M. Blackstone, 1 *Commentaries* °239.

106 William M. Blackstone, 2 *Commentaries* °2; Richard Doane, ed, 2 *Principles of Judicial Procedure, with the Outlines of a Procedure Code by Jeremy Betham* 501 (1837); Letter from Thomas Jefferson to John Tyler, June 17, 1812, in Albert E. Bergh, ed, 13 *The Writings of Thomas Jefferson* 166 (Thomas Jefferson Memorial Association 1903); Letter from Thomas Jefferson to Horatio G. Spafford, Mar 17, 1814, in H. A. Washington, ed, 6 *The Writings of Thomas Jefferson* 335 (Riker, Thorne 1854). See Bird Wilson, ed, 3 *The Works of the Honourable James Wilson, LLD* 199–246 (Lorenzo 1804).

107 The Federalist Fisher Ames complained, for example, that the press had "inspired ignorance . . . so that those who cannot be governed by reason are no longer to be awed by authority." Ames, 2 *Works of Fisher Ames* at 357 (cited in note 33)

108 Currie, *The Constitution in Congress* at 297 (cited in note 31). See Smith, *Freedom's Fetters* at 146–48 (cited in note 16); Chafee, *Free Speech in the United States* at 18–20 (cited in note 98).

109 8 *Annals of Congress* at 2133–34 (cited in note 36); id at 2103.

110 Id at 2171.

111 See Thomas Erskine May, 2 *The Constitutional History of England Since the Accession of George the Third, 1760–1860* 102–81 (Armstrong 1889); Stephen, 2 *History of the Criminal Law of England* at 298–395 (cited in note 103); Levy, *Emergence of a Free Press* at xi (cited in note 97); Smith, *Freedom's Fetters* at 129 (cited in note 16); Miller, *Crisis in Freedom* at 84 (cited in note 11).

112 10 *Annals of Congress* 917 (Gales and Seaton 1851).

113 *Communications*, Time Piece 2 (July 13, 1798).

114 For an exception, see Greenleaf's New Daily Advertiser (July 13, 1798), quoted in

Miller, *Crisis in Freedom* at 91 (cited in note 11).

[115] Aurora 3 (Jan 30, 1799); Aurora 3 (Feb 12, 1799).

[116] Sharp, *American Politics in the Early Republic* at 193–94 (cited in note 1).

[117] *The Virginia Report of 1799–1800, Touching the Alien and Sedition Laws; Together with the Virginia Resolutions of December 21, 1798, The Debates and Proceedings Thereon* 22–23 (Da Capo 1970).

[118] Frank Maloy Anderson, *Contemporary Opinion of the Virginia and Kentucky Resolutions*, 5 American Historical Review 46–47 (Oct 1899); *Answers of the Several State Legislatures*, in Jonathan Elliot, 4 *The Debates in the Several State Conventions on the Adoption of the Federal Constitution* 532–39 (Lippincott 2d ed 1901); Letter from Theodore Sedgwick to Rufus King, Jan 20, 1799, in King, ed, 2 *Life and Correspondence of Rufus King* at 518 (cited in note 55). See Adrienne Koch, *Jefferson and Madison: The Great Collaboration* 174–211 (Knopf 1950).

[119] James Madison, *The Virginia Report of 1799–1800*, in Levy, ed, *Free Press* at 198–212 (cited in note 97); James Madison, *Address of the General Assembly to the People of the Commonwealth of Virginia, January 23, 1799*, in Gaillard Hunt, ed, 6 *The Writings of James Madison* 339 (Putnam 1906).

[120] See Curtis, *Free Speech* at 62 (cited in note 80).

[121] Albany Centinel 1 (Oct 12, 1798); *New York, Nov 13*, New-York Gazette and General Advertiser (Nov 13, 1798).

[122] New York Commercial Advertiser 2 (Dec 29, 1798); Salem Gazette 3 (Dec 25, 1798).

[123] Smith, *Freedom's Fetters* at 181 (cited in note 16); Henry Cabot Lodge, *Studies in History* 183 (Houghton Mifflin 1884); Letter from Abigail Adams to Mary Cranch, Dec 11, 1799, in Stewart Mitchell, ed, *New Letters of Abigail Adams 1788–1801* 221 (Houghton Mifflin 1947); *From Timothy Pickering, to P. Johnson, Esquire, of Prince Edward County, Virginia*, Albany Centinel 2 (Oct 16, 1798).

[124] A writer at the time recalled that "spies were employed to report every action and word. No public company was free from these hired slaves of tyranny." John Wood, *The History of the Administration of John Adams* 162 (1802). See Frank M. Anderson, *The Enforcement of the Alien and Sedition Law*, in *Annual Report of the American Historical Association for the Year 1912* 115, 119 (1912).

[125] Miller, *Crisis in Freedom* at 87–89 (cited in note 11).

[126] Letter from Thomas Jefferson to John Taylor, June 1, 1798, in Ford, ed, 8 *Works of Thomas Jefferson* at 432 (cited in note 23). See Smith, *Freedom's Fetters* at 185–87 (cited in note 16); Pasley, *"Tyranny of Printers"* at 125 (cited in note 6). Among others, Republican editors of the New York *Time Piece*, the Boston *Independent Chronicle*, the Bennington *Vermont Gazette*, the New London, Connecticut, *Bee*, the New York *Mount Pleasant Register*, the New York *Argus*, and the Philadelphia *Aurora* were prosecuted under the Sedition Act. See Sharp, *American Politics in the Early Republic* at 218 (cited in note 1).

[127] Letter from Matthew Lyon to General Mason, "In Jail at Vergennes," Oct 14, 1798, in Wharton, *State Trials* at 342 (cited in note 17); Elkins and McKitrick, *Age of Federalism* at 706 (cited in note 26); Salem Gazette 3 (June 12, 1798); Albany Centinel 2 (July 31, 1798); *Extract of a Letter from New York, July 21*, Gazette of the United

States 3 (July 23, 1798).

[128] See Smith, *Freedom's Fetters* at 231 (cited in note 16).

[129] Wharton, *State Trials* at 333–34 (cited in note 17).

[130] Smith, *Freedom's Fetters* at 227 (cited in note 16); Scourge of Aristocracy and Repository of Important Political Truths 20 (Oct 1, 1798).

[131] See Kermit L. Hall, *The Oxford Companion to the Supreme Court of the United States* 145 (Oxford 1992).

[132] Country Porcupine (Oct 22, 1798), excerpted in Smith, *Freedom's Fetters* at 229 (cited in note 16). Although Justice Samuel Chase was the most aggressive judicial advocate of prosecutions under the Sedition Act, it was commonly the practice of the Federalist federal judges, and "especially Supreme Court justices on circuit, to charge grand juries with the duty of inquiring into all offenses against the Sedition Law." Id at 183.

[133] Wharton, *State Trials* at 335–37 (cited in note 17).

[134] See Austin, *Matthew Lyon* at 111 (cited in note 5).

[135] The jury was chosen from a panel of fourteen men. The prosecutor challenged one of the prospective jurors when a deputy sheriff testified that he had heard him say that he thought Lyon should not be condemned. Justice Paterson removed this man from the jury lists. Lyon challenged two jurors for their public opposition to him. Paterson sustained one of these objections, but not the other. See Wharton, *State Trials* at 333–35 (cited in note 17).

[136] Id at 336.

[137] Id at 336–37.

[138] Id at 341–42; Scourge of Aristocracy and Repository of Important Truths (Dec 15, 1798), excerpted in Austin, *Matthew Lyon* at 120 (cited in note 5). See J. Fairfax McLaughlin, *Matthew Lyon: The Hamden of Congress* 342–52 (Wynkoop Hallenbeck Crawford 1900).

[139] Letter from Matthew Lyons to Stevens T. Mason, Oct 14, 1798, in Wharton, *State Trials* at 339, 342 (cited in note 17).

[140] Albany Centinel 3 (Oct 23, 1798); *Comforting News*, Salem Gazette 3 (Oct 23, 1798); *By This Day's Mail*, Gazette of the United States 3 (Nov 2, 1798); Aurora 4 (Nov 1, 1798); Letter from Thomas Jefferson to John Taylor, Nov 26, 1798, in Andrew A. Lipscomb and Albert Ellery Bergh, eds, 10 *The Writings of Thomas Jefferson* 63 (Thomas Jefferson Memorial Association 1905).

[141] Miller, *Crisis in Freedom* at 109 (cited in note 11).

[142] Austin, *Matthew Lyon* at 123–24 (cited in note 5).

[143] Letter from Thomas Jefferson to James Madison, Jan 3, 1799, in Paul L. Ford, ed, 9 *The Works of Thomas Jefferson* 5 (Putnam 1904) (quoting Adams). Because the Reverend Ogden undertook this venture on Lyon's behalf, he was arrested and sentenced to jail in Litchfield, Connecticut, on his way back to Vermont. See Austin, *Matthew Lyon* at 125 (cited in note 5).

[144] Letter from Thomas Jefferson to James Madison, Jan 3, 1799, in Ford, ed, 9 *Works of Thomas Jefferson* at 4 (cited in note 143); *Lyon*, Commercial Advertiser 3 (Dec 28, 1798); M. Lyon, *To the Freemen of the Western District of Vermont*, Aurora 3 (Feb 8, 1799).

[145] Letter from Stevens T. Mason to Matthew Lyon, Nov 17, 1798, excerpted in Austin, *Matthew Lyon* at 120 (cited in note 5); Miller, *Crisis in Freedom* at 110–11 (cited in note 11). See Smith, *Freedom's Fetters* at 243 (cited in note 16).

[146] *Vergennes, (Ver.) February 14*, Connecticut Courant 2 (Mar 4, 1799).

[147] Pliny H. White, *The Life and Services of Matthew Lyon—An Address* 22 (Times Job Office 1858); John Spargo, *Anthony Haswell, Printer—Patriot—Ballader* 233 (Tuttle 1925).

[148] Porcupine's Gazette 3 (Feb 21, 1799); Miller, *Crisis in Freedom* at 111 (cited in note 11).

[149] 9 *Annals of Congress* 2963–64, 2970–72, 2973 (Gales and Seaton 1851). See Wharton, *State Trials* at 343 (cited in note 17).

[150] Miller, *Crisis in Freedom* at 203 (cited in note 11). See Smith, *Freedom's Fetters* at 308–11 (cited in note 16).

[151] Reading Weekly Advertiser (Oct 26, 1799), excerpted in Wharton, *State Trials* at 660 (cited in note 17). James Morton Smith speculates that Timothy Pickering either wrote the anonymous letter or furnished the information to the writer, "because he was the only man besides the president to have this data" about the original job application. Smith, *Freedom's Fetters* at 313 n 11 (cited in note 16).

[152] Wharton, *State Trials* at 659 (cited in note 17).

[153] Id at 662. See Smith, *Freedom's Fetters* at 318–19 (cited in note 16). The Federalists did not prosecute Cooper until five months after he published his reply to the anonymous message. What finally triggered the decision to indict Cooper under the Sedition Act was the role he played several months later in defending William Duane before the Senate. See infra at notes 184–92.

[154] Wharton, *State Trials* at 661, 664 (cited in note 17).

[155] Id.

[156] Id at 665.

[157] Id at 666–67.

[158] Id at 668.

[159] Thomas Cooper, *An Account of the Trial of Thomas Cooper, of Northumberland; on a Charge of Libel against the President of the United States* 39 (Bioren 1800).

[160] Wharton, *State Trials* at 670-76 (cited in note 17).

[161] Id at 672–73.

[162] Id at 675–76, 679.

[163] Id.

[164] Smith, *Freedom's Fetters* at 328 (cited in note 16).

[165] See id at 334.

[166] James T. Callender, *The American Annual Register, or Historical Memoirs of the United States for the Year 1796* 141 (Bioren and Badan 1797).

[167] Miller, *Crisis in Freedom* at 213 (cited in note 11); id at 214.

[168] Id at 215.

[169] *Callender*, Gazette of the United States 2 (Apr 24, 1798); Rosenfeld, *American Aurora* at 109 (cited in note 13).

[170] Wharton, *State Trials* at 688–90 (cited in note 17).

[171] 1 *The Trial of Samuel Chase* 372 (1805); Wharton, *State Trials* at 718 (cited in note 17).

[172] Letter from James Monroe to Thomas Jefferson, May 25, 1800, in Stanislaus Murray Hamilton, ed, 3 *The Writings of James Monroe* 180 (Putnam 1900); Albany Register (June 10, 1800), excerpted in Smith, *Freedom's Fetters* at 344 (cited in note 16).

[173] Wharton, *State Trials* at 692–95 (cited in note 17).

[174] Id at 707.

[175] 1 *Trial of Samuel Chase* at 176 (cited in note 171); id at 6.

[176] Worthington Chauncey Ford, ed, *Thomas Jefferson and James Thomson Callender* 23–24 (Historical Printing Club 1897).

[177] Smith, *Freedom's Fetters* at 357 (cited in note 16); James Callender, 2 *Prospect before Us* 76–77 (Jones for Pleasants and Field 1801); id at 47; Letter from James Callender to Thomas Jefferson, Oct 27, 1800, in Ford, ed, *Thomas Jefferson* at 30 (cited in note 176).

[178] Anderson, *Enforcement of the Alien and Sedition Laws* at 120 (cited in note 124).

[179] Wharton, *State Trials* at 684–87 (cited in note 17); Smith, *Freedom's Fetters* at 368–70 (cited in note 16). See generally id at 359–73.

[180] Chronicle (Nov 12, 1798), excerpted id at 250. See id at 257–60.

[181] Letter from Fisher Ames to Jeremiah Smith, Nov 22, 1798, in W. B. Allen, ed, 2 *Works of Fisher Ames as Published by Seth Ames* 1296–97 (Liberty Classics 1983); Letter from Fisher Ames to Christopher Gore, Dec 18, 1798, id at 1304; Smith, *Freedom's Fetters* at 262 (cited in note 16).

[182] Massachusetts Mercury 2 (June 21, 1799).

[183] See generally Curtis, *Free Speech* at 88–89 (cited in note 80); Smith, *Freedom's Fetters* at 257–70 (cited in note 16); Miller, *Crisis in Freedom* at 114–19 (cited in note 11).

[184] Pasley, *"Tyranny of Printers"* at 179 (cited in note 6).

[185] Aurora 2 (Aug 4, 1800).

[186] See Rosenfeld, *American Aurora* at 663–74 (cited in note 13).

[187] 10 *Annals of Congress* at 29–32 (cited in note 112).

[188] Aurora 2 (Feb 19, 1800).

[189] Id. Duane's account in the *Aurora* stated inaccurately that the bill had already passed the Senate and that the committee that drafted the bill had excluded its one Republican member from its deliberations. When these errors were pointed out, Duane corrected them. See Aurora 2 (Feb 22, 1800).

[190] Richmond Examiner (May 2, 1800), excerpted in Smith, *Freedom's Fetters* at 294 (cited in note 16); 10 *Annals of Congress* at 112 (cited in note 112).

[191] Aurora 2 (Mar 27, 1800). For especially engaging accounts of the ordeal of William Duane, see Miller, *Crisis in Freedom* at 194–202 (cited in note 11); Smith, *Freedom's Fetters* at 277–306 (cited in note 16); Pasley, *"Tyranny of Printers"* at 176–95 (cited in note 6).

[192] John P. Foley, 10 *The Jefferson Cyclopedia: A Comprehensive Collection of the Views of Thomas Jefferson* 368 (Funk and Wagnalls 1900).

[193] See Melvin I. Urofsky and Paul Finkelman, 1 A *March of Liberty: A Constitutional History of the United States* 183 (Oxford 2d ed 2002).

[194] Salem Gazette 2 (Mar 29, 1799).

[195] *Laocoon*, Boston Gazette (Apr 1799), reprinted in Ames, ed, 2 *Works of Fisher Ames* at

117 (cited in note 33).

196 Id at 109–28.

197 See Miller, *Crisis in Freedom* at 136 (cited in note 11).

198 James Iredell, *A Charge Delivered to the Grand Jury of the U. States*, Aurora 2 (May 28 and May 30, 1799).

199 Lawson, *Reign of Witches* at 43 (cited in note 35); Wharton, *State Trials* at 671 (cited in note 17).

200 1 *Trial of Samuel Chase* at 6 (cited in note 171). At Chase's trial before the Senate, the House managers told the Senate that by the proceedings the people "wish to teach a lesson of instruction to future judges, that when intoxicated by the spirit of party, they may recollect the scale of power may one day turn, and preserve the scales of justice equal." 2 *The Trial of Samuel Chase* 375–76 (Da Capo 1970).

201 See David P. Currie, *The Constitution in Congress: The Jeffersonians, 1801–1829* 31–36 (Chicago 2001).

202 See Sharp, *American Politics in the Early Republic* at 210–13 (cited in note 1).

203 See Miller, *Crisis in Freedom* at 153–59 (cited in note 11).

204 See Elkins and McKitrick, *Age of Federalism* at 727–43 (cited in note 26).

205 Letter from James McHenry to John Adams, May 31, 1800, in Harold Syrett, ed, 24 *The Papers of Alexander Hamilton* 557 (Columbia 1976); Letter from Theodore Sedgwick to Alexander Hamilton, May 13, 1800, id; Letter from Fisher Ames to Oliver Wolcott, June 12, 1800, in George Gibbs, ed, 2 *Memoirs of the Administrations of Washington and John Adams* 368 (Van Norden 1846).

206 Harold Syrett, ed, 25 *The Papers of Alexander Hamilton* 186, 190 (Columbia 1976); Noble E. Cunningham Jr., *The Jeffersonian Republicans: The Formation of Party Organization, 1789–1801* 230 (North Carolina 1957); *Alexander Hamilton versus John Adams*, Bee 3 (Oct 22, 1800).

207 Currie, *Constitution in Congress* at 126 (cited in note 31).

208 Letter from John Adams to James Lloyd, Jan 1815, in Charles Francis Adams, ed, 10 *The Works of John Adams* 113 (Little, Brown 1856).

209 Miller, *Crisis in Freedom* at 222 (cited in note 11); Worthington Chauncey Ford, *Jefferson and the Newspaper*, reprinted in 8 *Records of the Columbia Historical Society* 88 (Columbia Historical Society 1905).

210 Ironically, the act helped spawn a much stronger Republican press than that which existed before 1798. See Pasley, *"Tyranny of Printers"* at 105–6, 126–31, 153–75 (cited in note 6).

211 Larry D. Kramer, *The Supreme Court, 2000 Term—Foreword: We the Court*, 115 Harv L Rev 4, 15 (2001). See Learned Hand, *The Spirit of Liberty* 189–90 (Knopf 1952) ("Liberty lies in the hearts of men and women; when it dies there, no constitution, no law, no court can save it. . . . While it lies there, it needs no constitution, no law, no court to save it").

212 Urofsky and Finkelman, 1 *A March of Liberty* at 181 (cited in note 193). See Sharp, *American Politics in the Early Republic* at 8, 226–27 (cited in note 1).

213 Thomas Jefferson, *First Inaugural Address* (1801), reprinted in Melvin I. Urofsky, 1 *Documents of American Constitutional and Legal History* 171–74 (Knopf 1989).

[214] Miller, *Crisis in Freedom* at 231 (cited in note 11).

[215] Cong Globe, 26th Cong, 1st Sess 411 (1840). See 26 HR 80, 26th Cong, 1st Sess, Doc 86 (1840).

[216] 376 US 254 (1964).

[217] Id at 273, 276. David Currie has wisely observed that the "lamentable experience" of the Sedition Act also vividly demonstrates "how malleable the Constitution is, how much it leaves to the good faith of those whose conduct it governs and to their commitment to the principles it represents." Currie, *Constitution in Congress* at 297 (cited in note 31).

[218] *Gertz v. Robert Welch, Inc*, 418 US 323, 339 (1974).

[219] Id at 339–40.

[220] *Abrams v. United States*, 250 US 616, 630 (1919) (Holmes, J, dissenting).

[221] Id.

[222] See Geoffrey R. Stone, "Dialogue," in Lee C. Bollinger and Geoffrey R. Stone, eds, *Eternally Vigilant: Free Speech in the Modern Era* 29–31 (Chicago 2002).

[223] Letter from Matthew Lyon to John Adams, Mar 4, 1801, in McLaughlin, *Matthew Lyon* at 398 (cited in 138).

[224] Wharton, *State Trials* at 343 (cited in note 17).

[225] 14 *Annals of Congress* 1106, 1121–26 (Gales and Seaton 1851).

[226] Austin, *Matthew Lyon* at 149–50 (cited in note 5).

[227] Wharton, *State Trials* at 344 (cited in note 17).

CHAPTER II

[1] Cong Globe, 29th Cong, 2d Sess 122–24 (Jan 6, 1847).

[2] Cong Globe, 30th Cong, 1st Sess 64 (Dec 22, 1847).

[3] Cong Globe, 30th Cong, 1st Sess 156 (Jan 12, 1848). A treaty of peace was signed two weeks later.

[4] Albert J. Beveridge, 2 *Abraham Lincoln: 1809–1858* 134–35 (Houghton Mifflin 1928).

[5] *The Trial of Hon. Clement L. Vallandigham by a Military Commission* 11–12 (Rickey and Carroll 1863).

[6] James M. McPherson, *Battle Cry of Freedom: The Civil War Era* 8 (Oxford 1988).

[7] Charleston Mercury (Feb 1, 1858), excerpted in John McCardell, *The Idea of a Southern Nation: Southern Nationalists and Southern Nationalism, 1830–1860* 270–71 (Norton 1979).

[8] Dwight L. Dumond, *The Secession Movement, 1860–1861* 104 (Macmillan 1931).

[9] Letter from Abraham Lincoln to John B. Fry, Aug 15, 1860, in Roy P. Basler, ed, 4 *The Collected Works of Abraham Lincoln* 95 (Rutgers 1953).

[10] *The Terrors of Submission*, Charleston Mercury 1 (Oct 11, 1860).

[11] John W. Burgess, 1 *The Civil War and the Constitution, 1859–1865* 80 (Charles Scribner 1901).

[12] James Buchanan, *Fourth Annual Message, Dec 3, 1860*, in James D. Richardson, ed, 5 *A Compilation of the Messages and Papers of the Presidents, 1789–1897* 626, 635

(Government Printing Office 1897). See J. Matthew Gallman, *The North Fights the Civil War: The Home Front* 8 (Ivan R. Dee 1994); Daniel Farber, *Lincoln's Constitution* 93–101 (Chicago 2003).

13 *Going to Go*, New-York Tribune 4 (Nov 9, 1860). See Gallman, *North Fights the Civil War* at 10 (cited in note 12).

14 McPherson, *Battle Cry of Freedom* at 256 (cited in note 6).

15 See John G. Nicolay and John Hay, *Abraham Lincoln: A History* 50 (Chicago 1996) (Paul M. Angle, ed). One measure of Maryland's vulnerability is that Lincoln received less that 3 percent of the vote in Maryland in the 1860 presidential election. See William H. Rehnquist, *All the Laws But One: Civil Liberties in Wartime* 7 (Knopf 1998).

16 See James G. Randall, 1 *Lincoln the President: Springfield to Gettysberg* 288–91 (Vail-Ballou 1946).

17 *The Great Lincoln Escapade*, Sun 2 (Feb 25, 1861). For details of the threat of assassination, see Rehnquist, *All the Laws But One* at 6–7 (cited in note 15); Carl Sandburg, 2 *Abraham Lincoln: The War Years* 205–6 (Harcourt, Brace 1939).

18 See Rehnquist, *All the Laws But One* at 20–21 (cited in note 15). Several days earlier, Lincoln considered, but rejected, a proposal to arrest Maryland legislators who were planning to meet to discuss the possibility of secession. See id at 23–25.

19 See Mark E. Neely Jr., *The Fate of Liberty: Abraham Lincoln and Civil Liberties* 4 (Oxford 1991).

20 *Dred Scott v. Sandford*, 60 US 393 (1857).

21 Aileen S. Kraditor, *Means and Ends in American Abolitionism* 200 (Pantheon 1967).

22 Letter from Roger Taney to Franklin Pierce, June 12, 1861, excerpted in Carl Brent Swisher, *Roger B. Taney* 554 (Macmillian 1935).

23 *Ex parte Merryman*, 17 F Cases 144 (Cir Ct Md 1861). For further discussion of this case, see *infra* text accompanying notes 154–74.

24 *The Merriman Habeas Corpus Case*, Evening Star 2 (May 29, 1861); *Taney and Cadwallader*, New York Times 4–5 (May 29, 1861).

25 Lincoln even contemplated having Taney arrested if he pursued the matter further. See Harold M. Hyman, *A More Perfect Union: The Impact of the Civil War and Reconstruction on the Constitution* 84 n 8 (Knopf 1973).

26 Carl Sandburg, 1 *Abraham Lincoln: The War Years* 280 (Harcourt, Brace 1939).

27 See Rehnquist, *All the Laws But One* at 40 (cited in note 15).

28 See McPherson, *Battle Cry of Freedom* at 289 (cited in note 6).

29 See id at 290–93.

30 See Neely, *Fate of Liberty* at 32–50 (cited in note 19).

31 Interestingly, the least controversial portion of Frémont's order was "the novel idea of trying civilians by courts-martial in a loyal state of the Union . . . [which] would [then] spread across the nation. The use of military commissions during the Civil War would prove extremely damaging to Abraham Lincoln's historical reputation." Neely, *Fate of Liberty* at 34–35 (cited in note 19).

32 Letter from Abraham Lincoln to Orville H. Browning, Sept 22, 1861, in Basler, ed, 4 *Collected Works of Abraham Lincoln* at 531–32 (cited in note 9).

[33] See Neely, *Fate of Liberty* at 27 (cited in note 19).

[34] See Hyman, *More Perfect Union* at 69–71 (cited in note 25); Neely, *Fate of Liberty* at 127 (cited in note 19).

[35] Executive Order no. 1, Relating to Political Prisoners, Feb 14, 1862, in 2:2 *The War of the Rebellion: A Compilation of the Official Records of the Union and Confederate Armies* 222 (Government Printing Office 1902).

[36] See Shelby Foote, *The Civil War: A Narrative* 630 (Random House 1963).

[37] *The Return to Law and Liberty*, New York Tribune 4 (Feb 17, 1862).

[38] See McPherson, *Battle Cry of Freedom* at 308–12 (cited in note 6).

[39] Letter from William Lloyd Garrison to Oliver Johnson, Sept 9, 1862, excerpted id at 505; *Fourth of July Celebration at Himrods*, Douglas' Monthly 694 (Aug 1862). See William H. Hale, *Horace Greeley, Voice of the People* 257–61 (Harper 1950).

[40] Cong Globe, 37th Cong, 2d Sess 329 (Jan 14, 1862).

[41] See McPherson, *Battle Cry of Freedom* at 496 (cited in note 6).

[42] Cong Globe App, 37th Cong, 2d Sess 242 (June 3, 1962).

[43] McPherson, *Battle Cry of Freedom* at 508 (cited in note 6).

[44] Letter from Abraham Lincoln to Horace Greeley, Aug 22, 1862, in Roy P. Basler, ed, 5 *The Collected Works of Abraham Lincoln* 388 (Rutgers 1953).

[45] Abraham Lincoln, *Final Emancipation Proclamation*, Sept 22, 1862, in *Abraham Lincoln: Speeches and Writings, 1859–1865* 424 (Library of America 1989).

[46] Wood Gray, *The Hidden Civil War: The Story of the Copperheads* 115 (Viking 1942). See Frank L. Klement, *The Limits of Dissent: Clement L. Vallandigham and the Civil War* 106–7 (Fordham 1998).

[47] McPherson, *Battle Cry of Freedom* at 560 (cited in note 6).

[48] Crisis (Jan 14, 1863), excerpted in V. Jacque Voegeli, *Free But Not Equal: The Midwest and the Negro during the Civil War* 77 (Chicago 1967); Allan Nevins, 2 *The War for the Union* 394 (Charles Scribner 1960).

[49] David H. Donald, *Lincoln* 380 (Simon and Schuster 1995).

[50] Gallman, *North Fights the Civil War* at 128 (cited in note 12).

[51] See Peter J. Parish, *The American Civil War* 208–9 (Holmes and Meier 1975); Gallman, *North Fights the Civil War* at 49–50 (cited in note 12).

[52] See McPherson, *Battle Cry of Freedom* at 595–97 (cited in note 6).

[53] Abraham Lincoln, *Proclamation Calling Militia and Convening Congress*, Apr 15, 1861, in Basler, ed, 4 *Collected Works of Abraham Lincoln* at 332 (cited in note 9).

[54] Klement, *Limits of Dissent* at 61 (cited in note 46).

[55] Abraham Lincoln, *Proclamation Suspending the Writ of Habeas Corpus*, Sept 24, 1862, in Basler, ed, 5 *Collected Works of Abraham Lincoln* at 436 (cited in note 44).

[56] Robert E. Sterling, *Civil War Draft Resistance in the Middle West* 96–97 (unpublished PhD Dissertation, Northern Illinois University 1975), excerpted in McPherson, *Battle Cry of Freedom* at 493 (cited in note 6).

[57] See Foote, *Civil War* at 635 (cited in note 36); Gallman, *North Fights the Civil War* at 69–70 (cited in note 12).

[58] McPherson, *Battle Cry of Freedom* at 609 (cited in note 6).

[59] See Foote, *Civil War* at 635 (cited in note 36).

[60] See Gallman, *North Fights the Civil War* at 147–48 (cited in note 12); Robert S. Harper, *Lincoln and the Press* 270–76 (McGraw-Hill 1951).

[61] Foote, *Civil War* at 627, 629 (cited in note 36).

[62] Sandburg, 2 *Abraham Lincoln* at 143, 195 (cited in note 17).

[63] Foote, *Civil War* at 629 (cited in note 36).

[64] Id at 940. See Gallman, *North Fights the Civil War* at 162–64 (cited in note 12). Possible replacements included Treasury Secretary Salmon Chase, General Benjamin F. Butler, General Ulysses S. Grant, and John Charles Frémont, the party's 1856 presidential candidate.

[65] *More about the Niagara Peace Proposition*, Crisis 1 (Aug 3, 1864); MacPherson, *Battle Cry of Freedom* at 790 (cited in note 6).

[66] Edward McPherson, *The Political History of the United States during the Great Rebellion* 419–20 (Philp and Solomons 2d ed 1865).

[67] See Harper, *Lincoln and the Press* at 308–10 (cited in note 60).

[68] Carl Sandburg, 3 *Abraham Lincoln: The War Years* 203–4 (Harcourt, Brace 1939).

[69] Id.

[70] McPherson, *Battle Cry of Freedom* at 771 (cited in note 6). In a memo of August 23, Lincoln noted, "It seems exceedingly probable that this administration will not be re-elected." John G. Nicolay and John Hay, eds, 2 *Complete Works of Abraham Lincoln* 568 (Century 1894).

[71] See Michael Kent Curtis, *Free Speech, "The People's Darling Privilege"* 117–356 (Duke 2000).

[72] NC Stat ch 34, no 16 (1854), available in Bartholomew F. Moore and Asa Biggs, 34 *Revised Code of North Carolina* 16 (Little, Brown 1855).

[73] Act to Suppress the Circulation of Incendiary Publications, 1836 Va Acts ch 66.

[74] Richard H. Sewell, *Ballots for Freedom: Antislavery Politics in the United States, 1837–1860* 284 (Oxford 1976).

[75] Cong Globe, 36th Cong, 1st Sess 2321 (May 24, 1860).

[76] Philadelphia Inquirer (Aug 21, 1861), excerpted in Harper, *Lincoln and the Press* at 108 (cited in note 60). Similarly, the editor of the *Cleveland Leader* described Copperheads as "assassins" and "traitors." Klement, *Limits of Dissent* at 144 (cited in note 46). It was not uncommon for those sympathetic to the administration to try to "stop the flood of Southern propaganda by wrecking disloyal newspapers." Harper, *Lincoln and the Press* at 113 (cited in note 60). On occasion, "Republican ruffians" attempted "to intimidate Democrats or to mob Democratic newspaper offices." Klement, *Limits of Dissent* at 144 (cited in note 46).

[77] Sandburg, 1 *Abraham Lincoln* at 623 (cited in note 26).

[78] Id at 634.

[79] John G. Nicolay and John Hay, 7 *Abraham Lincoln: A History* 328 (Century 1914).

[80] Report of Major-General Ambrose E. Burnside, Nov 13, 1865, in 1:23:1 *The War of the Rebellion: A Compilation of the Official Records of the Union and Confederate Armies* 12 (Government Printing Office 1902).

[81] *Trial of Hon. Clement L. Vallandigham* at 7 (cited in note 5). A similar order was issued by General Milo Hascall in Indiana. See Curtis, *Free Speech* at 308–9 (cited in note 71); Harper, *Lincoln and the Press* at 251–57 (cited in note 60). Burnside's order was based on Lincoln's suspension of the writ of habeas corpus in Missouri in September 1862, when he declared that "during the existing insurrection and as a necessary measure for suppressing the same . . . all persons discouraging volunteer enlistments . . . or guilty of any disloyal practice . . . shall be subject to martial law and liable to trial and punishment." Abraham Lincoln, *Proclamation Suspending the Writ of Habeas Corpus*, Sept 24, 1862, in Basler, ed, 5 *Collected Works of Abraham Lincoln* at 436–37 (cited in note 44).

[82] Klement, *Limits of Dissent* at 19, 25 (cited in note 46).

[83] Letter from Clement Vallandigham to his wife, Dec 3, 1860, excerpted in James Vallandigham, A *Life of Clement L. Vallandigham* 144 (Turnbull Brothers 1872); Klement, *Limits of Dissent* at 67 (cited in note 46).

[84] Klement, *Limits of Dissent* at 63–67 (cited in note 46).

[85] McPherson, *Battle Cry of Freedom* at 591–92 (cited in note 6). See Klement, *Limits of Dissent* at ch 1–6 (cited in note 46).

[86] *The Record of Hon. C. L. Vallandigham on Abolition, the Union and the Civil War* 183, 189, 200 (J. Walter 1863). See Curtis, *Free Speech* at 304 (cited in note 71).

[87] Sandburg, 2 *Abraham Lincoln* at 127 (cited in note 17).

[88] *The Record of Hon. C. L. Vallandigham* at 137 (cited in note 86).

[89] Klement, *Limits of Dissent* at 135 (cited in note 46).

[90] Clement Vallandigham, *Letter to the Editor*, New York Times 1 (Mar 10, 1863).

[91] Rehnquist, *All the Laws But One* at 65 (cited in note 15). See Klement, *Limits of Dissent* at 138–40 (cited in note 46).

[92] Sandburg, 2 *Abraham Lincoln* at 161 (cited in note 17).

[93] The event was described in detail in the May 9 issue of the *Democratic Banner*, which was published in Mount Vernon, and in the May 2 issue of the *Columbus Crisis*. See Vallandigham, *Life of Clement L. Vallandigham* at 250–52 (cited in note 83).

[94] *Trial of Hon. Clement L. Vallandigham* at 11–12 (cited in note 5). This is not a verbatim transcript of the speech, which does not exist, but the specification of the charge against Vallandigham.

[95] Mount Vernon Democratic Banner (May 9, 1863), excerpted in Klement, *Limits of Dissent* at 154 (cited in note 46).

[96] *Ex parte Vallandigham*, 28 F Cases 874, 875 (Cir Ct Ohio 1863). For an account of the arrest, see Vallandigham, *Life of Clement L. Vallandigham* at 255–58 (cited in note 83).

[97] Transcript of the Trial of Clement L. Vallandigham before the Military Commission, May 6–7, 1863, id at 283.

[98] Id at 264 (this quotation is from the "specification" of the charge). One reason the commission did not want to put him before a firing squad was that it did not want to make him a martyr. See Klement, *Limits of Dissent* at 168 (cited in note 46).

[99] *Ex parte Vallandigham*, 28 F Cases at 876–77.

[100] President Lincoln and Secretary of War Stanton were concerned that without a spe-

cific suspension of the writ of habeas corpus in Ohio the local federal judge might grant Vallandigham's petition. On May 13, Stanton therefore prepared an order especially suspending the writ in Vallandigham's case. Lincoln, however, directed Stanton not to issue the order, because he was satisfied that neither of the local federal judges would be likely to grant Vallandigham's petition. See letter from Abraham Lincoln to Edwin M. Stanton, May 13, 1863, in Roy P. Basler, ed, 6 *The Collected Works of Abraham Lincoln* 215 (Rutgers 1953).

101 *Ex parte Vallandigham*, 28 F Cas at 921–22.

102 Id at 923–24.

103 Letter from Clement Vallandigham to the Democracy of Ohio, May 5, 1863, in Vallandigham, ed, *Life of Clement Vallandigham* at 260 (cited in note 83).

104 *The Arrest of Vallandigham*, Albany Argus 2 (May 8, 1863), excerpted in Curtis, *Free Speech* at 320 (cited in note 71); *The Military Discretion*, Detroit Free Press 2 (June 10, 1863).

105 *Ohio Democratic State Convention*, Cincinnati Daily Commercial 2 (June 12, 1863). See Curtis, *Free Speech* at 324–26 (cited in note 71).

106 *Order Thirty-eight*, Cincinnati Daily Commercial 2 (May 15, 1863); *Civil and Military Law*, Chicago Tribune 2 (June 12, 1863).

107 Hyman, *More Perfect Union* at 262 (cited in note 25).

108 *Vallandigham*, New-York Daily Tribune 4 (May 15, 1863); *The Voice of Reason*, National Intelligencer 3 (May 16, 1863) (reprinted from New York Evening Post), excerpted in Curtis, *Free Speech* at 326 (cited in note 71); *From the Bedford (Rep.) Standard*, Detroit Free Press 2 (May 27, 1863); *Senator Trumbull's Chicago Speech*, Cincinnati Daily Commercial 2 (June 11, 1863).

109 Harper, *Lincoln and the Press* at 257–58 (cited in note 60).

110 Chicago Times 2 (Sept 13, 1862).

111 *Mr. Vallandigham*, Chicago Times 2 (May 27, 1863); *The Feeling of the Army*, Chicago Times 2 (Apr 13, 1863).

112 Gen. Order no. 84, June 1, 1863, in 1:23:2 *The War of the Rebellion: A Compilation of the Official Records of the Union and Confederate Armies* 381 (Government Printing Office 1889).

113 Sandburg, 2 *Abraham Lincoln* at 128 (cited in note 17).

114 *Chicago Times Demonstration*, Cincinnati Daily Commercial 3 (June 4, 1863). See Curtis, *Free Speech* at 315 (cited in note 71).

115 *General Burnside's Orders*, Cincinnati Daily Commercial 1 (June 5, 1863).

116 See Foote, *Civil War* at 634 (cited in note 36).

117 Nicolay and Hay, 7 *Abraham Lincoln* at 338 (cited in note 79).

118 See Neely, *Fate of Liberty* at 67 (cited in note 19); James G. Randall, *The Civil War and Reconstruction* 397 (D. C. Heath 1937) (Lincoln was "embarrassed" by the arrest of Vallandigham). Chief Justice Rehnquist has observed, "The argument for detaining someone like John Merryman, who had helped to burn the railroad bridges that would bring troops through Baltimore to Washington, was much stronger than that for arresting and trying Vallandigham, who had simply expressed views strongly critical of the administration." Rehnquist, *All the Laws But One* at 73 (cited in note 15).

[119] Nicolay and Hay, 7 *Abraham Lincoln* at 338 (cited in note 79).

[120] See McPherson, *Battle Cry of Freedom* at 597 (cited in note 6).

[121] Nicolay and Hay, 7 *Abraham Lincoln* at 338 (cited in note 79).

[122] Abraham Lincoln, *Reply to the Ohio Democratic Convention*, June 29, 1868, in *Abraham Lincoln: Speeches and Writings* at 468 (cited in note 45).

[123] Klement, *Limits of Dissent* at 178–79 (cited in note 46); Donald, *Lincoln* at 420–21 (cited in note 49). In 1847–48, Lincoln was one of the most vehement critics of the Mexican War, challenging President Polk to prove that it was Mexico rather than the United States that initiated the conflict. See id at 122–28.

[124] *The Anti-Democratic Press Opposed the Arrest of Mr. Vallandigham*, Crisis 5 (May 27, 1863).

[125] Nicolay and Hay, 7 *Abraham Lincoln* at 340 (cited in note 79).

[126] Klement, *Limits of Dissent* at 181 (cited in note 46); *The Great Demonstration at Albany*, Cincinnati Daily Enquirer 1 (May 23, 1863); letter from Erastus Corning to Abraham Lincoln, May 29, 1863, excerpted in Klement, *Limits of Dissent* at 181 (cited in note 46). See id at 178–81; Harper, *Lincoln and the Press* at 246–48 (cited in note 60).

[127] Letter from Abraham Lincoln to Erastus Corning and Others, June 12, 1863, in *Abraham Lincoln: Speeches and Writings* at 459–60 (cited in note 45).

[128] Id.

[129] Id at 460.

[130] Lincoln added, in passing, "I do not know whether I would have ordered the arrest of Mr. Vallandigham," but "the commander in the field is the better judge of the necessity in any particular case." Id at 462.

[131] Id at 460–61.

[132] Id at 468–69.

[133] See chapter 4.

[134] See text at note 90.

[135] See Klement, *Limits of Dissent* at 135, 175 (cited in note 46).

[136] See *supra* text accompanying notes 88–90.

[137] Klement, *Limits of Dissent* at 183 (cited in note 46).

[138] See *Atkins v. Virginia*, 536 US 304 (2002) (holding that the execution of mentally retarded individuals violates the "cruel and unusual" punishment clause of the Eighth Amendment).

[139] *Butler v. Michigan*, 352 US 380, 383 (1957). See also *Reno v. ACLU*, 521 US 844, 875 (1997) (the "governmental interest in protecting children from harmful materials . . . does not justify an unnecessarily broad suppression of speech addressed to adults").

[140] See Donald, *Lincoln* at 444 (cited in note 49).

[141] Nicolay and Hay, 7 *Abraham Lincoln* at 349 (cited in note 79).

[142] It is not clear that Lincoln's prompt response was guided by a clear-cut sense of principle. Lincoln vacillated in making this decision. A year later, he recalled that he had been "'embarrassed with the question between what was due to the Military service on the one hand, and the Liberty of the Press on the other. . . .'" Letter from Abraham Lincoln to Isaac N. Arnold, May 25, 1864, in Roy P. Basler, ed, 7 *The Collected Works*

of Abraham Lincoln 361 (Rutgers 1953).

[143] Letter from Edwin Stanton to A. E. Burnside, June 1, 1863, in 2:5 The War of the Rebellion: A Compilation of the Official Records of the Union and Confederate Armies 724 (Government Printing Office 1902) (emphasis added).

[144] Although this action was generally applauded, it did not escape criticism. Joseph Medill of the Chicago Tribune protested Lincoln's revocation of Burnside's order as "a most unfortunate blunder." He called it "a triumph of treason." The Revocation, Chicago Tribune 1 (June 5, 1863). See Harper, Lincoln and the Press at 260–61 (cited in note 60).

[145] Clement L. Vallandigham, Address in Dayton, Ohio, June 15, 1864, in Vallandigham, Life of Clement L. Vallandigham at 357 (cited in note 83).

[146] Foote, Civil War at 634 (cited in note 36).

[147] See Sandburg, 2 Abraham Lincoln at 165 (cited in note 17). McPherson, Political History at 419–20 (cited in note 66). For a full account of Vallandigham's life after his conviction by the military commission, see Klement, Limits of Dissent at 190–213 (cited in note 46).

[148] See Harold H. Hyman, Election of 1864, in Arthur M. Schlesinger Jr. and Fred L. Israel, 3 History of American Presidential Elections 1172 (Chelsea House 1971).

[149] In many ways, the "most remarkable fact about the 1864 election is that it occurred" at all. Hyman, Election of 1864 at 1155 (cited in note 148).

[150] On the New Departure, see Vallandigham, Life of Clement L. Vallandigham at 436–51 (cited in note 83).

[151] See id at 515–35.

[152] See Jules Lobel, Emergency Power and the Decline of Liberalism, 98 Yale L J 1385, 1386 (1989).

[153] Harris v. Nelson, 394 US 286, 290–91 (1969). Ironically, in the years before the Civil War the writ was used frequently in the slavery controversy both to free blacks who were being detained as alleged runaway slaves and to return runaway slaves to their masters. See Neely, Fate of Liberty at xiv–xv (cited in note 19). See also Abelman v. Booth, 62 US 506 (1858).

[154] Letter from Lyman Trumbull to Abraham Lincoln, Apr 21, 1861, excerpted in Neely, Fate of Liberty at 6 (cited in note 19); letter from Orville Hickman Browning to Abraham Lincoln, Apr 22, 1861, excerpted id; John G. Nicolay and John Hay, 4 Abraham Lincoln: A History 151 (Century 1914).

[155] Neely, Fate of Liberty at 4 (cited in note 19). See James G. Randall, Constitutional Problems under Lincoln 123 (D. Appleton 1926) ("Few measures of the Lincoln administration were adopted with more reluctance than this [first] suspension of the citizen's safeguard against arbitrary arrest").

[156] 17 F Cases 144 (D Md 1861).

[157] Id at 148.

[158] 8 US (4 Cranch) 95, 101 (1807) ("If at any time the public safety should require the suspension of the powers vested by [the Habeas corpus Act] in the courts of the United States, it is for the legislature to say so").

[159] Joseph Story, 3 Commentaries on the Constitution § 676 (Hilliard Gray 1833) ("The

power is given to congress to suspend the writ of *habeas corpus*").

[160] *Merryman*, 17 F Cases at 148.

[161] Moreover, as Harold Hyman has observed, "punishment of Merryman exclusively through judicial processes" would have run "headlong into the solid fact that disloyalty was not a [federal] crime." The only relevant federal prohibition at the time was that for treason, but "the Constitution's arrangements and the conditions of 1861" made recourse to treason prosecutions "implausible." Hyman, *More Perfect Union* at 94–95 (cited in note 25).

[162] Abraham Lincoln, *Message to Congress in Special Session*, July 4, 1861, in *Abraham Lincoln: Speeches and Writings* at 250–53 (cited in note 45).

[163] As the Yale professor Henry Dutton argued at the time, "if the Constitution is destroyed, of what use" is the writ of habeas corpus? Henry Dutton, *Writ of Habeas Corpus*, 9 Am Law Reg 705, 716 (1860–61).

[164] Abraham Lincoln, *Message to Congress in Special Session*, July 4, 1861, in *Abraham Lincoln: Speeches and Writings* at 252 (cited in note 45).

[165] Letter from Abraham Lincoln to Erastus Corning and Others, June 12, 1863, id at 456–57.

[166] Id at 457.

[167] Id at 458; Abraham Lincoln, *Reply to Ohio Democrats*, June 29, 1863, id at 467.

[168] See letter from Abraham Lincoln to Erastus Corning and Others, June 12, 1863, id at 458–59. The day after Lincoln's address to Congress, Attorney General Bates issued a more thorough legal analysis that supported the president's conclusions. See *Suspension of the Privilege of the Writ of Habeas Corpus*, 10 Op Atty Gen 74–92 (1861).

[169] Letter from Abraham Lincoln to William H. Herndon, Feb 15, 1848, in Nathaniel Wright Stephenson, ed, *An Autobiography of Abraham Lincoln* 71 (Bobbs-Merrill 1926).

[170] Farber, *Lincoln's Constitution* at 161 (cited in note 12). Ultimately, however, Farber concludes that Lincoln's suspensions of the writ could be justified under current constitutional understandings as emergency military measures "in areas of insurrection or actual war." This, he reasons, would include the situation in Maryland in April 1861, but not necessarily some of the subsequent suspensions of the writ. Id at 163.

[171] Prior to this time, the writ of habeas corpus had "remained technically secure in most of the North." Only "administration insiders knew how hardened Abraham Lincoln's attitude on such constitutional issues had already become and thus how shaky was the legal status of the writ of *habeas corpus* everywhere in the country." Neely, *Fate of Liberty* at 51 (cited in note 19).

[172] Abraham Lincoln, *Proclamation Suspending the Writ of Habeas Corpus*, Sept 24, 1862, in Basler, ed, 5 *Collected Works of Abraham Lincoln* at 436–37 (cited in note 44). In fact, Stanton "had issued the orders on August 8, 1862, making the secretary of war rather than President Lincoln the first official to suspend the writ of *habeas corpus* across the whole United States." Stanton later swore that he had issued the orders under a verbal directive from Lincoln, and it would seem that the administration was testing the waters of public opinion. Although there was little public reaction, the "War Department proved incapable of controlling or coordinating so vast a system." Neely, *Fate of Liberty* at 53 (cited in note 19). See Hyman, *More Perfect Union* at

217–18 (cited in note 25).

173 An Act Relating to Habeas Corpus, and Regulating Judicial Proceedings in Certain Cases, 12 Stat 755 (Mar 3, 1863). The act provided that "during the present rebellion, the President of the United States, whenever, in his judgment, the public safety may require it, is authorized to suspend the privilege of the writ of habeas corpus in any case throughout the United States, or any part thereof."

174 Even after the far-reaching proclamation of 1862, the administration suspended the writ on several additional occasions. As Mark Neely has observed, the "administration lurched from problem to problem, drafting hasty proclamations and orders to meet the objective of the moment." Nonetheless, "military goals rather than political ones remained uppermost." Although these "orders and proclamations" were issued "piecemeal and unsystematically," they "were usually provoked by problems of military mobilization—first by obstructions of the routes to the underprotected capital and later by draft resistance." Neely, *Fate of Liberty* at 90–92 (cited in note 19).

The public continued to accept these tactics as appropriate. One of Lincoln's cabinet members reported, "I have never feared the popular pulse would not beat a healthful response even to a stringent measure in these times, if the public good demanded it." 1 *Diary of Gideon Welles, Secretary of the Navy under Lincoln and Johnson* 435 (Houghton Mifflin 1911). Even political leaders who had protested the president's actions wrote him to say that the suspension of habeas corpus "is a heavy blow but as it is right we can stand it." Letter from Andrew Curtain to Abraham Lincoln, Sept 18, 1863, excerpted in Neely, *Fate of Liberty* at 74 (cited in note 19).

175 Sandburg, 2 *Abraham Lincoln* at 154–55 (cited in note 17).

176 Record keeping in the war was inconsistent and incomplete. Prison officials were often unsure themselves why particular prisoners suddenly appeared in their prisons. See Neely, *Fate of Liberty* at 20, 23 (cited in note 19).

177 See Neely, *Fate of Liberty* at 113–38 (cited in note 19) (concluding that the best estimate is near the upper end of this range); Rehnquist, *All the Laws But One* at 49 (cited in note 15) (estimating 13,000); Foote, *Civil War* at 630–31 (cited in note 36) (noting that it is impossible to know how many of these individuals "had been fairly accused—and, if so, what their various offenses had been," because "not one of" them "was ever brought into a civil court for a hearing, although a few were sentenced by military tribunals"). According to Neely, the number of military arrests reached its height in the period between August 8 and September 8 of 1863, when the government was attempting to enforce the Conscription Act, prevent draft evasion and resistance to the draft, and meet the quota for draftees. See Neely, *Fate of Liberty* at 51–65 (cited in note 19).

178 Of 101 civilians tried by military commissions in Missouri between September 1861 and June 1862, only one was apprehended because of his political beliefs or expression. And although some newspapermen were arrested, such arrests were very much the exception. See Neely, *Fate of Liberty* at 44, 26–28, 131–38 (cited in note 19). Neely estimates that in the first ten months of the war, an average of only one civilian per month was subjected to military arrest in each of the states north of the border states. See id at 26–27.

[179] Id at 60; see id at 58–61.

[180] Abraham Lincoln, Memorandum: Military Arrests, May 17, 1861, in 4 *Collected Works of Abraham Lincoln* at 372 (cited in note 9).

[181] See Craig D. Tenney, *To Suppress or Not to Suppress: Abraham Lincoln and the Chicago Times* 27 Civil War History 249, 251 (1981) (Lincoln's failure early in the war to prohibit officials from moving against opposition speakers and publishers, and his preference for handling such matters on a "case-by-case" basis, was taken "as a tacit approval" of future actions against critics of the administration).

[182] Letter from Abraham Lincoln to John M. Schofield, July 13, 1863, in Basler, ed, 6 *Collected Works of Abraham Lincoln* at 326 (cited in note 100).

[183] Quantrill's raid left 182 unarmed men and boys dead. See McPherson, *Battle Cry of Freedom* at 785 (cited in note 6); Neely, *Fate of Liberty* at 46–47 (cited in note 19).

[184] Letter from Abraham Lincoln to John M. Schofield, Oct 1, 1863, in *Abraham Lincoln: Speeches and Writings* at 518 (cited in note 45).

[185] See Paul Finkelman, *Civil Liberties and Civil War: The Great Emancipator as Civil Libertarian*, 91 Mich L Rev 1353, 1376 (1993).

[186] Sandburg, 2 *Abraham Lincoln* at 155 (cited in note 17).

[187] 71 US (4 Wall) 2 (1866). The Supreme Court was unanimous in reversing Milligan's conviction, although the justices were divided on the rationale. Five justices held the military trial unconstitutional; four held that it violated the 1863 habeas corpus statute.

[188] Id at 127.

[189] Id at 120–21. For excellent discussions of *Ex parte Milligan*, see Rehnquist, *All the Laws But One* at 89–137 (cited in note 15); David P. Currie, *The Constitution in the Supreme Court: The First Hundred Years, 1789–1888* 288–92 (Chicago 1985). *Milligan* has been criticized for going too far in its protection of constitutional rights in wartime. See Charles Fairman, *History of the Supreme Court of the United States: Reconstruction and Reunion, 1864–1888* 182–253 (Macmillan 1971); Clinton Rossiter, *The Supreme Court and the Commander in Chief* 30–31 (Cornell 1976); Edward S. Corwin, *The President: Offices and Powers, 1787–1948* 165–66 (NYU 1940); Samuel Issacharoff and Richard H. Pildes, *Between Civil Libertarianism and Executive Unilateralism: An Institutional Process Approach to Rights during Wartime* (forthcoming 2004).

[190] Harper, *Lincoln and the Press* at 129 (cited in note 60). See id at 129–31.

[191] 2 *The American Annual Cyclopaedia and Register of Important Events of the Year 1862* 480–81 (Appleton 1869).

[192] 1 *The American Annual Cyclopaedia and Register of Important Events of the Year 1861* 329 (Appleton 1870).

[193] See Neely, *Fate of Liberty* at 27 (cited in note 19); Harper, *Lincoln and the Press* at 128–29, 148, 193, 198, 225, 298, 338, 341 (cited in note 60). For a detailed account of such an arrest, involving the publisher of the *Hagerstown Mail*, who was released upon taking an oath of allegiance to the Union, see Rehnquist, *All the Laws But One* at 46 (cited in note 15). One of the more peculiar newspaper cases involved the sup-

pression of the *New York World*. On May 18, 1864, the *World* "published a bogus presidential proclamation calling for a day of fasting and prayer and, more important, calling for a new draft of 400,000 men." Because this was false, and highly inflammatory, the president ordered the arrest of the *World*'s editors and publishers and the seizure of its offices by the military. Neely, *Fate of Liberty* at 104 (cited in note 19). See Farber, *Lincoln's Constitution* at 173–74 (cited in note 12).

[194] See Foote, *Civil War* at 635 (cited in note 36).

[195] Later in the war, a few local Missouri newspapers, such as the *Boone County Standard* and the *Platte City Conservator*, were closed and their editors subjected to either military arrest or banishment because they allegedly published "treasonable matter." See Harper, *Lincoln and the Press* at 141–48 (cited in 60).

[196] Daily Exchange 2 (Apr 15, 1861); Sidney T. Matthews, *Control of the Baltimore Press during the Civil War*, Maryland Historical Magazine 151 (June 1941); Daily Republican (July 31, 1861), excerpted id at 152. See Rehnquist, *All the Laws But One* at 46–47 (cited in note 15).

[197] Gray, *Hidden Civil War* at 122 (cited in note 46). See Harper, *Lincoln and the Press* at 148–51 (cited in note 60).

[198] Philadelphia Inquirer (Jan 31 and Feb 3, 1863), excerpted in Harper, *Lincoln and the Press* at 233–35 (cited in note 60).

[199] See Harper, *Lincoln and the Press* at 152–53, 189–91, 194, 197, 249 (cited in note 60).

[200] Neely, *Fate of Liberty* at xiii (cited in note 19). See Finkelman, *Civil Liberties and Civil War* at 1376 (cited in note 185) ("During the war a vigorous opposition press constantly criticized Lincoln, military policy, and the whole purpose of the war itself").

[201] *The News and President Lincoln*, New York Daily News 4 (May 23, 1864).

[202] See Sandburg, 3 *Abraham Lincoln* at 389–90 (cited in note 68).

[203] *The Lincoln Catechism*, in Arthur M. Schlesinger Jr. and Fred L. Israel, eds, 2 *History of American Presidential Elections 1789–1968* 1215–16, 1243 (Chelsea 1971).

[204] Cong Glob, 30th Cong 1st Sess 154–56. See Sandburg, 2 *Abraham Lincoln* at 146 (cited in note 17).

[205] *Lincoln Catechism* at 1236 (cited in note 203).

[206] *From the New York News: The Walpurigs Dance at Washington*, Crisis 7 (July 27, 1864).

[207] *The Conscription: The President Ill Advised*, New York Evening Express 2 (Aug 12, 1863); Harper, *Lincoln and the Press* at 270 (cited in note 60); Chicago Times (Mar 20, 1864), excerpted id at 263.

[208] Sandburg, 2 *Abraham Lincoln* at 138 (cited in note 17).

[209] Harper, *Lincoln and the Press* at 191–92 (cited in note 60); *From the Bangor (Maine) Democrat: A Plain Epistle to Uncle Abe*, Crisis 7 (May 13, 1863).

[210] Evening Journal, excerpted in *Paosecution [sic] of a Disloyal Editor*, Illinois Daily State Journal 2 (July 30, 1864).

[211] *An Editor Prosecuted for Criticising the Draft Proclamation*, Crisis 1 (Aug 10, 1864).

[212] Springfield Gazette, excerpted in *The President and His Critics*, Cincinnati Gazette 1 (Nov 29, 1862).

[213] See Hyman, *More Perfect Union* at 66, 69 (cited in note 25). See also Robert L. Breck,

The Habeas Corpus and Martial Law 9–10 (Richard H. Collins 1862) ("The American people are engaged in a great struggle in the process of which they begin to be, for the first time, thrown upon the serious discussion of the most fundamental and vital principles of . . . constitutional liberty. . . . They have lived so long in the almost unparalleled enjoyment of liberty, but have realized no occasion to study it, and have not analyzed or defined it").

[214] John Norton Pomeroy, *An Introduction to the Constitutional Law of the United States* 290 (Houghton, Osgood 5th ed 1880).

[215] See Edmund Wilson, *Patriotic Gore: Studies in the Literature of the American Civil War* (Oxford 1962); Gore Vidal, *Lincoln* (Random House 1984); Thomas J. DiLorenzo, *The Real Lincoln: A New Look at Abraham Lincoln, His Agenda, and an Unnecessary War* (Forum 2002). See also Dwight G. Anderson, *Abraham Lincoln: The Quest for Immortality* (Knopf 1982).

[216] See Hyman, *More Perfect Union* at 76–77 (cited in note 25). In support of his judgment that Lincoln was not a dictator, Hyman notes, among many other things, that "one of the most remarkable but least remarked aspects of the election [of 1864] was that it was held at all." Id at 278.

[217] See id at 72, 169; Randall, *Constitutional Problems under Lincoln* at 152–53 (cited in note 155).

[218] See Hyman, *More Perfect Union* at 46; Neely, *Fate of Liberty* at 227–28 (cited in note 19). See also Gallman, *North Fights the Civil War* at 145 (cited in note 12) ("Despite the troubling sacrifice of individual rights in a war fought to preserve the Constitution, perhaps more striking is the amount of open dissent permitted in the midst of a civil war"). For a more negative assessment, see Tenney, *To Suppress or Not to Suppress* at 249 (cited in note 181). Tenney argues, plausibly, that Lincoln could have "acted much earlier in the war" to protect the press and that his failure to do so could easily have been "viewed by cabinet officers, other bureaucrats and by generals in the field as a tacit approval of future repressive action against those publications and editors who bitterly opposed the administration and its war policies." He notes further that "Lincoln apparently never did anything generally to stifle such perceptions, choosing instead to handle such matters on a case-by-case basis."

[219] Curtis, *Free Speech* at 353 (cited in note 71).

[220] Neely, *Fate of Liberty* at 235 (cited in note 19); Abraham Lincoln, *Address at Gettysburg, Pennsylvania*, Nov 19, 1863, in *Abraham Lincoln: Speeches and Writings* at 536 (cited in note 45). (Lincoln saw the Civil War as dedicated to proving that a "nation, conceived in Liberty, and dedicated to the proposition that all men are created equal . . . can long endure" and to ensuring that "government of the people, by the people, for the people, shall not perish from the earth." Id.)

[221] See Hyman, *More Perfect Union* at 99–101 (cited in note 25); Randall, *Constitutional Problems under Lincoln* at 31 (cited in note 155) (arguing that it was fundamental to Americans during the Civil War "to admit that the Constitution is binding during war and yet to maintain that it sanctions extraordinary powers" when they are needed). For a more negative assessment, see Neely, *Fate of Liberty* at 73 (cited in note 19) (arguing that "questions of legal and constitutional form . . . took a back seat in the

Lincoln administration").

222 See Gallman, *North Fights the Civil War* at 194–95 (cited in note 12).

223 Hyman, *More Perfect Union* at 101 (cited in note 25).

CHAPTER III

1 See William H. Rehnquist, *All the Laws But One: Civil Liberties in Wartime* 171–72 (Knopf 1998); Harry N. Scheiber, *The Wilson Administration and Civil Liberties, 1917–1921* 2–3 (Cornell 1960).

2 Woodrow Wilson, Address to Joint Session of Congress, Apr 2, 1917, in Arthur S. Link, ed, 41 *The Papers of Woodrow Wilson* 520–21 (Princeton 1983).

3 65th Cong, 1st Sess, in 55 Cong Rec S 214 (Apr 4, 1917).

4 See Edward M. Coffman, *The War to End All Wars: The American Military Experience in World War I* 25 (Oxford 1968); Robert J. Goldstein, *Political Repression in Modern America: From 1870 to the Present* 105–7 (Schenkman 1978).

5 65th Cong, Spec Sess, in 55 Cong Rec S 104 (Apr 2, 1917).

6 Paul L. Murphy, *World War I and the Origin of Civil Liberties in the United States* 53 (Norton 1979).

7 Paul Avrich, *Anarchist Portraits* 214–28 (Princeton 1988). See generally Richard Polenberg, *Fighting Faiths: The Abrams Case, the Supreme Court, and Free Speech* (Viking 1987).

8 Woodrow Wilson, Third Annual Message to Congress, Dec 7, 1917, in Albert Shaw, ed, 1 *The Messages and Papers of Woodrow Wilson* 150–51 (Review of Reviews 1924). The president's address received merely a lukewarm reception. The *New York Times* reported that only "once" did Wilson evoke "unrestrained enthusiasm." *Congress Cheers as Wilson Urges Curb on Plotters*, New York Times 1 (Dec 8, 1915). This was in response to his statement that the legislature should purge the nation of the "corrupt distempers" of disloyal foreign-born citizens. Id. See Scheiber, *Wilson Administration* at 8 (cited in note 1). On the plight of German Americans during World War I, see Frederick C. Luebke, *The Bonds of Loyalty: German-Americans and World War I* (Northern Illinois 1974); Henry Landau, *The Enemy Within: The Inside Story of German Sabotage in America* (Putnam 1937).

9 Jane Addams, *Peace and Bread in Time of War* 62 (King's Crown 1945).

10 Elia Peattie, *Women of the Hour*, Harper's Bazaar 1003–8 (Oct 1904).

11 Jean Bethke Elshtain, *Jane Addams and the Dream of American Democracy* 92 (Basic 2002) (quoting Hull House charter).

12 Id at 226–35.

13 See Meirion Harries and Susie Harries, *The Last Days of Innocence: America at War, 1917–1918* 53–54 (Vintage 1997).

14 Bert Cochran, *The Achievement of Debs*, in Harvey Goldberg, ed, *American Radicals: Some Problems and Personalities* 163, 164–66 (Monthly Review 1957).

15 Eugene V. Debs, Speech in Canton, Ohio, June 16, 1918, in Arthur M. Schlesinger Jr., ed, *Writings and Speeches of Eugene V. Debs* 425 (Hermitage 1948).

16 See Polenberg, *Fighting Faiths* at 21–22 (cited in note 7).

[17] New York Sun (July 14, 1914), excerpted id at 22.

[18] See New York World (Apr 26, 1925).

[19] Emma Goldman, *Anarchism: What It Really Stands For*, in Emma Goldman, *Anarchism and Other Essays* 56 (Mother Earth 2d ed 1911).

[20] Leonard Abbott, *Emma Goldman as I Knew Her*, excerpted in Alice Wexler, *Emma Goldman: An Intimate Life* 231 (Pantheon 1984).

[21] Blast (June 1, 1917), excerpted in Polenberg, *Fighting Faiths* at 26 (cited in note 7).

[22] Richard Drinnon, *Rebel in Paradise: A Biography of Emma Goldman* 21 (Chicago 1961).

[23] Emma Goldman, *The Promoters of War Mania*, Mother Earth (Mar 1917).

[24] See Elshtain, *Jane Addams* at 245 (cited in note 11).

[25] James Weber Linn, *Jane Addams: A Biography* 347–48 (Appleton-Century 1935) (quoting Maude Royden).

[26] See John Lord O'Brian, *Civil Liberty in War Time*, 42 Rep NY St Bar Assn 275, 279 (1919) ("[T]his country, prior to our entry into the war, had on the statute books almost no protection against hostile activities").

[27] For an account of antiwar dissent in the War of 1812, the Mexican War, and the Spanish-American War, see Samuel Eliot Morison, Frederick Merk, and Frank Freidel, *Dissent in Three American Wars* (Harvard 1970).

[28] See Department of Justice, *Annual Report of the Attorney General of the United States for the Year 1918* 16–17 (Governmental Printing Office 1918).

[29] Murphy, *Origin of Civil Liberties* at 53 (cited in note 6). See also Wilson, Third Annual Message to Congress (cited in note 8).

[30] Woodrow Wilson, *Constitutional Government in the United States* 38 (Transaction 2002) (originally published in 1908 by Columbia University Press).

[31] See Murphy, *Origin of Civil Liberties* at 54–55 (cited in note 6) (discussing how the espionage bill passed the Senate prior to the nation's entry into war but was not voted on by the House until after). The Supreme Court unanimously upheld the constitutionality of the conscription law in January 1918. See *Selective Draft Law Cases*, 245 US 366 (1918).

[32] HR 291 tit I § 4, 65th Cong, 1st Sess, in 55 Cong Rec H 1695 (May 2, 1917).

[33] Report of the Committee on the Judiciary, HR Report No 30, 65th Cong, 1st Sess 9 (1917). See 54 Cong Rec S 3606–7 (Feb 19, 1917) (discussing the use of the word "disaffection"). Violations were punishable by fines of up to $10,000 and prison sentences of up to twenty years, or both.

[34] HR 291 § 1100, 65th Cong, 1st Sess, in 55 Cong Rec H 1595 (Apr 30, 1917).

[35] Resolutions of the American Newspaper Publishers' Association, 65th Cong, 1st Sess (Apr 25, 1917), in 55 Cong Rec S 1861 (May 5, 1917).

[36] *The Espionage Bill*, New York Times 12 (Apr 13, 1917).

[37] Milwaukee News (Apr 30, 1917), excerpted in Thomas F. Carroll, *Freedom of Speech and of the Press in War Time: The Espionage Act*, 17 Mich L Rev 621, 624 (1919).

[38] Philadelphia Evening Telegraph, excerpted in *Oppose Censorship as Now Proposed*, New York Times 7 (Apr 22, 1917). See also 65th Cong, 1st Sess in 55 Cong Rec H 1709–10 (May 2, 1917) (similar editorials from the *New York American*, the *Philadelphia Inquirer*, and the *Washington Times*).

[39] 65th Cong, 1st Sess in 55 Cong Rec H 1590–91 (Apr 30, 1917). See also id at 1695 (May 2, 1917) (Representative Morgan's observation that "in time of great national peril, it is necessary sometimes that individual citizens shall be willing to surrender some of the privileges which they have for the sake of the greater good").

[40] Id at 1590–91 (Apr 30, 1917). See also Carroll, 17 Mich L Rev at 627 (cited in note 37) (noting that an important defense of the provision was the argument that "the President, as Commander-in-Chief of the military forces, is the best judge" of whether such control of the press is "necessary to carry the war to a successful conclusion").

[41] Carroll, 17 Mich L Rev at 628 (cited in note 37).

[42] 65th Cong, 1st Sess, in 55 Cong Rec H 3137 (May 31, 1917).

[43] Id at 1591 (Apr 30, 1917).

[44] 65th Cong, 1st Sess, in 55 Cong Rec S 2097 (May 11, 1917).

[45] 65th Cong, 1st Sess, in 55 Cong Rec H 1594 (Apr 30, 1917).

[46] Id at 1773 (May 3, 1917).

[47] Id at 1775.

[48] Id at 1773.

[49] 65th Cong, 1st Sess, in 55 Cong Rec S 2119 (May 11, 1917). On another occasion, Senator Borah said that the act "has all the earmarks of a dictatorship. It suppresses free speech and does it all in the name of war and patriotism." Claudius O. Johnson, *Borah of Idaho* 214 (Longmans, Green 1936) (quoting a letter from Borah to a friend). See also Paul L. Murphy, *Communities in Conflict*, in Alan Reitman, ed, *The Pulse of Freedom: American Liberties, 1920–1970s* 23, 25 (Norton 1975) (quoting Borah: "I am charged with radicalism for opposing government repression").

[50] 65th Cong, 1st Sess, in 55 Cong Rec S 781 (Apr 18, 1917) (stating that the act would vest the censorship board with "a dangerous power").

[51] 65th Cong, 1st Sess, in 55 Cong Rec H 1606 (Apr 30, 1917). For another example, see 65th Cong, 1st Sess, in 55 Cong Rec S 2099 (May 11, 1917) (under this provision "it would be a violation of law for the newspapers of the country . . . to print the crop reports, which are intimately related to our military efficiency and the national defense") (remarks of Senator Smith). For a counterexample, see id at 2102 (it would be "the height of unwisdom to make public in the midst of war . . . the intention of this Government . . . to cover the North Sea with submerged floating mines") (remarks of Senator Stone).

[52] 65th Cong, 1st Sess, in 55 Cong Rec H 1593 (Apr 30, 1917).

[53] *Wilson Demands Press Censorship*, New York Times 1 (May 23, 1917) (quoting a letter from Woodrow Wilson to Representative Webb). The administration offered a "compromise" version of the press censorship provision, which failed of passage. See Conf Rep No 65, on HR 291, 65th Cong, 1st Sess, in 55 Cong Rec H 3124, 3125 (May 31, 1917) (amended press censorship provision in title I section 4).

[54] 65th Cong, 1st Sess, in 55 Cong Rec H 3134 (May 31, 1917).

[55] See *House Defeats Censorship Law by 184 to 144*, New York Times 1 (June 1, 1917) (stating that party lines were "shattered" in defeating the bill).

[56] The House instructed the conferees to strike the press censorship provision from the bill. See House of Representatives Report No 69, 65th Cong, 1st Sess 19 (1917). The

defeat of this part of the bill had unintended consequences, for once Wilson was "defeated on the censorship, press criticism and, indeed, press notice of the Espionage Act suddenly ceased. If it is true that 'after its elimination, a majority of the national lawmakers apparently believed that the bill could not be used to suppress critical opinion,' then these Congressmen were mistaken." Scheiber, *Wilson Administration* at 18–19 (cited in note 1) (quoting Horace C. Peterson and Gilbert C. Fite, *Opponents of War, 1917–1918* 16 [Wisconsin 1957]).

[57] 65th Cong, 1st Sess, in 55 Cong Rec S 2062 (May 10, 1917).

[58] 65th Cong, 1st Sess, in 55 Cong Rec H 1779 (May 3, 1917) (noting that while the press censorship provision was a menace to newspapers, the "nonmailability" provision was a "menace to all").

[59] 65th Cong, 1st Sess, in 55 Cong Rec S 2062 (May 10, 1917) (noting that similar attempts during the Civil War "wrought a greater evil than would [otherwise] have resulted"). See also id at 2118–19 (May 11, 1917) (Senator Borah: "There is not a single decision to be cited anywhere but holds that any law which undertakes to control the publication previous to its publication is in violation of the Constitution").

[60] 65th Cong, 1st Sess, in 55 Cong Rec H 1595–97 (Apr 30, 1917). The debate also touched upon "nihilism" and the views of Tolstoy and Emerson.

[61] Id at 1604 (noting that the opinion of the solicitor of the Post Office Department would "prevail without a trial").

[62] Id at 1607.

[63] Conf Rep No 65, on HR 291, 65th Cong, 1st Sess, in 55 Cong Rec H 3124, 3129 (May 29, 1917); 65th Cong, 1st Sess, in 55 Cong Rec H 3306 (June 7, 1917).

[64] Hearings on 291 before the House Committee on the Judiciary, 65th Cong, 1st Sess 36–43 (Apr 9 and 12, 1917).

[65] Id at 12–13.

[66] 65th Cong, 1st Sess, in 55 Cong Rec H 1594 (Apr 30, 1917) (Representative Webb).

[67] See Espionage Act of 1917, 40 Stat at 219.

[68] 65th Cong, 1st Sess, in 55 Cong Rec H 1594–95 (Apr 30, 1917). Congress also made a significant change in the mail exclusion provision. See *infra* text accompanying notes 57–63.

[69] Espionage Act of 1917, 40 Stat 217, 219.

[70] Id at 230–31. What I have labeled provision (c) was not in the original bill, but was added during the course of congressional deliberations. The government put in place several other significant internal security measures during this period. In February 1917, it enacted the Threats against the President Act, which forbade anyone "knowingly and willfully" to threaten the life of or bodily harm to the president. See 39 Stat 919. During the course of the war, the government prosecuted 60 cases under this act, leading to 35 convictions. For examples of such cases, see Department of Justice, *Annual Report of the Attorney General* at 56–57 (cited in note 28). On April 6, 1917, President Wilson issued the Alien Enemies proclamation, which established rules for the control of enemy aliens, restricting their movement and prohibiting them from doing anything to aid the enemies of the United States. Of approximately 3.5 million enemy aliens in the United States during the war, 2,300 were interned. See id at 26; Scheiber, *Wilson*

Administration at 45 (cited in note 1). On April 7, 1917, President Wilson issued a secret executive order that empowered federal "department heads to remove any employee deemed a loyalty risk 'by reason of his conduct, sympathies, or utterances, or because of other reasons growing out of the war.'" Id at 14–15 (quoting Confidential Executive Order Regarding Federal Employees, Apr 7, 1917, in Paul P. Van Riper, *History of the United States Civil Service* 266 [1958]). On October 6, 1917, Congress enacted the Trading with the Enemy Act, which enlarged the censorship powers of the postmaster general by requiring all foreign-language newspapers to obtain prior approval before mailing translated material relating to the war. See 40 Stat 411, 425–26.

[71] 65th Cong, 1st Sess, in 55 Cong Rec 1780 (May 3, 1917) (Representative London stating that he would support "every measure that will guard the military and naval secrets of the country," but nothing more).

[72] 65th Cong, 1st Sess, in 55 Cong Rec S 2116 (May 11, 1917). On the other hand, in the same speech, Senator Sterling also quoted approvingly an excerpt from a publication stating that if a newspaper "publishes statements the obvious effect and probable purpose of which are to give aid and comfort to the enemy, its editor should be liable to punishment." Id.

[73] 65th Cong, 1st Sess, 55 Cong Rec H 1596 (Apr 30, 1917).

[74] Thomas Gregory, *Suggestions of Attorney General Gregory to Executive Committee in Relation to the Department of Justice*, 4 ABA J 305, 306 (1918).

[75] New York Times 3 (Nov 21, 1917). See Goldstein, *Political Repression* at 108 (cited in note 4).

[76] Woodrow Wilson, *This Is a People's War*, Flag Day Address, June 14, 1917, in Roy S. Baker and William E. Dodd, eds, 5 *The Public Papers of Woodrow Wilson: The New Democracy* 60, 66 (Harper 1927).

[77] Creel described his mission as one of "driving home to the people the causes behind the war, and the great fundamental necessities that compelled a peace loving nation to take up arms to protect free institutions and preserve our liberties." George Creel, *Public Opinion in War Time*, 78 Annals of the Am Academy of Pol and Soc Sci 185–86 (1918).

[78] Frank Cobb, *The Press and Public Opinion*, New Republic 144 (Dec 31, 1919). For a similar evaluation, see Scheiber, *Wilson Administration* at 16 (cited in note 1) ("Creel mobilized journalists, artists, writers, advertisers, and professors in a campaign that often seemed geared to persuade the American people that every German soldier was a violent beast; that spies and saboteurs lurked behind every bush; that conscription, bond sales, and 'liberty cabbage' were the greatest national blessings since the Bill of Rights; and that Russian Bolsheviks were merely German agents").

[79] Creel was successful on both counts. The CPI succeeded in building a spirit of confidence and public support for the war, but its aggressive campaigning caused the loyalty of many innocent people to be impugned. At times, the CPI drowned "out the voices of those who took a more balanced and judicious view." Scheiber, *Wilson Administration* at 17 (cited in note 1).

[80] For a review of the nation's increasingly hostile treatment of immigrants in the years leading up to World War I, see William Preston Jr., *Aliens and Dissenters: Federal*

Suppression of Radicals, 1903–1933 2–10 (Harvard 1963).

[81] Robert La Follette, *Free Speech in America*, in Alex Barnett, *Words That Changed America* 165–69 (Lyons 2003).

[82] See Harries and Harries, *Last Days of Innocence* at 296 (cited in note 13); Peterson and Fite, *Opponents of War* at 194–207 (cited in note 56). See *Meyer v. Nebraska*, 255 US 390 (1923) (invalidating a law prohibiting the teaching of German); O. A. Hilton, *Public Opinion and Civil Liberties in Wartime, 1917–1919*, 28 Southwestern Soc Sci Q 201, 208–12 (1947).

[83] Murphy, *Origin of Civil Liberties* at 94–95 (cited in note 6). See Harries and Harries, *Last Days of Innocence* at 307 (cited in note 13).

[84] See Peterson and Fite, *Opponents of War* at 18 (cited in note 56); Goldstein, *Political Repression* at 111 (cited in note 4). On the American Patriot League, see generally Joan M. Jensen, *The Price of Vigilance* (Rand McNally 1968). On the effectiveness of government propaganda during World War I, see Hilton, 28 Southwestern Soc Sci Q 201 (cited in note 82).

[85] Gregory, 4 ABA J at 309 (cited in note 74). Gregory authorized the American Protective League, in its efforts to recruit members, to state on its letterhead, "Organized with the Approval, and Operating under the Direction of the United States Department of Justice, Bureau of Investigation." See Murphy, *Origin of Civil Liberties* at 89–90 (cited in note 6).

[86] Terry Teachout, *The Skeptic: A Life of H. L. Mencken* 144–45 (Harper Collins 2002).

[87] See Harries and Harries, *Last Days of Innocence* at 282–308 (cited in note 13); Murphy, *Origin of Civil Liberties* at 94–95 (cited in note 6); Hilton, 28 Southwestern Soc Sci Q at 202–12 (cited in note 82).

[88] Letter from Thomas W. Gregory to U.S. Attorneys, Oct 28, 1918, in Department of Justice, *Annual Report of the Attorney General* at 674 (cited in note 28).

[89] Murphy, *Origin of Civil Liberties* at 164–65 (cited in note 6).

[90] See id at 125.

[91] New York World 8 (Sept 6, 1918), excerpted in Murphy, *Origin of Civil Liberties* at 126 (cited in note 6).

[92] George Creel, *Rebel at Large: Recollections of Fifty Crowded Years* 196 (Putnam 1947). Creel attempted to maintain some measure of judgment in running his program. As a result, he was often harshly attacked by less tolerant members of Congress for not going even farther in his defense of the war effort. See 65th Cong, 2d Sess, in 56 Cong Rec S 4763–64, 4827–32 (Apr 8–9, 1918); Murphy, *Origin of Civil Liberties* at 107–16 (cited in note 6).

[93] Harries and Harries, *Last Days of Innocence* at 308 (cited in note 13).

[94] 65th Cong, 1st Sess, in 55 Cong Rec S 2062 (May 10, 1917).

[95] See Jerold S. Auerbach, *Unequal Justice: Lawyers and Social Change in Modern America* 104–5 (Oxford 1976); Murphy, *Origin of Civil Liberties* at 179–211 (cited in note 6). For the most part, lawyers during the war "permitted the dictates of patriotism to determine the contours of professionalism." See Polenberg, *Fighting Faiths* at 75–81 (cited in note 7); Murphy, *Origin of Civil Liberties* at 238–46 (cited in note 6); Thomas A. Lawrence, *Eclipse of Liberty: Civil Liberties in the United States during the*

First World War, 21 Wayne L Rev 33, 70–71 (1974). Federal judges who gave a speech-protective construction to the Espionage Act, such as Judge George Bourquin of Montana and Judge Charles Amidon of Missouri, were subjected to verbal abuse, ostracism, threats of impeachment, and worse. See Murphy, *Origin of Civil Liberties* at 198–211 (cited in note 6).

96 The Court did decide several pre–World War I cases involving the First Amendment. See, for example, *Patterson v. Colorado*, 205 US 454 (1907) (contempt of court); *Turner v. Williams*, 194 US 279 (1904) (deportation); *Ex parte Jackson*, 96 US 727 (1877) (lottery tickets). See generally David M. Rabban, *Free Speech in Its Forgotten Years* 132–41 (Cambridge 1997).

97 William Blackstone, 4 *Commentaries on the Laws of England* *151–52.

98 For illustrative decisions, see *Commonwealth v. Karvonen*, 219 Mass 30, 32, 106 NE 556, 557 (1914) (a law prohibiting the display of a red flag "cannot be stricken down as unconstitutional unless [it has] no tendency" to endanger public safety); *State v. Pioneer Press Co*, 100 Minn 173, 177, 110 NW 867, 868 (1907) (speech may be restricted if it "naturally tends to excite the public mind and thus indirectly affect the public good"); *State v. McKee*, 73 Conn 18, 46 A 409, 412 (1900) (speech may be restricted if it tends "to public demoralization"); *People v. Most*, 128 NY 108, 115–16, 27 NE 970 (1891) (an "incendiary" speech may be restricted where "dangerous . . . consequences . . . may result from [the] speech"). See Rabban, *Forgotten Years* at 129–76 (cited in note 96).

99 See id at 177–210.

100 Schofield, *Freedom of the Press in the United States*, 9 Am Soc Society Papers and Proceedings 67, 73, 83–88 (1914). For a contrary view at the time, see W. R. Vance, *Freedom of Speech and Press*, 2 Minn L Rev 239 (1918); Carroll, 17 Mich L Rev 621 (cited in note 37); G. P. Garrett, *Free Speech and the Espionage Act*, 10 Am Inst Crim L & Criminology J 71 (1919).

101 Thomas M. Cooley, *A Treatise on the Constitutional Limitations* 534–37 (Little, Brown 4th ed 1878).

102 Ernst Freund, *The Police Power: Public Policy and Constitutional Rights* 508–12, 516 (Callaghan 1904).

103 Judge Bourquin's opinion in *United States v. Hall* is reported in 65th Cong, 2d Sess, 56 Cong Rec S 4559–60 (Apr 4, 1918). Bourquin also dismissed the charge that Hall had willfully obstructed "the recruiting or enlistment service of the United States" because there was no evidence of actual obstruction and this clause of section 3 did not even cover "attempts to obstruct." He added that to the extent that statements like Hall's might cause a breach of the peace, they were a matter for state law.

104 Letter from Beulah Amidon Ratliff to Elwyn B. Robinson (Mar 26, 1956).

105 Letter from Charles Fremont Amidon to Theodore Roosevelt (Mar 15, 1909).

106 *United States v. Schutte*, 252 F 212, 214 (D ND 1918). See Walter Nelles, ed, *Espionage Act Cases* 90–92 (National Civil Liberties Bureau 1918); Murphy, *Origins of Civil Liberties* at 208 (cited in note 6).

107 The jury acquitted. *United States v. Wichek*, unreported opinion (D ND 1918), excerpted in Murphy, *Origin of Civil Liberties* at 208 (cited in note 6).

[108] *United States v. Brinton*, unreported opinion (D ND 1918), excerpted in Murphy, *Origins of Civil Liberties* at 205–6 (cited in note 6), citing U.S. Department of Justice, *Interpretation of War Statutes*, Bulletin No 132 (1919).

[109] 244 F 535 (SD NY 1917).

[110] Gerald Gunther, *Learned Hand: The Man and the Judge* 153 (Knopf 1994) (describing the character of the *Masses* and detailing its beginnings).

[111] William L. O'Neill, *The Last Romantic: A Life of Max Eastman* 40 (Oxford 1978).

[112] Murphy, *Origin of Civil Liberties* at 196 (cited in note 6).

[113] See *Masses*, 244 F at 542–43.

[114] The verse is reprinted in *Masses*, 244 F at 544.

[115] Id at 536–37.

[116] Gunther, *Learned Hand* at 155 (cited in note 110).

[117] *Masses*, 244 F at 539.

[118] Id at 540.

[119] See, for example, Rabban, *Forgotten Years* at 265 (cited in note 96) (stating that Hand's "confident assertion" that Congress did not intend to "invoke such power" with the Espionage Act was belied by the act's legislative history).

[120] *Masses*, 244 F at 540 (italics added).

[121] Id.

[122] Id.

[123] 65th Cong, 2d Sess, in 56 Cong Rec 4559–60 (Apr 4, 1918).

[124] Arnon Gutfeld, *The Ves Hall Case, Judge Bourquin, and the Sedition Act of 1918*, 37, Pacific Hist Rev 163, 170 (May 1968).

[125] Id.

[126] Act Defining the Crime of Sedition, 1918 (Special Sess) Mont Laws ch 11. See also 65th Cong, 2d Sess, in 56 Cong Rec S 4561 (Apr 4, 1918).

[127] See Murphy, *Origin of Civil Liberties* at 208–9 (cited in note 6).

[128] See Gregory, 4 ABA J at 305–7 (cited in note 74).

[129] *Masses Publishing Co. v. Patten*, 246 F 24 (2d Cir 1917). Judge Bourquin's opinion in *Hall* and Judge Amidon's opinions in *Schutte* and *Wichek* could not be overruled, because they could not be appealed by the government. The double jeopardy clause of the Fifth Amendment ordinarily prohibits the government from appealing a trial judge's grant of a defendant's motion for acquittal or a trial judge's instructions to a jury that returns a verdict of nonguilty.

[130] Letter from Learned Hand to Oliver Wendell Holmes, Nov 25, 1919, excerpted in Gunther, *Learned Hand* at 600–603 (cited in note 110).

[131] Letter from Learned Hand to Charles Burlingham, Oct 6, 1917, excerpted id at 161.

[132] The indictment of the editors and staff of the *Masses* was encouraged by the court of appeals. See *Court Finds Masses Unfit to be Mailed*, New York Times 10 (Nov 3, 1917) (noting that the Second Circuit's decision "clears the way for any criminal action the Department of Justice may wish to take"); *Seditious Editors Now Fear Prison*, id at 17 (Nov 4, 1917) (noting that the *Masses* decision spread "great alarm . . . among publishers and editors"). Immediately after the court of appeals "sustained the action of the postal authority," the "government prosecutor laid the facts before

the Grand Jury." *Indicts The Masses and 7 of its Staff*, id at 4 (Nov 20, 1917). On the trials, see Gunther, *Learned Hand* at 152 (cited in note 110) (detailing the ultimate demise of the *Masses*).

[133] For other decisions that narrowly construed section 3 of the Espionage Act, see, for example, *Grubl v. United States*, 264 F 44 (8th Cir 1920); *Fontana v. United States*, 262 F 283 (8th Cir 1919); *Harshfield v. United States*, 260 F 659 (8th Cir 1919); *Kammann v. United States*, 259 F 192 (7th Cir 1919); *Shilter v. United States*, 257 F 724 (9th Cir 1919); *Sandberg v. United States*, 257 F 643 (9th Cir 1919).

[134] See Lawrence, 21 Wayne L Rev at 70 (cited in note 95).

[135] See O'Brian, 42 Rep NY St Bar Assn at 299 (cited in note 26).

[136] See Murphy, *Origin of Civil Liberties* at 80 (cited in note 6); Rabban, *Forgotten Years* at 256 (cited in note 96); Department of Justice, *Annual Report of the Attorney General* at 47 (cited in note 28). More precisely, 2,168 individuals were prosecuted and 1,055 were convicted. See Scheiber, *Wilson Administration* at 46–47 (cited in note 1).

[137] See Murphy, *Origin of Civil Liberties* at 197–98 (cited in note 6).

[138] 255 F 886 (9th Cir 1919).

[139] Id at 887.

[140] Id at 887–89.

[141] See, for example, *Goldstein v. United States*, 258 F 908 (9th Cir 1919); *Coldwell v. United States*, 256 F 805 (1st Cir 1919); *Kirchner v. United States*, 255 F 301 (4th Cir 1918); *Deason v. United States*, 254 F 259 (5th Cir 1918); *Doe v. United States*, 253 F 903 (8th Cir 1918); *O'Hare v. United States*, 253 F 538 (8th Cir 1918); *Masses Publishing Co. v. Patten*, 246 F 24 (2d Cir 1917) (reversing Judge Hand's opinion); *United States v. Nagler*, 252 F 217 (WD Wis 1918); *United States v. Motion Picture Film "The Spirit of '76,"* 252 F 946 (SD Cal 1917). For additional citations, see Rabban, *Forgotten Years* at 256–59 (cited in note 96).

[142] Murphy, *Origin of Civil Liberties* at 190 (cited in note 6).

[143] *United States v. Stokes* (unreported) (D Mo 1918), revd 264 F 18 (8th Cir 1920), quoted in Zechariah Chafee, *Free Speech in the United States* 52–53 (Harvard 1941); Peterson and Fite, *Opponents of War* at 185–86 (cited in note 56). See *Mrs. Stokes Denies Assailing Red Cross*, New York Times 13 (May 22, 1918) (reporting Stokes's statements during her trial); *Mrs. Stokes Denies Disloyal Intent*, id (May 23, 1918) (reporting the conclusion of Stokes's trial and summation arguments by both attorneys); *Mrs. Rose R. Stokes Convicted of Disloyalty; Illegal to Impair National Morale, Says Judge*, id at 1 (May 24, 1918). On March 9, 1920, a federal court of appeals overturned Mrs. Stokes's conviction, ruling that that district judge had placed "too heavy a burden" on the defendant because of his inappropriate "partisan zeal." Stokes, 264 F at 26. See also *Ten-Year Sentence of Mrs. Rose Stokes Overruled by Federal Court in St. Louis*, New York Times 1 (Mar 10, 1920). On November 15, 1921, the government finally dismissed the charges against Stokes. *Mrs. Stokes Freed; Debs May Soon Be*, id at 5 (Nov 16, 1921).

[144] *United States v. Doe* (unreported) (D Colo 1918), affd, 253 F 903 (8th Cir 1918), excerpted in Chafee, *Free Speech* at 54–55 (cited in note 143).

[145] See *30 Germans Are Arrested in South Dakota for Opposing the War and the Draft Law*,

New York Times 1 (Aug 28, 1917) (reporting that the men were charged with "having signed a petition of intimidating character"). While the defendants' appeal was pending in the Supreme Court, the government offered a "confession of error." See *Baltzer v. United States*, 248 US 593, 593 (1918). For a full discussion of this prosecution, including Justice Holmes's unpublished opinion in the case, see Sheldon M. Novick, *The Unrevised Holmes and Freedom of Expression*, 1991 Sup Ct Rev 303, 331–35, 388.

146 *"The Spirit of '76,"* 252 F at 947–48 (confiscating the film and prohibiting its presentation without modification). See Peterson and Fite, *Opponents of War* at 185–86 (cited in note 56). The movie was finally screened at Town Hall in New York City in July of 1921. See *Revive "Spirit of '76," Film Barred in 1917*, New York Times 18 (July 14, 1921). After Goldstein's conviction, moviemakers quietly toed "the war-party line."

147 O'Brian, 42 Rep NY St Bar Assn at 299–300 (cited in note 26).

148 Chafee, *Free Speech* at 52 (cited in note 143).

149 O'Brian, 42 Rep NY St Bar Assn at 301 (cited in note 26).

150 Indeed, because the provision governing obstruction of the recruiting and enlistment service did not cover attempts, Congress amended the provision in 1918 at the request of the Department of Justice in order to clarify and expand the reach of this prohibition. See id at 275.

151 See Joel Prentiss Bishop, 1 *Criminal Law* § 725 (Little, Brown 5th ed 1872) (the law of attempts is "less understood by the courts" and "more obscure in the text-books" than any other branch of the criminal law). But see Glanville Williams, *Textbook on Criminal Law: Involvement in Crime* §§ 1–5 at 368–83 (Stevens 1978).

152 See, for example, *Glover v. Commonwealth*, 86 Va 382, 385–86 (1889) (an "attempt in criminal law" requires both the "intent to commit a crime" and "a direct act done towards its commission"); *People v. Mills*, 178 NY 274, 284–85 (1904) (an attempt requires both an "intent to commit a crime" and an "overt act . . . such as would naturally effect that result"); *State v. Thompson*, 31 Nev 209, 216 (1909) (an attempt requires "intent to commit the crime" and "performance of some act towards its commission"). See also Bishop, 1 *Criminal Law* at § 728 (cited in note 151) ("an attempt is . . . an intent to do a thing, combined with an act which falls short of thing intended"); William L. Clark and William L. Marshall, *A Treatise on the Law of Crimes* § 119 (Callaghan 2d ed 1912) ("to constitute an indictable attempt to commit a crime, there must be . . . an intent to commit that particular crime" and "an act done in pursuance of such intent, which falls short of the actual commission of the crime"); John Wilder May, *The Law of Crimes* § 183 (Little, Brown 3d ed 1905) ("it is necessary that some act should be done in pursuance of the intent, immediately and directly tending to the commission of the crime").

153 Joseph H. Beale Jr., *Criminal Attempts*, 16 Harv L Rev 491 (1902). See Blackstone, 4 *Commentaries* at °36 (cited in note 97) (no one can attempt "a crime without an intention to have it done"); Bishop, 1 *Criminal Law* at § 731 (cited in note 151) ("the intent in attempt must be specific").

154 See, for example, *Simpson v. State*, 59 Ala 1 (1877) (recklessness does not establish attempt); *Scott v. State*, 49 Ark 156 (1886) (same); *Pruitt v. State*, 20 Tex Ct App 129

(1886) (same). But see Oliver Wendell Holmes Jr., *The Common Law* 66–67 (Little, Brown 1951). Holmes argued that "the reason for punishing any act must generally be to prevent some harm which is foreseen as likely to follow that act under the circumstances in which it is done." Thus, "acts should be judged by their tendency under the known circumstances, not by the actual intent which accompanies them," and an act should be "punishable as an attempt, if, supposing it to have produced its natural and probable effect, it would have amounted to a substantive crime." Holmes acknowledged, however, that this was not the law. See Rabban, *Forgotten Years* at 285–98 (cited in note 96); Yosal Rogat, *The Judge as Spectator*, 31 U Chi L Rev 213 (1963). Moreover, his later writing clarified the role on intent in this context. See Oliver Wendell Holmes, *Privilege, Malice, and Intent*, 8 Harv L Rev 1 (1894).

155 Zechariah Chafee reported, "A lawyer who defended many Espionage Act cases tells me that there was much speculation among his clients as to whether they actually possessed the requisite criminal intent. A few of them admitted to him that they had it," but "most of the defendants had no real intention to cause trouble, and were only engaged in heated altercations or expounding economic doctrines." Chafee, *Free Speech* at 62 (cited in note 143).

156 See, for example, *Grubl v. United States*, 264 F 44 (8th Cir 1920); *Fontana v. United States*, 262 F 283 (8th Cir 1919); *Harshfield v. United States*, 260 F 659 (8th Cir 1919); *Kammann v. United States*, 259 F 192 (7th Cir 1919); *Shilter v. United States*, 257 F 724 (9th Cir 1919); *Sandberg v. United States*, 257 F 643 (9th Cir 1919).

157 Indeed, the law of attempt may be even more demanding than I have thus far suggested. Many courts have held, for example, that an individual cannot be held guilty of an attempt, regardless of other evidence of specific intent, unless the defendant's act is "of such a nature that it is itself evidence of the criminal intent with which it is done." John Salmond, *Jurisprudence* § 137 at 404 (Sweet and Maxwell 7th ed 1924). See, for example, *United States v. Cruz-Jiminez*, 977 F2d 95 (3d Cir 1992); *United States v. McDowell*, 714 F2d 106 (11th Cir 1983); *United States v. Everett*, 700 F2d 900 (3d Cir 1983). See generally Wayne R. LaFave, *Criminal Law* §§ 6.2–6.3 at 548–60 (West 3d ed 2000). Another, less rigid approach, exemplified by the Model Penal Code, holds that conduct cannot constitute an attempt "unless it is strongly corroborative of the actor's criminal purpose." See Model Penal Code § 5.01(2). Although this approach offers the prosecution somewhat more flexibility in proving specific intent, it is clearly a standard that could not be met by the Espionage Act prosecutions. See LaFave, *Criminal Law* § 6.2 at 550–52. Under this view, an attempt is constituted only if the accused "does an act . . . that can have *no other purpose* than the commission of that specific crime." J. W. Cecil Turner, *Attempts to Commit Crimes*, 5 Cambridge L J 230, 236 (1934) (original text all italicized). Although this standard can readily be satisfied in situations where, for example, the defendant puts poison in the drink or shoots directly at the intended victim, it is far from satisfied in the prosecutions brought under section 3 of the Espionage Act, where the acts of the defendants were almost always much more equivocal.

158 Chafee, *Free Speech* at ix (cited in note 143).

159 Letter from Charles Fremont Amidon to Zechariah Chafee, Aug 29, 1919, excerpted

id at 70.

[160] Hand noted that a speaker can arouse an audience to violate the law "as well by indirection as expressly," but nonetheless insisted that to violate the Espionage Act the prosecution must prove that the defendant engaged in "direct advocacy of resistance." *Masses*, 244 F 535, 540–41 535 (SD NY 1917). See also *United States v. Nearing*, 252 F 223, 228 (SD NY 1918), in which Judge Hand observed that "there may be language, as, for instance, Mark Antony's funeral oration, which can in fact counsel violence while it even expressly discountenances it."

[161] See Chafee, *Free Speech* at 45 (cited in note 143) (Hand wanted an "objective test" that could be "easily understood by the opponents of the war" so "[t]hey could safely engage in discussion of [the war and] its merits . . . so long as they refrained from urging violation of laws").

[162] Blackstone, 4 *Commentaries* at °37 (cited in note 97).

[163] *Nearing*, 252 F at 227.

[164] Under the government's theory in these cases, the defendants were "attempting" to obstruct the war effort by generating disaffection in the minds of others who would then commit unlawful acts of insubordination, refusal of duty, etc. Under the common law, however, it was almost unheard of for a court to sustain such a theory of "attempt." As Professor Joseph Beale wrote in 1902, one cannot attempt to commit an offense "by the solicitation of another to do an act." Beale, 16 Harv L Rev at 505 (cited in note 153). See also Francis Wharton, 1 *A Treatise on Criminal Law* § 179 at 200–202 (Kay and Brother 10th ed 1885); John W. Curran, *Solicitation: A Substantive Crime*, 17 Minn L Rev 499, 501–2 (1933). But see Bishop, 1 *Criminal Law* at § 768(c) (cited in note 151). For the contemporary view on this question, see LaFave, *Criminal Law* § 6.1 at 534–35 (cited in note 157).

The near-universal view was that in order for an individual who solicits another to commit a crime to be guilty of "attempt," the defendant must at the very least have undertaken some additional overt act, such as furnishing the person solicited with the equipment necessary to commit the crime. See, for example, *People v. Bush*, 4 Hill 133 (NY 1843); *Smith v. Commonwealth*, 54 Pa 209 (1867); *McDade v. People*, 29 Mich 50 (1874); *Stabler v. Commonwealth*, 95 Pa 318 (1880); *State v. Harney*, 101 Mo 470, 14 SW 657 (1890); *State v. Bowers*, 35 SC 262, 14 SE 488 (1892); *Ex parte Floyd*, 7 Cal App 588 (1908). For more recent decisions, see, for example, *State v. Davis*, 319 Mo 1222, 6 SW2d 609 (1928); *State v. Mandel*, 78 Ariz 226, 278 P2d 413 (1954); *Braham v. State*, 571 P2d 631 (Alaska 1977); *State v. Molasky*, 765 SW2d 597 (1989). See also Wharton, 1 *Criminal Law* at § 179 ("the question whether the solicitation is by itself the subject of penal prosecution must be answered in the negative"); Clark and Marshall, *Law of Crimes* at §§ 125, 133 ("the better opinion is that solicitation to commit a crime is not an attempt"); T. W. Hughes, *A Treatise on Criminal Law and Procedure* §§ 130, 139 (Bobbs-Merrill 1919) ("the weight of authority . . . sustains the view that solicitation to commit a crime may constitute an independent offense, but not a criminal attempt"); May, *Law of Crimes* at § 19 (cited in note 152) ("solicitation to commit a crime is not an attempt"). But see Bishop, 1 *Criminal Law* at § 768(c)(2) (cited in note 151) ("solicitation can be an indictable attempt . . . without any further . . . overt acts"). Given these limitations on the law of attempt, few, if any, of the defendants in the section 3 prosecutions should have been convicted of attempt.

Another relevant limitation in the law of attempt is that an effort to commit a crime that is dependent upon the cooperation of another individual who has not yet agreed to act ordinarily will not constitute an attempt. See, for example, *United States v. Stephens*, 12 F 52 (D Or 1882) (defendant's plan to have liquor sent unlawfully into Alaska does not constitute an attempt where no seller has yet agreed to ship the liquor); *People v. Murray*, 14 Cal 159 (1859) (defendant's plan to contract an incestuous marriage by marrying his niece does not constitute an attempt where no magistrate has yet agreed to perform the marriage). See Beale, 16 Harv L Rev at 503 (cited in note 153).

But even if the Espionage Act defendants were not guilty of attempt, perhaps they were guilty of the separate crime of solicitation. At the outset, it is important to note that section 3 prohibits "attempt," not "solicitation." This is not merely a technical distinction, and it is far from evident that it would be appropriate for federal courts to rewrite a statute to convert a prohibition of attempts into a prohibition of solicitations. More fundamentally, however, the crime of solicitation requires not only that the defendant specifically intend to bring about criminal conduct but also that he command, encourage, or request another to commit the crime. See Bishop,1 *Criminal Law* at §768(a) (cited in note 151) (referring to "direct solicitations"); Wharton, 1 *Criminal Law* at §179 (using such terms as "counseled," "advised," and "encouraged" to describe the crime of solicitation). See also Model Penal Code §5.02. The "essence of the crime of solicitation is 'asking a person to commit a crime.'" LaFave, *Criminal Law* § 6.1 at 531 (cited in note 157), citing *Gardner v. State*, 41 Md App 187, 396 A2d 303 (1979), affd 286 Md 520, 408 A2d 1317 (1979). See also Blackstone, 4 *Commentaries* at °36 (cited in note 97). Hence, Judge Hand's conclusion in *Masses* that in the absence of express advocacy of criminal conduct, there is no criminal offense of solicitation. Moreover, under the common law, a speaker ordinarily is guilty of solicitation to a crime only if he would have been indictable for the crime itself, had it been committed. See Beale, 16 Harv L Rev at 505 (cited in note 153). See also Chafee, *Free Speech* at 47 (cited in note 143). This would certainly not have been the case in most of the Espionage Act prosecutions.

[165] Beale, 16 Harv L Rev at 493, 496 (cited in note 153).

[166] See Joel Prentiss Bishop, 1 *Bishop on Criminal Law* § 669 (T. H. Flood 8th ed 1892) ("the difficulty is not a small one to lay down rules, readily applied"); LaFave, *Criminal Law* § 6.2 at 544–52 (cited in note 157).

[167] Beale, 16 Harv L Rev at 492 (cited in note 153).

[168] Id at 501.

[169] *Commonwealth v. Peaslee*, 177 Mass 267, 272, 59 NE 55, 56 (1901).

[170] Holmes, *Common Law* at 67 (cited in note 154). Most of the modern recodifications state that the defendant's conduct must "constitute a substantial step towards" the unlawful act. LaFave, *Criminal Law* § 6.2 at 545 n 108 (cited in note 157).

[171] *Commonwealth v. Kennedy*, 170 Mass 18, 22 48 NE 770, 771 (1897). Justice Holmes

also noted in *Kennedy* that because "the aim of the law is not to punish sins, but is to prevent certain external results, the act done must come pretty near to accomplishing that result before the law will notice it." Id at 770.

172 Chafee, *Free Speech* at 47 (cited in note 143).

173 For a detailed review of Congress's intent in enacting the Espionage Act, see Geoffrey R. Stone, *Judge Learned Hand and the Espionage Act of 1917: A Mystery Unraveled*, 70 U Chi L Rev 335 (2003).

174 In 1918, Congress enacted the Sedition Act of 1918, which made it unlawful for any person to utter, print, write, or publish any disloyal, profane, scurrilous, or abusive language intended to cause contempt or scorn for the form of government of the United States, the Constitution, or the flag; or to utter any words supporting the cause of any country at war with the Untied States or opposing the cause of the United States. Act of May 16, 1918, ch 75, § 1, 40 Stat 553.

175 See Chafee, *Free Speech* at 47–49 (cited in note 143):

[T]he rule has always been that, to establish criminal responsibility, the words uttered must constitute dangerous progress toward the consummation of the independent offense attempted and amount to procurement, counsel, or command to commit the forbidden acts. . . . [T]here is not a word in the 1917 Espionage Act to show that Congress did change the ordinary tests. . . . Every word used, "cause," "attempt," "obstruct," clearly involves proximate causation, a close and direct relation to actual interference with the operations of the army and navy, with enlistment and the draft.

176 Blackstone, 4 *Commentaries* at *35–37 (cited in note 97) (emphasis added).

177 Wharton, 1 *Criminal Law* at § 213 (cited in note 164).

178 Id at § 179.

179 For a detailed analysis tracing the precise origins of this confusion in the law of attempt, see Geoffrey R. Stone, *The Origins of the "Bad Tendency Test": Free Speech in Wartime*, 2002 Sup Ct Rev 411.

180 Espionage Act of 1917, 40 Stat at 230; *Burleson to Editor and Publisher*, New York World (Oct 31, 1917).

181 See Chafee, *Free Speech* at 97–100 (cited in note 143).

182 Letter from Theodore Roosevelt to Miles Poindexter, May 22, 1918, in Elting E. Morison, ed, 8 *The Letters of Theodore Roosevelt* 1323 (Harvard 1954).

183 Letter from Upton Sinclair to Woodrow Wilson, Oct 22, 1917, excerpted in Peterson and Fite, *Opponents of War* at 100 (cited in note 56). Professor Carl Swisher has observed that Burleson "exercised his power of censorship with a high hand" using "far-fetched lines of reasoning." Carl B. Swisher, *American Constitutional Development* 610 (Houghton Mifflin 1943).

184 New York World (Sept 22, 1918).

185 40 Stat 1012.

186 See *United States v. Wusterbarth*, 249 F 908 (DC NJ 1918).

187 Chafee, *Free Speech* at 204 (cited in note 143).

[188] See Elshtain, *Jane Addams* at 206 (cited in note 11).

[189] For examples of such legislation, see Murphy, *Origin of Civil Liberties* at 86 n 42 (cited in note 6).

[190] See Peterson and Fite, *Opponents of War* at 141–46 (cited in note 56).

[191] Murphy, *Origin of Civil Liberties* at 118 (cited in note 6). See also Robert K. Murray, *Red Scare: A Study in National Hysteria, 1919–1920* 13 (Minnesota 1955) (individuals and even towns with Germanic names changed them in "self-defense").

[192] Zechariah Chafee Jr., *Thirty-Five Years with Freedom of Speech* 4 (Baldwin Civil Liberties Foundation 1952). See Murphy, *Origin of Civil Liberties* at 134–35 (cited in note 6).

[193] *Address Delivered at the Boston Meeting: Address of the President*, 5 ABA J 527, 537 (1919). See David Cole, *Enemy Aliens* 107–15 (New 2003).

[194] *Theodore Schroeder: A Very Wise Man*, in Lesley Kuhn, ed, *Theodore Schroeder's Last Will* 25 (Psychological Library 1958) (quoting H. L. Mencken).

[195] Rabban, *Forgotten Years* at 76 (cited in note 96). On the demise of the Free Speech League, see id at 304–16.

[196] See Donald Johnson, *The Challenge to American Freedom: World War I and the Rise of the American Civil Liberties Union* 36–41 (Kentucky 1963).

[197] See *Not Cruel to Slackers*, New York Times 24 (Nov 20, 1918).

[198] See Johnson, *Challenge to American Freedom* at 60–61 (cited in note 196); Murphy, *Origin of Civil Liberties* at 164–65, 168 (cited in note 6); Scheiber, *Wilson Administration* at 33 (cited in note 1).

[199] See O'Brian, 42 Rep NY St Bar Assn at 275 (cited in note 26).

[200] Gregory, 4 ABA J at 306–7, 313, 316 (cited in note 74).

[201] Chafee, *Free Speech* at 41 (cited in note 143); Harry Kalven Jr., *A Worthy Tradition: Freedom of Speech in America* 89–90 (Harper and Row 1988).

[202] 65th Cong, 2d Sess, in 56 Cong Rec H 3003 (Mar 4, 1918) (Representative Gard). See also id ("It strikes me that . . . we have plenty of law now") (Rep Cox).

[203] See 65th Cong, 2d Sess, in 56 Cong Rec S 4838 (Apr 9, 1918).

[204] Id at 4559–60 (Apr 4, 1918).

[205] 40 Stat 553.

[206] 65th Cong, 2d Sess, in 56 Cong Rec S 4783 (Apr 8, 1918).

[207] Id at 4566 (Apr 4, 1918). In announcing that he would vote against the Sedition Act, Senator Hardwick of Georgia stated, "In taking this position, I am well aware that I will subject myself to bitter . . . criticism. It will be contended . . . that I am disloyal to the country." Id at 5940 (May 2, 1918).

[208] See, for example, id at 4640–41, 4648–51, 4713, 4759, 4763–65, 4775–76, 4833–34 (Apr 4–9, 1918).

[209] Senator Williams of Mississippi offered a different explanation:

Do you think you are fooling the American people? . . . Do you think they are going to be patient with you for camouflaging and wasting time here? You have had the opportunity every minute since this bill was reported either to vote it up or vote it down; . . . but you have chosen rather to waste time, talking, fooling, camouflaging, tweedleduming and tweedledeeing, splitting hairs at a time when the whole cause of liberty of the world is at stake. . . . Shall the right of the people to rule perish from the earth just simply in order that august Senators may split hairs upon the difference between "calculated" and "intended"? Who cares a cent which one of the two words you put into the statute?

Id at 4850 (Apr 9, 1918).

[210] Id at 4633 (Apr 5, 1918).

[211] See, for example, id at 4648 (Apr 5, 1918) (Senator Fall argues that if the courts do not do their job, "people will take the law into their own hands"); id at 4633 (Senator Borah warns that in the absence of this legislation it may become necessary to convene "military tribunals").

[212] Id at 4650.

[213] Id at 4647.

[214] Id at 4718 (Apr 6, 1918). See also id at 4571 (Apr 4, 1918) ("[W]e have reached a point now, and we reached it long ago, where any utterance tending to bring contempt upon the . . . United States or its form of government or the flag or the Constitution or the uniform of a soldier, whether uttered carelessly, willfully, or with . . . intent should be prohibited because . . . carelessness or ignorance may bring about as disastrous effect as any willful intent might bring about") (Senator Fall).

[215] Id at 4562 (Apr 4, 1918). See also id at 4764 (Apr 8, 1918) ("The object of this proposed law is to prevent violence. . . . It is for the sake of keeping the peace of this country, to prevent a breach of the peace, that it is necessary") (Senator Nelson); id at 4714 (Apr 6, 1918) ("The principal object of this bill . . . is to prevent mob law") (Senator Myers); id at 4633 (Apr 5, 1918) ("If we do not do our duty here, the impulses of loyal men and women will seek justice in rougher ways. . . . I shudder at the thought that this proud Republic is about to resort to the law of riot and disorder") (Senator Borah).

[216] Polenberg, *Fighting Faiths* at 31 (cited in note 7). A few members of Congress were skeptical about the real reason for the legislation. Senator Hardwick of Georgia saw no need for such "drastic" legislation in most parts of the country. He argued that "the real—in fact, practically the only—object" of the act was to deal with members of the International Workers of the World, who were causing a fuss "in a few of the Northwestern States." Hardwick resented being "confronted by a situation in which . . . we are asked to jeopardize the fundamental rights and liberties of 100,000,000 Americans" in order to address a local situation that has nothing to do with the proposed legislation. 65th Cong, 2d Sess, in 56 Cong Rec S 4638–39 (Apr 5, 1918). The International Workers of the World, also known as the IWW or the Wobblies, were deeply involved in free speech disputes from 1905 until the First World War. See Rabban, *Forgotten Years* at 77–128 (cited in note 96); Melvyn Dubofsky, *We Shall Be All: A History of the Industrial Workers of the World* (Chicago 1969).

[217] Id at 4714 (Apr 6, 1918) (Senator Myers reading Department of Justice statement); id at 4692.

[218] Id at 4769–70 (Apr 8, 1918).

[219] Id at 4651 (Apr 5, 1918).

220 Id at 4564 (Apr 4, 1918). See also id at 4651 (Apr 5, 1918) (Senator Thomas asking whether a lawyer who "defends" a person charged with violating the act violates the act himself because he "defends the act" prohibited by the legislation).

221 See id at 4634–46.

222 Id at 4633.

223 Id at 4637.

224 Id.

225 Id at 4711 (Apr 6, 1918).

226 Theodore Roosevelt, *Citizens or Subjects*, Kansas City Star (Apr 6, 1918), reprinted in *Roosevelt Denounces Provision in the Pending Disloyalty Bill*, Washington Post 3 (Apr 6, 1918).

227 Id. See also *Liberty of Criticism*, Wall Street Journal 1 (Apr 10, 1918) (editorializing against the Sedition Act of 1918 because "if passed in its present shape, incompetency and intrigue would no longer have much to fear from their worst enemy—a free and untrammeled press").

228 65th Cong, 2d Sess, in 56 Cong Rec S 4840 (Apr 9, 1918).

229 Id at 4835.

230 Id at 4826.

231 Letter from John Lord O'Brian to Representative Edwin Y. Webb, Apr 16, 1918, excerpted id at 5542 (Apr 24, 1918).

232 Id at 4835 (Apr 9, 1918) (This comment was actually made two weeks earlier when the Senate initially voted down the France amendment).

233 Id at 5544 (Apr 24, 1918).

234 Id at 6050 (May 4, 1918). In response to a similar assertion earlier in the debate, Senator Lodge observed, "This bill will not touch a single spy or a single German agent. . . . The spies or agents do not go around uttering, publishing, and writing. The dangerous men keep quiet." Id at 4562 (Apr 4, 1918).

235 Id at 6050–51 (May 4, 1918).

236 The lone dissenter was Meyer London, a Socialist from New York.

237 O'Brian, 42 Rep NY St Bar Assn at 304 (cited in note 26).

238 Memo from Attorney General Thomas Gregory to all United States Attorneys, May 23, 1918, excerpted in Murphy, *Origin of Civil Liberties* at 94 (cited in note 6). See also O'Brian, 42 Rep NY St Bar Assn at 305 (cited in note 26).

239 O'Brian, 42 Rep NY St Bar Assn at 305–6 (cited in note 26).

240 See Polenberg, *Fighting Faiths* at 198 (cited in note 7); David P. Currie, *The Constitution in the Supreme Court, The Second Century, 1886–1986* 126–30 (Chicago 1990); Murphy, *Origin of Civil Liberties* at 182–83 (cited in note 6); Robert Cover, *The Left, The Right and the First Amendment: 1918–1928*, 40 Md L Rev 349 (1981).

241 249 US 47 (1919).

242 249 US at 50–51 (the Court describing the contents of the pamphlet).

243 Id at 51.

244 Id at 52.

245 *Abrams v. United States*, 250 US 616, 222 (1919) (Holmes dissenting).

246 The Court had arguably applied some version of the "bad tendency" test (without an

independent requirement of specific intent) in several pre-*Schenck* decisions. See, for example, *Toledo Newspaper Co. v. United States*, 247 US 402, 420 (1918) (the freedom of the press, "as every other right enjoyed in human society, is subject to the restraints which separate right from wrongdoing"); *Fox v. Washington*, 236 US 273 (1915) (upholding a conviction for encouraging the commission of a crime); *Patterson v. Colorado*, 205 US 454 (1907) (upholding a contempt citation for criticizing judicial conduct in a pending case); *Turner v. Williams*, 194 US 279 (1904) (upholding the deportation of an alien for advocating anarchism); *Ex parte Jackson*, 96 US 727 (1877) (upholding a federal statute prohibiting the use of the mails for lottery advertisements). None of these decisions was cited in *Schenck*, however. For a full discussion of these decisions, see Rabban, *Forgotten Years* at 132–41 (cited in note 96).

[247] 249 US 204 (1919).

[248] 249 US 211 (1919).

[249] Id at 207–8.

[250] Id at 208–9.

[251] Debs, Speech in Canton, Ohio, June 16, 1918, in Schlesinger, ed, *Writings and Speeches of Eugene V. Debs* at 417–22 (cited in note 15) (parentheticals in original).

[252] See, for example, *Debs Arrested; Sedition Charged*, New York Times 1 (July 1, 1918); *Swears Debs Upheld Anti-War Program*, id at 8 (Sept 11, 1918); *E. V. Debs Declines to Offer Defense*, id at 8 (Sept 12, 1918); *Find Debs Guilty of Disloyal Act*, id at 4 (Sept 13, 1918); *Debs Case in High Court*, id at 4 (Jan 28, 1919).

[253] 249 US at 212–15.

[254] Id at 215–16.

[255] Kalven, *Worthy Tradition* at 135 (cited in note 201). Justice Holmes's prior opinions relating to free speech were consistent in spirit with his opinions in *Schenck*, *Frohwerk*, and *Debs*. See, for example, *Patterson v. Colorado*, 205 US 454 (1907) (upholding a contempt citation directed against newspaper articles that might "impede" the "orderly administration of justice"); *Fox v. Washington*, 236 US 273 (1915) (upholding a conviction for "encouraging . . . disrespect for law" of an individual who wrote a newspaper editorial critical of a town law against nude bathing). Those earlier cases both involved state laws, however, and it was not yet clear whether the protections of the First Amendment extended against state as well as federal government actions.

[256] Letter from Learned Hand to Oliver Wendell Holmes, June 22, 1918 excerpted in Gunther, *Learned Hand* at 163 (cited in note 110); letter from Oliver Wendell Holmes to Learned Hand, June 24, 1918, excerpted id. See *Jacobson v. Massachusetts*, 197 US 11 (1905) (upholding authority of state to compel vaccination).

[257] Holmes, *Common Law* 1 (cited in note 154).

[258] Oliver Wendell Holmes Jr., *The Law*, Feb 5, 1885, in Mark DeWolfe Howe, comp, *The Occasional Speeches of Justice Oliver Wendell Holmes* 20–21 (Belknap 1962).

[259] Owen Wister, *Roosevelt: The Story of a Friendship* 129 (Macmillan 1930).

[260] Walter Lippmann, *To Justice Holmes*, New Republic 156 (Mar 11, 1916).

[261] Letter from Oliver Wendell Holmes to Nina Gray, Feb 15, 1903, excerpted in Sheldon M. Novick, *Honorable Justice: The Life of Oliver Wendell Holmes* 249 (Little, Brown

1989); letter from Oliver Wendell Holmes to Ethel Scott, Apr 24, 1909, excerpted id.

262 Melvin I. Urofsky, *The Brandeis-Frankfurter Conversations*, 1985 Sup Ct Rev 299, 323–24 (1985).

263 Letter from Oliver Wendell Holmes to Learned Hand, Apr 19, 1918, excerpted in Liva Baker, *The Justice from Beacon Hill: The Life and Times of Oliver Wendell Holmes* 515 (Harper Collins 1991).

264 Learned Hand, *The Spirit of Liberty*, May 21, 1944, in Irving Dilliard, ed, *The Spirit of Liberty: Papers and Addresses of Learned Hand* 189, 190 (Knopf 1952).

265 Gunther, *Learned Hand* at 162 (cited in note 110).

266 Letters from Learned Hand to Oliver Wendell Holmes, Mar 3, 1933, and Mar 8, 1921, excerpted id at 162.

267 Gunther, *Learned Hand* at 162 (cited in note 110).

268 Holmes, *Common Law* at 43–44 (cited in note 154).

269 Letter from Learned Hand to Oliver Wendell Holmes, Mar 1919, in Gunther, *Learned Hand* at 164–66 (cited in note 110); letter from Oliver Wendell Holmes to Learned Hand, Feb 25, 1919, excerpted id; letter from Oliver Wendell Holmes to Learned Hand, Apr 3, 1919, excerpted id.

270 Ernst Freund, *The Debs Case and Freedom of Speech*, New Republic 13–15 (May 3, 1919). See also Harry Kalven Jr., *Professor Ernst Freund and Debs v. United States*, 40 U Chi L Rev 235 (1973). At about this same time, Judge Amidon indicated to Zechariah Chafee that he, too, had concluded that the line should be drawn at "language, either written or spoken, which directly advises men to resist or violate laws." Letter from Charles Fremont Amidon to Zechariah Chafee, Aug 29, 1919.

271 Polenberg, *Fighting Faiths* at 220 (cited in note 7).

272 Letter from Learned Hand to Ernst Freund, May 7, 1919, excerpted id at 220–21.

273 Letter and enclosure from Oliver Wendell Holmes to Harold Laski, May 13, 1919, in Mark DeWolfe Howe, ed, 1 *Holmes-Laski Letters: The Correspondence of Mr. Justice Holmes and Harold J. Laski, 1916–1935* 202–3 (Harold 1953).

274 Letter from Oliver Wendell Holmes to Frederick Pollock, April 5, 1919, in Mark DeWolfe Howe, ed, 2 *Holmes-Pollock Letters: The Correspondence of Mr. Justice Holmes and Sir Frederick Pollock, 1874–1932* 7 (Harvard 1941); letter from Holmes to John Wigmore, excerpted in Polenberg, *Fighting Faiths* at 221–22 (cited in note 7); letter from Holmes to Pollock, Oct 26, 1919, in Howe, ed, 2 *Holmes-Pollock Letters* at 28–29.

275 Zechariah Chafee, *Freedom of Speech in War Time*, 32 Harv L Rev 932, 930, 943–44, 960 (1919).

276 Harold J. Laski, *Authority in the Modern State* 56 (Yale 1919).

277 Letter from Learned Hand to Zechariah Chafee Jr., Jan 2, 1921, excerpted in Gunther, *Learned Hand* at 169 (cited in note 110). This note was actually sent several months later, after Justice Holmes's opinion in the *Abrams* case.

278 See Polenberg, *Fighting Faiths* at 227 (cited in note 7).

279 Letter from Oliver Wendell Holmes to Harold Laski, Oct 26, 1919, in Howe, ed, 1 *Holmes-Laski Letters* at 165 (cited in note 273).

[280] 250 US 616 (1919).

[281] Id at 620–22.

[282] Murphy, *Origin of Civil Liberties* at 234 (cited in note 6). For a fuller account of the judge and the trial, see Polenberg, *Fighting Faiths* at 95–153 (cited in note 7).

[283] Chafee, *Free Speech* at 127 (cited in note 143).

[284] On the trial, see generally id at 108–40; Polenberg, *Fighting Faiths* (cited in note 7); Lawrence, 21 Wayne L Rev 33 (cited in note 95).

[285] 250 US at 617–19.

[286] Id at 627–28.

[287] An interesting, and confusing, issue in the case concerned the intent of the defendants with respect to count 4 of the indictment. The Sedition Act of 1918 expressly prohibited any effort to curtail the protection of war materials "with intent [to] cripple or hinder the United States in the prosecution of the war." There was no question but that the defendant's motive was to support the Russian Revolution rather than to hinder the war effort against Germany. Indeed, the defendants made this perfectly clear in their leaflets. The Court in *Abrams* concluded that there was no legal distinction under the act between calling for a work stoppage to protest the sending of American troops into Russia, which the Court reasonably assumed to be part of the war against Germany, and calling for a work stoppage to protest the war against Germany. Justice Holmes, in a rather muddled part of his opinion, argued that because the defendants' motive was to help Russia rather than to help Germany, they did not have the specific intent to "hinder the United States in the prosecution of the war." Perhaps the key question in clarifying this matter is how one would deal under the act with a defendant who advocates a strike in a munitions plant in wartime in order to get better working conditions. Chafee assumes that such a defendant would not be covered by the act. See Chafee, *Free Speech* at 133 (cited in note 143).

[288] 250 US at 628. One difficulty Justice Holmes encountered was his puzzling assertion (in the light of the rest of his opinion) that an individual could be punished either for creating the present danger of an immediate evil or for intending to do so. The difficulty is that the defendants in *Abrams* clearly intended to incite an immediate general strike. Even if, as Holmes observed, there was no appreciable danger of harm to the government, the intent was clearly present. Justice Holmes attempted to escape this difficulty by arguing that the intent of the defendants was to prevent interference with the Russian Revolution rather than to undermine the war against Germany. Although this was technically true, it is not at all clear that it makes sense to disentangle the different motives quite so finely. Arguably, this was more appropriately a question of statutory construction (i.e., did the defendants violate the statute if they did not have the specific intent to hinder the war against Germany?) than a question of constitutional interpretation. See Kalven, *Worthy Tradition* at 141–44 (cited in note 201).

[289] 250 US at 629.

[290] Id at 630–31.

[291] Most commentators have concluded that "Holmes moved from a restrictive construction of the first amendment . . . in *Schenck, Frohwerk,* and *Debs* . . . to a libertarian position in his dissent in *Abrams.*" David M. Rabban, *The Emergence of Modern First*

Amendment Doctrine, 50 U Chi L Rev 1205, 1208–9 (1983). For a thoughtful analysis of the Holmes transformation, see id at 1311–17. For an especially critical view of Holmes in this period, see Fred D. Ragan, *Justice Oliver Wendell Holmes, Jr., Zechariah Chafee, Jr., and the Clear and Present Danger Test for Free Speech: The First Year, 1919*, 58 J Am Hist 24 (1971). Professor Zechariah Chafee argued that Holmes had intended all along to move to his *Abrams* understanding of clear and present danger, but this theory has been largely debunked. See Chafee, *Free Speech* at 86 (cited in note 143) (claiming that "Holmes was biding his time until the Court should have before it a conviction so clearly wrong as to let him speak out his deepest thoughts about the First Amendment"). For those who reject this "benign conspiracy" theory, see Kalven, *Worthy Tradition* at 136–38 (cited in note 201); Gunther, *Learned Hand* at 155–69 (cited in note 110); Rabban, *Forgotten Years* at 344–55 (cited in note 96); Polenberg, *Fighting Faiths* at 225 (cited in note 7). For a particularly thoughtful account of the various factors that may have influenced Holmes in the months between *Debs* and *Abrams*, see Rabban, *Forgotten Years* at 350–55 (cited in note 96) (noting as possible factors in this transformation the excesses of the Red Scare; the arguments of Chafee, Hand, and Freud; his readings that summer of Harold Laski's *Authority in the Modern State* and James Ford Rhodes's *History of the Civil War*). For a different view, arguing that Holmes did not change his views at all between *Debs* and *Abrams*, see Novick, 1991 S Ct Rev 303 (cited in note 145).

[292] John H. Wigmore, *Abrams v. U. S.: Freedom of Speech and Freedom of Thuggery in War-Time and Peace-Time*, 14 Ill L Rev 539 (1920).

[293] Id at 545, 549–50.

[294] Id at 552, 559–60.

[295] Letter from Oliver Wendell Holmes to Sir Frederick Pollock, Apr 25, 1920, in Howe, ed, 2 *Holmes-Pollock Letters* at 42 (cited in note 274). Edward Corwin of Princeton also wrote a critical review of *Abrams*. Corwin argued that Holmes's primary concern was that under the prevailing view of the Espionage Act juries were being permitted to infer specific intent from the mere tendency of the speech. Corwin acknowledged that this was so; he maintained, however, that because juries were not *directed* to find intent based only on possible bad tendency, but were merely *permitted* to draw such an inference, this did not amount to the reinstitution of the law of seditious libel. In his view, because juries could convict only if they found specific intent beyond a reasonable doubt, there was no constitutional objection to the fact that they were not *prohibited* from doing so based only on bad tendency. See Edward S. Corwin, *Freedom of Speech and Press under the First Amendment: A Resume*, 30 Yale L J 48 (1920). See also James Parker Hall, *Free Speech in War Time*, 21 Colum L Rev 526 (1921).

[296] Karl Llewellyn, *Free Speech in Time of Peace*, 29 Yale L J 337, 341 (1920). Llewellyn observed that both Holmes and Hand had accurately stated the test of "common-law incitement to crime." That is, "words are made punishable" only if they "produce or are intended to produce *a clear and imminent danger*" of harm. He acknowledged that both Holmes and Hand had departed from the "test of criminality which was upheld time and again" during World War I, but criticized that test, which would allow speech to be restricted because of the "*tendency* of the words used, in the circumstances in

which they were used," but without regard to whether the "tendencies may be remote or immediate." He noted that "it is somewhat hard to see how the most law-abiding citizen can agitate against a law to effect its repeal, without using words that have some possible tendency to induce violation of that law. And if such tendency can be made criminal in time of war, it can be made criminal in time of peace. In the *law* in war-time and peace-time there is in this matter no difference." Id at 338–39.

[297] See Elena Kagan, *Private Speech, Public Purpose: The Role of Governmental Motive in First Amendment Doctrine*, 63 U Chi L Rev 413 (1996); Geoffrey R. Stone, *Content Regulation and the First Amendment*, 25 Wm & Mary L Rev 189 (1983).

[298] Kalven, *Worthy Tradition* at 146–47 (cited in note 201). As Professor Robert Cover put the point, Holmes's opinion in *Abrams* transformed "the phrase 'clear and present danger' from an apology for repression into a commitment" to free expression. Cover, 40 Md L Rev at 373 (cited in note 240).

[299] 251 US 466 (1920).

[300] Id at 477–78, 481.

[301] Id at 493–95 (Brandeis dissenting).

[302] 252 US 239 (1920).

[303] Id at 246–47, 251; id at 269 (Brandeis dissenting). One of the first prosecutions under the Espionage Act also involved the distribution of *The Price We Pay*. In *United States v. Baker*, 247 F 124 (D Md 1917), Judge Rose directed a verdict of "not guilty." Judge Rose explained, "Anyone has a perfect right to any opinion he may see fit to form" and "to that end he may make *any argument* that commends itself to his reason and judgment against the policy of any particular law, whether it be the law for selective draft or any other. And *he is not answerable for the wisdom of his arguments.* He could not very well be so answerable and put on trial even for the *good faith* of some of them. I am afraid if he could that most of the political orators in every campaign would be put on trial for the good faith of what they said about the other party." Rose added, "[S]o far as I can see it is principally a circular intended to get people to subscribe to some newspaper and to get recruits for the Socialist Party. *I do not think that we ought to attempt to prosecute people for that kind of thing.*" 247 F at 124, excerpted in Brief of Gilbert Roe, as Amicus Curiae, *Debs v. United States*, No 714, *8–9 (filed Oct 1918) (available in Philip B. Kurland and Gerhard Casper, eds, 19 *Landmark Briefs and Arguments of the Supreme Court of the United States: Constitutional Law* 697, 709–10 [University Publications 1975]).

[304] 254 US 325 (1920).

[305] Id at 326–27, 333; id at 343 (Brandeis dissenting). Justice Holmes concurred in the result, but not in the opinion of the Court, because the First Amendment had not yet been held applicable to the states.

[306] Kalven, *Worthy Tradition* at 147 (cited in note 201).

[307] Id at 149.

[308] On several occasions, Attorney General Gregory attempted to limit the excessive zeal of his subordinates and members of the public; Assistant Attorney General O'Brian was "properly considered a sensitive civil libertarian in the context" of his times; and even George Creel sought to do his duty to the nation without violating the rights of

individuals. Murphy, *Origin of Civil Liberties* at 16 (cited in note 6).

309 As Professor Paul Murphy has observed, "[o]nce the spirit of intolerance was unleashed, . . . containing it was a difficult, if not impossible, task," and "careful distinctions between legitimate and illegitimate behavior quickly disappeared." Id at 72.

310 O'Brian, 42 Rep NY St Bar Assn at 277, 308 (cited in note 26).

311 Id at 308.

312 Id at 283, 213, 299, 306.

313 Id at 307–8; id at 308–9 n 15 (emphasis added).

314 Of course, in *Abrams*, Justice Holmes maintained that *Schenck*, *Frohwerk*, and *Debs* had been "rightly decided." 250 US at 627. The general consensus, however, is that Holmes's opinion in *Abrams* "belies" this claim. Rabban, *Forgotten Years* at 346 (cited in note 96). See Kalven, *Worthy Tradition* at 146 (cited in note 201); G. Edward White, *Justice Oliver Wendell Holmes: Law and the Inner Self* 414, 429 (Oxford 1993). Professor Sheldon Novick has offered a different hypothesis, based on his discovery of Justice Holmes's unpublished opinion in *Baltzer v. United States*. See Novick, 1991 Sup Ct Rev 303 (cited in note 145). Novick argues that Holmes's positions in all four of these decisions are premised on a consistent view of free speech and the common law. Although the discovery of Holmes's draft in *Baltzer* clearly suggests that Holmes was more attentive to First Amendment questions in the spring of 1919 than previously thought, I am nonetheless inclined to the view that he substantially changed his position in *Abrams*.

315 Brief for the United States, *Debs v. United States*, No 714, *72 (filed Oct 1918) (available in Kurland and Casper, eds, 19 *Landmark Briefs* at 677 [cited in note 303]). On the analogy to the Sedition Act of 1798, see Brief for the United States, *Frohwerk v. United States*, No 685, *22–23 (filed Oct 1918) (available in Kurland and Casper, eds, 19 *Landmark Briefs* at 535–36 [cited in note 303]); Brief for the United States in Reply to the Brief of Gilbert E. Roe, *Debs v. United States*, No 714, *8–9 (filed Oct 1918) (available in Kurland and Casper, eds, 19 *Landmark Briefs* at 763–64 [cited in note 303]).

316 Brief for the United States, *Debs v. United States* at *76–77 (cited in note 315) (quoting *Masses Publishing Co. v. Patten*, 246 F 24 [2d Cir 1917]).

317 Brief for the United States, *Schenck v. United States*, Nos 437 and 438, *12–13 (filed Oct 1917) (available in Philip B. Kurland and Gerhard Casper, eds, 18 *Landmark Briefs of the Supreme Court of the United States: Constitutional Law* 1037–38 [University Publications 1975]). Interestingly, Schenck also argued that this was the appropriate standard. Schenck's brief maintained that "the fair test of protection by the constitutional guarantee of free speech is whether an expression is made with sincere purpose to communicate honest opinion or belief, or whether it masks a primary intent to incite to forbidden action, or whether it does, in fact, incite to forbidden action." Brief of Charles T. Schenck and Elizabeth Baer, *Schenck v. United States*, Nos 437–38, *14–16 (filed Oct 1917) (available in Kurland and Casper, eds, 19 *Landmark Briefs* at 1002–4 [cited in note 303]). Schenck argued, however, that his circular did not meet this standard, because it was intended to persuade readers to sign a petition to repeal the Conscription Act, not to violate the law.

318 Brief for the United States, *Debs v. United States* at °75, 77 (cited in note 315). More-over, they point repeatedly to jury instructions in other cases in which the judge drew a clear distinction between specific intent and bad tendency.

319 In *Frohwerk*, the defendants failed to file a bill of exceptions. Thus, as O'Brian and Bettman noted in their brief to the Court, the "overruling of the demurrer to the evi-dence is not reviewable here." Accordingly, it was proper for the Court to assume that the evidence was sufficient to support the verdict. In such circumstances, O'Brian and Bettman argued persuasively that "the question raised under the First Amendment . . . therefore comes down to this—whether Congress has a constitutional power to provide punishment for deliberate attempts by means of publication of articles in a newspaper to interfere with the raising on an army and the faithful military service of those sub-ject thereto." They added that, in their view, "the constitutional guaranty of free press and speech . . . does not include the right to intentionally attempt to induce others to violate law, whether such attempts be couched in direct or indirect language," for "the right of the community to punish intentional incitement to violation of law is . . . well recognized." As in their briefs in *Schenck* and *Debs*, in *Frohwerk* they do not suggest that intent can be inferred from bad tendency. On the other hand, because the evi-dence is not properly before the Court, they do not discuss the evidence at trial that might otherwise have supported a finding of specific intent. This also explains the very cryptic nature of Justice Holmes's opinion on this question. Brief for the United States, *Frohwerk v. United States* at °11, 18–20 (cited in note 315).

320 For a somewhat different reading of these opinions, see Rabban, *Forgotten Years* at 285–93 (cited in note 96) (concluding that in these opinions Holmes "judged the intent requirement of the Espionage Act by the tendency of the words rather than through an effort to uncover the defendants' actual states of mind"). Although I had long shared this view, a closer reading of the briefs for the United States and the jury instructions has persuaded me that these opinions treat proof of intent as a separate and distinct requirement from proof of "bad tendency," although obviously the degree of probability that the speech will cause unlawful conduct is *relevant* to the question of intent. To the best of my knowledge, there is no definitive answer to this.

321 Beale, 16 Harv L Rev at 492 (cited in note 153).

322 Id at 501.

323 *Commonwealth v. Peaslee*, 177 Mass 267, 272, 59 NE 55, 56 (1901).

324 Chafee, *Free Speech* at 70 (cited in note 143). Chafee noted, "It is true that intention is material in other crimes, such as murder; but in dealing with an overt criminal act like killing the intention is evidenced by many other acts, which are a kind of fact with which the jurymen are familiar and capable of dealing. On the other hand, the inten-tion in making utterances is evidenced (1) by inferences drawn from the supposed bad tendency of the words themselves, and (2) by other utterances, which will also be viewed under the . . . test of bad tendency." Id at 61.

325 Brief of Gilbert E. Roe, as Amicus Curiae, *Debs v. United States* at °47–48 (cited in note 315).

326 Brief for the United States, in Reply to Brief of Gilbert E. Roe, as Amicus Curiae, *Debs v. United States*, No 714, °3–4 (filed Oct 1918) (available in Kurland and Casper, eds,

19 *Landmark Briefs* at 758–59 [cited in note 303]).

327 Id at 2.

328 Edward Corwin reached a conclusion similar to that of O'Brian and Bettman. See Corwin, 30 Yale L J 48 (cited in note 295).

329 Id at 530–31.

330 Id at 532 (emphasis added).

331 Id.

332 Id at 533.

333 Id at 534–35.

334 Id at 534.

335 Id at 535–36.

336 Id at 536.

337 See Murray, *Red Scare* at 9 (cited in note 191).

338 Alfred G. Gardiner, *Portraits and Portents* 13 (Harper 1926).

339 Murray, *Red Scare* at 36 (cited in note 191).

340 See Goldstein, *Political Repression* at 140–41 (cited in note 4).

341 *Bolshevism in the Northwest*, Cleveland Plain Dealer 4 (Feb 8, 1919); *The Seattle Soviet*, Chicago Tribune 6 (Feb 7, 1919); *Now Comes the Test of the Square Deal*, Seattle Star 1 (Feb 11, 1919). See Murray, *Red Scare* at 58–66 (cited in note 191).

342 *What Is Back of the Bombs?*, Literary Digest 9 (June 14, 1919); Washington Post (May 17, 1919). See Murray, *Red Scare* at 75–82 (cited in note 191); Paul D. Carrington, *Fearing Fear Itself: The Encounter of A. Mitchell Palmer with Louis F. Post*, 5 Green Bag 375, 378–79 (2002). The mutilation and hanging occurred in November 1919 in Centralia, Washington. See Murray, *Red Scare* at 181–89 (cited in note 191).

343 See *Senate Orders Reds Here Investigated*, New York Times 1 (Feb 5, 1919).

344 Murray, *Red Scare* at 97 (cited in note 191); New York Times 1 (Feb 12, 1919). See also *Radical Outrages Stir Washington; New Laws Needed*, id at 1 (May 3, 1919); *Palmer for Stringent Law*, id at 1 (Nov 16, 1919).

345 See *Assembly Approves Bolshevist Inquiry*, New York Times 8 (Mar 27, 1919).

346 *State Police in 3 Raids on Radicals*, New York Tribune 1 (June 22, 1919) (quoting Lusk).

347 See generally Goldstein, *Political Repression* at 147–48 (cited in note 4).

348 *The Irrepressible Conflict in Industry*, Literary Digest 11 (Nov 8, 1919) (quoting New York Tribune).

349 Letter from A. Mitchell Palmer to H. H. Hayhow, Feb 18, 1920, excerpted in Preston, *Aliens and Dissenters* at 193 (cited in note 80).

350 See Goldstein, *Political Repression* at 150 (cited in note 4).

351 Letter from FBI Director W. J. Flynn to All Special Agents and Employees, Aug 12, 1919, Exhibit No 5, in Investigation Activities of the Department of Justice, Sen Doc 153, 66th Cong, 1st Sess 30–34 (1919). Although the nativist hostility to "radical" aliens were especially virulent in this era, it is a long-standing theme of American history. See Lawrence, 21 Wayne L Rev 33 (cited in note 95).

352 New York World (Dec 23, 1919), excerpted in Louis F. Post, *The Deportations Delirium of Nineteen Twenty* (Kerr 1923); Portland Oregonian 10 (Dec 23, 1919), excerpted in Murray, *Red Scare* at 209 (cited in note 191). See also Goldstein, *Political Repression*

at 155 (cited in note 4).

353 Goldstein, *Political Repression* at 156–57 (cited in note 4).

354 *The Red Assassins*, Washington Post 26 (Jan 4, 1920).

355 Attorney General A. Mitchell Palmer on Charges Made against Department of Justice by Louis F. Post and Others, Hearings before the House Committee on Rules, 66th Cong, 2d Sess 27 (1920). See Murray, *Red Scare* at 219 (cited in note 191); Goldstein, *Political Repression* at 158 (cited in note 4). Mounds of fan mail poured into the offices of the Department of Justice, and the *New York Times* applauded Palmer's decisive actions. See New York Times (Jan 5, 1920).

356 See Murray, *Red Scare* at 231–35 (cited in note 191); Chafee, *Free Speech* at 159–68 (cited in note 143). The Supreme Court eventually considered the constitutionality of such legislation. See, for example, *Stromberg v. California*, 283 US 359 (1931) (invalidating California's red flag law because the law might be construed to prohibit "peaceful and orderly opposition to government by legal means"); *Whitney v. California*, 274 US 357 (1927) (upholding California's criminal syndicalism act); *Gitlow v. New York*, 268 US 652 (1925) (upholding New York's criminal anarchy statute).

357 Letter from Learned Hand to Oliver Wendell Holmes, Nov 25, 1919, excerpted in Gunther, *Learned Hand* at 348–49 (cited in note 110).

358 Murray, *Red Scare* at 237 (cited in note 191). The New York legislature voted to expel three of the five. The other two resigned rather than take the oath of office without their three colleagues. See id at 235–38.

359 263 F 110, 111–13 (D Montana 1920).

360 Palmer's proposal would have made it unlawful for any person to advocate or to justify the use of force as a means of changing any law of the United States. See Chafee, *Free Speech* at 168–70 (cited in note 143); Llewellyn, 29 Yale L J at 341–42 (cited in note 296).

361 See R. G. Brown et al, *To the American People: Report upon the Illegal Practices of the United States Department of Justice* (National Public Government League 1920).

362 Palmer on Charges Made against Department of Justice at 582 (cited in note 355).

363 *Colyer v. Skeffington*, 265 F 17, 44–47 (D Mass 1920).

364 For further discussion of the deportation saga, see Chafee, *Free Speech* at 196–240 (cited in note 143); Preston, *Aliens and Dissenters* at 181–207 (cited in note 80).

365 Christian Science Monitor 16 (June 25, 1920); Carrington, 5 Green Bag at 385 (cited in note 342).

366 Charles Evan Hughes, Address at Harvard Law School, June 21, 1920, excerpted in Chafee, *Free Speech* at 102 (cited in note 143).

367 See Lawrence, 21 Wayne L Rev at 33–43 (cited in note 95). See also John P. Roche, *The Quest for the Dream* (Macmillan 1963) (suggesting that wartime repression reflected an effort to Americanize a set of pluralistic communities through enforced patriotism).

368 See Harold M. Hyman, *To Try Men's Souls: Loyalty Tests in American History* 267–315 (California 1959) (recognizing the pressures placed on the Wilson administration by influential "superpatriots" to move against disloyalty).

369 Murphy, *Origin of Civil Liberties* at 252–53 (cited in note 6).

370 See Hyman, *To Try Men's Souls* at 267–315 (cited in note 368); Scheiber, *Wilson Administration* at 60 (cited in note 1) (Wilson's "abdication of personal responsibility left the fate of civil liberties to subordinate officials . . . at a time when few were inclined to be moderate"); Preston, *Aliens and Dissenters* at 128 (cited in note 80) (Wilson relied too often "on the opinions of the prosecuting officials—individuals not notorious for their objectivity in cases they have prepared").

371 According to the Department of Justice, many federal judges "imposed severe sentences as a means of fostering unity and bolstering morale." Scheiber, *Wilson Administration* at 43 n 7 (cited in note 1).

372 Kalven, *Worthy Tradition* at 147 (cited in note 201). See also Currie, *Constitution in the Supreme Court* at 127 (cited in note 240) (The Court's performance in these cases reflected "an extreme insensitivity to the values" of the First Amendment).

373 Letter from Alfred Bettman to Zechariah Chafee Jr., Sept 20, 1919, excerpted in Rabban, *Forgotten Years* at 327 (cited in note 96).

374 Letter from Alfred Bettman to Zechariah Chafee Jr., Oct 27, 1919, excerpted id at 328.

375 Letter from Alfred Bettman to Zechariah Chafee Jr., Sept 20, 1919, excerpted id.

376 *Do We Need More Sedition Laws? Testimony of Alfred Bettman and Swinburne Hale before the Committee on Rules of the House of Representatives* 4, 13–16 (Graphic 1920) (this is a reprinted copy of Bettman's statement before the Rules Committee of the House of Representatives on January 23, 1920).

377 Id at 4.

378 Id at 10 (quoting May, 2 Constitutional History ch 9).

379 See Rabban, *Forgotten Years* at 299 (cited in 96).

380 See John Dewey, *Conscription of Thought*, New Republic 128–30 (Sept 1, 1917); Henry F. May, *The End of American Innocence: A Study of the First Years of Our Own Time, 1912–1917* 373 (Knopf 1959); John C. Farrell, *John Dewey and World War I: Armageddon Tests a Liberal's Faith*, 9 Perspectives in Am Hist 299–340 (Harvard 1975).

381 John Dewey, *In Explanation of Our Lapse*, New Republic 13 (1917), reprinted in Jo Ann Boydston, ed, 10 *John Dewey: The Middle Works, 1899–1924* 292 (Southern Illinois 1980).

382 John Dewey, 2 *Characters and Events: Popular Essays in Social and Political Philosophy* 634 (Octagon 1970).

383 John Dewey and James H. Tufts, *Ethics* 401 (Holt 2d ed 1932).

384 John Dewey, *Liberalism and Civil Liberties*, in Jo Ann Boydston, ed, 2 *John Dewey: The Later Works, 1925–1953* 374 (Southern Illinois 1987).

385 See 66th Cong, 3d Sess, in 60 Cong Rec H 293–94 (Dec 13, 1920).

386 Max Lowenthal, *The Federal Bureau of Investigation* 298 (Sloane 1950).

387 See *March in Manacles, Plan of Radicals*, New York Times (Dec 16, 1919) (2,000 people marched in New York City in manacles to protest the imprisonment of "political prisoners").

388 *None Was a Spy—Profiteers Still Free*, Washington Times, reprinted in General Defense Committee, *Public Opinion: Where Does It Stand on the Question of Amnesty for Political Prisoners* 5–6 (1924).

389 See *Wilson Commutes Espionage Terms*, New York Times 9 (Mar 6, 1919); *Palmer*

Request Clemency for 52, id at 7 (Apr 12, 1919).

[390] Letter from Thomas Gregory to Woodrow Wilson, Mar 1, 1919, in Scheiber, *Wilson Administration* at 46 (cited in note 1).

[391] See *Wilson Refuses to Pardon Debs*, New York Times 1 (Feb 1, 1921). Debs was then sixty-five years old and in failing health. The *New York Times* applauded Wilson's decision. See *Debs*, id at 12 (Mar 26, 1921) ("Debs 'deserved ten years' imprisonment if any man ever deserved it. . . . This man tried to assassinate the United States Government").

[392] See *Nearing Attacks Holding Prisoners*, New York Times 18 (Feb 23, 1922) (the "joint amnesty committee" charged that the 112 individuals still in prison for Espionage Act violations were being held because of their efforts before the war "to attack the established industrial order"); *Urge House to Ask Pardons by Harding*, id at 4 (Mar 17, 1922) (in the face of "outspoken opposition," representatives of various "liberal organizations pleaded with the House Judiciary Committee" to ask the president to give "careful consideration to the propriety of giving immediate amnesty to 113 political prisoners serving long terms for violation of the Espionage Act"); *50 Congressmen Ask Harding for Amnesty*, id at 16 (Mar 22, 1922) (fifty congressmen from twenty-one states signed a petition asking President Harding to release all remaining prisoners convicted under the Espionage Act); *Convicts' Children Picket White House*, id at 20 (Apr 30, 1922) (a group of thirty-five women and children picketed the White House in support of amnesty for their still imprisoned husbands and fathers); *Clash with Parade of Amnesty Seekers*, id at 2 (Nov 12, 1922) (more than two hundred demonstrators carrying American flags marched on Armistice Day in Lafayette Square across from the White House in support of amnesty for the sixty-four remaining prisoners. When a small group of anti-amnesty protesters entered Lafayette Square carrying banners bearing such messages as "We Want Out, Too—Chicken Thieves Society," a ruckus broke out and the police had to restore order); *Wrangle in House on Amnesty Plea*, id at 23 (Dec 12, 1922) (a group of congressmen assailed other congressmen who had supported amnesty for individuals still imprisoned under the Espionage Act).

[393] See *Coolidge Releases All War Offenders as Christmas Gift*, id at 1–2 (Dec 16, 1923).

[394] Id.

[395] See Jerold S. Auerbach, *The Depression Decade*, in Reitman, ed, *Pulse of Freedom* at 67–68 (cited in note 49).

[396] See Avrich, *Anarchist Portraits* at 214–28 (cited in note 7); Polenberg, *Fighting Faiths* (cited in note 7).

CHAPTER IV

[1] See Richard W. Steele, *Free Speech in the Good War* 9 (St. Martin's 1999).

[2] See Paul L. Murphy, *World War I and the Origin of Civil Liberties in the United States* 30, 272 (Norton 1979); Jerold S. Auerbach, *The Depression Decade*, in Alan Reitman, ed, *The Pulse of Freedom: American Liberties, 1920–1970s* 65 (Norton 1975). There

were occasional prosecutions for seditious speech in the state courts during this period. For example, Israel Lazar was convicted of violating the Pennsylvania sedition law. During the 1928 presidential campaign, Lazar made a soapbox speech in support of the Communist Party candidate for president in which he declared, "This government murdered Sacco and Vanzetti. This is a strike-breaking government. Let us teach our young workers in time of war to shoot down people who ordered us to shoot other people." He was sentenced to serve from two to four years in prison. See *Lazar Conviction Upheld*, New York Times 26 (Dec 27, 1931); *Sedition Term Is Upheld*, id at 3 (June 29, 1932). In Chicago, the Illinois sedition act was invoked against twenty-six defendants who were arrested in Grant Park during a Communist meeting. See *26 Accused of Sedition*, id at 10 (Sept 10, 1929). Such incidents were rare, however.

3 268 US 652 (1925).

4 274 US 357 (1927).

5 *Gitlow*, 268 US at 664–65 (emphasis added).

6 See Harry Kalven Jr., *A Worthy Tradition: Freedom of Speech in America* 158 (Harper and Row 1988).

7 *Whitney*, 274 US at 375 (Brandeis concurring).

8 Id at 376–77.

9 *Whitney*, 274 US at 371 (majority); id at 377 (concurrence).

10 See *Schenck v. United States*, 249 US 47 (1919); *Frohwerk v. United States*, 249 US 204 (1919); *Debs v. United States*, 249 US 211 (1919); *Abrams v. United States*, 250 US 616 (1919); *Pierce v. United States*, 252 US 239 (1920); *Schaefer v. United States*, 251 US 466 (1920); *Gilbert v. Minnesota*, 254 US 325 (1920); *Gitlow v. New York*, 268 US 652 (1952), and *Whitney v. California*, 274 US 357 (1927).

11 See, for example, *Fiske v. Kansas*, 274 US 380 (1927) (invalidating the conviction under the Kansas criminal syndicalism statute of a member of the IWW); *Stromberg v. California*, 283 US 359 (1931) (invalidating California's "red flag" law); *Near v. Minnesota*, 283 US 697 (1931) (invalidating an injunction against speech); *Grosjean v. American Press Co*, 297 US 233 (1936) (invalidating a tax on newspapers); *De Jonge v. Oregon*, 299 US 353 (1937) (invalidating the conviction under the Oregon criminal syndicalism statute of a member of the Communist Party); *Herndon v. Lowry*, 301 US 242 (1937) (invalidating the conviction under a slave insurrection statute of an organizer for the Communist Party); *Lovell v. Griffin*, 303 US 444 (1938) (invalidating a standardless licensing ordinance); *Hague v. CIO*, 307 US 496 (1939) (invalidating a municipal ordinance prohibiting all public meetings in streets and other public places without a permit); *Thornhill v. Alabama*, 310 US 88 (1940) (invalidating a statute prohibiting picketing); *Cantwell v. Connecticut*, 310 US 296, 300 (1940) (invalidating the conviction of a Jehovah's Witness for "inciting a breach of the peace" by attacking the Catholic religion).

12 See Frank R. Strong, *Fifty Years of "Clear and Present Danger": From* Schenck *to* Brandenburg—*and Beyond*, 1969 S Ct Rev 41.

13 *Cantwell*, 310 US at 310–11.

14 *Bridges v. California*, 314 US 252, 266 (1941).

15 *Liberty and Tolerance*, New York Times 20 (Apr 29, 1938) (quoting Grenville Clark in

a speech to the American Publishers Association).

[16] Henry Steele Commager, *To Secure the Blessings of Liberty*, New York Times Magazine (Apr 9, 1939).

[17] Department of Justice, *Annual Report of the Attorney General of the United States for the Year 1939* 2 (Government Printing Office 1939). This new unit of the Department of Justice prosecuted several cases involving conspiracies intended to deny to individuals the free exercise of their right to free speech and free press. See, for example, id at 63; Department of Justice, *Annual Report of the Attorney General of the United States for the Year 1940* 77 (Government Printing Office 1940); Department of Justice, *Annual Report of the Attorney General of the United States for the Year 1941* 98–99 (Government Printing Office 1941).

[18] Department of Justice Release, Feb 3, 1939, excerpted in Sidney Fine, *Frank Murphy: The Washington Years* 79 (Michigan 1984). For an overview of the new Civil Liberties Unit and its work under Attorney General Murphy, see id at 76–98.

[19] Charles Seymour, *How Free Can Speech Be in Time of War?*, New York Times Magazine 13 (Apr 12, 1942).

[20] See Sidney Fine, *Frank Murphy: The Detroit Years* 1–17, 12 (Michigan 1975).

[21] Letter from Frank Murphy to Mary Brennan Murphy, Jan 28, 1917, excerpted id at 35.

[22] Letters from Frank Murphy to Mary Brennan Murphy, Feb–Apr, 1917, excerpted id at 37.

[23] Letters from Frank Murphy to Mary Brennan Murphy, Oct 2 and Nov 14, 1919, excerpted id at 66–67.

[24] Fine, *Detroit Years* at 69 (cited in note 20).

[25] David Lilienthal, *Has the Negro the Right of Self-Defense?*, Nation 725 (Dec 23, 1925), excerpted id at 163. The retrial, also presided over by Murphy, resulted in an acquittal.

[26] Fine, *Detroit Years* at 396–97 (cited in note 20).

[27] Executive Order, Feb 23, 1934, and Cabinet Minutes, Sept 11, 1935, both excerpted in Sidney Fine, *Frank Murphy: The New Deal Years* 87–88 (Chicago 1979).

[28] Fine, *New Deal Years* at 229, 239 (cited in note 27). Interestingly, when all was said and done Roosevelt carried the state by a greater margin than Murphy.

[29] *The President's Statement*, New York Times 1 (Oct 26, 1938).

[30] See Eugene C. Gerhart, *America's Advocate: Robert H. Jackson* 28–30 (Bobbs-Merrill 1958).

[31] Robert H. Jackson, *Tribute to Country Lawyers: A Review of* I Can Go Home Again *by Arthur Gray Powell*, 30 ABA J 136 (Mar 1944), excerpted in Gerhart, *America's Advocate* at 46 (cited in note 30).

[32] Gerhart, *America's Advocate* at 54 (cited in note 30).

[33] Francis Biddle, *In Brief Authority* 108 (Doubleday 1962).

[34] Letter from Felix Frankfurter to Eugene C. Gerhard, Sept 27, 1955, excerpted in Gerhart, *America's Advocate* at 191 (cited in note 30).

[35] James L. Vallandigham, *A Life of Clement L. Vallandigham* 294 (Turnbull Bros 1872).

[36] Francis Biddle, *A Casual Past* 300 (Doubleday 1961).

[37] Id at 356–57, 360.

[38] Biddle, *In Brief Authority* at 80, 164, 234 (cited in note 33). See Francis Biddle, *The Fear*

of Freedom 54–69 (Doubleday 1951).

[39] Those who opposed this bill argued not only that it was unnecessary but also that, like the Espionage Act of 1917, it would be misused to punish "the honest peacetime expression of opinions . . . by decent American citizens." Hanson W. Baldwin, *"Disaffection" Bill Draws Opposition*, New York Times E12 (Aug 11, 1935). See Steele, *Good War* at 29 (cited in note 1).

[40] See *Fascism in America*, Life 6 (Mar 6, 1939); Leo P. Ribuffo, *The Old Christian Right: The Protestant Far Right from the Great Depression to the Cold War* 180, 182 (Temple 1983).

[41] *Waging War against the Whole American Democratic Heritage*, New Republic (Oct 6, 1941). See Ribuffo, *Old Christian Right* at 178–84 (cited in note 40); Geoffrey Perrett, *Days of Sadness, Years of Triumph: The American People, 1939–1945* 100 (Wisconsin 1985).

[42] 75th Cong, 1st Sess, 81 Cong Rec H 3289 (Apr 8, 1937). See Robert J. Goldstein, *Political Repression in Modern America: From 1870 to the Present* 240 (Schenkman 1978).

[43] 75th Cong, 3rd Sess, 83 Cong Rec H 7574–77, 7575 (May 26, 1938) (Representative Maverick).

[44] Id at 7583–86 (May 26, 1938). Congressman O'Connor, for example, urged Congress to "save this country . . . from this horde of radicals, this horde of Communists, before the hour becomes too late." Id at 7586.

[45] House Resolution 282, 75th Cong, 3rd Sess, 83 Cong Rec H 6562 (May 10, 1938). See August Raymond Ogden, *The Dies Committee: A Study of the Special House Committee for the Investigation of Un-American Activities, 1938–1943* 43–45 (Murray and Heister 1944).

[46] See Donald S. Strong, *Organized Anti-Semitism in America: The Rise of Group Prejudice during the Decade 1930–1940* 21–23 (American Council on Public Affairs 1941).

[47] Geoffrey S. Smith, *To Save a Nation: American Countersubversives, the New Deal, and the Coming of World War II* 94 (Basic 1973).

[48] Strong, *Organized Anti-Semitism* at 29 (cited in note 46).

[49] See id at 29–37.

[50] Goldstein, *Political Repression* at 241 (cited in note 42).

[51] Auerbach, *Depression Decade* at 72, 87 (cited in note 2); Goldstein, *Political Repression* at 242 (cited in note 42); Ogden, *Dies Committee* at 74–75, 79, 83 (cited in note 45); Paul L. Murphy, *The Constitution in Crisis Times: 1918–1969* 214 (Harper and Row 1972).

[52] See Goldstein, *Political Repression* at 243–44 (cited in note 42); Ogden, *Dies Committee* at 53–65 (cited in note 45). James Cagney objected to the committee's reports that Hollywood was filled with Communists as "so exaggerated they are ridiculous." *Dies Clears Four Accused as Reds*, New York Times 21 (Aug 21, 1940).

[53] Ogden, *Dies Committee* at 77 (cited in note 45).

[54] Fine, *New Deal Years* at 504 (cited in note 27).

[55] *Dies Asserts "Isms" Hurt All Industry*, New York Times 14 (Nov 26, 1940).

[56] *Poppycock*, Washington Post 10 (Aug 24, 1938); St. Louis Post-Dispatch (Aug 28, 1938). See Ogden, *Dies Committee* at 67–68 (cited in note 45).

[57] *Dies Urges Ickes to Quit Cabinet*, New York Times 3 (Nov 25, 1938) ("radical associates"); *Dies Selects "Team" of "Hate Purveyors*," id at 12 (Nov 14, 1938) ("purveyors of class hatred"); Felix Belair Jr., *Campaign Reports Please Roosevelt*, id at 1 (Nov 2, 1938) ("Ho-hum"). See Ogden, *Dies Committee* at 85–88, 91–93 (cited in note 45). Harold Ickes responded more directly, stating that Dies was the "outstanding zany of our political history." *Name-Calling Led by Ickes and Dies*, New York Times 1 (Nov 24, 1938).

[58] *Dies Calls Chicago Isms Power House*, New York Times 19 (Oct 5, 1939).

[59] Ogden, *Dies Committee* at 157–58 (cited in note 45).

[60] *President Assails Issue of "Red List*," New York Times 16 (Oct 28, 1939).

[61] Goldstein, *Political Repression* at 242 (cited in note 42).

[62] Ogden, *Dies Committee* at 213 (cited in note 45).

[63] Report of the Federal Bureau of Investigation, HR Doc No 833, 77th Cong, 2d Sess 3–4 (Sept 3, 1943).

[64] *Dies Names 19 in the Government as Members of Communist Group*, New York Times 22 (Sept 25, 1942). See Ogden, *Dies Committee* at 270–71 (cited in note 45).

[65] See Ogden, *Dies Committee* at 113, 183 (cited in note 45).

[66] *The Dies Committee*, New York Times 16 (Dec 16, 1939). The *New York Times* described the committee's report in 1940 (one of several reports produced by the committee) as "astonishingly able and balanced." *The Dies Committee*, id at 15 (Jan 5, 1940). See Investigation of Un-American Propaganda Activities in the United States, HR No 1476, 76th Cong, 3d Sess (Jan 3, 1940).

[67] Walter Lippmann, *The Dies Committee*, Washington Post 9 (Jan 11, 1940). See Ogden, *Dies Committee* at 180 (cited in note 45).

[68] Auerbach, *Depression Decade* at 82 (cited in note 2).

[69] Frank J. Donner, *The Age of Surveillance: The Aims and Methods of America's Political Intelligence System* 53–54 (Knopf 1980).

[70] See Richard Gid Powers, *Secrecy and Power: The Life of J. Edgar Hoover* 239 (Free 1987).

[71] Donner, *Age of Surveillance* at 55 (cited in note 69).

[72] Goldstein, *Political Repression* at 253 (cited in note 42). See Athan Theoharis, *Spying on Americans: Political Surveillance from Hoover to the Huston Plan* 65–71 (Temple 1978).

[73] Theoharis, *Spying on Americans* at 71 (cited in note 72); Donner, *Age of Surveillance* at 56 (cited in note 69) (quoting a memorandum written by Hoover on Oct 10, 1938).

[74] See Steele, *Good War* at 27–33 (cited in note 1); Murphy, *Crisis Times* at 213 (cited in note 51).

[75] Goldstein, *Political Repression* at 248 (cited in note 42); Theoharis, *Spying on Americans* at 40–44 (cited in note 72).

[76] Goldstein, *Political Repression* at 248 (cited in note 42).

[77] Hearings before the House Committee on Appropriations 304–5 (Nov 30, 1939), excerpted in Final Report of the Select Committee to Study Governmental Operations with Respect to Intelligence Activities, S Rep No 94-755, 94th Cong, 2d Sess 405, 407–8 (Apr 23, 1976).

78 76th Cong, 3d Sess, in 86 Cong Rec S 5642 (May 7, 1940).

79 Id at 5643.

80 Goldstein, *Political Repression* at 248 (cited in note 42); Theoharis, *Spying on Americans* at 40–44 (cited in note 72).

81 See Ogden, *Dies Committee* at 134 (cited in note 45); Auerbach, *Depression Decade* at 88 (cited in note 2).

82 Dies charged that state guidebooks produced by the Federal Writers Project were filled with "communist phraseology." Another member of the committee, Representative Joe Starnes, in questioning the degree of Communist infiltration of the Federal Theater Project, asked whether Christopher Marlowe was a Communist. See Ogden, *Dies Committee* at 48, 62–64, 90, 96 (cited in note 45); Goldstein, *Political Repression* at 243–44 (cited in note 42).

83 Hatch Act, Pub L No 252, 53 Stat 1147 (1939).

84 Goldstein, *Political Repression* at 243–44 (cited in note 42). In June 1940 the Civil Service Commission declared ineligible for federal employment any "member of the Communist Party, the German-American Bund, or any other Communist or Fascist organization." Id at 250. The Selective Service Law of 1940, which reinstituted the draft, provided that "whenever a vacancy is caused in the employment rolls of any business or industry by reasons of induction into the service of the U.S.," that such vacancies should not be filled "by any person who is a member of the Communist Party or the German-American Bund." By 1941, all appropriations bills had a standard provision prohibiting payments to any persons advocating or belonging to any organization advocating the overthrow of government. See Goldstein, *Political Repression* at 246 (cited in note 42); Zechariah Chafee Jr., *Free Speech in the United States* 461 (Harvard 1941).

85 Espionage Act of 1917, 40 Stat 217 (1917), codified at 50 USC § 31, reenacted as Pub L No 443, 54 Stat 79 (1940). See Chafee, *Free Speech* at 464, 466 (cited in note 84); Goldstein, *Political Repression* at 244 (cited in note 42).

86 Steele, *Good War* at 75–77 (cited in note 1).

87 See id at 74–75; Goldstein, *Political Repression* at 257–62 (cited in note 42).

88 Alien Registration Act ("Smith Act"), Pub L No 670, 54 Stat 670, 671 (1940). The act also made it a crime to attempt to commit, or to conspire to commit, any of the acts prohibited, or to be a member of any organization that advocates or teaches the prohibited doctrine. On October 17, 1940, Congress passed the Voorhis Act, which required the registration of all organizations that had as one of their purposes the overthrow of the government of the United States. See Goldstein, *Political Repression* at 245–46 (cited in note 42).

89 See Chafee, *Free Speech* at 463 (cited in note 84).

90 Id at 443. The ACLU described the legislation as "unprecedented," and as the first federal peacetime sedition act since the Sedition Act of 1798. *Curbs on Freedom by States Feared*, New York Times 8 (Jan 2, 1941).

91 76th Cong, 3d Sess, in 86 Cong Rec 9035 (June 22, 1940).

92 76th Cong, 1st Sess, in 84 Cong Rec 10452 (July 29, 1939).

93 Donner, *Age of Surveillance* at 61 (cited in note 69).

[94] See Robert H. Jackson, *That Man: An Insider's Portrait of Franklin D. Roosevelt* 59–74 (Oxford 2003); Leo P. Ribuffo, *United States v. McWilliams: The Roosevelt Administration and the Far Right*, in Michael R. Belknap, ed, *American Political Trials* 179, 181–82 (Greenwood 1994).

[95] Steele, *Good War* at 82 (cited in note 1).

[96] Powers, *Secrecy and Power* at 239 (cited in note 70).

[97] Robert Jackson observed that the Dies Committee "was one long headache" for the Department of Justice. Fine, *Washington Years* at 99 (cited in note 18).

[98] Steele, *Good War* at 38 (cited in note 1); Fine, *Washington Years* at 119 (cited in note 18).

[99] Fine, *Washington Years* at 116–18 (cited in note 18).

[100] Perrett, *Days of Sadness* at 89 (cited in note 41); Steele, *Good War* at 44–46 (cited in note 1).

[101] See Fine, *Washington Years* at 125–26 (cited in note 18).

[102] 76th Cong, 3d Sess in 86 Cong Rec 4347 (Apr 11, 1940); *Jackson Condemns Attack by Bridges*, New York Times 7 (Apr 15, 1940).

[103] 76th Cong, 3d Sess (Mar 4, 1940), in 86 Cong Rec S A1840 (Apr 3, 1940).

[104] See Murphy, *Crisis Times* at 224–25 (cited in note 51).

[105] Francis Biddle, *The Power of Democracy: It Can Meet All Conditions*, excerpted in Patrick Washburn, *A Question of Sedition: The Federal Government's Investigation of the Black Press during World War II* 51 (Oxford 1986).

[106] Cabell Phillips, *No Witch Hunts*, New York Times Magazine 8 (Sept 21, 1941).

[107] Steele, *Good War* at 121 (cited in note 1).

[108] Id at 110.

[109] Id at 129–31; Murphy, *Crisis Times* at 225 n 339 (cited in note 51).

[110] Biddle, *In Brief Authority* at 150–52, 233–51 (cited in note 33). See *Dunne v. United States*, 138 F2d 137 (8th Cir 1943).

[111] Biddle, *In Brief Authority* at 211 (cited in note 33).

[112] See id at 235.

[113] Steele, *Good War* at 148 (cited in note 1).

[114] Biddle, *In Brief Authority* at 235 (cited in note 33).

[115] *Sedition Cases Dropped*, New York Times 21 (Apr 18, 1941). See Biddle, *In Brief Authority* at 234–35 (cited in note 33); Murphy, *Crisis Times* at 225 (cited in note 51); Goldstein, *Political Repression* at 264 (cited in note 42).

[116] Biddle, *In Brief Authority* at 236 (cited in note 33).

[117] Steele, *Good War* at 143–44 (cited in note 1).

[118] Id at 144.

[119] Biddle, *In Brief Authority* at 237–38 (cited in note 33).

[120] Ribuffo, *McWilliams* at 198 (cited in note 94).

[121] Freda Kirchway, *Curb the Fascist Press!*, Nation (Mar 28, 1942); Steele, *Good War* at 151 (cited in note 1). See Perrett, *Days of Sadness* at 227 (cited in note 41).

[122] See William Dudley Pelley, *Seven Minutes in Eternity*, American Magazine (Mar 1929), excerpted in Strong, *Organized Anti-Semitism* at 41 (cited in note 46).

[123] See Suzanne G. Ledeboer, *The Man Who Would Be Hitler: William Dudley Pelley and the Silver Legion*, 65 (2) Cal Hist 126, 127–28 (June 1986); Ribuffo, *Old Christian Right* at 25–33 (cited in note 40).

[124] See Ribuffo, *Old Christian Right* at 43–48 (cited in note 40).

[125] See Pelley, *Seven Minutes in Eternity* at 42–43 (cited in note 122); Smith, *To Save a Nation* at 55 (cited in note 47).

[126] See Smith, *To Save a Nation* at 55 (cited in note 47); Strong, *Organized Anti-Semitism* at 44 (cited in note 46).

[127] See Strong, *Organized Anti-Semitism* at 43–47 (cited in note 46); Smith, *To Save a Nation* at 58 (cited in note 47); Ledeboer, 65 (2) Cal Hist at 129–30 (cited in note 123).

[128] See Ribuffo, *Old Christian Right* at 63–64 (cited in note 40).

[129] Smith, *To Save a Nation* at 203 n 32, 60 (cited note 47).

[130] David H. Bennett, *The Party of Fear: From Nativist Movements to the New Right in American History* 246 (North Carolina 1988).

[131] Approximately 25 percent of the Silver League's members were women, most were middle-class, most lived in rural communities in the Pacific West, and many were ex-Klansmen.

[132] See Johan Smertenko, *Hitlerism Comes to America*, Harper's 660–70 (Nov 1933); Harold Loeb and Selden Rodman, *American Fascists in Embryo*, New Republic 185–87 (Dec 27, 1933); Ella Winter, *California's Littler Hitlers*, New Republic 188–90 (Dec 27, 1933), all excerpted in Ledeboer, 65 (2) Cal Hist at 155 n 34 (cited in note 123).

[133] *Pelley Is Jailed in Indianapolis*, New York Times 7 (Apr 6, 1942).

[134] Smith, *To Save a Nation* at 62 (cited in note 47). See Ribuffo, *Old Christian Right* at 66 (cited in note 40).

[135] Ledeboer, 65 (2) Cal Hist at 133–34 (cited in note 123).

[136] Smith, *To Save a Nation* at 85 (cited in note 47).

[137] See Ledeboer, 65 (2) Cal Hist at 134 (cited in note 123).

[138] See Smith, *To Save a Nation* at 86 (cited in note 47).

[139] Other such groups included Art J. Smith's Khaki Shirts and Gerald Winrod's Defenders of the Christian Faith. See Bennett, *Party of Fear* at 244–45 (cited in note 130); Ribuffo, *Old Christian Right* at 81, 88, 119 (cited in note 40).

[140] Investigation of Un-American Propaganda Activities in the United States, HR Rep No 1476, 76th Cong, 3d Sess 18–21 (Jan 3, 1940).

[141] Biddle, *In Brief Authority* at 189 (cited in note 33). See Perrett, *Days of Sadness* at 61–63 (cited in note 41).

[142] Charles Beard, *Giddy Minds and Foreign Quarrels*, Harper's (Sept 1939). See Perrett, *Days of Sadness* at 120, 158–61 (cited in note 41). For an excellent discussion of Lindbergh during this period, see Smith, *To Save a Nation* at 158–81 (cited in note 47).

[143] Franklin D. Roosevelt, *The Time Calls for Courage and More Courage*, in Samuel I. Rosenman, ed, 10 *The Public Papers and Addresses of Franklin D. Roosevelt* 86–87 (Harper 1950). See Perrett, *Days of Sadness* at 94, 100 (cited in note 41).

[144] Smith, *To Save a Nation* at 172 (cited in note 47).

[145] *President Defines Lindbergh's Niche*, New York Times 5 (Apr 26, 1941); Frank L. Kluckhohn, *Greenland Alarm*, New York Times 1 (Apr 26, 1941) ("He Likens Lindbergh to Civil War Copperhead"). In a June 24, 1938 "fireside chat," FDR expressly aligned himself with Abraham Lincoln and described his congressional critics as "Copperheads." See Jackson, *That Man* at 257 n 8 (cited in note 94).

[146] Ribuffo, *Old Christian Right* at 77 (cited in note 40); Smith, *To Save a Nation* at 141 (cited in note 47).

[147] William Dudley Pelley, *The Doughboy Blues*, Liberation (Sept 14, 1939), excerpted in Smith, *To Save a Nation* at 141 (cited in note 47).

[148] Ribuffo, *Old Christian Right* at 77 (cited in note 40).

[149] See id at 74.

[150] See Margaret A. Blanchard, *Revolutionary Sparks: Freedom of Expression in Modern America* 218 (Oxford 1992).

[151] *United States v. Pelley*, 132 F2d 170, 172–74 n 1, 175 n 2 (7th Cir 1942).

[152] See Charles A. Lindbergh, *The Wartime Journals of Charles A. Lindbergh* 683–89 (Harcourt Brace 1970).

[153] See Ribuffo, *Old Christian Right* at 78–79 (cited in note 40).

[154] *Pelley*, 132 F2d at 176–77, 179.

[155] See Ledeboer, 65 (2) Cal Hist at 136 (cited in note 123); Steele, *Good War* at 206–8 (cited in note 1). Pelley died on July 1, 1965, in Noblesville, Indiana.

[156] See chapter 1.

[157] *Abrams v. United States*, 250 US 616, 630 (1919).

[158] See chapter 3.

[159] In contemporary First Amendment jurisprudence, the Supreme Court has held that procedural rules should generally be framed to err on the side of First Amendment freedoms. See, for example, *Gooding v. Wilson*, 405 US 518 (1972) (overbreadth); *Smith v. Goguen*, 415 US 566 (1974) (vagueness); *New York Times v. Sullivan*, 376 US 254 (1964) (reckless disregard). In litigation over allegedly false statements of fact, the Court has held that the First Amendment requires the prosecution or civil plaintiff to bear the burden of proving falsity. See *Philadelphia Newspapers, Inc. v. Hepps*, 475 US 767 (1986).

[160] 8 *Annals of Congress* 2109–10, 2162 (Gales and Seaton 1851).

[161] Even the court of appeals seemed uneasy about this, noting that the government had "attempted" to prove these statements false, "apparently to the jury's satisfaction." *Pelley*, 132 F2d at 176.

[162] John J. Mearsheimer, *The Tragedy of Great Power Politics* 222–24 (Norton 2001). A similar phenomenon was evident during World War I, when courts often found "false" statements about the causes of the war that historians later endorsed. See, for example, *Pierce v. United States*, 252 US 239 (1920) (discussed in chapter 3); O. A. Hilton, *Public Opinion and Civil Liberties in Wartime, 1917–1919*, 28 Southwestern Soc Sci Q 201, 217 (1947) (citing cases during World War I in which courts held that statements attributing the American participation in the war to "economic or capitalistic factors" were "false").

[163] See, for example, *Stromberg v. California*, 283 US 359 (1931); *Herndon v. Lowry*, 301

US 242 (1937); *Bridges v. California*, 314 US 252 (1941).

[164] *Pelley*, 132 F2d, at 172, 176.

[165] 376 US 254 (1964).

[166] Id at 271–72 (citations omitted). The Court added that unless some account is taken of these realities, "critics of official conduct" will be "deterred from voicing their criticism, even though it is believed to be true and even though it is in fact true, because of doubt whether it can be proved in court or fear of the expense of having to do so." This will "dampen . . . the vigor" and limit "the variety of public debate." Id at 279.

[167] Id at 280.

[168] *Pelley*, 132 F2d at 177–78.

[169] Justice Brandeis argued for precisely this approach in his dissenting opinion in *Schaefer v. United States*, 251 US 466 (1920), in which the Court upheld a conviction during World War I under the "false statement" provision of the Espionage Act of 1917. Brandeis argued that even if speech is false it may not be punished unless it creates a clear and present danger. Id at 481.

[170] 315 US 568 (1942).

[171] Id at 571–72.

[172] See Cass R. Sunstein, *Pornography and the First Amendment*, 1986 Duke L J 589, 603–4.

[173] *Gertz v. Robert Welch, Inc*, 418 US 323, 340 (1974). Of course, one might argue that false statements of fact serve a positive function in that they trigger true statements and thus lead to a better understanding of the truth. But this sort of incidental beneficial effect does not count. By the same reasoning, there is positive value in the assassination of the president because it encourages better Secret Service protection in the future.

[174] Criminal prosecution for defamation of an individual is constitutionally permissible. See *Garrison v. Louisiana*, 379 US 64 (1964).

[175] This final twist highlights an additional concern in Pelley's prosecution: If we distinguished between criminal prosecutions of false statements that libel a public official and false statements that libel the government, how would we characterize Pelley's statements? Should those that refer to Roosevelt be subject to criminal prosecution even if the others are not? See *New York Times v. Sullivan*, 376 US 254, 291 (1964) ("[N]o court of last resort in this country has ever held . . . that prosecutions for libel on government have any place in the American system of jurisprudence").

[176] *Pelley*, 132 F2d at 172.

[177] Steele, *Good War* at 211–15 (cited in note 1); Ribuffo, *Old Christian Right* at 194–95 (cited in note 40). The ACLU divided on the case, with some directors believing that the prosecution was justified because some of the defendants "were cooperating with or acting on behalf of" the enemy. Ribuffo, *McWilliams* at 184 (cited in note 94).

[178] See Ribuffo, *McWilliams* at 183–84 (cited in note 94).

[179] Maximilian St. George and Lawrence Dennis, *A Trial on Trial: The Great Sedition Trial of 1944* 441–43 (National Civil Rights Committee 1946) (Government Exhibit no. 4295). Another example of their public statements is Government Exhibit no. 4348, an extract from the *Weckruf* of January 16, 1941, entitled "The Story behind the

Dies Committee":

The White House saw the possible utility of the Committee for warmongering purposes. It could provide war hysteria and smear isolationists. The purpose of the . . . smear tactics is purely to intimidate American or native isolationists. . . . The technique of the Dies smear is to identify opposition to American entry into the war with activities of German agents too terrible to particularize. German agents, good Germans and German sympathizers are guilty of the twin crimes of being German and opposing American entry into the war. Any American who opposes American entry into war is a fellow conspirator and a criminal. . . . The big idea is to damn, persecute or punish people for offenses which are not punishable under statutory laws.

Id at 441. Other statements of the defendants described Roosevelt as "a warmonger, liar, unscrupulous, and a pawn of the Jews, Communists and Plutocrats" and charged that the laws of the United States were "illegal, corrupt, traitorous and in direct violation of the Constitution." Id at 119.

180 See Lewis Wood, *28 Are Indicted on Sedition Charge*, New York Times 1 (July 24, 1942). According to the indictment, the defendants used various organizations to implement their conspiracy, including the Ku Klux Klan, the Black Legion, the America First Committee, the German-American Bund, and the National Committee to Keep America out of War. See id.

181 James Wechsler, *Sedition and Circuses*, Nation 530–31 (May 6, 1944), excerpted in Ribuffo, *Old Christian Right* at 199 (cited in note 40).

182 Goldstein, *Political Repression* at 268–69 (cited in note 42); Biddle, *In Brief Authority* at 239, 242 (cited in note 33). See also Ribuffo, *Old Christian Right* at 80–178 (cited in note 40).

183 Biddle, *In Brief Authority* at 241–42 (cited in note 33); Goldstein, *Political Repression* at 269 (cited in note 42); Perrett, *Days of Sadness* at 361–62 (cited in note 41).

184 Steele, *Good War* at 220–24, 195, 219 (cited in note 1). Interestingly, Rogge later represented several Communist defendants in Smith Act prosecutions during the Cold War. See Ribuffo, *McWilliams* at 199 (cited in note 94).

185 St. George and Dennis, *Trial on Trial* at 288–89 (cited in note 179).

186 Steele, *Good War* at 224 (cited in note 1).

187 Biddle, *In Brief Authority* at 243 (cited in note 33).

188 Preston, *Shadows of War and Fear* at 114 (cited in note 113). For an excellent account of the case, see Ribuffo, *Old Christian Right* at 193–215 (cited in note 40).

189 Smith, *To Save a Nation* at 12–13 (cited in note 47).

190 Bennett, *Party of Fear* at 254 (cited in note 130).

191 Fine, *New Deal Years* at 219–22 (cited in note 27). In Murphy's 1936 bid for reelection as governor of Michigan, Coughlin supported his opponent. See id at 248.

192 See Bennett, *Party of Fear* at 255–63 (cited in note 130).

193 See *WMCA Contradicts Coughlin on Jews*, New York Times 7 (Nov 21 1938); *Coughlin Defends Address on Jews*, id at 1 (Nov 28, 1938).

[194] See Strong, *Organized Anti-Semitism* at 59–63 (cited in note 46).

[195] See Smith, *To Save a Nation* at 129 (cited in note 47).

[196] FDR was responding, in part, to the fact that for several months the government had been "bombarded with requests 'to do something about *Social Justice*.' " Lewis Wood, *Attack on "Axis-Line" Press*, New York Times E7 (Apr 19, 1942).

[197] *Mailing Ban Put on Social Justice*, New York Times 1 (Apr 15, 1942). According to Lewis Wood, "[b]ecause of its prominence, *Social Justice* was singled out as the keystone in the arch of publications the government wants to demolish." "Drives against others," he reported, "will begin next week and be carried on continuously." Wood, *Attack on "Axis-Line" Press* at E7 (cited in note 196).

[198] See Biddle, *In Brief Authority* at 245 (cited in note 33).

[199] Id at 245–48.

[200] See Goldstein, *Political Repression* at 255–58 (cited in note 42).

[201] Id at 258–59. See Smith, *To Save a Nation* at 153–54 (cited in note 47).

[202] Biddle, *In Brief Authority* at 111 (cited in note 33).

[203] Harold M. Hyman, *To Try Men's Souls: Loyalty Tests in American History* 327–28 (California 1959).

[204] Frederick R. Barkley, *Crime Parley Puts Spy Issue up to FBI*, New York Times 2 (Aug 7, 1940). Much of the conference was devoted to ensuring that the FBI had primary control over the investigation of espionage and sabotage.

[205] The Supreme Court helped in this effort as well. See *Hines v. Davidowitz*, 312 US 52 (1941) (invalidating a Pennsylvania statute requiring aliens to register because federal law had preempted state action in this area).

[206] Biddle, *In Brief Authority* at 111–12 (cited in note 33).

[207] Goldstein, *Political Repression* at 264 (cited in note 42).

[208] Powers, *Secrecy and Power* at 253–55 (cited in note 70).

[209] See Perrett, *Days of Sadness* at 91–92 (cited in note 41); *Curbs on Freedom by States Feared*, New York Times at 8 (cited in note 90) (citing an ACLU report that from May through December 1940, more than 1,600 Jehovah's Witnesses were "forcibly interfered with, mobbed, tarred and feathered, or assaulted, with comparatively little restraint by local authorities"). See Blanchard, *Revolutionary Sparks* at 194–202 (cited in note 150).

[210] See Goldstein, *Political Repression* at 282–83 (cited in note 42).

[211] Elmer David, *Report to the President*, in Ronald T. Farrar, ed, 7 *Journalism Monographs* 16 (Aug 1968), excerpted in Blanchard, *Revolutionary Sparks* at 218 (cited in note 150).

[212] Blanchard, *Revolutionary Sparks* at 225 (cited in note 150).

[213] An illustration is *Action in the North Atlantic*, starring Humphrey Bogart, which depicted the Soviets as heroic.

[214] See Blanchard, *Revolutionary Sparks* at 118–227 (cited in note 150).

[215] 320 US 118 (1943).

[216] See Section 15 of the Act of June 29, 1906, Pub L No 338, 34 Stat 596, 601 (1906); Nationality Act of 1940, Pub L No 853, 54 Stat 1158 § 338, 1158–59 (1940), codified

at 8 USC § 738.

[217] Department of Justice, *Annual Report of the Attorney General of the United States for the Year 1943* 11 (Government Printing Office 1943).

[218] *Naturalized Foes to Lose Citizenship*, New York Times 25 (Mar 26, 1942).

[219] Department of Justice, *1943 Annual Report* at 11 (cited in note 217). See Steele, *Good War* at 189–204 (cited in note 1).

[220] *Schneiderman*, 320 US at 141, 157–59.

[221] 322 US 665 (1944).

[222] Id at 674, 677.

[223] For a full discussion of the denaturalization cases, see Kalven, *Worthy Tradition* at 423–36 (cited in note 6). The Court also overturned the decision to deport the labor leader Harry Bridges, ruling in 1945 that there was no evidence showing that Bridges had any connection with any organization advocating illegal overthrow of the government, except in "wholly lawful activities." *Bridges v. Wixon*, 326 US 135, 143 (1945). For a decision upholding a denaturalization order, see *Knauer v. United States*, 328 US 654 (1946) (holding that the defendant had falsely sworn loyalty to the United States).

[224] 319 US 583 (1943).

[225] Id at 586, 590.

[226] 322 US 680 (1944).

[227] Id at 683, 689. See also *Keegan v. United States*, 325 US 478 (1945) (overturning the convictions of twenty-four members of the Bund who had been charged with advocating draft evasion); *Viereck v. United States*, 318 US 236 (1943) (overturning the conviction of a German propaganda agent).

[228] See Murphy, *Crisis Times* at 227 (cited in note 51); Kalven, *Worthy Tradition* at 185–87 (cited in note 6); Blanchard, *Revolutionary Sparks* at 205–6 (cited in note 150). The federal courts upheld several treason prosecutions of individuals who had served as paid propaganda agents for the enemy. See, for example, *Gillars v. United States*, 182 F2d 962 (DC Cir 1950) (German broadcaster); *D'Aquino v. United States*, 192 F2d 338 (9th Cir 1951) ("Tokyo Rose"). See Blanchard, *Revolutionary Sparks* at 207–9 (cited in note 150); Stanley I. Kutler, *The American Inquisition: Justice and Injustice in the Cold War* 3–32 (Hill and Wang 1982)

[229] 310 US 586 (1940).

[230] 319 US 624 (1943).

[231] Id at 642.

[232] Steele, *Good War* at 156–58 (cited in note 1).

[233] See Blanchard, *Revolutionary Sparks* at 228 (cited in note 150). One noteworthy failure of the Supreme Court was its refusal to review the *Pelley* and *Dunne* cases. *Pelley v. United States*, 318 US 764 (1942) (cert denied); *Dunne v. United States*, 320 US 790 (1943) (cert denied). On *Dunne*, see text at notes 109–10, supra. See also Kalven, *Worthy Tradition* at 629 n 8 (cited in note 6). Robert Goldstein, who is generally critical of the nation's response to free speech issues during World War II, gives high marks to the Supreme Court, noting that to the extent the nation did well in this era, the Supreme Court "bears a good deal of the responsibility." Goldstein, *Political Repression* at 280

(cited in note 42). His overall view, however, is that in terms of the "'ratio' of repression to dissent," there "was probably more repression during World War II in *relation* to the amount of dissent voiced, than in any period in American history." Id at 284.

234 *Johnson v. Eisentrager*, 339 US 763, 772–73 (1950).

235 Alien Registration Act ("Smith Act"), Pub L No 670, 54 Stat 670, 673–76 (1940). One goal of the act was to supplant a variety of arbitrary state and local alien registration requirements that were springing up around the nation. This was thus another example of the Roosevelt administration's effort to coordinate state and federal efforts and to prevent state and local government from running amuck, as they had during World War I. See Biddle, *In Brief Authority* at 107–12 (cited in note 33).

236 Department of Justice, *1941 Annual Report* at 237 (cited in note 17).

237 Jackson, *That Man* at 61–62 (cited in note 94).

238 Id at 8.

239 Biddle, *In Brief Authority* at 107, 110, 111 (cited in note 33). See generally id at 106–19.

240 Department of Justice, *1941 Annual Report* at 8 (cited in note 17).

241 Alien Enemies Act of 1798, 1 Stat 577.

242 Biddle, *In Brief Authority* at 207–8 (cited in note 33).

243 Statement of the President, Sept 6, 1939, excerpted in Final Report of the Select Committee to Study Governmental Operations with Respect to Intelligence Activities, S Rep No 94-755, 94th Cong, 2d Sess 404 (Apr 23, 1976).

244 Hearings before the House Committee on Appropriations 304–5 (Nov 30, 1939), excerpted id at 405, 407–8.

245 See Powers, *Secrecy and Power* at 233 (cited in note 70).

246 Id at 239.

247 Department of Justice, *1943 Annual Report* at 9 (cited in note 217).

248 Eric K. Yamamoto et al, *Race, Rights and Reparation: Law and the Japanese American Internment* 39 n* (Aspen 2001). These data were extrapolated from information about the individuals who were still being detained in February 1942. A total of 653 individuals of Italian nationality were detained in this process. See Department of Justice, *1943 Annual Report* at 10 (cited in note 217).

249 Department of Justice, *Annual Report of the Attorney General of the United States for the Year 1942* 14 (Government Printing Office 1942).

250 Id.

251 Department of Justice, *Annual Report of the Attorney General of the United States for the Year 1944* 6 (Government Printing Office 1944).

252 Department of Justice, *1942 Annual Report* at 15 (cited in note 249); Department of Justice, *1943 Annual Report* at 10 (cited in note 217). This does not include the 228 Italian nationals who were still being detained as dangerous to the national security. Department of Justice, *1942 Annual Report* at 15 n 4 (cited in note 249).

253 See Ronald Takaki, *Double Victory: A Multicultural History of America in World War II* 131–32 (Little, Brown 2000).

254 3 CFR EO 9066 (1942). On March 21, 1942, Congress implicitly ratified the executive order by providing that violation of the order of a military commander was unlawful. Act of June 25, 1948, Pub L No 772, 62 Stat 683, 765, codified at 18 USC § 1383

(1974) (repealed by Pub L No 94-412, 90 Stat 1258 [1976]).

[255] See Commission on Wartime Relocation and Internment of Civilians, *Personal Justice Denied* 3 (1983). Anyone who was one-sixteenth Japanese was interned. See Perrett, *Days of Sadness* at 225 (cited in note 41).

[256] See *Terrace v. Thompson*, 266 US 197 (1923) (upholding Washington Alien Land Law); *Porterfield v. Webb*, 266 US 225 (1923) (upholding California Alien Land Law); *Ozawa v. United States*, 260 US 178 (1922) (upholding policy making Japanese immigrants ineligible for naturalized citizenship). In defense of the Alien Land laws, Attorney General Ulysses S. Webb argued to the Supreme Court in *Frick v. Webb*, 266 US 326, 330 (1923), "It was the purpose of those who understood the situation to prohibit the enjoyment or possession of, or dominion over, the agricultural lands of the State by aliens ineligible to citizenship,—in a practical way to prevent ruinous competition by the Oriental farmer against the American farmer." See Yamamoto et al, *Race, Rights and Reparation* at 57–90 (cited in note 248); Dudley O. McGovney, *The Anti-Japanese Land Laws of California and Ten Other States*, 35 Calif L Rev 7, 49 (1947); Roger Daniels, *Concentration Camps, North America: Japanese in the United States and Canada during World War II* 27–90 (Krieger 1981); Peter Irons, *Justice at War* 9–13 (Oxford 1983).

[257] Roosevelt had been raised in this climate, and although he was an advocate for peace between Japan and the United States, he supported most of the measures that were directed against people of Japanese descent, never overcoming his essential distrust of the Japanese "race." See Greg Robinson, *By Order of the President: FDR and the Internment of Japanese Americans* 8–53 (Harvard 2001).

[258] Id at 54.

[259] Id at 55–57. Years earlier, when Franklin Roosevelt was secretary of the navy, he wrote a memorandum observing, "One obvious thought occurs to me—that every Japanese citizen or non-citizen on the Island of Oahu who meets these Japanese ships or has any connection with their officers or men should be secretly but definitely identified and his or her name placed on a special list of those who would be the first to be placed in a concentration camp in the event of trouble." Memorandum for Chief of Naval Operations, PSF 197 (Japan), excerpted id at 55–56.

[260] Robinson, *By Order of the President* at 61 (cited in note 257).

[261] FBI Memorandum, Nov 15, 1940, excerpted id at 62.

[262] Yamamoto et al, *Race, Rights and Reparation* at 96 (cited in note 248). See Robinson, *By Order of the President* at 64–65 (cited in note 257).

[263] See Yamamoto et al, *Race, Rights and Reparation* at 96–97 (cited in note 248).

[264] Id at 97; Robinson, *By Order of the President* at 65–67 (cited in note 257). It is not known whether FDR ever read the entire report, or whether he just read a summary prepared by John Franklin Carter. If the latter, Carter's summary was misleading in that it "minimized and distorted Munson's endorsement of community loyalty." Id at 69.

[265] Ted Lyons, *Lancer's Column*, Rafu Shimpo 3 (Dec 7, 1941), excerpted in Robinson, *By Order of the President* at 71 (cited in note 257); Jerome Frank, *Red-White-and-Blue Herring*, Satevepost (Dec 6, 1941), excerpted in Perrett, *Days of Sadness* at 217 (cited in note 41).

[266] Department of Justice, *1942 Annual Report* at 14 (cited in note 249).

[267] 77th Cong, 1st Sess, 87 Cong Rec H A5554 (Dec 8, 1941); Commission on Wartime Relocation, *Personal Justice Denied* at 48 (cited in note 255).

[268] Commission on Wartime Relocation, *Personal Justice Denied* at 257 (cited in note 255).

[269] See Yamamoto et al, *Race, Rights and Reparation* at 97 (cited in note 248).

[270] See Biddle, *In Brief Authority* at 214 (cited in note 33); Robinson, *By Order of the President* at 89 (cited in note 257).

[271] See Irons, *Justice at War* at 26–27 (cited in note 256).

[272] Ed Cray, *Chief Justice: A Biography of Earl Warren* 115 (Simon and Schuster 1997).

[273] Yamamoto et al, *Race, Rights and Reparation* at 97–98 (cited in note 248); Robinson, *By Order of the President* at 84–85 (cited in note 257); Irons, *Justice at War* at 26–27, 280–84 (cited in note 256); Perrett, *Days of Sadness* at 216 (cited in note 41).

[274] See Robinson, *By Order of the President* at 77–78 (cited in note 257); Cray, *Chief Justice* at 115–17 (cited in note 272).

[275] Yamamoto et al, *Race, Rights and Reparation* at 98 (cited in note 248).

[276] Commission on Wartime Relocation, *Personal Justice Denied* at 67–68 (cited in note 255); Jacobus tenBroek, Edward N. Barnhart, and Floyd W. Matson, *Prejudice, War and the Constitution* 71–80 (California 1954).

[277] Cray, *Chief Justice* at 117 (cited in note 272); Irons, *Justice at War* at 38 (cited in note 256).

[278] San Francisco Examiner (Jan 29, 1942), excerpted in Yamamoto et al, *Race, Rights and Reparation* at 99 (cited in note 248).

[279] Cray, *Chief Justice* at 117 (cited in note 272).

[280] Id at 118, 121; Irons, *Justice at War* at 29–41 (cited in note 256).

[281] Yamamoto et al, *Race, Rights and Reparation* at 100 (cited in note 248). See Biddle, *In Brief Authority* at 215–16 (cited in note 33); Irons, *Justice at War* at 59 (cited in note 256) (quoting DeWitt's final report).

[282] Transcript of meeting in General DeWitt's office, Jan 4, 1942, and testimony before House Naval Affairs Subcommittee, Apr 13, 1943, excerpted in Commission on Wartime Relocation, *Personal Justice Denied* at 65–66 (cited in note 255); Yamamoto et al, *Race, Rights and Reparation* at 99 (cited in note 248); Fine, *Washington Years* at 437 (cited in note 18).

[283] Frank J. Taylor, *The People Nobody Wants*, Saturday Evening Post 24, 66 (May 9, 1942), excerpted in *Korematsu v. United States*, 323 US 214, 239 n 12 (1944) (Murphy dissenting). During January and February of 1942, Roosevelt was flooded with petitions and letters urging evacuation.

[284] Powers, *Secrecy and Power* at 249 (cited in note 70); Don Whitehead, *The FBI Story: A Report to the People* 188 (Random House 1956); Biddle, *In Brief Authority* at 215–17 (cited in note 33).

[285] Biddle, *In Brief Authority* at 215–17 (cited in note 33).

[286] Irons, *Justice at War* at 53 (cited in note 256).

[287] Biddle, *In Brief Authority* at 218–24 (cited in note 33).

[288] Id; Powers, *Secrecy and Power* at 249 (cited in note 70); Irons, *Justice at War* at 23, 28

(cited in note 256).

[289] Irons, *Justice at War* at 55–56 (cited in note 256).

[290] Walter Lippmann, *The Fifth Column on the Coast*, Washington Post 9 (Feb 12, 1942).

[291] Biddle, *In Brief Authority* at 217–18 (cited in note 33).

[292] Cray, *Chief Justice* at 120 (cited in note 272); Irons, *Justice at War* at 72 (cited in note 256).

[293] Cray, *Chief Justice* at 120 (cited in note 272).

[294] Irons, *Justice at War* at 61 (cited in note 256).

[295] Id at 62.

[296] Biddle, *In Brief Authority* at 219 (cited in note 33).

[297] For a detailed account of how this decision was reached in the White House, see Irons, *Justice at War* at 56–65 (cited in note 256).

[298] For a sharp critique of DeWitt's report, see Biddle, *In Brief Authority* at 221–23 (cited in note 33). See also Irons, *Justice at War* at 278–310 (cited in note 256).

[299] Robinson, *By Order of the President* at 109–10 (cited in note 257); Irons, *Justice at War* at 51–52 (cited in note 256); Stetson Conn, *The Army and Japanese Evacuation*, in Stetson Conn, Rose C. Engelman, and Byron Fairchild, *Guarding the United States and Its Outposts*, 12 (2) Western Hemisphere Subseries of *The United States Army in World War II* (Office of the Chief of Military History, Dept of the Army 1964), excerpted in Biddle, *In Brief Authority* at 222, 220 n 1 (cited in note 33).

[300] See Tetsuden Kashima, *Judgment without Trial: Japanese American Imprisonment during World War II* 67–87 (Washington 2003); Harry N. Scheiber and Jane L. Scheiber, *Constitutional Liberty in World War II: Army Rule and Martial Law in Hawaii, 1941–1946*, 3 Western Legal Hist 341, 344 (1990); Harry N. Scheiber and Jane L. Scheiber, *Bayonets in Paradise: A Half-Century Retrospective on Martial Law in Hawai'i, 1941–1946*, 19 U Hawaii L Rev 477, 481–82 (1997).

[301] In 1943, in a two-volume report on the relocation of Japanese Americans, J. Edgar Hoover again described the internment as "extremely unfortunate" and unnecessary. See Powers, *Secrecy and Power* at 250 (cited in note 70).

[302] Jackson, *That Man* at 59, 68, 74 (cited in note 94).

[303] See id at 59–74.

[304] Biddle, *In Brief Authority* at 219 (cited in note 33). James Rowe, who actually shepherded the executive order to Roosevelt's desk, recalled in 1981, "It's a terrible thing to say, but it was a minor problem with the President." Irons, *Justice at War* at 365 (cited in note 256).

[305] See Biddle, *In Brief Authority* at 214, 219, 223 (cited in note 33). Several years later, Stimson acknowledged that "to loyal citizens this forced evacuation was a personal injustice." Henry L. Stimson and McGeorge Bundy, *On Active Service in Peace and War* 406 (Harper 1948).

[306] See Dennis J. Hutchinson, *"The Achilles Heel" of the Constitution: Justice Jackson and the Japanese Exclusion Cases*, 2002 Sup Ct Rev 455. On the response of the ACLU, see Irons, *Justice at War* at 106–18, 128–38, 168–75, 186–92, 194–95, 254–55, 257–61, 267–68 (cited in note 256); Perrett, *Days of Sadness* at 223–24 (cited in note 41).

[307] Irons, *Justice at War* at 42 (cited in note 256).

[308] See Yamamoto et al, *Race, Rights and Reparation* at 90 (cited in note 248).

[309] Actually, Hirabayashi intended to challenge the exclusion order, but when he turned himself in to the FBI it discovered a diary in his briefcase that make clear he had violated the curfew order. See Irons, *Justice at War* at 89–92 (cited in note 256).

[310] 320 US 81 (1943). See also *Yasui v. United States*, 320 US 115 (1943) (also upholding the constitutionality of the curfew order).

[311] Fine, *Washington Years* at 438 (cited in note 18).

[312] *Hirabayashi*, 320 US at 93–95, 99–101 (internal citations omitted).

[313] Id at 109–11, 113.

[314] See Irons, *Justice at War* at 93–96 (cited in note 256).

[315] 323 US 214 (1944).

[316] Id at 218–20, 223–24 (internal citations omitted).

[317] Id at 226.

[318] Id at 244–46, 248. Interestingly, Justice Jackson's dissenting opinion in *Korematsu* was a revised version of a draft opinion he had written, but never circulated or published, in *Hirabayashi*. In the original draft, Jackson expressly recalled Lincoln's excesses during the Civil War, but he omitted those passages from his eventual dissenting opinion in *Korematsu*. See Hutchinson, 2002 Sup Ct Rev 445 (cited in note 306).

[319] Id at 233–35, 241–42 (internal citations omitted).

[320] 323 US 283 (1944).

[321] Id at 297, 300, 302, 304. In separate concurring opinions, Justices Murphy and Roberts attacked the Court for sidestepping what they regarded as the central issue in the case: whether it was constitutional for the United States to detain a loyal citizen who had committed no crime. Murphy and Roberts argued that this was plainly unconstitutional. For an interesting recent account of *Endo*, see Patrick O. Gudridge, *Remember Endo?*, 116 Harv L Rev 1933 (2003).

[322] Yamamoto et al, *Race, Rights and Reparation* at 174–75 (cited in note 248). See Irons, *Justice at War* at 344–45 (cited in note 256).

[323] Irons, *Justice at War* at 273–77 (cited in note 256).

[324] Evacuation Claims Act of 1948, Pub L No 886, 62 Stat 1231.

[325] Yamamoto et al, *Race, Rights and Reparation* at 240–41 (cited in note 248).

[326] See, for example, *Terrace v. Thompson*, 266 US 197 (1923) (upholding Washington Alien Land Law); *Porterfield v. Webb*, 266 US 225 (1923) (upholding California Alien Land Law); *Ozawa v. United States*, 260 US 178 (1922) (upholding policy making Japanese immigrants ineligible for naturalized citizenship).

[327] 334 US 410 (1948).

[328] Id at 420.

[329] 332 US 633 (1948).

[330] Id at 646.

[331] 327 US 304 (1946).

[332] See Irons, *Justice at War* at 72 (cited in note 256).

[333] Biddle, *In Brief Authority* at 212, 226 (cited in note 33).

[334] Wiley B. Rutledge to Harlan Fiske Stone, June 12, 1943, excerpted in Alpheus Thomas Mason, *Harlan Fiske Stone: Pillar of the Law* 676 (Viking 1956); Fowler V. Harper,

Justice Rutledge and the Bright Constellation 173 (Bobbs-Merrill 1965).

335 *Justice Black, Champion of Civil Liberties for 34 Years on the Court, Dies at 85,* New York Times 76 (Sept 26, 1971).

336 William O. Douglas, *The Autobiography of William O. Douglas: The Court Years, 1939–1975* 38–39, 279–80 (Random House 1980).

337 Earl Warren, *The Bill of Rights and the Military,* 37 NYU L Rev 181, 191–92 (1962).

338 Earl Warren, *The Memoirs of Earl Warren* 149 (Doubleday 1977).

339 See Cray, *Chief Justice* at 520 (cited in note 272).

340 See Biddle, *In Brief Authority* at 216–19 (cited in note 33); Irons, *Justice at War* at 119 (cited in note 256).

341 John D. Weaver, *Warren: The Man, the Court, the Era* 113 (Little, Brown 1967).

342 3 CFR Proc 4417, An American Promise, Feb 19, 1976.

343 Commission on Wartime Relocation, *Personal Justice Denied* at 5, 8 (cited in note 255).

344 A third petition was filed by Minoru Yasui, whose conviction for violating the curfew rules had also been upheld by the Supreme Court.

345 *Korematsu v. United States,* 584 F Supp 1406 (ND Cal 1984).

346 See Yamamoto et al, *Race, Rights and Reparation* at 293–330 (cited in note 248); Irons, *Justice at War* at 206–18 (cited in note 256); Peter Irons, *Fancy Dancing in the Marble Palace,* 3 Const Commen 35, 39–41 (1986). A draft of the United States's brief to the Supreme Court in *Korematsu* included a footnote that expressly conceded, "The recital in the Final Report of circumstances justifying the evacuation as a matter of military necessity . . . is in several respects, particularly with reference to the use of illegal radio transmitters and shore-to-ship signaling by persons of Japanese ancestry, in conflict with the views of this Department. We, therefore, do not ask the Court to take judicial notice of the recital of those facts contained in the Report." The War Department objected to this wording because it would reveal the misstatements in DeWitt's report and undermine the military case for internment. Over the objections of several officials in the Department of Justice, the War Department insisted on compromise language that obfuscated the issue and did not alert the Court to the inaccuracies in DeWitt's report. The final version of the footnote substituted the following language in place of the language of the draft quoted above: "We have specifically recited in this brief the facts relating to the justification for the evacuation, of which we ask the Court to take judicial notice, and we rely upon the Final Report only to the extent that it relates to such facts." 584 F Supp at 1417–18. See Yamamoto et al, *Race, Rights and Reparation* at 293–330 (cited in note 248); Irons, *Justice at War* at 206–18 (cited in note 256); Irons, 3 Const Commen at 39–41.

347 *Korematsu,* 584 F Supp at 1420.

348 *Hirabayashi v. United States,* 828 F2d 591 (9th Cir 1987).

349 See Irons, *Justice at War* at 206–18, 278–310 (cited in note 256).

350 *Hirabayashi,* 828 F2d at 598, 603–4.

351 Civil Liberties Act of 1988, Pub L No 100-383, 102 Stat 903, codified at 50 USC App § 1989(b) (1996).

352 Id at 903–4. On the stigma inflicted upon internees, see Kashima, *Judgment without*

Trial at 216–20 (cited in note 300).

[353] See Eugene V. Rostow, *The Japanese American Cases—A Disaster*, 54 Yale L J 489, 507, 520 (1945); Morton Grodzins, *Americans Betrayed: Politics and the Japanese Evacuation* (Chicago 1949); tenBroek, Barnhart, and Matson, *Prejudice, War and the Constitution* (cited in note 276); Roger Daniels, *The Politics of Prejudice: The Anti-Japanese Movement in California and the Struggle for Japanese Exclusion* (California 1962).

[354] Joel B. Grossman, *The Japanese American Cases and the Vagaries of Constitutional Adjudication in Wartime: An Institutional Perspective* 19 U Hawaii L Rev 649, 685 (1997).

[355] See Hutchinson, 2002 Sup Ct Rev at 485 n 99 (cited in note 306).

[356] Jackson advised the president that Murphy "would not be an appropriate appointment," because he was "not interested in legal problems," he had no curiosity about "the law as a philosophy" and he "was not a man of studious habits." Biddle regarded Murphy's appointment to the Supreme Court as a "bad appointment." Indeed, according to Biddle, "Murphy knew it, and everyone knew it." Murphy himself wanted to be secretary of war, a position Roosevelt could not give him, because he had "no administrative competence." To escape objections from Murphy to his nomination as a justice of the Supreme Court, the president publicly announced his appointment without telling him in advance. Biddle, *In Brief Authority* at 93 (cited in note 33). See Jackson, *That Man* at 24–25 (cited in note 94). Personally, Biddle had no use for Murphy, whom he described as a "windbag." According to Biddle, Murphy was "vain, self-conscious, and avid for publicity." He adds, "I have no idea why the President liked Frank Murphy, but he did. Frank had no humor, he preached at you, he must have been a bore as a companion. He was like a ham actor, beating his chest, stepping aside, throwing his head up, darting a piercing look. Perhaps all this amused the President." Although Murphy "saw always in values of black and white, knew no intervening shades, disentangled none of [the] complexities," Biddle admired his "unfaltering" support of "civil liberties and individual rights." Id at 307, 93–94. For Roosevelt's view of this appointment, see Fine, *Washington Years* at 132–37 (cited in note 18).

[357] Gerhart, *America's Advocate* at 183 (cited in note 30).

[358] 320 US 118, 157 (1943).

[359] 323 US 214, 233 (1944).

[360] *Remarks of Professor Paul A. Freund*, in *Robert Houghwout Jackson* 52 (1955), excerpted in Gerhart, *America's Advocate* at 302 (cited in note 30).

[361] 319 US 624 (1943).

[362] 323 US at 243.

[363] Jackson's commitment to free speech was not unflagging. See, for example, *Dennis v. United States*, 341 US 494 (1951) (upholding the convictions of leaders of the Communist Party under the Smith Act) (Jackson concurring); *Terminiello v. Chicago*, 337 US 1 (1949) (invalidating the prosecution of a fascist speaker) (Jackson dissenting).

[364] *Youngstown Sheet & Tube Co. v. Sawyer*, 343 US 579, 643–44 (1952). See James M. Marsh, *Robert H. Jackson*, in Clare Cushman, ed, *The Supreme Court Justices* 408–10

(Cong Quarterly 2d ed 1995).

365 Biddle, *In Brief Authority* at 194–95 (cited in note 33).

366 Id at 364–65, 432, 434, 483.

CHAPTER V

1 William M. Wiecek, *The Legal Foundations of Domestic Anticommunism: The Background of Dennis v. United States*, 2001 Sup Ct Rev 375, 417.

2 See id at 428–29.

3 Earl Mazo and Stephen Hess, *Nixon: A Political Portrait* 40 (Harper 1968); David Caute, *The Great Fear: The Anti-Communist Purge under Truman and Eisenhower* 26 (Simon and Schuster 1978); David M. Oshinsky, *Senator Joseph McCarthy and the American Labor Movement* 52–53 (Missouri 1976). See Robert Griffith, *The Politics of Fear: Joseph R. McCarthy and the Senate* 10–11 (Kentucky 1970); Thomas C. Reeves, *The Life and Times of Joe McCarthy* 100 (Stein and Day 1982); Robert J. Goldstein, *Political Repression in Modern America: 1870 to the Present* 295–96 (Schenkman 1978); Arthur Herman, *Joseph McCarthy: Reexamining the Life and Legacy of America's Most Hated Senator* 39 (Free 2000).

4 Caute, *Great Fear* at 15, 27–28 (cited in note 3); Alan D. Harper, *The Politics of Loyalty: The White House and the Communist Issue, 1946–1952* 76 (Greenwood 1969).

5 Subversive Activities Control Act of 1950, 64 Stat 987, codified at 50 USC § 671 .

6 Richard M. Fried, *Electoral Politics and McCarthyism: The 1950 Campaign*, in Robert Griffith and Athan Theoharis, eds, *The Specter: Original Essays on the Cold War and the Origins of McCarthyism* 192, 196 (New Viewpoints 1974). For a discussion of Smathers's smear campaign against Pepper, see Thomas G. Paterson, *The Dissent of Senator Claude Pepper*, in Thomas G. Paterson, ed, *Cold War Critics: Alternatives to American Foreign Policy in the Truman Years* 114 (Quadrangle 1971).

7 Caute, *Great Fear* at 429 (cited in note 3)

8 Communist Control Act of 1954, Pub L No 637, 68 Stat 775.

9 Irving Howe, *The Shame of U.S. Liberalism*, Dissent 308 (Autumn 1954).

10 See generally Ralph S. Brown, *Loyalty and Security: Employment Tests in the United States* (Yale 1958); Caute, *Great Fear* (cited in note 3); Frank J. Donner, *The Age of Surveillance: The Aims and Methods of America's Political Intelligence System* (Knopf 1980); Athan Theoharis, *Spying on Americans: Political Surveillance from Hoover to the Huston Plan* (Temple 1978).

11 See Alan Barth, *The Loyalty of Free Men* 9 (Viking 1952).

12 John Lord O'Brian, *Loyalty Tests and Guilt by Association*, 61 Harv L Rev 592, 607 (1948).

13 Fulton J. Sheen, *Communism and the Conscience of the West* iii (Garden City 1951)

14 Mary Ann Dzuback, *Robert M. Hutchins: Portrait of an Educator* 26 (Chicago 1991).

15 Letter from John H. Wigmore to James R. Angell, Apr 1, 1927, excerpted id at 54.

16 Harry S. Ashmore, *Unreasonable Truths: The Life of Robert Maynard Hutchins* 47 (Lit-

tle, Brown 1989).

[17] Frederick Rudolph, *The American College and University: A History* 349 (Vintage 1962).

[18] Ashmore, *Unreasonable Truths* at 77 (cited in note 16).

[19] William H. McNeill, *Hutchins' University: A Memoir of the University of Chicago, 1929–1950* 20 (Chicago 1991). Katharine Graham recalled that in the late 1930s it was a photo of the "young, handsome, dynamic" Hutchins that led her to enroll as a student in the University of Chicago. Katharine Graham, *Personal History* 80 (Knopf 1997).

[20] Edward Shils, *Robert Maynard Hutchins*, in Edward Shils, ed, *Remembering the University of Chicago: Teachers, Scientists, and Scholars* 185–86 (Chicago 1991).

[21] Ashmore, *Unreasonable Truths* at 113 (cited in note 16).

[22] Id at 114.

[23] *Midway Man*, Time 33, 38 (June 24, 1935).

[24] Robert Maynard Hutchins, Address to the American Association of University Professors, Nov 27, 1931, excerpted in Ashmore, *Unreasonable Truths* at 128–29 (cited in note 16).

[25] John W. Boyer, *Academic Freedom and the Modern University: The Experience of the University of Chicago*, University of Chicago Record 2, 5 (Dec 5, 2002).

[26] Ashmore, *Unreasonable Truths* at 129 (cited in note 16).

[27] Robert Hutchins, *The President's Report to the Alumni at the Midwinter Dinner*, University of Chicago Magazine 171–72 (Mar 1935).

[28] Letter from Charles Walgreen to Robert Maynard Hutchins, Apr 13, 1935, excerpted in McNeill, *Hutchins' University* at 63 (cited in note 19); Boyer, *Academic Freedom* at 7 (cited in note 25).

[29] Illinois House Joint Resolution No 21, reprinted in *The Great Investigation: An Account of the Investigation of the University of Chicago by the State Seditious Activity Investigation Committee in the Spring of 1949* 1 (All-Campus Committee Opposing the Broyles Bills and the Broyles Investigation 1949); Robert M. Hutchins, Radio Address, Apr 18, 1935, excerpted in McNeill, *Hutchins' University* at 65 (cited in note 19).

[30] Boyer, *Academic Freedom* at 7 (cited in note 25).

[31] Ashmore, *Unreasonable Truths* at 131 (cited in note 16).

[32] *Midway Man*, Time at 40 (cited in note 23). See Boyer, *Academic Freedom* at 8 (cited in note 25).

[33] Barth, *Loyalty of Free Men* at 20–24 (cited in note 11).

[34] In the 1924 presidential election, the Communist Party candidate received 33,361 votes; in 1928, 48,770 votes; in 1932, 102,991 votes; in 1936, 80,159 votes; and in 1940, 46,251 votes. In 1944, there was no Communist Party candidate for president, and in 1948 the party supported the Progressive Party candidate, Henry Wallace. See Barth, *Loyalty of Free Men* at 24–25 (cited in note 11); Caute, *Great Fear* at 185–86 (cited in note 3). The original two Communist parties in the United States fused into the CPUSA in 1923.

[35] Caute, *Great Fear* at 187 (cited in note 3).

[36] See Herman, *Joseph McCarthy* at 107 (cited in note 3).

[37] Eugene Lyons, *The Red Decade* 191 (Arlington House 1941), excerpted in Herman, *Joseph McCarthy* at 65 (cited in note 3).

[38] See Athan Theoharis, *Seeds of Repression: Harry S. Truman and the Roots of McCarthyism* 7 (Quadrangle 1971); Herman, *Joseph McCarthy* at 65 (cited in note 3).

[39] See Harvey Klehr, *The Heyday of American Communism: The Depression Decade* (Basic 1984); Joseph R. Starobin, *American Communism in Crisis, 1943–1957* 20–47 (Harvard 1972); Fraser M. Ottanelli, *The Communist Party of the United States: From the Depression to World War II* (Rutgers 1991); Reeves, *Joe McCarthy* at 206 (cited in note 3); Barth, *Loyalty of Free Men* at 33–34, 59–60 (cited in note 11).

[40] See Barth, *Loyalty of Free Men* at 28–31 (cited in note 11). For an excellent study of communism during this era, see generally Klehr, *Heyday of American Communism* (cited in note 39).

[41] Theoharis, *Seeds of Repression* at 7 (cited in note 38).

[42] James MacGregor Burns, *Roosevelt: The Soldier of Freedom* 416 (Harcourt Brace 1970). See Goldstein, *Political Repression* at 287–88 (cited in note 3); Richard M. Freeland, *The Truman Doctrine and the Origins of McCarthyism* 38–39 (Knopf 1972).

[43] See Theoharis, *Seeds of Repression* at 9, 29–30 (cited in note 38).

[44] Amendment of National Labor Relations Act, 49 Stat 449, codified at 29 USC §§ 155–66 (1947). See Goldstein, *Political Repression* at 290–91 (cited in note 3). On the Taft-Hartley Act generally, see Margaret A. Blanchard, *Revolutionary Sparks: Freedom of Expression in Modern America* 241–42 (Oxford 1992).

[45] See Goldstein, *Political Repression* at 291–92 (cited in note 3); David H. Bennett, *The Party of Fear: From Nativist Movements to the New Right in American History* 275–76 (North Carolina 1988).

[46] Bennett, *Party of Fear* at 274 (cited in note 45).

[47] Theoharis, *Seeds of Repression* at 57 (cited in note 38).

[48] See id at 57–58.

[49] Id at 41.

[50] Id at 55–56.

[51] Bennett, *Party of Fear* at 288 (cited in note 45).

[52] Goldstein, *Political Repression* at 292–93 (cited in note 3). See Griffith, *Politics of Fear* at 35–38, 98–99 (cited in note 3); Caute, *Great Fear* at 55–56 (cited in note 3). In the *Amerasia* case, the grand jury found in June 1950 that there was no evidence of official misconduct and that "the American people have been poorly served by the compounding of confusion through disclosures of half-truths [and] contradictory statements." Edward Razal, *Jurors Clear U.S. in Amerasia Case; Ask Further Study*, New York Times 1, 2 (June 16, 1950). See generally Harvey Klehr and Ronald Radosh, *The Amerasia Spy Case: Prelude to McCarthyism* (North Carolina 1996).

[53] Thomas I. Emerson and David M. Helfeld, *Loyalty among Government Employees*, 58 Yale L J 1, 17 (1948).

[54] Reeves, *Joe McCarthy* at 101 (cited in note 3). See Goldstein, *Political Repression* at 295 (cited in note 3); Oshinsky, *Senator Joseph McCarthy* at 52–53 (cited in note 3); Peter

H. Irons, *American Business and the Origins of McCarthyism: The Cold War Crusade of the United States Chamber of Commerce*, in Griffith and Theoharis, eds, *Specter* at 72–89 (cited in note 6).

55 Reeves, *Joe McCarthy* at 101 (cited in note 3). See generally Donald F. Crosby, *The Politics of Religion: American Catholics and the Anti-Communist Impulse*, in Griffith and Theoharis, eds, *Specter* at 18–38 (cited in note 6); Robert I. Gannon, *The Cardinal Spellman Story* 336–50 (Doubleday 1962); Eric F. Goldman, *The Crucial Decade: America, 1945–1955* 129–31 (Knopf 1956); Fulton J. Sheen, *Communism and the Conscience of the West* 48–158 (Bobbs-Merrill 1948); Bennett, *Party of Fear* at 287–88 (cited in note 45).

56 John D. Morris, *House Body Maps Exposing of Reds in Labor Unions, Schools, and Films*, New York Times 1 (Jan 23, 1947). See Robert K. Carr, *The House Committee on Un-American Activities* 37–38 (Cornell 1952); Goldstein, *Political Repression* at 296 (cited in note 3).

57 See Thomas G. Paterson, *Introduction: American Critics of the Cold War and Their Alternatives*, in Paterson, ed, *Cold War Critics* at 3–15 (cited in note 6); Goldstein, *Political Repression* at 297 (cited in note 3); Reeves, *Joe McCarthy* at 123 (cited in note 3). For a detailed discussion of Henry Wallace's stand on Truman's Cold War policies, see Ronald Radosh and Leonard P. Liggio, *Henry A. Wallace and the Open Door*, in Paterson, ed, *Cold War Critics* at 76–113 (cited in note 6) (arguing that Truman's portrayal of Wallace as "a naïve defender of Stalinist Russia" was deeply misleading and an "abuse of Wallace's ideas").

58 See George F. Kennan, *The Sources of Soviet Conduct*, Foreign Affairs 566, 582 (July 1947).

59 Theoharis, *Seeds of Repression* at 60 (cited in note 38).

60 Wiecek, 2001 Sup Ct Rev at 423 (cited in note 1). According to Richard Freeland, the basic approach of the Truman Doctrine was "to invert reality by imputing the urgency of a political crisis in the United States to the movement of events in the international sphere." Freeland, *Truman Doctrine* at 94 (cited in note 42).

61 See Robert J. Donovan, *Conflict and Crisis: The Presidency of Harry S Truman, 1945–1948* 293–98 (Norton 1977); Caute, *Great Fear* at 27 (cited in note 3).

62 Goldstein, *Political Repression* at 298–99 (cited in note 3). See Theoharis, *Seeds of Repression* at 103–4 (cited in note 38).

63 Executive Order No 9835, Prescribing Procedures for the Administration of an Employees Loyalty Program in the Executive Branch of the Government, 12 Fed Reg 1935 (Mar 21, 1947). See generally Brown, *Loyalty and Security* (cited in note 10); Goldstein, *Political Repression* at 299–302 (cited in note 3); Reeves, *Joe McCarthy* at 124–25 (cited in note 3). For historical background of the Federal Employee Program, see Freeland, *Truman Doctrine* at 117–20 (cited in note 42).

64 Henry Steele Commager, *Freedom and Order: A Commentary on the American Political Scene* 73–74 (Braziller 1966).

65 Harry S. Truman, 2 *Memoirs: Years of Trial and Hope* 272, 280 (Doubleday 1956). See also Eleanor Bontecou, *The Federal Loyalty-Security Program* at 30–33 (Cornell

1953).

[66] See Theoharis, *Seeds of Repression* at 106–7 (cited in note 38); Goldstein, *Political Repression* at 309 (cited in note 3).

[67] See Freeland, *Truman Doctrine* at 215–16 (cited in note 42); Goldstein, *Political Repression* at 310 (cited in note 3). For an extensive discussion of the attorney general's list, see Bontecou, *Federal Loyalty-Security Program* at 157–204 (cited in note 65). The list is reprinted id at 352–58.

[68] See Eric Bentley, *Thirty Years of Treason: Excerpts from Hearings before the House Committee on Un-American Activities 1938–1968* 110–244 (Viking 1971); Goldstein, *Political Repression* at 307–8 (cited in note 3); Caute, *Great Fear* at 487–520 (cited in note 3).

[69] On the deportation arrests, see Caute, *Great Fear* at 233–44 (cited in note 3); Freeland, *Truman Doctrine* at 294–98 (cited in note 42).

[70] See *Dennis v. United States*, 341 US 494 (1951).

[71] Reeves, *Joe McCarthy* at 212 (cited in note 3).

[72] Barton J. Bernstein and Allen J. Matusow, eds, *The Truman Administration: A Documentary History* 385–86 (Harper and Row 1966). See Harper, *Politics of Loyalty* at 71 (cited in note 4); Bennett, *Party of Fear* at 289–90 (cited in note 45); Griffith, *Politics of Fear* at 44–45 (cited in note 3).

[73] American Civil Liberties Union, *Annual Report 1942–1943* 3, excerpted in Goldstein, *Political Repression* at 312–14 (cited in note 3); Caute, *Great Fear* at 32 (cited in note 3).

[74] Alistair Cooke, *Witch-Hunting Contest*, Manchester Guardian 5 (May 31, 1948).

[75] See Goldstein, *Political Repression* at 312–14 (cited in note 3). On the influence of the Communists on the Progressives, see Caute, *Great Fear* at 32 (cited in note 3). For a discussion of prominent liberals who opposed Truman's Cold War policies and consequently faced political backlash and accusations of Communist sympathies, see generally Paterson, ed, *Cold War Critics* (cited in note 6) (discussing, among others, Henry Wallace, Claude Pepper, and Glen Taylor).

[76] See Theoharis, *Seeds of Repression* at 20–21 (cited in note 38).

[77] Goldstein, *Political Repression* at 316 (cited in note 3). See Harper, *Politics of Loyalty* at 72–76 (cited in note 4); Emerson and Helfeld, 58 Yale L J at 24–25 (cited in note 53). As David Caute has observed, Truman seemed not to notice the irony. After bragging that he had imposed upon the federal civil service the most stringent "loyalty program in the 'Free World,'" he then turned around and defended it against his "Republican critics as 'the most loyal' in the world." Caute, *Great Fear* at 33 (cited in note 3).

[78] Theoharis, *Seeds of Repression* at 133 (cited in note 38).

[79] Chambers explained that he had hidden the microfilm in the dumbwaiter of a relative's apartment in Brooklyn "as a lifesaver against potential Communist threats on his life." Caute, *Great Fear* at 60 (cited in note 3).

[80] See Bennett, *Party of Fear* at 290 (cited in note 45); Caute, *Great Fear* at 58–62 (cited in note 3); Goldstein, *Political Repression* at 316–17 (cited in note 3).

[81] Coplon was convicted of espionage. See Caute, *Great Fear* at 61–62 (cited in note 3). Coplon's conviction was overturned on appeal because of illegal FBI wiretapping.

See Goldstein, *Political Repression* at 317 (cited in note 3).

82 See Theoharis, *Seeds of Repression* at 106 (cited in note 38).

83 Bennett, *Party of Fear* at 291–92 (cited in note 45).

84 See Goldstein, *Political Repression* at 319 (cited in note 3); Allen J. Matusow, ed, *Joseph R. McCarthy* 8 (Prentice-Hall 1970). On Taft's criticisms of Truman's foreign policy, see Henry W. Berger, *Senator Robert A. Taft Dissents from Military Escalation*, in Paterson, ed, *Cold War Critics* at 167 (cited in note 6).

85 See Theoharis, *Seeds of Repression* at 98–99 (cited in note 38).

86 American Civil Liberties Union, *In the Shadow of Fear: American Liberties, 1948–1949* 3 (1949).

87 On the Hiss prosecution, see generally Alistair Cooke, *A Generation on Trial: U.S.A. v. Alger Hiss* (Knopf 1950); Allen Weinstein, *Perjury: The Hiss-Chambers Case* (Vintage 1978); Whittaker Chambers, *Witness* 539–784 (Random House 1952); Alger Hiss, *In the Court of Public Opinion* (Knopf 1957).

88 Reeves, *Joe McCarthy* at 221 (cited in note 3); Herman, *Joseph McCarthy* at 94 (cited in note 3).

89 Goldstein, *Political Repression* at 320 (cited in note 3). See Matusow, ed, *Joseph R. McCarthy* at 8–9 (cited in note 84); Walter Trohan, *Sees Struggle over "Liberty or Socialism,"* Chicago Tribune 1, 4 (Feb 7, 1950); *540,000 Reds in U.S., Hoover Tells Senators*, Chicago Tribune 3 (Feb 8, 1950); Reeves, *Joe McCarthy* at 221–22 (cited in note 3); Bennett, *Party of Fear* at 291–92 (cited in note 45). On the Rosenbergs, see Ronald Radosh and Joyce Milton, *The Rosenberg File: A Search for the Truth* (Holt, Reinhart and Winston 1983); Walter Schneir and Miriam Schneir, *Invitation to an Inquest* (Doubleday 1965); Robert Meeropol and Michael Meeropol, *We Are Your Sons* (Houghton Mifflin 1975).

90 Reeves, *Joe McCarthy* at 223–26 (cited in note 3). See also Griffith, *Politics of Fear* at 48–51 (cited in note 3); John W. Caughey, *McCarthyism Rampant*, in Alan Reitman, ed, *The Pulse of Freedom* 159 (Norton 1975).

91 The origins of McCarthy mysterious figures are traced in Griffith, *Politics of Fear* at 41–42, 49–51 (cited in note 3).

92 Reeves, *Joe McCarthy* at 230–33 (cited in note 3).

93 *Senate Inquiry Set on Acheson Staff*, New York Times 26 (Feb 26, 1950).

94 State Department Employee Loyalty Investigation, Hearings before a Subcommittee of the Committee on Foreign Relations Pursuant to S Res 231, 81st Cong, 2d Sess 11, 18, 31 (1950) (hereafter Tydings Committee Hearings); Reeves, *Joe McCarthy* at 251 (cited in note 3); Tydings Committee Hearings at 176–214. See also Reeves, *Joe McCarthy* 250–60 (cited in note 3); Griffith, *Politics of Fear* at 67–69 (cited in note 3).

95 State Department Employee Loyalty Investigations, Report of the Committee on Foreign Relations Pursuant to S Res 231, S Rep 2108, 81st Cong, 2d Sess 151–52, 167 (July 20, 1950).

96 Reeves, *Joe McCarthy* at 322 (cited in note 3). See id at 315–26.

97 William S. White, *Wherry Says Blood of G.I.'s in Korean War Is on Acheson*, New York Times 1 (Aug 17, 1950); William S. White, *Congress Votes Marshall Bill in Unusually Bitter Sessions*, New York Times 1 (Sept 16, 1950); Cabell Phillips, *The Truman*

Presidency: The History of a Triumphant Succession 374 (Penguin 1969). See Goldstein, *Political Repression* at 325 (cited in note 3); Griffith, *Politics of Fear* at 115–16 (cited in note 3).

[98] Internal Security Act of 1950, 64 Stat 987. See Stefan Kanfer, *A Journal of the Plague Years* 151 (Atheneum 1973); Goldstein, *Political Repression* at 359 (cited in note 3).

[99] Internal Security Act, 64 Stat at 987; Goldstein, *Political Repression* at 323 (cited in note 3). See id at 322–23; Griffith, *Politics of Fear* at 117–22 (cited in note 3).

[100] Veto Message from the President of the United States, 81st Cong, 2d Sess, in 96 Cong Rec H 15629–32 (Sept 22, 1950). See generally Theoharis, *Seeds of Repression* at 116–17, 120–21 (cited in note 38); William R. Tanner and Robert Griffith, *Legislative Politics and "McCarthyism": The Internal Security Act of 1950*, in Griffith and Theoharis, eds, *Specter* at 174–89 (cited in note 6); Milton R. Konvitz, *Expanding Liberties: Freedom's Gains in Postwar America* 140–41 (Viking 1966). For a critical view of Truman's unwillingness to "expend political capital . . . to protect individual liberties," see Athan Theoharis, *The Threat to Civil Liberties*, in Paterson, ed, *Cold War Critics* at 283–93 (cited in note 6).

[101] 81st Cong, 2d Sess, in 96 Cong Rec S 15736 (Sept 23, 1950) (Senate vote); 81st Cong, 2d Sess in 96 Cong Rec H 15632 (Sept 22, 1950) (House vote). On the Internal Security Act, see Blanchard, *Revolutionary Sparks* at 248–53 (cited in note 44).

[102] Goldstein, *Political Repression* at 325 (cited in note 3); Earl Mazo, *Richard Nixon: A Political and Personal Portrait* 78–79 (Harper 1959); David McCullough, *Truman* 814 (Simon and Schuster 1992); Reeves, *Joe McCarthy* at 332–34 (cited in note 3). See also Griffith, *Politics of Fear* at 122–23 (cited in note 3).

[103] Bennett, *Party of Fear* at 300 (cited in note 45). See also Reeves, *Joe McCarthy* at 315–46 (cited in note 3). The extent of McCarthy's actual political influence, as distinct from his perceived political influence, has often been questioned. See Griffith, *Politics of Fear* at 195, 239–42 (cited in note 3).

[104] Harry Truman, Address at a Dinner of the Federal Bar Association, Apr 24, 1950, in *Public Papers of the Presidents of the United States: Harry S. Truman, 1950* 267, 268, 271–72 (Government Printing Office 1965); *Senators Will Ask Bundenz to Identify Secret Communists*, New York Times 1 (Apr 16, 1950); Max Lowenthal, *The Federal Bureau of Investigation* 448, 450 (Sloane 1950).

[105] Griffith, *Politics of Fear* at 115 (cited in note 3).

[106] Truman, 2 *Memoirs* at 286 (cited in note 65).

[107] See Harper, *Politics of Loyalty* at 174–85 (cited in note 4); Goldstein, *Political Repression* at 328 (cited in note 3).

[108] Executive Order 10241, 16 Fed Reg 3690 (Apr 28, 1951). See Reeves, *Joe McCarthy* at 354–56 (cited in note 3); Athan Theoharis, *The Escalation of the Loyalty Program*, in Barton J. Bernstein, ed, *Politics and Policies of the Truman Administration* 242, 256–59 (Quadrangle 1970).

[109] McCullough, *Truman* at 764 (cited in note 102).

[110] Id at 824–25, 832–33. See Dean Rusk, *As I Saw It* 170 (Norton 1990); Truman, 2 *Memoirs* at 436–38 (cited in note 65).

[111] 82d Cong, 1st Sess, 97 Cong Rec S 6602 (June 14, 1951). See Bennett, *Party of Fear* at

301–2 (cited in note 45); Reeves, *Joe McCarthy* at 372 (cited in note 3). Marshall had long been a target of the China lobby and of right-wing Republicans. Twenty Republican senators had tried to defeat his appointment as secretary of defense, and eleven voted against his confirmation. See Reeves, *Joe McCarthy* at 372 (cited in note 3); Herman, *Joseph McCarthy* at 189 (cited in note 3). McCarthy later wrote a book denouncing Marshall. See Joseph R. McCarthy, *America's Retreat from Victory: The Story of George Catlett Marshall* 4 (Devin-Adair 1951).

112 Reeves, *Joe McCarthy* at 372 (cited in note 3). For negative press reaction to the speech, see McCarthy, *America's Retreat* at 174–80 (cited in note 111).

113 Fred J. Cook, *The Nightmare Decade: The Life and Times of Senator Joe McCarthy* 347 (Random House 1971); Reeves, *Joe McCarthy* at 379–80 (cited in note 3). See Goldstein, *Political Repression* at 329 (cited in note 3); William S. White, *Democrats' Heavy Fire Is Trained on M'Carthy*, New York Times B7 (Sept 9, 1951).

114 Reeves, *Joe McCarthy* at 380, 426 (cited in note 3).

115 Goldstein, *Political Repression* at 327 (cited in note 3). See Herbert S. Parmet, *Eisenhower and the American Crusades* 97 (Macmillan 1972); Mazo and Hess, *Nixon* at 76–89 (cited in note 3).

116 Richard M. Fried, *Men against McCarthy* at 244–45 (Columbia 1976); Reeves, *Joe McCarthy* at 450 (cited in note 3); Caute, *Great Fear* at 46 (cited in note 3). See also Richard H. Rovere, *Senator Joe McCarthy* 181–83 (Harcourt Brace 1959).

117 William S. White, *M'Carthy Senate Power Now Deeply Entrenched*, New York Times E4 (Jan 18, 1953). See Brown, *Loyalty and Security* at 363 (cited in note 10).

118 Griffith, *Politics of Fear* at 210–11 (cited in note 3); William S. White, *Citadel: The Story of the United States Senate* 258 (Harper 1956).

119 *Text of Address by Truman Explaining to Nation His Actions in the White Case*, New York Times 26 (Nov 17, 1953); *President's Brother Scores McCarthy*, id at 6 (July 25, 1953). See William S. White, *Joe McCarthy: The Man with the Power*, Look 30 (June 16, 1953); Reeves, *Joe McCarthy* at 493–94 (cited in note 3).

120 Reeves, *Joe McCarthy* at 474 (cited in note 3); Walter Johnson, *1600 Pennsylvania Avenue: Presidents and the People, 1929–1959* 292 (Little, Brown 1960).

121 See Goldman, *Crucial Decade* at 252–53 (cited in note 55); Goldstein, *Political Repression* at 334–37 (cited in note 3).

122 Goldstein, *Political Repression* at 339 (cited in note 3). See generally id at 337–40. The Eisenhower administration also expanded the use of mail openings and wiretaps in subversive activity investigations and signed legislation revoking the citizenship of citizens convicted under the Smith Act. See Frank Donner, *Electronic Surveillance: The National Security Game*, 2 Civ Lib Rev 15, 20–22 (1975); Harold W. Chase, *Security and Liberty: The Problem of Native Communists, 1947–1955* 33–34 (Doubleday 1955); Goldstein, *Political Repression* at 339–40 (cited in note 3).

123 Robert Dallek, *An Unfinished Life: John F. Kennedy, 1917–1963* 188 (Little, Brown 2003).

124 Communist Control Act of 1954, Pub L 637, 68 Stat 775, 776 (1954).

125 Act Concerning Sedition, 1918 Conn Pub Acts 312; Act Concerning Public Offenses and Declaring an Emergency, Ind Code Ann § 226 (Michie 1951). See Caute, *Great*

Fear at 70–73 (cited in note 3); Goldstein, *Political Repression* at 349–51 (cited in note 3); Walter Gellhorn, *A General View*, in Walter Gellhorn, ed, *The States and Subversion* 364 (Cornell 1952).

[126] Edward L. Barrett Jr., *The Tenney Committee: Legislative Investigation of Subversive Activities in California* 68, 301 (Cornell 1951). See also Caute, *Great Fear* at 78–81 (cited in note 3); Milton R. Konvitz, *First Amendment Freedoms: Selected Cases on Freedom of Religion, Speech, Press, Assembly* 692 (Cornell 1963); Vern Countryman, *Un-American Activities in the State of Washington* (Cornell 1951).

[127] See Goldstein, *Political Repression* at 352–59 (cited in note 3); Brown, *Loyalty and Security* at 92–118 (cited in note 10); Robert E. Cushman, *Civil Liberties in the United States: A Guide to Current Problems and Experience* 174 (Cornell 1956); Caute, *Great Fear* at 180–84, 339–45 (cited in note 3); Caughey, *McCarthyism Rampant* at 170 (cited in note 90); Kanfer, *Plague Years* at 151 (cited in note 98); Francis Biddle, *The Fear of Freedom* 31–36 (Doubleday 1952).

[128] See Barth, *Loyalty of Free Men* at 96 (cited in note 11); Brown, *Loyalty and Security* at 333–39, 478–82 (cited in note 10).

[129] During World War I, the Civil Service Commission, acting under wartime orders, conducted 3,672 loyalty investigations. The procedures were informal and haphazard. During the war, a total of 660 individuals were denied federal employment because of questionable loyalty. See Harold M. Hyman, *To Try Men's Souls: Loyalty Tests in American History* 269 (California 1960); Caute, *Great Fear* at 267 (cited in note 3). See Barth, *Loyalty of Free Men* at 97 (cited in note 11).

[130] Act to Prevent Pernicious Political Activities, 53 Stat 1148, sec 9A (Aug 2, 1939). See Bontecou, *Federal Loyalty-Security Program* at 10–13 (cited in note 65).

[131] See Bontecou, *Federal Loyalty-Security Program* at 10 (cited in note 65); Caute, *Great Fear* at 267–68 (cited in note 3).

[132] Emerson and Helfeld, 58 Yale L J at 17 (cited in note 53).

[133] For a sharply critical view of Truman's motives, see Freeland, *Truman Doctrine* at 127–28 (cited at note 42).

[134] See Theoharis, *Threat to Civil Liberties* (cited in note 100).

[135] Letter from Attorney General Thomas Clark to A. Devitt Vanech, Chairman of the President's Temporary Commission on Employee Loyalty, Feb 14, 1947, reprinted in Bontecou, *Federal Loyalty-Security Program* at 307 (cited in note 65); Harper, *Politics of Loyalty* at 35 (cited in note 4); Theoharis, *Seeds of Repression* at 103 (cited in note 38). See generally Bontecou, *Federal Loyalty-Security Program* at 23–28 (cited in note 65)

[136] 12 Fed Reg at 1935 (cited in note 63). See Barth, *Loyalty of Free Men* at 101 (cited in note 11).

[137] 12 Fed Reg at 1935 (cited in note 63). See Goldstein, *Political Repression* at 299–305 (cited in note 3); Reeves, *McCarthy* at 124–25 (cited in note 3).

[138] Theoharis, *Seeds of Repression* at 102 (cited in note 38).

[139] See Brown, *Loyalty and Security* at 24–27 (cited in note 10).

[140] 12 Fed Reg at 1935 (cited in note 63). See Caute, *Great Fear* at 268–72 (cited in note 3).

[141] 12 Fed Reg at 1935 (cited in note 63). The executive order stated that mere membership in a listed organization should not be regarded as conclusive proof of disloyalty, but in practice this proved illusory, especially with respect to present membership. See Caute, *Great Fear* at 269 (cited in note 3).

[142] See Caute, *Great Fear* at 169, 581 n 18 (cited in note 3).

[143] Freeland, *Truman Doctrine* at 210–11 (cited in note 42); Goldstein, *Political Repression* at 309 (cited in note 3).

[144] Barth, *Loyalty of Free Men* at 106 (cited in note 11).

[145] See Bontecou, *Federal Loyalty-Security Program* at 204 (cited in note 65); Goldstein, *Political Repression* at 310–11 (cited in note 3).

[146] 12 Fed Reg at 1935 (cited in note 63); Barth, *Loyalty of Free Men* at 101 (cited in note 11).

[147] See Theoharis, *Seeds of Repression* at 102–3 (cited in note 38).

[148] See Blanchard, *Revolutionary Sparks* at 253 (cited in note 44); Emerson and Helfeld, 58 Yale L J at 71 (cited in note 53).

[149] Theoharis, *Seeds of Repression* at 109–10 (cited in note 38); Barth, *Loyalty of Free Men* at 158, 109 (cited in note 11). See Caute, *Great Fear* at 115–16 (cited in note 3). See generally Bontecou, *Federal Loyalty-Security Program* at 82–95 (cited in note 65).

[150] Goldstein, *Political Repression* at 302 (cited in note 3). See also Barth, *Loyalty of Free Men* at 49 (cited in note 11).

[151] See Caute, *Great Fear* at 279–81 (cited in note 3); Goldstein, *Political Repression* at 302 (cited in note 3); Walter Gellhorn, *Security, Loyalty and Science* 152–53 (Cornell 1950). See Emerson and Helfeld, 58 Yale L J at 72, 74 (cited in note 53).

[152] Barth, *Loyalty of Free Men* at 117–18 (cited in note 11).

[153] Id at 111–15. See Caute, *Great Fear* at 276–77 (cited in note 3); Bontecou, *Federal Loyalty-Security Program* at 226 (cited in note 65).

[154] See Brown, *Loyalty and Security* at 487–91 (cited in note 10); Caute, *Great Fear* at 592–93 n 15 (cited in note 3); Barth, *Loyalty of Free Men* at 125–26 (cited in note 11); Bennett, *Party of Fear* at 286 (cited in note 45).

[155] It was not at all unusual for the entire loyalty process to last two full years, during which time employees were typically suspended without pay. See Brown, *Loyalty and Security* at 48, 188 (cited in note 10).

[156] See Caute, *Great Fear* at 271 (cited in note 3).

[157] Id at 277–78 (cited in note 26); Bontecou, *Federal Loyalty-Security Program* at 129 (cited in note 65).

[158] O'Brian, 61 Harv L Rev at 598 (cited in note 12). For the impact on scientific research, see Gellhorn, *Security, Loyalty and Science* at 157–67 (cited in note 151).

[159] Letter from L. A. Nikoloric to Sheila N. Schwartz, Apr 28, 1950, excerpted in Laura Kalman, *Abe Fortas: A Biography* 132 (Yale 1990); letter from Abe Fortas to Norman P. Moore, July 25, 1953, excerpted id.

[160] Caute, *Great Fear* at 276 (cited in note 3). See also Barth, *Loyalty of Free Men* at 127 (cited in note 11); Brown, *Loyalty and Security* at 183–93 (cited in note 10).

[161] See supra text accompanying note 108.

[162] Moreover, the new executive order granted all agencies summary-dismissal authority

and directed federal agencies to reopen all cases in which there had previously been a full-field investigation to determine whether employees who had been cleared under the 1951 standard could pass muster under the 1953 standard.

163 Executive Order 10450, Security Requirements for Government Employment, 18 Fed Reg 2489 (1953). See Caute, *Great Fear* at 274 (cited in note 3).

164 Goldstein, *Political Repression* at 337–38 (cited in note 3). See Caute, *Great Fear* at 273–75 (cited in note 3).

165 Earl Latham, *The Communist Controversy in Washington: From the New Deal to McCarthy* 369 (Harvard 1966); Herman, *Joseph McCarthy* at 4 (cited in note 3); James Rorty and Moshe Decter, *McCarthy and the Communists* 23 (Beacon 1954).

166 For a discussion of the various rationales for loyalty testing, and the conclusion that this program achieved none of them well, see Brown, *Loyalty and Security* at 333–56, 478 (cited in note 10).

167 See Barth, *Loyalty of Free Men* at 134–35 (cited in note 11).

168 See, for example, Henry Mayer, *How the Loyalty-Security Program Affects Private Employment*, 15 Lawyers Guild Review 119, 122 (Winter 1955–56).

169 See generally Brown, *Loyalty and Security* at 4–8 (cited in note 10); John H. Schaar, *Loyalty in America* (California 1957); Henry Steele Commager, *Freedom, Loyalty, Dissent* 135–55 (Oxford 1954).

170 Barth, *Loyalty of Free Men* at 6 (cited in note 11). On the inability to define "loyalty," see Brown, *Loyalty and Security* at 4–12 (cited in note 10) (concluding that the word "loyalty" in this context clearly took on political meaning far removed from legitimate concerns about security); Emerson and Helfeld, 58 Yale L J at 36–53 (cited in note 53) (concluding that the loyalty program was designed to determine not which employees were disloyal but which had the *potential* to be disloyal). Interestingly, in a reply to Emerson and Helfeld, J. Edgar Hoover implied that they wrote their article with the intention of supporting communism. J. Edgar Hoover, *A Comment on the Article "Loyalty among Government Employees,"* 58 Yale L J 401, 410 (1948). Emerson and Helfeld responded that they were "satisfied to leave to the reader . . . the decision as to whether Mr. Hoover's innuendos regarding our motives are justified." Thomas I. Emerson and David M. Helfeld, *Reply by the Authors*, 58 Yale L J 412, 412 (1948).

171 See Goldstein, *Political Repression* at 343 (cited in note 3). See generally Alan Barth, *Government by Investigation* (Viking 1955); Telford Taylor, *Grand Inquest: The Story of Congressional Investigations* (Simon and Schuster 1955).

172 Communist Espionage in the United States Government, Hearings before the House Committee on Un-American Activities, 80th Cong, 2d Sess 1–2 (Aug 28, 1948).

173 See Carr, *House Committee* at 3–7 (cited in note 56). See generally Ernest J. Eberling, *Congressional Investigations: A Study of the Origin and Development of the Power of Congress to Investigate and Punish for Contempt* (Columbia 1928); Marshall Edward Dimock, *Congressional Investigating Committees* (Johns Hopkins 1929); M. Nelson McGeary, *The Developments of Congressional Investigative Power* (Columbia 1940). See also *Congressional Investigations: A Symposium*, 18 U Chi L Rev 421–685 (1951).

174 Gerald D. Morgan, *Congressional Investigations and Judicial Review: Kilbourn v.*

Thompson Revisited, 37 Cal L Rev 556, 556 (1949).

[175] 103 US 168 (1880).

[176] 273 US 135 (1927).

[177] Id at 176. See also *Sinclair v. United States*, 279 US 263, 292 (1929) ("[F]ew if any of the rights of the people guarded by fundamental law are of greater importance . . . than the right to be exempt from all unauthorized, arbitrary, or unreasonable inquiries . . . in respect of their personal and private affairs").

[178] H Res 282, 75th Cong, 3d Sess, in 83 Cong Rec H 7568 (May 26, 1938).

[179] Investigation of Un-American Activities and Propaganda, Report of the Special Committee on Un-American Activities Pursuant to H Res 282, HR Rep No 2, 75th Cong, 1st Sess 13 (1939).

[180] Investigation of Un-American Propaganda Activities in the United States, Report of the Special Committee on Un-American Activities Pursuant to H Res 282 and H Res 26, HR Rep No 1476, 76th Cong, 3rd Sess 24 (1940).

[181] Martin Dies, *The Trojan Horse in America* 355, 361–62 (Dodd, Mead 1940). See Barth, *Loyalty of Free Men* at 51–55, 61 (cited in note 11). On the Dies Committee, see generally August Raymond Ogden, *The Dies Committee: A Study of the Special House Committee for the Investigation of Un-American Activities, 1938–1944* (Catholic 1945).

[182] Carr, *House Committee* at 17–22 (cited in note 56).

[183] 80th Cong, 1st Sess, in 93 Cong Rec H 1131 (Feb 18, 1947); 79th Cong, 1st Sess, in 91 Cong Rec H 7737 (July 18, 1945). See Walter Goodman, *The Committee: The Extraordinary Career of the House Committee on Un-American Activities* 167–89 (Farrar, Straus and Giroux 1968); Carr, *House Committee* at 220–23 (cited in note 56); Caute, *Great Fear* at 90 (cited in note 3).

[184] Carr, *House Committee* at 216 (cited in note 56).

[185] Edward A. Harris, *Sidelights on Movie-Like Hearing on Hollywood Reds*, St. Louis Post-Dispatch 7 (Oct 21, 1947). See Carr, *House Committee* at 265 (cited in note 56); Caute, *Great Fear* at 93 (cited in note 3).

[186] John D. Morris, *House Body Maps Exposing of Reds in Labor Unions, Schools, and Films*, New York Times 1 (Jan 23, 1947). See also Freeland, *Truman Doctrine* at 132–33 (cited in note 42).

[187] Robert E. Stripling, *The Red Plot against America* 23 (Bell 1949). See Carr, *House Committee* at 260 (cited in note 56).

[188] Carr, *House Committee* at 357–60 (cited in note 56). See also Caute, *Great Fear* at 101 (cited in note 3).

[189] Stripling, *Red Plot* at 60 (cited in note 187); Testimony of Ruth Fischer before the House Committee on Un-American Activities, Feb 6, 1947, excerpted in Bentley, ed, *Thirty Years of Treason* 61, 67 (cited in note 68).

[190] See Testimony of Gerhart Eisler before the House Committee on Un-American Activities, Feb 6, 1947, excerpted in Bentley, ed, *Thirty Years of Treason* at 57–59 (cited in note 68); *Gerhart Eisler, Top Communist Who Fled U.S. Prosecution, Dies*, New York Times 47 (Mar 22, 1968).

[191] Testimony of Hanns Eisler before the House Committee on Un-American Activities,

Sept 24, 1947, excerpted in Bentley, ed, *Thirty Years of Treason* at 75 (cited in note 68).

[192] Id at 77–78.

[193] Id at 96–98.

[194] Id at 86.

[195] Id at 80–81.

[196] Id at 82, 84.

[197] Id at 93.

[198] Id at 93–94.

[199] Id at 94–95.

[200] *Rankin Charges Subversive Plot in Film Capital*, New York Herald Tribune 7 (July 1, 1945).

[201] 79th Cong, 1st Sess, in 91 Cong Rec H 7372, 7386 (July 9, 1945). See Caute, *Great Fear* at 90 (cited in note 3).

[202] Extension of Remarks of Hon J. Parnell Thomas, 80th Cong, 1st Sess, in 93 Cong Rec H A2687 (June 6, 1947). See Carr, *House Committee* at 56–57 (cited in note 56); Cabell Phillips, *Un-American Committee Puts On Its "Big Show,"* New York Times E7 (Oct 26, 1947).

[203] See Carr, *House Committee* at 58 (cited in note 56).

[204] See Barth, *Loyalty of Free Men* at 63–64 (cited in note 11).

[205] Carr, *House Committee* at 59 (cited in note 56).

[206] Hearings Regarding the Communist Infiltration of the Motion Picture Industry before the House Committee on Un-American Activities, 80th Cong, 1st Sess 233 (Oct 1947) (hereafter cited as Motion Picture Hearings) .

[207] Carr, *House Committee* at 60–61 (cited in note 56).

[208] Motion Picture Hearings at 10 (cited in note 206).

[209] Id at 71. The committee also failed to prove that the White House had improperly pressured Hollywood to make pro-Soviet films. Robert Taylor repudiated his earlier claim that he had been coerced into making *Song of Russia*. Id at 167. See Carr, *House Committee* at 68–69 (cited in note 56).

[210] Motion Picture Hearings at 83 (cited in note 206).

[211] Id at 84, 87.

[212] Id at 92, 95, 96, 100, 104.

[213] Id at 166–70.

[214] Id at 219–20, 224.

[215] Id at 215–18.

[216] See Barth, *Loyalty of Free Men* at 63–64 (cited in note 11).

[217] Motion Picture Hearings at 290–95 (cited in note 206).

[218] See Carr, *House Committee* at 72–73 (cited in note 56).

[219] 80th Cong, 1st Sess, in 93 Cong Rec H 10771 (Nov 24, 1947).

[220] Barth, *Loyalty of Free Men* at 63 (cited in note 11). See Carr, *House Committee* at 75 (cited in note 56).

[221] Barth, *Loyalty of Free Men* at 65–66 (cited in note 11); Blanchard, *Revolutionary Sparks* at 236 (cited in note 44).

[222] Hollywood Life (Mar 30, 1951), excerpted in Bentley, ed, *Thirty Years of Treason* at

305–6 (cited in note 68).

223 Ferrer's ad said, "I attest, and will so swear under oath, that I am not, have never been, and could not be, a member of the Communist party; nor, specifically, am I a sympathizer with any Communist aim, a fellow traveler, or in any way an encourager of any Communist party concept or objective." Bentley, ed, *Thirty Years of Treason* at 297 (cited in note 68). Ferrer's testimony before HUAC is excerpted id at 407–34 (May 22, 1951).

224 See generally Caute, *Great Fear* at 487–520, 557–60 (cited in note 3). For excerpts from the testimony of some of these individuals before HUAC, see Bentley, ed, *Thirty Years of Treason* at 348–76 (Sterling Hayden), 484–95 (Elia Kazan), 496–98 (Edward G. Robinson), 498–531 (Clifford Odets), 625–34 (Jerome Robbins), 653–66 (Lee J. Cobb) (cited in note 68). On the blacklist in radio, television, and theater, see Merle Miller, *The Judges and the Judged* (Doubleday 1952); Caute, *Great Fear* at 521–38, 617–18 n 7 (cited in note 3); Brown, *Loyalty and Security* at 157–63 (cited in note 10); Kanfer, *Plague Years* (cited in note 98).

225 Barth, *Loyalty of Free Men* at 65 (cited in note 11).

226 See Caute, *Great Fear* at 56 (cited in note 3); Emerson and Helfeld, 58 Yale L J at 22–23 (cited in note 53). Chambers and Bentley were only two of many "professional" ex-Communist witnesses. Among the others who were most influential were Louis Francis Budenz, a former managing editor of the *Daily Worker*, John Lautner and Benjamin Gitlow, who had gained fame as the defendant in *Gitlow v. New York*, 268 US 652 (1925). See Caute, *Great Fear* at 122–38 (cited in note 3).

227 Carr, *House Committee* at 80 (cited in note 56); Caute, *Great Fear* at 56 (cited in note 3).

228 Elizabeth Bentley, *Out of Bondage* 4 (Devin-Adair 1951); Hearings Regarding Communist Espionage in the United States Government before the Committee on Un-American Activities, 80th Cong, 2d Sess 539–40 (1948) (hereafter cited as Communist Espionage Hearings); Bentley, *Out of Bondage* at 7, 22.

229 Communist Espionage Hearings at 522 (cited in note 228).

230 Bentley, *Out of Bondage* at 271, 278, 281, 284–85 (cited in note 228).

231 See Caute, *Great Fear* at 56–57 (cited in note 3); Barth, *Loyalty of Free Men* at 76–77 (cited in note 11); Reeves, *Joe McCarthy* at 211 (cited in note 3). It was primarily on the basis of Bentley's testimony that the reactionary Senate Internal Security Subcommittee issued its report, *Interlocking Subversion in Government Departments*, which purported to trace Communist penetration of the New Deal administration. See Interlocking Subversion in Government Departments, Report of the Subcommittee to Investigate the Administration of the Internal Security Act and Other Internal Security Laws, 83d Cong, 1st Sess 49 (July 30, 1953). See Caute, *Great Fear* at 57 (cited in note 3).

232 Caute, *Great Fear* at 58 (cited in note 3).

233 Bentley, *Out of Bondage* at 178–79 (cited in note 228). Bentley later recalled that Remington "was one of the most frightened people" with whom she had ever had to deal and that "he often resorted to elaborate . . . subterfuges to avoid doing his Communist duties." Remington would always "deprecate the value of the information that he

gave, saying that it wasn't worth bothering with." Id at 180.

[234] See Carr, *House Committee* at 194–98 (cited in note 56); Caute, *Great Fear* at 287–89 (cited in note 3); Edward Ranzal, *Remington's Guilt Upheld on Appeal*, New York Times 6 (Nov 25, 1953); *United States v. Remington*, 191 F2d 246 (2d Cir 1951); *United States v. Remington*, 208 F2d 567 (2d Cir 1953). For a lively account of Judge Hand's struggles with the *Remington* case, see Gerald Gunther, *Learned Hand: The Man and the Judge* 612–25 (Knopf 1994).

[235] See Caute, *Great Fear* at 56, 289 (cited in note 3) (on Bentley's credibility); Reeves, *Joe McCarthy* at 211 (cited in note 3) (on results of Bentley's testimony). Arthur Herman, on the other hand, reports that "virtually everything Bentley said would later turn out to be true." See Herman, *Joseph McCarthy* at 57 (cited in note 3).

[236] Bentley, *Out of Bondage* at 310–11 (cited in note 228).

[237] Communist Espionage Hearings at 564–66 (cite in note 228).

[238] See Cooke, *Generation on Trial* at 8 (cited in note 87); Carr, *House Committee* at 99 (cited in note 56).

[239] Communist Espionage Hearings at 585–86, 643 (cited in note 206)

[240] Id at 988. See Carr, *House Committee* at 101–9 (cited in note 56).

[241] See Blanchard, *Revolutionary Sparks* at 239 (cited in note 44).

[242] Carr, *House Committee* at 167–69 (cited in note 56).

[243] Frank J. Donner, *The Un-Americans* 64 (Ballantine 1961). See Goldstein, *Political Repression* at 345–46, 376 (cited in note 3); Caute, *Great Fear* at 96–100 (cited in note 3).

[244] *United States v. Lovett*, 328 US 303 (1946).

[245] See Reeves, *Joe McCarthy* at 210 (cited in note 3); Goldstein, *Political Repression* at 346 (cited in note 3).

[246] Caute, *Great Fear* at 100 (cited in note 3).

[247] Carr, *House Committee* at 273, 344, 455–59 (cited in note 56); Barth, *Government by Investigation* at 160 (cited in note 171). See Goldstein, *Political Repression* at 343–44 (cited in note 3).

[248] See Carr, *House Committee* at x (cited in note 56).

[249] See Herbert Block, *The Herblock Book* 144–45 (Beacon 1952). Block sometimes struggled with Philip Graham, the publisher of the *Washington Post*, over just how far Graham would let him go in attacking McCarthy. See Graham, *Personal History* at 203–4 (cited in note 19).

[250] See generally Griffith, *Politics of Fear* at 2–12 (cited in note 3); Reeves, *Joe McCarthy* at 1–61 (cited in note 3); David M. Oshinsky, *A Conspiracy So Immense: The World of Joe McCarthy*, 8–52 (Free 1983); Rovere, *Senator Joseph McCarthy* at 79–98 (cited in note 116); Bennett, *Party of Fear* at 294–96 (cited in note 45); Herman, *Joseph McCarthy* at 21–26 (cited in note 3).

[251] Reeves, *Joe McCarthy* at 85, 104–5 (cited in note 3); Herman, *Joseph McCarthy* 26–27, 30–38 (cited in note 3) (offering a more sympathetic view of McCarthy deceits).

[252] See Oshinsky, *Conspiracy So Immense* at 54–84, 107 (cited in note 250); Herman, *Joseph McCarthy* 51–56 (cited in note 3); Griffith, *Politics of Fear* at 12–16 (cited in

note 3); Bennett, *Party of Fear* at 296 (cited in note 45); Reeves, *Joe McCarthy* at 161–200 (cited in note 3). The Father Walsh story may be apocryphal. See Herman, *Joseph McCarthy* at 96–97 (cited in note 3).

253 On McCarthy's speech in Wheeling, see Bennett, *Party of Fear* at 293–94 (cited in note 45); Oshinsky, *Conspiracy So Immense* at 108–10 (cited in note 250); Rovere, *Senator Joe McCarthy* at 124–26 (cited in note 116). The full text of the Wheeling speech can be found at 81st Cong, 2d Sess, in 96 Cong Rec S 1954 (Feb 20, 1950).

254 Reeves, *Joe McCarthy* at 233 (cited in note 3). In fact, McCarthy's "new information" was derived from old lists that had been vetted in the past and were well known. It wasn't until he finally began disclosing his information, however, that this became apparent. See *Acheson Defends His Department, Terms It No Haven of Disloyalty*, New York Times 6 (Feb 25, 1950); Reeves, *Joe McCarthy* at 241–43 (cited in note 3); Griffith, *Politics of Fear* at 48–51 (cited in note 3).

255 81st Cong, 2d Sess, in 96 Cong Rec S 1952–81 (Feb 20, 1950). See Reeves, *Joe McCarthy* at 236–40 (cited in note 3); Griffith, *Politics of Fear* at 54–57 (cited in note 3).

256 *Mr. M'Carthy's Campaign*, New York Times 28 (Feb 22, 1950).

257 See Griffith, *Politics of Fear* at 62–65, 102–3 (cited in note 3); Blanchard, *Revolutionary Sparks* at 246 (cited in note 44).

258 S R 231, 81st Cong, 2d Sess, in 96 Cong Rec S 2150 (Feb 22, 1950).

259 In another illustrative instance, McCarthy waved before the Senate a purported "FBI chart" supposedly revealing that at least three "Communist agents" were still employed by the State Department. In fact, there was no such FBI chart. Even so, some senators and many citizens were taken in by his deceit. See Tydings Committee Hearings at 1252–53 (cited in note 94); Clayton Knowles, *State Department Quickly Denies New Charges Made by McCarthy*, New York Times 20 (June 7, 1950); Griffith, *Politics of Fear* at 99–100 (cited in note 3).

260 Rovere, *Senator Joseph McCarthy* at 151 (cited in note 116); Tydings Committee Hearings at 417–86, 558–70 (cited in note 94). See Jay Walz, *Lattimore Named as "Top Soviet Spy" Cited by M'Carthy*, New York Times 1 (Mar 27, 1950); Reeves, *Joe McCarthy* at 267–74 (cited in note 3); Bennett, *Party of Fear* at 297–98 (cited in note 45); Caute, *Great Fear* at 317–21 (cited in note 3); Oshinsky, *Conspiracy So Immense* at 136–38, 147–48 (cited in note 250); Griffith, *Politics of Fear* at 76–87 (cited in note 3); Stanley I. Kutler, *The American Inquisition: Justice and Injustice in the Cold War* 183–214 (Hill and Wang 1982).

261 See Herman, *Joseph McCarthy* at 119–28 (cited in note 3).

262 *M'Carthy Labels Marshall "Unfit,"* New York Times 3 (Apr 21, 1950); Reeves, *Joe McCarthy* at 299 (cited in note 3). See Edwin R. Bayley, *McCarthy Scores Acheson, Again Calls for His Removal*, Milwaukee Journal 1 (June 9, 1950); Griffith, *Politics of Fear* at 89–90 (cited in note 3).

263 State Department Employee Loyalty Investigation, Report of the Committee on Foreign Relations Pursuant to S Res 231, S Rep 2108, 81st Cong, 2d Sess 151–52 (1950). See also Reeves, *Joe McCarthy* at 304–7 (cited in note 3); William S. White, *Tydings*

Charges M'Carthy Perjured Himself at Inquiry, New York Times 1 (July 21, 1950). In expressing his "Individual Views," Republican Senator Henry Cabot Lodge complained that the investigation had been "superficial and inconclusive." *The M'Carthy Charges*, New York Times 28 (July 18, 1950). Even McCarthy apologists like William F. Buckley Jr. conceded that McCarthy could legitimately have been censured for lying about the source and nature of his information. See William F. Buckley Jr. and L. Brent Bozell, *McCarthy and His Enemies: The Record and Its Meaning* 60 (Regner 1954).

264 William S. White, *Red Charges by M'Carthy Ruled False*, New York Times 1 (July 18, 1950).

265 William S. White, *"Hideous" Cover-Up Is Laid to Tydings in Reply by Jenner*, New York Times 1 (July 22, 1950). See also Richard L. Strout, *Senator Roars with Debate over McCarthy Spy Issues*, Christian Science Monitor 3 (July 22, 1950); 81st Cong, 2d Sess, in 96 Cong Rec S 10686–89, 10691–717 (July 20, 1950).

266 William S. White, *Nazi Tactics Laid to M'Carthy Foes*, New York Times 1 (July 25, 1950); White, *Tydings Charges M'Carthy*, id at 1 (cited in note 263); Joseph Alsop and Stewart Alsop, *Why Has Washington Gone Crazy?*, Saturday Evening Post 20 (July 29, 1950); Reeves, *Joe McCarthy* at 314 (cited in note 3).

267 81st Cong, 2d Sess in 96 Cong Rec S 16641 (Dec 15, 1950); *Demagogue*, Washington Post 4B (Dec 24, 1950). See 81st Cong, 2d Sess, in 96 Cong Rec S 16634–41 (Dec 15, 1950); Reeves, *Joe McCarthy* at 348–50 (cited in note 3).

268 Maryland Senatorial Election of 1950, Report of the Senate Committee on Rules and Administration, Subcommittee on Privileges and Election Pursuant to S Res 250, HR Rep No 647, 82nd Cong, 1st Sess (1951). The report added that other Republicans had also played a role in the anti-Tydings campaign. See generally Fried, *Men against McCarthy* at 141–53 (cited in note 116).

269 *Benton Demands M'Carthy Resign*, New York Times 6 (Aug 7, 1951). See *Democrats Fume at McCarthy, But He Has Them Terrorized*, Newsweek 19 (Aug 20, 1951); Harlan Trott, *Benton Appeals to Senate to Remove McCarthy*, Christian Science Monitor 3 (Aug 7, 1951); 82nd Cong, 1st Sess 9498–501 (Aug 6, 1951). See also Reeves, *Joe McCarthy* at 375 (cited in note 3); Jack Anderson and Ronald W. May, *McCarthy: The Man, the Senator, the "Ism"* 316 (Beacon 1952). On the remarkable career of William Benton, see Sidney Hyman, *The Lives of William Benton* (Chicago 1969).

270 82nd Cong, 2d Sess, 98 Cong Rec S 3934 (Apr 10, 1952). See Reeves, *Joe McCarthy* at 386–400 (cited in note 3).

271 Herman, *Joseph McCarthy* at 199 (cited in note 3).

272 Griffith, *Politics of Fear* at 176 (cited in note 3).

273 *M'Carthy, Benton Exchange Charges*, New York Times 5 (July 4, 1952). See Reeves, *Joe McCarthy* at 404 (cited in note 3).

274 Reeves, *Joe McCarthy* at 455 (cited in note 3).

275 See Investigations of Senators Joseph R. McCarthy and William Benton, Report of the Subcommittee on Privileges and Elections to the Committee on Rules and Administration Pursuant to S Res 187 and S Res 304, 82d Cong, 2d Sess (1952).

276 John B. Oaks, *Inquiry into McCarthy's Status*, New York Times Magazine 9 (Apr 12,

1953); Griffith, *Politics of Fear* at 206 (cited in note 3). See William S. White, *The Professional: Lyndon B. Johnson* 48–50 (Houghton Mifflin 1964). By 1953, the only Democratic senator willing to take on McCarthy directly was Herbert H. Lehman of New York. See Griffith, *Politics of Fear* at 222 (cited in note 3).

277 Reeves, *Joe McCarthy* at 463–66 (cited in note 3).

278 Id at 479–80, 485. See C. P. Trussell, *Voice Must Drop Works of Leftists*, New York Times 9 (Feb 20, 1953); Wayne Phillips, *Harassing Feared by "Voice" Suicide*, id at 10 (Mar 7, 1953); *New Hearings Set on "Red" Book Issue*, id at 16 (June 24, 1953); Martin Merson, *The Private Diary of a Public Servant* 14–16 (Macmillian 1955); James A. Wechsler, *The Age of Suspicion* 264 (Random House 1953); Caute, *Great Fear* at 321–24 (cited in note 3).

279 *Text of Senator McCarthy's Speech Accusing Truman of Aiding Suspected Red Agents*, New York Times 5 (Nov 25, 1953); *News Summary & Index*, id at 32 (Nov 26, 1953).

280 Peter Kihss, *Army Drops Guard Called Pro-Stalin*, New York Times 13 (Sept 3, 1953). See also Peter Kihss, *M'Carthy Accuses 2 Army Employees*, id at 9 (Sept 1, 1953); Peter Kihss, *M'Carthy "Orders" Army Bare Files*, id at 4 (Sept 2, 1953).

281 See Army Signal Corps Subversion and Espionage, Hearings before the Permanent Subcommittee on Investigations of the Committee on Government Operations Pursuant to S Res 40, 83d Cong, 1st and 2d Sess (1953–54).

282 Communist Infiltration in the Army, Hearings before the Permanent Subcommittee on Investigations of the Committee on Government Operations Pursuant to S Res 40, 83d Cong, 2d Sess 147, 153 (1954). The dentist, Irving Peress, had lied on his army application about whether he had ever been a member of the Communist Party. The Army loyalty screeners had failed to catch the lie. See Herman, *Joseph McCarthy* at 247–50 (cited in note 3).

283 *The Real Issue*, New York Times 26 (Feb 23, 1954). See James Reston, *Officers Ordered to Defy M'Carthy and Not Testify*, id at 1 (Feb 21, 1954).

284 *Monitored Records of Telephone Calls between McCarthy and Stevens*, New York Times 42 (June 6, 1954).

285 *The Real Issue*, New York Times at 26 (cited in note 283). See also *McCarthy and Zwicker*, Chicago Tribune 14 (Feb 25, 1954) (stating that McCarthy's behavior toward Zwicker was unjustified and that McCarthy needed to distinguish "the role of investigator from the role of avenging angel").

286 Robert A. Caro, *The Years of Lyndon Johnson: Master of the Senate* 551 (Knopf 2002); Bob Edwards, *Edward R. Murrow and the Birth of Broadcast Journalism* 105–23 (Wiley, 2004); Edward Bliss Jr., ed, *In Search of Light: The Broadcasts of Edward R. Murrow, 1938–1961* 247 (Knopf 1967). See Bennett, *Party of Fear* at 307 (cited in note 45); Reeves, *Joe McCarthy* at 564–65 (cited in note 3); Blanchard, *Revolutionary Sparks* at 261–62 (cited in note 44). For a critical analysis of Murrow's broadcast, asserting that it employed "exactly the same techniques of 'partial truth and innuendo' that critics accused McCarthy of using," see Herman, *Joseph McCarthy* at 253 (cited in note 3). McCarthy responded to the broadcast by threatening to "expose" Murrow's (nonexistent) Communist "affiliations" and by pressuring his sponsors to cut their ties to the program.

[287] James Reston, *Stevens Case Stuns Capital; Pentagon Bitter and Gloomy*, New York Times 1 (Feb 26, 1954). See Griffith, *Politics of Fear* at 247–48 (cited in note 3); Reeves, *Joe McCarthy* at 552 (cited in note 3).

[288] Walter Lippmann, *Today and Tomorrow: The McCarthy-Stevens Affair*, Washington Post 9 (Mar 1, 1954); Madison Capital Times (March 3, 1954).

[289] W. H. Lawrence, *President Chides M'Carthy on "Fair Play" at Hearings; Senator Defiant in Retort*, New York Times 1 (Mar 4, 1954); James Reston, *Other Cheek Is Struck*, id at 14 (Mar 4, 1954).

[290] Emmet John Hughes, *The Ordeal of Power: A Political Memoir of the Eisenhower Years* 42 (Atheneum 1963). See Dwight D. Eisenhower, *The White House Years: Mandate for Change, 1953–1956* 317–19 (Doubleday 1963).

[291] Eisenhower, *Mandate for Change* at 318 (cited in note 290); Sherman Adams, *Firsthand Report: The Story of the Eisenhower Administration* 30–32 (Harper 1961). See Parmet, *Eisenhower* at 130–32 (cited in 115); Hughes, *Ordeal of Power* at 41–43 (cited in note 290); Reeves, *Joe McCarthy* at 438–39 (cited in note 3); Griffith, *Politics of Fear* at 191–94 (cited in note 3); W. H. Lawrence, *Eisenhower Scores President on Reds; Supports M'Carthy*, New York Times 1 (Oct 4, 1952).

[292] See Leonard Mosley, *Marshall: Organizer of Victory* 506–7 (Hearst 1982); Bennett, *Party of Fear* at 302 (cited in note 45).

[293] See Reeves, *Joe McCarthy* at 536–37 (cited in note 3); Bennett, *Party of Fear* at 305–7 (cited in note 45).

[294] See *Text of Army Report Charging Threats by McCarthy and Cohn in Interceding for Schine*, New York Times A9 (Mar 12, 1954).

[295] See W. H. Lawrence, *M'Carthy Charges Army "Blackmail,"* New York Times 1 (Mar 13, 1954).

[296] *Text of Nixon Reply to Stevenson Attack on the Administration*, New York Times 44 (Mar 14, 1954); Madison Capital Times (Mar 15, 1954); Reeves, *Joe McCarthy* at 578 (cited in note 3).

[297] Roy Cohn, *McCarthy* 208 (New American 1968).

[298] See Reeves, *Joe McCarthy* at 588–89 (cited in note 3).

[299] Charges and Countercharges Involving: Secretary of the Army Robert T. Stevens, John G. Adams, H. Struve Hensel, and Senator Joe McCarthy, Roy M. Cohn, and Francis P. Carr, Hearings before the Senate Special Subcommittee on Investigations Pursuant to S Res 189, 83d Cong, 2d Sess 372 (Apr 22, 1954) (hereafter Army-McCarthy Hearings). See W. H. Lawrence, *Stevens Swears M'Carthy Falsified*, New York Times 1 (Apr 23, 1954).

[300] Army-McCarthy Hearings at 2426–30 (cited in note 299). See W. H. Lawrence, *Exchange Bitter*, New York Times 1 (June 10, 1954).

[301] See Charges and Countercharges Involving: Secretary of the Army Robert T. Stevens, John G. Adams, H. Struve Hensel, and Senator Joe McCarthy, Roy M. Cohn, and Francis P. Carr, Report of the Special Senate Subcommittee on Investigations Pursuant to S Res 189, S Rep 2507, 83d Cong, 2d Sess 79 (1954); Reeves, *Joe McCarthy* at 635 (cited in note 3); Bennett, *Party of Fear* at 308–9 (cited in note 45).

[302] George Gallup, *Group of Those Undecided about McCarthy up by 6%*, Washington

Post 29 (Nov 12, 1954). See Robert M. Hallett, *Results of McCarthy Investigations into Communist Activities Analyzed*, Christian Science Monitor 3 (Aug 24, 1954); Reeves, *Joe McCarthy* at 641 (cited in note 3).

[303] See 83d Cong, 2d Sess, in 100 Cong Rec S 8032–33 (June 11, 1954); C. P. Trussells, *Flanders Moves in Senate to Strip McCarthy of Posts*, New York Times 1 (June 12, 1954). For Senator Flanders's account of the events surrounding the censure, see Ralph E. Flanders, *Senator from Vermont* 250–68 (Little, Brown 1961). See also Griffith, *Politics of Fear* at 270–77 (cited in note 3); Blanchard, *Revolutionary Sparks* at 261 (cited in note 44).

[304] Letter from James Reston to John Howe, Sept 29, 1954, excerpted in Griffith, *Politics of Fear* at 278 (cited in note 3).

[305] Report of the Select Committee to Study Censure Charges against Joseph R. McCarthy Pursuant to S Res 301, S Rep 2508, 83d Cong, 2d Sess 30–31, 60–61 (1954).

[306] 83d Cong, 2d Sess, in 100 Cong Rec S 15988 (Nov 12, 1954); id at 16059 (Nov 16, 1954); id at 16018–19 (Nov 15, 1954); id at 16292 (Dec 1, 1954). See Griffith, *Politics of Fear* at 307–15 (cited in note 3); Herman, *Joseph McCarthy* at 291 (cited in note 3).

[307] 83d Cong, 2d Sess in 100 Cong Rec S 15953 (Nov 10, 1954); id at 16392 (Dec 2, 1954). See Griffith, *Politics of Fear* at 314 (cited in note 3).

[308] Caro, *Master of the Senate* at 545 (cited in note 286); Dallek, *Unfinished Life* at 188 (cited in note 123);

[309] Stewart Alsop, *The Center: People and Power in Political Washington* 8 (Harper and Row 1968).

[310] Reeves, *Joe McCarthy* at xv (cited in note 3). See Cohn, *McCarthy* at 262–64 (cited in note 297).

[311] Herman, *Joseph McCarthy* at 100 (cited in note 3). See Ann Coulter, *Slander: Liberal Lies about the American Right* 118 (Three Rivers 2002) (describing McCarthyism as "liberals' favorite mythological event").

[312] Herman, *Joseph McCarthy* at 100, 172–75, 142 (cited in note 3).

[313] Biddle, *Fear of Freedom* (cited in note 127).

[314] Id at 2, 7–8, 18–19, 28, 254, 247–49, 253.

[315] John Lord O'Brian, *National Security and Individual Freedom* (Harvard 1955).

[316] Id at 7, 13, 21.

[317] Id at 22, 24, 41.

[318] Id at 49–50.

[319] Id at 50, 70–71, 79, 80, 82, 46.

[320] John Lord O'Brian, *New Encroachments on Individual Freedom*, 66 Harv L Rev 1, 3–4, 26 (1952). See also John Lord O'Brian, *Changing Attitudes toward Freedom*, 9 Wash & Lee L Rev 157 (1952).

[321] 341 US 494 (1951).

[322] See Caute, *Great Fear* at 187–99 (cited in note 3). One of the twelve defendants, W. Z. Foster, was later severed from the case because of ill health.

[323] See Harry Kalven Jr., *A Worthy Tradition: Freedom of Speech in America* 191 (Harper and Row 1988); Martin Shapiro, *Freedom of Speech: The Supreme Court and Judicial*

Review 63–64 (Prentice-Hall 1966).

[324] Michael R. Belknap, *Cold War in the Courtroom: The Foley Square Communist Trial*, in Michael R. Belknap, ed, *American Political Trials* 208, 211 (Greenwood 1994).

[325] Washington Post (July 24, 1948). See Belknap, *Cold War in the Courtroom* at 211–14 (cited in note 324).

[326] See *United States v. Dennis*, 183 F2d 201, 206 (2d Cir 1950).

[327] See Caute, *Great Fear* at 189–90 (cited in note 3).

[328] Id at 191–93 (cited in note 26) (emphasis added); Belknap, *Cold War in the Courtroom* at 219 (cited in note 324). Judge Medina sentenced one of the defendants to only three years in prison because of his war record.

[329] Gunther, *Learned Hand* at 276 (cited in note 234).

[330] Letters from Learned Hand to Bernard Berenson, Aug 2, 1947, Jan 8, 1950, Sept 20, 1950, excerpted id at 578, 581; Learned Hand, *A Plea for the Open Mind and Free Discussion*, in Irving Dilliard, ed, *The Spirit of Liberty: Papers and Addresses of Learned Hand* 272, 284 (Knopf 3d ed 1960); letter from Learned Hand to Felix Frankfurter, Oct 30, 1952, excerpted in Gunther, *Learned Hand* at 589 (cited in note 234).

[331] See Caute, *Great Fear* at 193–94 (cited in note 3).

[332] *Dennis*, 183 F2d at 206–7.

[333] Id at 207.

[334] Id at 207, 212.

[335] Id at 212–13.

[336] Letter from Learned Hand to Felix Frankfurter, June 8, 1951, excerpted in Gunther, *Learned Hand* at 604 (cited in note 234); letter from Learned Hand to Elliot Richardson, Feb 29, 1952, excerpted id.

[337] Letter from Learned Hand to Irving Dilliard, Apr 3, 1952, excerpted id at 605; letter from Learned Hand to Bernard Berenson, June 11, 1951, excerpted id at 603; letter from Learned Hand to Felix Frankfurter, June 8,1951, excerpted id. See Kalven, *Worthy Tradition* at 631 n 15 (cited in note 323).

[338] *Masses Publishing Co. v. Patten*, 244 F 535, 540 (SD NY 1917).

[339] *Dennis*, 183 F2d at 206–7, 213.

[340] Letter from Learned Hand to Felix Frankfurter, June 8, 1951, excerpted in Gunther, *Learned Hand* at 604 (cited in note 234); letter from Learned Hand to Elliot Richardson, Feb 29, 1952, excerpted id at 605.

[341] Kalven, *Worthy Tradition* at 190 (cited in note 323).

[342] For Truman, Vinson was the person best able to unify the Court and improve its public image. See Richard Kirkendall, *Fred M. Vinson*, in Leon Friedman and Fred L. Israel, eds, 4 *The Justices of the United States Supreme Court, 1789–1969* 2639, 2641 (Chelsea 1969).

[343] Joseph P. Lash, ed, *From the Diaries of Felix Frankfurter* 274 (Norton 1975) (Frankfurter's diary entry for Oct 19, 1946).

[344] See William O. Douglas, *The Court Years: 1937–1975* 226 (Random House 1980).

[345] See James E. St. Clair and Linda C. Gugin, *Chief Justice Fred M. Vinson of Kentucky: A Political Biography* 190–230 (Kentucky 2002); Robert J. Donovan, *Tumultuous*

Years: The Presidency of Harry S Truman, 1949–1953 386 (Norton 1982).

[346] Only eight justices participated because Justice Tom Clark, who had initiated the prosecution when he was Truman's attorney general, recused himself from the case.

[347] *Dennis v. United States*, 341 US 494, 501–2 (1951).

[348] Id at 507.

[349] Id at 508–9.

[350] Id at 510–11.

[351] Id at 539, 542, 544–45 (Frankfurter concurring).

[352] Letter from Learned Hand to Elliot Richardson, Feb 29, 1952, excerpted in Gunther, *Learned Hand* at 604 (cited in note 234); letter from Learned Hand to Felix Frankfurter, June 8, 1951, excerpted id.

[353] *Dennis*, 341 US at 549 (Frankfurter concurring).

[354] Id.

[355] Id at 550.

[356] Id at 568–71 (Jackson concurring).

[357] Id at 582–83, 588–89 (Douglas dissenting).

[358] Id at 589.

[359] Roger K. Newman, *Hugo Black: A Biography* 402–3 (Pantheon 1994) (emphasis added).

[360] *Dennis*, 341 US at 581 (Black dissenting).

[361] See Shapiro, *Freedom of Speech* at 63–64 (cited in note 323); Kalven, *Worthy Tradition* at 191–93 (cited in note 323).

[362] For discussion of such an approach, see Richard A. Posner, *The Speech Market and the Legacy of Schenck*, in Lee C. Bollinger and Geoffrey R. Stone, eds, *Eternally Vigilant: Free Speech in the Modern Era* 120 (Chicago 2002); John Hart Ely, *Democracy and Distrust: A Theory of Judicial Review* 108 (Harvard 1980); Richard A. Posner, *Free Speech in an Economic Perspective*, 20 Suffolk U L Rev 1 (1986).

[363] See Geoffrey R. Stone, *Content Regulation and the First Amendment*, 25 Wm & Mary L Rev 189 (1983).

[364] See Harvey Klehr, John Earl Haynes, and Fridrikh Igorevich Firsov, *The Secret World of American Communism* 16 (Yale 1995); Harvey Klehr, John Earl Haynes, and Kyrill M. Anderson, *The Soviet World of American Communism* 4–5 (Yale 1998); Allen Weinstein and Alexander Vassiliev, *The Haunted Wood: Soviet Espionage in America — The Stalin Era* (Random House 1999).

[365] Justice Clark, one of Truman's four appointees, did not participate in *Dennis*. Justice Wiley Rutledge, a Roosevelt appointee, joined the Truman appointees and Justices Frankfurter and Jackson to form the six-justice majority.

[366] See Wiecek, 2001 Sup Ct Rev at 379 (cited in note 1).

[367] Consider the "legislative findings" in the McCarran Internal Security Act of 1950, which was enacted only a few months before the decision in *Dennis*. The act posited a "world Communist movement" that achieved its goals by "treachery, deceit, infiltration, . . . espionage, sabotage, [and] terrorism." Individual members of the Communist Party of the United States are "rigidly and ruthlessly disciplined," and such

persons "repudiate their allegiance to the United States." The act declared further that the party was actively preparing for its moment of opportunity, its moment to launch a violent revolution, "when the United States may be so far extended by foreign engagements, so far divided in counsel, or so far in industrial or financial straits" that it would be vulnerable to such an effort. The act thus announced that the Communist Party posed "a clear and present danger to the security of the United States and to the existence of free American institutions." Subversive Activities Control Act of 1950, Pub L 831, 64 Stat 987.

368 Id at 429.

369 *The Smith Act Upheld*, New York Times 30 (June 5, 1951); *Freedom with Security*, Washington Post 12 (June 6, 1951); *What the Court Destroyed*, New Republic 5 (June 18, 1951); St. Clair and Gugin, *Chief Justice Fred M. Vinson* at 246 (cited in note 345). As soon as the Court's decision was announced, four of the eleven defendants in *Dennis* jumped bail. Two were captured by the FBI by 1953; two remained in hiding until 1956, when they decided to surrender to the police. See Caute, *Great Fear* at 205 (cited in note 3).

370 Caute, *Great Fear* at 195, 201 (cited in note 3). See id at 195–208.

371 341 US 716 (1951).

372 Id at 720–21. *Garner* was a 5-to-4 decision. Justices Black, Frankfurter, Douglas, and Burton dissented, arguing variously that the act was unconstitutional because it was a bill of attainder (Black and Douglas), reached back in time and left "no room for a change of heart" (Burton), and did not satisfy the *scienter* requirement (Frankfurter).

373 342 US 485 (1952).

374 Id at 487 n 3, 488 n 4, 493. *Adler* was a 6-to-3 decision. Justices Black, Douglas, and Frankfurter dissented. Later that year, in *Wieman v. Updegraff*, 344 US 183 (1952), the Court unanimously invalidated an oath requirement because, unlike the programs upheld in *Garner* and *Adler*, the challenged act disqualified even individuals who did not know of the organization's proscribed advocacy.

375 342 US 580 (1952).

376 Justices Black and Douglas dissented. See also *Galvan v. Press*, 347 US 522 (1954) (upholding the deportation of an individual who had been in the United States for thirty-one years because he had been a member of the Communist Party from 1944 to 1946, whether or not the government could prove that the individual knew of the party's unlawful advocacy).

377 Newman, *Hugo Black* at 411 (cited in note 359).

378 See also *American Communications Association v. Douds*, 339 US 382 (1950) (upholding section 9(h) of the Labor-Management Relations Act of 1950, which prohibited the NLRB from enforcing employee representation rights of an labor union whose officers failed to execute affidavits that they were not members of the Communist Party); *Gerende v. Board of Supervisors of Elections*, 341 US 56 (1951) (upholding a Maryland law requiring candidates for public office to "make oath that he is not a person who is engaged 'in one way or another in the attempt to overthrow the government by force or violence,' and that he is not knowingly a member of an organization engaged in such an attempt"). One of the few speech-protective decisions of this era

was *Joint Anti-Fascist Refugee Committee v. McGrath*, 341 US 123 (1951) (holding unconstitutional the attorney general's listing of the Joint Anti-Fascist Refugee Committee as a subversive organization under President Truman's 1947 executive order establishing the federal loyalty program because on the state of pleadings there was insufficient evidence to justify the attorney general's designation of the organization as subversive). Several years later the Court upheld an order requiring the Communist Party to register under the Subversive Activities Control Act. See *Communist Party v. Subversive Activities Control Board*, 367 US 1 (1961).

[379] Douglas, *Court Years* at 96 (cited in note 344).

[380] See Kalven, *Worthy Tradition* at 211 (cited in note 323).

[381] 354 US 298 (1957). The other three decisions were *Watkins v. United States*, 354 US 178 (1957) (limiting HUAC's investigative activities); *Sweezy v. New Hampshire*, 354 US 234 (1957) (limiting state investigative activities); *Service v. Dulles* 354 US 363 (1957) (limiting loyalty-security dismissals).

[382] See Caute, *Great Fear* at 200–201 (cited in note 3). The Supreme Court later held that the bail was excessive and had not been set by the proper standards. *Stack v. Boyle*, 342 US 1 (1951).

[383] Justices Brennan and Whittaker did not participate. Justice Clark dissented.

[384] Kalven, *Worthy Tradition* at 211 (cited in note 323). Kalven credits this allusion to Philip Kurland. See id at 632 n 5.

[385] *Yates*, 354 US at 318–19, 321, 324–25.

[386] Id at 327–28.

[387] *U.S. Court Clears 9 California Reds*, New York Times 54 (Dec 3, 1957). See Caute, *Great Fear* at 208 (cited in note 3).

[388] 367 US 203 (1961).

[389] Id at 219, 229. See also *Noto v. United States*, 367 US 290 (1961) (holding that "mere abstract teaching of communist theory" is not within scope of Smith Act and that membership provision of the act requires evidence of "present illegal [communist] party advocacy").

[390] 384 US 11 (1966).

[391] Id at 13, 17, 19. In dissent, Justice White, joined by Justices Clark, Harlan, and Stewart, argued that the public employment situation is completely different from the criminal prosecution situation and that the government should not be compelled to hire individuals who knowingly join organizations that are dedicated "to the overthrow of the government by any illegal means necessary to achieve this end." Id at 21 (White, dissenting).

[392] See *Aptheker v. Secretary of State*, 378 US 500 (1964) (passports); *Nowak v. United States*, 356 US 660 (1958) (denaturalization); *Maisenberg v. United States*, 356 US 670 (1958) (denaturalization); *Speiser v. Randal*, 357 US 513 (1958) (property tax exemptions); *Lamont v. Postmaster General*, 381 US 301 (1965) (mail).

[393] 357 US 449 (1958).

[394] Id at 462–63. See also *Shelton v. Tucker*, 364 US 479 (1960) (holding unconstitutional an Arkansas statute requiring every public school teacher to file an affidavit listing every organization to which he had belonged or contributed within the preceding

five years).

395 See *Quinn v. United States*, 349 US 155 (1955); *Emspak v. United States*, 349 US 190 (1955); *Bart v. United States*, 349 US 219 (1955).

396 354 US 178 (1957).

397 Id at 197, 200. See also *Sweezy v. New Hampshire*, 354 US 234 (1957) (invalidating a conviction for contempt of a state investigating committee because the delegation of authority to the state attorney general was unconstitutionally broad).

398 360 US 109 (1959).

399 Id at 130, 134. Harlan distinguished *NAACP v. Alabama* on the ground that, unlike the NAACP, the Communist Party is not "an ordinary political" organization because of its historical "nexus" to the "violent overthrow of government."

400 Id at 144, 153 (Black dissenting). See also *Uphaus v. Wyman*, 360 US 72 (1959) (upholding a contempt citation arising out of a state investigation of Communist activities); *Wilkinson v. United States*, 365 US 399 (1961) (upholding a HUAC contempt citation); *Braden v. United States*, 365 US 431 (1961) (upholding a HUAC contempt citation). But see *Deutch v. United States*, 367 US 456 (1961) (invalidating a HUAC contempt citation on grounds of pertinency); *Russell v. United States*, 369 US 749 (1962) (invalidating a HUAC contempt citation because of a defect in the indictments).

401 372 US 539 (1963).

402 Id at 545, 551 (emphasis added). The Court distinguished *Barenblatt* on the rather tenuous ground that *Barenblatt* involved an inquiry into Communist Party membership, whereas *Gibson* involved an inquiry into whether members of the Communist Party were members of the NAACP. See also *Yellin v. United States*, 374 US 109 (1963) (invalidating a HUAC contempt citation); *DeGregory v. Attorney General of New Hampshire*, 383 US 825 (1966) (invalidating a state contempt citation); *Gojack v. United States*, 384 US 702 (1966) (invalidating a HUAC contempt citation).

403 For an excellent review the Court's decisions in this era, see Kalven, *Worthy Tradition* at 190–587 (cited in note 323).

404 Cf Paul Lazarsfeld and Wagner Thielens Jr., *The Academic Mind: Social Scientists in a Time of Crisis* (Free 1958) (dealing with the attitudes of academics).

405 *Text of President's Speech at Dedication of New Legion Building*, Washington Post 7 (Aug 15, 1951). See Reeves, *Joseph McCarthy* at 379–80 (cited in note 3).

406 Madison Capital Times (July 30, Aug 2, 1951). There was good evidence to suggest that the public's confidence in democratic values and freedom of expression deteriorated significantly during this era. See O'Brian, *National Security* at 69–70 (cited in note 315).

407 Newman, *Hugo Black* at 401 (cited in note 359).

408 Goldstein, *Political Repression* at 380–81 (cited in note 3).

409 Norman Mailer, *The White Negro*, excerpted in Massimo Teodori, ed, *The New Left: A Documentary History* 10 (Bobbs-Merrill 1969).

410 See Caute, *Great Fear* at 12 (cited in note 3).

411 Max Ascoli, *The American Politburo*, Reporter 4–5 (July 10, 1951); Sidney Hook, *Political Power and Personal Freedom* 293–94 (Criterion 1959), both excerpted in Caute,

Great Fear at 52–53 (cited in note 3).

[412] Caute, *Great Fear* at 39 (cited in note 3).

[413] Kutler, *American Inquisition* at 154 (cited in note 260); John P. Frank, *The United States Supreme Court, 1950–51*, 19 U Chi L Rev 165, 200 (1952).

[414] See Mary S. McAuliffe, *The Politics of Civil Liberties: The American Civil Liberties Union during the McCarthy Years*, in Griffith and Theoharis, eds, *Specter*, at 154–70 (cited in note 6); Jerold Auerbach, *The Depression Decade*, in Reitman, ed, *Pulse of Freedom* at 83–104 (cited in note 90); Brown, *Loyalty and Security* at 109–16 (cited in note 10); Goldstein, *Political Repression* at 363–68 (cited in note 3). Several cases involving admission to the bar reached the Supreme Court in this era. See, for example, *Konigsberg v. State Bar*, 366 US 36 (1961) (upholding a state bar's decision to deny an individual membership in the bar because he refused to answer questions concerning membership in the Communist Party); *In re Anastoplo*, 366 US 82 (1961) (similar); *Schware v. Board of Bar Examiners of New Mexico*, 353 US 232 (1957) (invalidating an exclusion from the bar).

[415] Kalman, *Abe Fortas* at 132 (cited in note 159).

[416] Id at 136. See generally id at 129–51.

[417] *Adler*, 342 US at 493; *More Enemy Kings Here, Hoover Says*, New York Times 32 (Apr 5, 1953); Christian Science Monitor 11 (Mar 10, 1954); Goodman, *Committee* at 332 (cited in note 183); *The Danger Signals*, Time 85–86 (Apr 13, 1953); Biddle, *Fear of Freedom* at 180–81 (cited in note 127). See Caute, *Great Fear* at 428–29 (cited in note 3); Goldstein, *Political Repression* at 354–55 (cited in note 3).

[418] Barth, *Loyalty of Free Men* at 224 (cited in note 11).

[419] Id at 219–20. See id at 218–21.

[420] Goldstein, *Political Repression* at 363 (cited in note 3). See Goodman, *Committee* at 325–32 (cited in note 183); Goldstein, *Political Repression* at 355, 362–63 (cited in note 3); Barth, *Loyalty of Free Men* at 223 (cited in note 11); Biddle, *Fear of Freedom* at 155–81 (cited in note 127); *Academic Freedom and Tenure in the Quest for National Security*, 42 Bulletin of the American Association of University Professors 49 (1956).

[421] See Blanchard, *Revolutionary Sparks* at 255–57 (cited in note 44); Caute, *Great Fear* at 11 (cited in note 3).

[422] *Great Investigation* at 68 (cited in note 29).

[423] Id at 66. See Boyer, *Academic Freedom* at 10 (cited in note 25). In total, about 350 students went to Springfield from the University of Chicago and Roosevelt University.

[424] Id at 66. See Geoffrey R. Stone, *Academic Freedom and Responsibility*, in John W. Boyer, ed, *The Aims of Education* 233, 249 (Chicago 1997).

[425] Robert Maynard Hutchins, Testimony before the Subversive Activities Committee of the Illinois State Legislature (Apr 21, 1949), in *Great Investigation* at 2–4 (cited in note 29). See Barth, *Loyalty of Free Men* at 226–27 (cited in note 11).

[426] Hutchins, Testimony before the Subversive Activities Committee at 2–3, 10–18 (cited in note 425).

[427] Id at 10–18, 27.

[428] *Great Investigation* at 65 (cited in note 29); Stone, *Academic Freedom and Responsibility* at 251 (cited in note 424).

[429] See Boyer, *Academic Freedom* at 11 (cited in note 25). On this episode, see E. Houston Harsha, *Illinois: The Broyles Commission*, in Gellhorn, ed, *States and Subversion* 54, 95–108 (cited in note 125).

[430] Robert Maynard Hutchins, *Education for Freedom* 100–105 (Louisiana State 1943).

[431] See Shils, *Robert Maynard Hutchins* at 194–96 (cited in note 20).

[432] On Hutchins from 1951 to 1977, see Dzuback, *Robert M. Hutchins* at 229–83 (cited in note 14); Ashmore, *Unreasonable Truths* at 311–541 (cited in note 16).

CHAPTER VI

[1] See Charles DeBenedetti, *An American Ordeal: The Antiwar Movement of the Vietnam Era* 2 (Syracuse 1990).

[2] William L. O'Neill, *Coming Apart: An Informal History of America in the 1960's* (Quadrangle 1977).

[3] Robert Dallek, *An Unfinished Life: John F. Kennedy, 1917–1963* 186–87 (Little, Brown 2003).

[4] See, for example, Hans J. Morgenthau, *Vietnam—Another Korea?*, Commentary 369, 374 (May 1962).

[5] Leslie H. Gelb and Richard K. Betts, *The Irony of Vietnam: The System Worked* 70 (Brookings 1979).

[6] On Kennedy's reluctance to expand the American military involvement in Vietnam, see Dallek, *Unfinished Life* at 447–50, 709–10 (cited in note 3); Adam Garfinkle, *Telltale Hearts: The Origins and Impact of the Vietnam Antiwar Movement* 54–55 (St. Martin's 1995); William Manchester, *The Glory and the Dream: A Narrative History of America: 1932–1972* 925 (Little, Brown 1973).

[7] Arthur Krock, *Memoirs: Sixty Years on the Firing Line* 358 (Funk and Wagnalls 1968); Arthur M. Schlesinger Jr., *A Thousand Days: John F. Kennedy in the White House* 547 (Houghton Mifflin 1965).

[8] David Wise and Thomas B. Ross, *The Invisible Government* 159–64 (Random House 1964). See also DeBenedetti, *American Ordeal* at 81–91 (cited in note 1).

[9] See Todd Gitlin, *The Sixties: Years of Hope, Days of Rage* 242 (Bantam 1993). See also Loren Baritz, *Backfire: A History of How American Culture Led Us into Vietnam and Made Us Fight the Way We Did* 145, 176 (Morrow 1985); Stanley Karnow, *Vietnam: A History* 512 (Penguin 1984); William H. Chafe, *The Unfinished Journey: America Since World War II* 289–90 (Oxford 2003); Gabriel Kolko, *Anatomy of a War: Vietnam, the United States, and the Modern Historical Experience* 145 (Pantheon 1985).

[10] Lawrence M. Baskir and William A. Strauss, *The Draft and Who Escaped It*, in Andrew J. Rotter, ed, *Light at the End of the Tunnel: A Vietnam War Anthology* 457 (St. Martin's 1991).

[11] David Dellinger, *From Yale to Jail: The Life Story of a Moral Dissenter* 11–16 (Pantheon 1993). See Nancy Zaroulis and Gerald Sullivan, *Who Spoke Up? American Protest against the War in Vietnam, 1963–1975* 7–8 (Doubleday 1984).

[12] Dellinger, *From Yale to Jail* at 21–25 (cited in note 11).

[13] Id at 23–55.

[14] Id at 61–86. See Michael Ferber and Staughton Lynd, *The Resistance* 6 (Beacon 1971).

[15] See Zaroulis and Sullivan, *Who Spoke Up?* at 7–8 (cited in note 11).

[16] DeBenedetti, *American Ordeal* at 25 (cited in note 1); Dellinger, *From Yale to Jail* at 145–50 (cited in note 11).

[17] Dellinger, *From Yale to Jail* at 189–90 (cited in note 11).

[18] *Post War World Council Newsletter* 3 (Feb 1955), excerpted in DeBenedetti, *American Ordeal* at 15 (cited in note 1). See Linus Pauling, *No More War!* 11–13 (Victor Gollancz 1958); DeBenedetti, *American Ordeal* at 9–15 (cited in note 1); Fred Halstead, *Out Now! A Participant's Account of the American Movement Against the Vietnam War* 7–14 (Monad 1978).

[19] C. Wright Mills christened the SPU the "New Left." See C. Wright Mills, *Letter to the New Left*, in Priscilla Long, ed, *The New Left: A Collection of Essays* 25 (Porter Sargent 1969).

[20] Amy Swerdlow, *"Not My Son, Not Your Son, Not Their Sons": Mothers against the Vietnam Draft*, in Melvin Small and William D. Hoover, eds, *Give Peace a Chance: Exploring the Vietnam Antiwar Movement* 159 (Syracuse 1992); Penny Blum, *Invitation to Women*, Nation 20 (Jan 13, 1962). WSP played a unique role in the pantheon of antiwar groups. As an organization of respectable women, it was able to achieve a special level of credibility at "a time when Cold War dissenters were dismissed by the press, the public, and political leaders as either subversives or deviants. . . . By mid-decade, WSP had moved from antinuclear activism to militant protest against U.S. intervention in Vietnam." Swerdlow, *Not My Son* at 159–60, 163. On the role of women in the New Left, see Barbara L. Tischler, *The Refiner's Fire: Anti-war Activism and Emerging Feminism in the Late 1960s*, in Marc Jason Gilbert, ed, *The Vietnam War on Campus: Other Voices, More Distant Drums* 54, 58–59 (Praeger 2001).

[21] See Irwin Unger, *The Movement: A History of the American New Left, 1959–1972* 82–83 (Harper and Row 1974); DeBenedetti, *American Ordeal* at 57 (cited in note 1).

[22] Allan Nevins, ed, *The Burden and the Glory* 57 (Harper and Row 1964).

[23] Dallek, *Unfinished Life* at 619–20, 629 (cited in note 3).

[24] *First Step—To Where?*, Bulletin of Atomic Scientists 2–3 (Oct 1963). Earlier that year, at a march in support of nuclear disarmament, those carrying signs denouncing U.S. involvement in Vietnam were asked to remove their signs because some peace leaders did not want to divide an already weak "peace community" by criticizing President Kennedy's policy in Vietnam. See Zaroulis and Sullivan, *Who Spoke Up?* at 8–9 (cited in note 11).

[25] Garfinkle, *Telltale Hearts* at 66 (cited in note 6).

[26] See Maurice Isserman, *You Don't Need a Weatherman But a Postman Can Be Helpful: Thoughts on the History of SDS and the Antiwar Movement*, in Small and Hoover, eds, *Give Peace a Chance* at 22–34 (cited in note 20); DeBenedetti, *American Ordeal* at 63–67 (cited in note 1); Kirkpatrick Sale, *SDS* 15–17 (Random House 1973); Garfinkle, *Telltale Hearts* at 61 (cited in note 6).

[27] Gitlin, *Sixties* at 121 (cited in note 9). See also Zaroulis and Sullivan, *Who Spoke Up?* at 29–31 (cited in note 11).

[28] Port Huron Statement, reprinted in James Miller, *Democracy Is in the Streets: From Port Huron to the Siege of Chicago* (Simon and Schuster 1987). See Garfinkle, *Telltale Hearts* at 62–63 (cited in note 6).

[29] See DeBenedetti, *American Ordeal* at 66-68 (cited in note 1); Sale, *SDS* at 49–54 (cited in note 26); Halstead, *Out Now!* at 24–28 (cited in note 18).

[30] David Dellinger, *Growing Pains in the Anti-war Movement*, Liberation 7, 14 (Apr 1962), excerpted in DeBenedetti, *American Ordeal* at 59 (cited in note 1). One of the first public demonstrations against the Vietnam War took place in October 1963 when a handful of SDS members protested the visit to the United States of Mme Ngo Dinh Nhu, the sister-in-law of South Vietnam's dictatorial leader. See Robert Justin Goldstein, *Political Repression in Modern America: From 1870 to the Present* 435 (Schenkman 1978).

[31] This is derived from Charles DeBenedetti's very insightful analysis on this issue. See DeBenedetti, *American Ordeal* at 73–76 (cited in note 1).

[32] Erich Fromm, *The Sane Society* 357 (Holt, Rinehart and Winston 1955);

[33] Allen Ginsberg, *Howl*, in Allen Ginsberg, *Collected Poems, 1947–1980* 126 (Harper and Row 1984).

[34] Lewis Mumford, *The Morals of Extermination*, Atlantic Monthly 38, 40 (Oct 1959); Stephen Carey and Robert Pickus, *Reply to the Critics*, Progressive 19, 24 (Oct 1955). See DeBenedetti, *American Ordeal* at 73 (cited in note 1).

[35] Thomas Merton, *Introduction*, in *Breakthrough to Peace* 10 (New Directions 1962).

[36] DeBenedetti, *American Ordeal* at 76 (cited in note 1).

[37] Garfinkle, *Telltale Hearts* at 48 (cited in note 6).

[38] Sale, *SDS* at 20 (cited in note 26).

[39] See Goldstein, *Political Repression* at 434–35 (cited in note 30). See Sale, *SDS* at 162–69 (cited in note 26); Seymour Martin Lipset and Sheldon S. Wolins, eds, *The Berkeley Student Revolt: Facts and Interpretations* (Doubleday 1965); Paul Jacobs and Saul Landau, *The New Radicals: A Report with Documents* 59–64 (Random House 1966).

[40] See Eric F. Goldman, *The Tragedy of Lyndon Johnson* 164–75 (Knopf 1969).

[41] Id at 175–76.

[42] DeBenedetti, *American Ordeal* at 89 (cited in note 1).

[43] 88th Cong, 2d Sess, in 110 Cong Rec S 12399 (June 2, 1964). Morse also replied to a statement made by Secretary of State Dean Rusk, who attacked the country's "quitters," accusing them of "playing into the hands" of the nation's enemies. Morse said that Rusk was equating criticism with treason, as the "late unlamented Senator [Joseph] McCarthy had done." Zaroulis and Sullivan, *Who Spoke Up?* at 16–17 (cited in note 11).

[44] 88th Cong, 2d Sess, in 110 Cong Rec S 4835 (Mar 10, 1964).

[45] See Zaroulis and Sullivan, *Who Spoke Up?* at 18–19 (cited in note 11); Gitlin, *Sixties* at 179 (cited in note 9); Sale, *SDS* at 36 (cited in note 26). Although the SDS had not yet embraced a strong antiwar position, the Progressive Labor Party sponsored a "We Won't Go" pledge against the Vietnam War in the spring of 1964. See Ferber and

Lynd, *Resistance* at 50–51 (cited in note 14). Other early expressions of antiwar sentiment included an ad in the New York *Herald Tribune* in May 1964, declaring that the
149 signers "would not fight if called to do so in Vietnam," and an antiwar petition
signed by five thousand college and university professors that was delivered to the
State Department on July 10, 1964. See Zaroulis and Sullivan, *Who Spoke Up?* at
19–21 (cited in note 11).

[46] See Goldman, *Tragedy* at 175–76 (cited in note 40). At the time of the U.S. retaliatory
airstrike, Johnson explained to the American public, "Aggression by terror against the
peaceful villages of South Vietnam has now been joined by open aggression on the
high seas against the United States of America. . . . Yet our response, for the present,
will be limited and fitting. We Americans know, although others appear to forget, the
risks of spreading conflict. We still seek no wider war." Id.

[47] *Message and Draft Text in Congress*, New York Times 8 (Aug 6, 1964). See Melvin
Small, *Johnson, Nixon, and the Doves* 28 (Rutgers 1988). The Senate vote was 88 to
2. Only Senators Morse and Gruening voted no. See Zaroulis and Sullivan, *Who
Spoke Up?* at 22–23 (cited in note 11).

[48] See David Halberstam, *The Best and the Brightest* 408–14 (Random House 1972);
Goldman, *Tragedy* at 177–83, 253–56 (cited in note 40); DeBenedetti, *American
Ordeal* at 92–99 (cited in note 1).

[49] See Halberstam, *Best and Brightest* at 537–43, 579–80 (cited in note 48); Small, *Doves*
at 29–31 (cited in note 47).

[50] DeBenedetti, *American Ordeal* at 100 (cited in note 1).

[51] The challenges facing SDS as it found itself at the forefront of a loosely organized antiwar movement are traced in Sale, *SDS* at 173–79, 198–99 (cited in note 26). The civil
rights movement still preoccupied much of the national attention and activist energy.
March 1965 marked Martin Luther King Jr.'s Selma–Montgomery march and the face-
off with Governor George Wallace, which required federal troops to secure the safety
of the marchers. Although Lyndon Johnson fully supported the aim of the marchers,
he was "no enthusiast of mass demonstrations." In his view, such activists would better serve their cause by working directly with politicians to enact legislation. Goldman, *Tragedy* at 310–14 (cited in note 40). His aversion to mass demonstrations as an
appropriate means of political action did not abate when the antiwar movement
moved in this direction.

[52] See DeBenedetti, *American Ordeal* at 99–102 (cited in note 1).

[53] Doris Kearns, *Lyndon Johnson and the American Dream* 251 (Harper and Row 1976).

[54] Goldman, *Tragedy* at 378–79 (cited in note 40).

[55] Halberstam, *Best and Brightest* at 298 (cited in note 48).

[56] See DeBenedetti, *American Ordeal* at 103–6 (cited in note 1). Even critics of the government's policy in Vietnam within the Johnson administration were effectively
muted. Vice President Hubert Humphrey, for example, advised the president that, in
his view, there should be "more effort at a political solution" and informed him of his
doubts about "the wisdom of trying to bomb the North Vietnamese to the negotiating
table." But Humphrey made these points to Johnson in "strict confidence"; he did not

express them publicly. Goldman, *Tragedy* at 263–64 (cited in note 40). By 1965, although the administration was still confident of its ability to manage its critics, most of the president's advisers agreed that "if the war dragged on too long, the dissenters might become an important domestic political problem." Small, *Doves* at 25 (cited in note 47).

57 Caroline Page, *U.S. Official Propaganda during the Vietnam War, 1965–1973* 53–54 (Leicester 1996).

58 See DeBenedetti, *American Ordeal* at 104 (cited in note 1); Goldman, *Tragedy* at 403–5 (cited in note 40).

59 Larry Berman, *Planning A Tragedy: The Americanization of the War in Vietnam* 121 (Norton 1982).

60 See George C. Herring, *LBJ Goes to War*, in Rotter, ed, *End of Tunnel* at 147 (cited in note 10).

61 3 *The Pentagon Papers: The Defense Department History of United States Decisionmaking on Vietnam* 477 (Beacon 1971) (Senator Gravel edition).

62 "*We Have to Finish the Job,*" Newsweek 27 (Sept 20, 1965). An article in the *New York Herald Tribune* referred to the "credibility gap," and an article in the *Washington Post* observed that there was "growing doubt and cynicism concerning Administration pronouncements," which it too termed a "credibility gap." Goldman, *Tragedy* at 409 (cited in note 40). Contributing to Johnson's credibility problem was also his approach to the press, which reflected his view that a president had to "protect his options" even to the point of wanting to cut off press speculation about his possible decisions. James Reston observed,

> If all presidential options are to be protected from speculation until the very last minute, what redress will there be the day after the President has opted to dispatch the Marines, or bomb Hanoi, or publish a decision to wage war . . . as he deems necessary? These are hard questions, and the answers are not that the Commander in Chief must telegraph all his punches in advance. But at the same time, the doctrine of no-speculation-before-official-publication . . . is something new in the catalogue of presidential privilege.

Id at 413.

63 See *A Grasp of Vietnam by Public Indicated*, New York Times 1 (July 30, 1965).

64 Halberstam, *Best and Brightest* at 591, 623 (cited in note 48).

65 See Laurence Stern, *3000 Hear U.S. Viet Policy Attacked and Supported at "Teach-In" Here*, Washington Post A1 (May 16, 1965); Richard E. Peterson, *The Scope of Organized Student Protest in 1964–1965* 11–35, 41–48 (Educational Testing Service 1966); Sales, *SDS* at 183–85 (cited in note 26); Garfinkle *Telltale Hearts* at 72 (cited in note 6); DeBenedetti, *American Ordeal* at 108 (cited in note 1); Goldman, *Tragedy* at 430–31 (cited in note 40); Zaroulis and Sullivan, *Who Spoke Up?* at 37 (cited in note 11); Halstead, *Out Now!* at 45–54, 69 (cited in note 18). The Johnson administration dispatched a "truth team" from the State Department to travel to various cam-

puses in an effort to counter the anti-administration line taken by the teach-ins. This effort lasted about three weeks, before the "hostile receptions" drove home the point that it was "too little too late." Dean Rusk criticized the teach-ins, lamenting the "gullibility of educated men and the disregard of plain facts." Zaroulis and Sullivan, *Who Spoke Up?* at 37–38, 42 (cited in note 11).

66 See Garfinkle, *Telltale Hearts* at 74 (cited in note 6); Sale, *SDS* at 185–91 (cited in note 26); Halstead, *Out Now!* at 35–44 (cited in note 18); Melvin Small, *Covering Dissent: The Media and the Anti-Vietnam War Movement* 35–37 (Rutgers 1994); *Viet-Nam War Protest Is Staged by 16,000*, Washington Post A1 (Apr 18, 1965); *15,000 White House Pickets Denounce Vietnam War*, New York Times 1 (Apr 18, 1965).

67 See DeBenedetti, *American Ordeal* at 112 (cited in note 1); Peter Bart, *33-Hour Teach-in Attracts 10,000*, New York Times 26 (May 23, 1965); Raymond Daniell, *U.S. Assailed on Vietnam Policy before 17,000 at a Garden Rally*, id at 4 (June 9, 1965).

68 See Goldman, *Tragedy* at 430–31 (cited in note 40); DeBenedetti, *American Ordeal* at 113–15 (cited in note 1). The criticism by the intellectual and artistic elite provoked an especially strong reaction from Johnson over the subject of the White House Festival of the Arts on June 8, 1965. When several of the invited artists publicly declined to attend, citing their dismay with recent foreign policy developments, Johnson threw a fit. Over time, Johnson's inability to accept such criticism graciously became a wall between him and the nation's intellectual and cultural elite. In 1965, however, he still kept these reactions largely private, and that the festival went on despite these protests led the *New York Times* to note that, "by tolerating dissent within its own precincts, the White House raised its own and the nation's stature." Goldman, *Tragedy* at 444–75 (cited in note 40). See also Zaroulis and Sullivan, *Who Spoke Up?* at 44–45 (cited in note 11).

69 See Ferber and Lynd, *Resistance* at 34–38 (cited in note 14); Isserman, *Don't Need a Weatherman* at 26–27 (cited in note 26); DeBenedetti, *American Ordeal* at 116–17 (cited in note 1); Sale, *SDS* at 213–15 (cited in note 26); Jacobs and Landau, *New Radicals* at 66, 75 (cited in note 39).

70 See Small, *Doves* at 46 (cited in note 47).

71 *Show of Support on Vietnam Gains Strength in U.S.*, New York Times 1 (Oct 21, 1965).

72 89th Cong, 1st Sess, in 111 Cong Rec S 27253 (Oct 18, 1965).

73 DeBenedetti, *American Ordeal* at 118 (cited in note 1).

74 Lady Bird Johnson, *A White House Diary* 262 (Holt, Rinehart and Winston 1970).

75 Goldman, *Tragedy* at 413–14 (cited in note 40).

76 Id.

77 DeBenedetti, *American Ordeal* at 119 (cited in note 1).

78 *Straws in the Wind*, Nation 514 (Dec 27, 1965). See DeBenedetti, *American Ordeal* at 122–38. A particularly ugly display by counterdemonstrators took place at a rally on November 6, 1965. A few days earlier, Norman Morrison, a thirty-two-year-old Quaker and father of three, burned himself to death in front of the Pentagon in protest against the war. At the November 6 rally in Union Square in New York City, antiwar protesters observed a moment of silence for Morrison, as counterdemonstra-

tors carried signs reading, "Burn Yourself Instead of Your Card" and "Thanks Pinkos, Queers, Cowards, Draft Dodgers—Mao Tse-Tsung," while chanting, "Drop Dead, Red." Ferber and Lynd, *Resistance* at 24–25 (cited in note 14). See also Zaroulis and Sullivan, *Who Spoke Up?* at 61 (cited in note 11).

[79] Ted Finman and Stewart Macaulay, *Freedom to Dissent: The Vietnam Protests and the Worlds of Public Officials*, 1966 Wisc L Rev 632, 676–77. See also Goldstein, *Political Repression* at 435–36 (cited in note 30); *Vietnam War Protests Held Red-Dominated*, Washington Post A17 (Oct 15, 1965).

[80] Finman and Macaulay, 1966 Wisc L Rev at 675–76 (cited in note 79); Goldstein, *Political Repression* at 436 (cited in note 30). These accusations were bolstered when the *New York Times* ran a front-page story by Seymour Topping on the October march with the subhead "Asian Communists Sure Public Opinion in U.S. Will Force War's End." New York Times 1 (Nov 28, 1965). *Time* magazine ran an editorial explaining that "the Vietniks, by encouraging the Communist hope and expectation that the U.S. does not have the stomach to fight it out in Vietnam, are probably achieving what they would least like: prolonging the war and adding to the casualty lists on both sides." *The Vietniks: Self-defeating Dissent*, Time 44, 45 (Oct 29, 1965).

[81] Goldstein, *Political Repression* at 436 (cited in note 30). See Halberstam, *Best and Brightest* at 453, 623–24 (cited in note 48).

[82] Goldman, *Tragedy* at 499–500 (cited in note 40). See Goldstein, *Political Repression* at 436–37, 454–57 (cited in note 30).

[83] Small, *Doves* at 64–65 (cited in note 47).

[84] Louis Harris, *Confidence in Johnson on War Back to 42%*, Washington Post A2 (Sept 20, 1966).

[85] See Garfinkle, *Telltale Hearts* at 85 (cited in note 6).

[86] *T.R.B. from Washington*, New Republic 4 (June 25, 1966). The military was also beginning to experience increasing difficulty in convincing soldiers of the justness of the war. Captain Howard Levy, a physician, refused to train Special Forces medics to serve in Vietnam. He argued that the war was wrong, that the Green Berets were participating in war crimes, and that black soldiers should refuse to serve in Vietnam. The army court-martialed him and one month before his discharge date sentenced him to three years of hard labor. Levy argued that this penalty violated his rights under the First Amendment. The case finally reached the Supreme Court in 1974, when the Court upheld his conviction, explaining that although "members of the military are not excluded from the protection granted by the First Amendment, the different character of the military community and of the military mission requires a different application of those protections." *Parker v. Levy*, 417 US 733, 758 (1974). See Terry H. Anderson, *The GI Movement and the Response from the Brass*, in Small and Hoover, eds, *Give Peace a Chance* at 93, 96 (cited in note 20).

[87] Ferber and Lynd, *Resistance* at 29–33 (cited in note 14). In July 1965, the Freedom Democratic Party issued an antiwar statement (anticipating later SNCC statements) that argued that blacks should not "be in any war fighting for America." In response to objections that those in Vietnam were fighting for "Freedom" or "Democracy," the statement charged, "[T]hat's what we are fighting for here in Mississippi . . .—we

don't know anything about Communism, socialism, and all that, but we do know that Negroes have caught hell here under this *American Democracy*." Jacobs and Landau, *New Radicals* at 249–50 (cited in note 39).

[88] See DeBenedetti, *American Ordeal* at 153–54, 166–67 (cited in note 1); Sale, *SDS* at 255–63 (cited in note 26). For a recounting of the events that led to the pledge, and the text of the antidraft resolution, see Ferber and Lynd, *Resistance* at 59–65 (cited in note 14).

[89] In July 1965, a delegation of ten American women, organized by Women Strike for Peace, met with representatives of the North Vietnamese and NLF in Indonesia. In December 1965, Tom Hayden and Staughton Lynd, an assistant professor of history at Yale, became the first Americans to visit Hanoi during the war. See Tom Hayden and Staughton Lynd, *The Other Side* (New American Library 1966); DeBenedetti, *American Ordeal* at 168–71 (cited in note 1); Garfinkle, *Telltale Hearts* at 82–83 (cited in note 6). In 1966, the *New York Times* began publishing reports by Harrison Salisbury from Hanoi. Salisbury reported that the official Washington communiqués on American bombings of North Vietnam had been "deliberately obfuscating" and that American bombs, "despite all claims for 'surgical precision,' had killed civilians and destroyed churches, schools, homes, and factories in Hanoi and other North Vietnamese cities." Zaroulis and Sullivan, *Who Spoke Up?* at 98 (cited in note 11).

[90] Goldstein, *Political Repression* at 437 (cited in note 30). See Walter Goodman, *The Committee: The Extraordinary Career of the House Committee on Un-American Activities* 473–81 (Farrar, Straus and Giroux 1968).

[91] Homer Bigart, *Fulbright Warns of "Fatal" Course by U.S. in Vietnam*, New York Times 1 (Apr 29, 1966); David S. Broder, *Goldwater Says Johnson Plays Politics with War*, id at 6 (May 6, 1966). See DeBenedetti, *American Ordeal* at 151 (cited in note 1); Garfinkle, *Telltale Hearts* at 89 (cited in note 6).

[92] See Louis Harris, *How the U.S. Public Now Feels about Vietnam*, Newsweek 24 (Feb 27, 1967); DeBenedetti, *American Ordeal* at 168–71 (cited in note 1).

[93] DeBenedetti, *American Ordeal* at 172 (cited in note 1). See Zaroulis and Sullivan, *Who Spoke Up?* at 108–9 (cited in note 11); Douglas Robinson, *Dr. King Proposes a Boycott of War*, New York Times 1 (Apr 5, 1967); Leroy F. Aarons, *King Urges Cease-fire and End of Bombing, Denounces U.S. Role*, Washington Post A1 (Apr 5, 1967).

[94] Memorandum from John Roche to Lyndon B Johnson, Apr 5, 1967, excerpted in DeBenedetti, *American Ordeal* at 173 (cited in note 1). See Small, *Doves* at 100 (cited in note 47).

[95] See Small, *Covering Dissent* at 68 (cited in note 66).

[96] See Sale, *SDS* at 335 (cited in note 26) (Sale notes that, in many ways, the demonstrations were a success, but that within SDS these demonstrations represented the end of the effort to change national policy through peaceful protest); Douglas Robinson, *100,000 Rally at U.N. against Vietnam War*, New York Times 1 (Apr 16, 1967); Leroy F. Aarons, *125,000 Marchers Protest War*, Washington Post A1 (Apr 16, 1967); Paul Hofmann, *50,000 at San Francisco Peace Rally*, New York Times 3 (Apr 16, 1967).

[97] Goldstein, *Political Repression* at 437 (cited in note 30). See also Max Frankel, *F.B.I. Is Watching "Anti-war" Effort, President Says*, New York Times 1 (Apr 16, 1967); id at 9

(Apr 17, 1967); Goodman, *Committee* at 483 (cited in note 90); Thomas I. Emerson, *The System of Freedom of Expression* 91 (Random House 1970); Michael Parenti, *The Anti-Communist Impulse* 13 (Random House 1969).

[98] See Gitlin, *Sixties* at 271 (cited in note 9).

[99] See DeBenedetti, *American Ordeal* at 192–94 (cited in note 1); Gitlin, *Sixties* at 264–74 (cited in note 9).

[100] Louis Harris, *A New Sophistication*, Newsweek 20 (July 10, 1967).

[101] Tom Hayden, *Rebellion and Repression* 30 (Meridian 1969).

[102] Ferber and Lynd, *Resistance* at 1 (cited in note 14).

[103] *Militant* (Jan 8, 1968), excerpted in Halstead, *Out Now!* at 406–7 (cited in note 18). See Gitlin, *Sixties* at 289 (cited in note 9).

[104] Zaroulis and Sullivan, *Who Spoke Up?* at 112–13 (cited in note 11). See Ferber and Lynd, *Resistance* at 68–76 (cited in note 14).

[105] See Mary McCarthy, *Vietnam* 106 (Harcourt 1967); Noam Chomsky, *American Power and the New Mandarins* 324–35, 358–59 (Pantheon 1967).

[106] See Lawrence M. Baskir and William A. Strauss, *Chance and Circumstance: The Draft, the War and the Vietnam Generation* 5, 69 (Knopf 1978); Gitlin, *Sixties* at 291 (cited in note 9).

[107] Ferber and Lynd, *Resistance* at 129 (cited in note 14); Zaroulis and Sullivan, *Who Spoke Up?* at 136 (cited in note 11).

[108] *Rap Brown Praises Rioters in Detroit*, New York Times 60 (Aug 28, 1967); *Carmichael Asks Revolution in U.S.*, id at 17 (Aug 18, 1967).

[109] See DeBenedetti, *American Ordeal* at 187 (cited in note 1).

[110] Don Obendorfer, *46 Million See War as a Mistake: Gallup*, Washington Post A2 (Oct 17, 1967).

[111] *The Escalation of Dissent*, Commonweal 86 (Oct 17, 1967).

[112] See Jerome H. Skolnick, *The Politics of Protest* 60 (Simon and Schuster 1969); Goldstein, *Political Repression* at 509–10 (cited in note 30); DeBenedetti, *American Ordeal* at 196 (cited in note 1); Garfinkle, *Telltale Hearts* at 150 (cited in note 6). For an account of the planning that led to the attempt to block induction centers, and the subsequent violence, see Ferber and Lynd, *Resistance* at 140–47 (cited in note 14).

[113] See David Farber, *The Counterculture and the Antiwar Movement*, in Small and Hoover, eds, *Give Peace a Chance* at 7, 16–21 (cited in note 20); Halstead, *Out Now!* at 313–34 (cited in note 18); Garfinkle, *Telltale Hearts* at 64 (cited in note 6).

[114] See DeBenedetti, *American Ordeal* at 188 (cited in note 1); Farber, *Counterculture* at 16–17 (cited in note 113).

[115] Garfinkle, *Telltale Hearts* at 152 (cited in note 6).

[116] Norman Mailer, *The Armies of the Night* 255–56 (New American Library 1968).

[117] See id at 262; Goldstein, *Political Repression* at 439 (cited in note 30); DeBenedetti, *American Ordeal* at 197–98 (cited in note 1) Sale, *SDS* at 383–86 (cited in note 26); Zaroulis and Sullivan, *Who Spoke Up?* at 137–42 (cited in note 11); Halstead, *Out Now!* at 334–40 (cited in note 18); William Chapman, *GIs Repel Pentagon Charge; 50,000 Rally against War*, Washington Post A1 (Oct 22, 1967); Joseph A. Loftus, *Guards Repulse War Protesters at the Pentagon*, New York Times 1 (Oct 22, 1967);

William Chapman, *Anti-war Protest Recedes*, Washington Post A1 (Oct 23, 1967); Ben A. Franklin, *War Protesters Defying Deadline Seized in Capital*, New York Times 1 (Oct 23, 1967).

[118] Goldstein, *Political Repression* at 439 (cited in note 30). See Jessica Mitford, *The Trial of Dr. Spock* 53–54 (Knopf 1969)

[119] DeBenedetti, *American Ordeal* at 198 (cited in note 1); *207 Critics of War Are Seized at Peaceful Protest in Oakland*, New York Times 8 (Dec 19, 1967). See also Zaroulis and Sullivan, *Who Spoke Up?* at 147 (cited in note 11) (discussing a mid-December Harris Poll that showed that more than 75 percent of Americans believed that antiwar demonstrations "encouraged the Communists to fight all the harder" and 70 percent believed that they were "acts of disloyalty" to the soldiers fighting the war).

[120] See Kenneth J. Heineman, *American Schism: Catholic Activists, Intellectuals, and Students Confront the Vietnam War*, in Gilbert, ed, *Vietnam War on Campus* at 89, 100 (cited in note 20); Rodney Stark, *Police Riots: Collective Violence and Law Enforcement* 4–5, 32–54 (Wadsworth 1972); Skolnick, *Politics of Protest* at 69 (cited in note 112); Goldstein, *Political Repression* at 510–11 (cited in note 30); Ferber and Lynd, *Resistance* at 201–2 (cited in note 14).

[121] See Goldstein, *Political Repression* at 510 (cited in note 30); Sale, *SDS* at 371–73 (cited in note 26); Skolnick, *Politics of Protest* at 69 (cited in note 112); Ed Cray, *The Enemy in the Streets: Police Malpractice in America* 226–28 (Doubleday 1972); Thomas Powers, *The War at Home: Vietnam and the American People, 1964-1968* 244–49 (Grossman 1973); Stark, *Police Riots* at 6, 22–32, 53–54 (cited in note 120).

[122] Lyndon B. Johnson and Doris Kearns Goodwin, 2 *The Johnson Presidential Press Conferences* 870 (Coleman 1978). See also DeBenedetti, *American Ordeal* at 204 (cited in note 1).

[123] Thomas Powers, *The Man Who Kept the Secrets: Richard Helms and the CIA* 315 (Knopf 1979); Gitlin, *Sixties* at 264 (cited in note 9); DeBenedetti, *American Ordeal* at 205 (cited in note 1).

[124] *Man-made Misery and God's Promise*, Christian Century 1643, 1644 (Dec 27, 1967).

[125] Zaroulis and Sullivan, *Who Spoke Up?* at 124 (cited in note 11). On reactions to McCarty's candidacy within various parts of the left, see Garfinkle, *Telltale Hearts* at 164–65 (cited in note 6).

[126] James Reston, *Washington: The Flies That Captured the Flypaper*, New York Times 46 (Feb 7, 1968). See Gitlin, *Sixties* at 298–301 (cited in note 9); DeBenedetti, *American Ordeal* at 209–10 (cited in note 1); Larry Berman, *The Tet Offensive*, in Rotter, ed, *End of Tunnel* at 158–59 (cited in note 10); Halstead, *Out Now!* at 382–83 (cited in note 18).

[127] Don Oberdorfer, *Tet!* 158 (Doubleday 1971). See Zaroulis and Sullivan, *Who Spoke Up?* at 150–52 (cited in note 11).

[128] Halberstam, *Best and Brightest* at 640 (cited in note 48).

[129] Harry McPherson, *A Political Education* 434 (Little, Brown 1972).

[130] Townsend Hoopes, *The Limits of Intervention: An Inside Account of How the Johnson Policy of Escalation in Vietnam Was Reversed* 204 (McKay 1973).

[131] Id at 215–16. On the wise men, see also Theodore H. White, *The Making of the Presi-*

dent, 1968 111–13 (Atheneum 1969); Herbert Y. Schandler, *The Unmaking of a President: Lyndon Johnson and Vietnam* 254–55, 259–65 (Princeton 1977); Merle Miller, *Lyndon: An Oral History* 613 (Ballantine 1980) (In his victory statement the morning after the election, Nixon declared that "a great objective" of his administration would be "to bring the American people together."); Gitlin, *Sixties* at 303–4 (cited in note 9); Garfinkle, *Telltale Hearts* at 157–58 (cited in note 6).

[132] Miller, *Lyndon* at 503 (cited in note 131). See Zaroulis and Sullivan, *Who Spoke Up?* at 160 (cited in note 11).

[133] Gitlin, *Sixties* at 304 (cited in note 9). See Zaroulis and Sullivan, *Who Spoke Up?* at 162–63 (cited in note 11).

[134] Jason Epstein, *The Great Conspiracy Trial: An Essay on Law, Liberty and the Constitution* 70–71 (Random House 1970). See also DeBenedetti, *American Ordeal* at 217–18 (cited in note 1).

[135] See David Bird, *300 Protesting Columbia Students Barricade Office of College Dean,* New York Times 1 (Apr 24, 1968); Murray Schumach, *Columbia Closed as Efforts to End Dispute Continue,* id at 1 (Apr 29, 1968); Sylvan Fox, *Students Invade a Columbia Hall; Police Oust Them,* id at 1 (May 22, 1968).

[136] Rowland Evans Jr. and Robert D. Novak, *Nixon in the White House: The Frustration of Power* 271 (Random House 1971).

[137] See Gitlin, *Sixties* at 306–9 (cited in note 9); Ferber and Lynd, *Resistance* at 233–38 (cited in note 14); Sale, *SDS* at 430–47 (cited in note 26); Zaroulis and Sullivan, *Who Spoke Up?* at 165–68 (cited in note 11); Halstead, *Out Now!* at 386–88 (cited in note 18).

[138] See DeBenedetti, *American Ordeal* at 218 (cited in note 1).

[139] Ray Reed, *Humphrey Calls for End of War "Without Humiliation or Defeat,"* New York Times 29 (Apr 25, 1968).

[140] DeBenedetti, *American Ordeal* at 220 (cited in note 1).

[141] See Walter Goodman, *Liberals vs. Radicals—War in the Peace Camp,* New York Times 319 (Dec 3, 1967).

[142] Gitlin, *Sixties* at 293–94, 261 (cited in note 9).

[143] Id at 261, 263.

[144] Garfinkle, *Telltale Hearts* at 160–61 (cited in note 6).

[145] Tom Buckley, *The Battle of Chicago: From the Yippies' Side,* New York Times Magazine 28 (Sept 15, 1968). See DeBenedetti, *American Ordeal* at 223-24 (cited in note 1).

[146] Gitlin, *Sixties* at 235 (cited in note 9).

[147] Abbie Hoffman, *Revolution for the Hell of It* 102 (Dial 1968) (Hoffman published under the pen name Free). See Gitlin, *Sixties* at 235 (cited in note 9); Halstead, *Out Now!* at 406 (cited in note 18).

[148] See Gitlin, *Sixties* at 322–24 (cited in note 9); Zaroulis and Sullivan, *Who Spoke Up?* at 183–84 (cited in note 11).

[149] See Donald Janson, *"Militant" War Protest Slated outside Democratic Convention,* New York Times 24 (Aug 6, 1968); Donald Janson, *In Chicago the Scene May Be Wilder,* id at E2 (Aug 11, 1968); J. Anthony Lukas, *Dissenters Focusing on Chicago,* id

at 1 (Aug 18, 1968).

150 See Abbie Hoffman, *Soon to Be a Major Motion Picture* 152–54 (Putnam 1980); Richard Harris, *Justice: The Crisis of Law, Order, and Freedom in America* 67–70 (Dutton 1970); Daniel Walker, *Rights in Conflict: 7 Brutal Days: The Violent Confrontation of Demonstrators and Police in the Parks and Streets of Chicago during the Week of the Democratic National Convention of 1968* 40 (Grosset and Dunlap 1968); Gitlin, *Sixties* at 321–22 (cited in note 9).

151 *Hundreds of Protesters Block Traffic in Chicago*, New York Times 25 (Aug 26, 1968); Donald Johnson, *Police Assaults on 21 Newsmen in Chicago Are Denounced by Officials and Papers*, id at 36 (Aug 28, 1968); J. Anthony Lukas, *Police Battle Demonstrators in Streets*, id at 1 (Aug 29, 1968). See Epstein, *Great Conspiracy Trial* at 82–85 (cited in note 134); James W. Ely Jr., "The Chicago Conspiracy Case," in Michael R. Belknap, ed, *American Political Trials* 233, 239 (Greenwood 1994); DeBenedetti, *American Ordeal* at 227 (cited in note 1).

152 DeBenedetti, *American Ordeal* at 227 (cited in note 1). On the convention, see Lewis Chester, Godfrey Hodgson, and Bruce Page, *An American Melodrama: The Presidential Campaign of 1968* 503–604 (Viking 1969); Tom Hayden, *Reunion: A Memoir* 293–326 (Random House 1988); Gitlin, *Sixties* at 322–36 (cited in note 9).

153 Norman Mailer, *Miami and the Siege of Chicago: An Informal History of the Republican and Democratic Conventions of 1968* 116 (World Publishing 1968).

154 Hayden, *Rebellion and Repression* at 163 (cited in note 101).

155 White, *Making of President* at 369–73 (cited in note 131). See also Gitlin, *Sixties* at 326–34 (cited in note 9); Walker, *Rights in Conflict* at 158–86 (cited in note 150); Chester, Hodgson, and Page, *American Melodrama* at 582–83 (cited in note 152); Zaroulis and Sullivan, *Who Spoke Up?* at 193–96 (cited in note 11).

156 Mailer, *Siege of Chicago* at 172 (cited in note 153).

157 Goldstein, *Political Repression* at 509 (cited in note 30); Halstead, *Out Now!* at 410–15 (cited in note 18).

158 Walker, *Rights in Conflict* at vii (cited in note 150). Tom Wicker observed after the convention, "The truth is that these were our children in the streets, and the Chicago police beat them up." Walter Schneier, ed, *Telling It Like It Was: The Chicago Riots* (Signet 1969), excerpted in Dellinger, *From Yale to Jail* at 337 (cited in note 11).

159 *When a 2-Party System Becomes a 1-Party Rubber Stamp*, I. F. Stone's Weekly 1, 3 (Sept 9, 1968). See DeBenedetti, *American Ordeal* at 228 (cited in note 1).

160 David Dellinger, *More Power Than We Know: The People's Movement toward Democracy* 125 (Anchor 1975). At the end of September, as antiwar protests around the globe drew hundreds of thousands of demonstrators, and long-awaited peace talks faltered in Paris, HUAC initiated hearings to investigate alleged Communist involvement in the Chicago convention protests. The hearings produced no evidence of such involvement. Zaroulis and Sullivan, *Who Spoke Up?* at 203–5 (cited in note 11).

161 The Gallup poll showed that 56 percent of Americans approved the actions of the police, with only 31 percent disapproving. See 3 *The Gallup Poll* 2160 (Random House 1972); Gitlin, *Sixties* at 471 (cited in note 9).

162 Sale, *SDS* at 476–77 (cited in note 26).

[163] Nixon received only 43.4 percent of the vote, Humphrey 42.7 percent, and Governor George Wallace of Alabama 13.5 percent. It is noteworthy that the two most stalwart antiwar senators Ernest Gruening and Wayne Morse, were both defeated for reelection.

[164] Evans and Novak, *Nixon in White House* at 33, 76, 80–83 (cited in note 136); Halberstam, *Best and Brightest* at 661 (cited in note 48); Jonathan Schell, *The Time of Illusion* 18–22 (Knopf 1976).

[165] See Seymour M. Hersh, *The Price of Power: Kissinger in the Nixon White House* 51 (Summit 1983); Karnow, *Vietnam* at 601 (cited in note 9); Baritz, *Backfire* at 200 (cited in note 9); Gitlin, *Sixties* at 377–78 (cited in note 9).

[166] Schell, *Time of Illusion* at 36–38 (cited in note 164).

[167] See Gitlin, *Sixties* at 342–43 (cited in note 9); Sale, *SDS* at 512–13, 632–33 (cited in note 26); Manchester, *Glory and Dream* at 1198 (cited in note 6); Goldstein, *Political Repression* at 430-31 (cited in note 30).

[168] Harold Jacobs, ed, *Weatherman* 7–8, 166, 167–72 (Ramparts 1970); Garfinkle, *Telltale Hearts* at 112–15 (cited in note 6). See also John Kifner, *That's What the Weathermen Are Supposed to Be . . . "Vandals in the Mother Country,"* New York Times 182 (Jan 4, 1970). On the Weathermen's split from SDS, see Andrew Kopkind, *The Real SDS Stands Up*, in Jacobs, ed, *Weatherman* at 15–28 (cited in note 168); Zaroulis and Sullivan, *Who Spoke Up?* at 251–56 (cited in note 11).

[169] Gitlin, *Sixties* at 385–86 (cited in note 9). See Garfinkle, *Telltale Hearts* at 183–85 (cited in note 6).

[170] Shin'ya Ono, *A Weatherman: You Do Need a Weatherman to Know Which Way the Wind Blows*, in Jacobs, ed, *Weatherman* at 254 (cited in note 168). On other groups that took extreme positions during these years, such as the yippies, the crazies, and the Up Against the Wall Motherfuckers, see Farber, *Counterculture* at 19 (cited in note 113).

[171] Tom Hayden, *Trial* 92 (Holt, Rinehart and Winston 1970); Tom Hayden, *Justice in the Streets*, in Jacobs, ed, *Weatherman* at 296–97 (cited in note 168). See Sale, *SDS* at 603–4 (cited in note 26); Garfinkle, *Telltale Hearts* at 177 (cited in note 6).

[172] See Sale, *SDS* at 606–8 (cited in note 26); Goldstein, *Political Repression* at 512 (cited in note 30); Gitlin, *Sixties* at 393 (cited in note 9); Tom Thomas, *The Second Battle of Chicago 1969*, in Jacobs, ed *Weatherman* at 196–225 (cited in note 168); John Kifner, *300 in S.D.S. Clash with Chicago Police*, New York Times 1 (Oct 9, 1968); William Chapman and Robert M. Krim, *300 Rampage after Rally in Chicago*, Washington Post A1 (Oct 9, 1969). The violent outcome was not totally unexpected by the Weatherman participants, who anticipated the possibility that the government's response might be harsh and that "hundreds of people might well be arrested and/or hurt, and . . . that a few people might even get killed." Ono, *You Do Need a Weatherman* at 249, 251 (cited in note 170).

[173] Gitlin, *Sixties* at 397 (cited in note 9).

[174] Small, *Doves* at 182 (cited in note 47); David McReynolds, *Pacifists and the Vietnam Antiwar Movement*, in Small and Hoover, eds, *Give Peace a Chance* at 53, 65 (cited in note 20). See also Zaroulis and Sullivan, *Who Spoke Up?* at 264–73 (cited in note 11);

Halstead, *Out Now!* at 488–90 (cited in note 18); Schell, *Time of Illusion* at 52–53 (cited in note 164); John Herbers, *Vietnam Moratorium Observed Nationwide by Foes of the War*, New York Times 1 (Oct 16, 1969). See also Chalmers M. Roberts, *Moratorium Activities Peaceful*, Washington Post A1 (Oct 16, 1969).

175 Evans and Novak, *Nixon in White House* at 85–86 (cited in note 136); Schell, *Time of Illusion* at 62–66 (cited in note 164); Small, *Covering Dissent* at 92–95, 269–79 (cited in note 66).

176 Memorandum from Alexander P. Butterfield to Richard M. Nixon: Game Plan for Post-Speech Activities—Second Post-Speech Up-dating . . . Covers Period Nov 10–Dec 31, excerpted in Bruce Oudes, ed, *From: The President: Richard Nixon's Secret Files* 65–69 (Harper and Row 1989).

177 See Goldstein, *Political Repression* at 497–98 (cited in note 30); Richard Harwood, *War Protest Walk Begins on Quiet Note*, Washington Post A1 (Nov 14, 1969); David E. Rosenbaum, *"March against Death" Begun by Thousands in Washington*, New York Times 1 (Nov 14, 1969); Joseph Lelyveld, *Nationwide Protest on War Opens with Light Turnout*, id at 1 (Nov 14, 1969).

178 See Garfinkle, *Telltale Hearts* at 180 (cited in note 6); Richard Harwood, *Largest Rally in Washington History Demands Rapid End to Vietnam War*, Washington Post 1 (Nov 16, 1969). The Weathermen mocked the "peaceful" part of the demonstration, arguing, "It's crazy to think that because we walked in front of their houses with a peace sign, the rich fuckers in power would somehow see how they rip people off." Harold Jacobs, *Washington, November 15, 1969*, excerpted in Jacobs, ed, *Weatherman* at 275 (cited in note 168). See also Halstead, *Out Now!* at 515–21 (cited in note 18).

179 John Kifner, *That's What the Weathermen Are Supposed to Be*, New York Times 182 (Jan 4, 1970). See Gitlin, *Sixties* at 394 (cited in note 9).

180 *"Bloodbath" Remark by Gov. Reagan*, San Francisco Chronicle 1 (Apr 8, 1970). See Goldstein, *Political Repression* at 432, 512 (cited in note 30); Manchester, *Glory and Dream* at 1199–200, 1212 (cited in note 6).

181 See Karnow, *Vietnam* at 618 (cited in note 9).

182 Evans and Novak, *Nixon in White House* at 254–55 (cited in note 136).

183 William Safire, *Before the Fall: An Inside View of the Pre-Watergate White House* 190 (Doubleday 1975); DeBenedetti, *American Ordeal* at 279 (cited in note 1).

184 Henry Kissinger, *White House Years* 487 (Little, Brown 1979). See DeBenedetti, *American Ordeal* at 279 (cited in note 1).

185 Juan de Onis, *Nixon Puts "Bums" Label on Some College Radicals*, New York Times 1 (May 2, 1970). See Evans and Novak, *Nixon in White House* at 275–76 (cited in note 136); Theodore H. White, *Breach of Faith: The Fall of Richard Nixon* 129 (Atheneum 1975).

186 See Schell, *Time of Illusion* at 97–98 (cited in note 164). For background on the tradition of student activism at Kent State, and the political and campus events that led up to the killing, see Kenneth J. Heineman, *"Look Out Kid, You're Gonna Get Hit!": Kent State and the Vietnam Antiwar Movement*, in Small and Hoover, eds, *Give Peace a Chance* at 201–22 (cited in note 20); Sale, *SDS* at 635–36 (cited in note 26); Halstead, *Out Now!* at 537–39 (cited in note 18); Karnow, *Nixon's War* at 188 (cited in

note 181).

187 Evans and Novak, *Nixon in White House* at 277 (cited in note 136); Schell, *Time of Illusion* at 98 (cited in note 164); Jules Witcover, *White Knight: The Rise of Spiro Agnew* 336 (Random House 1972).

188 DeBenedetti, *American Ordeal* at 279–80 (cited in note 1). See Evans and Novak, *Nixon in White House* at 277 (cited in note 136); Garfinkle, *Telltale Hearts* at 191–92 (cited in note 6).

189 DeBenedetti, *American Ordeal* at 280 (cited in note 1); Gitlin, *Sixties* at 409–10 (cited in note 9).

190 *The Report of the President's Commission on Campus Unrest* 1 (Government Printing Office 1971). See White, *Breach of Faith* at 129–31 (cited in note 185).

191 Kissinger, *White House Years* at 513 (cited in note 184). See Gitlin, *Sixties* at 409–10 (cited in note 9).

192 Evans and Novak, *Nixon in White House* at 289–90 (cited in note 136); Garfinkle, *Telltale Hearts* at 188 (cited in note 6); Schell, *Time of Illusion* at 101 (cited in note 164).

193 John W. Finney, *President Assailed by Fulbright Panel*, New York Times 1 (May 5, 1970).

194 See DeBenedetti, *American Ordeal* at 286 (cited in note 1).

195 See *Poll Finds Favor for Asian Policy*, New York Times 8 (May 4, 1970).

196 See DeBenedetti, *American Ordeal* at 281–82 (cited in note 1).

197 *Two Gatherings*, New Yorker 23, 24 (May 30, 1970).

198 Evans and Novak, *Nixon in White House* at 285 (cited in note 136); Kissinger, *White House Years* at 968–69 (cited in note 184); Karl E. Meyer, *Agnew Attacks "Charlatan" of Peace, Freedom*, Washington Post A9 (June 4, 1970); Safire, *Before the Fall* at 308 (cited in note 183).

199 John R. Coyne Jr., *The Impudent Snobs: Agnew vs. the Intellectual Establishment* 259 (Arlington House 1972).

200 See DeBenedetti, *American Ordeal* at 281–85 (cited in note 1); Schell, *Time of Illusion* at 101–2 (cited in note 164).

201 Richard M. Nixon, *RN: The Memoirs of Richard Nixon, 1970* 492–93 (Grosset and Dunlap 1978).

202 Schell, *Time of Illusion* at 130 (cited in note 164).

203 See DeBenedetti, *American Ordeal* at 293 (cited in note 1).

204 Id at 297. See Gitlin, *Sixties* at 379 (cited in note 9); Ferber and Lynd, *Resistance* at 230–33 (cited in note 14). On the role of women in the antiwar movement and the shift of some of them to the cause of women's liberation, see Alice Echols, *"Women Power" and Women's Liberation: Exploring the Relationship between the Antiwar Movement and the Women's Liberation Movement*, in Small and Hoover, eds, *Give Peace a Chance* at 171–81 (cited in note 20); Nina S. Adams, *The Women Who Left Them Behind*, in Small and Hoover, eds, *Give Peace a Chance* at 182, 185 (cited in note 20); Cathy Wilkerson, *Toward a Revolutionary Women's Militia*, in Jacobs, ed, *Weatherman* at 91–96 (cited in note 168).

205 James A. Wechsler, *A Time of Numbness*, American Report 4 (Feb 26, 1971).

[206] See Evans and Novak, *Nixon in White House* at 383–90 (cited in note 136).

[207] Oudes, ed, *From: The President* at 199 (cited in note 176).

[208] See William F. Crandell, *They Moved the Town: Organizing Vietnam Veterans against the War*, in Small and Hoover, eds, *Give Peace a Chance* at 141, 148–51 (cited in note 20); Halstead, *Out Now!* at 605–7 (cited in note 18); *Veterans Discard Medals in War Protest at Capitol*, New York Times 1 (Apr 24, 1971).

[209] DeBenedetti, *American Ordeal* at 309–10 (cited in note 1).

[210] Id at 305. See also McReynolds, *Pacifists* at 67–69 (cited in note 174).

[211] *The Biggest Bust*, Newsweek 24 (May 17, 1971). See also Halstead, *Out Now!* at 617–23 (cited in note 18).

[212] Charles W. Colson, *Born Again* 45 (Chosen Books 1976). See George W. Hopkins, *"May Day" 1971: Civil Disobedience and the Vietnam Antiwar Movement*, in Small and Hoover, eds, *Give Peace a Chance* at 71, 77–78 (cited in note 20). On other protests connected to the May Day demonstrations in Washington, see David Cortright, *GI Resistance during the Vietnam War*, in Small and Hoover, eds, *Give Peace a Chance* at 116, 124–25 (cited in note 20).

[213] Goldstein, *Political Repression* at 462 (cited in note 30).

[214] See DeBenedetti, *American Ordeal* at 310 (cited in note 1).

[215] Id at 307.

[216] Goldstein, *Political Repression* at 462 (cited in note 30). See generally J. Anthony Lukas, *Nightmare: The Underside of the Nixon Years* (Viking 1976); Schell, *Time of Illusion* (cited in note 164); Evans and Novak, *Nixon in White House* (cited in note 136); White, *Breach of Faith* (cited in note 185).

[217] Zaroulis and Sullivan, *Who Spoke Up?* at 58 (cited in note 11).

[218] 89th Cong, 1st Sess, in 111 Cong Rec H 19871 (Aug 10, 1965); 89th Cong, 1st Sess, in 111 Cong Rec S 20433 (Aug 13, 1965); 89th Cong, 1st Sess, in 111 Cong Rec H 19871 (Aug 10, 1965).

[219] See Universal Military Training and Service Act of 1948, 50 USC § 462(b) (1965). See also Ferber and Lynd, *Resistance* at 23–24 (cited in note 14).

[220] See *Stomberg v. California*, 283 US 359 (1931) (holding unconstitutional a state law declaring unlawful the display of a red flag as a symbol of opposition to organized government).

[221] *State Board of Education v. Barnette*, 319 US 624, 632 (1943).

[222] 391 US 367 (1968).

[223] Id at 370.

[224] Id at 375.

[225] Id at 380–82.

[226] Lawrence R. Velvel, *Freedom of Speech and the Draft Card Burning Cases*, 16 U Kan L Rev 149, 153 (1968). See Vincent Blasi, *The Checking Value in First Amendment Theory*, 1977 Am B Found Res J 521, 640 (the "communication achieved by the wave of draft-card burnings at the height of the United States involvement in Vietnam represents a paradigm example" of the kind of speech that can "activate the political conscience" of the people "by transcending rationality and appealing to more primitive,

more basic instincts").

[227] *O'Brien*, 391 US at 389 (Harlan concurring).

[228] John Hart Ely, *Flag Desecration: A Case Study in the Roles of Categorization and Balancing in First Amendment Analysis*, 88 Harv L Rev 1482, 1489–90 (1975).

[229] Dean Alfange Jr., *Free Speech and Symbolic Content: The Draft-Card Burning Case*, 1968 Sup Ct Rev 1, 23, 25.

[230] On the problem of incidental restrictions, see Geoffrey R. Stone, *Content-Neutral Restrictions*, 54 U Chi L Rev 46, 99–114 (1987); Elena Kagan, *Private Speech, Public Purpose: The Role of Governmental Motive in First Amendment Doctrine*, 63 U Chi L Rev 413, 494–508 (1996); Michael C. Dorf, *Incidental Burdens on Fundamental Rights*, 109 Harv L Rev 1175 (1996); Jeb Rubenfeld, *The First Amendment's Purpose*, 53 Stan L Rev 767 (2001). For examples of "extraordinary circumstances," see, for instance, *NAACP v. Alabama*, 357 US 449 (1958) (invalidating as applied to the NAACP an Alabama statute requiring all out-of-state corporations operating in Alabama to discuss the names and addresses of all members because the compelled disclosure of NAACP membership lists would have a severe impact on the ability of the NAACP and its members to pursue their constitutional rights).

[231] *O'Brien*, 391 US at 382–84.

[232] Alfange, 1968 Sup Ct Rev at 15 (cited in note 229).

[233] On the problem of government motivation and the First Amendment, see Kagan, 63 U Chi L Rev 413 (cited in note 230); Rubenfeld, 53 Stan L Rev 767 (cited in note 230); Stone, 54 U Chi L Rev at 55–56, 106–7 (cited in note 230).

[234] Mitford, *Dr. Spock* at 4–5 (cited in note 118).

[235] Id at 255–59.

[236] Id. See also John F. Bannan and Rosemary S. Bannan, *Law, Morality and Vietnam: The Peace Militants and the Courts* 91 (Indiana 1974).

[237] Mitford, *Dr. Spock*, at 263–67 (cited in note 118).

[238] Id at 267–69 (cited in note 118).

[239] *Abrams v. United States*, 250 US 616, 630 (1919) (Holmes dissenting).

[240] *Gitlow v. New York*, 268 US 652, 673 (1925) (Holmes dissenting).

[241] *Whitney v. California*, 274 US 357, 376 (1927) (Brandeis concurring).

[242] Id.

[243] See Goldstein, *Political Repression* at 441 (cited in note 30); Charles Goodell, *Political Prisoners in America* 226 (Random House 1973); Mitford, *Dr. Spock* at 65–71, 191 (cited in note 118).

[244] Learned Hand called conspiracy the prosecutor's "darling," *Harrison v. United States*, 7 F2d 259, 263 (2d Cir 1925), for as one of the most commonly charged federal crimes, it can be applied to a variety of situations, while courts tend to construe it broadly. *United States v. Reynolds*, 929 F2d 435, 439 (7th Cir 1990) ("rare is the case omitting such a charge"). Conspiracy can be proven: without a formal agreement, and on only circumstantial evidence (*Glasser v. United States*, 315 US 60, 80 [1942]); without the actors' knowledge or intention that the conspiracy violates the law (*United States v. Virgen-Moreno*, 265 F3d 276, 284 [5th Cir 2001]); and without anything more than a defendant's "slight connection" to the conspiracy, in order to prove

their "knowing participation." (*United States v. Leahy*, 82 F3d 624 [5th Cir 1996]). Furthermore, in proving that a co-conspirator committed an "overt act" to further the conspiracy, that overt act need not be unlawful. *United States v. Hurley*, 957 F2d 1, 3 (1st Cir 1992). These rather loosely defined requirements to prove conspiracy raise a host of other problems. For example, special evidentiary rules—such as the co-conspirator hearsay rule—have been developed to deal with the issue of conspiracy. *Bourjaily v. United States*, 483 US 171, 179–80 (1987) (holding that the two traditional requirements to the admittance of hearsay evidence—unavailability and independent indicia of reliability—are no longer necessary).

245 *Krulewitch v. United States*, 336 US 440, 446 (1949).

246 Mitford, *Dr. Spock* at 62 (cited in note 118).

247 Id at 61.

248 See id at 206–9; Zaroulis and Sullivan, *Who Spoke Up?* at 172–73 (cited in note 11).

249 *United States v. Spock*, 416 F2d 165 (1st Cir 1969) (holding that criminal intent in a conspiracy prosecution must be judged *strictissimi juris* to avoid the danger of punishing an individual for his constitutionally protected activities and that the use of special questions to the jury was improper and prejudicial). See Goldstein, *Political Repression* at 441 (cited in note 30); Goodell, *Political Prisoners* at 226 (cited in note 243); Bannan and Bannan, *Law, Morality and Vietnam* at 102–6 (cited in note 236).

250 Francine du Plessix Gray, *Divine Disobedience: Profiles in Catholic Radicalism* 47 (Knopf 1970).

251 Bannan and Bannan, *Law, Morality and Vietnam* at 124–50 (cited in note 236); Howard Zinn, *A People's History of the United States* 479 (Harper and Row 1980).

252 See generally Jack Nelson and Ronald J. Ostrow, *The FBI and the Berrigans* (Coward, McGann and Geoghegan 1972). See also Goldstein, *Political Repression* at 488–91 (cited in note 30).

253 Federal Riot Act, 18 USC § 2101 (1970). See Epstein, *Great Conspiracy Trial* at 31–33 (cited in note 134); Ely, *Chicago Conspiracy Case* at 237 (cited in note 151); Emerson, *System of Free Expression* at 408–9 (cited in note 97); Goldstein, *Political Repression* at 441–42 (cited in note 30); Zaroulis and Sullivan, *Who Spoke Up?* at 164 (cited in note 11).

254 Milton Viorst, *Attorney General Mitchell's Philosophy Is "The Justice Department Is an Institution for Law Enforcement, Not Social Improvement,"* New York Times Magazine 10 (Aug 10, 1969). See also Dellinger, *From Yale to Jail* at 339 (cited in note 11); Harris, *Justice* at 152 (cited in note 150).

255 See Goldstein, *Political Repression* at 487–88 (cited in note 30);

256 Epstein, *Great Conspiracy Trial* at 92–95, 101 (cited in note 134); Ely, *Chicago Conspiracy Case* at 240 (cited in note 151); Dellinger, *From Yale to Jail* at 341 (cited in note 11).

257 Walker, *Rights in Conflict* at 10, 11 (cited in note 150); David Dellinger, *Revolutionary Nonviolence* 315 (Bobbs-Merrill 1970); Ely, *Chicago Conspiracy Case* at 238 (cited in note 151).

258 See Epstein, *Great Conspiracy Trial* at 95 (cited in note 134).

259 Ely, *Chicago Conspiracy Case* at 243 (cited in note 151); Goldstein, *Political Repression* at 487–88 (cited in note 30). See *United States v. Seale*, 461 F2d 345, 373–89

(7th Cir 1972).

260 Ely, *Chicago Conspiracy Case* at 246 (cited in note 151).

261 Goldstein, *Political Repression* at 487–88 (cited in note 30); Ely, Chicago *Conspiracy Case* at 242–48 (cited in note 151).

262 Ely, *Chicago Conspiracy Case* at 248 (cited in note 151).

263 See Athan Theoharis, *Spying on Americans: Political Surveillance from Hoover to the Huston Plan* 135–36 (Temple 1978).

264 See Intelligence Activities: Senate Resolution 21, Hearings before the Select Committee to Study Government Operations with Respect to Intelligence Activities of the United States Senate, 94th Cong, 1st Sess, Volume 6: Federal Bureau of Investigations 18–19 (1976) (hereafter FBI Hearings); Supplementary Detailed Staff Reports of the Intelligence Activities and the Rights of Americans: Book III, Final Report of the Select Committee to Study Governmental Operations with Respect to Intelligence Activities, United States Senate, 94th Cong, 2d Sess 59, 72 (Apr 23, 1976) (hereafter Final Report III); Goldstein, *Political Repression* at 487–88 (cited in note 30).

265 See Final Report III at 139, 475-83 (cited in note 264); Intelligence Activities and the Rights of Americans: Book II, Final Report of the Select Committee to Study Governmental Operations with Respect to Intelligence Operations, United States Senate, 94th Cong, 2d Sess 71 (Apr 26, 1976) (hereafter Final Report II); Goldstein, *Political Repression* at 445–47 (cited in note 30); Theoharis, *Spying on Americans* at 136–48, 172–75 (cited in note 263); Ward Churchill and Jim Vander Wall, *The COINTEL-PRO Papers: Documents from the FBI's Secret Wars against Dissent in the United States* 166–67 (South End 1990); Frank J. Donner, *The Age of Surveillance: The Aims and Methods of America's Political Intelligence System* 211 (Knopf 1980). Another major focus of FBI surveillance and COINTELPRO in the late 1960s were "Black Nationalist" groups, including SCLC, SNCC, the Nation of Islam, H. Rap Brown, Elijah Muhammad, and Malcolm X. See FBI Hearings at 383–92 (cited in note 264); Final Report III at 179–80 (cited in note 264); Final Report II at 87–88 (cited in note 265); Goldstein, *Political Repression* at 449–51 (cited in note 30); Donner, *Age of Surveillance* at 212–13 (cited in note 265).

266 See Sanford Ungar, *FBI* 288–89 (Little, Brown 1976); Goldstein, *Political Repression* at 445 (cited in note 30); Donner, *Age of Surveillance* at 256–57 (cited in note 265).

267 See Churchill and Vander Wall, *COINTELPRO Papers* at 172 (cited in note 265); Small, *Doves* at 103–4 (cited in note 47); Goldstein, *Political Repression* at 448–49 (cited in note 30).

268 Goldstein, *Political Repression* at 448–49 (cited in note 30); Finman and Macaulay, 1966 Wisc L Rev at 676 (cited in note 79); Sale, *SDS* at 275 (cited in note 26).

269 James Kirkpatrick Davis, *Assault on the Left: The FBI and the Sixties Antiwar Movement* 31 (Praeger 1997) (emphasis in original).

270 See Sale, *SDS* at 275–76, 328–29, 407, 499–500 (cited in note 26); Goldstein, *Political Repression* at 449 (cited in note 30); Davis, *Assault on Left* at 29–30 (cited in note 269).

271 See Final Report II at 119–20, 227–30 (cited in note 265); FBI Hearings at 476–79, 638–40, 718–20 (cited in note 264); Goldstein, *Political Repression* at 448–49 (cited

in note 30); Donner, *Age of Surveillance* at 252–53 (cited in note 265).

272 See Memorandum from FBI Boston Field Office to FBI Headquarters, Jan 22, 1966, excerpted in Davis, *Assault on Left* at 32 (cited in note 269).

273 FBI Hearings at 393 (cited in note 264); Department of Justice News Release, Nov 18, 1974, excerpted in Goldstein, *Political Repression* at 451 (cited in note 30). See DeBenedetti, *American Ordeal* at 225 (cited in note 1); Theoharis, *Spying on Americans* at 148 (cited in note 263); Churchill and Vander Wall, *COINTELPRO Papers* at 176–77 (cited in note 265).

274 Memorandum from FBI Philadelphia Field Office to FBI Headquarters, May 29, 1968, excerpted in Davis, *Assault on Left* at 51 (cited in note 269).

275 See Memorandum from SAC/Cincinnati to J. Edgar Hoover, June 3, 1968, excerpted in DeBenedetti, *American Ordeal* at 225 (cited in note 1).

276 Memorandum from San Antonio SAG to SOG, Aug 27, 1968, excerpted in DeBenedetti, *American Ordeal* at 226 (cited in note 1).

277 Memorandum from SAC, Detroit to J. Edgar Hoover, Oct, 1970, excerpted in Churchill and Vander Wall, *COINTELPRO Papers* at 212 (cited in note 265). See Memorandum from SAC, Los Angeles to J. Edgar Hoover, June 17, 1970, excerpted id at 214 (attacking Jane Fonda); Memorandum from SAC, Los Angeles to J. Edgar Hoover, Apr 27, 1970, excerpted id at 216–17 (attacking Jean Seberg). See also David Wise, *The American Police State: The Government against the People* 316 (Random House 1976).

278 See Cathy Perkus, ed, *COINTELPRO: The FBI's Secret War on Political Freedom* (Monado 1975); Final Report III at 3–77 (cited in note 264); Goldstein, *Political Repression* at 452, 470–71 (cited in note 30).

279 See Final Report III at 510–12 (cited in note 264); Goldstein, *Political Repression* at 453–54 (cited in note 30); Memorandum, FBI Headquarters to Field Offices, Jan 30, 1968, excerpted in Davis, *Assault on Left* at 43 (cited in note 269); Memorandum from C. D. Brennan to W. C. Sullivan, May 9, 1968, excerpted in Davis, *Assault on Left* at 43 (cited in note 269); Churchill and Vander Wall, *COINTELPRO Papers* at 175 (cited in note 265); Wise, *American Police State* at 313 (cited in note 277).

280 See Final Report III at 561–677 (cited in note 264); Intelligence Activities: Senate Resolution 21, Hearings before the Select Committee to Study Governmental Operations with Respect to Intelligence Activities, 94th Cong, 1st Sess, Volume 4: Mail Opening (1975); Goldstein, *Political Repression* at 454–55 (cited in note 30).

281 In fact, the CIA delivered four separate reports to President Johnson on this question. None found any appreciable foreign involvement. Nonetheless, Operation CHAOS steadily expanded, focusing increasingly on domestic matters. After Nixon succeeded Johnson, he too insisted that the anti-war movement was the product of foreign influence, and in June 1969 he ordered yet another report. Once again, the CIA found no appreciable foreign involvement in the antiwar movement. But this did not bring CHAOS to an end. To the contrary, the Nixon administration linked CHAOS administratively to other domestic security programs in order to produce a more powerful, more efficient investigative program. A young White House aide, acting under Nixon's orders, noted, "We do not want news media to be alerted to what we are

attempting to do or how we are operating because the disclosure of such information might embarrass the Administration." Schell, *Time of Illusion* at 60–61 (cited in note 164).

[282] *The Nelson Rockefeller Report to the President by the Commission on CIA Activities within the United States* 130–59 (Manor 1975). See also Final Report III at 681–732 (cited in note 264); Goldstein, *Political Repression* at 454–57 (cited in note 30); Lukas, *Nightmare* at 28–30 (cited in note 216); Theoharis, *Spying on Americans* at 178 (cited in note 263).

[283] See Goldstein, *Political Repression* at 458 (cited in note 30).

[284] See id at 457–59; Theoharis, *Spying on Americans* at 178–79 (cited in note 263).

[285] Theoharis, *Spying on Americans* at 121–22 (cited in note 263).

[286] Goldstein, *Political Repression* at 461 (cited in note 30). See Zaroulis and Sullivan, *Who Spoke Up?* at 218–23 (cited in note 11).

[287] Goldstein, *Political Repression* at 465–67 (cited in note 30). See Final Report III at 508, 527–28 (cited in note 264).

[288] Lukas, *Nightmare* at 29 (cited in note 216). See Wise, *American Police State* at 192–94 (cited in note 277); Zaroulis and Sullivan, *Who Spoke Up?* at 221–22 (cited in note 11).

[289] Goldstein, *Political Repression* at 480 (cited in note 30). See also Donner, *Age of Surveillance* at 162–67, 232–33 (cited in note 265); Powers, *Man Who Kept Secrets* at 246–47 (cited in note 123); Todd Gitlin, *The Whole World Is Watching: Mass Media in the Making and Unmaking of the New Left* 269–79 (Berkeley 1980); Geoffrey Rips, *The Campaign against the Underground Press*, in Anne Janowitz and Nancy J. Peters, eds, *UnAmerican Activities* 55–135 (City Lights 1981); Churchill and Vander Wall, *COINTELPRO Papers* at 165–230 (cited in note 265); Gitlin, *Sixties* at 378 (cited in note 9).

[290] See Epstein, *Great Conspiracy Trial* at 111–12 (cited in note 134).

[291] Lukas, *Nightmare* at 22 (cited in note 216); Theoharis, *Spying on Americans* at 188–89 (cited in note 263); Churchill and Vander Wall, *COINTELPRO Papers* at 208 (cited in note 265).

[292] Jerry J. Berman and Morton H. Halperin, eds, *The Abuses of the Intelligence Agencies* 90–92 (Center for National Security Studies 1975). See Goldstein, *Political Repression* at 480–83 (cited in note 30); Lukas, *Nightmare* at 22–23 (cited in note 216); Final Report II at 850–52, 876–90 (cited in note 265).

[293] See Lukas, *Nightmare* at 12–13 (cited in note 216).

[294] Stanley I. Kutler, ed, *Abuse of Power: The New Nixon Tapes* 8, 507 (Simon and Schuster 1997); White, *Breach of Faith* at 126 (cited in note 185). See Gitlin, *Sixties* at 413–14 (cited in note 9); Theoharis, *Spying on Americans* at 16–17 (cited in note 263); Lukas, *Nightmare* at 32–33 (cited in note 216).

[295] Wise, *American Police State* at 154–55 (cited in note 277); Lukas, *Nightmare* at 33 (cited in note 216); DeBenedetti, *American Ordeal* at 288 (cited in note 1); Theoharis, *Spying on Americans* at 21–26 (cited in note 263); Donner, *Age of Surveillance* at 265 (cited in note 265); Schell, *Time of Illusion* at 112 (cited in note 164).

[296] See Goldstein, *Political Repression* at 485–86 (cited in note 30); DeBenedetti, *Ameri-

can Ordeal at 288 (cited in note 1); Wise, *American Police State* at 155–56 (cited in note 277); Donner, *Age of Surveillance* 266 (cited in note 265); Gitlin, *Sixties* at 413–14 (cited in note 9); Peter Schrag, *Test of Loyalty: Daniel Ellsberg and the Rituals of Secret Government* 76–77 (Simon and Schuster 1974). In a conversation in 1973, Nixon admitted that he had approved the Huston Plan. For a series of conversations on May 16, 1973, where he repeatedly speaks of approving the Huston Plan, "approved . . . illegal activities," see Kutler, ed, *Abuse of Power* at 507–20 (cited in note 294).

[297] See Lukas, *Nightmare* at 36–37 (cited in note 216).

[298] Henry Steele Commager, *Is Freedom Dying in America?*, Look 16–17 (July 14, 1970).

[299] Theoharis, *Spying on Americans* at 148–49 (cited in note 263). See Wise, *American Police State* at 281 (cited in note 277); DeBenedetti, *American Ordeal* at 288 (cited in note 1).

[300] *Mitchell Issues Plea on F.B.I. Files*, New York Times 24 (Mar 24, 1971). See Theoharis, *Spying on Americans* at 149 (cited in note 263).

[301] *What Is the FBI Up To?*, Washington Post A20 (Mar 25, 1971).

[302] Goldstein, *Political Repression* at 452, 463–65 (cited in note 30). See Berman and Halperin, eds, *Abuses of Intelligence Agencies* at 2 (cited in note 292); Churchill and Vander Wall, *COINTELPRO Papers* at 229 (cited in note 265).

[303] Final Report II at 5–6 (cited in note 265).

[304] Army Surveillance of Civilians: A Documentary Analysis by the Staff of the Subcommittee on Constitutional Rights, Committee on the Judiciary, United States Senate, 92d Cong, 2d Sess 97 (1971). See Goldstein, *Political Repression* at 459, 480 (cited in note 30); Final Report III at 789, 806 (cited in note 264).

[305] San Diego Union (May 23, 1976), excerpted in Goldstein, *Political Repression* at 540–42 (cited in note 30).

[306] The Levi guidelines have since been modified, and relaxed, by a succession of attorneys general, including William French Smith, Richard Thornburgh, and John Ashcroft. See conclusion, infra. See also Nancy Chang, *Silencing Political Dissent* 32–37 (Seven Stories 2002).

[307] *Katz v. United States*, 389 US 347 (1967).

[308] *Bates v. City of Little Rock*, 361 US 516, 523 (1960). See also *Shelton v. Tucker*, 364 US 479 (1960) (holding unconstitutional a state law requiring teachers to disclose all organizations with which they were affiliated).

[309] See Geoffrey R. Stone, *The Scope of the Fourth Amendment: Privacy and the Police Use of Spies, Secret Agents, and Informers*, 4 Am B Found Res J 1193, 1230, 1240 (1976); *Hoffa v. United States*, 385 US 293 (1966) (individuals assume a risk that friends and associates, acting in their private capacities, may betray confidences); *United States v. White*, 401 US 745, 749, 751, 752 (1971) (plurality opinion).

[310] Max Lowenthal, *The Federal Bureau of Investigation* 298 (Sloane 1950).

[311] In *Laird Secretary of Defense v. Tatum*, 408 US 1 (1972), the Court declined to rule on the constitutionality of Army domestic intelligence activities, including the monitoring of public meetings, because the complainants lacked "standing." That is, they could not show that information gathered by the Army had actually been used to harm them.

The Court held that the mere fact that their First Amendment activities would be "chilled" by the continuation of such activities was not sufficient to allow them to challenge the constitutionality of the surveillance. See *New Alliance Party v. Federal Bureau of Investigation*, 858 F Supp 425 (SD NY 1994) (same with respect to a challenge to FBI surveillance activities). On the question whether government surveillance has a chilling effect on the willingness of individuals to engage in controversial First Amendment activities, see Goldstein, *Political Repression* at 530–37 (cited in note 30); Sale, *SDS* at 503 (cited in note 26); Frank Donner, *Political Informers*, in Pat Watters and Stephen Gillers, eds, *Investigating the FBI* 338–68 (Doubleday 1973).

[312] Gitlin, *Sixties* at 415 (cited in note 9). See Goldstein, *Political Repression* at 530–37 (cited in note 30).

[313] Sanford J. Ungar, *The Papers and the Papers: An Account of the Legal and Political Battle over the Pentagon Papers* 23–27 (Dutton 1972).

[314] Halberstam, *Best and Brightest* at 633 (cited in note 48); David Rudenstine, *The Pentagon Papers Case: Rediscovering its Meaning Twenty Years Later*, 12 Cardoza L Rev 1869 (1991).

[315] See Ungar, *Papers* at 32–34 (cited in note 313).

[316] 1 *The Pentagon Papers: The Defense Department History of United States Decision-making on Vietnam* xi, xii (Beacon 1971) (Senator Gravel edition).

[317] See Daniel Ellsberg, *Secrets: A Memoir of Vietnam and the Pentagon Papers* 48–87 (Penguin 2002); Schrag, *Test of Loyalty* at 24–28 (cited in note 296).

[318] Ellsberg, *Secrets* at 185 (cited in note 317). See Schrag, *Test of Loyalty* at 28–55 (cited in note 296).

[319] Ellsberg, *Secrets* at 255–56 (cited in note 317).

[320] Id at 272.

[321] Ellsberg did not give Sheehan the final four volumes, which dealt with diplomatic negotiations to end the war and to secure the release of American prisoners of war, because he considered this the "most sensitive" part of the report. Ungar, *Papers* at 83 (cited in note 313).

[322] Id at 14.

[323] See Ellsberg, *Secrets* at 428 (cited in note 317).

[324] Ungar, *Papers* at 114–16 (cited in note 313). In an April Los Angeles speech, Agnew called the media society's "most rabid critics." *Agnew Assails Media on Vietnam Coverage*, Washington Post A27 (Apr 8, 1971). In a June 1971 speech to broadcasters, Agnew charged that the news media was beset by a "wave of paranoia" concerning the Nixon administration, noting that "if anyone is 'paranoid with fear, suspicion and loathing,' it is not the Administration but rather those who keep voicing fear, suspicion and loathing." *Agnew Deplores Media "Paranoia,"* New York Times 42 (June 2, 1971).

[325] Ungar, *Papers* at 119–20 (cited in note 313). See Schrag, *Test of Loyalty* at 83–84 (cited in note 296).

[326] Max Frankel, *Court Step Likely*, New York Times 1 (June 15, 1971).

[327] Ungar, *Papers* at 122 (cited in note 313). See Schrag, *Test of Loyalty* at 85 (cited in note 296).

[328] *United States v. New York Times Co*, 328 F Supp 324, 325 (SD NY 1971). See Ungar,

Papers at 124–25 (cited in note 313).

329 William M. Blackstone, 4 *Commentaries on the Laws of England* °151.

330 James Madison, *The Virginia Report of 1799–1800*, in Leonard W. Levy, ed, *Freedom of the Press: From Zenger to Jefferson* 213 (Bobbs-Merrill 1966); James Madison, *Address of the General Assembly to the People of the Commonwealth of Virginia*, January 23, 1799, in Gaillard Hunt, ed, 6 *The Writings of James Madison: 1790–1802* 334–36 (Putnam 1906).

331 See, for example, *Commonwealth v. Karvonen*, 219 Mass 30, 32–33, 106 NE 556, 557 (1914) (permissible to punish speech if it is "likely to provoke turbulence or to menace the safety of travelers or citizens in general, or otherwise interfere with the common welfare)"; *State v. Pioneer Press Co*, 100 Minn 173, 176–77, 110 NW 867, 868 (1907) (permissible to regulate speech that "naturally tends to excite the public mind and thus indirectly affect the public good"); *State v. McKee*, 73 Conn 18, 26, 46 A 409, 412 (1900) (permissible to restrict speech "calculated to induce" immorality).

332 See, for example, Henry Schofield, *Freedom of the Press in the United States*, 9 American Sociological Society Papers and Proceedings 67 (1914); Thomas M. Cooley, *Constitutional Limitations* 525–28 (Little, Brown 6th ed 1883); Ernst Freund, *The Police Power: Public Policy and Constitutional Rights* 508–12, 516 (Callaghan 1904).

333 *Schenck v. United States*, 249 US 47, 51–52 (1919).

334 283 US 697 (1931).

335 Id at 719, 720.

336 Blackstone, 4 *Commentaries* at °151–52 (cited in note 329).

337 See Alexander M. Bickel, *The Morality of Consent* 61 (Yale 1975). See also Stephen R. Barnett, *The Puzzle of Prior Restraint*, 29 Stan L Rev 539 (1977); Vincent Blasi, *Toward a Theory of Prior Restraint: The Central Linkage*, 66 Minn L Rev 11, 23 (1981);

338 Ellsberg, *Secrets* at 394 (cited in note 317).

339 Id at 400–401.

340 Ungar, *Papers* at 139–46 (cited in note 313). See Katharine Graham, *Personal History* 447–51 (Vintage 1997).

341 Ungar, *Papers* at 152–53 (cited in note 313).

342 Milwaukee News (Apr 30, 1917), excerpted in Thomas F. Carroll, *Freedom of Speech and of the Press in War Time: The Espionage Act*, 17 Mich L Rev 621, 624 (1919). Congress's rejection of the press censorship provision is discussed in detail in chapter 3.

343 Ungar, *Papers* at 155–58 (cited in note 313).

344 *United States v. New York Times*, 328 F Supp 324, 330 (SD NY 1971). See Ungar, *Papers* at 168–69.

345 *New York Times v. United States*, 403 US 713 (1971).

346 Id at 714 (citation omitted).

347 Id at 715, 717, 719 (Black concurring).

348 Id at 722–23, 724 (Douglas concurring).

349 Id at 725–27 (Brennan concurring).

[350] 347 US 483 (1954).

[351] Id at 742, 745 (Marshall concurring).

[352] Id at 727, 728, 730 (Stewart concurring).

[353] Id at 731 (White concurring).

[354] Id at 748, 750, 752 (Burger dissenting).

[355] Id at 753, 758 (Harlan dissenting), quoting *Chicago & Southern Air Lines v. Waterman Steamship Corp*, 333 US 103, 111 (1948) (opinion of Justice Jackson).

[356] Id at 762–63 (Blackmun concurring), quoting *United States v. Washington Post*, 446 F2d 1327, 1330 (DC Cir 1971) (Judge Wilkie).

[357] Ungar, *Papers* at 14, 19 (cited in note 313).

[358] Halberstam, *Best and Brightest* at 409 (cited in note 48).

[359] Memorandum from Charles W. Colson to H. R Haldeman, June 25, 1971, excerpted in Oudes, ed, *From: The President* at 283–84 (cited in note 176); Kutler, *Abuse of Power* at 6, 20 (cited in note 294).

[360] Ellsberg, *Secrets* at 438 (cited in note 317); Theoharis, *Spying on Americans* at 190–92 (cited in note 263). On May 16, 1973, Nixon recalled in a conversation in the Oval Office with Fred Buzhardt and Haig, "We set up in the White House an independent group under Bud Krogh to cover the problems of leaks involving, at the time, of the Goddamn Pentagon papers, right? Remember we called it . . . the plumbers operation." Kutler, ed, *Abuse of Power* at 514 (cited in note 294). See also Wise, *American Police State* at 13–14 (cited in note 277); Theoharis, *Spying on Americans* at 190–91 (cited in note 263).

[361] See Schrag, *Test of Loyalty* at 100–105 (cited in note 296). See generally Ungar, *Papers* (cited in note 313).

[362] Barry Sussman, *The Great Coverup: Nixon and the Scandal of Watergate* 214 (Signet 1974); Goldstein, *Political Repression* at 489–91 (cited in note 30); Ellsberg, *Secrets* at 455–57 (cited in note 317); letter from Earl Silbert to Assistant Attorney General Henry E. Petersen, Apr 16, 1973, excerpted id at 444.

[363] Kutler, ed, *Abuse of Power* at 35 (cited in note 294) (conversation in the Oval Office between Richard Nixon, H. R. Haldeman, John Mitchell, John Erlichman, and Charles Colson on Sept 19, 1971).

[364] Ellsberg, *Secrets* at 415–16, 420 (cited in note 317). See Ungar, *Papers* at 301–2 (cited in note 313).

[365] Ungar, *Papers* at 236 (cited in note 313).

[366] 393 US 503 (1969).

[367] Id at 510–11, 508.

[368] 398 US 58 (1970).

[369] Id at 63.

[370] See Churchill and Vander Wall, *COINTELPRO Papers* at 191 (cited in note 265).

[371] 415 US 566 (1974).

[372] Id at 568–69, 573–74.

[373] 418 US 405 (1974).

[374] Id at 407, 410, 406.

[375] Gerald Gunther, *Learned Hand and the Origins of Modern First Amendment Doctrine: Some Fragments of History*, 27 Stan L Rev 719, 749 (1975).

[376] 385 US 116 (1966).

[377] Id at 120, 133, 134.

[378] 395 US 444 (1969).

[379] 274 US 357 (1927). For a discussion of *Whitney*, see chapter 4.

[380] *Brandenburg*, 395 US at 444–45, 447.

[381] Gunther, 27 Stan L Rev at 754–55 (cited in note 375).

[382] See Bernard Schwartz, *Holmes versus Hand: Clear and Present Danger or Advocacy of Unlawful Action?*, 1994 Sup Ct Rev 209, 240–41.

[383] See John Hart Ely, *Democracy and Distrust: A Theory of Judicial Review* 115 (Harvard 1980).

[384] See, for example, *Healy v. James*, 408 US 169 (1972) (invalidating the refusal of a public university to deny recognition to SDS because it advocated a "philosophy of violence"); *NAACP v. Claiborne Hardware Co*, 458 US 886 (1982) (invalidating a civil judgment because the speech at issue did not meet the requirements of *Brandenburg*); *Communist Party of Indiana v. Whitcomb*, 414 US 441, 443 n 1 (1974) (invalidating a statute that denied a place on the ballot to any party that failed to file "an affidavit . . . that it does not advocate the overthrow of . . . government by force or violence"). See also *Watts v. United States*, 394 US 705, 706 (1969) (invalidating the conviction of an individual who, at a public rally, said "if they ever make me carry a rifle the first man I want to get in my sights is LBJ"); *Hess v. Indiana*, 414 US 105, 107 (1973) (invalidating the conviction of an individual who, during an antiwar demonstration, shouted, "We'll take the fucking street later"). The Court did not invalidate every restriction of dissident speech during the Vietnam War, however. Recall *O'Brien*, for example, and the issue of draft card burning. Also, in *Parker v. Levy*, 417 US 733 (1974), the Court upheld a military court martial of a soldier who urged black soldiers not to go to Vietnam "if ordered to do so." The Court explained that "the different character of the . . . military mission" requires a different application of First Amendment principles and that in the military "no question can be left open as to the . . . duty of obedience in the soldier." Id at 758, 744.

[385] Lee C. Bollinger, *Epilogue*, in Lee C. Bollinger and Geoffrey R. Stone, *Eternally Vigilant: Free Speech in the Modern Era* 312–13 (Chicago 2002).

[386] *Masses Publishing Co. v. Patten*, 244 F 535, 540 (SD NY 1917); *New York Times v. Sullivan*, 376 US 254, 270, 273 (1964).

[387] Harry Kalven Jr., *A Worthy Tradition: Freedom of Speech in America* 232 (Harper and Row 1988).

[388] Richard A. Posner, *Pragmatism versus Purposivism in First Amendment Analysis*, 54 Stan L Rev 737, 741 (2002).

[389] Dellinger, *From Yale to Jail* at 329, 333, 335 (cited in note 11).

[390] Id at 381–83.

[391] *Activists Share Struggle at Allen*, Daily Illini Online (Mar 1, 2000), online at http://www.dailyillini.com/mar_00/mar1/news/news10.html (visited Jan 26, 2004). See Henry Allen, *All-American Dissenter*, Washington Post B1 (Apr 28, 1980).

CONCLUSION

[1] Robert H. Jackson, *Wartime Security and Liberty under Law*, 1 Buff L Rev 103, 116 (1951).

[2] On the problem of hindsight, see Jeffrey J. Rachlinski, *A Positive Psychological Theory of Judging in Hindsight*, 65 U Chi L Rev 571 (1998). Psychologists have found that people tend to overstate the predictability of past events. See, for example, Baruch Fischhoff, *Hindsight ≠ Foresight: The Effect of Outcome Knowledge on Judgment under Uncertainty*, 1 J Exp Psych: Human Perception and Performance 288 (1975).

[3] See W. Kip Viscusi, *Alarmist Decisions with Divergent Risk Information*, 107 Econ J 1657, 1657–59 (1997); Paul Slovic, *The Perception of Risk* 220–31 (Earthscan 2000); Christina E. Wells, *Discussing the First Amendment*, 101 U Mich L Rev 2901, 2920 (2003); Susan E. Jackson and Jane E. Dutton, *Discerning Threats and Opportunities*, 33 Admin Sci Q 370, 384–86 (1988); Richard M. Doty, Bill E. Peterson, and David G. Winter, *Threat and Authoritarianism in the United States, 1978–1987*, 61 J Personality & Social Psych 629 (1991); Arne Öhman, Daniel Lundquist, and Francisco Esteves, *The Face in the Crowd Revisited: A Threat Advantage with Schematic Stimuli*, 80 J Personality & Social Psych 381 (2001); Andrew J. Tomarken, Susan Mineka, and Michael Cook, *Fear-Relevant Selective Associations and Covariation Bias*, 98 J of Abnor Psych 381 (1989).

[4] On the phenomenon of cascades, see Cass R. Sunstein, *Why Societies Need Dissent* 54–73 (Harvard 2003); Timur Kuran and Cass R. Sunstein, *Availability Cascades and Risk Regulation*, 51 Stan L Rev 683 (1999). Chip Heath, Chris Bell, and Emily Sternberg, *Emotional Selection in Memes: The Case of Urban Legends*, 81 J Personality & Social Psych 1028 (2001).

[5] John Keane, *Fear and Democracy*, in Kenton Worcester, Sally Avery Bermanzohn, and Mark Ungar, eds, *Violence and Politics: Globalization's Paradox* 226, 235 (Routledge 2002)

[6] Zechariah Chafee Jr., *Free Speech in the United States* 70 (Harvard 1948).

[7] Cass R. Sunstein, *The Laws of Fear*, 115 Harv L Rev 1119, 1127 (2002). For commentary on these behavioral phenomena, see Amos Tversky and Daniel Kahneman, *Judgment under Uncertainty: Heuristics and Biases*, in Daniel Kahneman et al, eds, *Judgment under Uncertainty: Heuristics and Biases* 3 (Cambridge 1982); Slovic, *Perception of Risk* (cited in note 3); Cass R. Sunstein, *Beyond the Precautionary Principle*, 151 U Pa L Rev 1003 (2003); Cass R. Sunstein, *Probability Neglect: Emotions, Worst Cases, and Law*, 112 Yale L J 61 (2002); Kuran and Sunstein, *Availability Cascades* (cited in note 4); Roger G. Noll and James E. Krier, *Some Implications of Cognitive Psychology for Risk Regulation*, 19 J Legal Stud 747, 769–71 (1990). For an excellent discussion of these issue in the context of the Supreme Court's decision in *Dennis*, see Christina E. Wells, *Fear and Loathing in Consitutional Decision-making: A Case Study of Dennis v. United States* (forthcoming).

[8] "One of the most destructive . . . problems facing contemporary society is the pervasive tendency of people to respond with hostility and disdain toward those who are differ-

ent. . . . This tendency to reject those who are different is well documented in the literature on prejudice." Jeff Greenberg et al, *Evidence for Terror Management Theory II: The Effects of Mortality Salience on Reactions to Those Who Threaten or Bolster the Cultural Worldview*, 58 J of Personality & Social Psych 308 (1990). See H. Tajfel, *Social Psychology of Intergroup Relations*, in M. R. Rosensweig and L. W. Porter, eds, 33 *Annual Review of Psychology* 1 (Stanford 1982); Leon Festinger, *A Theory of Social Comparison Processes*, 7 Human Relations 117 (1954); David A. Wilder and John E. Thompson, *Assimilation and Contrast Effects in the Judgments of Groups*, 54 J of Personality & Social Psych 62–73 (1988); Joachim Krueger and Russel W. Clement, *The Truly False Consensus Effect: An Ineradicable and Egocentric Bias in Social Perception*, id at 596–610 (1994); John L. Sullivan, James Pierson, and George E. Marcus, *Political Tolerance and American Democracy* 251 (Chicago 1982); John Mueller, *Trends in Political Tolerance*, 52 Pub Op Q 1, 16–17 (1988); Donald R. Kinder, *Opinion and Action in the Realm of Politics*, in Daniel T. Gilbert, Susan T. Fiske, and Gardner Lindzey, eds, 2 *The Handbook of Social Psychology* 778, 789–93 (McGraw-Hill 4th ed 1998); Dennis Chong, *How People Think, Reason and Feel about Rights and Liberties*, 37 Am J Pol Sci 867, 885–88 (1993); James H. Kuklinski et al, *The Cognitive and Affective Bases of Political Tolerance Judgments*, 35 Am J Pol Sci 1 (1991).

[9] See Eric A. Posner and Adrian Vermeule, *Accommodating Emergencies*, 56 Stan L Rev 605, 626–35 (2003).

[10] See Arne Öhman, *Fear and Anxiety as Emotional Phenomena: Clinical Phenomenology, Evolutionary Perspectives, and Information-Processing Mechanisms*, in Michael Lewis and Jeannette M. Haviland, eds, *Handbook of Emotions* 520 (Guilford 1993). I am grateful to Joshua Walker for introducing me to much of this literature in his student paper, *The Fortress of Expression: Threat Bias in First Amendment Judicial Decision Making* (Apr 15, 2002).

[11] See 65th Cong, 2d Sess, in Cong Rec S 4633, 4637 (April 5, 1918) (statements of Senators France and Poindexter).

[12] 323 US at 219.

[13] Sunstein, *Why Societies Need Dissent* at 8 (cited in note 4). See Luther Gulick, *Administrative Reflections from World War II* 121–29 (Alabama 1948).

[14] For competing views on the question of progress over time in the constitutional protection of civil liberties, compare Posner and Vermeule, 56 Stan L Rev at 622–25 (cited in note 9) (skeptical about claim of progress) with William H. Rehnquist, *All the Laws But One: Civil Liberties in Wartime* 221 (Vintage 2000) (progress); Jack Goldsmith and Cass R. Sunstein, *Military Tribunals and Legal Culture: What a Difference Sixty Years Makes*, 19 Const Comment 261 (2002) (progress); and Mark V. Tushnet, *Defending Korematsu? Reflections on Civil Liberties in Wartime*, 2003 Wis L Rev 273 (progress).

[15] 8 *Annals of Congress* 1484, 1961, 1677 (Gales and Seaton 1851).

[16] 65th Cong, Spec Sess, in 55 Cong Rec S 104 (Apr 2, 1917).

[17] *All Disloyal Men Warned by Gregory*, New York Times 3 (Nov 21, 1917).

[18] Act of May 16, 1918, ch 75, § 1, 40 Stat 553.

[19] Richard M. Fried, *Men against McCarthy* 244–45 (Columbia 1976); Robert J. Goldstein, *Political Repression in Modern America: 1870 to the Present* 327 (Schenkman 1978). See also Thomas C. Reeves, *The Life and Times of Joe McCarthy* 450 (Stein and Day 1982); David Caute, *The Great Fear: The Anti-Communist Purge under Truman and Eisenhower* 46 (Simon and Schuster 1978).

[20] William S. White, *Red Charges by M'Carthy Ruled False*, New York Times 1 (July 18, 1950). See also Richard H. Rovere, *Senator Joe McCarthy* 181–83 (Harcourt Brace 1959); *Text of McCarthy Reply*, New York Times 16 (July 18, 1950).

[21] That the particularly harsh restrictions on dissent in these eras were motivated at least in part by ulterior political interests lends support to the after-the-fact judgment that these restrictions were not essential to the national security, as the government claimed, but were means of achieving other, quite different goals.

[22] See Posner and Vermeule, 56 Stan L Rev at 637 (cited in note 9) ("People feel fear because they perceive a threat; they cannot step outside of themselves and doubt their own beliefs because they know that fear can interfere with cognition").

[23] Learned Hand, *The Spirit of Liberty*, in Irving Dillard, ed, *The Spirit of Liberty: Papers and Addresses of Learned Hand* 189–90 (Knopf 1974). See Larry B. Kramer, *The People Themselves: Popular Constitutionalism and Judicial Review* (Oxford 2004).

[24] Sunstein, *Why Societies Need Dissent* at 128 (cited in note 4).

[25] *Abrams v. United States*, 250 US 616, 630 (1919) (Holmes dissenting).

[26] Hand, *Spirit of Liberty* at 190 (cited in note 23).

[27] Steven H. Shiffrin, *The First Amendment, Democracy, and Romance* 159 (Harvard 1990). See Henry Steele Commager, *"To Secure the Blessings of Liberty,"* New York Times Magazine 3 (Apr 9, 1939).

[28] See Sunstein, 151 U Pa L Rev at 1057 (cited in note 7); Roger E. Kasperson et al, *The Social Amplification of Risk: A Conceptual Framework*, 8 Risk Analysis 177, 183–84 (1988); Yuval Rottenstreich and Christopher K. Hsee, *Money, Kisses, and Electric Shocks: On the Affective Psychology of Risk*, 12 Psychological Sci 185, 186–88 (2001); Jeffrey Rosen, *Naked Terror*, New York Times Magazine 10 (Jan 4, 2004).

[29] See Sunstein, 112 Yale L J at 95 (cited in note 7) (the only effective way to reduce fear of a low probability risk may be to "[c]hange the subject").

[30] See Oren Gross, *Chaos and Rules: Should Responses to Violent Crises Always Be Constitutional?*, 112 Yale L J 1011, 1033 (2003).

[31] Id at 1022–23, 1069–96. On legislation that takes effect only upon a declaration of war or a presidential proclamation or executive order under the National Emergencies Act, 50 USC §§ 1601, 1621 (1994), see id at 1065–66.

[32] For a skeptical view of such rules, see Posner and Vermeule, 56 Stan L R at 637–39 (cited in note 9).

[33] 65th Cong, 2d Sess, in 56 Cong Rec S 4826 (Apr 9, 1918).

[34] *Gitlow v. New York*, 268 US 652 (1925) (upholding New York criminal anarchy statute forbidding any person to advocate, advise, or teach "the duty, necessity and propriety of overthrowing . . . organized government by force [or] violence").

[35] *Whitney v. California*, 274 US 357, 360 (1927) (upholding California criminal syndicalism statute prohibiting any person from knowingly becoming a member of any

organization that advocates "the commission of crime, sabotage, or unlawful acts of force and violence or unlawful methods of terrorism as a means of accomplishing a change in industrial ownership . . . or effecting any political change").

[36] *Yates v. United States*, 354 US 298 (1957) (adopting a narrow construction of the Smith Act in order to avoid doubts about its constitutionality).

[37] As the Supreme Court has developed a more robust constitutional jurisprudence, Congress has, if anything, tended to be too passive in making its own independent judgments about when potential legislation may be unconstitutional. See Abner J. Mikva and Joseph R. Lundy, *The 91 Congress and the Constitution*, 38 U Chi L Rev 449, 458–59, 473–74, 497–99 (1971).

[38] Sunstein, *Why Societies Need Dissent* at 11 (cited in note 4). See also id at 8, 27; David Myers and Helmut Lamm, *The Group Polarization Phenomenon*, 83 Psych Bull 602 (1976).

[39] Jackson, 1 Buff L Rev at 115 (cited in note 1).

[40] See Rehnquist, *All the Laws But One* at 221–25 (cited in note 14).

[41] *Brandenburg v. Ohio*, 395 US 444 (1969).

[42] See Posner and Vermeule, 56 Stan L R at 605–7 (cited in note 9); Rehnquist, *All the Laws But One* at 205 (cited in note 14) ("Judicial inquiry, with its restrictive rules of evidence, orientation towards resolution of factual disputes in individual cases, and long delays, is ill-suited to determine an issue such as 'military necessity' ").

[43] Anthony Lewis, *Security and Liberty: Preserving the Values of Freedom*, in Richard C. Leone and Greg Anrig Jr., eds, *The War on Our Freedoms: Civil Liberties in an Age of Terrorism* 47, 67 (Century Foundation 2003).

[44] *Terminiello v. City of Chicago*, 337 US 1, 37 (1949) (Jackson, dissenting).

[45] Rehnquist, *All the Laws But One* at 221 (cited in note 14).

[46] For the argument that in periods of crisis courts have tended to use a "process-based/institutionally oriented approach," rather than an individual rights–oriented approach, and that this is a preferable way for the courts to review the legality of governmental action in emergency situations, see Samuel Issacharoff and Richard H. Pildes, *Between Civil Libertarianism and Executive Unilateralism: An Institutional Process Approach to Rights during Wartime*, 5 Theor Inquiries in Law 1, 3 (2004). Under this view, courts tend to shift difficult constitutional decisions in such periods away from themselves by insisting on *joint* legislative and executive action. This is a thoughtful and interesting analysis. It should be used to supplement rather than supplant the individual rights approach.

[47] Richard A. Posner, *Law, Pragmatism, and Democracy* 303–4, 296 (Harvard 2003).

[48] Id at 298–99. For a critical view of Posner's analysis in this respect, see Michael Sullivan and Daniel J. Solove, *Can Pragmatism Be Radical? Richard Posner and Legal Pragmatism*, 113 Yale L J 687, 710 (2003).

[49] Posner, *Law, Pragmatism, and Democracy* at 299 (cited in note 47).

[50] Francis Biddle, *In Brief Authority* 219 (Doubleday 1962).

[51] Rehnquist, *All the Laws But One* at 224 (cited in note 14).

[52] Id at 222.

[53] See Wells, *Discussing the First Amendment* at 2921–22 (cited in note 3).

[54] See Vincent Blasi, *The Pathological Perspective and the First Amendment*, 85 Colum L Rev 449, 452–59, 506–14 (1985); Gross, 112 Yale L J at 1048 (cited in note 30); Wells, *Fear and Loathing* at (cited in note 7). For a critical view, see Posner and Vermeule, *Accommodating Emergencies* at 643 (cited in note 9) ("It is perverse for a government to commit itself not to respond vigorously to emergencies").

[55] Tushnet, 2003 *Defending Korematsu?* at 292 (cited in note 14). See William J. Brennan Jr., *The Quest to Develop a Jurisprudence of Civil Liberties in Times of Security Crises*, 18 Isr Y B Hum Rts 11 (1988); Posner and Vermeule, *Accommodating Emergencies* at 624–25 (cited in note 9); Gross, *Chaos and Rules* at 1020 (cited in note 30).

[56] Clinton L. Rossiter, *The Supreme Court and the Commander-in-Chief* 54 (Cornell 1951).

[57] See *Schneiderman v. United States*, 320 US 118, 154, 157 (1943) (the government cannot constitutionally denaturalize an American citizen because of his membership in the Communist Party unless it can prove by "clear, unequivocal and convincing" evidence that he had personally endorsed the use of "present violent action which creates a clear and present danger of public disorder or other substantive evil"); *Baumgartner v. United States*, 322 US 665, 677 (1944) (the government cannot constitutionally denaturalize a former member of the German-American Bund for making "sinister" statements); *Taylor v. Mississippi*, 319 US 583, 586 (1943) (the government cannot constitutionally punish an individual for stating that "it was wrong for our President to send our boys . . . [to be] shot down for no purpose at all"); *Hartzel v. United States*, 322 US 680, 683 (1944) (the government cannot constitutionally punish an individual for distributing pamphlets that depicted the war as a "gross betrayal of America," denounced "our English allies and the Jews," and assailed the "patriotism of the President"); *Keegan v. United States*, 325 US 478 (1945) (overturning the convictions of twenty-four members of the Bund who had been charged with advocating draft evasion).

[58] *West Virginia Board of Education v. Barnette*, 319 US 624 (1943).

[59] *Duncan v. Kahanamoku*, 327 US 304 (1946).

[60] *Ex parte Endo*, 323 US 283 (1944).

[61] *Youngstown Sheet & Tube Co. v. Sawyer*, 343 US 579 (1952).

[62] *Yates v. United States*, 354 US 298 (1967)

[63] *New York Times Co. v. United States*, 403 US 713 (1971). See also *United States v. United States District Court (Keith)*, 407 US 297 (1972) (unanimously rejecting the government's claim of power to conduct national security wiretaps without judicial approval).

[64] For a more pessimistic view, see Edward S. Corwin, *Total War and the Constitution* 177 (Knopf 1947) ("In total war the Court necessarily loses some part of its normal freedom of decision and becomes assimilated . . . to the mechanism of the national defense").

[65] See Rehnquist, *All the Laws But One* at 221, 224–25 (cited in note 14) (noting that an important part of the progress the nation has made in its protection of civil liberties in wartime is due to the "fact that the First Amendment had come into its own," and that in future wartime situations it is both "desirable and likely" that courts will more carefully scrutinize "the government's claims of necessity as a basis for curtailing

civil liberty").

66 Lewis, *Security and Liberty* at 50 (cited in note 43); Richard C. Leone, *The Quiet Republic: The Missing Debate about Civil Liberties after 9/11*, in Leone and Anrig, eds, *War on our Freedoms* at 8 (cited in note 43); Although the Bush administration did not issue such comments as frequently as the Adams and Wilson administrations, the nature of mass communication has made that unnecessary. The point was made.

67 Leone, *Quiet Republic* at 5 (cited in note 66).

68 See Danny Hakim, *States Are Told to Keep Detainee Information Secret*, New York Times A14 (Apr 19, 2002); Katharine Q. Seelye, *Moscow, Seeking Extradition, Says 3 Detainees Are Russian*, id at A13 (Apr 3, 2002); Tamar Lewin, *Rights Groups Press for Names of Muslims Held in New Jersey*, id at A9 (Jan 23, 2002); Dan Eggen and Susan Schmidt, *Count of Released Detainees Is Hard to Pin Down*, Washington Post A10 (Nov 6, 2002); Office the Inspector General, U.S. Dept of Justice, *The September 11 Detainees: A Review of the Treatment of Aliens Held on Immigration Charges in Connection with the Investigation of the September 11 Attacks* (June 2, 2003).

69 See George Lardner Jr, *U.S. Will Monitor Call to Lawyers*, Washington Post A1 (Nov 9, 2001); 29 CFR § 501.3 (d).

70 *Padilla v. Rumsfeld*, 352 F3d 695 (2d cir 2003). See also *Hamdi v. Rumsfeld*, 316 F3d 450 (4th Cir 2003) (upholding the executive's declaration that an individual was an "enemy combatant").

71 See Homeland Security Act of 2002, Pub L No 107-296, 116 Stat 2135, codified at 6 USCA § 122 (2002).

72 See Stephen J. Schulhofer, *The Enemy Within: Intelligence Gathering, Law Enforcement, and Civil Liberties in the Wake of September 11* 2–3 (Century Foundation 2002); Gross, 112 Yale L J at 1017–18 (cited in note 30).

73 Uniting and Strengthening America by Providing Appropriate Tools Required to Intercept and Obstruct Terrorism (USA PATRIOT) Act of 2001, Pub L No 107–56, 115 Stat 272.

74 Leone, *Quiet Republic* at 8 (cited in note 66). See David Cole and James X. Dempsey, *Terrorism and the Constitution: Sacrificing Civil Liberties in the Name of National Security* 151 (First Amendment Foundation 2002). See Nancy Chang, *Silencing Political Dissent: How Post–September 11 Anti-Terrorism Measures Threaten Our Civil Liberties* 43 (Seven Stories 2002). The PATRIOT Act passed the Senate by a vote of 99 to 1. The only senator to vote against the legislation was Russ Feingold, Democrat of Wisconsin. Thereafter, several other senators told him privately that they agreed with him but were afraid to appear to the public as " 'soft' on terrorism." Timothy Lynch, *Breaking the Vicious Cycle: Preserving Our Liberties While Fighting Terrorism*, 443 Policy Analysis 1, 7 (June 26, 2002); Robert E. Pierre, *Wisconsin Senator Emerges as a Maverick*, Washington Post A8 (Oct 27, 2001). In the House, the vote was 356 to 66.

75 See Stephen J. Schulhofer, *No Checks, No Balances: Discarding Bedrock Constitutional Principles*, in Leone and Anrig, eds, *War on our Freedoms* at 74, 76–77 (cited in note 43); Chang, *Silencing Political Dissent* at 43–66 (cited in note 74). For defenses of the PATRIOT Act, see Orin S. Kerr, *Internet Surveillance Law after the USA Patriot Act: The Big Brother That Isn't*, 97 Nw U L Rev 607 (2003); Eric Posner and John Yoo, *The*

PATRIOT Act under Fire, Wall Street Journal A26 (Dec 9, 2003).

76 Among the Republicans who opposed Operation TIPS was House Majority Leader Dick Armey of Texas. See Jackie Koszczuk, *Ashcroft Drawing Criticism from Both Sides of the Aisle*, Cong Q Weekly 2286 (Sept 7, 2002).

77 Leone, *Quiet Republic* at 9–10 (cited in note 66). See also Kathleen M. Sullivan, *Under a Watchful Eye: Incursions on Personal Privacy*, in Leone and Anrig, eds, *War on Our Freedoms* at 128, 132–33 (cited in note 66); Jonathan Riehl, *Lawmakers Likely to Limit New High-Tech Eavesdropping*, Cong Q 406 (Feb 15, 2003).

78 *Alliance to End Repression v. City of Chicago*, 237 F3d 799 (7th Cir 2001).

79 A number of Republicans, including Senators Larry Craig of Idaho, Mike Crapo of Idaho, Lisa Murkowski of Alaska, and John Sununu of New Hamshpire, are among those who condemned PATRIOT Act II. See Jesse J. Holland, *Bush Aims to Expand USA Patriot Act*, Guardian (Jan 22, 2004). For the text of the proposed legislation, see http://www.dailyrotten.com/source-docs/patriot2draft.html.

80 Jeffrey Rosen, *Privacy Pleas: Why Congress Is Brave and the Courts Aren't*, New Republic 19 (May 26, 2003). See Issacharoff and Pildes, *Between Civil Libertarianism and Executive Unilateralism* at 45 (cited in note 46).

81 Posner, *Law, Pragmatism, and Democracy* at 304 (cited in note 47).

82 James Goodby and Kenneth Weisbrode, *Bush's Corrosive Campaign of Fear*, Financial Times (Nov 19, 2003).

83 Max Lowenthal, *The Federal Bureau of Investigation* 298 (Sloane 1950).

84 See Chang, *Silencing Political Dissent* at 32–37 (cited in note 74).

85 The Attorney General's Guidelines on General Crimes, Racketeering Enterprise and Terrorism Enterprise Investigations VI(a)–(b) (2002), online at http://www.usdoj.gov/olp/generalcrimes2.pdf (visited March 14, 2004). See Neil A. Lewis, *Ashcroft Permits F.B.I. to Monitor Internet and Public Activities*, New York Times A20 (May 31, 2002).

86 Eric Lichtblau, *F.B.I. Scrutinizes Antiwar Rallies*, New York Times 1 (Nov 23, 2003).

87 Department of Justice, Fact Sheet, *Attorney General's Guidelines: Detecting and Preventing Terrorist Attacks* (May 30, 2002), cited in Schulhofer, *Enemy Within* at 62 (cited in note 72).

88 The Levi, Smith, and Thornburgh guidelines required senior Justice Department approval *prior* to investigating political and religious groups. In announcing the new guidelines, Attorney General Ashcroft criticized this requirement as "unnecessary procedural red tape." The Ashcroft guidelines thus decentralize this decision making, granting much greater independence to the fifty-six local FBI field offices. As we have seen repeatedly, however, whether in the Civil War (with Lincoln's generals), World War I (with the Justice Department's U.S. attorneys), or during the Vietnam War (with the FBI's local agents), such decentralization invariably leads to a greater suppression of civil liberties. What Ashcroft calls red tape, Levi rightly understood to be essential to government accountability. Remarks of Attorney General John Ashcroft, Attorney General Guidelines (May 30, 2002), online at http://www.usdoj.gov/ag/speeches/2002/53002agpreparedremarks.htm (visited Mar 14, 2004).

89 John Podesta, *Need to Know: Governing in Secret*, in Leone and Anrig, eds, *War on Our*

Freedoms at 220, 227 (cited in note 43).

90 Id at 221–25; Leone, *Quiet Republic* at 9 (cited in note 66); John F. Stacks, *Watchdogs on a Leash: Closing Doors on the Media*, in Leone and Anrig, eds, *War on Our Freedoms* at 237 (cited in note 43).

91 Schulhofer, *No Checks, No Balances* at 91 (cited in note 75). See Podesta, *Need to Know* at 221–25 (cited in note 89); Leone, *Quiet Republic* at 9 (cited in note 66); Stacks, *Watchdogs on a Leash* at 237 (cited in note 90); Schulhofer, *Enemy Within* at 4, 11–13 (cited in note 72). On the secrecy of deportation hearings, compare *Detroit Free Press v. Ashcroft*, 303 F3d 681 (6th Cir 2002) (closed hearing unconstitutional) with *North Jersey Media Group, Inc. v. Ashcroft*, 308 F3d 198 (3d Cir 2002) (closed hearing constitutional).

92 Podesta, *Need to Know* at 225 (cited in note 89).

93 *Whitney v. California*, 274 US 357, 375 (1927) (Brandeis concurring).

INDEX

Page numbers in *italics* refer to illustrations.